ISBN: 978129007202

Published by:
HardPress Publishing
8345 NW 66TH ST #2561
MIAMI FL 33166-2626

Email: info@hardpress.net
Web: http://www.hardpress.net

hichester

COLLECTION

OF

ANCIENT AND MODERN

BRITISH AUTHORS.

VOL. CCCCXLIX.

LIVES OF MAHOMET

AND

HIS SUCCESSORS

PARIS.—PRINTED BY E. THUNOT AND Co.
Rue Racine, 26, near the Odeon.

LIVES

OF

MAHOMET

AND

HIS SUCCESSORS.

BY

WASHINGTON IRVING.

PARIS,

BAUDRY'S EUROPEAN LIBRARY, | A. AND W. GALIGNANI AND Co.,
3, QUAI MALAQUAIS, AU 1ᵉʳ ÉTAGE. | 18, RUE VIVIENNE.

———

1850

PREFACE.

Some apology may seem necessary for presenting a life of Mahomet at the present day, when no new fact can be added to those already known concerning him. Many years ago, during a residence in Madrid, the author projected a series of writings illustrative of the domination of the Arabs in Spain. These were to be introduced by a sketch of the life of the founder of the Islam Faith, and the first mover of Arabian conquest. Most of the particulars for this were drawn from Spanish sources, and from Gagnier's translation of the Arabian historian Abulfeda, a copy of which the author found in the Jesuits' Library of the Convent of St. Isidro, at Madrid.

Not having followed out, in its extent, the literary plan devised, the manuscript life lay neglected among the author's papers until the year 1831, when he revised and enlarged it for the Family Library of Mr. John Murray. Circumstances prevented its publication at that time, and it again was thrown aside for years.

During his last residence in Spain, the author beguiled the tediousness of a lingering indisposition, by again revising the manuscript, profiting in so doing by recent lights thrown on the subject by different writers, and particularly by Dr. Gustav Weil, the very intelligent and learned librarian of the University of Heidelberg, to whose industrious researches and able disquisitions he acknowledges himself greatly indebted.[1]

Such is the origin of the work now given to the public; on which the author lays no claim to novelty of fact, nor profundity of research. It still bears the type of a work intended for a Family Library; in constructing which the whole aim of the writer has been to digest into an easy, perspicuous, and flowing narrative, the admitted facts concerning Mahomet, together with such legends and traditions as have been wrought into the whole system of oriental literature; and at the same time to give such a summary of his faith as might be sufficient for the general reader. Under such circumstances he has not thought it worth while to encumber his pages with a scaffolding of references and citations, nor to depart from the old English nomenclature of oriental names.

W. I.

SUNNYSIDE, 1849.

[1] Mohammed der Prophet, sein Leben und seine Lehre. Stuttgart. 1843.

CONTENTS.

LIFE OF MAHOMET.

CONTENTS.

LIVES OF THE SUCCESSORS OF MAHOMET.

CONTENTS.

MAHOMET AND HIS SUCCESSORS.

CHAPTER I.

Preliminary notice of Arabia and the Arabs.

During a long succession of ages, extending from the earliest period of recorded history down to the seventh century of the Christian era, that great chersonese or peninsula formed by the Red Sea, the Euphrates, the Gulf of Persia, and the Indian Ocean, and known by the name of Arabia, remained unchanged and almost unaffected by the events which convulsed the rest of Asia, and shook Europe and Africa to their centre. While kingdoms and empires rose and fell; while ancient dynasties passed away; while the boundaries and names of countries were changed, and their inhabitants were exterminated or carried into captivity, Arabia, though its frontier provinces experienced some vicissitudes, preserved in the depths of its deserts its primitive character and independence, nor had its nomadic tribes ever bent their haughty necks to servitude.

The Arabs carry back the traditions of their country to the highest antiquity. It was peopled, they say, soon after the deluge, by the progeny of Shem the son of Noah, who gradually formed themselves into several tribes, the most noted of which are the Adites and Thamudites. All these primitive tribes are said to have been either swept from the earth in punishment of their iniquities, or obliterated in subsequent modifications of the races, so that little remains concerning them but shadowy traditions and a few passages in the Koran. They are occasionally mentioned in oriental history as the "old primitive Arabians,"—the "lost tribes."

The permanent population of the peninsula is ascribed, by the same authorities, to Kahtan or Joctan, a descendant in the fourth generation from Shem. His posterity spread over the southern part of the peninsula and along the Red Sea. Yarab, one of his sons, founded the kingdom of Yemen, where the territory of Araba was called after him; whence the Arabs derive the names of themselves and their country. Jurham, another son, founded the kingdom of Hedjaz, over which his descendants bore sway for many

1

generations.   Among these people Hagar and her son Ishmael were
kindly received, when exiled from their home by the patriarch
Abraham.   In the process of time Ishmael married the daughter
of Modâd, a reigning prince of the line of Jurham; and thus a
stranger and a Hebrew became grafted on the original Arabian
stock.   It proved a vigorous graft.   Ishmael's wife bore him twelve
sons, who acquired dominion over the country, and whose prolific
race, divided into twelve tribes, expelled or overran and obliterated
the primitive stock of Joctan.

Such is the account given by the peninsular Arabs of their origin;[1] and Christian writers cite it as containing the fulfilment of
the covenant of God with Abraham, as recorded in Holy Writ.
"And Abraham said unto God, O that Ishmael might live before
thee!   And God said, As for Ishmael, I have heard thee.   Behold,
I have blessed him, and will make him fruitful, and will multiply
him exceedingly : *twelve princes* shall he beget, and I will make
him a great nation."   (Genesis xvii. 18, 20.)

These twelve princes with their tribes are further spoken of in
the Scriptures (Genesis xxv. 18) as occupying the country "from
Havilah unto Shur, that is before Egypt, as thou goest towards
Assyria;" a region identified by sacred geographers with part of
Arabia.   The description of them agrees with that of the Arabs of
the present day.   Some are mentioned as holding towns and castles,
others as dwelling in tents, or having villages in the wilderness.
Nebaioth and Kedar, the two first-born of Ishmael, are most noted
among the princes for their wealth in flocks and herds, and for the
fine wool of their sheep.   From Nebaioth came the Nabathai who
inhabited Stony Arabia; while the name of Kedar is occasionally
given in Holy Writ to designate the whole Arabian nation.   "Woe
is me," says the Psalmist, "that I sojourn in Mesech, that I dwell
in the tents of Kedar."   Both appear to have been the progenitors
of the wandering or pastoral Arabs; the free rovers of the desert.
"The wealthy nation," says the prophet Jeremiah, "that dwelleth
without care; which have neither gates nor bars, which dwell alone."

A strong distinction grew up in the earliest times between the
Arabs who " held towns and castles," and those who " dwelt in
tents."   Some of the former occupied the fertile wadies, or valleys,
scattered here and there among the mountains, where these towns
and castles were surrounded by vineyards and orchards, groves of
palm-trees, fields of grain, and well-stocked pastures.   They were
settled in their habits, devoting themselves to the cultivation of the
soil and the breeding of cattle.

Others of this class gave themselves up to commerce, having
ports and cities along the Red Sea; the southern shores of the pe-

---

[1] Beside the Arabs of the peninsula, who were all of the Shemitic race, there were
others called Cushites, being descended from Cush the son of Ham.   They inhabited the
banks of the Euphrates and the Persian Gulf.   The name of Cush is often given in
Scripture to the Arabs generally as well as to their country.   It must be the Arabs of
this race who at present roam the deserted regions of ancient Assyria, and have been
employed recently in disinterring the long-buried ruins of Nineveh.   They are sometimes distinguished as the Syro-Arabians.   The present work relates only to the Arabs
f the peninsula, or Arabia Proper.

ninsula and the Gulph of Persia, and carrying on foreign trade by means of ships and caravans. Such especially were the people of Yemen, or Arabia the Happy, that land of spices, perfumes and frankincense; the Sabæa of the poets; the Sheba of the sacred Scriptures. They were among the most active mercantile navigators of the eastern seas. Their ships brought to their shores the myrrh and balsams of the opposite coast of Berbera, with the gold, the spices, and other rich commodities of India and tropical Africa. These, with the products of their own country, were transported by caravans across the deserts to the semi-Arabian states of Ammon, Moab, and Edom or Idumea, to the Phœnician ports of the Mediterranean, and thence distributed to the western world.

The camel has been termed the ship of the desert, the caravan may be termed its fleet. The caravans of Yemen were generally fitted out, manned, conducted and guarded by the nomadic Arabs, the dwellers in tents, who, in this respect, might be called the navigators of the desert. They furnished the innumerable camels required, and also contributed to the freight by the fine fleeces of their countless flocks. The writings of the prophets show the importance, in scriptural times, of this inland chain of commerce by which the rich countries of the south, India, Ethiopia, and Arabia the Happy, were linked with ancient Syria.

Ezekiel, in his lamentations for Tyre, exclaims, "Arabia, and all the princes of Kedar, they occupied with thee in lambs, and rams, and goats; in these were they thy merchants. The merchants of Sheba and Raamah occupied in thy fairs with chief of all spices, and with all precious stones and gold. Haran, and Canneh, and Eden, [1] the merchants of Sheba, Asshur, and Chelmad, were thy merchants." And Isaiah, speaking to Jerusalem, says—"The multitude of camels shall cover thee; the dromedaries of Midian and Ephah; all they from Sheba shall come; they shall bring gold and incense. * * * * All the flocks of Kedar shall be gathered together unto thee; the rams of Nebaioth shall minister unto thee." (Isaiah lx. 6, 7.)

The agricultural and trading Arabs, however, the dwellers in towns and cities, have never been considered the true type of the race. They became softened by settled and peaceful occupations, and lost much of their original stamp by an intercourse with strangers. Yemen, too, being more accessible than the other parts of Arabia, and offering greater temptation to the spoiler, had been repeatedly invaded and subdued.

. It was among the other class of Arabs, the rovers of the desert, the " dwellers in tents," by far the most numerous of the two, that the national character was preserved in all its primitive force and freshness. Nomadic in their habits, pastoral in their occupations, and acquainted by experience and tradition with all the hidden resources of the desert, they led a wandering life, roaming from place to place in quest of those wells and springs which had been the resort of their forefathers since the days of the patriarchs; encamping wherever they could find date-trees for shade, and

---

[1] Haran, Canna, and Aden, ports on the Indian Sea.

sustenance and pasturage for their flocks, and herds, and camels; and shifting their abode whenever the temporary supply was exhausted.

These nomadic Arabs were divided and subdivided into innumerable petty tribes or families, each with its Sheikh or Emir, the representative of the patriarch of yore, whose spear, planted beside his tent, was the ensign of command.   His office, however, though continued for many generations in the same family, was not strictly hereditary; but depended upon the good-will of the tribe.   He might be deposed, and another of a different line elected in his place.   His power, too, was limited, and depended upon his personal merit and the confidence reposed in him.   His prerogative consisted in conducting negotiations of peace and war ; in leading his tribe against the enemy; in choosing the place of encampment and in receiving and entertaining strangers of note.   Yet, even in these and similar privileges, he was controlled by the opinions and inclinations of his people. [1]

However numerous and minute might be the divisions of a tribe, the links of affinity were carefully kept in mind by the several sections.   All the Sheikhs of the same tribe acknowledge a common chief called the Sheikh of Sheikhs, who, whether ensconced in a rock-built castle, or encamped amid his flocks and herds in the desert, might assemble under his standard all the scattered branches on any emergency affecting the common weal.

The multiplicity of these wandering tribes, each with its petty prince and petty territory, but without a national head, produced frequent collisions.   Revenge, too, was almost a religious principle among them.   To avenge a relative slain was the duty of his fa-

---

[1] In summer the wandering Arabs, says Burckhardt, seldom remain above three or four days on the same spot; as soon as their cattle have consumed the herbage near a watering place, the tribe removes in search of pasture, and the grass again springing up, serves for a succeeding camp.   The encampments vary in the number of tents, from six to eight hundred ; when the tents are but few, they are pitched in a circle; but more considerable numbers in a straight line, or a row of single tents, especially along a rivulet, sometimes three or four behind as many others.   In winter, when water and pasture never fail, the whole tribe spreads itself over the plain in parties of three or four tents each, with an interval of half an hour's distance between each party.   The Sheikh's tent is always on the side on which enemies or guests may be expected.   To oppose the former, and to honour the latter, is the Sheikh's principal business.   Every father of a family sticks his lance into the ground by the side of his tent, and ties his horse in front.   There also his camels repose at night —*Burckhardt, Notes on Bedouins,* vol. i. p. 33.

The following is descriptive of the Arabs of Assyria, though it is applicable, in a great degree, to the whole race.

"It would be difficult to describe the appearance of a large tribe when migrating to new pastures.   We soon found ourselves in the midst of wide-spreading flocks of sheep and camels.   As far as the eye could reach, to the right, to the left, and in front, still the same moving crowd.   Long lines of asses and bullocks, laden with black tents, huge caldrons, and variegated carpets ; aged women and men, no longer able to walk, tied on the heap of domestic furniture; infants crammed into saddlebags, their tiny heads thrust through the narrow opening, balanced on the animal's back by kids or lambs tied on the opposite side; young girls clothed only in the close-fitting Arab shirt, which displayed rather than concealed their graceful forms; mothers with their children on their shoulders; boys driving flocks of lambs; horsemen armed with their long tufted spears, scouring the plain on their fleet mares; riders urging their dromedaries with their short-hooked sticks, and leading their high-bred steeds by the halter; colts galloping among the throng; such was the motley crowd through which we had to wend our way."—*Layard's Nineveh,* i. 4.

mily, and often involved the honour of his tribe; and these debts of blood sometimes remained unsettled for generations, producing deadly feuds.

The necessity of being always on the alert to defend his flocks and herds, made the Arab of the desert familiar from his infancy with the exercise of arms. None could excel him in the use of the bow, the lance and the scimitar, and the adroit and graceful management of the horse. He was a predatory warrior also ; for though at times he was engaged in the service of the merchant, furnishing him with camels and guides and drivers for the transportation of his merchandise, he was more apt to lay contributions on the caravan or plunder it outright in its toilful progress through the desert. All this he regarded as a legitimate exercise of arms; looking down upon the gainful sons of traffic as an inferior race, debased by sordid habits and pursuits.

Such was the Arab of the desert, the dweller in tents, in whom was fulfilled the prophetic destiny of his ancestor Ishmael. "He will be a wild man; his hand will be against every man, and every man's hand against him."[1] Nature had fitted him for his destiny. His form was light and meagre, but sinewy and active, and capable of sustaining great fatigue and hardship. He was temperate and even abstemious, requiring but little food, and that of the simplest kind. His mind like his body was light and agile. He eminently possessed the intellectual attributes of the Shemitic race, penetrating sagacity, subtle wit, a ready conception, and a brilliant imagination. His sensibilities were quick and acute, though not lasting; a proud and daring spirit was stamped on his sallow visage and flashed from his dark and kindling eye. He was easily aroused by the appeals of eloquence, and charmed by the graces of poetry. Speaking a language copious in the extreme, the words of which have been compared to gems and flowers, he was naturally an orator; but he delighted in proverbs and apothegms, rather than in sustained flights of declamation, and was prone to convey his ideas in the oriental style by apologue and parable.

Though a restless and predatory warrior, he was generous and hospitable. He delighted in giving gifts; his door was always open to the wayfarer, with whom he was ready to share his last morsel ; and his deadliest foe, having once broken bread with him, might repose securely beneath the inviolable sanctity of his tent.

In religion the Arabs, in what they term the Days of Ignorance, partook largely of the two faiths, the Sabean and the Magian, which at that time prevailed over the eastern world. The Sabean, however, was the one to which they most adhered. They pretended to derive it from Sabi the son of Seth, who, with his father and his brother Enoch, they suppose to be buried in the pyramids. Others derive the name from the Hebrew word, Saba, or the Stars, and trace the origin of the faith to the Assyrian shepherds, who as they watched their flocks by night on their level plains, and beneath their cloudless skies, noted the aspects and movements of the heavenly bodies, and formed theories of their good and evil influences on

1 Genesis xvi. 12.

human affairs; vague notions which the Chaldean philosophers and priests reduced to a system, supposed to be more ancient even than that of the Egyptians.

By others it is derived from still higher authority, and claimed to be the religion of the antediluvian world. It survived, say they, the deluge, and was continued among the patriarchs. It was taught by Abraham, adopted by his descendants, the children of Israel, and sanctified and confirmed in the tablets of the law delivered unto Moses, amid the thunder and lightning of Mount Sinai.

In its original state the Sabean faith was pure and spiritual; inculcating a belief in the unity of God, the doctrine of a future state of rewards and punishments, and the necessity of a virtuous and holy life to obtain a happy immortality. So profound was the reverence of the Sabeans for the Supreme Being, that they never mentioned his name, nor did they venture to approach him, but through intermediate intelligences or angels. These were supposed to inhabit and animate the heavenly bodies, in the same way as the human body is inhabited and animated by a soul. They were placed in their respective spheres to supervise and govern the universe in subserviency to the Most High. In addressing themselves to the stars and other celestial luminaries, therefore, the Sabeans did not worship them as deities, but sought only to propitiate their angelic occupants as intercessors with the Supreme Being ; looking up through these created things to God the great creator.

By degrees this religion lost its original simplicity and purity, and became obscured by mysteries, and degraded by idolatries. The Sabeans, instead of regarding the heavenly bodies as the habitations of intermediate agents, worshipped them as deities; set up graven images in honour of them, in sacred groves and in the gloom of forests; and at length enshrined these idols in temples, and worshipped them as if instinct with divinity. The Sabean faith too underwent changes and modifications in the various countries through which it was diffused. Egypt has long been accused of reducing it to the most abject state of degradation; the statues, hieroglyphics, and painted sepulchres of that mysterious country, being considered records of the worship, not merely of celestial intelligences, but of the lowest order of created beings, and even of inanimate objects. Modern investigation and research, however, are gradually rescuing the most intellectual nation of antiquity from this aspersion, and as they slowly lift the veil of mystery which hangs over the tombs of Egypt, are discovering that all these apparent objects of adoration were but symbols of the varied attributes of the one Supreme Being, whose name was too sacred to be pronounced by mortals. Among the Arabs the Sabean faith became mingled with wild superstitions, and degraded by gross idolatry. Each tribe worshipped its particular star or planet, or set up its particular idol. Infanticide mingled its horrors with their religious rites. Among the nomadic tribes the birth of a daughter was considered a misfortune, her sex rendering her of little service in a wandering and predatory life, while she might bring disgrace upon her family by misconduct or captivity. Motives of unnatural policy, therefore, may have mingled with their religious feelings, in offering up female infants as sacrifices to their idols, or in burying them alive.

The rival sect of Magians or Guebres (fire worshippers), which as we have said, divided the religious empire of the East, took its rise in Persia, where, after a while, its oral doctrines were reduced to writing by its great prophet and teacher Zoroaster, in his volume of the Zendavesta. The creed, like that of the Sabeans, was originally simple and spiritual, inculcating a belief in one supreme and eternal God, in whom and by whom the universe exists: that he produced, through his creating word, two active principles, Ormusd, the principle or angel of light or good, and Ahriman, the principle or angel of darkness or evil: that these formed the world out of a mixture of their opposite elements, and were engaged in a perpetual contest in the regulation of its affairs. Hence the vicissitudes of good and evil, accordingly as the angel of light or darkness has the upper hand: this contest would continue until the end of the world, when there would be a general resurrection and a day of judgment: the angel of darkness and his disciples would then be banished to an abode of woful gloom, and their opponents would enter the blissful realms of ever during light.

The primitive rites of this religion were extremely simple. The Magians had neither temples, altars, nor religious symbols of any kind, but addressed their prayers and hymns directly to the Deity, in what they conceived to be his residence, the sun. They reverenced this luminary as being his abode, and as the source of the light and heat of which all the other heavenly bodies were composed; and they kindled fires upon the mountain tops to supply light during its absence. Zoroaster first introduced the use of temples, wherein sacred fire, pretended to be derived from heaven, was kept perpetually alive through the guardianship of priests, who maintained a watch over it night and day.

In process of time this sect, like that of the Sabeans, lost sight of the divine principle in the symbol, and came to worship light or fire, as the real Deity, and to abhor darkness as Satan or the devil. In their fanatic zeal the Magians would seize upon unbelievers and offer them up in the flames to propitiate their fiery deity.

To the tenets of these two sects reference is made in that beautiful text of the wisdom of Solomon: "Surely vain are all men by nature who are ignorant of God, and could not, by considering the work, acknowledge the work master; but deemed either fire, or wind, or the swift air, or the circle of the stars, or the violent water, or the lights of heaven, to be gods, which govern the world."

Of these two faiths the Sabean, as we have before observed, was much the most prevalent among the Arabs; but in an extremely degraded form, mingled with all kinds of abuses, and varying among the various tribes. The Magian faith prevailed among thoses tribes which, from their frontier position, had frequent intercourse with Persia; while other tribes partook of the superstitions and idolatries of the nations on which they bordered.

Judaism had made its way into Arabia at an early period, but very vaguely and imperfectly. Still many of its rites and ceremonies, and fanciful traditions, became implanted in the country. At a later day, however, when Palestine was ravaged by the Romans, and the city of Jerusalem taken and sacked, many of the Jews took refuge among the Arabs; became incorporated with the native tribes; formed themselves into communities; acquired possession of fertile tracts; built castles and strongholds, and rose to considerable power and influence.

The Christian religion had likewise its adherents among the Arabs. St. Paul himself declares in his epistle to the Galatians, that soon after he had been called to preach Christianity among the heathens, he " went into Arabia." The dissensions, also, which rose in the Eastern church, in the early part of the third century, breaking it up into sects, each persecuting the others as it gained the ascendency, drove many into exile into remote parts of the East; filled the deserts of Arabia with anchorites, and planted the Christian faith among some of the principal tribes.

The foregoing circumstances, physical and moral, may give an idea of the causes which maintained the Arabs for ages in an unchanged condition. While their isolated position and their vast deserts protected them from conquest, their internal feuds, and their want of a common tie, political or religious, kept them from being formidable as conquerors. They were a vast aggregation of distinct parts; full of individual vigour, but wanting coherent strength. Although their nomadic life rendered them hardy and active; although the greater part of them were warriors from infancy, yet their arms were only wielded against each other, excepting some of the frontier tribes, which occasionally engaged as mercenaries in external wars. While, therefore, the other nomadic races of Central Asia, possessing no greater aptness for warfare, had, during a course of ages, successively overrun and conquered the civilized world, this warrior race, unconscious of its power, remained disjointed and harmless in the depths of its native deserts.

The time at length arrived when its discordant tribes were to be united in one creed, and animated by one common cause; when a mighty genius was to arise, who should bring together these scattered limbs, animate them with his own enthusiastic and daring spirit, and lead them forth, a giant of the desert, to shake and overturn the empires of the earth.

CHAPTER II.

Birth and parentage of Mahomet.—His infancy and childhood.

Mahomet, the great founder of the faith of Islam, was born in Mecca, in April, in the year 569 of the Christian era. He was of the valiant and illustrious tribe of Koreish, of which there were two branches, descended from two brothers, Haschem and Abd

Schems. Haschem, the progenitor of Mahomet, was a great benefactor of Mecca. This city is situated in the midst of a barren and stony country, and in former times was often subject to scarcity of provisions. At the beginning of the sixth century Haschem established two yearly caravans, one in the winter to South Arabia or Yemen; the other in the summer to Syria. By these means abundant supplies were brought to Mecca, as well as a great variety of merchandise. The city became a commercial mart, and the tribe of Koreish, which engaged largely in these expeditions, became wealthy and powerful. Haschem, at this time, was the guardian of the Caaba, the great shrine of Arabian pilgrimage and worship, the custody of which was confided to none but the most honourable tribes and families, in the same manner as in old times, the temple of Jerusalem was intrusted only to the care of the Levites. In fact the guardianship of the Caaba was connected with civil dignities and privileges, and gave the holder of it the control of the sacred city.

On the death of Haschem, his son, Abd al Motâlleb, succeeded to his honours, and inherited his patriotism. He delivered the holy city from an invading army of troops and elephants, sent by the Christian princes of Abyssinia, who at that time held Yemen in subjection. These signal services rendered by father and son, confirmed the guardianship of the Caaba in the line of Haschem; to the great discontent and envy of the line of Abd Schems.

Abd al Motâlleb had several sons and daughters. Those of his sons who figure in history were, Abu Taleb, Abu Lâhab, Abbas, Hamza, and Abdallah. The last named was the youngest and best beloved. He married Amina, a maiden of a distant branch of the same illustrious stock of Koreish. So remarkable was Abdallah for personal beauty and those qualities which win the affections of women, that, if Moslem traditions are to be credited, on the night of his marriage with Amina, two hundred virgins of the tribe of Koreish died of broken hearts.

Mahomet was the first and only fruit of the marriage thus sadly celebrated. His birth, according to similar traditions with the one just cited, was accompanied by signs and portents announcing a child of wonder. His mother suffered none of the pangs of travail. At the moment of his coming into the world, a celestial light illumined the surrounding country, and the new-born child, raising his eyes to heaven, exclaimed : " God is great! There is no God but God, and I am his prophet."

Heaven and earth, we are assured, were agitated at his advent. The Lake Sawa shrank back to its secret springs, leaving its borders dry; while the Tigris, bursting its bounds, overflowed the neighbouring lands. The palace of Khosru the king of Persia shook to its foundations, and several of its towers were toppled to the earth. In that troubled night the Kadhi, or Judge of Persia, beheld, in a dream, a ferocious camel conquered by an Arabian courser. He related his dream in the morning to the Persian monarch, and inter preted it to portend danger from the quarter of Arabia.

In the same eventful night the sacred fire of Zoroaster, which, guarded by the Magi, had burned without interruption for upwards of a thousand years, was suddenly extinguished, and all the idols in the world fell down.   The demons, or evil genii, which lurk in the stars and the signs of the zodiac, and exert a malignant influence over the children of men, were cast forth by the pure angels, and hurled, with their arch leader, Eblis, or Lucifer, into the depths of the sea.

The relatives of the new-born child, say the like authorities, were filled with awe and wonder.   His mother's brother, an astrologer, cast his nativity, and predicted that he would rise to vast power, found an empire, and establish a new faith among men.   His grandfather, Abd al Motâlleb, gave a feast to the principal Koreishites, the seventh day after his birth, at which he presented this child, as the dawning glory of their race, and gave him the name of Mahomet (or Muhamed), indicative of his future renown.

Such are the marvellous accounts given by Moslem writers of the infancy of Mahomet, and we have little else than similar fables about his early years.   He was scarce two months old when his father died, leaving him no other inheritance than five camels, a few sheep, and a female slave of Ethiopia, named Barakat.   His mother, Amina, had hitherto nurtured him, but care and sorrow dried the fountains of her breast, and the air of Mecca being unhealthy for children, she sought a nurse for him among the females of the neighbouring Bedouin tribes.   These were accustomed to come to Mecca twice a year, in spring and autumn, to foster the children of its inhabitants; but they looked for the offspring of the rich, where they were sure of ample recompense, and turned with contempt from this heir of poverty. At length Ilalêma, the wife of a Saadite shepherd, was moved to compassion, and took the helpless infant to her home.   It was in one of the pastoral valleys of the mountains. [1]

Many were the wonders related by Halêma of her infant charge. On the journey from Mecca, the mule which bore him became miraculously endowed with speech, and proclaimed aloud that he bore on his back the greatest of prophets, the chief of ambassadors, the favourite of the Almighty.   The sheep bowed to him as he passed; as he lay in his cradle and gazed at the moon, it stooped to him in reverence.

The blessing of heaven, say the Arabian writers, rewarded the charity of Halêma.   While the child remained under her roof, every thing around her prospered.   The wells and springs were never dried up; the pastures were always green; her flocks and herds increased tenfold; a marvellous abundance reigned over her fields, and peace prevailed in her dwelling.

The arabian legends go on to extol the almost supernatural powers, bodily and mental, manifested by this wonderfuld child at a very early age.   He could stand alone when three months old ; run abroad when he was seven, and at ten could join other children

---

[1] The Beni Sad (or children of Sad) date from the most remote antiquity, and, with the Katan Arabs, are the only remnants of the primitive tribes of Arabia.   Their valley is among the mountains which range southwardly from the Tayef.—*Burckhardt on the Bedouins*, vol. ii. p. 47.

in their sports with bows and arrows. At eight months he could speak so as to be understood; and in the course of another month could converse with fluency, displaying a wisdom astonishing to all who heard him.

At the age of three years, while playing in the fields with his foster brother, Masroud, two angels in shining apparel appeared before them. They laid Mahomet gently upon the ground, and Gabriel, one of the angels, opened his breast, but without inflicting any pain. Then taking forth his heart, he cleansed it from all impurity, wringing from it those black and bitter drops of original sin, inherited from our forefather Adam, and which lurk in the hearts of the best of his descendants, inciting them to crime. When he had thoroughly purified it, he filled it with faith and knowledge and prophetic light, and replaced it in the bosom of the child. Now, we are assured by the same authorities, began to emanate from his countenance that mysterious light which had continued down from Adam, through the sacred line of prophets, until 'the time of Isaac and Ishmael; but which had lain dormant in the descendants of the latter, until it thus shone forth with renewed radiance from the features of Mahomet.

At this supernatural visitation, it is added, was impressed between the shoulders of the child the seal of prophecy, which continued throughout life the symbol and credential of his divine mission; though unbelievers saw nothing in it but a large mole, the size of a pigeon's egg.

When the marvellous visitation of the angel was related to Halêma and her husband, they were alarmed lest some misfortune should be impending over the child, or that his supernatural visitors might be of the race of evil spirits or genii, which haunt the solitudes of the desert, wreaking mischief on the children of men. His Saadite nurse, therefore, carried him back to Mecca, and delivered him to his mother Amina.

He remained with his parent until his sixth year, when she took him with her to Medina, on a visit to her relatives of the tribe of Adij, but on her journey homeward she died, and was buried at Ahwa, a village between Medina and Mecca. Her grave it will be found, was a place of pious resort and tender recollection to her son, at the latest period of his life.

The faithful Abyssinian slave Barakat, now acted as a mother to the orphan child, and conducted him to his grand-father Abd al Motâlleb, in whose household he remained for two years, treated with care and tenderness. Abd al Motâlleb was now well stricken in years; having outlived the ordinary term of human existence. Finding his end approaching, he called to him his eldest son Abu Taleb, and bequeathed Mahomet to his especial protection. The good Abu Taleb took his nephew to his bosom, and ever afterwards was to him as a parent. As the former succeeded to the guardianship of the Caaba at the death of his father, Mahomet continued for several years in a kind of sacerdotal household, where the rites and ceremonies of the sacred house were rigidly observed. And here we deem it necessary to give a more especial notice of the alleged origin of the Caaba, and of the rites and traditions and superstitions connected with it, closely interwoven as they are with the faith of Islam and the story of its founder.

CHAPTER III.

Traditions concerning Mecca and the Caaba.

When Adam and Eve were cast forth from Paradise, say Arabian traditions, they fell in different parts of the earth; Adam on a mountain of the island of Serendib, or Ceylon; Eve in Arabia on the borders of the Red Sea, where the port of Joddah is situated. For two hundred years they wandered separate and lonely about the earth, until, in consideration of their penitence and wretchedness, they were permitted to come together again on Mount Arafat, not far from the present city of Mecca. In the depth of his sorrow and repentance, Adam, it is said, raised his hands and eyes to heaven, and implored the clemency of God; entreating that a shrine might be vouchsafed to him similar to that at which he had worshipped when in Paradise, and round which the angels used to move in adoring processions.

The supplication of Adam was effectual. A tabernacle or temple formed of radiant clouds was lowered down by the hands of angels, and placed immediately below its prototype in the celestial paradise. Towards this heaven-descended shrine, Adam thenceforth turned when in prayer, and round it he daily made seven circuits in imitation of the rites of the adoring angels.

At the death of Adam, say the same traditions, the tabernacle of clouds passed away, or was again drawn up to heaven; but another, of the same form and in the same place, was built of stone and clay by Seth, the son of Adam. This was swept away by the deluge. Many generations afterwards, in the time of the patriarchs, when Hagar and her child Ishmael were near perishing with thirst in the desert, an angel revealed to them a spring or well of water, near to the ancient site of the tabernacle. This was the well of Zem Zem, held sacred by the progeny of Ishmael to the present day. Shortly afterwards two individuals of the gigantic race of the Amalekites, in quest of a camel which had strayed from their camp, discovered this well, and, having slaked their thirst, brought their companions to the place. Here they founded the city of Mecca, taking Ishmael and his mother under their protection. They were soon expelled by the proper inhabitants of the country, among whom Ishmael remained. When grown to man's estate, he married the daughter of the ruling prince, by whom he had a numerous progeny, the ancestors of the Arabian people. In process of time, by God's command he undertook to rebuild the Caaba, on the precise site of the original tabernacle of clouds. In this pious work he was assisted by his father Abraham. A miraculous stone served Abraham as a scaffold, rising and sinking with him as he built the walls of the sacred edifice. It still remains there an inestimable relic, and the print of the patriarch's foot is clearly to be perceived on it by all true believers.

While Abraham and Ishmael were thus occupied, the angel Gabriel brought them a stone, about which traditional accounts are a little at variance; by some it is said to have been one of the precious stones of Paradise, which fell to the earth with Adam, and was afterwards lost in the slime of the deluge, until retrieved by the angel Gabriel. The more received tradition is, that it was originally the guardian angel appointed to watch over Adam in Paradise, but changed into a stone and ejected thence with him at his fall, as a punishment for not having been more vigilant. This stone Abraham and Ishmael received with proper reverence, and inserted it in a corner of the exterior wall of the Caaba, where it remains to the present day, devoutly kissed by worshippers each time they make a circuit of the temple. When first inserted in the wall it was, we are told, a single jacinth of dazzling whiteness, but became gradually blackened by the kisses of sinful mortals. At the resurrection it will recover its angelic form, and stand forth a testimony before God in favour of those who have faithfully performed the rites of pilgrimage.

Such are the Arabian traditions, which rendered the Caaba and the well of Zem Zem, objects of extraordinary veneration from the remotest antiquity among the people of the East, and especially the descendants of Ishmael. Mecca, which incloses these sacred objects within its walls, was a holy city many ages before the rise of Mahometanism, and was the resort of pilgrims from all parts of Arabia. So universal and profound was the religious feeling respecting this observance, that four months in every year were devoted to the rites of pilgrimage, and held sacred from all violence and warfare. Hostile tribes then laid aside their arms; took the heads from their spears; traversed the late dangerous deserts in security; thronged the gates of Mecca clad in the pilgrim's garb; made their seven circuits round the Caaba in imitation of the angelic host; touched and kissed the mysterious black stone; drank and made ablutions at the well Zem Zem in memory of their ancestor Ishmael; and having performed all the other primitive rites of pilgrimage returned home in safety, again to resume their weapons and their wars.

Among the religious observances of the Arabs in these their "days of ignorance;" that is to say, before the promulgation of the Moslem doctrines, fasting and prayer had a foremost place. They had three principal fasts within the year; one of seven, one of nine, and one of thirty days. They prayed three times each day: about sunrise, at noon, and about sunset; turning their faces in the direction of the Caaba, which was their kebla, or point of adoration. They had many religious traditions, some of them acquired in early times from the Jews, and they are said to have nurtured their devotional feelings with the book of Psalms, and with a book said to be by Seth, and filled with moral discourses.

Brought up, as Mahomet was, in the house of the guardian of the Caaba, the ceremonies and devotions connected with the sacred edifice may have given an early bias to his mind, and inclined it to those speculations in matters of religion by which it eventually became engrossed.   Though his Moslem biographers would fain persuade us his high destiny was clearly foretold in his childhood by signs and prodigies, yet his education appears to have been as much neglected as that of ordinary Arab children ; for we find that he was not taught either to read or write.   He was a thoughtful child, however ; quick to observe, prone to meditate on all that he observed, and possessed of an imagination fertile, daring, and expansive.   The yearly influx of pilgrims from distant parts made Mecca a receptacle for all kinds of floating knowledge, which he appears to have imbibed with eagerness and retained in a tenacious memory ; and as he increased in years, a more extended sphere of observation was gradually opened to him.

CHAPTER IV.

First journey of Mahomet with the caravan to Syria.

Mahomet was now twelve years of age, but, as we have shown, he had an intelligence far beyond his years.   The spirit of inquiry was awake within him, quickened by intercourse with pilgrims from all parts of Arabia.   His uncle Abu Taleb, too, beside his sacerdotal character as guardian of the Caaba, was one of the most enterprising merchants of the tribe of Koreish, and had much to do with those caravans set on foot by his ancestor Haschem, which traded to Syria and Yemen.   The arrival and departure of those caravans, which thronged the gates of Mecca and filled its streets with pleasing tumult, were exciting events to a youth like Mahomet, and carried his imagination to foreign parts.   He could no longer repress the ardent curiosity thus aroused ; but once, when his uncle was about to mount his camel to depart with the caravan for Syria, clung to him, and entreated to be permitted to accompany him : " For who, oh my uncle," said he, " will take care of me when thou art away ? "

The appeal was not lost upon the kind-hearted Abu Taleb.   He bethought him, too, that the youth was of an age to enter upon the active scenes of Arab life, and of a capacity to render essential service in the duties of the caravan ; he readily, therefore, granted his prayer, and took him with him on the journey to Syria.

The route lay through regions fertile in fables and traditions, which it is the delight of the Arabs to recount in the evening halts of the caravan   The vast solitudes of the desert, in which that wandering people pass so much of their lives, are prone to engender superstitious fancies ; they have accordingly peopled them with good and evil genii, and clothed them with tales of enchantment, mingled up with wonderful events which happened in days of old.   In these evening halts of the caravan, the youthful mind of Mahomet doubtless imbibed many of those superstitions of the desert which ever afterwards dwelt in his memory, and had a powerful influence over his imagination. We may especially note two traditions which he must have heard at this time, and which we find recorded by him in after years in the Koran. One related to the mountainous district of Hedjar. Here, as the caravan wound its way through silent and deserted valleys, caves were pointed out in the sides of the mountains once inhabited by the Beni Thamud, or children of Thamud, one of the "lost tribes" of Arabia; and this was the tradition concerning them.

They were a proud and gigantic race, existing before the time of the patriarch Abraham. Having fallen into blind idolatry, God sent a prophet of the name of Saleh, to restore them to the right way. They refused, however, to listen to him, unless he should prove the divinity of his mission by causing a camel, big with young, to issue from the entrails of a mountain. Saleh accordingly prayed, and lo! a rock opened, and a female camel came forth, which soon produced a foal. Some of the Thamudites were convinced by the miracle, and were converted by the prophet from their idolatry; the greater part, however, remained in unbelief. Saleh left the camel among them as a sign, warning them that a judgment from heaven would fall on them, should they do her any harm. For a time the camel was suffered to feed quietly in their pastures, going forth in the morning, and returning in the evening. It is true, that when she bowed her head to drink from a brook or well, she never raised it until she had drained the last drop of water; but then in return she yielded milk enough to supply the whole tribe. As, however, she frightened the other camels from the pasture, she became an object of offence to the Thamudites, who hamstrung and slew her. Upon this there was a fearful cry from heaven, and great claps of thunder, and in the morning all the offenders were found lying on their faces, dead. Thus the whole race was swept from the earth, and their country was laid for ever afterward under the ban of heaven.

This story made a powerful impression on the mind of Mahomet, insomuch that, in after years, he refused to let his people encamp in the neighbourhood, but hurried them away from it as an accursed region.

Another tradition, gathered on this journey, related to the city of Eyla, situated near the Red Sea. This place, he was told, had been inhabited in old times by a tribe of Jews, who lapsed into idolatry and profaned the Sabbath, by fishing on that sacred day; whereupon the old men were transformed into swine, and the young men into monkeys.

We have noted these two traditions especially because they are both cited by Mahomet as instances of divine judgment on the crime of idolatry, and evince the bias his youthful mind was already taking on that important subject.

Moslem writers tell us, as usual, of wonderful circumstances which attended the youth throughout this journey, giving evidence of the continual guardianship of heaven. At one time, as he traversed the burning sands of the desert, an angel hovered over him unseen, sheltering him with his wings; a miracle, however, which evidently does not rest on the evidence of an eye-witness; at another time he was protected by a cloud which hung over his head during the noontide heat; and on another occasion, as he sought the scanty shade of a withered tree, it suddenly put forth leaves and blossoms.

After skirting the ancient domains of the Moabites and the Ammonites, often mentioned in the sacred Scriptures, the caravan arrived at Bosra, or Bostra, on the confines of Syria, in the country of the tribe of Manasseh, beyond the Jordan.   In Scripture days it had been a city of the Levites, but now was inhabited by Nestorian Christians.   It was a great mart, annually visited by the caravans; and here our wayfarers came to a halt, and encamped near a convent of Nestorian monks.

By this fraternity Abu Taleb and his nephew were entertained with great hospitality.   One of the monks, by some called Sergius, by others Bahira, [1] on conversing with Mahomet, was surprised at the precocity of his intellect, and interested by his eager desire for information, which appears to have had reference, principally, to matters of religion.   They had frequent conversations together on such subjects, in the course of which the efforts of the monk must have been mainly directed against that idolatry in which the youthful Mahomet had hitherto been educated; for the Nestorian Christians were strenuous in condemning not merely the worship of images, but even the casual exhibition of them; indeed, so far did they carry their scruples on this point, that even the cross, that general emblem of Christianity, was in a great degree included in this prohibition.

Many have ascribed that knowledge of the principles and traditions of the Christian faith displayed by Mahomet in after life, to those early conversations with this monk; it is probable, however, that he had further intercourse with the latter in the course of subsequent visits which he made to Syria.

Moslem writers pretend that the interest taken by the monk in the youthful stranger, arose from his having accidentally perceived between his shoulders the seal of prophecy.   He warned Abu Taleb, say they, when about to set out on his return to Mecca, to take care that his nephew did not fall into the hands of the Jews; foreseeing with the eye of prophecy the trouble and opposition he was to encounter from that people.

It required no miraculous sign, however, to interest a sectarian monk anxious to make proselytes, in an intelligent and inquiring youth, nephew of the guardian of the Caaba, who might carry back with him to Mecca the seeds of Christianity sown in his tender mind; and it was natural that the monk should be eager to prevent his hoped-for convert, in the present unsettled state of his religious opinions, from being beguiled into the Jewish faith.

Mahomet returned to Mecca, his imagination teeming with the wild tales and traditions picked up in the desert, and his mind deeply impressed with the doctrines imparted to him in the Nestorian convent.   He seems ever afterwards to have entertained a

---

[1] Some assert that these two names indicate two monks, who held conversations with Mahomet.

mysterious reverence for Syria, probably from the religious impressions received there. It was the land whither Abraham the patriarch had repaired from Chaldea, taking with him the primitive worship of the one true God. "Verily," he used to say in after years, " God has ever maintained guardians of his word in Syria; forty in number; when one dies another is sent in his room; and through them the land is blessed." And again—" Joy be to the people of Syria, for the angels of the kind God spread their wings over them. " [1]

NOTE.—The conversion of Abraham from the idolatry into which the world had fallen after the deluge, is related in the Sixth Chapter of the Koran. Abraham's father, Azer, or Zerah, as his name is given in the Scriptures, was a statuary and an idolater.

"And Abraham said unto his father Azer, ' Why dost thou take graven images for gods? Verily, thou and thy people are in error.'

" Then was the firmament of heaven displayed unto Abraham, that he might see how the world was governed.

"When night came, and darkness overshadowed the earth, he beheld a bright star shining in the firmament, and cried out to his people who were astrologers : ' This, according to your assertions, is the Lord.'

" But the star set: and Abraham said, ' I have no faith in gods that set.'

" He beheld the moon rising, and exclaimed, ' Assuredly, this is the Lord.' But the moon likewise set, and he was confounded, and prayed unto God, saying, ' Direct me, lest I become as one of these people, who go astray.'

"When he saw the sun rising, he cried out, ' This is the most glorious of all ; this of a certainty is the Lord.' But the sun also set. Then said Abraham, ' I believe not, oh my people, in those things which ye call gods. Verily, I turn my face unto Him, the Creator, who hath formed both the heavens and the earth.' "

CHAPTER V.

Commercial occupations of Mahomet.—His marriage with Cadijah

Mahomet was now completely launched in active life, accompanying his uncles in various expeditions. At one time, when about sixteen years of age, we find him with his uncle Zobier, journeying with the caravan to Yemen; at another time acting as armour-bearer to the same uncle, who led a warlike expedition of Koreishites in aid of the Kenanites against the tribe of Hawazan. This is cited as Mahomet's first essay in arms, though he did little else than supply his uncle with arrows in the heat of the action, and shield him from the darts of the enemy. It is stigmatized among Arabian writers as al Fadjar, or the impious war, having been carried on during the sacred months of pilgrimage.

As Mahomet advanced in years, he was employed by different persons as commercial agent or factor in caravan journeys to Syria, Yemen, and elsewhere; all which tended to enlarge the

[1] Mishcât-ul-Masâbih, vol. ii, p. 812.

sphere of his observation, and to give him a quick insight into character and a knowledge of human affairs.

He was a frequent attender of fairs also, which, in Arabia, were not always mere resorts of traffic, but occasionally scenes of poetical contests between different tribes, where prizes were adjudged to the victors, and their prize poems treasured up in the archives of princes. Such, especially, was the case with the fair of Ocadh; and seven of the prize poems adjudged there, were hung up as trophies in the Caaba. At these fairs, also, were recited the popular traditions of the Arabs, and inculcated the various religious faiths which were afloat in Arabia. From oral sources of this kind, Mahomet gradually accumulated much of that varied information as to creeds and doctrines which he afterwards displayed.

There was at this time residing in Mecca a widow, named Cadijah (or Khadijah), of the tribe of Koreish. She had been twice married. Her last husband, a wealthy merchant, had recently died, and the extensive concerns of the house were in need of a conductor. A nephew of the widow, named Chuzima, had become acquainted with Mahomet in the course of his commercial expeditions, and had noticed the ability and integrity with which he acquitted himself on all occasions. He pointed him out to his aunt as a person well qualified to be her factor. The personal appearance of Mahomet may have strongly seconded this recommendation; for he was now about twenty-five years of age, and extolled by Arabian writers for his manly beauty and engaging manners. So desirous was Cadijah of securing his services, that she offered him double wages to conduct a caravan which she was on the point of sending off to Syria. Mahomet consulted his uncle Abu Taleb, and by his advice, accepted the offer. He was accompanied and aided in the expedition by the nephew of the widow, and by her slave Maïsara, and so highly satisfied was Cadijah with the way in which he discharged his duties, that, on his return, she paid him double the amount of his stipulated wages. She afterwards sent him to the southern parts of Arabia on similar expeditions, in all which he gave like satisfaction.

Cadijah was now in her fortieth year, a woman of judgment and experience. The mental qualities of Mahomet rose more and more in her estimation, and her heart began to yearn toward the fresh and comely youth. According to Arabian legends, a miracle occurred most opportunely to confirm and sanctify the bias of her inclinations. She was one day with her handmaids, at the hour of noon, on the terraced roof of her dwelling, watching the arrival of a caravan conducted by Mahomet. As it approached, she beheld, with astonishment, two angels overshadowing him with their wings to protect him from the sun. Turning, with emotion, to her handmaids, "Behold!" said she, "the beloved of Allah, who sends two angels to watch over him!"

Whether or not the handmaidens looked forth with the same eyes of devotion as their mistress, and likewise discerned the angels, the legend does not mention. Suffice it to say, the widow was filled with a lively faith in the superhuman merits of her youthful steward, and forthwith commissioned her trusty slave, Maïsara, to offer him her hand. The negotiation is recorded with simple brevity. "Mahomet," demanded Maïsara, "why dost thou not marry?" "I have not the means," replied Mahomet. "Well, but if a wealthy dame should offer thee her hand : one also who is handsome and of high birth?" "And who is she?" "Cadijah!" "How is that possible?" "Let me manage it." Maïsara returned to his mistress and reported what had passed. An hour was appointed for an interview, and the affair was brought to a satisfactory arrangement with that promptness and sagacity which had distinguished Mahomet in all his dealings with the widow. The father of Cadijah made some opposition to the match, on account of the poverty of Mahomet, following the common notion that wealth should be added to wealth : but the widow wisely considered her riches only as the means of enabling her to follow the dictates of her heart. She gave a great feast, to which were invited her father and the rest of her relatives, and Mahomet's uncles Abu Taleb and Hamza, together with several other of the Koreishites. At this banquet wine was served in abundance, and soon diffused good humour round the board. The objections to Mahomet's poverty were forgotten; speeches were made by Abu Taleb on the one side, and by Waraka, a kinsman of Cadijah, on the other, in praise of the proposed nuptials; the dowry was arranged, and the marriage formally concluded

Mahomet then caused a camel to be killed before his door, and the flesh distributed among the poor. The house was thrown open to all comers; the female slaves of Cadijah danced to the sound of timbrels, and all was revelry and rejoicing. Abu Taleb, forgetting his age and his habitual melancholy, made merry on the occasion. He had paid down from his purse a dower of twelve-and-a-half okks of gold, equivalent to twenty young camels. Halêma, who had nursed Mahomet in his infancy, was summoned to rejoice at his nuptials, and was presented with a flock of forty sheep, with which she returned, enriched and contented, to her native valley, in the desert of the Saadites.

CHAPTER VI.

Conduct of Mahomet after his marriage.—Becomes anxious for religious reform.—His habits of solitary abstraction.—The vision of the cave.—His annunciation as a prophet.

The marriage with Cadijah placed Mahomet among the most wealthy of his native city. His moral worth also gave him great influence in the community. Allah, says the historian Abulfeda, had endowed him with every gift necessary to accomplish and adorn an honest man; he was so pure and sincere; so free from every evil thought, that he was commonly known by the name of Al.Almin, or the Faithful.

The great confidence reposed in his judgment and probity, caused him to be frequently referred to as arbiter in disputes between his townsmen. An anecdote is given as illustrative of his sagacity on such occasions. The Caaba having been injured by fire, was undergoing repairs, in the course of which the sacred black stone was to be replaced. A dispute arose among the chiefs of the various tribes, as to which was entitled to perform so august an office, and they agreed to abide by the decision of the first person who should enter by the gate al Harâm. That person happened to be Mahomet. Upon hearing their different claims, he directed that a great cloth should be spread upon the ground, and the stone laid thereon; and that a man from each tribe should take hold of the border of the cloth. In this way the sacred stone was raised equally and at the same time by them all to a level with its allotted place, in which Mahomet fixed it with his own hands.

Four daughters and one son, were the fruit of the marriage with Cadijah. The son was named Kasim, whence Mahomet was occasionally called Abu Kasim, or the father of Kasim, according to Arabian nomenclature. This son, however, died in his infancy.

For several years after his mariage he continued in commerce, visiting the great Arabian fairs, and making distant journeys with the caravans. His expeditions were not as profitable as in the days of his stewardship, and the wealth acquired with his wife diminished, rather than increased in the course of his operations. That wealth, in fact, had raised him above the necessity of toiling for subsistence, and given him leisure to indulge the original bias of his mind; a turn for reverie and religious speculation, which he had evinced from his earliest years. This had been fostered in the course of his journeyings, by his intercourse with Jews and Christians, originally fugitives from persecution, but now gathered into tribes, or forming part of the population of cities. The Arabian deserts too, rife as we have shown them with fanciful superstitions, had furnished aliment for his enthusiastic reveries. Since his marriage with Cadijah, also, he had a household oracle to influence him in his religious opinions. This was his wife's cousin Waraka, a man of speculative mind and flexible faith; originally a Jew; subsequently a Christian; and withal a pretender to astrology. He is worthy of note as being the first on record to translate parts of the Old and New Testament into Arabic. From him Mahomet is supposed to have derived much of his information respecting those writings, and many of the Mishnu and the Talmud, on which he draws so copiously in his Koran.

The knowledge thus variously acquired and treasured up in an uncommonly retentive memory, was in direct hostility to the gross idolatry prevalent in Arabia, and practised at the Caaba. That sacred edifice had gradually become filled and surrounded by idols, to the number of three hundred and sixty, being one for every day of the Arab year. Hither had been brought idols from various parts, the deities of other nations, the chief of which, Hobal, was from Syria, and supposed to have the power of giving rain. Among these idols too, were Abraham and Ishmael, once revered as prophets and progenitors, now represented with divining arrows in their hands, symbols of magic.

Mahomet became more and more sensible of the grossness and absurdity of this idolatry, in proportion as his intelligent mind contrasted it with the spiritual religions, which had been the subjects of his inquiries. Various passages in the Koran show the ruling idea which gradually sprang up in his mind, until it engrossed his thoughts and influenced all his actions. That idea was a religious reform. It had become his fixed belief, deduced from all that he had learnt and meditated, that the only true religion had been revealed to Adam at his creation, and been promulgated and practised in the days of innocence. That religion inculcated the direct and spiritual worship of one true and only God, the creator of the universe.

It was his belief, furthermore, that this religion, so elevated and simple, had repeatedly been corrupted and debased by man, and especially outraged by idolatry; wherefore a succession of prophets each inspired by a revelation from the Most High, had been sent from time to time, and at distant periods, to restore it to its original purity. Such was Noah, such was Abraham, such was Moses, and such was Jesus Christ. By each of these, the true religion had been reinstated upon earth, but had again been vitiated by their followers. The faith as taught and practised by Abraham when he came out of the land of Chaldea, seems especially to have formed a religious standard in his mind, from his veneration for the patriarch as the father of Ishmael, the progenitor of his race.

It appeared to Mahomet that the time for another reform was again arrived. The world had once more lapsed into blind idolatry. It needed the advent of another prophet, authorized by a mandate from on high, to restore the erring children of men to the right path, and to bring back the worship of the Caaba to what it had been in the days of Abraham and the patriarchs. The probability of such an advent, with its attendant reforms, seems to have taken possession of his mind, and produced habits of reverie and meditation, incompatible with the ordinary concerns of life and the bustle of the world. We are told that he gradually absented himself from society, and sought the solitude of a cavern on Mount Hara, about three leagues north of Mecca, where, in emulation of the Christian anchorites of the desert, he would remain days and nights together, engaged in prayer and meditation. In this way he always passed the month of Ramadhan, the holy month of the Arabs. Such intense occupation of the mind on one subject, accompanied by fervent enthusiasm of spirit, could not but have a powerful effect upon his frame. He became subject to dreams, to ectasies and trances. For six months successively, according to one of his historians, he had constant dreams bearing on the subject of his waking thoughts. Often he would lose all cousciousness of surrounding objects, and lie upon the ground as if insensible. Cadijah, who was sometimes the faithful companion of his solitude, beheld these paroxyms with anxious solicitude, and entreated to know the cause; but he evaded her inquiries, or answered them mysteriously. Some of his adversaries have attributed them to epilepsy, but devout Moslems declare them to have been the workings of prophecy; for already, say they, the intimations of the Most High began to dawn, though vaguely, on his spirit; and his mind laboured with conceptions too great for mortal thought. At length, say they, what had hitherto been shadowed out in dreams, was made apparent and distinct by an angelic apparition and a divine annunciation.

It was in the fortieth year of his age, when this famous revelation took place. Accounts are given of it by Moslem writers as if received from his own lips, and it is alluded to in certain passages of the Koran. He was passing, as was his wont, the month of Ramadhan in the cavern of Mount Hara, endeavouring by fasting, prayer, and solitary meditation, to elevate his thoughts to the contemplation of divine truth. It was on the night called by Arabs Al Kader, or the Divine Decree; a night in which, according to the Koran, angels descend to earth, and Gabriel brings down the decrees of God. During that night there is peace on earth, and a holy quiet reigns over all nature until the rising of the morn.

As Mahomet, in the silent watches of the night, lay wrapped in his mantle, he heard a voice calling upon him; uncovering his head, a flood of light broke upon him of such intolerable splendour that he swooned away. On regaining his senses, he beheld an angel in a human form, which, approaching from a distance, displayed a silken cloth covered with written characters. "Read!" said the angel.

"I know not how to read!" replied Mahomet.

"Read!" repeated the angel, "in the name of the Lord, who has created all things; who created man from a clot of blood. Read in the name of the Most High, who taught man the use of the pen; who sheds on his soul the ray of knowledge, and teaches him what before he knew not."

Upon this Mahomet instantly felt his understanding illumined with celestial light, and read what was written on the cloth, which contained the decrees of God, as afterwards promulgated in the Koran. When he had finished the perusal, the heavenly messenger announced, "Oh Mahomet, of a verity, thou art the prophet of God! and I am his angel Gabriel."

Mahomet, we are told, came trembling and agitated to Cadijah in the morning, not knowing whether what he had heard and seen was indeed true, and that he was a prophet decreed to effect that reform so long the object of his meditations; or whether it might not be a mere vision, a delusion of the senses, or worse than all, the apparition of an evil spirit.

Cadijah, however, saw every thing with the eye of faith, and the credulity of an affectionate woman. She saw in it the fruition of her husband's wishes, and the end of his paroxyms and privations. "Joyful tidings dost thou bring!" exclaimed she. "By him, in whose hand is the soul of Cadijah, I will henceforth regard thee as the prophet of our nation. Rejoice," added she, seeing him still cast down; "Allah will not suffer thee to fall to shame. Hast thou not been loving to thy kinsfolk, kind to thy neighbours, charitable to the poor, hospitable to the stranger, faithful to thy word, and ever a defender of the truth?"

Cadijah hastened to communicate what she had heard to her cousin Waraka, the translator of the Scriptures; who, as we have shown, had been a household oracle of Mahomet in matters of religion. He caught at once, and with eagerness, at this miraculous annunciation. "By him in whose hand is the soul of Waraka," exclaimed he; "thou speakest true, oh Cadijah! The angel who has appeared to thy husband is the same who, in days of old, was sent to Moses the son of Amram. His annunciation is true. Thy husband is indeed a prophet!"

The zealous concurrence of the learned Waraka, is said to have had a powerful effect in fortifying the dubious mind of Mahomet.

NOTE.—Dr. Gustav Weil, in a note to *Mohammed der Prophet*, discusses the question of Mahomet's being subject to attacks of epilepsy; which has generally been represented as a slander of his enemies and of Christian writers. It appears, however, to have been asserted by some of the oldest Moslem biographers, and given on the authority of persons about him. He would be seized, they said, with violent trembling, followed by a kind of swoon, or rather convulsion, during which perspiration would stream from his forehead in the coldest weather; he would lie with his eyes closed, foaming at the mouth and bellowing like a young camel. Ayesha one of his wives, and Zeid one of his disciples, are among the persons cited as testifying to that effect. They considered him at such times as under the influence of a revelation. He had such attacks, however, in Mecca, before the Koran was revealed to him. Cadijah feared that he was possessed by evil spirits, and would have called in the aid of a conjurer to exorcise them, but he forbade her. He did not like that any one should see him during these paroxysms. His visions, however, were not always preceded by such attacks. Hareth Ibn Haschem, it is said, once asked him in what manner the revelations were made. "Often," replied he, "the angel appears to me in a human form, and speak to me. Sometimes I hear sounds like the tinkling of a bell, but see nothing. [A ringing in the ears is a symptom of epilepsy.] When the invisible angel has departed, I am possessed of what he has revealed." Some of his revelations he professed to receive direct from God, others in dreams; for the dreams of prophets, he used to say, are revelations.

The reader will find this note of service in throwing some degree of light upon the enigmatical career of this extraordinary man.

CHAPTER VII.

Mahomet inculcates his doctrines secretly and slowly.—Receives further revelations and commands.—Announces it to his kindred.—Manner in which it was received.— Enthusiastic devotion of Ali.—Christian portents.

For a time Mahomet confided his revelations merely to his own household. One of the first to avow himself a believer, was his servant Zeid, an Arab of the tribe of Kalb. This youth had been captured in childhood by a freebooting party of Koreishites, and had come by purchase or lot into the possession of Mahomet. Several years afterwards his father, hearing of his being in Mecca,

repaired thither and offered a considerable sum for his ransom.
" If he chooses to go with thee," said Mahomet, " he shall go
without ransom : but if he chooses to remain with me, why should
I not keep him ? " Zeid preferred to remain, having ever, he said,
been treated more as a son than as a slave. Upon this, Mahomet
publicly adopted him and he had ever since remained with him
in affectionate servitude. Now, on embracing the new faith he
was set entirely free, but it will be found that he continued through
life that devoted attachment which Mahomet seems to have had
the gift of inspiring in his followers and dependents.

The early steps of Mahomet in his prophetic career, were perilous and doubtful, and taken in secrecy. He had hostility to apprehend on every side ; from his immediate kindred, the Koreishites
of the line of Haschem, whose power and prosperity were identified with idolatry ; and still more from the rival line of Abd
Schems, who had long looked with envy and jealousy on the
Haschemites, and would eagerly raise the cry of heresy and impiety to dispossess them of the guardianship of the Caaba. At the
head of this rival branch of Koreish was Abu Sofian, the son of
Harb, grandson of Omeya, and great grandson of Abd Schems.
He was an able and ambitious man, of great wealth and influence,
and will be found one of the most persevering and powerful opponents of Mahomet.[1]

Under these adverse circumstances the new faith was propagated
secretly and slowly, insomuch that for the first three years the
number of converts did not exceed forty ; these, too, for the most
part, were young persons, strangers, and slaves. Their meetings
for prayer were held in private, either at the house of one of the
initiated, or in a cave near Mecca. Their secrecy, however, did
not protect them from outrage. Their meetings were discovered ;
a rabble broke into their cavern and a scuffle ensued. One of the
assailants was wounded in the head by Saad, an armourer, thenceforth renowned among the faithful, as the first of their number
who shed blood in the cause of Islam.

One of the bitterest opponents of Mahomet, was his uncle Abu
Lahab, a wealthy man, of proud spirit and irritable temper. His
son Otha had married Mahomet's third daughter, Rokaia, so that
they were doubly allied. Abu Lahab, however, was also allied to
the rival line of Koreish, having married Omm Jemil, sister of Abu
Sofian, and he was greatly under the control of his wife and his
brother-in-law. He reprobated what he termed the heresies of
his nephew, as calculated to bring disgrace upon their immediate
line, and to draw upon it the hostilities of the rest of the tribe of
Koreish. Mahomet was keenly sensible of the rancorous opposition of this uncle, which he attributed to the instigations of his
wife, Omm Jemil. He especially deplored it, as he saw that it
affected the happiness of his daughter Rokaia, whose inclination

---

[1] Niebuhr (Travels, vol. ii.) speaks of the tribe of Harb, which possessed several
cities and a number of villages in the highlands of Hedjas, a mountainous range between
Mecca and Medina. They have castles on precipitous rocks, and harass and lay under
contribution the caravans. It is presumed that this tribe takes its name from the father
of Abu Sofian ; as did the great line of the Omeyades from his grandfather.

to his doctrines brought on her the reproaches of her husband and his family.

These and other causes of solicitude preyed upon his spirits, and increased the perturbation of his mind. He became worn and haggard, and subject more and more to fits of abstraction. Those of his relatives who were attached to him, noticed his altered mien, and dreaded an attack of illness; others scoffingly accused him of mental hallucination; and the foremost among these scoffers was his uncle's wife, Omm Jemil, the sister of Abu Sofian.

The result of this disordered state of mind and body was another vision, or revelation, commanding him to " arise, preach, and magnify the Lord." He was now to announce, publicly and boldly, his doctrines, beginning with his kindred and tribe.   Accordingly, in the fourth year of what is called his mission, he summoned all the Koreishites of the line of Haschem to meet him on the hill of Safa, in the vicinity of Mecca, when he would unfold matters important to their welfare. They assembled there, accordingly, and among them came Mahomet's hostile uncle Abu Lahab, and with him his scoffing wife, Omm Jemil. Scarce had the prophet begun to discourse of his mission, and to impart his revelations, when Abu Lahab started up in a rage, reviled him for calling them together on so idle an errand, and catching up a stone, would have hurled it at him. Mahomet turned upon him a withering look; cursed the hand thus raised in menace, and predicted his doom to the fire of Jehennam; with the assurance that his wife, Omm Jemil, would bear the bundle of thorns with which the fire would be kindled.

The assembly broke up in confusion. Abu Lahab and his wife, exasperated at the curse dealt out to them, compelled their son, Otha, to repudiate his wife, Rokaia, and sent her back weeping to Mahomet. She was soon indemnified, however, by having a husband of the true faith, being eagerly taken to wife by Mahomet's zealous disciple, Othman Ibn Affan.

Nothing discouraged by the failure of his first attempt, Mahomet called a second meeting of the Haschemites at his own house, where, having regaled them with the flesh of a lamb, and given them milk to drink, he stood forth and announced, at full length, his revelations received from heaven, and the divine command to impart them to those of his immediate line.

" Oh children of Abd al Motâlleb," cried he, with enthusiasm, "to you, of all men, has Allah vouchsafed these most precious gifts.   In his name I offer you the blessings of this world, and endless joys hereafter.   Who among you will share the burden of my offer.   Who will be my brother : my lieutenant, my vizier?"

All remained silent; some wondering; others smiling with incredulity and derision. At length Ali, starting up with youthful zeal, offered himself to the service of the prophet, though modestly acknowledging his youth and physical weakness [1]. Mahomet threw his arms round the generous youth, and pressed him to his

---

[1] By an error of translators, Ali is made to accompany his offer of adhesion by an extravagant threat against all who should oppose Mahomet.

bosom. "Behold my brother, my vizier, my vicegerent," exclaimed he; "let all listen to his words, and obey him."

The outbreak of such a stripling as Ali, however, was answered by a scornful burst of laughter of the Koreishites; who taunted Abu Taleb, the father of the youthful proselyte, with having to bow down before his son, and yield him obedience.

But though the doctrines of Mahomet were thus ungraciously received by his kindred and friends, they found favour among the people at large, especially among the women, who are ever prone to befriend a persecuted cause. Many of the Jews, also, followed him for a time, but when they found that he permitted his disciples to eat the flesh of the camel, and of other animals forbidden by their law, they drew back and rejected his religion as unclean.

Mahomet now threw off all reserve, or rather was inspired with increasing enthusiasm, and went about openly and earnestly proclaiming his doctrines, and giving himself out as a prophet, sent by God to put an end to idolatry, and to mitigate the rigour of the Jewish and the Christian law. The hills of Safa and Kubeis, sanctified by traditions concerning Hagar and Ishmael, were his favourite places of preaching, and Mount Hara was his Sinai, whither he retired occasionally, in fits of excitement and enthusiasm, to return from its solitary cave with fresh revelations of the Koran.

The good old Christian writers, on treating of the advent of one whom they denounce as the Arab enemy of the church, make superstitious record of divers prodigies which occurred, about this time, awful forerunners of the troubles about to agitate the world. In Constantinople, at that time the seat of Christian empire, were several monstrous births and prodigious apparitions, which struck dismay into the hearts of all beholders. In certain religious processions in that neighbourhood, the crosses on a sudden moved of themselves, and were violently agitated, causing astonishment and terror. The Nile, too, that ancient mother of wonders, gave birth to two hideous forms, seemingly man and woman, which rose out of its waters, gazed about them for a time with terrific aspect, and sank again beneath the waves. For a whole day the sun appeared to be diminished to one-third of its usual size, shedding pale and baleful rays. During a moonless night a furnace light glowed throughout the heavens, and bloody lances glittered in the sky.

All these, and sundry other like marvels, were interpreted into signs of coming troubles. The ancient servants of God shook their heads mournfully, predicting the reign of anti-Christ at hand; with vehement persecution of the Christian faith, and great desolation of the churches; and to such holy men who have passed through the trials and troubles of the faith, adds the venerable Padre Jayme Bleda, it is given to understand and explain these mysterious portents, which forerun disasters of the church; even as it is given to ancient mariners to read in the signs of the air, the heavens and the deep, the coming tempest which is to overwhelm their bark.

Many of these sainted men were gathered to glory before the completion of their prophecies. There, seated securely in the empyreal heavens, they may have looked down with compassion upon the troubles of the Christian world; as men on the serene heights of mountains look down upon the tempests which sweep the earth and sea, wrecking tall ships, and rending lofty towers.

CHAPTER VIII.

Outlines of the Mahometan Faith.

Though it is not intended in this place to go fully into the doctrines promulgated by Mahomet, yet it is important to the right appreciation of his character and conduct, and of the events and circumstances set forth in the following narrative, to give their main features.

It must be particularly borne in mind, that Mahomet did not profess to set up a new religion; but to restore that derived in the earliest times, from God himself. "We follow," says the Koran, "the religion of Abraham the orthodox, who was no idolater. We believe in God and that which hath been sent down to us, and that which hath been sent down unto Abraham and Ishmael, and Isaac and Jacob and the tribes, and that which was delivered unto Moses and Jesus, and that which was delivered unto the prophets from the Lord : we make no distinction between any of them, and to God we are resigned." [1]

The Koran, [2] which was the great book of his faith, was delivered in portions from time to time, according to the excitement of his feelings, or the exigency of circumstances. It was not given as his own work, but as a divine revelation; as the very words of God. The Deity is supposed to speak in every instance. "We have sent thee down the book of truth, confirming the scripture which was revealed before it, and preserving the same in its purity." [3]

The law of Moses, it was said, had for a time been the guide and rule of human conduct. At the coming of Jesus Christ it was superseded by the Gospel; both were now to give place to the Koran, which was more full and explicit than the preceding codes, and intended to reform the abuses which had crept into them through the negligence or the corruptions of their professors. It was the completion of the law; after it there would be no more divine revelations. Mahomet was the last, as he was the greatest, of the line of prophets sent to make known the will of God.

The unity of God was the corner stone of this reformed religion. "There is no God but God," was its leading dogma. Hence, it received the name of the religion of Islam, [4] an Arabian word,

[1] Koran, chap. ii.
[2] Derived from the Arabic word Kora, to read or teach.
[3] Koran, chap. v.
[4] Some Etymologists derive Islam from Salem or Aslama, which signifies salvation.

implying submission to God. To this leading dogma, was added, "Mahomet is the prophet of God;" an addition authorized, as it was maintained, by the divine annunciation, and important to procure a ready acceptation of his revelations.

Beside the unity of God, a belief was incalculated in his angels or ministering spirits; in his prophets; in the resurrection of the body; in the last judgment and a future state of rewards and punishments, and in predestination. Much of the Koran may be traced to the Bible, the Mishnu and the Talmud of the Jews,[1] especially its wild though often beautiful traditions concerning the angels, the prophets, the patriarchs, and the good and evil genii. He had at an early age imbibed a reverence for the Jewish faith, his mother, it is suggested, having been of that religion.

The system laid down in the Koran, however, was essentially founded on the Christian doctrines inculcated in the New Testament; as they had been expounded to him by the Christian sectarians of Arabia. Our Saviour was to be held in the highest reverence as an inspired prophet, the greatest that had been sent before the time of Mahomet, to reform the law; but all idea of his divinity was rejected as impious, and the doctrine of the Trinity was denounced as an outrage on the unity of God. Both were pronounced errors and interpolations of the expounders; and this, it will be observed, was the opinion of some of the Arabian sects of Christians.

The worship of saints and the introduction of images and paintings representing them, were condemned as idolatrous lapses from the pure faith of Christ, and such, we have already observed, were the tenets of the Nestorians with whom Mahomet is known to have had much communication.

All pictures representing living things were prohibited. Mahomet used to say, that the angels would not enter a house in which there were such pictures, and that those who made them would be sentenced in the next world, to find souls for them, or be punished.

Most of the benignant precepts of our Saviour were incorporated in the Koran. Frequent alms-giving was enjoined as an imperative duty, and the immutable law of right and wrong, "Do

---

The Christians form from it the term Islamism, and the Jews have varied it into Ismailism, which they intend as a reproach, and an allusion to the origin of the Arabs as descendants of Ishmael.

From Islam the Arabians drew the terms Moslem or Muslem, and Musulman, a professor of the faith of Islam. These terms are in the singular number and make Musliman in the dual, and Muslimen in the plural. The French and some other nations follow the idioms of their own languages in adopting or translating the Arabic terms, and form the plural by the addition of the letter s; writing Musulman and Musulmans. A few English writters, of whom Gibbon is the chief, have imitated them, imagining that they were following the Arabian usage. Most English authors, however, follow the idiom of their own language, writing Moslem and Moslems, Musulman and Musulmen; this usage is also the more harmonious.

[1] *The Mishnu* of the Jews like the Sonna of the Mahometans, is a collection of traditions forming the Oral law. It was compiled in the second century by Judah Hakkodish, a learned Jewish Rabbi, during the reign of Antonius Pius, the Roman Emperor.

The Jerusalem Talmud and the Babylonish Talmud, are both commentaries on the Mishnu. The former was compiled at Jerusalem, about three hundred years after Christ, and the latter in Babylonia, about two centuries later. The Mishnu is the most ancient record possessed by the Jews except the Bible.

unto another, as thou wouldst he should do unto thee," was given for the moral conduct of the faithful.

"Deal not unjustly with others," says the Koran, "and ye shall not be dealt with unjustly. If there be any debtor under a difficulty of paying his debt, let his creditor wait until it be easy for him to do it; but if he remit it in alms, it will be better for him."

Mahomet inculcated a noble fairness and sincerity in dealing. "Oh merchants!" would he say, "falsehood and deception are apt to prevail in traffic, purify it therefore with alms; give something in charity as an atonement; for God is incensed by deceit in dealing, but charity appeases his anger. He who sells a defective thing, concealing its defect, will provoke the anger of God and the curses of the angels.

"Take not advantage of the necessities of another to buy things at a sacrifice; rather relieve his indigence.

"Feed the hungry; visit the sick, and free the captive if confined unjustly.

"Look not scornfully upon thy fellow man; neither walk the earth with insolence; for God loveth not the arrogant and vainglorious. Be moderate in thy pace, and speak with a moderate tone; for the most ungrateful of all voices, is the voice of asses." [1]

Idolatry of all kinds was strictly forbidden; indeed it was what Mahomet held in most abhorrence. Many of the religious usages, however, prevalent since time immemorial among the Arabs, to which he had been accustomed from infancy, and which were not incompatible with the doctrine of the unity of God, were still retained. Such was the pilgrimage to Mecca, including all the rites connected with the Caaba, the well of Zem Zem, and other sacred places in the vicinity; apart from any worship of the idols by which they had been profaned.

The old Arabian rite of prayer, accompanied or rather preceded by ablution, was still continued. Prayers indeed were enjoined at certain hours of the day and night; they were simple in form and phrase addressed directly to the Deity with certain inflexions, or at times a total prostration of the body, and with the face turned towards the Kebla, or point of adoration.

At the end of each prayer, the following verse from the second chapter of the Koran was recited. It is said to have great beauty

---

[1] The following words of Mahomet, treasured up by one of his disciples, appear to have been suggested by a passage in Matthew xxv. 35-45 :

"Verily, God will say at the day of resurrection,' Oh sons of Adam! I was sick, and ye did not visit me.' Then they will say, 'How could we visit thee? for thou art the Lord of the universe, and art free from sickness.' And God will reply, 'Knew ye not that such a one of my servants was sick, and ye did not visit him? Had you visited that servant, it would have been counted to you as righteousness.' And God will say, 'Oh sons of Adam! I asked you for food, and ye gave it me not." And the sons of Adam will say, 'How could we give thee food, seeing thou art the sustainer of the universe, and art free from hunger?' And God will say, 'Such a one of my servants asked you for bread, and ye refused it. Had you given him to eat, ye would have received your reward from me.' And God will say, 'Oh sons of Adam, I asked you for water, and ye gave it me not.' They will reply, 'Oh, our supporter! How could we give thee water, seeing thou art the sustainer of the universe, and not subject to thirst?' And God will say, 'Such a one of my servants asked you for water, and ye did not give it to him. Had ye done to, ye would have received your reward from me.'"

in the original Arabic, and is engraved on gold and silver ornaments, and on precious stones worn as amulets.   "God! There is no God but He, the living, the ever living; he sleepeth not, neither doth he slumber.   To him belongeth the heavens, and the earth, and all that they contain.   Who shall intercede with him unless by his permission?   He knoweth the past and the future, but no one can comprehend any thing of his knowledge but that which he revealeth. His sway extendeth over the heavens and the earth, and to sustain them both is no burthen to him.   He is the High, the Mighty!"

Mahomet was strenuous in enforcing the importance and efficacy of prayer.   "Angels," said he, come among you both by night and day; after which those of the night ascend to heaven, and God asks them how they left his creatures.   We found them, say they, at their prayers, and we left them at their prayers."

The doctrines in the Koran respecting the resurrection and final judgment, were in some respects similar to those of the Christian religion, but were mixed up with wild notions derived from other sources; while the joys of the Moslem heaven, though partly spiritual, were clogged and debased by the sensualities of earth, and infinitely below the ineffable purity and spiritual blessedness of the heaven promised by our Saviour.

Nevertheless, the description of the last day, as contained in the eighty-first chapter of the Koran, and which must have been given by Mahomet at the outset of his mission at Mecca, as one of the first of his revelations, partakes of sublimity.

"In the name of the all merciful God! a day shall come when the sun will be shrouded, and the stars will fall from the heavens.

"When the camels about to foal will be neglected, and wild beasts will herd together through fear.

"When the waves of the ocean will boil, and the souls of the dead again be united to the bodies.

"When the female infant that has been buried alive will demand, for what crime was I sacrificed? and the eternal books will be laid open.

"When the heavens will pass away like a scroll, and hell will burn fiercely; and the joys of paradise will be made manifest.

"On that day shall every soul make known that which it hath performed.

"Verily, I swear to you by the stars which move swiftly and are lost in the brightness of the sun, and by the darkness of the night, and by the dawning of the day, these are not the words of an evil spirit, but of an angel of dignity and power, who possesses the confidence of Allah, and is revered by the angels under his command.   Neither is your companion, Mahomet, distracted.   He beheld the celestial messenger in the light of the clear horizon, and the words revealed to him are intended as an admonition unto all creatures."

NOTE.—To exhibit the perplexed maze of controversial doctrines from which Mahomet had to acquire his notions of the Christian faith, we subjoin the leading points of the jarring sects of oriental Christians alluded to in the foregoing article ; all of which have been pronounced heretical or schismatic.

The Sabellians, so called from Sabellius, a Lybian priest of the third century, believed in the unity of God, and that the Trinity expressed but three different states or relations, Father, Son, and Holy Ghost, all forming but one substance, as a man consists of body and soul.

The Arians, from Arius, an ecclesiastic of Alexandria in the fourth century, affirmed Christ to be the Son of God, but distinct from him and inferior to him, and denied the Holy Ghost to be God.

The Nestorians, from Nestorius, Bishop of Constantinople in the fifth century, maintained that Christ had two distinct natures, divine and human; that Mary was only his mother, and Jesus a man, and that it was an abomination to style her, as was the custom of the church, the Mother of God.

The Monophysites maintained the single nature of Christ, as their name betokens. They affirmed that he was combined of God and man, so mingled and united as to form but one nature.

The Eutychians, from Eutyches, abbot of a convent in Constantinople in the fifth century, were a branch of the Monophysites, expressly opposed to the Nestorians. They denied the double nature of Christ, declaring that he was entirely God previous to the incarnation, and entirely man during the incarnation.

The Jacobites, from Jacobus, Bishop of Edessa, in Syria, in the sixth century, were a very numerous branch of the Monophysites, varying but little from the Eutychians. Most of the Christian tribes of Arabs were Jacobites.

The Mariamites, or worshippers of Mary, regarded the Trinity as consisting of God the Father, God the Son, and God the Virgin Mary.

The Collyridians were a sect of Arabian Christians, composed chiefly of females. They worshipped the Virgin Mary as possessed of divinity, and made offerings to her of a twisted cake, called collyris, whence they derived their name.

The Nazaræans, or Nazarenes, were a sect of Jewish Christians who considered Christ as the Massiah, as born of a Virgin by the Holy Ghost, and as possessing something of a divine nature; but they conformed in all other respects to the rites and ceremonies of the Mosaic law.

The Ebionites, from Ebion, a converted Jew, who lived in the first century, were also a sect of judaizing Christians, little differing from the Nazaræans. They believed Christ to be a pure man, the greatest of the prophets, but denied that he had any existence previous to being born of the Virgin Mary. This sect, as well as that of the Nazaræans, had many adherents in Arabia.

Many other sects might be enumerated, such as the Corinthians, Maronites, and Marcionites, who took their names from learned and zealous leaders; and the Docetes and Gnostics, who were subdivided into various sects of subtle enthusiasts. Some of these asserted the immaculate purity of the Virgin Mary, affirming that her conception and delivery were effected like the transmission of the rays of light through a pane of glass, without impairing her virginity; an opinion still maintained strenuously in substance by Spanish Catholics.

Most of the Docetes asserted that Jesus Christ was of a nature entirely divine; that a phantom, a mere form without substance, was crucified by the deluded Jews, and that the crucifixion and resurrection were deceptive mystical exhibitions at Jerusalem for the benefit of the human race.

The Carpocratians, Basilidians, and Valentinians, named after three Egyptian controversialists, contented that Jesus Christ was merely a wise and virtuous mortal, the son of Joseph and Mary, selected by God to reform and instruct mankind; but that a divine nature was imparted to him at the maturity of his age, and period of his baptism, by St. John. The former part of this creed, which is that of the Ebionites, has been revived, and is professed by some of the Unitarian Christians, a numerous and increasing sect of Protestants of the present day.

It is sufficient to glance at these dissensions, which we have not arranged in chronological order, but which convulsed the early Christian church, and continued to prevail at the era of Mahomet, to acquit him of any charge of conscious blasphemy in the opinions he inculcated concerning the nature and mission of our Saviour.

CHAPTER IX.

Ridicule cast on Mahomet and his doctrines.—Demand for miracles.—Conduct of Abu Taleb.—Violence of the Koreishites.—Mahomet's daughter Rokaia, with her uncle Othman, and a number of disciples take refuge in Abyssinia.—Mahomet in the house of Orkham.—Hostility of Abu Jahl; his punishment.

The greatest difficulty with which Mahomet had to contend at the outset of his prophetic career, was the ridicule of his opponents. Those who had known him from his infancy—who had seen him a boy about the streets of Mecca; and afterwards occupied in all the ordinary concerns of life, scoffed at his assumption of the apostolic character. They pointed with a sneer at him as he passed, exclaiming. "Behold the grandson of Abd al Motálleb, who pretends to know what is going on in heaven!" Some who had witnessed his fits of mental excitement and ecstasy, considered him insane; others declared that he was possessed with a devil, and some charged him with sorcery and magic.

When he walked the streets he was subject to those jeers, and taunts, and insults which the vulgar are apt to vent upon men of eccentric conduct and unsettled mind. If he attempted to preach, his voice was drowned by discordant noises and ribald songs: nay, dirt was thrown upon him when he was praying in the Caaba.

Nor was it the vulgar and ignorant alone who thus insulted him. One of his most redoubtable assailants was a youth named Amru; and as he subsequently made a distinguished figure in Mahometan history, we would impress the circumstances of this, his first appearance, upon the mind of the reader. He was the son of a courtezan of Mecca; who seems to have rivalled in fascination the Phrynes and Aspasias of Greece, and to have numbered some of the noblest of the land among her lovers. When she gave birth to this child, she mentioned several of the tribe of Koreish who had equal claims to the paternity. The infant was declared to have most resemblance to Aass, the oldest of her admirers, whence, in addition to his name of Amru, he received the designation of Ibn al Aass, the son of Aass.

Nature had lavished her choicest gifts upon this natural child, as if to atone for the blemish of his birth. Though young, he was already one of the most popular poets of Arabia, and equally distinguished for the pungency of his satirical effusions and the captivating sweetness of his serious lays.

When Mahomet first announced his mission, this youth assailed him with lampoons and humorous madrigals; which, falling in with the poetic taste of the Arabs, were widely circulated, and proved greater impediments to the growth of Islamism than the bitterest persecution.

Those who were more serious in their opposition demanded of Mahomet supernatural proofs of what he asserted. "Moses and Jesus, and the rest of the prophets," said they, "wrought miracles to prove the divinity of their missions. If thou art indeed a prophet, greater than they, work the like miracles."

The reply of Mahomet may be gathered from his own words in the Koran. "What greater miracle could they have than the Koran itself: a book revealed by means of an unlettered man; so elevated in language, so incontrovertible in argument, that the united skill of men and devils could compose nothing comparable. What greater proof could there be that it came from none but God himself? The Koran itself is a miracle."

They demanded, however, more palpable evidence; miracles addressed to the senses; that he should cause the dumb to speak, the deaf to hear, the blind to see; the dead to rise; or that he should work changes in the face of nature; cause fountains to gush forth; change a sterile place into a garden, with palm-trees, and vines, and running streams; cause a palace of gold to rise, decked with jewels and precious stones; or ascend by a ladder into heaven in their presence. Or, if the Koran did indeed, as he affirmed, come down from heaven; that they might see it as it descended, or behold the angel who brought it; and then they would believe.

Mahomet replied sometimes by arguments, sometimes by denunciations. He claimed to be nothing more than a man sent by God as an apostle. Had angels, said he, walked familiarly on earth, an angel had assuredly been sent on this mission; but woful had been the case of those who, as in the present instance, doubted his word. They would not have been able, as with me, to argue, and dispute, and take time to be convinced; their perdition would have been instantaneous. "God," added he, "needs no angel to enforce my mission. He is a sufficient witness between you and me. Those whom he shall dispose to be convinced, will truly believe; those whom he shall permit to remain in errour, will find none to help their unbelief. On the day of resurrection they will appear blind, and deaf, and dumb, and grovelling on their faces. Their abode will be in the eternal flames of Jehennam. Such will be the reward of their unbelief.

"You insist on miracles. God gave to Moses the power of working miracles. What was the consequence? Pharaoh disregarded his miracles, accused him of sorcery, and sought to drive him and his people from the land; but Pharaoh was drowned, and with him all his host. Would ye tempt God to miracles, and risk the punishment of Pharaoh?"

It is recorded by Al Maalem, an Arabian writer, that some of Mahomet's disciples at one time joined with the multitude in this cry for miracles, and besought him to prove, at once, the divinity of his mission, by turning the hill of Safa into gold. Being thus closely urged, he betook himself to prayer; and having finished, assured his followers that the angel Gabriel had appeared to him, and informed him that, should God grant his prayer, and work the desired miracle, all who disbelieved it would be exterminated. In pity to the multitude, therefore, who appeared to be a stiff-necked generation, he would not expose them to destruction : so the hill of Safa was permitted to remain in its pristine state.

Other Moslem writers assert that Mahomet departed from his self-prescribed rule, and wrought occasional miracles, when he found his hearers unusually slow of belief. Thus we are told that, at one time, in presence of a multitude, he called to him a bull, and took from his horns a scroll containing a chapter of the Koran, just sent down from heaven. At another time, while discoursing in public, a white dove hovered over him, and, alighting on his shoulder, appeared to whisper in his ear ; being, as he said, a messenger from the Deity. On another occasion he ordered the earth before him to be opened, when two jars were found, one filled with honey, the other with milk, which he pronounced emblems of the abundance promised by heaven to all who should obey his law.

Christian writers have scoffed at these miracles ; suggesting that the dove had been tutored to its task, and sought grains of wheat which it had been accustomed to find in the ear of Mahomet ; that the scroll had previously been tied to the horns of the bull, and the vessels of milk and honey deposited in the ground. The truer course would be to discard these miraculous stories altogether, as fables devised by mistaken zealots ; and such they have been pronounced by the ablest of the Moslem commentators.

There is no proof that Mahomet descended to any artifices of the kind to enforce his doctrines or establish his apostolic claims. He appears to have relied entirely on reason and eloquence, and to have been supported by religious enthusiasm in this early and dubious stage of his career. His earnest attacks upon the idolatry which had vitiated and superseded the primitive worship of the Caaba, began to have a sensible effect, and alarmed the Koreishites. They urged Abu Taleb to silence his nephew or to send him away ; but finding their entreaties unavailing, they informed the old man that if this pretended prophet and his followers persisted in their heresies, they should pay for them with their lives.

Abu Taleb hastened to inform Mahomet of these menaces, imploring him not to provoke against himself and family such numerous and powerful foes.

The enthusiastic spirit of Mahomet kindled at the words. " Oh my uncle !" exclaimed he, " though they should array the sun against me on my right hand, and the moon on my left, yet, until God should command me, or should take me hence, would I not depart from my purpose."

He was retiring with dejected countenance, when Abu Taleb called him back. The old man was as yet unconverted, but he was struck with admiration of the undaunted firmness of his nephew, and declared that, preach what he might, he would never abandon him to his enemies. Feeling that of himself he could not yield sufficient protection, he called upon the other descendants of Haschem and Abd al Motâlleb to aid in shielding their kinsman from the persecution of the rest of the tribe of Koreish ; and so strong is the family tie among the Arabs, that though it was pro-

tecting him in what they considered a dangerous heresy, they all
consented excepting his uncle Abu Lahab.

The animosity of the Koreishites became more and more virulent,
and proceeded to personal violence. Mahomet was assailed and
nearly strangled in the Caaba, and was rescued with difficulty by
Abu Beker, who himself suffered personal injury in the affray. His
immediate family became objects of hatred, especially his daughter
Rokaia and her husband Othman Ibn Affan. Such of his disciples
as had no powerful friends to protect them were in peril of their
lives. Full of anxiety for their safety, Mahomed advised them to
leave his dangerous companionship for the present, and take
refuge in Abyssinia. The narrowness of the Red Sea made it easy
to reach the African shore. The Abyssinians were Nestorian Christians, elevated by their religion above their barbarous neighbours.
Their najashee or king was reputed to be tolerant and just. With
him Mahomet trusted his daughter and his fugitive disciples would
find refuge.

Othmann Ibn Affan was the leader of this little band of Moslems,
consisting of eleven men and four women. They took the way by
the sea-coast to Jodda, a port about two days' journey to the east
of Mecca, where they found two Abyssinian vessels at anchor, in
which they embarked, and sailed for the land of refuge.

This event, which happened in the fifth year of the mission of
Mahomet, is called the first Hegira or Flight, to distinguish it from
the second Hegira, the flight of the prophet himself from Mecca to
Medina. The kind treatment experienced by the fugitives induced
others of the same faith to follow their example, until the number
of Moslem refugees in Abyssinia amounted to eighty-three men
and eighteen women, besides children.

The Koreishites finding that Mahomet was not to be silenced,
and was daily making converts, passed a law banishing all who
should embrace his faith. Mahomet retired before the storm,
and took refuge in the house of a disciple named Orkham, situated
on the hill of Safa. This hill, as has already been mentioned, was
renowned in Arabian tradition as the one on which Adam and Eve
were permitted to come once more together, after the long solitary wandering about the earth which followed their expulsion from
paradise. It was likewise connected in tradition with the fortunes
of Hagar and Ishmael.

Mahomet remained for a month in the house of Orkham, continuing his revelations and drawing to him sectaries from various
parts of Arabia. The hostility of the Koreishites followed him to
his retreat. Abu Jahl, an Arab of that tribe, sought him out,
insulted him with opprobrious language, and even personally
maltreated him. The outrage was reported to Hamza an uncle of
Mahomet, as he returned to Mecca from hunting. Hamza was no
proselyte to Islamism, but he was pledged to protect his nephew.
Marching with his bow unstrung in his hand to an assemblage of
the Koreishites, where Abu Jahl was vaunting his recent triumph,
he dealt the boaster a blow over the head, that inflicted a grievous
wound. The kinsfolk of Abu Jahl rushed to his assistance, but
the brawler stood in awe of the vigorous arm and fiery spirit of

Hamza, and sought to pacify him. "Let him alone," said he to his kinsfolk; " in truth I have treated his nephew very roughly." He alleged in palliation of his outrage the apostasy of Mahomet; but Hamza was not to be appeased. "Well!" cried he, fiercely and scornfully, "I also do not believe in your gods of stone; can you compel me?" Anger produced in his bosom what reasoning might have attempted in vain. He forthwith declared himself a convert; took the oath of adhesion to the prophet, and became one of the most zealous and valiant champions of the new faith.

CHAPTER X.

Omar Ibn al Khattâb, nephew of Abu Jahl, undertakes to revenge his uncle by slaying Mahomet.—His wonderful conversion to the faith.—Mahomet takes refuge in a castle of Abu Taleb.—Abu Sofian, at the head of the rival branch of Koreishites, persecutes Mahomet and his followers.—Obtains a decree of non-intercourse with them.—Mahomet leaves his retreat and makes converts during the month of pilgrimage.—Legend of the conversion of Habib the Wise.

The hatred of Abu Jahl to the prophet was increased by the severe punishment received at the hands of Hamza. He had a nephew named Omar Ibn al Khattâb; twenty-six years of age; of gigantic stature, prodigious strength, and great courage. His savage aspect appalled the bold, and his very walking-staff struck more terror into beholders than another man's sword. Such are the words of the Arabian historian, Abu Abdallah Mohamed Ibn Omal Alwakedi, and the subsequent feats of this warrior prove that they were scarce chargeable with exaggeration.

Instigated by his uncle Abu Jahl, this fierce Arab undertook to penetrate to the retreat of Mahomet. who was still in the house of Orkham, and to strike a poniard to his heart. The Koreishites are accused of having promised him one hundred camels and one thousand ounces of gold for this deed of blood; but this is improbable, nor did the vengeful nephew of Abu Jahl need a bribe.

As he was on his way to the house of Orkham he met a Koreishite, to whom he imparted his design. The Koreishite was a secret convert to Islamism, and sought to turn him from his bloody errand. "Before you slay Mahomet," said he, " and draw upon yourself the vengeance of his relatives, see that your own are free from heresy." "Are any of mine guilty of backsliding?" demanded Omar with astonishment. "Even so," was the reply; "thy sister Amina and her husband Seid."

Omar hastened to the dwelling of his sister, and, entering it abruptly, found her and her husband reading the Koran. Seid attempted to conceal it, but his confusion convinced Omar of the truth of the accusation, and heightened his fury. In his rage he struck Seid to the earth; placed his foot upon his breast, and would have plunged his sword into it, had not his sister interposed. A blow on the face bathed her visage in blood. "Enemy of Allah!"

sobbed Amina, "dost thou strike me thus for believing in the only true God? In despite of thee and thy violence, I will persevere in the true faith. Yes," added she with fervour, "'There is no God but God, and Mahomet is his prophet:'—And now, Omar, finish thy work!"

Omar paused; repented of his violence, and took his foot from the bosom of Seid.

"Show me the writing," said he. Amina, however, refused to let him touch the sacred scroll until he had washed his hands. The passage which he read, is said to have been the twentieth chapter of the Koran, which thus begins:

"In the name of the most merciful God! We have not sent down the Koran to inflict misery on mankind, but as a monitor, to teach him to believe in the true God, the creator of the earth and the lofty heavens.

"The all merciful is enthroned on high, to him belongeth whatsoever is in the heavens above, and in the earth beneath, and in the regions under the earth.

"Dost thou utter thy prayers with a loud voice? know that there is no need. God knoweth the secrets of thy heart; yea, that which is most hidden.

"Verily, I am God; there is none beside me. Serve me serve none other. Offer up thy prayer to none but me."

The words of the Koran sank deep into the heart of Omar. He read farther, and was more and more moved; but when he came to the parts treating of the resurrection and of judgment, his conversion was complete.

He pursued his way to the house of Orkham, but with an altered heart. Knocking humbly at the door, he craved admission. "Come in, son of al Khattâb," exclaimed Mahomet. "What brings thee hither?"

"I come to enroll my name among the believers of God and his prophet." So saying, he made the Moslem profession of faith.

He was not content until his conversion was publicly known. At his request, Mahomet accompanied him instantly to the Caaba, to perform openly the rites of Islamism. Omar walked on the left hand of the prophet, and Hamza on the right, to protect him from injury and insult, and they were followed by upwards of forty disciples. They, passed in open day through the streets of Mecca, to the astonishment of the inhabitants. Seven times did they make the circuit of the Caaba, touching each time the sacred black stone, and complying with all the other ceremonials. The Koreishites regarded this procession with dismay, but dared not approach nor molest the prophet, being deterred by the looks of those terrible men of battle Hamza and Omar; who, it is said, glared upon them like two lions that had been robbed of their young.

Fearless and resolute in every thing, Omar went by himself the next day to pray as a Moslem in the Caaba, in open defiance of the Koreishites. Another Moslem, who entered the temple, was interrupted in his worship, and rudely treated; but no one molested Omar, because he was the nephew of Abu Jahl. Omar repaired to his uncle. "I renounce thy protection," said he. I will not be better off than my fellow-believers." From that time he cast his lot with the followers of Mahomet, and was one of his most strenuous defenders.

Such was the wonderful conversion of Omar, afterwards the most famous champion of the Islam faith. So exasperated were the Koreishites by this new triumph of Mahomet, that his uncle Abu Taleb feared they might attempt the life of his nephew, either by treachery, or open violence. At his earnest entreaties, therefore, the latter, accompanied by some of his principal disciples, withdrew to a kind of castle, or stronghold, belonging to Abu Taleb, in the neighbourhood of the city.

" The protection thus given by Abu Taleb, the head of the Haschemites, and by others of his line, to Mahomet and his followers, although differing from them in faith, drew on them the wrath of the rival branch of the Koreishites, and produced a schism in the tribe. Abu Sofian, the head of that branch, availed himself of the heresies of the prophet to throw discredit, not merely upon such of his kindred as had embraced his faith, but upon the whole line of Haschem, which, though dissenting from his doctrines, had, through mere clannish feelings, protected him. 'It is evident the hostility of Abu Sofian arose, not merely from personal hatred or religious scruples, but from family feud. He was ambitious of transferring to his own line the honours of the city so long engrossed by the Haschemites. The last measure of the kind-hearted Abu Taleb, in placing Mahomet beyond the reach of persecution, and giving him a castle as a refuge, was seized upon by Abu Sofian and his adherents, as a pretext for a general ban of the rival line. They accordingly issued a decree, forbidding the rest of the tribe of Koreish from intermarrying, or holding any intercourse, even of bargain or sale, with the Haschemites, until they should deliver up their kinsman, Mahomet, for punishment. This decree, which took place in the seventh year of what is called the mission of the prophet, was written on parchment, and hung up in the Caaba. It reduced Mahomet and his disciples to great straits, being almost famished at times in the stronghold in which they had taken refuge. The fortress was also beleaguered occasionally by the Koreishites, to enforce the ban in all its rigour, and to prevent the possibility of supplies.

The annual season of pilgrimage, however, when hosts of pilgrims repair from all parts of Arabia to Mecca, brought transient relief to the persecuted Moslems. During that sacred season, according to immemorial law and usage among the Arabs, all hostilities were suspended, and warring tribes met in temporary peace to worship at the Caaba. At such times Mahomet and his disciples would venture from their stronghold and return to Mecca. Protected also by the immunity of the holy month, Mahomet would mingle among the pilgrims and preach and pray; propound his doctrines, and proclaim his revelations. In this way he made many converts, who, on their return to their several homes, carried with them the seeds of the new faith to distant regions. Among these converts were occasionally the princes or heads of tribes, whose example had an influence on their adherents. Arabian legends

give a pompous and extravagant account of the conversion of one
of these princes; which, as it was attended by some of the most
noted miracles recorded of Mahomet, may not be unworthy of an
abbreviated insertion.

The prince in question was Habib Ibn Malec, surnamed the Wise
on account of his vast knowledge and erudition; for he is represented as deeply versed in magic and the sciences, and acquainted
with all religions, to their very foundations, having read all that
had been written concerning them, and also acquired practical information, for he had belonged to them all by turns, having been
Jew, Christian, and one of the Magi.   It is true, he had had more
than usual time for his studies and experience, having, according
to Arabian legend, attained to the age of one hundred and forty
years.   He now came to Mecca at the head of a powerful host of
twenty thousand men, bringing with him a youthful daughter, Satiha, whom he must have begotten in a ripe old age; and for whom
he was putting up prayers at the Caaba, she having been struck
dumb, and deaf, and blind, and deprived of the use of her limbs.

Abu Sofian and Abu Jahl, according to the legend, thought the
presence of this very powerful, very idolatrous, and very wise old
prince, at the head of so formidable a host, a favourable opportunity to effect the ruin of Mahomet.   They accordingly informed
Habib the Wise of the heresies of the pretended prophet; and prevailed upon the venerable prince to summon him into his presence,
at his encampment in the Valley of Flints, there to defend his doctrines; in the hope that his obstinacy in errour would draw upon
him banishment or death.

The legend gives a magnificent account of the issuing forth of
the idolatrous Koreishites, in proud array, on horseback and on
foot, led by Abu Sofian and Abu Jahl, to attend the grand inquisition in the Valley of Flints; and of the oriental state in which they
were received by Habib the Wise, seated under a tent of crimson,
on a throne of ebony, inlaid with ivory and sandal-wood, and
covered with plates of gold.

Mahomet was in the dwelling of Cadijah when he received a
summons to this formidable tribunal.   Cadijah was loud in her expressions of alarm; and his daughters hung about his neck, weeping
and lamenting, for they thought him going to certain death; but
he gently rebuked their fears, and bade them trust in Allah.

Unlike the ostentatious state of his enemies, Abu Sofian and Abu
Jahl, he approached the scene of trial in simple guise, clad in a white
garment with a black turban, and a mantle which had belonged to
his grandfather Abd al Motâlleb, and was made of the stuff of Aden.
His hair floated below his shoulders, the mysterious light of prophecy beamed from his countenance; and though he had not
anointed his beard, nor used any perfumes, excepting a little musk
and camphor for the hair of his upper lip, yet wherever he passed
a bland odour diffused itself around, being, say the Arabian writers,
the fragrant emanations from his person.

He was preceded by the zealous Abu Beker, clad in a scarlet
vest and a white turban; with his mantle gathered up under his
arms, so as to display his scarlet slippers.

A silent awe, continues the legend, fell upon the vast assemblage as the prophet approached. Not a murmur, not a whisper was to be heard. The very brute animals were charmed to silence; and the neighing of the steed, the bellowing of the camel, and the braying of the ass were mute.

The venerable Habib received him graciously: his first question was to the point. "They tell thou dost pretend to be a prophet sent from God? Is it so?"

"Even so;" replied Mahomet. "Allah has sent me to proclaim the veritable faith."

"Good," rejoined the wary sage, "but every prophet has given proof of his mission by signs and miracles. Noah had his rainbow: Solomon his mysterious ring: Abraham the fire of the furnace, which became cool at his command: Isaac the ram, which was sacrificed in his stead: Moses his wonder-working rod, and Jesus brought the dead to life, and appeased tempests with a word. If, then, thou art really a prophet, give us a miracle in proof."

The adherents of Mahomet trembled for him when they heard this request, and Abu Jahl clapped his hands and extolled the sagacity of Habib the Wise. But the prophet rebuked him with scorn. "Peace! dog of thy race!" exclaimed he; "disgrace of thy kindred, and of thy tribe." He then calmly proceeded to execute the wishes of Habib.

The first miracle demanded of Mahomet was to reveal what Habib had within his tent, and why he had brought it to Mecca.

Upon this, says the legend, Mahomet bent toward the earth and traced figures upon the sand. Then raising his head, he replied, "Oh Habib! thou hast brought hither thy daughter, Satiha, deaf and dumb, and lame and blind, in the hope of obtaining relief of Heaven. Go to thy tent; speak to her, and hear her reply, and know that God is all powerful."

The aged prince hastened to his tent. His daughter met him with light step and extended arms, perfect in all her faculties, her eyes beaming with joy, her face clothed with smiles, and more beautous than the moon in an unclouded night.

The second miracle demanded by Habib was still more difficult. It was that Mahomet should cover the noontide heaven with supernatural darkness, and cause the moon to descend and rest upon the top of the Caaba.

The prophet performed this miracle as easily as the first. At his summons, a darkness blotted out the whole light of day. The moon was then seen straying from her course and wandering about the firmament. By the irresistible power of the prophet, she was drawn from the heavens and rested on the top of the Caaba. She then performed seven circuits about it, after the manner of the pilgrims, and having made a profound reverence to Mahomet, stood before him with lambent wavering motion, like a flaming sword; giving him the salutation of peace, and hailing him as a prophet.

Not content with this miracle, pursues the legend, Mahomet compelled the obedient luminary to enter by the right sleeve of his mantle, and go out by the left; then to divide into two parts, one of which went towards the east, and the other towards the west.

and meeting in the centre of the firmament reunited themselves into a round and glorious orb.

It is needless to say that Habid the Wise was convinced, and converted by these miracles, as were also four hundred and seventy of the inhabitants of Mecca. Abu Jahl, however, was hardened in unbelief, exclaiming that all was illusion and enchantement produced by the magic of Mahomet.

NOTE.—The miracles here recorded are not to be found in the pages of the accurate Abulfeda, nor are they maintained by any of the graver of the Moslem writers; but they exist in tradition, and are set forth with great prolixity by apocryphal authors, who insist that they are alluded to in the fifty-fourth chapter of the Koran. They are probably as true as many other of the wonders related of the prophet. It will be remembered that he himself claimed but one miracle, "the Koran."

CHAPTER XI.

The ban of non-intercourse mysteriously destroyed.—Mahomet enabled to return to Mecca.—Death of Abu Taleb; of Cadijah.—Mahomet betroths himself to Ayesha.—Marries Sawda.—The Koreishites renew their persecution.—Mahomet seeks an asylum in Tayef.—His expulsion thence.—Visited by genii in the desert of Naklah.

Three years had elapsed since Mahomet and his disciples took refuge in the castle of Abu Taleb. The ban or decree still existed in the Caaba, cutting them off from all intercourse with the rest of their tribe. The sect, as usual, increased under persecution. Many joined it in Mecca; murmurs arose against the unnatural feud engendered among the Koreishites, and Abu Sofian was made to blush for the lengths to which he had carried his hostility against some of his kindred.

All at once it was discovered that the parchment in the Caaba, on which the decree had been written, was so substantially destroyed, that nothing of the writing remained but the initial words, "In thy name, Oh Almighty God!" The decree was, therefore, declared to be annulled, and Mahomet and his followers were permitted to return to Mecca unmolested. The mysterious removal of this legal obstacle has been considered by pious Moslems, another miracle wrought by supernatural agency in favour of the prophet; though unbelievers have surmised that the document, which was becoming embarrassing in its effects to Abu Sofian himself, was secretly destroyed by mortal hands.

The return of Mahomet and his disciples to Mecca, was followed by important conversions, both of inhabitants of the city and of pilgrims from afar. The chagrin experienced by the Koreishites from the growth of this new sect, was soothed by tidings of victories of the Persians over the Greeks, by which they conquered Syria and a part of Egypt. The idolatrous Koreishites exulted in the defeat of the Christian Greeks, whose faith, being opposed to the worship of idols, they assimilated to that preached by Mahomet. The latter replied to their taunts and exultations, by producing the thirtieth chapter of the Koran, opening with these words : "The Greeks have been overcome by the Persians, but they shall overcome the latter in the course of a few years."

The zealous and believing Abu Beker, made a wager of ten camels, that this prediction would be accomplished within three years. "Increase the wager, but lengthen the time," whispered Mahomet. Abu Beker staked one hundred camels, but made the time nine years. The prediction was verified and the wager won. This anecdote is confidently cited by Moslem doctors, as a proof that the Koran came down from heaven, and that Mahomet possessed the gift of prophecy. The whole, if true, was no doubt a shrewd guess into futurity, suggested by a knowledge of the actual state of the warring powers.

Not long after his return to Mecca, Mahomet was summoned to close the eyes of his uncle Abu Taleb, then upwards of fourscore years of age, and venerable in character as in person. As the hour of death drew nigh, Mahomet exhorted his uncle to make the profession of faith necessary, according to the Islam creed, to secure a blissful resurrection.

A spark of earthly pride lingered in the breast of the dying patriarch. "Oh son of my brother!" replied he, "should I repeat those words, the Koreishites would say, I did so through fear of death."

Abulfeda, the historian, insists that Abu Taleb actually died in the faith. Al Abbas, he says, hung over the bed of his expiring brother, and perceiving his lips to move, approached his ear to catch his dying words. They were the wished-for confession. Others affirm that his last words were, "I die in the faith of Abd al Motâlleb." Commentators have sought to reconcile the two accounts, by asserting that Abd al Motâlleb, in his latter days renounced the worship of idols, and believed in the unity of God.

Scarce three days had elapsed from the death of the venerable Abu Taleb, when Cadijah, the faithful and devoted wife of Mahomet, likewise sank into the grave. She was sixty-five years of age. Mahomet wept bitterly at her tomb, and clothed himself in mourning for her, and for Abu Taleb, so that this year was called the year of mourning. He was comforted in his affliction, says the Arabian author, Abu Horaira, by an assurance from the angel Gabriel, that a silver palace was allotted to Cadijah in Paradise, as a reward for her great faith and her early services to the cause.

Though Cadijah had been much older than Mahomet at the time of their marriage, and past the bloom of years when women are desirable in the East, and though the prophet was noted for an amorous temperament, yet he is said to have remained true to her to the last; nor ever availed himself of the Arabian law, permitting a plurality of wives, to give her a rival in his house. When, however, she was laid in the grave, and the first transport of his grief had subsided, he sought to console himself for her loss, by entering anew into wedlock; and henceforth indulged in a plurality of wives. He permitted, by his law, four wives to each of his followers; but did not limit himself to that number; for he observed that a prophet, being peculiarly gifted and privileged, was not bound to restrict himself to the same laws as ordinary mortals.

His first choice was made within a month after the death of Cadijah, and fell upon a beautiful child named Ayesha, the daughter of his faithful adherent, Abu Beker. Perhaps he sought, by this alliance, to grapple Abu Beker still more strongly to his side; he being one of the bravest and most popular of his tribe. Ayesha, however, was but seven years of age, and, though females soon bloom and ripen in those eastern climes, she was yet too young to enter into the married state. He was merely betrothed to her, therefore, and postponed their nuptials for two years, during which time he caused her to be carefully instructed in the accomplishments proper to an Arabian maiden of distinguished rank.

Upon this wife, thus chosen in the very blossom of her years, the prophet doted more passionately than upon any of those whom he subsequently married. All these had been previously experienced in wedlock; Ayesha, he said, was the only one who came a pure unspotted virgin to his arms.

Still, that he might not be without due solace while Ayesha was attaining the marriageable age, he took, as a wife, Sawda, the widow of Sokran, one of his followers. She had been nurse to his daughter Fatima, and was one of the faithful who fled into Abyssinia from the early persecutions of the people of Mecca. It is pretended that, while in exile, she had a mysterious intimation of the future honour which awaited her; for she dreamt that Mahomet laid his head upon her bosom. She recounted the dream to her husband Sokran, who interpreted it as a prediction of his speedy death, and of her marriage, with the prophet.

The marriage, whether predicted or not, was one of mere expediency. Mahomet never loved Sawda with the affection he manifested for his other wives. He would even have put her away in after years, but she implored to be allowed the honour of still calling herself his wife; proffering that, whenever it should come to her turn to share the marriage bed, she would relinquish her right to Ayesha. Mahomet consented to an arrangement which favoured his love for the latter, and Sawda continued, as long as she lived, to be nominally his wife.

Mahomet soon became sensible of the loss he had sustained in the death of Abu Taleb; who had been not merely an affectionate relative, but a steadfast and powerful protector, from his great influence in Mecca. At his death there was no one to check and counteract the hostilities of Abu Sofian and Abu Jahl; who soon raised up such a spirit of persecution among the Koreishites, that Mahomet found it unsafe to continue in his native place. He set out, therefore, accompanied by his freedman Zeid, to seek a refuge at Tayef, a small walled town, about seventy miles from Mecca, inhabited by the Thakifites, or Arabs of the tribe of Thakeef. It was one of the favoured places of Arabia, situated among vineyards and gardens. Here grew peaches and plums, melons and pomegranates; figs, blue and green, the nebeck-tree producing the lotus, and palm-trees with their clusters of green and golden fruit. So fresh were its pastures and fruitful its fields, contrasted with the sterility of the neighbouring deserts, that the Arabs fabled it to have originally been a part of Syria, broken off and floated hither at the time of the deluge.

Mahomet entered the gates of Tayef with some degree of confidence, trusting for protection to the influence of his uncle Al Abbas, who had possessions there. He could not have chosen a worse place of refuge. Tayef was one of the strongholds of idolatry. Here was maintained in all its force the worship of El Làt, one of the female idols already mentioned. Her image of stone was covered with jewels and precious stones, the offerings of her votaries; it was believed to be inspired with life, and the intercession of El Làt was implored as one of the daughters of God.

Mahomet remained about a month in Tayef, seeking in vain to make proselytes among its inhabitants. When he attempted to preach his doctrines, his voice was drowned by clamours. More than once he was wounded by stones thrown at him, and which the faithful Zeid endeavoured in vain to ward-off. So violent did the popular fury become at last, that he was driven from the city, and even pursued for some distance beyond the walls by an insulting rabble of slaves and children.

Thus driven ignominiously from his hoped-for place of refuge, and not daring to return openly to his native city, he remained in the desert until Zeid should procure a secret asylum for him among his friends in Mecca. In this extremity, he had one of those visions or supernatural visitations which appear always to have occurred in lonely or agitated moments, when we may suppose him to have been in a state of mental excitement. It was after the evening prayer, he says, in a solitary place in the valley of Naklah, between Mecca and Tayef. He was reading the Koran, when he was overheard by a passing company of Gins or Genii. These are spiritual beings, some good, others bad, and liable like man to future rewards and punishments. "Hark! give ear!" said the Genii one to the other. They paused and listened as Mahomet continued to read. "Verily," said they at the end, "we have heard an admirable discourse, which directeth unto the right institution; wherefore we believe therein."

This spiritual visitation consoled Mahomet for his expulsion from Tayef, showing that though he and his doctrines might be rejected by men, they were held in reverence by spiritual intelligences. At least so we may infer from the mention he makes of it in the forty-sixth and seventy-second chapters of the Koran. Thenceforward, he declared himself sent for the conversion of these genii as well as of the human race.

NOTE.—The belief in genii was prevalent throughout the East, long before the time of Mahomet. They were supposed to haunt solitary places, particularly toward nightfall; a superstition congenial to the habits and notions of the inhabitants of lonely and desert countries. The Arabs supposed every valley and barren waste to have its tribe of genii, who were subject to a dominant spirit, and roamed forth at night to beset the pilgrim and the traveller. Whenever, therefore, they entered a lonely valley toward the close of evening, they used to supplicate the presiding spirit or lord of the place, to protect them from the evil genii under his command.

Those columns of dust raised by whirling eddies of wind, and which sweep across the desert, are supposed to be caused by some evil genius or sprite of gigantic size.

The serpents which occasionally infest houses were thought to be often genii, some infidels and some believers. Mahomet cautioned his followers to be slow to kill a house serpent. " Warn him to depart; if he do not obey, then kill him, for it is a sign that he is a mere reptile or an infidel genius."

It is fabled that in earlier times, the genii had admission to heaven, but were expelled on account of their meddling propensities. They have ever since been of a curious and prying nature, often attempting to clamber up to the constellations; thence to peep into heaven, and see and overhear what is going on there. They are, however, driven thence by angels with flaming swords; and those meteors called shooting stars are supposed by Mahometans to be darted by the guardian angels at these intrusive genii.

Other legends pretend that the earth was originally peopled by these genii, but they rebelled against the Most High, and usurped terrestrial dominion, which they maintained for two thousand years. At length, Azazil, or Lucifer, was sent against them and defeated them, overthrowing their mighty king Gian ben Gian, the founder of the pyramids; whose magic buckler of talismanic virtue fell subsequently into the hands of king Solomon the Wise, giving him power over the spells and charms of magicians and evil genii. The rebel spirits, defeated and humiliated, were driven into an obscure corner of the earth. Then it was that God created man, with less dangerous faculties and powers, and gave him the world for a habitation.

The angels according to Moslem notions were created from bright gems; the genii from fire without smoke, and Adam from clay.

Mahomet, when in the seventy-second chapter of the Koran, he alludes to the visitation of the genii in the valley of Naklah, makes them give the following frank account of themselves:

"We formerly attempted to pry into what was transacting in heaven, but we found the same guarded by angels with flaming darts; and we sat on some of the seats thereof to hear the discourse of its inhabitants; but whoso listeneth now finds a flame prepared to guard the celestial confines. There are some among us who are Moslems, and there are others who swerve from righteousness. Whoso embraceth Islamism seeketh the true direction; but those who swerve from righteousness shall be fuel for the fire of Jehennam."

CHAPTER XII.

Night journey of the prophet from Mecca to Jerusalem; and thence to the seventh heaven.

An asylum being provided for Mahomet in the house of Mutem Ibn Adi, one of his disciples, he ventured to return to Mecca. The supernatural visitation of genii in the valley of Naklah, was soon followed by a vision or revelation far more extraordinary, and which has ever since remained a theme of comment and conjecture among devout Mahometans. We allude to the famous night journey to Jerusalem, and thence to the seventh heaven. The particulars of it, though given as if in the very words of Mahomet, rest merely on tradition ; some, however, cite texts corroborative of it, scattered here and there in the Koran.

We do not pretend to give this vision or revelation in its amplitude and wild extravagance, but will endeavour to seize upon its most essential features.

The night on which it occurred, is described as one of the darkest and most awfully silent that had ever been known. There was no crowing of cocks nor barking of dogs; no howling of wild beasts nor hooting of owls. The very waters ceased to murmur, and the winds to whistle ; all nature seemed motionless and dead. In the mid watches of the night, Mahomet was roused by a voice crying, " Awake, thou sleeper! " The angel Gabriel stood before him. His forehead was clear and serene, his complexion white as snow, his hair floated on his shoulders ; he had wings of many dazzling hues, and his robes were sown with pearls and embroidered with gold.

He brought Mahomet a white steed of wonderful form and qualities, unlike any animal he had ever seen ; and. in truth, it differs from any animal ever before described. It had a human face, but the cheeks of a horse : its eyes were as jacinths and radiant as stars. It had eagle's wings all glittering with rays of light ; and its whole form was resplendent with gems and precious stones. It was a female, and from its dazzling splendour and incredible velocity was called Al Borak, or Lightning.

Mahomet prepared to mount this supernatural steed, but as he extended his hand, it drew back and reared.

" Be still, Oh Borak! " said Gabriel ; "respect the prophet of God. Never wert thou mounted by mortal man more honoured of Allah."

" Oh Gabriel! " replied Al Borak, who at this time was miraculously endowed with speech ; " did not Abraham of old, the friend of God, bestride me when he visited his son Ishmael? Oh Gabriel! is not this the mediator, the intercessor, the author of the profession of faith ? "

" Even so, Oh Borak, this is Mahomet Ibn Abdallah, of one of the tribes of Arabia the Happy, and of the true faith. He is chief of the sons of Adam, the greatest of the divine legates, the seal of the prophets. All creatures must have his intercession before they can enter paradise. Heaven is on his right hand, to be the reward of those who believe in him ; the fire of Jehennam is on his left hand, into which all shall be thrust who oppose his doctrines."

" Oh Gabriel! " entreated Al Borak ; " by the faith existing between thee and him, prevail on him to intercede for me at the day of the resurrection "

" Be assured, Oh Borak! " exclaimed Mahomet, " that through my intercession thou shalt enter paradise."

No sooner had he uttered these words, than the animal approached and submitted to be mounted, then rising with Mahomet on its back, it soared aloft far above the mountains of Mecca.

As they passed like lightning between heaven and earth, Gabriel cried aloud, " Stop, Oh Mahomet! descend to the earth, and make the prayer with two inflections of the body."

They alighted on the earth, and having made the prayer—

" Oh friend and well beloved of my soul!" said Mahomet; "why dost thou command me to pray in this place?"

" Because it is Mount Sinai, on which God communed with Moses."

Mounting aloft, they again passed rapidly between heaven and earth, until Gabriel called out a second time, "Stop, Oh Mahomet! descend, and make the prayer with two inflections."

They descended, Mahomet prayed, and again demanded, "Why didst thou command me to pray in this place?"

" Because it is Bethlehem, where Jesus the Son of Mary was born."

They resumed their course through the air, until a voice was heard on the right, exclaiming, "Oh Mahomet, tarry a moment, that I may speak to thee; of all created beings I am most devoted to thee."

But Borak pressed forward, and Mahomet forbore to tarry, for he felt that it was not with him to stay his course, but with God the all-powerful and glorious.

Another voice was now heard on the left, calling on Mahomet in like words to tarry; but Borak still pressed forward, and Mahomet tarried not. He now beheld before him a damsel of ravishing beauty, adorned with all the luxury and riches of the earth. She beckoned him with alluring smiles: "Tarry a moment, Oh Mahomet, that I may talk with thee. I, who, of all beings, am the most devoted to thee." But still Borak pressed on, and Mahomet tarried not; considering that it was not with him to stay his course, but with God the all-powerful and glorious.

Addressing himself, however, to Gabriel, "What voices are those I have heard?" said he; "and what damsel is this who has beckoned to me?"

" The first, Oh Mahomet, was the voice of a Jew; hadst thou listened to him, all thy nation would have been won to Judaism.

" The second was the voice of a Christian: hadst thou listened to him, thy people would have inclined to Christianity.

" The damsel was the world, with all its riches, its vanities, and allurements; hadst thou listened to her, thy nation would have chosen the pleasures of this life, rather than the bliss of eternity, and all would have been doomed to perdition."

Continuing their aerial course, they arrived at the gate of the holy temple at Jerusalem, where, alighting from Al Borak, Mahomet fastened her to the rings where the prophets before him had fastened her. Then entering the temple, he found there Abraham, and Moses, and Isa (Jesus), and many more of the prophets. After he had prayed in company with them for a time, a ladder of light was let down from heaven, until the lower end rested on the Shakra, or foundation-stone of the sacred house, being the stone of Jacob. Aided by the angel Gabriel, Mahomet ascended this ladder with the rapidity of lightning.

Being arrived at the first heaven, Gabriel knocked at the gate. Who is there? was demanded from within. Gabriel. Who is with thee? Mahomet. Has he received his mission? He has. Then he is welcome! and the gate was opened.

This first heaven was of pure silver, and in its resplendent vault the stars are suspended by chains of gold. In each star an angel is placed sentinel, to prevent the demons from scaling the sacred abodes. As Mahomet entered, an ancient man approached him, and Gabriel said, "Here is thy father Adam, pay him reverence." Mahomet did so, and Adam embraced him, calling him the greatest among his children, and the first among the prophets.

In this heaven were innumerable animals of all kinds, which Gabriel said were angels, who, under these forms, interceded with Allah for the various races of animals upon earth. Among these was a cock of dazzling whiteness, and of such marvellous height, that his crest touched the second heaven, though five hundred years' journey above the first. This wonderful bird saluted the ear of Allah each morning with his melodious chant. All creatures on earth, save man, are awakened by his voice, and all the fowls of his kind chant hallelujahs in emulation of his note. [1]

They now ascended to the second heaven. Gabriel, as before, knocked at the gate; the same questions and replies were exchanged; the door opened and they entered.

This heaven was all of polished steel, and dazzling splendour. Here they found Noah; who, embracing Mahomet, hailed him as the greatest among the prophets.

Arrived at the third heaven, they entered with the same ceremonies. It was all studded with precious stones, and too brilliant for mortal eyes. Here was seated an angel of immeasurable height, whose eyes were seventy thousand days' journey apart. He had at his command a hundred thousand battalions of armed men. Before him was spread a vast book, in which he was continually writing and blotting out.

"This, Oh Mahomet," said Gabriel, "is Asrael, the angel of death, who is in the confidence of Allah. In the book before him he is continually writing the names of those who are to be born, and blotting out the names of those who have lived their allotted time, and who, therefore, instantly die."

They now mounted to the fourth heaven, formed of the finest silver. Among the angels who inhabited it was one five hundred days' journey in height. His countenance was troubled, and rivers of tears ran from his eyes. "This," said Gabriel, "is the angel of tears, appointed to weep over the sins of the children of men, and to predict the evils which await them."

---

[1] There are three to which, say the Moslem doctors, God always lends a willing ear: the voice of him who reads the Koran; of him who prays for pardon; and of this cock who crows to the glory of the Most High. When the last day is near, they add, Allah will bid this bird to close his wings and chant no more. Then all the cocks on earth will cease to crow, and their silence will be a sign that the great day of judgment is impending.

The Reverend Doctor Humphrey Prideaux, Dean or Norwich, in his life of Mahomet, accuses him of having stolen this wonderful cock from the tract Bava Bartha of the Babylonish Talmud, "wherein," says he, "we have a story of such a prodigious bird, called Zig, which, standing with his feet on the earth, reacheth up to the heavens with his head, and with the spreading of his wings, darkeneth the whole orb of the sun, and causeth a total eclipse thereof. This bird the Chaldee paraphrast on the Psalms says is a cock, and that he crows before the Lord; and the Chaldee paraphrast on Job tell us of his crowing every morning before the Lord, and that God giveth him wisdom for that purpose."

The fifth heaven was of the finest gold. Here Mahomet was received by Aaron with embraces and congratulations. The avenging angel dwells in this heaven, and presides over the element of fire. Of all the angels seen by Mahomet, he was the most hideous and terrific. His visage seemed of copper, and was covered with wens and warts. His eyes flashed lightning, and he grasped a flaming lance. He sat on a throne surrounded by flames, and before him was a heap of red-hot chains. Were he to alight upon earth in his true form, the mountains would be consumed, the seas dried up, and all the inhabitants would die with terror. To him, and the angels his ministers, is intrusted the execution of divine vengeance on infidels and sinners.

Leaving this awful abode, they mounted to the sixth heaven, composed of a transparent stone, called Hasala, which may be rendered carbuncle. Here was a great angel, composed half of snow and half of fire; yet the snow melted not, nor was the fire extinguished. Around him a choir of lesser angels continually exclaimed, "Oh Allah! who hast united snow and fire, unite all thy faithful servants in obedience to thy law."

"This," said Gabriel, "is the guardian angel of heaven and earth. It is he who despatches angels unto individuals of thy nation, to incline them in favour of thy mission, and call them to the service of God; and he will continue to do so until the day of resurrection."

Here was the prophet Musa (Moses), who,·however, instead of welcoming Mahomet with joy, as the other prophets had done, shed tears at sight of him.

"Wherefore dost thou weep?" inquired Mahomet. "Because I behold a successor, who is destined to conduct more of his nation into paradise than ever I could of the backsliding children of Israel."

Mounting hence to the seventh heaven, Mahomet was received by the patriarch Abraham. This blissful abode is formed of divine light, and of such transcendent glory that the tongue of man cannot describe it. One of its celestial inhabitants will suffice to give an idea of the rest. He surpassed the whole earth in magnitude, and had seventy thousand heads; each head seventy thousand mouths; each mouth seventy thousand tongues; each tongue spoke seventy thousand different languages, and all these were incessantly employed in chanting the praises of the Most High.

While contemplating this wonderful being, Mahomet was suddenly transported aloft to the lotus-tree, called Sedrat, which flourishes on the right hand of the invisible throne of Allah. The branches of this tree extend wider than the distance between the sun and the earth. Angels more numerous than the sands of the sea-shore, or of the beds of all the streams and rivers, rejoice beneath its shade. The leaves resemble the ears of an elephant; thousands of immortal birds sport among its branches, repeating the sublime verses of the Koran. Its fruits are milder than milk and sweeter than honey. If all the creatures of God were assembled, one of these fruits would be sufficient for their sustenance. Each seed incloses a houri, or celestial virgin, provided for the felicity of true

4

believers.   From this tree issue four rivers; two flow into the interior of paradise, two issue beyond it, and become the Nile and Euphrates.

Mahomet and his celestial guide now proceeded to Al Mamour, or the House of Adoration; formed of red jacinths or rubies, and surrounded by innumerable lamps, perpetually burning.   As Mahomet entered the portal, three vases were offered him, one containing wine, another milk, and the third, honey.   He took and drank of the vase containing milk.

"Well hast thou done; auspicious is thy choice," exclaimed Gabriel.   "Hadst thou drunk of the wine, thy people had all gone astray."

The sacred house resembles in form the Caaba at Mecca, and is perpendicularly above it in the seventh heaven.   It is visited every day by seventy thousand angels of the highest order.   They were at this very time making their holy circuit, and Mahomet, joining with them, walked round it seven times.

Gabriel could go no further.   Mahomet now traversed, quicker than thought, an immense space : passing through two regions of dazzling light, and one of profound darkness.   Emerging from this utter gloom, he was filled with awe and terror at finding himself in the presence of Allah, and but two bow-shots from his throne. The face of the Deity was covered with twenty thousand veils, for it would have annihilated man to look upon its glory.   He put forth his hands, and placed one upon the breast and the other upon the shoulder of Mahomet, who felt a freezing chill penetrate to his heart and to the very marrow of his bones.   It was followed by a feeling of estatic bliss, while a sweetness and fragrance prevailed around, which none can understand, but those who have been in the divine presence.

Mahomet now received from the Deity himself, many of the doctrines contained in the Koran; and fifty prayers were prescribed as the daily duty of all true believers.

When he descended from the divine presence and again met with Moses, the latter demanded what Allah had required " That I should make fifty prayers every day."

"And thinkest thou to accomplish such a task?   I have made the experiment before thee.   I tried it with the children of Israel, but in vain ; return, then, and beg a diminution of the task."

Mahomet returned accordingly, and obtained a diminution of ten prayers; but when he related his success to Moses, the latter made the same objection to the daily amount of forty.   By his advice Mahomet returned repeatedly, until the number was reduced to five.

Moses still objected.   " Thinkest thou to exact five prayers daily from thy people ? By Allah! I have had experience with the children of Israel, and such a demand is vain ; return, therefore, and entreat still further mitigation of the task."

"No," replied Mahomet, "I have already asked indulgence until I am ashamed."   With these words he saluted Moses and departed.

By the ladder of light he descended to the temple of Jerusalem, where he found Borak fastened as he had left her, and mounting, was borne back in an instant to the place whence he had first been taken.

This account of the vision, or nocturnal journey, is chiefly according to the words of the historians Abulfeda, Al Bokhari, and Abu Horeira, and is given more at large in the Life of Mahomet, by Gagnier. The journey itself has given rise to endless commentaries and disputes among the doctors. Some affirm that it was no more than a dream or vision of the night; and support their assertion by a tradition derived from Ayesha, the wife of Mahomet, who declared that, on the night in question, his body remained perfectly still, and it was only in spirit that he made his nocturnal journey. In giving this tradition, however, they did not consider that at the time the journey was said to have taken place, Ayesha was still a child, and, though espoused, had not become the wife of Mahomet.

Others insist that he made the celestial journey bodily, and that the whole was miraculously effected in so short a space of time, that, on his return, he was able to prevent the complete overturn of a vase of water, which the angel Gabriel had struck with his wing on his departure.

Others say that Mahomet only pretended to have made the nocturnal journey to the temple of Jerusalem, and that the subsequent ascent to heaven was a vision. According to Ahmed ben Joseph, the nocturnal visit to the temple was testified by the patriarch of Jerusalem himself. "At the time," says he, "that Mahomet sent an envoy to the emperor Heraclius, at Constantinople, inviting him to embrace Islamism, the patriarch was in the presence of the emperor. The envoy having related the nocturnal journey of the prophet, the patriarch was seized with astonishment, and informed the emperor of a circumstance coinciding with the narrative of the envoy. 'It is my custom,' said he, 'never to retire to rest at night until I have fastened every door of the temple. On the night here mentioned, I closed them according to my custom, but there was one which it was impossible to move. Upon this, I sent for the carpenters, who, having inspected the door, declared that the lintel over the portal, and the edifice itself, had settled to such a degree, that it was out of their power to close the door. I was obliged, therefore, to leave it open. Early in the morning, at the break of day, I repaired thither, and behold, the stone placed at the corner of the temple was perforated, and there were vestiges of the place where Al Borak had been fastened. Then, said I, to those present, this portal would not have remained fixed unless some prophet had been here to pray.'"

Traditions go on to say, that when Mahomet narrated his nocturnal journey to a large assembly in Mecca, many marvelled yet believed, some were perplexed with doubt, but the Koreishites laughed it to scorn. "Thou sayest that thou hast been to the temple of Jerusalem," said Abu Jahl; "prove the truth of thy words, by giving a description of it."

For a moment Mahomet was embarrassed by the demand, for he had visited the temple in the night, when its form was not discernible; suddenly, however, the angel Gabriel stood by his side, and placed before his eyes an exact type of the sacred edifice, so that he was enabled instantly to answer the most minute questions.

The story still transcended the belief even of some of his disciples, until Abu Beker, seeing them wavering in their faith, and in danger of backsliding, roundly vouched for the truth of it; in reward for which support, Mahomet gave him the title of Al Seddek, or the Testifier to the Truth, by which he was thenceforth distinguished.

As we have already observed, this nocturnal journey rests almost entirely upon tradition, though some of its circumstances are vaguely alluded to in the Koran. The whole may be a fanciful superstructure of Moslem fanatics on one of these visions or ecstasies to which Mahomet was prone, and the relation of which caused him to be stigmatized by the Koreishites as a madman.

CHAPTER XIII.

Mahomet makes converts of pilgrims from Medina.—Determines to fly to that city.—A plot to slay him.—His miraculous escape.—His Hegira, or flight.—His reception at Medina.

The fortunes of Mahomet were becoming darker and darker in his native place. Cadijah, his original benefactress, the devoted companion of his solitude and seclusion, the zealous believer in his doctrines, was in her grave : so also was Abu Taleb, once his faithful and efficient protector. Deprived of the sheltering influence of the latter, Mahomet had become, in a manner, an outlaw in Mecca; obliged to conceal himself, and remain a burthen on the hospitality of those whom his own doctrines had involved in persecution. If wordly advantage had been his object, how had it been attained? Upwards of ten years had elapsed since first he announced his prophetic mission; ten long years of enmity, trouble, and misfortune. · Still he persevered, and now, at a period of life when men seek to enjoy in repose the fruition of the past, rather than risk all in new schemes for the future, we find him, after having sacrificed ease, fortune, and friends, prepared to give up home and country also, rather than his religious creed.

As soon as the privileged time of pilgrimage arrived, he emerged once more from his concealment, and mingled with the multitude assembled from all parts of Arabia. His earnest desire was to find some powerful tribe, or the inhabitants of some important city, capable and willing to receive him as a guest, and protect him in the enjoyment and propagation of his faith.

His quest was for a time unsuccessful. Those who had come to worship at the Caaba, drew back from a man stigmatized as an apostate; and the worldly-minded were unwilling to befriend one proscribed by the powerful of his native place.

At length, as he was one day preaching on the hill Al Akaba, a little to the north of Mecca, he drew the attention of certain pilgrims from the city of Yathreb. This city, since called Medina, was about two hundred and seventy miles north of Mecca. Many of its inhabitants were Jews and heretical Christians. The pilgrims in question were pure Arabs of the ancient and powerful tribe of Khazradites, and in habits of friendly intercourse with the Kenedites and Naderites, two Jewish tribes inhabiting Mecca, who claimed to be of the sacerdotal line of Aaron. The pilgrims had often heard their Jewish friends explain the mysteries of their faith, and talk of an expected Messiah. They were moved by the eloquence of Mahomet, and struck with the resemblance of his doctrines to those of the Jewish law; insomuch that when they heard him proclaim himself a prophet, sent by heaven to restore the ancient faith, they said, one to another, "Surely this must be the promised Messiah of which we have been told." The most they listened, the stronger became their persuasion of the fact, until in the end they avowed their conviction, and made a final profession of the faith.

As the Khazradites belonged to one of the most powerful tribes of Yathreb, Mahomet sought to secure their protection, and proposed to accompany them on their return; but they informed him that they were at deadly feud with the Awsites, another powerful tribe of that city, and advised him to defer his coming until they should be at peace. He consented; but on the return home of the pilgrims, he sent with them Musab Ibn Omeir, one of the most learned and able of his disciples, with instructions to strengthen them in the faith, and to preach it to their townsmen. Thus were the seeds of Islamism first sown in the city of Medina. For a time they thrived but slowly. Musab was opposed by the idolaters, and his life threatened; but he persisted in his exertions, and gradually made converts among the principal inhabitants. Among these were Saad Ibn Maads, a prince or chief of the Awsites; and Osaid Ibn Hodheir, a man of great authority in the city. Numbers of the Moslems of Mecca also, driven away by persecution, took refuge in Medina, and aided in propagating the new faith among its inhabitants, until it found its way into almost every household.

Feeling now assured of being able to give Mahomet an asylum in the city, upwards of seventy of the converts of Medina, led by Musab Ibn Omeir, repaired to Mecca with the pilgrims in the holy month of the thirteenth year of "the mission," to invite him to take up his abode in their city. Mahomet gave them a midnight meeting on the hill Al Akaba. His uncle Al Abbas, who like the deceased Abu Taleb, took an affectionate interest in his welfare, though no convert to his doctrines, accompanied him to this secret conference, which he feared might lead him into danger. He entreated the pilgrims from Medina not to entice his nephew to their city until more able to protect him: warning them that their open adoption of the new faith would bring all Arabia in arms against them. His warnings and entreaties were in vain: a solemn compact was made between the parties. Mahomet demanded that they should abjure idolatry, and worship the one true God openly and fearlessly. For himself he exacted obedience in weal and woe; and for the disciples who might accompany him, protection; even such as they would render to their own wives and children. . On these terms he offered to bind himself to remain among them, to be the friend of their friends, the enemy of their enemies. "But, should we perish in your cause," asked they, "what will be our reward?" "Paradise!" replied the prophet.

. The terms were accepted; the emissaries from Medina placed their hands in the the hands of Mahomet, and swore to abide by the compact. The latter then singled out twelve from among them, whom he designated as his apostles; in imitation, it is supposed, of the example of our Saviour. Just then a voice was heard from the summit of the hill, denouncing them as apostates, and menacing them with punishment. The sound of this voice, heard in the darkness of the night, inspired temporary dismay. "It is the voice of the fiend Iblis," said Mahomet, scornfully; "he is the foe of God : fear him not." It was probably the voice of some spy or evesdropper of the Koreishites; for the very next morning they manifested a knowledge of what had taken place in the night; and treated the new confederates with great harshness as they were departing from the city.

It was this early accession to the faith, and this timely aid proffered and subsequently afforded to Mahomet and his disciples, which procured for the Moslems of Medina the appellation of Ansarians, or auxiliaries, by which they were afterwards distinguished.

After the departure of the Ansarians, and the expiration of the holy month, the persecutions of the Moslems were resumed with increased virulence, insomuch that Mahomet, seeing a crisis was at hand, and being resolved to leave the city, advised his adherents generally to provide for their safety. For himself, he still lingered in Mecca with a few devoted followers.

Abu Sofian, his implacable foe, was at this time governor of the city. He was both incensed and alarmed at the spreading growth of the new faith, and held a meeting of the chief of the Koreishites to devise some means of effectually putting a stop to it. Some advised that Mahomet should be banished the city; but it was objected that he might gain other tribes to his interest, or perhaps the people of Medina, and return at their head to take his revenge. Others proposed to wall him up in a dungeon, and supply him with food until he died; but it was surmised that his friends might effect his escape. All these objections were raised by a violent and pragmatical old man, a stranger from the province of Nedja, who, say the Moslem writers, was no other than the devil in disguise, breathing his malignant spirit into those present. At length it was declared by Abu Jahl, that the only effectual check on the growing evil was to put Mahomet to death. To this all agreed, and as a means of sharing the odium of the deed, and withstanding the vengeance it might awaken among the relatives of the victim, it was arranged that a member of each family should plunge his sword into the body of Mahomet.

It is to this conspiracy that allusion is made in the eighth chapter of the Koran. "And call to mind how the unbelievers plotted against thee, that they might either detain thee in bonds, or put thee to death, or expel thee the city; but God laid a plot against them; and God is the best layer of plots."

In fact, by the time the murderers arrived before the dwelling of Mahomet, he was apprised of the impending danger. As usual, the warning is attributed to the angel Gabriel, but it is probable it was given by some Koreishite, less bloody-minded than his confederates. It came just in time to save Mahomet from the hands of his enemies. They paused at his door, but hesitated to enter. Looking through a crevice they beheld, as they thought, Mahomet wrapped in his green mantle, and lying asleep on his couch. They waited for a while, consulting whether to fall on him while sleeping, or wait until he should go forth. At length they burst open the door and rushed toward the couch. The sleeper started up; but, instead of Mahomet, Ali stood before them. Amazed and confounded, they demanded, " Where is Mahomet?" " I know not," replied Ali, sternly, and walked forth; nor did any one venture to molest him. Enraged at the escape of their victim, however, the Koreishites proclaimed a reward of a hundred camels to any one who should bring them Mahomet alive or dead.

Divers accounts are given of the mode in which Mahomet made his escape from the house afer the faithful Ali had wrapped himself in his mantle and taken his place upon the couch. The most miraculous account is, that he opened the door silently, as the Koreishites stood before it, and, scattering a handful of dust in the air, cast such blindness upon them, that he walked through the midst of them without being perceived. This, it is added, is confirmed by the verse of the 30th chapter of the Koran : " We have thrown blindness upon them, that they shall not see."

The most probable account is, that he clambered over the wall in the rear of the house, by the help of a servant, who bent his back for him to step upon it.

He repaired immediately to the house of Abu Beker, and they arranged for instant flight. It was agreed that they should take refuge in a cave in Mount Thor, about an hour's distance from Mecca, and wait there until they could proceed safely to Medina : and in the meantime the children of Abu Beker should secretly bring them food. They left Mecca while it was yet dark, making their way on foot by the light of the stars, and the day dawned as they found themselves at the foot of Mount Thor. Scarce were they within the cave, when they heard the sound of pursuit. Abu Beker, though a brave man, quaked with fear. " Our pursuers," said he, " are many, and we are but two." " Nay," replied Mahomet, " there is a third; God is with us !" And here the Moslem writers relate a miracle, dear to the minds of all true believers. By the time, say they, that the Koreishites reached the mouth of the cavern, an acacia tree had sprung up before it, in the spreading branches of which a pigeon had made its nest, and laid its eggs, and over the whole a spider had woven its web. When the Koreishites beheld these signs of undisturbed quiet, they concluded that no one could recently have entered the cavern ; so they turned away, and pursued their search in another direction.

Whether protected by miracle or not, the fugitives remained for three days undiscovered in the cave, and Asama, the daughter of Abu Beker, brought them food in the dusk of the evenings.

On the fourth day, when they presumed the ardour of pursuit had abated, the fugitives ventured forth, and set out for Medina, on camels which a servant of Abu Beker ·had brought in the night for them. Avoiding the main road usually taken by the caravans, they bent their course nearer to the coast of the Red Sea. They had not proceeded far, however, before they were overtaken by a troop of horse, headed by Soraka Ibn Malec. Abu Beker was again dismayed by the number of their pursuers; but Mahomet repeated the assurance, " Be not troubled ; Allah is with us." Soraka was a grim warrior, with shagged iron-gray locks, and naked sinewy arms rough with hair. As he overtook Mahomet, his horse reared and fell with him. His superstitious mind was struck with it as an evil sign. Mahomet perceived the state of his feelings, and by an eloquent appeal wrought upon him to such a degree, that Soraka, filled with awe, entreated his forgiveness; and turning back with his troop, suffered him to proceed on his way unmolested.

The fugitives continued their journey without further interruption, until they arrived at Koba, a hill about two miles from Medina. It was a favourite resort of the inhabitants of the city, and a place to which they sent their sick and infirm, for the air was pure and salubrious. Hence, too, the city was supplied with fruit; the hill and its environs being covered with vineyards, and with groves of the date and lotus; with gardens producing citrons, oranges, pomegranates, figs, peaches, and apricots; and being irrigated with limpid streams.

On arriving at this fruitful spot, Al Kaswa, the camel of Mahomet, crouched on her knees, and would go no further. The prophet interpreted it as a favourable sign, and determined to remain at Koba, and prepare for entering the city. The place where his camel knelt is still pointed out by pious Moslems, a mosque named Al Takwa having been built there to commemorate the circumstance. Some affirm that it was actually founded by the prophet. A deep well is also shown in the vicinity, beside which Mahomet reposed under the shade of the trees, and into which he dropped his seal ring. It is believed still to remain there, and has given sanctity to the well; the waters of which are conducted by subterraneous conduits to Medina. At Koba he remained four days, residing in the house of an Awsite named Colthum Ibn Hadem. While at this village he was joined by a distinguished chief, Boreida Ibn Hoseib, with seventy followers, all of the tribe of Saham. These made profession of faith between the hands of Mahomet.

Another renowned proselyte who repaired to the prophet at this village, was Salman al Parsi (or the Persian). He is said to have been a native of a small place near Ispahan, and that, on passing one day by a Christian church, he was so much struck by the devotion of the people, and the solemnity of the worship, that he became digusted with the idolatrous faith in which he had been brought up. He afterwards wandered about the east, from city to city, and convent to convent, in quest of a religion, until an ancient monk, full of years and infirmities, told him of a prophet who had arisen in Arabia to restore the pure faith of Abraham.

This Salman rose to power in after years, and was reputed by the unbelievers of Mecca to have assisted Mahomet in compiling his doctrine. This is alluded to in the sixteenth chapter of the Koran. "Verily, the idolaters say, that a certain man assisted to compose the Koran; but the language of this man is Ajami (or Persian), and the Koran is indited in the pure Arabian tongue." [1]

The Moslems of Mecca, who had taken refuge some time before in Medina, hearing that Mahomet was at hand, came forth to meet him at Koba; among these was the early convert ·Talha, and Zobeir, the nephew of Cadijah. These, seing the travel-stained garments of Mahomet and Abu Beker, gave them white mantles, with which to make their entrance into Medina. Numbers of the Ansarians, or auxiliaries, of Medina, who had made their compact with Mahomet in the preceding year, now hastened to renew their vow of fidelity.

Learning from them that the number of proselytes in the city was rapidly augmenting, and that there was a general disposition to receive him favourably, he appointed Friday, the Moslem sabbath, the sixteenth day of the month Rabi, for his public entrance.

Accordingly, on the morning of that day he assembled all his followers to prayer; and after a sermon, in which he expounded the main principles of his faith, he mounted his camel Al Kaswa, and set forth for that city which was to become renowned in after ages as his city of refuge.

Boreida Ibn al Hoseib, with his seventy horsemen of the tribe of Saham, accompanied him as a guard. Some of the disciples took turns to hold a canopy of palm-leaves over his head, and by his side rode Abu Beker. "Oh apostle of God!" cried Boreida, "thou shalt not enter Medina without a standard," so saying, he unfolded his turban, and tying one end of it to the point of his lance, bore it aloft before the prophet.

The city of Medina was fair to approach, being extolled for beauty of situation, salubrity of climate, and fertility of soil; for the luxuriance of its palm-trees, and the fragrance of its shrubs and flowers. At a short distance from the city a crown of new proselytes to the faith, came forth in sun and dust to meet the cavalcade. Most of them had never seen Mahomet, and paid reverence to Abu Beker through mistake; but the latter put aside the screen of palm-leaves, and pointed out the real object of homage, who was greeted with loud acclamations.

In this way did Mahomet, so recently a fugitive from his native city, with a price upon his head, enter Medina, more as a conqueror in triumph than an exile seeking an asylum. He alighted at the house of a Khazradite, named Abu Ayub, a devout Moslem, to

---

[1] The renowned and learned Humphrey Prideaux, Doctor of Divinity and Dean of Norwich, in his Life of Mahomet, confounds this Salman the Persian with Abdallah Ibn Salam, a learned Jew; by some called Abdias Ben Salan in the Hebrew dialect, and by others Abdallah Salen; who is accused by Christian writers of assisting Mahomet in fabricating his revelations.

whom moreover he was distantly related; here he was hospitably received, and took up his abode in the basement story.

Shortly after his arrival he was joined by the faithful Ali, who had fled from Mecca, and journeyed on foot, hiding himself in the day and travelling only at night, lest he should fall into the hands of the Koreishites. He arrived weary and wayworn, his feet bleeding with the roughness of the journey.

Within a few days more came Ayesha, and the rest of Abu Beker's household, together with the family of Mahomet, conducted by his faithful freedman Zeid, and by Abu Beker's servant Abdallah.

Such is the story of the memorable Hegira, or "Flight of the prophet;" — the era of the Arabian kalendar from which time is calculated by all true Moslems: it corresponds to the 622d year of the Christian era.

CHAPTER XIV.

Moslems in Medina, Mohadjerins and Ansarians.—The party of Abdallah Ibn Obba and the Hypocrites.—Mahomet builds a mosque; preaches; makes converts among the Christians.—The Jews slow to believe.—Brotherhood established between fugitives and allies.

Mahomet soon found himself at the head of a numerous and powerful sect in Medina; partly made up of those of his disciples who had fled from Mecca, and were thence called Mohadjerins or Fugitives, and partly of inhabitants of the place, who on joining the faith were called Ansarians or Auxiliaries. Most of these latter were of the powerful tribes of the Awsites and Khazradites, which, though descended from two brothers, Al Aws and Al Khazraj, had for a hundred and twenty years distracted Medina by their inveterate and mortal feuds, but had now become united in the bonds of faith. With such of these tribes as did not immediately adopt his doctrines he made a covenant.

The Khazradites were very much under the sway of a prince or chief, named Abdallah Ibn Obba; who, it is said, was on the point of being made king, when the arrival of Mahomet and the excitement caused by his doctrines gave the popular feeling a new direction. Abdallah was stately in person, of a graceful demeanour, and ready and eloquent tongue; he professed great friendship for Mahomet, and with several companions of his own type and character, used to attend the meetings of the Moslems. Mahomet was captivated at first by their personal appearance, their plausible conversation, and their apparent deference; but he found in the end that Abdallah was jealous of his popularity and cherished secret animosity against him, and that his companions were equally false in their pretended friendship; hence, he stamped them with the name of "The Hypocrites." Abdallah Ibn Obba long continued his political rival in Medina.

Being now enabled publicly to exercise his faith and preach his doctrines, Mahomet proceeded to erect a mosque. The place chosen was a graveyard or burying ground, shaded by date-trees. He is said to have been guided in his choice by what he considered a favourable omen; his camel having knelt opposite to this place on his public entry into the city. The dead were removed, and the trees cut down to make way for the intended edifice. It was simple in form and structure, suited to the unostentatious religion which he professed, and to the scanty and precarious means of its votaries. The walls were of earth and brick; the trunks of the palm-trees recently felled, served as pillars to support the roof, which was framed of their branches and thatched with their leaves. It was about a hundred ells square, and had three doors; one to the south, where the Kebla was afterwards established, another called the gate of Gabriel, and the third the gate of Mercy. A part of the edifice, called Soffat, was assigned as a habitation to such of the believers as were without a home.

Mahomet assisted with his own hands in the construction of this mosque. With all his foreknowledge, he little thought that he was building his own tomb and monument; for in that edifice his remains are deposited. It has in after times been repeatedly enlarged and beautified, but still bears the name Mesjed al Nebi (the Mosque of the Prophet), from having been founded by his hands. He was for some time at a loss in what manner his followers should be summoned to their devotions; whether with the sound of trumpets, as among the Jews, or by lighting fires on high places, or by the striking of timbrels. While in this perplexity, a form of words to be cried aloud, was suggested by Abdallah, the son of Zeid, who declared that it was revealed to him in a vision. It was instantly adopted by Mahomet, and such is given as the origin of the following summons, which is to this day heard from the lofty minarets throughout the East, calling the Moslems to the place of worship : " God is great ! God is great ! There is no God but God. Mahomet is the apostle of God. Come to prayers ! come to prayers ! God is great! God is great. There is no God but God." To which at dawn of day is added the exhortation, " Prayer is better than sleep ! Prayer is better than sleep ! "

Every thing in this humble mosque was at first conducted with great simplicity. At night it was lighted up by splinters of the date-tree; and it was some time before lamps and oil were introduced. The prophet stood on the ground and preached, leaning with his back against the trunk of one of the date-trees, which served as pillars. He afterwards had a pulpit or tribune erected, to which he ascended by three steps, so as to be elevated above the congregation. Tradition asserts, that when he first ascended this pulpit, the deserted date-tree uttered a groan; whereupon, as a consolation, he gave it the choice either to be transplanted to a garden again to flourish, or to be transferred to paradise, there to yield fruit, in after life, to true believers. The date-tree wisely chose the latter, and was subsequently buried beneath the pulpit, there to await its blissful resurrection.

Mahomet preached and prayed in the pulpit, sometimes sitting, sometimes standing and leaning on a staff. His precepts as yet were all peaceful and benignant, inculcating devotion to God and humanity to man.   He seems to have emulated for a time the benignity of the Christian faith.   "He who is not affectionate to God's creatures, and to his own children," would he say, "God will not be affectionate to him.   Every Moslem who clothes the naked of his faith, will be clothed by Allah in the green robes of paradise."

In one of his traditional sermons transmitted by his disciples, is the following apologue on the subject of charity: "When God created the earth it shook and trembled, until he put mountains upon it, to make it firm.   Then the angels asked, ' Oh God, is there any thing of thy creation stronger than these mountains?'   And God replied, ' Iron is stronger than the mountains; for it breaks them.'   ' And is there any thing of thy creation stronger than iron?'   ' Yes; fire is stronger than iron, for it melts it.'   ' Is there any thing of thy creation stronger than fire?'   ' Yes; water, for it quenches fire.'   ' Oh Lord, is there any thing of thy creation stronger than water?'   ' Yes, wind; for it overcomes water and puts it in motion.'   ' Oh, our Sustainer ! is there any thing of thy creation stronger than wind?'   ' Yes, a good man giving alms; if he give with his right hand and conceal it from his left, he overcomes all things.' "

His definition of charity embraced the wide circle of kindness.   Every good act, he would say, is charity.   Your smiling in your brother's face is charity; an exhortation of your fellow man to virtuous deed is equal to alms-giving; your putting a wanderer in the right road is charity; your assisting the blind is charity; your removing stones and thorns and other obstructions from the road is charity; your giving water to the thirsty is charity.

A man's true wealth hereafter is the good he does in this world to his fellow man.   When he dies, people will say, What property has he left behind him?   But the angels, who examine him in the grave, will ask, ' What good deeds hast thou sent before thee?"

"Oh prophet!" said one of his disciples, "my mother, Omm-Sad, is dead; what is the best alms I can send for the good of her soul?"   "Water!" replied Mahomet, bethinking himself of the panting heats of the desert.   "Dig a well for her, and give water to the thirsty."   The man digged a well in his mother's name, and said, "This well is for my mother, that its rewards may reach her soul."

Charity of the tongue, also, that most important and least cultivated of charities, was likewise earnestly inculcated by Mahomet.   Abu Jaraiya, an inhabitant of Basrah, coming to Medina, and being persuaded of the apostolical office of Mahomet, entreated him some great rule of conduct.   "Speak evil of no one," answered the prophet.   "From that time," says Abu Jaraiya, "I never did abuse any one, whether freeman or slave."

The rules of Islamism extended to the courtesies of life.   Make a salam (or salutation) to a house on entering and leaving it.   Return the salute of friends and acquaintances, and wayfarers on the road.   He who rides must be the first to make the salute to him who walks; he who walks to him who is sitting; a small party to a large party, and the young to the old.

On the arrival of Mahomet at Medina, some of the Christians of the city promptly enrolled themselves among his followers; they were probably of those sectarians who held to the human nature of Christ, and found nothing repugnant in Islamism; which venerated Christ as the greatest among the prophets. The rest of the Christians resident there showed but little hostility to the new faith, considering it far better than the old idolatry. Indeed, the schims and bitter dissensions among the Christians of the East had impaired their orthodoxy, weakened their zeal, and disposed them easily to be led away by new doctrines.

The Jews, of which there were rich and powerful families in Medina and its vicinity, showed a less favourable disposition. With some of them Mahomet made covenants of peace, and trusted to gain them in time to accept him as their promised Messiah or prophet. Biased, perhaps unconsciously, by such views, he had modelled many of his doctrines on the dogmas of their religion, and observed certain of their fasts and ordinances. He allowed such as embraced Islamism, to continue in the observance of their Sabbath, and of several of the Mosaic laws and ceremonies. It was the custom of the different religions of the East, to have each a Kebla or sacred point towards which they turned their faces in the act of adoration; the Sabeans toward the North Star; the Persian fire-worshipper towards the east, the place of the rising sun; the Jews toward their holy city of Jerusalem. Hitherto Mahomet had prescribed nothing of the kind; but now, out of deference to the Jews, he made Jerusalem the Kebla, toward which all Moslems were to turn their faces when in prayer.

While new converts were daily made among the inhabitants of Medina, sickness and discontent began to prevail among the fugitives from Mecca. They were not accustomed to the climate; many suffered from fevers, and in their sickness and debility languished after the home whence they were exiled.

To give them a new home, and link them closely with their new friends and allies, Mahomet established a brotherhood between fifty-four of them and as many of the inhabitants of Médina. Two persons thus linked together, were pledged to stand by each other in weal and woe; it was a tie which knit their interests more closely even than that of kindred, for they were to be heirs to each other in preference to blood relations.

This institution was one of expediency, and lasted only until the new comers had taken firm root in Medina; extended merely to those of the people of Mecca who had fled from persecution; and is alluded to in the following verse of the eighth chapter of the Koran: "They who have believed and have fled their country, and employed their substance and their persons in fighting for the faith, and they who have given the prophet a refuge among them, and have assisted him, these shall be deemed the one nearest of kin to the other."

In this shrewd, but simple way, were laid the foundations of that power which was soon to attain stupendous strength, and to shake the mightiest empires of the world.

CHAPTER XV.

Marriage of Mahomet with Ayesha.—Of his daughter Fatima with Ali.—Their household
arrangements.

. The family relations of Mahomet had been much broken up by
the hostility brought upon him by his religious zeal. His daughter
Rokaia was still an exile with her husband, Othman Ibn Affan,
in Abyssinia; his daughter Zeinab had remained in Mecca with
her husband, Abul Aass, who was a stubborn opposer of the
new faith. The family with Mahomet in Medina consisted of his
recently wedded wife Sawda, and Fatima and Um Colthum,
daughters of his late wife Cadijah. · He had a heart prone to
affection, and subject to female influence, but he had never entertained much love for Sawda; and though he always treated her
with kindness, he felt the want of some one to supply the place of
his deceased wife Cadijah.

"Oh Omar," said he one day, "the best of man's treasures is
a virtuous woman, who acts by God's orders, and is obedient and
pleasing to her husband : he regards her personal and mental
beauties with delight; when he orders her to do any thing she
obeys him; and when he is absent she guards his right in property
and honour."

He now turned his eyes upon his betrothed spouse Ayesha, the
beautiful daughter of Abu Beker. Two years had elapsed since
they were betrothed, and she had now attained her ninth year;
an infantine age it would seem, though the female form is
wonderfully precocious in the quickening climates of the East.
Their nuptials took place a few months 'after their arrival in
Medina, and were celebrated with great simplicity; the wedding
supper was of milk, and the dowry of the bride was twelve okk
of silver.

· The betrothing of Fatima, his youngest daughter, with his loyal
disciple Ali, followed shortly after, and their marriage at a somewhat
later period. Fatima was between fifteen and sixteen years of age,
of great beauty, and extolled by Arabian writers as one of the four
perfect women with whom Allah has deigned to bless the earth.
The age of Ali was about twenty-two.

Heaven and earth, say the Moslem writers, joined in paying honour
to these happy espousals. Medina resounded with festivity, and
blazed with illuminations, and the atmosphere was laden with aro-
matic odours. As Mahomet, on the nuptial night, conducted his
daughter to her bridegroom, heaven sent down a celestial pomp to
attend her : on her right hand was the archangel Gabriel, on her
left was Michael, and she was followed by a train of seventy thousand
angels, who all night kept watch round the mansion of the youthful
pair.

Such are the vaunting exaggerations with which Moslem writers are prone to overlay every event in the history of the prophet, and destroy the real grandeur of his career, which consists in its simplicity. A more reliable account states that the wedding feast was of dates and olives; that the nuptial couch was a sheep-skin; that the portion of the bride consisted of two skirts, one head-tire, two silver armlets, one leathern pillow stuffed with palm-leaves, one beaker or drinking cup, one handmill, two large jars for water, and one pitcher. All this was in unison with the simplicity of Arab housekeeping, and with the circumstances of the married couple; and to raise the dowry required of him, Ali, it is said, had to sell several camels and some shirts of mail.

The style of living of the prophet himself was not superior to that of his disciple. Ayesha, speaking of it in after years, observed: "For a whole month together we did not light a fire to dress victuals; our food was nothing but dates and water, unless any one sent us meat. The people of the prophet's household never got wheat-bread two successive days."

His food, in general, was dates and barley-bread, with milk and honey. He swept his chamber, lit his fire, mended his clothes, and was, in fact, his own servant. For each of his two wives he provided a separate house adjoining the mosque. He resided with them by turns, but Ayesha ever remained his favourite.

Mahomet has been extolled by Moslem writers for the chastity of his early life; and it is remarkable that, with all the plurality of wives indulged in by the Arabs, and which he permitted himself in subsequent years, and with all that constitutional fondness which he evinced for the sex, he remained single in his devotion to Cadijah to her dying day, never giving her a rival in his house, nor in his heart. Even the fresh and budding charms of Ayesha, which soon assumed such empire over him, could not obliterate the deep and mingled feeling of tenderness and gratitude for his early benefactress. Ayesha was piqued one day at hearing him indulge in these fond recollections: "Oh, apostle of God," demanded the youthful beauty, "was not Cadijah stricken in years? Has not Allah given thee a better wife in her stead?"

"Never!" exclaimed Mahomet, with an honest burst of feeling—"never did God give me a better! When I was poor, she enriched me; when I was pronounced a liar, she believed in me; when I was opposed by all the world, she remained true to me!"

CHAPTER XVI.

The sword announced as the instrument of faith.—First foray against the Koreishites.—Surprisal of a caravan.

We come now to an important era in the career of Mahomet. Hitherto he had relied on argument and persuasion to make proselytes; enjoining the same on his disciples. His exhortations to them to bear with patience and long-suffering the violence of their enemies, almost emulated the meek precept of our Saviour, "if they smite thee on the one cheek, turn to them the other also." He now arrived at a point where he completely diverged from the celestial spirit of the Christian doctrines, and stamped his religion with the alloy of fallible mortality. His human nature was not capable of maintaining the sublime forbearance he had hitherto inculcated. Thirteen years of meek endurance had been rewarded by nothing but aggravated injury and insult. His greatest persecutors had been those of his own tribe, the Koreishites, especially those of the rival line of Abd Schems; whose vindictive chief, Abu Sofian, had now the sway at Mecca. By their virulent hostility his fortunes had been blasted; his family degraded, impoverished, and dispersed, and he himself driven into exile. All this he might have continued to bear with involuntary meekness, had not the means of retaliation unexpectedly sprung up within his reach. He had come to Medina a fugitive seeking an asylum, and craving merely a quiet home. In a little while, and probably to his own surprise, he found an army at his command : for among the many converts daily made in Medina; the fugitives flocking to him from Mecca, and proselytes from the tribes of the desert; were men of resolute spirit, skilled in the use of arms, and fond of partisan warfare. Human passions and mortal resentments were awakened by this sudden accession of power. They mingled with that zeal for religious reform, which was still his predominant motive. In the exaltations of his enthusiastic spirit he endeavoured to persuade himself, and perhaps did so effectually, that the power thus placed within his reach was intended as a means of effecting his great purpose, and that he was called upon by divine command to use it. Such, at least, is the purport of the memorable manifesto which he issued at this epoch, and which changed the whole tone and fortunes of his faith.

"Different prophets," said he, "have been sent by God to illustrate his different attributes : Moses his clemency and providence; Solomon his wisdom, majesty, and glory; Jesus Christ his righteousness, omniscience, and power;—his righteousness by purity of conduct; his omniscience by the knowledge he displayed of the secrets of all hearts; his power by the miracles he wrought. None of these attributes, however, have been sufficient to enforce conviction, and even the miracles of Moses and Jesus have been treated with unbelief. I, therefore, the last of the prophets, am sent with the sword! Let those who promulgate my faith enter into no argument nor discussion; but slay all who refuse obedience to the law. Whoever fights for the true faith, whether he fall or conquer, will assuredly receive a glorious reward."

"The sword," added he, "is the key of heaven and hell; all who draw it in the cause of the faith will be rewarded with temporal advantages; every drop shed of their blood, every peril and hardship endured by them, will be registered on high as more meritorious than even fasting or praying. If they fall in battle, their sins will at once be blotted out, and they will be transported to paradise, there to revel in eternal pleasures in the arms of black-eyed houris."

Predestination was brought to aid these belligerent doctrines. Every event, according to the Koran, was predestined from eternity, and could not be avoided. No man could die sooner or later than his allotted hour, and when it arrived, it would be the same, whether the angel of death should find him in the quiet of his bed, or amid the storm of battle.

Such were the doctrines and revelations which converted Islamism of a sudden from a religion of meekness and philanthropy, to one of violence and the sword. They were peculiarly acceptable to the Arabs, harmonizing with their habits, and encouraging their predatory propensities. Virtually pirates of the desert, it is not to be wondered at that, after this open promulgation of the Religion of the Sword, they should flock in crowds to the standard of the prophet. Still no violence was authorized by Mahomet against those who should persist in unbelief, provided they should readily submit to his temporal sway, and agree to pay tribute; and here we see the first indication of worldly ambition and a desire for temporal dominion dawning upon his mind. Still it will be found, that the tribute thus exacted was subsidiary to his ruling passion, and mainly expended by him in the extension of the faith.

The first warlike enterprises of Mahomet betray the lurking resentment we have noted. They were directed against the caravans of Mecca, belonging to his implacable enemies the Koreishites. The three first were headed by Mahomet in person, but without any material result. The fourth was confided to a Moslem, named Abdallah Ibn Jasch; who was sent out with eight or ten resolute followers on the road toward South Arabia. As it was now the holy month of Radjab, sacred from violence and rapine, Abdallah had sealed orders, not to be opened until the third day. These orders were vaguely yet significantly worded. Abdallah was to repair to the valley of Naklah, between Mecca and Tayef (the same in which Mahomet had the revelation of the Genii), where he was to watch for an expected caravan of the Koreishites. "Perhaps," added the letter of instructions shrewdly,—"perhaps thou mayest be able to bring us some tidings of it."

Abdallah understood the true meaning of the letter, and acted up to it. Arriving in the valley of Naklah, he descried the caravan, consisting of several camels laden with merchandise, and conducted by four men. Following it at a distance, he sent one of his men, disguised as a pilgrim, to overtake it. From the words of the latter the Koreishites supposed his companions to be like himself, pilgrims bound to Mecca. Beside, it was the month of Radjab, when the desert might be travelled in security. Scarce had they come to a halt, however, when Abdallah and his comrades fell on them; killed one and took two prisoners; the fourth escaped. The victors then returned to Medina with their prisoners and booty.

All Medina was scandalized at this breach of the holy month. Mahomet, finding that he had ventured too far, pretended to be angry with Abdallah, and refused to take the share of the booty offered to him. Confiding in the vagueness of his instructions, he insisted that he had not commanded Abdallah to shed blood, or commit any violence during the holy month.

The clamour still continuing, and being echoed by the Koreishites of Mecca, produced the following passage of the Koran:

"They will ask thee concerning the sacred month, whether they may make war therein. Answer: To war therein is grievous; but to deny God, to bar the path of God against his people, to drive true believers from his holy temple, and to worship idols, are sins far more grievous than to kill in the holy months."

Having thus proclaimed divine sanction for the deed, Mahomet no longer hesitated to take his share of the booty. He delivered one of the prisoners on ransom; the other embraced Islamism.

The above passage of the Koran, however satisfactory it may have been to devout Moslems, will scarcely serve to exculpate their prophet in the eyes of the profane. The expedition of Abdallah Ibn Jasch was a sad practical illustration of the new religion of the sword. It contemplated not merely an act of plunder and revenge, a venial act in the eyes of Arabs, and justified by the new doctrines by being exercised against the enemies of the faith, but an outrage also on the holy month, that period sacred from time immemorial against violence and bloodshed, and which Mahomet himself professed to hold in reverence. The craft and secrecy also with which the whole was devised and conducted, the sealed letter of instructions to Abdallah, to be opened only at the end of three days, at the scene of projected outrage; and couched in language vague, equivocal, yet sufficiently significant to the agent; all were in direct opposition to the conduct of Mahomet in the earlier part of his career, when he dared openly to pursue the path of duty, "though the sun should be arrayed against him on the right hand, and the moon on the left;" all showed that he was conscious of the turpitude of the act he was authorizing. His disavowal of the violence committed by Abdallah, yet his bringing the Koran to his aid to enable him to profit by it with impunity, give still darker shades to this transaction; which altogether shows how immediately and widely he went wrong the moment he departed from the benevolent spirit of Christianity, which he at first endeavoured to emulate. Worldly passions and worldly interests were fast getting the ascendency over that religious enthusiasm which first inspired him. As has well been observed, "the first drop of blood shed in his name in the Holy Week, displayed him a man, in whom the slime of earth had quenched the holy flame of prophecy."

CHAPTER XVII.

The Battle of Beder.

In the second year of the Hegira Mahomet received intelligence that his arch foe, Abu Sofian, with a troop of thirty horsemen, was conducting back to Mecca a caravan of a thousand camels, laden with the merchandise of Syria. Their route lay through the country of Medina, between the range of mountains and the sea. Mahomet determined to intercept them. About the middle of the month Ramadhan, therefore, he sallied forth with three hundred and fourteen men, of whom eighty-three were Mohadjerins, or exiles from Mecca; sixty-one Awsites, and a hundred and seventy Khazradites. Each troop had its own banner. There were but two horses in this litle army,[1] but there were seventy fleet camels, which the troop mounted by turns, so as to make a rapid march without much fatigue.

Othman Ibn Affan, the son-in-law of Mahomet, was now returned with his wife Rokaia from their exile in Abyssinia, and would have joined the enterprise, but his wife was ill almost unto death, so that he was obliged reluctantly to remain in Medina.

Mahomet for a while took the main road to Mecca, then leaving it to the left, turned toward the Red Sea and entered a fertile valley, watered by the brook Beder. Here he laid in wait near a ford, over which the caravans were accustomed to pass. He caused his men to dig a deep trench, and to divert the water therein, so that they might resort thither to slake their thirst out of reach of the enemy.

In the meantime, Abu Sofian having received early intelligence that Mahomet had sallied forth to waylay him with a superior force, despatched a messenger named Omair, on a fleet dromedary, to summon instant relief from Mecca. The messenger arrived at the Caaba haggard and breathless. Abu Jahl mounted the roof and sounded the alarm. All Mecca was in confusion and consternation. Henda, the wife of Abu Sofian, a woman of a fierce and intrepid nature, called upon her father Otha, her brother Al Walid, her uncle Shaiba, and all the warriors of her kindred, to arm and hasten to the relief of her husband. The brothers, too, of the Koreishite slain by Abdallah Ibn Jasch, in the valley of Naklah, seized their weapons to avenge his death. Motives of interest were

---

1 "The Arabs of the desert," says Burckhardt, "are not rich in horses. Among the great tribes on the Red Sea, between Akaba and Mecca, and to the south and southeast of Mecca, as far as Yemen, horses are very scarce, especially among those of the mountainous districts. The settled inhabitants of Hedjaz and Yemen are not much in the habit of keeping horses. The tribes most rich in horses are those who dwell in the comparatively fertile plains of Mesopotamia, on the banks of the river Euphrates, and on the Syrian plains."—*Burckhardt*, II. 50.

mingled with eagerness for vengeance, for most of the Koreishites had property embarked in the caravan. In a little while a force of one hundred horse and seven hundred camels hurried forward on the road toward Syria. It was led by Abu Jahl, now threescore and ten years of age, a veteran warrior of the desert, who still retained the fire, and almost the vigour and activity of youth, combined with the rancour of old age.

While Abu Jahl, with his forces, was hurrying on in one direction, Abu Sofian was approaching in another. On arriving at the region of danger, he preceded his caravan a considerable distance, carefully regarding every track and footprint. At length he came upon the track of the little army of Mahomet. He knew it from the size of the kernels of the dates, which the troops had thrown by the wayside as they marched,—those of Medina being remarkable for their smallness. On such minute signs do the Arabs depend in tracking their foes through the deserts.

Observing the course Mahomet had taken, Abu Sofian changed his route, and passed along the coast of the Red Sea until he considered himself out of danger. He then sent another messenger to meet any Koreishites that might have sallied forth, and to let them know that the caravan was safe, and they might return to Mecca.

The messenger met the Koreishites when in full march. On hearing that the caravan was safe, they came to a halt and held council. Some were for pushing forward and inflicting a signal punishment on Mahomet and his followers; others were for turning back. In this dilemma, they sent a scout to reconnoitre the enemy. He brought back word that they were about three hundred strong; this increased the desire of those who were for battle. Others remonstrated. "Consider," said they, "these are men who have nothing to lose; they have nothing but their swords; not one of them will fall without slaying his man. Beside, we have relatives among them; if we conquer, we will not be able to look each other in the face, having slain each other's relatives." These words were producing their effect, but the brothers of the Koreishite who had been slain in the valley of Naklah, were instigated by Abu Jahl to cry for revenge. That fiery old Arab seconded their appeal. "Forward!" cried he; "let us get water from the brook Beder for the feast with which we shall make merry over the escape of our caravan." The main body of the troops, therefore, elevated their standards and resumed their march, though a considerable number turned back to Mecca.

The scouts of Mahomet brought him notice of the approach of this force. The hearts of some of his followers failed them; they had come forth in the expectation of little fighting and much plunder, and were dismayed at the thoughts of such an overwhelming host; but Mahomet bade them be of good cheer, for Allah had promised him an easy victory.

The Moslems posted themselves on a rising ground, with water at the foot of it. A hut, or shelter of the branches of trees, had been hastily erected on the summit for Mahomet, and a dromedary stood before it, on which he might fly to Medina in case of defeat.

The vanguard of the enemy entered the valley panting with thirst, and hastened to the stream to drink; but Hamza, the uncle of Mahomet, set upon them with a number of his men, and slew the leader with his own hand. Only one of the vanguard escaped, who was afterwards converted to the faith.

The main body of the enemy now approached with sound of trumpet. Three Koreishite warriors advancing in front, defied the bravest of the Moslems to equal combat. Two of these challengers were Otha, the father-in-law of Abu Sofian, and Al Walid, his brother-in-law. The third challenger was Shaiba, the brother of Otha. These it will be recollected had been instigated to sally forth from Mecca, by Henda, the wife of Abu Sofian. They were all men of rank in their tribe.

Three warriors of Medina stepped forward and accepted their challenge; but they cried, "No! Let the renegades of our own city of Mecca, advance, if they dare." Upon this Hamza and Ali, the uncle and cousin of Mahomet, and Obeidah Ibn al Hareth, undertook the fight. After a fierce and obstinate contest, Hamza and Ali each slew his antagonist. They then went to the aid of Obeidah, who was severely wounded and nearly overcome by Otha. They slew the Koreishite and bore away their associate, but he presently died of his wounds.

The battle now became general. The Moslems, aware of the inferiority of their number, at first merely stood on the defensive, maintaining their position on the rising ground, and galling the enemy with flights of arrows whenever they sought to slake their intolerable thirst at the stream below. Mahomet remained in his hut on the hill, accompanied by Abu Beker, and earnestly engaged in prayer. In the course of the battle he had a paroxysm, or fell into a kind of trance. Coming to himself, he declared that God in a vision had promised him the victory. Rushing out of the hut, he caught up a handful of dust and cast it into the air toward the Koreishites, exclaiming, "May confusion light upon their faces." Then ordering his followers to charge down upon the enemy: "Fight, and fear not," cried he; "the gates of paradise are under the shade of swords. He will assuredly find instant admission, who falls fighting for the faith."

In the shock of battle which ensued, Abu Jahl, who was urging his horse into the thickest of the conflict, received a blow of a scimetar in the thigh, which brought him to the ground. Abdallah Ibn Masoud put his foot upon his breast, and while the fiery veteran was still uttering imprecations and curses on Mahomet, severed his head from his body.

The Koreishites now gave way and fled. Seventy remained dead on the field, and nearly the same number were taken prisoners. Fourteen Moslems were slain, whose names remain on record as martyrs to the faith.

This signal victory was easily to be accounted for on natural principles; the Moslems being fresh and unwearied, and having the advantage of a rising ground, and a supply of water; while the Koreishites were fatigued by a hasty march, parched with thirst, and diminished in force, by the loss of numbers who had turned back to Mecca. Moslem writers, however, attribute this early triumph of the faith to supernatural agency. When Mahomet scattered dust in the air, say they, three thousand angelic warriors in white and yellow turbans, and long dazzling robes, and mounted on black and white steeds, came rushing like a blast, and swept the Koreishites before them. Nor is this affirmed on Moslem testimony alone, but given on the word of an idolater, a peasant who was attending sheep on an adjacent hill. " I was with a companion, my cousin," said the peasant, " upon the fold of the mountain watching the conflict, and waiting to join with the conquerors and share the spoil. Suddenly, we beheld a great cloud sailing toward us, and within it were the neighing of steeds and braying of trumpets. As it approached, squadrons of angels sallied forth, and we heard the terrific voice of the archangel as he urged his mare Haizum, 'Speed! speed! Oh Haizum!" At which awful sound the heart of my companion burst with terror, and he died on the spot; and I had well nigh shared his fate." [1]

When the conflict was over Abdallah Ibn Masoud brought the head of Abu Jahl to Mahomet, who eyed the grisly trophy with exultation, exclaiming, " This man was the Pharaoh of our nation." The true name of this veteran warrior was Amru Ibn Hasham. The Koreishites had given him the surname of Abu 'lhoem, or Father of Wisdom, on account of his sagacity. The Moslems had changed it to Abu Jahl, Father of Folly. The latter appellation has adhered to him in history, and he is never mentioned by true believers without the ejaculation, " may he be accursed of God."

The Moslems who had fallen in battle were honourably interred; as to the bodies of the Koreishites, they were contemptuously thrown into a pit which had been digged for them. The question was how to dispose of the prisoners. Omar was for striking off their heads; but Abu Beker advised that they should be given up on ransom. Mahomet observed that Omar was like Noah, who prayed for the destruction of the guilty by the deluge; but Abu Beker was like Abraham, who interceded for the guilty. He decided on the side of mercy. But two of the prisoners were put to death; one, named Nadhar, for having ridiculed the Koran as a collection of Persian tales and fables; the other, named Okba, for the attempt upon the life of Mahomet when he first preached in the Caaba, and when he was rescued by Abu Beker. Several of the prisoners who were poor, were liberated on merely making oath never again to take up arms against Mahomet or his followers. The rest were detained until ransoms should be sent by their friends.

Among the most important of the prisoners, was Al Abbas, the

---

[1] This miraculous aid is repeatedly mentioned in the Koran, e. g.:

"God had already given you the victory at Beder, when ye were inferior in number. When thou saidst unto the faithful, Is it not enough for you that your Lord should assist you with three thousand angels, sent down from heaven? Verily, if ye persevere, and fear God, and your enemies come upon you suddenly, your Lord will assist you with five thousand angels, distinguished by their horses and attire—

"O true believers, ye slew not those who were slain at Beder yourselves, but God slew them. Neither didst thou, O Mahomet, cast the gravel into their eyes, when thou didst seem to cast it; but God cast it."—*Sale's Koran,* chap. iii.

uncle of Mahomet. He had been captured by Abu Yaser, a man of small stature. As the bystanders scoffed at the disparity of size, Al Abbas pretended that he really had surrendered to a horseman of gigantic size, mounted on a steed the like of which he had never seen before. Abu Yaser would have steadily maintained the truth of his capture, but Mahomet, willing to spare the humiliation of his uncle, intimated that the captor had been aided by the angel Gabriel.

Al Abbas would have excused himself from paying ransom, alleging that he was a Moslem in heart, and had only taken part in the battle on compulsion; but his excuse did not avail. It is thought by many that he really had a secret understanding with his nephew, and was employed by him as a spy in Mecca, both before and after the battle of Beder.

Another prisoner of great importance to Mahomet was Abul Aass, the husband of his daughter Zeinab. The prophet would fain have drawn his son-in-law to him and enrolled him among his disciples, but Abul Aass remained stubborn in unbelief. Mahomet then offered to set him at liberty on condition of his returning to him his daughter. To this the infidel agreed; and Zeid, the faithful freedman of the prophet, was sent with several companions to Mecca, to bring Zeinab to Medina; in the meantime, her husband Abul Aass, remained a hostage for the fulfilment of the compact.

Before the army returned to Medina there was a division of the spoil; for, though the caravan of Abu Sofian had escaped, yet considerable booty of weapons and camels had been taken in the battle, and a large sum of money would accrue from the ransom of the prisoners. On this occasion, Mahomet ordered that the whole should be equally divided among all the Moslems engaged in the enterprise; and though it was a long-established custom among the Arabs to give a fourth part of the booty to the chief, yet he contented himself with the same share as the rest. Among the spoil which fell to his lot was a famous sword of admirable temper, called Dhul Fakar, or the Piercer. He ever afterwards bore it when in battle; and his son-in-law Ali inherited it at his death.

This equal distribution of the booty caused great murmurs among the troops. Those who had borne the brunt of the fight, and had been most active in taking the spoil, complained that they had to share alike with those who had stood aloof from the affray; and with the old men who had remained to guard the camp. The dispute, observes Sale, resembles that of the soldiers of David in relation to spoils taken from the Amalekites; those who had been in the action insisting that they who tarried by the stuff should have no share of the spoil. The decision was the same—that they should share alike. (1 Samuel, ch. xxx. 24-25.) Mahomet, from his knowledge of bible history, may have been guided by this decision. The division of the spoils was an important point to settle, for a leader about to enter on a career of predatory warfare. Fortunately, he had timely revelation shortly after his return to Mecca, regulating for the future the division of all booty gained in fighting for the faith.

Such are the particulars of the famous battle of Beder, the first victory of the Saracens under the standard of Mahomet; inconsiderable, perhaps in itself, but stupendous in its results; being the commencement of a career of victories which changed the destinies of the world.

CHAPTER XVIII.

Death of the prophet's daughter Rokaia.—Restoration of his daughter Zeinab.—Effect of the prophet's malediction on Abu Lahab and his family.—Frantic rage of Henda, the wife of Abu Sofian.—Mahomet narrowly escapes assassination.—Embassy of the Koreishites.—The King of Abyssinia.

Mahomet returned in triumph to Medina with the spoils and prisoners taken in his first battle. His exultation, however, was checked by domestic grief. Rokaia, his beloved daughter, so recently restored from exile, was no more. The messenger who preceded Mahomet with tidings of his victory, met the funeral train at the gate of the city, bearing her body to the tomb.

The affliction of the prophet was soothed shortly afterward by the arrival from Mecca of his daughter Zeinab, conducted by the faithful Zeid. The mission of Zeid had been attended with difficulties. The people of Mecca were exasperated by the late defeat, and the necessity of ransoming the prisoners. Zeid remained, therefore, without the walls, and sent in a message to Kenanah, the brother of Abul Aass, informing him of the compact, and appointing a place where Zeinab should be delivered into his hands. Kenanah set out to conduct her thither in a litter. On the way he was beset by a throng of Koreishites, determined to prevent the daughter of Mahomet from being restored to him. In the confusion one Habbar Ibn Aswad made a thrust at the litter with a lance, which, had not Kenanah parried it with his bow, might have proved fatal to Zeinab. Abu Sofian was attracted to the place by the noise and tumult, and rebuked Kenanah for restoring Mahomet's daughter thus publicly, as it might be construed into a weak concession; Zeinab was taken back, therefore, to her home, and Kenanah delivered her up secretly to Zeid in the course of the following night.

Mahomet was so exasperated at hearing of the attack on his daughter, that he ordered whoever should take Habbar, to burn him alive. When his rage had subsided he modified this command. "It is for God alone," said he, "to punish man with fire. If taken let Habbar be put to death with the sword."

The recent triumph of the Moslems at Beder struck the Koreishites of Mecca with astonishment and mortification. The man so recently driven a fugitive from their walls, had suddenly started up a powerful foe. Several of their bravest and most important men had fallen beneath his sword; others were his captives, and awaited a humiliating ransom. Abu Lahab, the uncle of Mahomet, and always his vehement opposer, had been unable, from illness, to take the field. He died a few days afer hearing of the victory, his death being hastened by the exasperation of his spirits. Pious Moslems, however, attribute it to the curse pronounced by Mahomet aforetime on him and his family, when he raised his hand to hurl a stone at the prophet on the hill of Safa. That curse, say they, fell heavily also on his son Otho, who had repudiated the prophet's daughter Rokaia; he was torn to pieces by a lion, in the presence of a whole caravan, when on a journey to Syria.

By no one was the recent defeat at Beder felt so severely as by Abu Sofian. He reached Mecca in safety with his caravan, it is true; but it was to hear of the triumph of the man he detested, and to find his home desolate. His wife Henda met him with frantic lamentations for the death of her father, her uncle, and her brother. Rage mingled with her grief, and she cried night and day for vengeance on Hamza and Ali, by whose hands they had fallen. [1]

Abu Sofian summoned two hundred fleet horsemen, each with a sack of meal at his saddle-bow, the scanty provisions of an Arab for a foray; as he sallied forth he vowed neither to anoint his head, perfume his beard, nor approach a female, until he had met Mahomet face to face. Scouring the country to within three miles of the gates of Medina, he slew two of the prophet's followers, ravaged the fields, and burnt the date-trees.

Mahomet sallied forth to meet him at the head of a superior force. Abu Sofian, regardless of his vow, did not await his approach, but turned bridle and fled. His troop clattered after him, throwing off their sacks of meal in the hurry of their flight; whence this scampering affair was derisively called "The war of the meal sacks."

Moslem writers record an imminent risk of the prophet, while yet in the field on this occasion. He was one day sleeping alone at the foot of a tree, at a distance from his camp, when he was awakened by a noise, and beheld Durthur, a hostile warrior, standing over him with a drawn sword. "Oh Mahomet," cried he, "who is there now to save thee?" "God!" replied the prophet. Struck with conviction, Durthur let fall his sword, which was instantly seized upon by Mahomet. Brandishing the weapon, he exclaimed in turn, "Who is there now to save thee, Oh Durthur?" "Alas, no one!" replied the soldier. "Then learn from me to be merciful." So saying, he returned the sword. The heart of the warrior was overcome; he acknowledged Mahomet as the prophet of God, and embraced the faith.

[1] It is a received law among all the Arabs, that whoever sheds the blood of a man, owes blood on that account to the family of the slain person. This ancient law is sanctioned by the Koran. "O true believers, the law of retaliation is ordained to you for the slain; the free shall die for the free" The blood revenge, or Thar, as it is termed in Arabic, is claimed by the relatives of all who have been killed in open war, and not merely of the actual homicide, but of all his relations. For those killed in wars between two tribes, the price of blood is required from the persons who were known to have actually killed them.

The Arab regards this blood revenge as one of his most sacred rights, as well as duties; no earthly consideration could induce him to give it up. He has a proverbial saying, "Were hell-fire to be my lot, I would not relinquish the Thar."—See *Burckhardt*, v. i. 314, Notes.

As if the anecdote were not sufficiently marvellous, other devout Moslems affirm that the delivrance of Mahomet was through the intervention of the angel Gabriel, who, at the moment Durthur was about to strike, gave him a blow on the breast with his invisible hand, which caused him to let fall his sword.

About this time the Koreishites of Mecca bethought themselves of the relatives and disciples of Mahomet who had taken refuge from their persecutions in Abyssinia; most of whom still remained there under the protection of the Najashee or Abyssinian king. To this potentate the Koreishites sent an embassy to obtain the persons of the fugitives. One of the ambassadors was Abdallah Ibn Rabia; another was Amru Ibn Al Aass, the distinguished poet who had assailed Mahomet at the outset of his mission with lampoons and madrigals. He was now more matured in years, and as remarkable for his acute sagacity as for his poetic talents. He was still a redoubtable opponent of the faith of Islam, of which in after years he was to prove one of the bravest and most distinguished champions.

Amru and Abdallah opened their embassy in the oriental style by the parade of rich presents, and then requested, in the name of the Koreish authorities of Mecca, that the fugitives might be delivered up to them. The king was a just man, and summoned the Moslems before him to explain this new and dangerous heresy of which they were accused. Among their number was Giafar, or Jaffar, the son of Abu Taleb, and brother of Ali, consequently the cousin of Mahomet. He was a man of persuasive eloquence and a most prepossessing appearance. He stood forth on this occasion, and expounded the doctrines of Islam with zeal and power. The king; who, as has been observed, was a Nestorian Christian, found these doctrines so similar in many respects to those of his sect, and so opposed to the gross idolatry of the Koreishites, that, so far from giving up the fugitives, he took them more especially into favour and protection, and returning to Amru and Abdallah the presents they had brought, dismissed them from his court.

CHAPTER XIX.

The battle of Beder had completely changed the position of Mahomet; he was now a triumphant chief of a growing power. The idolatrous tribes of Arabia were easily converted to a faith which flattered their predatory inclinations with the hope of spoil, and which, after all, professed but to bring them back to the primitive religion of their ancestors; the first cavalcade, therefore, which entered the gates of Medina with the plunder of a camp, made converts of almost all its heathen inhabitants, and gave Mahomet the control of the city. His own tone now became altered, and he spoke as a lawgiver and a sovereign. The first evidence of this change of feeling was in his treatment of the Jews, of whom there were three principal and powerful families in Medina.

All the concessions made by him to that stiff-necked race had proved fruitless; they not only remained stubborn in unbelief, but treated him and his doctrines with ridicule. Assma, the daughter of Merwan, a Jewish poetess, wrote satires against him. She was put to death by one of his fanatic disciples. Abu Afak, an Israelite, one hundred and twenty years of age, was likewise slain for indulging in satire against the prophet. Kaab Ibn Aschraf, another Jewish poet, repaired to Mecca after the battle of Beder, and endeavoured to stir up the Koreishites to vengeance, reciting verses in which he extolled the virtues and bewailed the death of those of their tribe who had fallen in the battle. Such was his infatuation, that he recited these verses in public, on his return to Medina, and in the presence of some of the prophet's adherents who were related to the slain. Stung by this invidious hostility, Mahomet one day exclaimed in his anger, "Who will rid me of this son of Aschraf?" Within a few days afterwards, Kaab paid for his poetry with his life; being slain by a zealous Ansarian of the Awsite tribe.

An event at length occurred, which caused the anger of Mahomet against the Jews to break out in open hostility. A damsel of one of the pastoral tribes of Arabs who brought milk to the city, was one day in the quarter inhabited by the Beni Kainoka, or children of Kainoka, one of the three principal Jewish families. Here she was accosted by a number of young Israelites, who having heard her beauty extolled, besought her to uncover her face. The damsel refused an act contrary to the laws of propriety among her people. A young goldsmith, whose shop was hard by, secretly fastened the end of her veil to the bench on which she was sitting, so that when she rose to depart, the garment remained, and her face was exposed to view. Upon this there was laughter and scoffing among the young Israelites, and the damsel stood in the midst confounded and abashed. A Moslem present, resenting the shame put upon her, drew his sword, and thrust it through the body of the goldsmith; he in his turn was instantly slain by the Israelites. The Moslems from a neighbouring quarter flew to arms, the Beni Kainoka did the same, but being inferior in numbers, took refuge in a stronghold. Mahomet interfered to quell the tumult; but, being generally exasperated against the Israelites, insisted that the offending tribe should forthwith embrace the faith. They pleaded the treaty which he had made with them on his coming to Medina, by which they were allowed the enjoyment of their religion; but he was not to be moved. For some time the Beni Kainoka refused to yield, and remained obstinately shut up in their stronghold; but famine compelled them to surrender. Abdallah Ibn Obba Solul, the leader of the Khazradites, who was a protector of this Jewish tribe, interfered in their favour, and prevented their being put to the sword; but their wealth and effects were confiscated, and they were banished to Syria, to the number of seven hundred men.

The arms and riches accruing to the prophet and his followers from this confiscation, were of great avail in the ensuing wars of the faith. Among the weapons which fell to the share of Mahomet, are enumerated three swords; Medham, the Keen, al Battar, the Trenchant, and Hatef, the Deadly. Two lances, al Monthari, the Disperser, and al Monthawi, the Destroyer. A cuirass of silver, named al Fadha, and another named al Saadia, said to have been given by Saul to David, when about to encounter Goliath. There was a bow, too, called al Çatûm, or the Strong, but it did not answer to its name, for in the first battle in which the prophet used it, he drew it with such force that he broke it in pieces. In general, he used the Arabian kind of bow, with appropriate arrows and lances, and forbade his followers to use those of Persia.

Mahomet now sought no longer to conciliate the Jews; on the contrary, they became objects of his religious hostility. He revoked the regulation by which he had made Jerusalem the Kebla or point of prayer, and established Mecca in its place; towards which, ever since, the Mahometans turn their faces when performing their devotions.

The death of the prophet's daughter Rokaia had been properly deplored by her husband Othman. To console the latter for his loss, Omar, his brother in arms, offered him, in the course of the year, his daughter Hafza for wife. She was the widow of Hobash, a Suhamite, eighteen-years of age, and of tempting beauty, yet Othman declined the match. Omar was indignant at what he conceived a slight to his daughter and to himself, and complained of it to Mahomet. "Be not grieved, Omar," replied the prophet, "a better wife is destined for Othman, and a better husband for thy daughter." He in effect gave his own daughter Omm Kolthum to Othman; and took the fair Hafza to wife himself. By these politic alliances he grappled both Othman and Omar more strongly to his side, while he gratified his own inclinations for female beauty. Hafza, next to Ayesha, was the most favoured of his wives; and was intrusted with the coffer containing the chapters and verses of the Koran as they were revealed.

CHAPTER XX.

Henda incites Abu Sofian and the Koreishites to revenge the death of her relations slain in the battle of Beder.—The Koreishites sally forth, followed by Henda and her female companions.—Battle of Ohod.—Ferocious triump of Henda.—Mahomet consoles himself by marrying Hend, the daughter of Omeya.

As the power of Mahomet increased in Medina, the hostility of the Koreishites in Mecca augmented in virulence. Abu Sofian held command in the sacred city, and was incessantly urged to warfare by his wife Henda, whose fierce spirit could take no rest, until "blood revenge" had been wreaked on those by whom her father and brother had been slain   Akrema, also, a son of Abu Jahl, and who inherited his father's hatred of the prophet, clamoured for vengeance   In the third year of the. Hegira, therefore, the year after the battle of Beder, Abu Sofian took the field at the head of three thousand men, most of them Koreishites, though there were also Arabs of the tribes of Kanana and Tehama.   Seven hundred were armed with corselets. and two hundred were horsemen.   Akrema was one of the captains, as was also Kaled Ibn al Waled, a warrior of indomitable valour, who afterwards rose to great renown.   The banners were borne in front by the race of Abd al Dar, a branch of the tribe of Koreish, who had a hereditary right to the foremost place in council, the foremost rank in battle, and to bear the standard in the advance of the army.

In the rear of the host folloyed the vindictive Henda, with fifteen principal women of Mecca, relatives of those slain in the battle of Beder; sometimes filling the air with wailings and lamentations for the dead; at other times animating the troops with the sound of timbrels and warlike chants.   As they passed through the village of Abwa, where Amina the mother of Mahomet was interred, Henda was with difficulty prevented from tearing the mouldering bones out of the grave.

Al Abbas, the uncle of Mahomet, who still resided in Mecca, and was considered hostile to the new faith, seeing that destruction threatened his nephew should that army come upon him by surprise, sent secretly a swift messenger to inform him of his danger. Mahomet was at the village of Koba, when the message reached him.   He immediately hastened back to Medina, and called a council of his principal adherents.   Representing the insufficiency of their force to take the field, he gave it as his opinion that they should await an attack in Medina, where the very women and children could aid them by hurling stones from the house-tops. The elder among his followers joined in his opinion; but the young men, of heady valour at all times, and elated by the late victory at Beder, cried out for a fair fight in the open field.

Mahomet yielded to their clamours, but his forces, when mustered, were scarce a thousand men ; one hundred only had cuirasses, and but two were horsemen.   The hearts of those recently so clamorous to sally forth, now misgave them, and they would fain await the encounter within the walls   "No," replied Mahomet, "it becomes not a prophet when once he has drawn the sword to sheathe it; nor when once he has advanced, to turn back, until God has decided between him and the foe."   So saying, he led forth his army.   Part of it was composed of Jews and Khazradites, led by Abdallah Ibn Obba Solûl.   Mahomet declined the assistance of the Jews, unless they embraced the faith of Islam, and as they refused, he ordered them back to Medina; upon which their protector, Abdallah, turned back also with his Khazradites; thus reducing the army to about seven hundred men.

With this small force Mahomet posted himself upon the hill of Ohod, about six miles from Medina. His position was partly defended by rocks and the asperities of the hill, and archers were stationed to protect him in flank and rear from the attacks of cavalry. He was armed with a helmet and two shirts of mail. On his sword was engraved, "Fear brings disgrace; forward lies honour. Cowardice saves no man from his fate." As he was not to take an active part in battle, he confided his sword to a brave warrior, Abu Dudjana, who swore to wield it as long as it had edge and temper. For himself, he, as usual, took a commanding stand whence he might overlook the field.

The Koreishites, confident in their numbers, came marching to the foot of the hill with banners flying. Abu Sofian led the centre; there were a hundred horsemen on each wing; the left commanded by Akrema, the son of Abu Jahl, the right by Khaled Ibn al Waled. As they advanced, Henda and her companions struck their timbrels and chanted their war song; shrieking out at intervals the names of those who had been slain in the battle of Beder. "Courage, sons of Abd al Dar!" cried they to the standard-bearers. "Forward to the fight! close with the foe! strike home and spare not. Sharp be your swords and pitiless your hearts!"

Mahomet restrained the impatience of his stroops; ordering them not to commence the fight, but to stand firm and maintain their advantage of the rising ground. Above all, the archers were to keep to their post, let the battle go as it might, lest the cavalry should fall upon his rear.

The horsemen of the left wing, led by Akrema, now attempted to take the Moslems in flank, but were repulsed by the archers, and retreated in confusion. Upon this Hamza set up the Moslem war-cry, Amit! amit! (Death! death!) and rushed down with his forces upon the centre. Abu Dudjana was at his right hand, armed with the sword of Mahomet, and having a red band round his head, on which was written, "Help comes from God! victory is ours!"

The enemy were staggered by the shock. Abu Dudjana dashed into the midst of them, dealing deadly blows on every side, and exclaiming. "The sword of God and his prophet!" Seven standard-bearers, of the race of Abd el Dar, were, one after the other, struck down, and the centre began to yield. The Moslem archers, thinking the victory secure, forgot the commands of Mahomet, and leaving their post, dispersed in quest of spoil, crying "Booty! booty!" Upon this Khaled, rallying the horse, got possession of the ground abandoned by the archers, attacked the Moslems in rear, put some to flight, and threw the rest in confusion. In the midst of the confusion a horseman, Obbij Ibn Chalaf by name, pressed through the throng, crying, "Where is Mahomet? There is no safety while he lives." But Mahomet, seizing a lance from an attendant, thrust it through the throat of the idolater, who fell dead from his horse. "Thus," says the pious Al Jannabi, "died this enemy of God, who, some years before, had menaced the prophet, saying, 'I shall find a day to slay thee.' 'Have a care,' was the reply; 'if it please Allah, thou thyself shall fall beneath my hand.'"

In the midst of the melee a stone from a sling struck Mahomet on the mouth, cutting his lip and knocking out one of his front teeth; he was wounded in the face also by an arrow, the iron head of which, remained in the wound. · Hamza, too, while slaying a Koreishite, was transfixed by the lance of Waksa, an Ethiopian slave, who had been promised his freedom if he should revenge the death of his master, slain by Hamza in the battle of Beder. Mosaab Ibn Omair, also, who bore the standard of Mahomet, was laid low, but Ali seized the sacred banner and bore it aloft amidst the storm of battle.

As Mosaab resembled the prophet in person, a shout was put up by the enemy that Mahomet was slain. The Koreishites were inspired with redoubled ardour at the sound; the Moslems fled in despair, · bearing with them Abu Beker and Omar, who were wounded. Raab, the son of Malek, however, beheld Mahomet lying among the wounded in a ditch, and knew him by his armour. " Oh believers!" cried he, " the prophet of God yet lives. To the rescue! to the rescue!" Mahomet was drawn forth and borne up the hill to the summit of a rock, where the Moslems prepared for a desperate defence. The Koreishites, however, thinking Mahomet slain, forbore to pursue them, contenting themselves with plundering and mutilating the dead. Henda and her female companions were foremost in the savage work of vengeance; and the ferocious heroine sought to tear out and devour the heart of Hamza. Abu Sofian bore a part of the mangled body upon his lance, and descending the hill in triumph, exclaimed, exultingly, "War has its vicissitudes. The battle of Ohod succeeds to the battle of Beder."

The Koreishites having withdrawn, Mahomet descended from the rock and visited the field of battle. At sight of the body of his uncle Hamza, so brutally mangled and mutilated, he vowed to inflict like outrage on seventy of the enemy when in his power. His grief, we are told, was soothed by the angel Gabriel, who assured him that Hamza was enregistered an inhabitant of the seventh heaven, by the title of "The lion of God and of his prophet."

The bodies of the slain were interred two and two, and three and three, in the places where they had fallen. Mahomet forbade his followers to mourn for the dead by cutting off their hair, rending their garments, and the other modes of lamentation usual among the Arabs; but he consented that they should weep for the dead, as tears relieve the overladen heart.

The night succeeding the battle was one of great disquietude, lest the Koreishites should make another attack; or should surprise Medina. On the following day he marched in the direction of that city, hovering near the enemy, and on the return of night lighting numerous watch-fires. Abu Sofian, however, had received intelligence that Mahomet was still alive. He felt himself too weak to attack the city, therefore, while Mahomet was in the field, and might come to its assistance; and he feared that the latter might be reinforced by its inhabitants, and seek him with superior numbers. Contenting himself, therefore, with the recent victory, he made a truce with the Moslems for a year, and returned in triumph to Mecca.

Mahomet sought consolation for this mortifying defeat by taking to himself another wife, Hend, the daughter of Omeyà, a man of great influence. She was a widow, and had, with her husband, been among the number of the fugitives in Abyssinia. She was now twenty-eight years of age, and had a son named Salma, whence, she was commonly called Omm Salma, or the Mother of Salma. Being distinguished for grace and beauty, she had been sought by Abu Beker and Omar, but without success. Even Mahomet at first met with difficulty. "Alas!" said she, "what happiness can the prophet of God expect with me? I am no longer young; I have a son, and I am of a jealous disposition." "As to thy age," replied Mahomet, "thou art much younger than I. As to thy son, I will be a father to him : as to thy jealous disposition, I will pray Allah to root it from thy heart."

A separate dwelling was prepared for the bride, adjacent to the mosque. The household goods, as stated by a Moslem writer, consisted of a sack of barley, a hand-mill, a pan, and a pot of lard or butter. Such were as yet the narrow means of the prophet; or rather, such the frugality of his habits and the simplicity of Arab life.

CHAPTER XXI.

Treachery of certain Jewish tribes ; their punishment.— Devotion of the prophet's freed-man Zeid; divorces his beautiful wife Zeinab, that she may become the wife of the prophet.

The defeat of Mahomet at the battle of Ohod, acted for a time unfavourably to his cause among some of the Arab and Jewish tribes, as was evinced by certain acts of perfidy. The inhabitants of two towns, Adhal and Kara, sent a deputation to him, professing an inclination to embrace the faith, and requesting missionaries to teach them its doctrines. He accordingly sent six disciples to accompany the deputation; but on the journey, while reposing by the brook Radje within the boundaries of the Hodseitites, the deputies fell upon the unsuspecting Moslems, slew four of them, and carried the other two to Mecca, where they gave them up to the Koreishites, who put them to death.

A similar act of treachery was practised by the people of the province of Nadjed. Pretending to be Moslems, they sought succour from Mahomet against their enemies. He sent a number of his followers to their aid, who were attacked by the Beni Suleim or Suleimites, near the brook Manna, about four day's journey from Medina, and slain almost to a man. One of the Moslems, Amru Ibn Omeya, escaped the carnage and made for Medina. On the way he met two unarmed Jews of the Beni Amir ; either mistaking these for enemies, or provoked to wanton rage by the death of his comrades, he fell upon them and slew them. The tribe, who were at peace with Mahomet, called upon him for redress. He referred the matter to the mediation of another Jewish tribe, the Beni

Nadher, who had rich possessions and a castle, called Zohra, within three miles of Medina. This tribe had engaged by treaty, when he came a fugitive from Mecca, to maintain a neutrality between him and his opponents. The chief of this tribe being now applied to as a mediator, invited Mahomet to an interview. He went, accompanied by Abu Beker, Omar, Ali, and a few others. A repast was spread in the open air before the mansion of the chief. Mahomet, however, received private information that he had been treacherously decoyed hither, and was to be slain as he sat at the repast: it is said that he was to be crushed by a mill-stone, flung from the terraced roof of the house. Without intimating his knowledge of the treason, he left the company abruptly, and hastened back to Medina.

His rage was now kindled against the whole race of Nadher, and he ordered them to leave the country within ten days on pain of death. They would have departed, but Abdallah the Khazradite secretly persuaded them to stay by promising them aid. He failed in his promise. The Beni Nadher, thus disappointed by the " Chief of the Hypocrites," shut themselves up in their castle of Zohra, where they were besieged by Mahomet, who cut down and burnt the date-trees, on which they depended for supplies. At the end of six days they capitulated, and were permitted to depart, each with a camel load of effects, arms excepted. Some were banished to Syria, others to Khaïbar, a strong Jewish city and fortress, distant several days' journey from Medina. As the tribe was wealthy, there was great spoil, which Mahomet took entirely to himself. His followers demurred that this was contrary to the law of partition revealed in the Koran; but he let them know that according to another revelation, all booty gained, like the present, without striking a blow, was not won by man, but was a gift from God, and must be delivered over to the prophet to be expended by him in good works, and the relief of orphans, of the poor, and the traveller. Mahomet in effect did not appropriate it to his own benefit, but shared it among the Mohadjerins, or exiles from Mecca; two Nadherite Jews who had embraced Islamism, and two or three Ansarians or Auxiliaries of Medina, who had proved themselves worthy, and were poor.

We forbear to enter into details of various petty expeditions of Mahomet about this time, one of which extended to the neighbourhood of Tabuk, on the Syrian frontier, to punish a horde which had plundered the caravans of Medina. These expeditions were checkered in their results, though mostly productive of booty ; which now began to occupy the minds of the Moslems, almost as much as the propagation of the faith. , The spoils thus suddenly gained may have led to riot and debauchery, as we find a revelation of the passage of the Koran, forbidding wine and games of hazard, those fruitful causes of strife and insubordination in predatory camps.

During this period of his career, Mahomet in more than one instance narrowly escaped falling by the hand of an assassin. He himself is charged with the use of insidious means to rid himself of an enemy; for it is said that he sent Amru Ibn Omeya on a secret

6

errand to Mecca, to assassinate Abu Sofian, but that the plot was discovered, and the assassin only escaped by rapid flight. The charge, however, is not well substantiated, and is contrary to his general character and conduct.

If Mahomet had relentless enemies, he had devoted friends, an instance of which we have in the case of his freedman and adopted son Zeid Ibn Horeth. He had been one of the first converts to the faith, and one of its most valiant champions. Mahomet consulted him on all occasions, and employed him in his domestic concerns. One day he entered his house with the freedom with which a father enters the dwelling of a son. Zeid was absent, but Zeinab his wife, whom he had recently married, was at home. She was the daughter of Djasch, of the country of Kaiba, and considered the fairest of her tribe. In the privacy of home she had laid aside her veil and part of her attire, so that her beauty stood revealed to the gaze of Mahomet on his sudden entrance. He could not refrain from expressions of wonder and admiration, to which she made no reply, but repeated them all to her husband on his return. Zeid knew the amorous susceptibility of Mahomet, and saw that he had been captivated by the beauty of Zeinab. Hastening after him, he offered to repudiate his wife; but the prophet forbade it as contrary to the law. The zeal of Zeid was not to be checked; he loved his beautiful wife, but he venerated the prophet, and he divorced himself without delay. When the requisite term of separation had elapsed, Mahomet accepted, with gratitude, this pious sacrifice. His nuptials with Zeinab surpassed in splendour all his other marriages. His doors were thrown open to all comers; they were feasted with the flesh of sheep and lambs, with cakes of barley, with honey, and fruits, and favourite beverages; so they ate and drank their fill and then departed—railing against the divorce as shameful, and the marriage as incestuous.

At this critical juncture was revealed that part of the thirty-third chapter of the Koran, distinguishing relatives by adoption from relatives by blood, according to which there was no sin in marrying one who had been the wife of an adopted son. This timely revelation pacified the faithful; but, to destroy all shadow of a scruple, Mahomet revoked his adoption, and directed Zeid to resume his original appellation of Ibn Hareth, after his natural father. The beautiful Zeinab, however, boasted thenceforth a superiority over the other wives of the prophet on the score of the revelation, alleging that her marriage was ordained by heaven.[1]

---

[1] This was Mahomet's second wife of the name of Zeinab; the first, who had died some time previous, was the daughter of Chuzeima.

CHAPTER XXII.

Expedition of Mahomet against the Beni Mostalek.—He espouses Barra, a captive.—
Treachery of Abdallah Ibn Obba.—Ayesha slandered.—Her vindication.—Her innocence proved by a revelation.

Among the Arab tribes which ventured to take up arms against
Mahomet after his defeat at Ohod, were the Beni Mostalek, a powerful race of Koreishite origin.   Mahomet received intelligence of
their being assembled in warlike guise under their prince Al Hareth,
near the wells of Moraïsi, in the territory of Kedaid, and within
five miles of the Red Sea.   He immediately took the field at the
head of a chosen band of the faithful, accompanied by numbers of
the Khazradites, led by their chief Abdallah Ibn Obba.   By a rapid
movement he surprised the enemy; Al Hareth was killed at the
onset by the flight shot of an arrow; his troops fled in confusion
after a brief resistance, in which a few were slain.   Two hundred
prisoners, five thousand sheep, and one thousand camels, were the
fruits of this easy victory.   Among the captives was Barra the
daughter of Al Hareth, and wife to a young Arab of her kin.   In
the division of the spoil she fell to the lot of Thabet Ibn Reis, who
demanded a high ransom.   The captive appealed to Mahomet
against this extortion, and prayed that the ransom might be miti-
gated.   The prophet regarded her with eyes of desire, for she was
fair to look upon.   "I can serve thee better," said he, "than by
abating thy ransom : be my wife."   The beautiful Barra gave ready
consent; her ransom was paid by the prophet to Thabet; her
kindred were liberated by the Moslems, to whose lot they had
fallen; most of them embraced the faith, and Barra became the wife
of Mahomet after his return to Medina.

After the battle, the troops crowded round the wells of Moraïsi
to assuage their thirst.   In the press a quarrel rose between some
of the Mohadjerins, or exiles of Mecca, and the Khazradites, in
which one of the latter received a blow.   His comrades rushed to
revenge the insult, and blood would have been shed but for the interference of Mahomet.   The Khazradites remained incensed, and
other of the people of Medina made common cause with them.
Abdallah Ibn Obba, eager to take advantage of every circumstance
adverse to the rising power of Mahomet, drew his kindred and
townsfolk apart.   "Behold," said he, "the insults you have
brought upon yourselves by harbouring these fugitive Koreishites.
You have taken them to your houses, and given them your goods,
and now they turn upon and maltreat you.   They would make
themselves your masters even in your own house; but by Allah,
when we return to Medina, we will see which of us is strongest."

Secret word was brought to Mahomet of this seditious speech.
Omar counselled him at once to make way with Abdallah; but the

prophet feared to excite the vengeance of the kindred and adherents of the powerful Khazradite. To leave no time for mutiny, he set off immediately on the homeward march, although it was in. the heat of the day, and continued on throughout the night, nor halted until the following noon, when the wearied soldiery cared for nothing but repose.

On arriving at Medina, he called Abdallah to account for his seditious expressions. He flatly denied them, pronouncing the one who had accused him a liar. A revelation from heaven, however, established the charge against him and his adherents. "These are the men," says the Koran, "who say to the inhabitants of Medina, do not bestow any thing on the refugees who are with the apostle of God, that they may be compelled to separate from him. They say, verily, if we return to Medina, the worthier will expel thence the meaner. God curse them! how are they turned aside from the truth."

Some of the friends of Abdallah, convinced by this revelation, advised him to ask pardon of the prophet; but he spurned their counsel. "You have already," said he, "persuaded me to give this man my countenance and friendship, and now you would have me put myself beneath his very feet."

Nothing could persuade him that Mahomet was not an idolater at heart, and his revelations all imposture and deceit. He considered him, however, a formidable rival, and sought in every way to injure and annoy him. To this implacable hostility is attributed a scandalous story which he propagated about Ayesha, the favourite wife of the prophet.

It was the custom with Mahomet always to have one of his wives with him, on his military expeditions, as companion and solace; she was taken by lot, and on the recent occasion the lot had fallen on Ayesha. She travelled in a litter, inclosed by curtains, and borne on the back of a camel, which was led by an attendant. On the return homeward the army, on one occasion, coming to a halt, the attendants of Ayesha were astonished to find the litter empty. Before they had recovered from their surprise, she arrived on a camel, led by a youthful Arab named Safwan Ibn al Moattel. This circumstance having come to the knowledge of Abdallah, he proclaimed it to the world after his return to Medina, affirming that Ayesha had been guilty of wantonness with the youthful Safwan.

The story was eagerly caught up and circulated by Hamna, the sister of the beautiful Zeinab, whom Mahomet had recently espoused, and who hoped to benefit her sister by the downfall of her deadly rival Ayesha; it was echoed also by Mistah, a kinsman of Abu Beker, and was celebrated in satirical verses by a poet named Hasan.

It was some time before Ayesha knew of the scandal thus circulating at her expense. Sickness had confined her to the house on her return to Medina, and no one ventured to tell her of what she was accused. She remarked, however, that the prophet was stern and silent, and no longer treated her with his usual tenderness. On her recovery, she heard with consternation the crime alleged against her, and protested her innocence. The following is her version of the story.

The army, on its homeward march, had encamped not far from Medina, when orders were given in the night to march. The attendants, as usual, brought a camel before the tent of Ayesha, and placing the litter on the ground, retired until she could take her seat within it. As she was about to enter, she missed her necklace, and returned into the tent to seek it. In the meantime the attendants lifted the litter upon the camel and strapped it fast not perceiving that it was empty; she being slender and of little weight. When she returned from seeking the necklace, the camel was gone, and the army was on the march; whereupon she wrapped herself in her mantle and sat down, trusting that, when her absence should be discovered, some persons would be sent back in quest of her.

While thus seated, Safwan Ibn al Moattel, the young Arab, being one of the rear-guard, came up, and, recognizing her, accosted her with the usual Moslem salutation. "To God we belong, and to God we must return ! Wife of the prophet, why dost thou remain behind ?"

Ayesha made no reply, but drew her veil closer over her face. Safwan then alighted, aided her to mount the camel, and, taking the bridle, hastened to rejoin the army. The sun had risen, however, before he overtook it, just without the walls of Medina.

This account, given by Ayesha, and attested by Safwan Ibn al Moattel, was satisfactory to her parents and particular friends; but was scoffed at by Abdallah and his adherents, "the Hypocrites." Two parties thus arose on the subject, and great strife ensued. As to Ayesha, she shut herself up within her dwelling, refusing all food, and weeping day and night in the bitterness of her soul.

Mahomet was sorely troubled in mind, and asked counsel of Ali in his perplexity. The latter made light of the affair, observing that his misfortune was the frequent lot of man. The prophet was but little consoled by this suggestion. He remained separated from Ayesha for a month; but his heart yearned toward her; not merely on account of her beauty, but because he loved her society. In a paroxysm of grief, he fell into one of those trances, which unbelievers have attributed to epilepsy; in the course of which he received a seasonable revelation, which will be found in a chapter of the Koran. It was to this effect.

They who accuse a reputable female of adultery, and produce not four witnesses of the fact, shall be scourged with fourscore stripes, and their testimony rejected. As to those who have made the charge against Ayesha, have they produced four witnesses thereof? If they have not, they are liars in the sight of God. Let them receive, therefore, the punishment of their crime.

The innocence of the beautiful Ayesha being thus miraculously made manifest, the prophet took her to his bosom with augmented affection. Nor was he slow in dealing the prescribed castigation. It is true, Abdallah Ibn Obba was too powerful a personage to be subjected to the scourge, but it fell the heavier on the shoulders of his fellow calumniators. The poet Hasan was cured for some time of his propensity to make satirical verses, nor could Hamna, though a female, and of great personal charms, escape the infliction of stripes; for, Mahomet observed that such beauty should have been accompanied by a gentler nature.

The revelation at once convinced the pious Ali of the purity of Ayesha; but she never forgot nor forgave that he had doubted; and the hatred thus implanted in her bosom, was manifested to his great detriment in many of the most important concerns of his after life.

CHAPTER XXIII.

The battle of the Moat.—Bravery of Saad Ibn Moad.—Defeat of the Koreishites.—Capture of the Jewish castle of Koraida.—Saad decides as to the punishment of the Jews.— Mahomet espouses Rehana, a Jewish captive.—His life endangered by sorcery: saved by a revelation of the angel Gabriel.

During the year of truce which succeeded the battle of Ohod, Abu Sofian, the restless chief of the Koreishites, formed a confederacy with the Arab tribe of Ghatafan and other tribes of the desert, as well as with many of the Jews of the race of Nadher, whom Mahomet had driven from their homes. The truce being ended, he prepared to march upon Medina, with these confederates, their combined forces amounting to ten thousand men.

Mahomet had early intelligence of the meditated attack, but his late reverse at Ohod made him wary of taking the field against such numbers; especially as he feared the enemy might have secret allies in Medina; where he distrusted the Jewish inhabitants and the Hypocrites, the partisans of Abdallah Ibn Obba, who were numerous and powerful.

Great exertions were now made to put the city in a state of defence. Salmân the Persian, who had embraced the faith, advised that a deep moat should be digged at some distance beyond the wall, on the side on which the enemy would approach. This mode of defence, hitherto unused in Arabia, was eagerly adopted by Mahomet; who set a great number of men to dig the moat, and even assisted personally in the labour. Many miracles are recorded of him during the progress of this work. At one time, it is said, he fed a great multitude from a single basket of dates; which remained full after all were satisfied. At another time he feasted a thousand men upon a roasted lamb and a loaf of barley bread; yet enough remained for all his fellow-labourers in the moat. Nor must we omit to note the wonderful blows which he gave to a rock, with an iron mallet; striking off sparks which in one direction lighted up all Yemen, or Arabia the Happy; in another, revealed the imperial palace of Constantinople; and in a third, illumined the towers of the royal residence of Persia; all signs and portents of the future conquests of Islam.

Scarcely was the moat completed when the enemy appeared in great force on the neighbouring hills. Leaving Ibn Omm Mactum,

a trusty officer, to command in the city, and keep a vigilant eye on
the disaffected, Mahomet sallied forth with three thousand men,
whom he formed in battle array, having the deep moat in front.
Abu Sofian advanced confidently with his combined force of Koreishites and Ghatafanites, but was unexpectedly checked by the
moat, and by a galling fire from the Moslems drawn up beyond it.
The enemy now encamped; the Koreishites in the lower part of
the valley, and the Ghatafanites in the upper; and for some days
the armies remained on each side of the moat, keeping up a distant
combat with slings and stones, and flights of arrows.

In the meantime, spies brought word to Mahomet that a Jewish
tribe, the Beni Koraida, who had a strong castle near the city,
and had made a covenant of peace with him, were in secret league
with the enemy. He now saw the difficulty, with his scanty forces,
to man the whole extent of the moat; to guard against a perfidious
attack from the Koraidites; and to maintain quiet in the city where
the Jews must have secret confederates. Summoning a council
of war, he consulted with his captains on the policy of bribing the
Ghatafanites to a separate peace, by offering them a third of the
date-harvest of Medina. Upon this, Saad Ibn Moad, a stout leader
of the Awsites of Medina, demanded : " Do you propose this by the
command of Allah, or is it an idea of your own ?"   " If it had
been a command of Allah," replied Mahomet, " I should never
have asked your advice. I see you pressed by enemies on every
side, and I seek to break their confederacy."   " Oh prophet of
God!" rejoined Saad, " when we were fellow-idolaters with these
people of Ghatafan, they got none of our dates without paying for
them : and shall we give them up gratuitously now that we are of
the true faith, and led by thee? No, by Allah ! if they want our
dates they must win them with their swords."

The stout Saad had his courage soon put to the proof. A
prowling party of Koreishite horsemen, among whom was Akrema
the son of Abu Jahl, and Amru, uncle of Mahomet's first wife
Cadijah, discovered a place where the moat was narrow, and
putting spurs to their steeds succeeded in leaping over, followed
by some of their comrades. They then challenged the bravest of
the Moslems to equal combat. The challenge was accepted by
Saad Ibn Moad, by Ali, and several of their companions. Ali had
a close combat with Amru; they fought on horseback and on foot,
until, grappling with each other, they rolled in the dust. In the
end, Ali was victorious and slew his foe. The general conflict
was maintained with great obstinacy; several were slain on both
sides, and Saad Ibn Moad was severely wounded. At length the
Koreishites gave way, and spurred their horses to recross the moat.
The steed of one of them, Nawfal Ibn Abdallah, leaped short; his
rider was assailed with stones while in the moat, and defied the
Moslems to attack him with nobler weapons, In an instant Ali
sprang down into the moat, and Nawfal soon fell beneath his
sword. Ali then joined his companions in pursuit of the retreating
foe, and wounded Akrema with a javelin. This skirmish was dignified with the name of the Battle of the Moat.

Mahomet, still unwilling to venture a pitched battle, sent Rueim, a secretly converted Arab of the tribe of Ghatafan, to visit the camps of the confederates and artfully to sow dissensions among them. Rueim first repaired to the Koraidites, with whom he was in old habits of friendship. "What folly is this," said he, "to suffer yourselves to be drawn by the Koreishites of Mecca into their quarrel. Bethink you how different is your situation from theirs. If defeated, they have only to retreat to Mecca, and be secure. Their allies from the desert will also retire to their distant homes, and you will be left to bear the whole brunt of the vengeance of Mahomet and the people of Medina. Before you make common cause with them, therefore, let them pledge themselves and give hostages, never to draw back until they have broken the power of Mahomet."

He then went to the Koreishites and the tribe of Ghatafan, and warned them against confiding in the Jews of Koraida, who intended to get hostages from them, and deliver them up into the hands of Mahomet.

The distrust thus artfully sown among the confederates soon produced its effects. Abu Sofian sent word on Friday evening, to the Koraidites, to be ready to join next morning in a general assault. The Jews replied, that the following day was their Sabbath, on which they could not engage in battle; at the same time they declined to join in any hostile act, unless their allies should give hostages to stand by them to the end.

The Koreishites and Ghatafanites were now convinced of the perfidy of the Koraidites, and dared not venture upon the meditated attack, lest these should fall upon them in the rear. While they lay idly in their camp a cold storm came on, with drenching rain and sweeping blasts from the desert. Their tents were blown down; their camp-fires were extinguished; in the midst of the uproar, the alarm was given that Mahomet had raised the storm by enchantment, and was coming upon them with his forces. All now was panic and confusion, Abu Sofian, finding all efforts vain to produce order, mounted his camel in despair, and gave the word to retreat. The confederates hurried off from the scene of tumult and terror, the Koreishites towards Mecca, the others to their homes in the desert.

Abu Sofian, in rage and mortification, wrote a letter to Mahomet, upbraiding him with his cowardice in lurking behind a ditch, a thing unknown in Arabian warfare; and threatening to take his revenge on some future day, when they might meet in open fight, as in the field of Ohod. Mahomet hurled back a defiance, and predicted that the day was approaching when he would break in pieces the idols of the Koreishites.

The invaders having disappeared, Mahomet turned to take vengeance on the Beni Koraida; who shut themselves up in their castle, and withstood a siege of many days. At length, pinched by famine, they implored the intercession of their ancient friends and protectors, the Awsites. The latter entreated the prophet to grant these Hebrews the same terms he had formerly granted to the Beni Kainoka, at the prayer of Abdallah the Khazradite. Mahomet reflected a moment, and offered to leave their fate to the decision of

Saad Ibn Moad, the Awsite chief. The Koraidites gladly agreed, knowing him to have been formerly their friend. They accordingly surrendered themselves, to the number of seven hundred, and were conducted in chains to Medina. Unfortunately for them, Saad considered their perfidious league with the enemy as one cause of the recent hostility. He was still smarting with the wound received in the battle of the Moat, and in his moments of pain and anger had repeatedly prayed that his life might be spared to see vengeance wreaked on the Koraidites. Such was the state of his feelings when summoned to decide upon their fate.

Being a gross, full-blooded man, he was with difficulty helped upon an ass, propped up by a leathern cushion, and supported in his seat until he arrived at the tribunal of justice. Before ascending it, he exacted an oath from all present to abide by his decision. The Jews readily took it, anticipating a favourable sentence. No sooner was he helped into the tribunal, than, extending his hand, he condemned the men to death, the women and children to slavery, and their effects to be shared among the victors.

The wretched Jews looked aghast, but there was no appeal. They were conducted to a public place since called the Market of the Koraidites, where great graves had been digged. Into these they were compelled to descend, one by one, their prince Hoyai Ibn Ahktab among the number, and were successively put to death. Thus the prayer of Saad Ibn Moad for vengeance on the Koraidites was fully gratified. He witnessed the execution of the men he had condemned, but such was his excitement that his wound broke out afresh, and he died shortly afterwards.

In the Castle of Koraida was found a great quantity of pikes, lances, cuirasses, and other armour; and its lands were covered with flocks and herds and camels. In dividing the spoil each foot-soldier had one lot, each horseman three; two for his horse, and one for himself. A fifth part of the whole was set apart for the prophet.

The most precious prize in the eyes of Mahomet was Rihana, daughter of Simeon, a wealthy and powerful Jew; and the most beautiful female of her tribe. He took her to himself, and, having converted her to the faith, added her to the number of his wives.

But, though thus susceptible of the charms of the Israelitish women, Mahomet became more and more vindictive in his hatred of the men; no longer putting faith in their covenants, and suspecting them of the most insidious attempts upon his life. Moslem writers attribute to the spells of Jewish sorcerers a long and languishing illness, with which he was afflicted about this time, and which seemed to defy all remedy. They describe the very charm by which it was produced. It was prepared, say they, by a Jewish necromancer from the mountains, aided by his daughters, who were equally skilled in the diabolic art. They formed a small waxen effigy of Mahomet; wound round it some of his hair, and thrust through it eleven needles. They then made eleven knots in a bow-string, blowing with their breaths on each; and, winding the string round the effigy, threw the whole into a well

Under the influence of this potent spell Mahomet wasted away, until his friend, the angel Gabriel, revealed the secret to him in a vision. On awaking, he sent Ali to the well, where the image was discovered. When it was brought to Mahomet, continues the legend, he repeated over it the two last chapters of the Koran, which had been communicated to him in the recent vision. They consist of eleven verses, and are to the following purport.

In the name of the all merciful God! I will fly for refuge to the Lord of the light of day.

That he may deliver me from the danger of beings and things created by himself.

From the dangers of the darksome night, and of the moon when in eclipse.

From the danger of sorcerers, who tie knots and blow on them with their breath.

From the danger of the envious, who devise deadly harm.

I will fly for refuge to Allah, the Lord of men.

To Allah, the King of men.

To Allah, the God of men.

That he may deliver me from the evil spirit who flies at the mention of his holy name.

Who suggests evil thoughts into the hearts of the children of men.

And from the evil Genii, and men who deal in magic.

At the repetition of each one of these verses, says the legend, a knot of the bow-string came loose, a needle fell from the effigy, and Mahomet gained strength. At the end of the eleventh verse he rose, renovated in health and vigour, as one restored to freedom, after having been bound with cords.

The two final chapters of the Koran, which comprise these verses, are entitled the amulets, and considered by the superstitious Moslems effectual talismans against sorcery and magic charms.

The conduct of Mahomet in the affair narrated in this chapter, has been censured as weak and vacillating, and deficient in military decision, and his measures as wanting in true greatness of mind, and the following circumstances are adduced to support these charges. When threatened with violence from without, and perfidy from within, he is for bribing a part of his confederate foes to a separate peace; but suffers himself to be, in a manner, hectored out of this crafty policy by Saad Ibn Moad; yet, subsequently, he resorts to a scheme still more subtle and crafty, by which he sows dissension among his enemies. Above all, his conduct towards the Jews has been strongly reprobated. His referring the appeal of the Beni Koraida for mercy, to the decision of one whom he knew to be bent on their destruction, has been stigmatized as cruel mockery; and the massacre of those unfortunate men in the market-place of Medina, is pronounced one of the darkest pages of his history. In fact, his conduct towards this race from the time that he had power in his hands, forms an exception to the general tenour of his disposition, which was forgiving and humane. He may have been especially provoked against them by proofs of treachery and deadly rancour on their part, but we see in this, as in other parts of his policy in this part of his career, instances of that worldly alloy which at times was debasing his spirit, now that he had become the Apostle of the religion of the Sword.

CHAPTER XXIV.

Mahomet undertakes a pilgrimage to Mecca.—Evades Khaled and a troop of horse sent against him.—Encamps near Mecca.—Negotiates with the Koreishites for permission to enter and complete his pilgrimage.—Treaty for ten years, by which he is permitted to make a yearly visit of three days.—He returns to Medina.

Six years had now elapsed since the flight of Mahomet from Mecca. As that city was sacred in the eyes of the Arabs and their great point of pilgrimage, his long exile from it, and his open warfare with the Koreishites, who had charge of the Caaba, prejudiced him in the opinion of many of the tribes, and retarded the spread of his doctrines. His followers, too, who had accompanied him in his flight, languished once more to see their native home, and there was danger of their faith becoming enfeebled under a protracted exile.

Mahomet felt more and more the importance of linking the sacred city with his religion, and maintaining the ancient usages of his race. Besides, he claimed but to be a reformer, anxious to restore the simplicity and purity of the patriarchal faith. The month Doul Kaada was at hand, the month of pilgrimage, when there was a truce to warfare, and enemies might meet in peace within the holy boundaries. A timely vision assured Mahomet that he and his followers might safely avail themselves of the protection of this venerable custom to revisit the ancient shrines of Arabian worship. The revelation was joyfully received by his followers, and in the holy month he set forth from Medina on his pilgrimage, at the head of fourteen hundred men; partly Mohadjerins or Fugitives, and partly Ansarians or Auxiliaries. They took with them seventy camels to be slain in sacrifice at the Caaba. To manifest publicly that they came in peace and not in war, they halted at Dsu Huleifa, a village about a day's journey from Medina, where they laid aside all their weapons, excepting their sheathed swords, and thence continued on in pilgrim garb.

In the meantime a confused rumour of this movement had reached Mecca. The Koreishites, suspecting hostilities, sent forth Khaled Ibn Waled with a powerful troop of horse, to take post in a valley about two days' journey from Mecca, and check the advance of the Moslems.

Mahomet, hearing that the main road was thus barred against him, took a rugged and difficult route through the defiles of the mountains, and, avoiding Khaled and his forces, descended into the plain near Mecca; where he encamped at Hodeïba, within the sacred boundaries. Hence he sent assurances to the Koreishites of his peaceable intentions, and claimed the immunities and rights of pilgrimage.

Envoys from the Koreishites visited his camp to make observations. They were struck with the reverence with which he was regarded by his followers. The water with which he performed his ablutions became sanctified; a hair falling from his head, or the paring of a nail, was caught up as a precious relic. One of the envoys, in the course of conversation, unconsciously touched the flowing beard of the prophet; he was thrust back by the disciples, and warned of the impiety of the act. In making his report to the Koreishites on his return, " I have seen the king of Persia, and the emperor of Constantinople, surrounded by their courts;" said he, "but never did I behold a sovereign so revered by his subjects, as is Mahomet by his followers."

The Koreishites were the more loth to admit into their city an adversary to their sect, so formidable in his influence over the minds and affections of his fellow-men. Mahomet sent repeated missions to treat for a safe access to the sacred shrines, but in vain. Othman Ibn Affan, his son-in-law, was his last envoy. Several days elapsed without his return, and it was rumoured that he was slain. Mahomet determined to revenge his fall. Standing under a tree, and summoning his people around him, he exacted an oath to defend him even to the death, and never to desert the standard of the faith. This ceremony is known among Mahometans, by the name of the Spontaneous Inauguration.

The reappearance of Othman in the camp, restored tranquillity. He was accompanied by Solhail, an ambassador from the Koreishites, to arrange a treaty of peace. They perceived the impolicy of warring with a man whose power was incessantly increasing, and who was obeyed with such fanatic devotion. The treaty proposed was for ten years; during which time Mahomet and his adherents were to have free access to Mecca as pilgrims, there to remain, three days at a time, in the exercise of their religious rites. The terms were readily accepted, and Ali was employed to draw up the treaty. Mahomet dictated the words. "Write," said he, "these are the conditions of peace made by Mahomet the apostle of God." " Hold!" cried Solhail, the ambassador, "had I believed thee to be the apostle of God, I should never have taken up arms against thee. Write, therefore, simply thy name, and the name of thy father." Mahomet was fain to comply, for he felt he was not sufficiently in force at this moment to contend about forms; so he merely denominated himself in the treaty, Mahomet Ibn Abdallah (Mahomet the son of Abdallah), an abnegation which gave some little scandal to his followers. Their discontent was increased when he ordered them to shave their heads, and to sacrifice on the spot the camels brought to be offered up at the Caaba,-as it showed he had not the intention of entering Mecca; these rites being properly done at the conclusion of the ceremonials of pilgrimage. They reminded him of his vision which promised a safe entrance of the sacred city; he replied, that the present treaty was an earnest of its fulfilment, which would assuredly take place on the following year. With this explanation they had to content themselves; and having performed the ceremony, and made the sacrifice prescribed, the camp was broken up, and the pilgrim host returned, somewhat disappointed and dejected, to Medina.

CHAPTER XXV.

Expedition against the city of Khaïbar; siege. —Exploits of Mahomet's captains.— Battle of Ali and Marhab.—Storming of the citadel.—Ali makes a buckler of the gate.— Capture of the place.—Mahomet poisoned; he marries Safiya, a captive; also Omm Habiba, a widow.

To console his followers for the check their religious devotion had experienced at Mecca, Mahomet now set on foot an expedition calculated to gratify that love of plunder, which began to rival fanaticism in attaching them to his standard

About five days' journey to the northeast of Medina, was situated the city of Khaïbar, and its dependent territory. It was inhabited by Jews, who had grown wealthy by commerce, as well as agriculture. Their rich domain was partly cultivated with grain, and planted with groves of palm-trees; partly devoted to pasturage and covered with flocks and herds; and it was fortified by several castles. So venerable was its antiquity, that Abulfeda, the Arabian historian, assures us that Moses, after the passage of the Red Sea, sent an army against the Amalekites, inhabiting Gothreb (Medina), and the strong city of Khaïbar.

This region had become a place of refuge for the hostile Jews, driven by Mahomet from Medina and its environs, and for all those who had made themselves obnoxious to his vengeance. These circumstances, together with its teeming wealth, pointed it out as a fit and ripe object for that warfare which he had declared against all enemies of the faith.

In the beginning of the seventh year of the Hegira, he departed on an expedition against Khaïbar, at the head of twelve hundred foot and two hundred horse, accompanied by Abu Beker, by Ali, by Omar, and other of his principal officers. He had two standards; one represented the sun, the other a black eagle; which last became famous in after years as the standard of Khaled.

Entering the fertile territory of Khaïbar, he began his warfare by assailing the inferior castles with which it was studded. Some of these capitulated without making resistance; in which cases, being considered "gifts from God," the spoils went to the prophet, to be disposed of by him in the way before mentioned. Others of more strength, and garrisoned by stouter hearts, had to be taken by storm.

After the capture of these minor fortresses, Mahomet advanced against the city of Khaïbar. It was strongly defended by outworks, and its citadel, Al Kamus, built on a steep rock, was deemed impregnable, insomuch that Kenana Ibn al Rabi, the chief or king of the nation, had made it the depository of all his treasures.

The siege of this city was the most important enterprise the Moslems had yet undertaken. When Mahomet first came in sight of its strong and frowning walls, and its rock-built citadel, he is said to have put up the following prayer:

"Oh Allah! Lord of the seven heavens, and of all things which they cover! Lord of the seven earths, and all which they sustain! Lord of the evil spirits, and of all whom they lead astray! Lord of the winds, and of all whom they scatter and disperse! We supplicate thee to deliver into our hands this city, and all that it contains, and the riches of all its lands. To thee we look for aid against this people, and against all the perils by which we are environed."

To give more solemnity to his prayers, he chose as his place of worship a great rock, in a stony place called Mansela, and, during all the time that he remained encamped before Khaïbar, made daily seven circuits round it, as are made round the Caaba. A mosque was erected on this rock in after times in memorial of this devout ceremonial, and it became an object of veneration to all pious Moslems.

The siege of the citadel lasted for some time, and tasked the skill and patience of Mahomet and his troops; as yet but little practised in the attack of fortified places. They suffered too from want of provisions, for the Arabs in their hasty expeditions seldom burden themselves with supplies, and the Jews on their approach had laid waste the level country, and destroyed the palm-trees round their capital.

Mahomet directed the attacks in person : the besiegers protected themselves by trenches, and brought battering-rams to play upon the walls; a breach was at length effected, but for several days every attempt to enter was vigorously repelled. Abu Beker at one time led the assault, bearing the standard of the prophet; but, after fighting with great bravery, was compelled to retreat. The next attack was headed by Omar Ibn Khattab, who fought until the close of day with no better success. A third attack was led by Ali, whom Mahomet armed with his own scimetar, called Dhu'l-Fakâr, or the Trenchant. On confiding to his hands the sacred banner, he pronounced him "a man who loved God and his prophet; and whom God and his prophet loved. A man who knew not fear, nor ever turned his back upon a foe."

And here it may be well to give a traditional account of the person and character of Ali. He was of the middle height, but robust and square, and of prodigious strength. He had a smiling countenance, exceedingly florid, with a bushy beard. He was distinguished for an amiable disposition, sagacious intellect, and religious zeal; and, from his undaunted courage, was surnamed the Lion of God.

Arabian writers dwell with fond exaggeration on the exploits, at Khaïbar, of this their favourite hero. He was clad, they say, in a scarlet vest, over which was buckled a cuirass of steel. Scrambling with his followers up the great heap of stones and rubbish in front of the breach, he planted his standard on the top, determined never to recede until the citadel was taken. The Jews sallied forth to drive down the assailants. In the conflict which ensued, Ali fought hand to hand with the Jewish commander, Al Hareth, whom he slew. The brother of the slain advanced to revenge his death. He was of gigantic stature ; with a double cuirass, a double turban, wound round a helmet of proof, in front of which sparkled an immense diamond. He had a sword girt to each side, and brandished a three-pronged spear, like a trident. The warriors measured each other with the eye, and accosted each other in boasting oriental style.

"I," said the Jew, "am Marhab; armed at all points, and terrible in battle."

"And I am Ali, whom his mother, at his birth, surnamed Al Haidara (the rugged lion)."

The Moslem writers make short work of the Jewish champion. He made a thrust at Ali with his three-pronged lance, but it was dexterously parried; and before he could recover himself, a blow from the scimetar Dhu'l-Fakâr divided his buckler, passed through the helm of proof, through doubled turban and stubborn skull, cleaving his head even to his teeth. His gigantic form fell lifeless to the earth.

The Jews now retreated into the citadel, and a general assault took place. In the heat of the action the shield of Ali was severed from his arm, leaving his body exposed: wrenching a gate, however, from its hinges, he used it as a buckler through the remainder of the fight. Abu Râfe, a servant of Mahomet, testifies to the fact. "I afterwards," says he, "examined this gate in company with seven men, and all eight of us attempted in vain to wield it "[1]

The citadel being captured, every vault and dungeon was ransacked for the wealth said to be deposited there by Kenana the Jewish prince. None being discovered, Mahomet demanded of him where he had concealed his treasure. He declared that it had all been expended in the subsistence of his troops, and in preparations for defence. One of his faithless subjects, however, revealed the place where a great amount had been hidden. It did not equal the expectations of the victors, and Kenana was put to the torture to reveal the rest of his supposed wealth. He either could not or would not make further discoveries, so he was delivered up to the vengeance of a Moslem, whose brother he had crushed to death by a piece of a millstone hurled from the wall, and who struck off his head with a single blow of his sabre.[2]

While in the citadel of Khaïbar, Mahomet came near falling a victim to Jewish vengeance. Demanding something to eat, a shoulder of lamb was set before him. At the first mouthful he perceived something unusual in the taste, and spat it forth, but instantly felt acute internal pain. One of his followers, named Baschar, who had eaten more freely, fell down and expired in convulsions. All now was confusion and consternation; on diligent inquiry, it was found that the lamb had been cooked by Zaïnab, a

[1] This stupendous feat is recorded by the historian Abulfeda, c. 24. "Abu Rafe," observes Gibbon, "was an eye-witness; but who will be witness for Abu Rafe?" We join with the distinguished historian in his doubt; yet if we scrupulously question the testimony of an eye-witness, what will become of history?

[2] The Jews inhabiting the tract of country called Khaïbar, are still known in Arabia by the name of Beni Kheibar. They are divided into three tribes, under independent Sheikhs, the Beni Messiad, Beni Schahan, and Beni Anaesse. They are accused of pillaging the caravans.—*Niebuhr*, v. ii. p. 43.

female captive, niece to Marhab, the gigantic warrior slain by Ali. Being brought before Mahomet, and charged with having infused poison into the viand, she boldly avowed it, vindicating it as a justifiable revenge for the ills he had brought upon her tribe and her family. "I thought," said she, "if thou wert indeed a prophet, thou wouldst discover thy danger; if but a chieftain, thou wouldst fall, and we should be delivered from a tyrant."

Arabian writers are divided as to the fate of this heroine. According to some, she was delivered up to the vengeance of the relatives of Baschar, who had died of the poison. According to others, her beauty pleaded in her behalf, and Mahomet restored her unharmed to her family.

The same writers seldom permit any remarkable event of Mahomet's life to pass without a miracle. In the present instance, they assure us that the poisoned shoulder of lamb became miraculously gifted with speech, and warned Mahomet of his danger. If so, it was rather slow of speech, for he had imbibed sufficient poison to injure his constitution throughout the remainder of his life; affecting him often with paroxysms of pain; and in his last moments he complained that the veins of his heart throbbed with the poison of Khaïbar. He experienced kinder treatment at the hands of Safiya (or Sophia), another female captive, who had still greater motives for vengeance than Zaïnab; for she was the recently espoused wife of Kenana, who had just been sacrificed for his wealth, and she was the daughter of Hoya Ibn Akhtab, prince of the Beni Koraida, who, with seven hundred of his people, had been put to death in the square of Medina, as has been related.

This Safiya was of great beauty; it is not surprising, therefore, that she should find instant favour in the eyes of Mahomet, and that he should seek, as usual, to add her to his harem; but it may occasion surprise that she should contemplate such a lot with complacency. Moslem writers, however, explain this by assuring us that she was surpernaturally prepared for the event.

While Mahomet was yet encamped before the city, and carrying on the siege, she had a vision of the night, in which the sun descended from the firmament and nestled in her bosom. On recounting her dream to her husband Kenana in the morning, he smote her on the face, exclaiming, "Woman, you speak in parables of this Arab chief who has come against us."

The vision of Safiya was made true, for having converted her with all decent haste to the faith of Islam, Mahomet took her to wife before he left Khaïbar. Their nuptials took place on the homeward march, at Al Sahba, where the army halted for three days Abu Ayub, one of the prophet's most ardent disciples and marshal of his household, patrolled around the nuptial tent throughout the night, sword in hand. Safiya was one the most favoured wives of Mahomet whom she survived for forty years of widowhood.

Besides the marriages of affection which we have recorded, the prophet, about this time, made another of policy. Shortly after his return to Medina, he was gladdened by the arrival, from Abyssinia, of the residue of the fugitives. Among these was a comely widow, thirty years of age, whose husband, Abdallah, had died while in exile. She was generally known by the name of Omm Habiba, the mother of Habiba, from a daughter to whom she had given birth. This widow was the daughter of Mahomet's arch enemy, Abu Sofian; and the prophet conceived that a marriage with the daughter might soften the hostility of the father; a politic consideration, which is said to have been either suggested or sanctioned by a revelation of a chapter of the Koran.

When Abu Sofian heard of the espousals, "By heaven," exclaimed he, " this camel is so rampant, that no muzzle can restrain him."

CHAPTER XXVI.

Missions to various Princes; to Heraclius; to Khosru II; to the Prefect of Egypt.— Their result.

During the residue of the year, Mahomet remained at Medina, sending forth his trusty disciples, by this time experienced captains, on various military expeditions; by which refractory tribes were rapidly brought into subjection. His views as a statesman widened as his territories increased. Though he professed, in cases of necessity, to propagate his religion by the sword, he was not neglectful of the peaceful measures of diplomacy, and sent envoys to various princes and potentates, whose dominions bordered on his political horizon, urging them to embrace the faith of Islam; which was in effect, to acknowledge him, through his apostolic office, their superior.

Two of the most noted of these missions, were to Khosru II, king of Persia, and Heraclius, the Roman emperor, at Constantinople. The wars between the Romans and the Persians, for the dominion of the East, which had prevailed from time to time through several centuries, had been revived by these two potentates with varying fortunes, and for several years past had distracted the eastern world. Countries had been overrun by either power; states and kingdoms had changed hands under alternate invasions, and according to the conquets and defeats of the warring parties. At one time, Khosru with three armies, one vauntingly called the Fifty Thousand Golden Spears, had wrested Palestine, Cappadocia, Armenia, and several other great and wealthy provinces from the Roman emperor; had made himself master of Jerusalem, and carried off the Holy Cross to Persia; had invaded Africa, conquered Libya and Egypt, and extended his victories even to Carthage.

In the midst of his triumphant career, a Moslem envoy arrived bearing him a letter from Mahomet. Khosru sent for his secretary or interpreter, and ordered him to read it. The letter began as follows:

"In the name of the most merciful God! Mahomet, son of Abdallah, and apostle of God, to Khosru king of Persia."

"What!" cried Khosru, starting up in haughty indignation, "does one who is my slave, dare to put his name first in writing to me?" So saying, he seized the letter and tore it in pieces, without seeking to know its contend. He then wrote to his viceroy in Yemen, saying, "I am told there is in Medina a madman, of the tribe of Koreish, who pretends to be a prophet. Restore him to his senses; or if you cannot, send me his head."

When Mahomet was told how Khosru had torn his letter, "Even so," said he, "shall Allah rend his empire in pieces."

The letter from the prophet to Heraclius, was more favourably received, reaching him probably during his reverses. It was signed in characters of silver, Mahomet Azzarel, Mahomet the messenger of God, and invited the emperor to renounce Christianity, and embrace the faith of Islam. Heraclius, we are told, deposited the epistle respectfully upon his pillow, treated the envoy with distinction, and dismissed him with magnificent presents. Engrossed, however, by his Persian wars, he paid no further attention to this mission, from one whom he probably considered a mere Arab fanatic; nor attached sufficient importance to his military operations, which may have appeared mere predatory forays of the wild tribes of the desert.

Another mission of Mahomet was to the Mukowkis, or governor of Egypt, who had originally been sent there by Heraclius to collect tribute ; but who, availing himself of the confusion produced by the wars between the Romans and Persians, had assumed sovereign power, and nearly thrown off all allegiance to the emperor. He received the envoy with signal honour, but evaded a direct reply to the invitation to embrace the faith, observing that it was a grave matter requiring much consideration. In the meantime, he sent presents to Mahomet of precious jewels; garments of Egyptian linen; exquisite honey and butter; a white she-ass, called Yafur; a white mule, called Daldal, and a fleet horse called Lazlos, or the Prancer. The most acceptable of his presents, however, were two Coptic damsels, sisters, called Mariyah (or Mary), and Shiren.

The beauty of Mariyah caused great perturbation in the mind of the prophet. He would fain have made her his concubine, but was impeded by his own law in the seventeenth chapter of the Koran, ordaining that fornication should be punished with stripes.

He was relieved from his dilemma, by another revelation revoking the law in regard to himself alone, allowing him intercourse with his handmaid. It remained in full force, however, against all other Moslems. Still, to avoid scandal, and above all, not to excite the jealousy of his wives, he carried on his intercourse with the beautiful Mariyah in secret; which may be one reason why she remained long a favourite.

CHAPTER XXVII.

Mahomet's pilgrimage to Mecca; his marriage with Maimuna.—Khaled Ibn al Waled and Amru Ibn al Aass become proselytes.

The time had now arrived when, by treaty with the Koreishites, Mahomet and his followers were permitted to make a pilgrimage to Mecca, and pass three days unmolested at the sacred shrines. He departed accordingly with a numerous and well-armed host, and seventy camels for sacrifices. His old adversaries would fain. have impeded his progress, but they were overawed, and on his approach withdrew silently to the neighbouring hills. On entering the bounds of Mecca, the pilgrims, according to compact and usage, laid aside all their warlike accoutrements excepting their swords, which they carried sheathed.

Great was their joy on beholding once more the walls and towers of the sacred city. They entered the gates in pilgrim garb, with devout and thankful hearts, and Mahomet performed all the ancient and customary rites, with a zeal and devotion which gratified beholders, and drew to him many converts. When he had complied with all the ceremonials he threw aside the Iram or pilgrim's garb, and withdrew to Sarif, a hamlet two leagues distant, and without the sacred boundaries. Here he had a ceremonial of a different kind to perform, but one in which he was prone to act with unfeigned devotion. It was to complete his marriage with Maimuna, the daughter of Al Hareth, the Helalite. He had become betrothed to her on his arrival at Mecca, but had postponed the nuptials until after he had concluded the rites of pilgrimage. This was doubtless another marriage of policy, for Maimuna was fifty-one years of age, and a widow, but the connexion gained him two powerful proselytes. One was Khaled Ibn al Waled, a nephew of the widow, an intrepid warrior who had come near destroying Mahomet at the battle of Ohod. He now became one of the most victorious champions of Islamism, and by his prowess obtained the appellation of "The Sword of God."

The other proselyte was Khaled's friend Amru Ibn al Aass; the same who assailed Mahomet with poetry and satire at the commencement of his prophetic career; who had been an ambassador from the Koreishites to the king of Abyssinia, to obtain the surrender of the fugitive Moslems, and who was henceforth destined with his sword to carry victoriously into foreign lands, the faith he had once so strenuously opposed.

Note.—Maimuna was the last spouse of the prophet, and, old as she was at her marriage, survived all his other wives. She died many years after him, in a pavilion at Serif, under the same tree in the shade of which her nuptial tent had been pitched, and was there interred. The pious historian, Al Jannabi, who styles himself "a poor servant of Allah, hoping for the pardon of his sins through the mercy of God," visited her tomb on returning from a pilgrimage to Mecca, in the year of the Hegira, 963, A. D. 1555. "I saw there," said he, "a dome of black marble erected in memory of Maimuna, on the very spot on which the apostle of God had reposed with her. God knows the truth! and also the reason of the black colour of the stone. There is a place of ablution, and an oratory; but the building has fallen to decay."

CHAPTER XXVIII.

A Moslem envoy slain in Syria.—Expedition to avenge his death.—Battle of Muta.— Its results.

Among the different missions which had been sent by Mahomet beyond the bounds of Arabia to invite neighbouring princes to embrace his religion, was one to the governor of Bosra, the great mart on the confines of Syria, to which he had made his first caravan journey in the days of his youth. Syria had been alternately under Roman and Persian domination, but was at that time subject to the emperor, though probably in a great state of confusion. The envoy of Mahomet was slain at Muta, a town about three days' journey eastward from Jerusalem. The one who slew him was an Arab of the Christian tribe of Gassan, and son to Shorhail, an emir, who governed Muta in the name of Heraclius.

To revenge the death of his legate, and to insure respect to his envoys in future, Mahomet prepared to send an army of three thousand men against the offending city. It was a momentous expedition, as it might, for the first time, bring the arms of Islam in collision with those of the Roman Empire; but Mahomet presumed upon his growing power, the energy of his troops, and the disordered state of Syrian affairs. The command was intrusted to his freedman Zeid, who had given such signal proof of devotion in surrendering to him his beautiful wife Zeinab. Several chosen officers were associated with him. One was Mahomet's cousin Jaafar, son of Abu Taleb, and brother of Ali; the same who, by his eloquence, had vindicated the doctrines of Islam before the king of Abyssinia, and defeated the Koreish embassy. He was now in the prime of life, and noted for great courage and manly beauty. Another of the associate officers was Abdallah Ibn Kawaha, the poet, but who had signalized himself in arms as well as poetry. A third was the new proselyte Khaled, who joined the expedition as a volunteer, being eager to prove by his sword the sincerity of his conversion.

The orders to Zeid were to march rapidly, so as to come upon Muta by surprise, to summon the inhabitants to embrace the faith, and to treat them with lenity. Women, children, monks, and the blind, were to be spared at all events; nor were any houses to be destroyed, nor trees cut down.

The little army sallied from Medina in the full confidence of coming upon the enemy unawares. On their march, however, they learned that a greatly superior force of Romans, or rather Greeks and Arabs, was advancing to meet them.   A council of war was called.   Some were for pausing, and awaiting further orders from Mahomet : but Abdallah, the poet, was for pushing fearlessly forward without regard to numbers.   " We fight for the faith! " cried he ; " if we fall, paradise is our reward.   On, then, to victory or martyrdom ! "

All caught a spark of the poet's fire, or rather, fanaticism. They met the enemy near Muta, and encountered them ·with fury rather than valour.   In the heat of the conflict Zeid received a mortal wound.   The sacred banner was falling from his grasp, but was seized and borne aloft by Jaafar.   The battle thickened round him, for the banner was the object of fierce contention. He defended it with desperate valour.   The hand by which he held it was struck off; he grasped it with the other.   That, too, was severed; he embraced it with his bleeding arms.   A blow from a scimetar cleft his skull; he sank dead upon the field, still clinging to the standard of the faith.   Abdallah the poet next reared the banner; but he too fell beneath the sword.   Khaled, the new convert, seeing the three Moslem leaders slain, now grasped the fatal standard, but in his hand it remained aloft.   His voice rallied the wavering Moslems : his powerful arm cut its way through the thickest of the enemy.   If his own account may be credited, and he was one whose deeds needed no exaggeration, nine scimetars were broken in his hand by the fury of the blows given by him in this deadly conflict.

Night separated the combatants.   In the morning Khaled, whom the army acknowledged as their commander, proved himself as wary as he was valiant.   By dint of marches and counter-marches, he presented his forces in so many points of view, that the enemy were deceived as to his number, and supposed he had received a strong reinforcement.   At his first charge, therefore, they retreated : their retreat soon became a flight; in which they were pursued with great slaughter.   Khaled then plundered their camp, in which was found great booty.   Among the slain in the field of battle was found the body of Jaafar, covered with wounds, but all in front.   Out of respect to his valour, and to his relationship with the prophet, Khaled ordered that his corpse should not be buried on the spot, but borne back for honourable interment at Medina.

The army, on its return, though laden with spoil, entered the city more like a funeral train than a triumphant pageant, and was received with mingled shouts and lamentations.   While the people rejoiced in the success of their arms, they mourned the loss of three of their favourite generals.   All bewailed the fate of Jaafar, brought home a ghastly corpse to that city whence they had so recently seen him sally forth in all the pride of valiant manhood, the admiration of every beholder.   He had left behind a beautiful wife and infant son.   The heart of Mahomet was touched by her affliction.   He took the orphan child in his arms and bathed it with his tears.   But most he was affected when he beheld the young daughter of his faithful Zeid approaching him.   He fell on her neck and wept in speechless emotion.   A bystander expressed surprise that he should give way to tears for a death which, according to

Moslem doctrine, was but a passport to paradise. "Alas!" replied the prophet, "these are the tears of friendship for the loss of a friend!"

The obsequies of Jaafar were performed on the third day after the arrival of the army. By that time Mahomet had recovered his self-possession, and was again the prophet. He gently rebuked the passionate lamentations of the multitude, taking occasion to inculcate one of the most politic and consolatory doctrines of his creed. "Weep no more," said he, "over the death of this my brother. In place of the two hands lost in defending the standard of the faith, two wings have been given him to bear him to paradise; there to enjoy the endless delights insured to all believers who fall in battle."

It was in consequence of the prowess and generalship displayed by Khaled in this perilous fight, that he was honoured by Mahomet with the appellation of "The Sword of God," by which he was afterwards renowned.

CHAPTER XXIX.

Designs upon Mecca.—Mission of Abu Sofian.—Its result.

Mahomet, by force either of arms or eloquence, had now acquired dominion over a great number of the Arabian tribes. He had many thousand warriors under his command; sons of the desert inured to hunger, thirst, and the scorching rays of the sun, and to whom war was a sport, rather than a toil. He had corrected their intemperance, disciplined their valour, and subjected them to rule. Repeated victories had given them confidence in themselves and in their leader; whose standard they followed with the implicit obedience of soldiers, and the blind fanaticism of disciples.

The views of Mahomet expanded with his means, and a grand enterprise now opened upon his mind. Mecca, his native city, the abode of his family for generations, the scene of his happiest years, was still in the hands of his implacable foes. The Caaba, the object of devotion and pilgrimage to all the children of Ishmael, the shrine of his earliest worship, was still profaned by the emblems and rites of idolatry. To plant the standard of the faith on the walls of his native city; to rescue the holy house from profanation; restore it to the spiritual worship of the one true God, and make it the rallying point of Islamism, formed now the leading object of his ambition.

The treaty of peace existing with the Koreishites was an impediment to any military enterprise; but some casual feuds and skirmishings soon gave a pretext for charging them with having violated the treaty stipulations. The Koreishites had by this time learned to appreciate and dread the rapidly increasing power of the Moslems, and were eager to explain away, or atone for, the quarrels and misdeeds of a few heedless individuals. They even prevailed on their leader, Abu Sofian, to repair to Medina as ambassador of peace, trusting that he might have some influence with the prophet through his daughter Omm Habiba.

It was a sore trial to this haughty chief to come almost a suppliant to the man whom he had scoffed at as an impostor, and treated with inveterate hostility; and his proud spirit was doomed to still further mortification, for Mahomet, judging from his errand of the weakness of his party, and being secretly bent on war, vouchsafed him no reply.

Repressing his rage, Abu Sofian sought the intermediation of Abu Beker, of Omar, and Ali; but they all rebuked and repulsed him; for they knew the secret wishes of Mahomet. He next endeavoured to secure the favour of Fatima, the daughter of Mahomet and wife of Ali, by flattering a mother's pride, entreating her to let her son Hasan, a child but six years old, be his protector; but Fatima answered haughtily, " My son is too young to be a protector; and no protection can avail against the will of the prophet of God." Even his daughter, Omm Habiba, the wife of Mahomet, on whom Abu Sofian had calculated for influence, added to his mortification, for on his offering to seat himself on a mat in her dwelling, she hastily folded it up, exclaiming, " It is the bed of the prophet of God, and too sacred to be made the resting-place of an idolater."

The cup of humiliation was full to overfloving, and in the bitterness of his heart Abu Sofian cursed his daughter. He now turned again to Ali, beseeching, his advice in the desperate state of his embassy.

"I can advise nothing better," replied Ali, "than for thee to promise, as the head of the Koreishites, a continuance of thy protection; and then to return to thy home."

" But thinkest thou, that promise will be of any avail?"

" I think not," replied Ali dryly; " but I know not to the contrary."

In pursuance of this advice, Abu Sofian repaired to the mosque, and made public declaration, in behalf of the Koreishites, that on their part the treaty of peace should be faithfully maintained; after which he returned to Mecca, deeply humiliated by the imperfect result of his mission. He was received with scoffs by the Koreishites, who observed that his declaration of peace availed nothing without the concurrence of Mahomet.

CHAPTER XXX.

Surprise and Capture of Mecca.

Mahomet now prepared for a secret expedition to take Mecca by surprise. His allies were summoned from all quarters to Medina; but no intimation was given of the object he had in view. All the roads leading to Mecca were barred to prevent any intelligence of his movements being carried to the Koreishites.   With all his precautions the secret came near being discovered.   Among his followers, fugitives from Mecca, was one named Hateb, whose family had remained behind, and were without connexions or friends to take an interest in their welfare.   Hateb now thought to gain favour for them among the Koreishites, by betraying the plans of Mahomet. He accordingly wrote a letter revealing the intended enterprise, and gave it in charge to a singing woman, named Sara, a Haschemite slave, who undertook to carry it to Mecca.

She was already on the road when Mahomet was apprised of the treachery.   Ali and five others, well mounted, were sent in pursuit of the messenger.   They soon overtook her, but searched her person in vain.   Most of them would have given up the search and turned back, but Ali was confident that the prophet of God could not be mistaken nor misinformed.   Drawing his scimetar, he swore to strike off the head of the messenger, unless the letter were produced.   The threat was effectual.   She drew forth the letter from among her hair.

Hateb on being taxed with his perfidy, acknowledged it ; but pleaded his anxiety to secure favour for his destitute family, and his certainty that the letter would be harmless, and of no avail against the purposes of the apostle of God.   Omar spurned at his excuses and would have struck off his head ; but Mahomet, calling to mind that Hateb had fought bravely in support of the faith in the battle of Beder, admitted his excuses and forgave him.

The prophet departed with ten thousand men on this momentous enterprise.   Omar, who had charge of regulating the march, and appointing the encampments, led the army by lonely passes of the mountains ; prohibiting the sound of attabal or trumpet, or any thing else that could betray their movements.   While on the march, Mahomet was joined by his uncle Al Abbas, who had come forth with his family from Mecca, to rally under the standard of the faith. Mahomet received him graciously, yet with a hint at his tardiness. "Thou art the last of the emigrants," said he, "as I am the last of the prophets."   Al Abbas sent his family forward to Medina, while he turned and accompanied the expedition.   The army reached the valley of Marr Azzahran, near to the sacred city, without being discovered.   It was nightfall when they silently pitched their tents, and now Omar for the first time permitted them to light their watch-fires.

In the meantime, though Al Abbas had joined the standard of the faith in all sincerity, yet he was sorely disquieted at seeing his nephew advancing against Mecca, with such a powerful force and such hostile intent ; and feared the entire destruction of the Koreishites, unless they could be persuaded in time to capitulate.   In the dead of the night, he mounted Mahomet's white mule Fadda, and rode forth to reconnoitre.   In skirting the camp, he heard the tramp of men and sound of voices.   A scouting party were bringing in two prisoners captured near the city.   Al Abbas approached, and found the captives to be Abu Sofian, and one of his captains. They were conducted to the watch-fire of Omar, who recognized

Abu Sofian by the light. "God be praised," cried he, "that I have such an enemy in my hands, and without conditions." His ready scimetar might have given fatal significance to his words, had not Al Abbas stepped forward and taken Abu Sofian under his protection, until the will of the prophet should be known. Omar rushed forth to ascertain that will, or rather to demand the life of the prisoner; but Al Abbas, taking the latter up behind him, put spurs to his mule, and was the first to reach the tent of the prophet, followed hard by Omar, clamouring for the head of Abu Sofian.

Mahomet thus beheld in his power his inveterate enemy, who had driven him from his home and country, and persecuted his family and friends; but he beheld in him the father of his wife Omm Habiba, and felt inclined to clemency. He postponed all decision in the matter until morning; giving Abu Sofian in charge of Al Abbas.

When the captain was brought before him on the following day: "Well, Abu Sofian," cried he, "is it not at length time to know that there is no other God but God?"

"That I already knew," replied Abu Sofian.

"Good! and is it not time for thee to acknowledge me as the apostle of God?"

"Dearer art thou to me than my father and my mother," replied Abu Sofian, using an oriental phrase of compliment; "but I am not yet prepared to acknowledge thee a prophet."

"Out upon thee!" cried Omar, "testify instantly to the truth, or thy head shall be severed from thy body."

To these threats were added the counsels and entreaties of Al Abbas, who showed himself a real friend in need. The rancour of Abu Sofian had already been partly subdued by the unexpected mildness of Mahomet; so, making a merit of necessity, he acknowledged the divinity of his mission; furnishing an illustration of the Moslem maxim, "To convince stubborn unbelievers, there is no argument like the sword."

Having now embraced the faith, Abu Sofian obtained favourable terms for the people of Mecca, in case of their submission. None were to be harmed who should remain quietly in their houses; or should take refuge in the houses of Abu Sofian and Hakim; or under the banner of Abu Rawaiha.

That Abu Sofian might take back to the city a proper idea of the force brought against it, he was stationed with Al Abas at a narrow defile where the whole army passed in review. As the various Arab tribes marched by with their different arms and ensigns, Al Abbas explained the name and country or each. Abu Sofian was surprised at the number, discipline, and equipment of the troops; for the Moslems had been rapidly improving in the means and art of war; but when Mahomet approached, in the midst of a chosen guard, armed at all points and glittering with steel, his astonishment passed all bounds. "There is no withstanding this!" cried he to Al Abas, with an oath—"truly thy nephew wields a mighty power."

"Even so," replied the other; "return then to thy people; provide for their safety, and warn them not to oppose the apostle of God."

Abu Sofian hastened back to Mecca, and assembling the inhabitants, told them of the mighty host at hand, led on by Mahomet; of the favourable terms offered in case of their submission, and of the vanity of all resistance. As Abu Sofian had been the soul of the opposition to Mahomet and his doctrines, his words had instant effect in producing acquiescence in an event which seemed to leave no alternative. The greater part of the inhabitants, therefore, prepared to witness, without resistance, the entry of the prophet.

Mahomet, in the meantime, who knew not what resistance he might meet with, made a careful distribution of his forces as he approached the city. While the main body marched directly forward, strong detachments advanced over the hills on each side. To Ali, who commanded a large body of cavalry, was confided the sacred banner, which he was to plant on Mount Hadjun, and maintain it there until joined by the prophet. Express orders were given to all the generals to practise forbearance, and in no instance to make the first attack; for it was the earnest desire of Mahomet to win Mecca by moderation and clemency, rather than subdue it by violence. It is true, all who offered armed resistance were to be cut down, but none were to be harmed who submitted quietly. Overhearing one of his captains exclaim, in the heat of his zeal, that "no place was sacred on the day of battle," he instantly appointed a cooler-headed commander in his place.

The main body of the army advanced without molestation. Mahomet brought up the rear-guard, clad in a scarlet vest, and mounted on his favourite camel Al Kaswa. He proceeded but slowly, however; his movements being impeded by the immense multitude which thronged around him. Arrived on Mount Hadjun, where Ali had planted the standard of the faith, a tent was pitched for him. Here he alighted, put off his scarlet garment, and assumed the black turban and the pilgrim garb. Casting a look down into the plain, however, he beheld, with grief and indignation, the gleam of swords and lances, and Khaled, who commanded the left wing, in a full career of carnage. His troops, composed of Arab tribes converted to the faith, had been galled by a flight of arrows from a body of Koreishites; whereupon the fiery warrior charged into the thickest of them with sword and lance; his troops pressed after him; they put the enemy to flight, entered the gates of Mecca pell-mell with them, and nothing but the swift commands of Mahomet preserved the city from a general massacre.

The carnage being stopped, and no further opposition manifested, the prophet descended from the mount and approached the gates, seated on his camel, accompanied by Abu Beker on his right hand, and followed by Osama, the son of Zeid. The sun was just rising as he entered the gates of his native city, with the glory of a conqueror, but the garb and humility of a pilgrim. He entered, repeating verses of the Koran, which he said had been revealed to him at Medina, and were prophetic of the event. He triumphed in the spirit of a religious zealot, not of a warrior. "Unto God," said he, "belong the hosts of heaven and earth, and God is mighty and wise. Now hath God verified unto his apostle the vision, wherein he said, ye shall surely enter the holy temple of Mecca in full security."

Without dismounting, Mahomet repaired directly to the Caaba, the scene of his early devotions, the sacred shrine of worship since the days of the patriarchs, and which he regarded as the primitive temple of the one true God. Here he made the seven circuits round the sacred edifice, a reverential rite from the days of religious purity; with the same devout feeling he each time touched the black stone with his staff; regarding it as a holy relic. He would have entered the Caaba, but Othman Ibn Talha, the ancient custodian, locked the door. Ali snatched the keys, but Mahomet caused them to be returned to the venerable officer, and so won him by his kindness, that he not merely threw open the doors, but subsequently embraced the faith of Islam; whereupon he was continued in his office.

Mahomet now proceeded to execute the great object of his religious aspirations, the purifying of the sacred edifice from the symbols of idolatry, with which it was crowded. All the idols in and about it, to the number of three hundred and sixty, were thrown down and destroyed. Among these, the most renowned was Hobal, an idol brought from Balka, in Syria, and fabled to have the power of granting rain. It was, of course, a great object of worship among the inhabitants of the thirsty desert. There were statues of Abraham and Ishmael also, represented with divining arrows in their hands; "an outrage on their memories," said Mahomet, "being symbols of a diabolical art which they had never practised." In reverence of their memories, therefore, these statues were demolished. There were paintings, also, depicting angels in the guise of beautiful women. "The angels," said Mahomet, indignantly, "are no such beings. There are celestial houris provided in paradise for the solace of true believers; but angels are ministering spirits of the Most High, and of too pure a nature to admit of sex." The paintings were accordingly obliterated.

Even a dove, curiously carved of wood, he broke with his own hands, and cast upon the ground, as savouring of idolatry.

From the Caaba he proceeded to the well of Zem Zem. It was sacred in his eyes, from his belief that it was the identical well revealed by the angel to Hagar and Ishmael, in their extremity; he considered the rite connected with it as pure and holy, and continued it in his faith. As he approached the well, his uncle Al Abbas presented him a cruise of the water, that he might drink, and make the customary ablution. In commemoration of this pious act, he appointed his uncle guardian of the cup of the well; an office of sacred dignity, which his descendants retain to this day.

At noon one of his followers, at his command summoned the people to prayer from the top of the Caaba, a custom continued ever since throughout Mahometan countries, from minarets or towers provided in every mosque. He also established the Kebla, toward which the faithful in every part of the world should turn their faces in prayer.

He afterwards addressed the people in a kind of sermon, setting forth his principal doctrines, and announcing the triumph of the faith as a fulfiment of prophetic promise. Shouts burst from the multitude in reply. "Allah Achbar! God is great!" cried they. "There is no God but God, and Mahomet is his prophet."

The religious ceremonials being ended, Mahomet took his station on the hill Al Safa, and the people of Mecca, male and female passed before him, taking the oath of fidelity to him as the prophet of God, and renouncing idolatry. This was in compliance with a revelation in the Koran : "God hath sent his apostle with the direction, and the religion of truth, that he may exalt the same over every religion. Verily, they who swear fealty to him, swear fealty unto God; the hand of God is over their hands." In the midst of his triumph, however, he rejected all homage paid exclusively to himself, and all regal authority. "Why dost thou tremble?" said he, to a man who approached with timid and faltering steps. "Of what dost thou stand in awe? I am no king, but the son of a Koreishite woman, who ate flesh dried in the sun."

His lenity was equally conspicuous. The once haughty chiefs of the Koreishites appeared with abject countenances before the man they had persecuted, for their lives were in his power.

" What can you expect at my hands?" demanded he sternly.

"Mercy, oh generous brother! Mercy, oh son of a generous line!"

"Be it so!" cried he, with a mixture of scorn and pity "Away! begone! ye are free!"

Some of his followers who had shared his persecutions, were disappointed in their anticipations of a bloody revenge, and murmured at his clemency; but he persisted in it, and established Mecca as an inviolable sanctuary, or place of refuge, so to continue until the final resurrection. He reserved to himself, however, the right on the present occasion, and during that special day to punish a few of the people of the city, who had grievously offended, and been expressly proscribed; yet even these, for the most part, were ultimately forgiven.

Among the Koreishite women who advanced to take the oath, he descried Henda, the wife of Abu Sofian ; the savage woman who had animated the infidels at the battle of Ohod, and had gnawed the heart of Hamza, in revenge for the death of her father. On the present occasion she had disguised herself to escape detection; but seeing the eyes of the prophet fixed on her, she threw herself at his feet, exclaiming, "I am Henda : pardon! pardon!" Mahomet pardoned her—and was requited for his clemency by her making his doctrines the subject of contemptuous sarcasms.

Among those destined to punishment, was Wacksa, the Ethiopian, who had slain Hamza; but he had fled from Mecca on the entrance of the army. At a subsequent period he presented himself before the prophet, and made the profession of faith before he was recognized. He was forgiven, and made to relate the particulars of the death of Hamza; after which Mahomet dismissed him with an injunction, never again to come into his presence. He survived until the time of the Caliphat of Omar, during whose reign he was repeatedly scourged for drunkenness.

Another of the proscribed, was Abdallah Ibn Saad, a young

Koreishite, distinguished for wit and humour, as well as for warlike accomplishments.. As he held the pen of a ready writer, Mahomet had employed him to reduce the revelations of the Koran to writing. In so doing, he had often altered and amended the text; nay, it was discovered that, through carelessness or design, he had occasionally falsified it, and rendered it absurd. He had even made his alterations and amendments matter of scoff and jest among his companions, observing that if the Koran proved Mahomet to be a prophet, he himself must be half a prophet. His interpolations being detected he had fled from the wrath of the prophet, and returned to Mecca, where he relapsed into idolatry. On the capture of the city his foster-brother concealed him in his house, until the tumult had subsided, when he led him into the presence of the prophet, and supplicated for his pardon. This was the severest trial of the lenity of Mahomet. The offender had betrayed his confidence; held him up to ridicule; questioned his apostolic mission, and struck at the very foundation of his faith. For some time he maintained a stern silence; hoping, as he afterwards declared, some zealous disciple might strike off the offender's head. No one, however, stirred; so, yielding to the entreaties of Othman, he granted a pardon. Abdallah instantly renewed his profession of faith; and continued a good Mussulman. His name will be found in the wars of the Caliphs. He was one of the most dexterous horsemen of his tribe, and evinced his ruling passion to the last, for he died repeating the hundredth chapter of the Koran, entitled "The war-steeds." Perhaps it was one which had experienced his interpolations.

Another of the proscribed, was Akrema Ibn Abu Jahl, who on many occasions had manifested a deadly hostility to the prophet, inherited from his father. On the entrance of Mahomet into Mecca, Akrema threw himself upon a fleet horse, and escaped by an opposite gate, leaving behind him a beautiful wife, Omm Hakem, to whom he was recently married. She embraced the faith of Islam, but soon after learnt that her husband, in attempting to escape by sea to Yemen, had been driven back to port. Hastening to the presence of the prophet, she threw herself on her knees before him, loose, dishevelled, and unveiled, and implored grace for her husband. The prophet, probably more moved by her beauty than her grief, raised her gently from the earth, and told her her prayer was granted. Hurrying to the seaport, she arrived just as the vessel in which her husband had embarked was about to sail. She returned, mounted behind him, to Mecca, and brought him, a true believer, into the presence of the prophet. On this occasion, however, she was so closely veiled that her dark eyes alone were visible. Mahomet received Akrema's profession of faith; made him commander of a battalion of Hawazenites, as the dower of his beautiful and devoted wife, and bestowed liberal donations on the youthful couple. Like many other converted enemies, Akrema proved a valiant soldier in the wars of the faith, and after signalizing himself on various occasions, fell in battle, hacked and pierced by swords and lances.

The whole conduct of Mahomet on gaining possession of Mecca, showed that it was a religious, more than a military triumph. His heart, too, softened toward his native place, now that it was in his power; his resentments were extinguished by success, and his inclinations were all toward forgiveness.

The Ansarians, or Auxiliaries of Medina, who had aided him in his campaign, began to fear that its success might prove fatal to their own interests. They watched him anxiously, as one day, after praying on the hill Al Safa, he sat gazing down wistfully upon Mecca, the scene of his early struggles and recent glory : " Verily," said he, "thou art the best of cities, and the most beloved of Allah ! Had I not been driven out from thee by my own tribe, never would I have left thee ! " On hearing this, the Ansarians said, one to another, " Behold ! Mahomet is conqueror and master of his native city; he will, doubtless, establish himself here, and forsake Medina !" Their words reached his ear, and he turned to them with reproachful warmth : "No !" cried he, " when you plighted to me your allegiance, I swore to live and die with you. I should not act as the servant of God, nor as his ambassador, were I to leave you."

He acted according to his words, and Medina, which had been his city of refuge, continued to be his residence to his dying day.

Mahomet did not content himself with purifying the Caaba, and abolishing idolatry from his native city; he sent forth his captains at the head of armed bands, to cast down the idols of different tribes set up in the neighbouring towns and villages, and to convert their worshippers to his faith.

Of all these military apostles, none was so zealous as Khaled; whose spirit was still fermenting with recent conversion. Arriving at Naklah, the resort of the idolatrous Koreishites to worship at the shrine of Uzza, he penetrated the sacred grove, laid waste the temple, and cast the idol to the ground. A horrible hag, black and naked, with dishevelled hair, rushed forth, shrieking and wringing her hands ; but Khaled severed her through the middle with one blow of his scimetar. He reported the deed to Mahomet, expressing a doubt whether she were priestess or evil spirit. " Of a truth," replied the prophet, " it was Uzza herself whom thou hast destroyed."

On a similar errand into the neighbouring province of Tehama, Khaled had with him three hundred and fifty men, some of them of the tribe of Suleim, and was accompanied by Abda'lrahman, one of the earliest proselytes of the faith. His instructions from the prophet were to preach peace and good will, to inculcate the faith, and to abstain from violence, unless assailed. When about two days' journey on his way to Tehama, he had to pass through the country of the tribe of Jadsima. Most of the inhabitants had embraced the faith, but some were still of the Sabean religion. On a former occasion this tribe had plundered and slain an uncle of Khaled, also the father of Abda'lrahman, and several Suleimites, as they were returning from Arabia Felix. Dreading that Khaled and his host might take vengeance for these misdeeds,-they armed themselves on their approach.

Khaled was secretly rejoiced at seeing them ride forth to meet him in this military array. Hailing them with an imperious tone, he demanded whether they were Moslems or infidels. They replied, in faltering accents, "Moslems." "Why, then, come ye forth to meet us with weapons in your hands?" "Because we have enemies among some of the tribes who may attack us unawares."

Khaled sternly ordered them to dismount and lay by their weapons. Some complied, and were instantly seized and bound; the rest fled. Taking their flight as a confession of guilt, he pursued them with great slaughter; laid waste the country, and in the effervescence of his zeal even slew some of the prisoners.

Mahomet, when he heard of this unprovoked outrage, raised his hands to heaven, and called God to witness that he was innocent of it. Khaled, when upbraided with it on his return, would fain have shifted the blame on Abda'lrahman, but Mahomet rejected indignantly an imputation against one of the earliest and worthiest of his followers. The generous Ali was sent forthwith to restore to the people of Jadsima what Khaled had wrested from them, and to make pecuniary compensation to the relatives of the slain. It was a mission congenial with his nature, and he executed it faithfully. Inquiring into the losses and sufferings of each individual, he paid him to his full content. When every loss was made good, and all blood atoned for, he distributed the remaining money among the people, gladdening every heart by his bounty. So Ali received the thanks and praises of the prophet, but the vindictive Khaled was rebuked even by those whom he had thought to please.

"Behold!" said he, to Abda'lrahman, "I have avenged the death of thy father." "Rather say," replied the other, indignantly, "thou hast avenged the death of thine uncle. Thou hast disgraced the faith by an act worthy of an idolater."

CHAPTER XXXI.

Hostilities in the Mountains.— Enemy's camp in the valley of Autas.—Battle at the pass of Honein.—Capture of the enemy's camp.—Interview of Mahomet with the nurse of his childhood.—Division of spoil.—Mahomet at his mother's grave.

While the military apostles of Mahomet were spreading his doctrines at the point of the sword in the plains, a hostile storm was gathering in the mountains. A league was formed among the Thakefites, the Hawazins, the Joshmites, the Saadites, and several other of the hardy mountain tribes of Bedouins, to check a power which threatened to subjugate all Arabia. The Saadites, or Beni Sad, here mentioned, are the same pastoral Arabs among whom Mahomet had been nurtured in his childhood; and in whose valley, according to tradition, his heart had been plucked forth and purified by an angel. The Thakefites, who were foremost in the league, were a powerful tribe, possessing the strong mountain town of Tayef and its productive territory. They were bigoted idolaters; maintaining at their capital the far-famed shrine of the female idol

Al Lat. The reader will remember the ignominious treatment of
Mahomet, when he attempted to preach his doctrines at Tayef;
being stoned in the public square, and ultimately driven with insult
from the gates. It was probably a dread of vengeance at his
hands, which now made the Thakefites so active in forming a league
against him.

Malec Ibn Auf, the chief of the Thakefites, had the general command of the confederacy. He appointed the valley of Autas, between Honein and Tayef, as the place of assemblage and encampment; and as he knew the fickle nature of the Arabs, and their
proneness to return home on the least caprice, he ordered them
to bring with them their families and effects. They assembled,
accordingly, from various parts, to the number of four thousand
fighting men; but the camp was crowded with women and children,
and encumbered with flocks and herds.

The expedient of Malec Ibn Auf to secure the adhesion of the
warriors, was strongly disapproved by Doraïd, the chief of the
Joshmites. This was an ancient warrior, upwards of a hundred
years old; meagre as a skeleton, almost blind, and so feeble that
he had to be borne in a litter on the back of a camel. Still,
though unable to mingle in battle, he was potent in council from
his military experience. This veteran of the desert advised that
the women and children should be sent home forthwith, and the
army relieved from all unnecessary incumbrances. His advice was
not taken; and the valley of Autas continued to present rather the
pastoral encampment of a tribe, than the hasty levy of an army.

In the meantime Mahomet, hearing of the gathering storm, had
sallied forth to anticipate it, at the head of about twelve thousand
troops, partly fugitives from Mecca, and auxiliaries from Medina,
partly Arabs of the desert, some of whom had not yet embraced
the faith.

In taking the field he wore a polished cuirass and helmet, and
rode his favourite while mule Daldal, seldom mounting a charger,
as he rarely mingled in actual fight. His recent successes and his
superiority in numbers, making him confident of an easy victory,
he entered the mountains without precaution, and pushing forward
for the enemy's camp at Mutas, came to a deep gloomy valley on
the confines of Honein. The troops marched without order through
the rugged defile, each one choosing his own path. Suddenly they
were assailed by showers of darts, stones, and arrows, which lay
two or three of Mahomet's soldiers dead at his feet, and wounded
several others. Malec, in fact, had taken post with his ablest warriors about the heights commanding this narrow gorge. Every cliff
and cavern was garrisoned with archers and slingers, and some
rushed down to contend at close quarters.

Struck with a sudden panic, the Moslems turned and fled. In
vain did Mahomet call upon them as their general, or appeal to
them as the prophet of God. Each man sougth but his own safety,
and an escape from this horrible valley.

For a moment all seemed lost, and some recent but unwilling
converts betrayed an exultation in the supposed reverse of fortune
of the prophet.

"By heavens!" cried Abu Sofian, as he looked after the flying Moslems, "nothing will stop them until they reach the sea."

"Ay," exclaimed another, "the magic power of Mahomet is at an end!"

A third, who cherished a lurking revenge for the death of his father, slain by the Moslems in the battle of Ohod, would have killed the prophet in the confusion, had he not been surrounded and protected by a few devoted followers. Mahomet himself, in an impulse of desperation, spurred his mule upon the enemy; but Al Abbas seized the bridle, stayed him from rushing to certain death, and at the same time put up a shout that echoed through the narrow valley. Al Abbas was renowned for strength of lungs, and at this critical moment it was the salvation of the army. The Moslems rallied when they heard his well-known voice, and finding they were not pursued, returned to the combat. The enemy had descended from the heights, and now a bloody conflict ensued in the defile. "The furnace is kindling," cried Mahomet exultingly, as he saw the glitter of arms and flash of weapons. Stooping from his saddle, and grasping a handful of dust, he scattered it in the air toward the enemy. "Confusion on their faces!" cried he, "may this dust blind them!" They were blinded accordingly, and fled in confusion, say the Moslem writers; though their defeat may rather be attributed to the Moslem superiority of force, and the zeal inspired by the exclamations of the prophet. Malec and the Thakefites took refuge in the distant city of Tayef, the rest retreated to the camp in the valley of Autas.

While Mahomet remained in the valley of Honein, he sent Abu Amir with a strong force, to attack the camp. The Hawazins made a brave defence. Abu Amir was slain; but his nephew, Abu Musa, took the command, and obtained a complete victory, killing many of the enemy. The camp afforded great booty and many captives, from the unwise expedient of Malec Ibn Auf, in encumbering it with the families and effects, the flocks and herds of the confederates; and from his disregard of the sage advice of the veteran Doraid. The fate of that ancient warrior of the desert is worthy of mention. While the Moslem troops, scattered through the camp, were intent on booty, Rabia Ibn Rafi, a young Suleimite, observed a litter born off on the back of a camel, and pursued it, supposing it to contain some beautiful female. On overtaking it and drawing the curtain, he beheld the skeleton form of the ancient Doraid. Vexed and disappointed, he struck at him with his sword, but the weapon broke in his hand. "Thy mother," said the old man sneeringly, "has furnished thee with wretched weapons; thou wilt find a better one hanging behind my saddle."

The youth seized it, but as he drew it from the scabbard, Doraid perceiving that he was a Suleimite, exclaimed, "Tell thy mother thou hast slain Doraid Ibn Simma, who has protected many women of her tribe in the day of battle." The words were ineffectual; the skull of the veteran was cloven with his own scimetar. When Rabia, on his return to Mecca, told his mother of the deed, "Thou hast indeed slain a benefactor of thy race," said she reproachfully.

" Three women of thy family has Doraid Ibn Simma freed from captivity."

Abu Musa returned in triumph to Mahomet, making a great display of the spoils of the camp of Autas, and the women and children whom he had captured.   One of the female captives threw herself at the feet of the prophet, and implored his mercy as his foster-sister Al Shima, the daughter of his nurse Halêma, who had nurtured him in the Saadite valley.   Mahomet sought in vain to recognize in her withered features the bright playmate of his infancy, but she laid bare her back, and showed a scar where he had bitten her in their childish gambols. He no longer doubted; but treated her with kindness, giving her the choice either to remain with him and under his protection, or to return to her home and kindred.

A scruple rose among the Moslems with respect to their female captives.   Could they take to themselves such as were married, without committing the sin of adultery?   The revelation of a text of the Koran put an end to the difficulty, " Ye shall not take to wife free women who are married, unless your right hand shall have made them slaves. "   According to this all women taken in war may be made the wives of the captors, though their former husbands be living.   The victors of Honein failed not to take immediate advantage of this law.

Leaving the captives and the booty in a secure place, and properly guarded, Mahomet now proceeded in- pursuit of the Thakefites who had taken refuge in Tayef.   A sentiment of vengeance mingled with his pious ardour as he approached this idolatrous place, the scene of former injury and insult, and beheld the gate whence he had once been ignominiously driven forth.   The walls were too strong however to be stormed, and there was a protecting castle; for the first time, therefore, he had recourse to cata-pults, battering-rams, and other engines used in sieges, but unknown in Arabian warfare.   These were prepared under the direction of Salmân al Farsi, the converted Persian.

The besieged, however, repulsed every attack, galling the assailants with darts and arrows, and pouring down melted iron upon the shields of bull-hides, under covert of which they approached the walls.   Mahomet now laid waste the fields, the orchards, and vineyards, and proclaimed freedom to all slaves who should desert from the city.   For twenty days he carried on an ineffectul siege —daily offering up prayers midway between the tents of his wives Omm Salama and Zeinab, to whom it had fallen by lot to accompany him in this campaign.   His hopes of success began to fail, and he was further discouraged by a dream, which was unfavourably interpreted by Abu Beker, renowned for his skill in expounding visions.   He would have raised the siege, but his troops murmured; whereupon he ordered an assault upon one of the gates.   As usual, it was obstinately defended; numbers were slain on both sides; Abu Sofian, who fought valiantly on the occasion, lost an eye, and the Moslems were finally repulsed.

Mahomet now broke up his camp, promising his troops to renew the siege at a future day, and proceeded to the place where were collected the spoils of his expedition.   These, say Arabian writers, amounted to twenty-four thousand camels, forty thousand sheep, four thousand ounces of silver, and six thousand captives.

In a little while appeared a deputation from the Hawazins, declaring the submission of their tribe, and begging the restoration of their families and effects. With them came Halêma, Mahomet's foster-nurse, now well stricken in years. The recollections of his childhood again pleaded with his heart. "Which is dearest to you," said he to the Hawazins, "your families or your goods?" They replied, "Our families."

"Enough," rejoined he, "as far as it concerns Al Abbas and myself, we are ready to give up our share of the prisoners; but there are others to be moved. Come to me after noontide prayer, and say, ' we implore the ambassador of God that he counsel his followers to return us our wives and children; and we implore his followers that they intercede with him in our favour."

The envoys did as he advised. Mahomet and Al Abbas immediately renounced their share of the captives; their example was followed by all excepting the tribes of Tamim and Fazara, but Mahomet brought them to consent by promising them a sixfold share of the prisoners taken in the next expedition. Thus the intercession of Halêma procured the deliverance of all the captives of her tribe. A traditional anecdote shows the deference with which Mahomet treated this humble protector of his infancy. "I was sitting with the prophet," said one of his disciples, "when all of a sudden a woman presented herself, and he rose and spread his cloth for her to sit down upon. When she went away, it was observed, ' that woman suckled the prophet.'"

Mahomet now sent an envoy to Malec, who remained shut up in Tayef, offering the restitution of all the spoils taken from him at Honein, and a present of one hundred camels, if he would submit and embrace the faith. Malec was conquered and converted by this liberal offer, and brought several of his confederate tribes with him to the standard of the prophet. He was immediately made their chief; and proved, subsequently, a severe scourge in the cause of the faith to his late associates the Thakefites.

The Moslems now began to fear that Mahomet, in these magnanimous impulses, might squander away all the gains of their recent battles; thronging round him, therefore, they clamoured for a division of the spoils and captives. Regarding them, indignantly, "Have you ever," said he, "found me avaricious, or false, or disloyal?" Then plucking a hair from the back of a camel, and raising his voice, "By Allah!" cried he, "I have never taken from the common spoil the value of that camel's hair more than my fifth; and that fifth has always been expended for your good."

He then shared the booty as usual; four-fifths among the troops; but his own fifth he distributed among those whose fidelity he wished to insure. The Koreishites he considered dubious allies; perhaps he had overheard the exultation of some of them in anticipation of his defeat; he now sought to rivet them to him by gifts. To Abu Sofian he gave one hundred camels and forty okks of silver, in compensation for the eye lost in the attack on the gate of Tayef. To Akrema Ibn Abu Jahl, and others of like note, he gave in due proportions, and all from his own share.

Among the lukewarm converts thus propitiated, was Abbas Ibn Mardas, a poet. He was dissatisfied with his share, and vented his discontent in satirical verses. Mahomet overheard him. "Take that man hence," said he, "and cut out his tongue." Omar, ever ready for rigorous measures, would have executed the sentence literally, and on the spot; but others, better instructed in the prophet's meaning, led Abbas, all trembling, to the public square where the captured cattle were collected, and bade him choose what he liked from among them.

"What!" cried the poet, joyously, relieved from the horrors of mutilation, "is this the way the prophet would silence my tongue? By Allah! I will take nothing." Mahomet, however, persisted in his politic generosity, and sent him sixty camels. From that time forward the poet was never weary of chanting the liberality of the prophet.

While thus stimulating the good-will of lukewarm proselytes of Mecca, Mahomet excited the murmurs of his auxiliaries of Medina. "See," said they, "how he lavishes gifts upon the treacherous Koreishites, while we, who have been loyal to him through all dangers, receive nothing but our naked share. What have we done that we should be thus thrown into the background?"

Mahomet was told of their murmurs, and summoned their leaders to his tent. "Hearken, ye men of Medina," said he; "were ye not in discord among yourselves, and have I not brought you into harmony? Were ye not in error, and have I not brought yo into the path of truth? Were ye not poor, and have I not made you rich?"

- They acknowledged the truth of his words. "Look ye!" continued he, "I came among you stigmatized as a liar, yet you believed in me; persecuted, yet you protected me; a fugitive, yet you sheltered me; helpless, yet you aided me. Think you I do not feel all this? Think you I can be ungrateful? You complain that I bestow gifts upon these people, and give none to you. It is true, I give them worldly gear, but it is to win their worldly hearts. To you, who have been true, I give—myself! They return home with sheep and camels; ye return with the prophet of God among you. For, by him in whose hands is the soul of Mahomet, though the whole world should go one way and ye another, I would remain with you! Which of you, then, have I most rewarded?"

The auxiliaries were moved even to tears by this appeal. "Oh, prophet of God," exclaimed they, "we are content with our lot!"

The booty being divided, Mahomet returned to Mecca, not with the parade and exultation of a conqueror, but in pilgrim garb, to complete the rites of his pilgrimage. All these being scrupulously performed, he appointed Moad Ibn Jabal as iman, or pontiff, to instruct the people in the doctrines of Islam, and gave the government of the city into the hands of Otab, a youth but eighteen years of age; after which he bade farewell to his native place, and set out with his troops on the return to Medina.

Arriving at the village of Al Abwa, where his mother was buried, his heart yearned to pay a filial tribute to her memory, but his own revealed law forbade any respect to the grave of one who had died in unbelief. In the strong agitation of his feelings he implored from heaven a relaxation of this law. If there was any deception on an occasion of this kind, one would imagine it must have been self-deception, and that he really believed in a fancied intimation from heaven relaxing the law, in part, in the present instance, and permitting him to visit the grave. He burst into tears on arriving at this trying place of the tenderest affections; but tears were all the filial tribute he was permitted to offer. "I asked leave of God," said he, mournfully, "to visit my mother's grave, and it was granted; but when I asked leave to pray for her, it was denied me."

CHAPTER XXXII.

Death of the prophet's daughter Zeinab.—Birth of his son Ibrahim.—Deputations from distant tribes.—Poetical contest in presence of the prophet.—His susceptibility to the charms of poetry.—Reduction of the city of Tayef; destruction of its idols.—Negotiation with Amir Ibn Tafiel, a proud Bedouin chief; independent spirit of the latter.—Interview of Adi, another chief, with Mahomet.

Shortly after his return to Medina, Mahomet was afflicted by the death of his daughter Zeinab, the same who had been given up to him in exchange for her husband Abul Aass, the unbeliever, captured at the battle of Beder. The domestic affections of the prophet were strong, and he felt deeply this bereavement; he was consoled, however, by the birth of a son, by his favourite concubine Mariyah. He called the child Ibrahim, and rejoiced in the hope, that this son of his old age, his only male issue living, would continue his name to after generations.

His fame, either as a prophet or a conqueror, was now spreading to the uttermost parts of Arabia, and deputations from distant tribes were continually arriving at Medina, some acknowledging him as a prophet and embracing Islamism; others submitting to him as a temporal sovereign, and agreeing to pay tribute. The talents of Mahomet rose to the exigency of the moment; his views expanded with his fortunes, and he now proceeded with statesmanlike skill to regulate the fiscal concerns of his rapidly growing empire. Under the specious appellation of alms, a contribution was levied on true believers, amounting to a tithe of the productions of the earth, where it was fertilized by brooks and rain; and a twentieth part where its fertility was the result of irrigation. For every ten camels, two sheep were required; for forty head of cattle, one cow; for thirty head, a two year's calf; for every forty sheep, one; whoever contributed more than at this rate, would be considered so much the more devout, and would gain a proportionate favour in the eyes of God.

The tribute exacted from those who submitted to temporal sway, but continued in unbelief, was at the rate of one dinar in money or goods, for each adult person, bond or free.

Some difficulty occurred in collecting the charitable contributions; the proud tribe of Tamim openly resisted them, and drove away the collector. A troop of Arab horse was sent against them, and brought away a number of men, women and children, captives. A deputation of the Tamimites came to reclaim the prisoners. Four of the deputies were renowned as orators and poets, and instead of humbling themselves before Mahomet, proceeded to declaim in prose and verse, defying the Moslems to a poetical contest.

"I am not sent by God as a poet," replied Mahomet, "neither do I seek fame as an orator."

Some of his followers, however, accepted the challenge, and a war of ink ensued, in which the Tamimites acknowledged themselves vanquished. So well pleased was Mahomet with the spirit of their defiance, with their poetry, and with their frank acknowledgment of defeat, that he not merely gave them up the prisoners, but dismissed them with presents.

Another instance of his susceptibility to the charms of poetry, is recorded in the case of Caab Ibn Zohair, a celebrated poet of Mecca, who had made him the subject of satirical verses, and had consequently been one of the proscribed; but had fled on the capture of the sacred city. Caab now came to Medina to make his peace, and approaching Mahomet when in the mosque began chanting his praises in a poem afterwards renowned among the Arabs as a master-piece. He concluded by especially extolling his clemency, "for with the prophet of God, the pardon of injuries is, of all his virtues, that on which one can rely with the greatest certainty."

Captivated with the verse, and soothed by the flattery, Mahomet made good the poet's words, for he not merely forgave him, but taking off his own mantle, threw it upon his shoulders. The poet preserved the sacred garment to the day of his death, refusing golden offers for it. The Caliph Moawyah purchased it of his heirs for ten thousand drachmas, and it continued to be worn by the Caliphs in processions and solemn ceremonials, until the thirty-sixth Caliphat, when it was torn from the back of the Caliph Al-Most'asem Billah, by Holâgu, the Tartar conqueror, and burnt to ashes.

While town after town, and castle after castle of the Arab tribes were embracing the faith, and professing allegiance to Mahomet, Tayef, the stronghold of the Thakefites, remained obstinate in the worship of its boasted idol Al Lat. The inhabitants confided in their mountain position, and in the strength of their walls and castle. But, though safe from assault, they found themselves gradually hemmed in and isolated by the Moslems, so that at length they could not stir beyond their walls without being attacked. Thus threatened and harassed, they sent ambassadors to Mahomet to treat for peace.

The prophet cherished a deep resentment against this stiff-necked and most idolatrous city, which had at one time ejected him from its gates, and at another time repulsed him from its walls. His terms were conversion and unqualified submission. The ambassadors readily consented to embrace Islamism themselves, but pleaded

the danger of suddenly shocking the people of Tayef, by a demand
to renounce their ancient faith. In their name, therefore, they
entreated permission for three years longer, to worship their ancient idol Al Lat.   The request was peremptorily denied.   They
then asked at least one month's delay, to prepare the public mind.
This likewise was refused, all idolatry being incompatible with the
worship of God.   They then entreated to be excused from the
observance of the daily prayers.

"There can be no true religion without prayer," replied Mahomet.   In fine, they were compelled to make an unconditional
submission.

Abu Sofian Ibn Harb, and Al Mogheira, were sent to Tayef, to
destroy the idol Al Lat, which was of stone.   Abu Sofian struck at
it with a pick-axe, but missing his blow fell prostrate on his face.
The populace set up a shout, considering it a good augury, but Al
Mogheira demolished their hopes, and the statue, at one blow of
a sledge-hammer.   He then stripped it of the costly robes, the bracelets, the necklace, the ear-rings, and other ornaments of gold
and precious stones wherewith it had been decked by its worshippers, and left it in fragments on the ground, with the women of
Tayef weeping and lamenting over it. [1]

Among those who still defied the power of Mahomet, was the Bedouin chief Amir Ibn Tufiel, head of the powerful tribe of Amir.
He was renowned for personal beauty and princely magnificence;
but was of a haughty spirit; and his magnificence partook of ostentation.   At the great fair of Okaz, between Tayef and Naklah, where
merchants, pilgrims, and poets, were accustomed to assemble from
all parts of Arabia; a herald would proclaim: "Whoso wants a
beast of burden, let him come to Amir; is any one hungry, let
him come to Amir, and he will be fed; is he persecuted, let him
fly to Amir, and he will be protected."

Amir had dazzled every one by his generosity, and his ambition
had kept pace with his popularity.   The rising power of Mahomet
inspired him with jealouly.   When advised to make terms with
him; "I have sworn," replied he haughtily, "never to rest until I
had won all Arabia; and shall I do homage to this Koreishite?"

The recent conquests of the Moslems, however, brought him to
listen to the counsels of his friends.   He repaired to Medina, and
coming into the presence of Mahomet, demanded frankly, "Wilt
thou be my friend?"

"Never, by Allah!" was the reply, "unless thou dost embrace
the faith of Islam."

"And if I do; wilt thou content thyself with the sway over the
Arabs of the cities, and leave to me the Bedouins of the deserts?"

Mahomet replied in the negative.

"What then will I gain by embracing thy faith?"

"The fellowship of all true believers."

[1] The Thakefites continue a powerful tribe to this day; possessing the same fertile
region on the eastern declivity of the Hedjas chain of mountains. Some inhabit the
ancient town of Tayef, others dwell in tents and have flocks of goats and sheep. They
can raise two thousand match-locks, and defended their stronghold of Tayef in the
wars with the Wahabys.—*Burckhardt, Notes*, v. 2.

"I covet no such fellowship!" replied the proud Amir; and with a warlike menace he returned to his tribe.

A Bedouin chieftain of a different character was Adi, a prince of the tribe of Taï. His father Hatim had been famous, not merely for warlike deeds, but for boundless generosity, insomuch that the Arabs were accustomed to say, "as generous as Hatim." Adi the son was a Christian; and however he might have inherited his father's generosity, was deficient in his valour. Alarmed at the ravaging expeditions of the Moslems, he ordered a young Arab, who tended his camels in the desert, to have several of the strongest and fleetest at hand, and to give instant notice of the approach of an enemy.

It happened that Ali, who was scouring that part of the country with a band of horsemen, came in sight, bearing with him two banners, one white, the other black. The young Bedouin beheld them from afar, and ran to Adi, exclaiming, "The Moslems are at hand. I see their banners at a distance!" Adi instantly placed his wife and children on the camels, and fled to Syria. His sister, surnamed Saffana, or the Pearl, fell into the hands of the Moslems, and was carried with other captives to Medina. Seeing Mahomet pass near to the place of her confinement, she cried to him:

"Have pity upon me, oh ambassador of God! My father is dead, and he who should have protected has abandoned me. Have pity upon me, oh ambassador of God, as God may have pity upon thee!"

"Who is thy protector?" asked Mahomet.

"Adi, the son of Hatim."

"He is a fugitive from God and his prophet," replied Mahomet, and passed on.

On the following day, as Mahomet was passing by, Ali, who had been touched by the woman's beauty and her grief, whispered to her to arise and entreat the prophet once more. She accordingly repeated her prayer. "Oh prophet of God! my father is dead; my brother, who should have been my protector, has abandoned me. Have mercy upon me, as God will have mercy upon thee."

Mahomet turned to her benignantly. "Be it so," said he; and he not only set her free, but gave her raiment and a camel, and sent her by the first caravan bound to Syria.

Arriving in presence of her brother, she upbraided him with his desertion. He acknowledged his fault, and was forgiven. She then urged him to make his peace with Mahomet; "he is truly a prophet," said she, "and will soon have universal sway; hasten, therefore, in time to win his favour."

The politic Adi listened to her counsel, and hastening to Medina, greeted the prophet, who was in the mosque. His own account of the interview presents a striking picture of the simple manners and mode of life of Mahomet, now in the full exercise of sovereign power, and the career of rapid conquest. "He asked me," says Adi, "my name, and when I gave it, invited me to accompany him to his home. On the way a weak emaciated woman accosted him. He stopped and talked to her of her affairs. This, thought I to myself, is not very kingly. When we arrived at his house, he gave me a leathern cushion stuffed with palm-leaves to sit upon, while he sat upon the bare ground. This, thought I, is not very princely!

"He then asked me three times to embrace Islamism. I replied, I have a faith of my own. 'I know thy faith,' said he, 'better than thou dost thyself. As prince, thou takest one-fourth of the booty from thy people. Is this Christian doctrine?' By these words I perceived him to be a prophet, who knew more than other men.

"'Thou dost not incline to Islamism,' continued he, 'because thou seest we are poor. The time is at hand when true believers will have more wealth than they will know how to manage. Perhaps thou art deterred, by seeing the small number of the Moslems in comparison with the hosts of their enemies. By Allah! in a little while a Moslem woman will be able to make a pilgrimage on her camel, alone and fearless, from Kadesia to God's temple at Mecca. Thou thinkest, probably, that the might is in the hands of the unbelievers; know that the time is not far off when we will plant our standards on the white castles of Babylon.'" [1]

The politic Adi believed in the prophecy, and forthwith embraced the faith.

CHAPTER XXXIII.

Preparations for an expedition against Syria. — Intrigues of Abdallah Ibn Obba,—Contributions of the faithful.—March of the army.—The accursed region of Hajar.—Encampment at Tabuc.—Subjugation of the neighbouring provinces.—Khaled surprises Okaidor and his castle.—Return of the army to Medina.

Mahomet had now, either by conversion or conquest, made himself sovereign of almost all Arabia. The scattered tribes, heretofore dangerous to each other, but by their disunion powerless against the rest of the world, he had united into one nation, and thus fitted for external conquest. His prophetic character gave him absolute control of the formidable power thus conjured up in the desert, and he was now prepared to lead it forth for the propagation of the faith, and the extension of the Moslem power in foreign lands.

His numerous victories, and the recent affair at Muta, had at length, it is said, roused the attention of the Emperor Heraclius, who was assembling an army on the confines of Arabia to crush this new enemy. Mahomed determined to anticipate his hostilities, and to carry the standard of the faith into the very heart of Syria.

Hitherto he had undertaken his expeditions with secrecy; imparting his plans and intentions to none but his most confidential officers, and beguiling his followers into enterprises of danger. The present campaign, however, so different from the brief predatory excursions of the Arabs, would require great preparations; an unusual

[1] Weil's Mohammed, p. 247.

force was to be assembled, and all kinds of provisions made for distant marches, and a long absence. He proclaimed openly, therefore, the object and nature of the enterprise.

There was not the usual readiness to flock to his standard. Many remembered the disastrous affair of Muta, and dreaded to come again in conflict with disciplined Roman troops. The time of year also was unpropitious for such a distant and prolonged expedition. It was the season of summer heat; the earth was parched, and the springs and brooks were dried up. The date-harvest too was approaching, when the men should be at home to gather the fruit, rather than abroad on predatory enterprises.

All these things were artfully urged upon the people by Abdallah Ibn Obba, the Khazradite, who continued to be the covert enemy of Mahomet, and seized every occasion to counteract his plans. " A fine season, this," would he cry, " to undertake such a distant march in defiance of dearth and drought, and the fervid heat of the desert! Mahomet seems to think a war with Greeks quite a matter of sport; trust me, you will find it very different from a war of Arab against Arab. By Allah! methinks I already see you all in chains."

By these and similar scoffs and suggestions, he wrought upon the fears and feelings of the Khazradites, his partisans, and rendered the enterprise generally unpopular. Mahomet, as usual, had resort to revelation. " Those who would remain behind, and refuse to devote themselves to the service of God," said a timely chapter of the Koran, " allege the summer heat as an excuse. Tell them the fire of hell is hotter! They may hug themselves in the enjoyment of present safety, but endless tears will be their punishment hereafter?"

Some of his devoted adherents manifested their zeal at this lukewarm moment. Omar, Al Abbas, and Abda'lrahman, gave large sums of money; several female devotees brought their ornaments and jewels. Othman delivered one thousand, some say ten thousand, dinars to Mahomet, and was absolved from his sins, past, present, or to come. Abu Beker gave four thousand drachmas; Mahomet hesitated to accept the offer, knowing it to be all that he possessed. " What will remain," said he, " for thee and thy family?" " God and his prophet," was the reply.

These devout examples had a powerful effect; yet it was with much difficulty that an army of ten thousand horse and twenty thousand foot was assembled. Mahomet now appointed Ali governor of Medina during his absence, and guardian of both their families. He accepted the trust with great reluctance, having been accustomed always to accompany the prophet, and share all his perils. All arrangements being completed. Mahomet marched forth from Medina on this momentous expedition. A part of his army was composed of Khazradites and their confederates, led by Abdallah Ibn Obba. This man, whom Mahomet had well denominated the Chief of the Hypocrites, encamped separately with his adherents at night, at some distance in the rear of the main army; and when the latter marched forward in the morning, lagged behind and led his troops back to Medina. Repairing to Ali, whose dominion in the city was irksome to him and his adherents, he endeavoured to make him discontented with his position, alleging that Mahomet had left him in charge of Medina solely to ride himself of an incumbrance. Stung by the suggestion, Ali hastened after Mahomet, and demanded if what Abdallah and his followers said were true.

"These men, replied Mahomet, " are liars. They are the party of Hypocrites and Doubters, who would breed sedition in Medina. I left thee behind to keep watch over them, and to be a guardian to both our families. I would have thee to be to me what Aaron was to Moses; excepting that thou canst not be, like him, a prophet; I being the last of the prophets." With this explanation, Ali returned contented to Medina.

Many have inferred from the foregoing, that Mahomet intended Ali for his Caliph or successor; that being the signification of the Arabic word used to denote the relation of Aaron to Moses.

The troops who had continued on with Mahomet soon began to experience the difficulties of braving the desert in this sultry season. Many turned back on the second day; and others on the third and fourth. Whenever word was brought to the prophet of their desertion, " Let them go," would be the reply; " if they are good for any thing God will bring them back to us; if they are not, we are relieved from so many incumbrances."

While some thus lost heart upon the march, others who had remained at Medina repented of their faint-heartedness. One, named Abu Khaithama, entering his garden during the sultry heat of the day, beheld a repast of viands and fresh water spread for him by his two wives in the cool shade of a tent. Pausing at the threshold, " At this moment," exclaimed he, " the prophet of God is exposed to the winds and heats of the desert, and shall Khaithama sit here in the shade beside his beautiful wives? By Allah ! I will not enter the tent !" He immediately armed himself with sword and lance, and, mounting his camel, hastened off to join the standard of the faith.

In the meantime the army, after a weary march of seven days, entered the mountainous district of Hajar, inhabited in days of old by the Thamudites, one of the lost tribes of Arabia. It was the accursed region, the tradition concerning which has already been related. The advance of the army, knowing nothing of this tradition, and being heated and fatigued, beheld, with delight, a brook running through a verdant valley, and cool caves cut in the sides of the neighbouring hills, once the abodes of the heaven-smitten Thamudites. Halting along the brook, some prepared to bathe, others began to cook and make bread, while all promised themselves cool quarters for the night in the caves.

Mahomet, in marching, had kept, as was his wont, in the rear of the army to assist the weak; occasionally taking up a wayworn laggard behind him. Arriving at the place where the troops had halted, he recollected-it of old, and the traditions concerning it, which had been told to him when he passed here in the days of his boyhood. Fearful of incurring the ban which hung over the neighbourhood, he ordered his troops to throw away the meat

cooked with the water of the brook, to give the bread kneaded
with it to the camels, and to hurry away from the heaven-accursed
place.   Then wrapping his face in the folds of his mantle, and
setting spurs to his mule, he hastened through that sinful region;
the army following him as if flying from an enemy.

The succeeding night was one of great suffering; the army had
to encamp without water; the weather was intensely hot, with a
parching wind from the desert; an intolerable thirst prevailed
throughout the camp, as though the Thamudite ban still hung
over it.   The next day, however, an abundant rain refreshed and
invigorated both man and beast.   The march was resumed with
new ardour, and the army arrived, without further hardship, at
Tabuc, a small town on the confines of the Roman empire, about
half way between Medina and Damascus, and about ten days'
journey from either city.

Here Mahomet pitched his camp in the neighbourhood of a
fountain, and in the midst of groves and pasturage.   Arabian traditions affirm that the fountain was nearly dry; insomuch that,
when a small vase was filled for the prophet, not a drop was left:
having assuaged his thirst, however, and made his ablutions,
Mahomet threw what remained in the vase back into the fountain;
whereupon a stream gushed forth sufficient for the troops and all
the cattle.

From this encampment Mahomet sent out his captains to proclaim and enforce the faith, or to exact tribute.   Some of the
neighbouring princes sent embassies, either acknowledging the divinity of his mission, or submitting to his temporal sway.   One of
these was Johanna Ibn Ruba, prince of Eyla, a Christian city, near
the Red Sea.   This was the same city about which the tradition
is told, that in days of old, when its inhabitants were Jews, the
old men were turned into swine, and the young men into monkeys,
for fishing on the Sabbath, a judgment solemnly recorded in the
Koran.

The prince of Eyla made a covenant of peace with Mahomet,
agreeing to pay an annual tribute of three thousand dinars or
crowns of gold.   The form of the covenant became a precedent
in treating with others powers.

Among the Arab princes who professed the Christian faith, and
refused to pay homage to Mahomet, was Okaïder Ibn Malec, of the
tribe of Kenda.   He resided in a castle at the foot of a mountain, in
the midst of his domain.   Khaled was sent with a troop of horse to
bring him to terms.   Seeing the castle was too strong to be carried
by assault, he had recourse to stratagem.   One moonlight night, as
Okaïder and his wife were enjoying the fresh air on the terraced
roof of the castle, they beheld an animal grazing, which they supposed to be a wild ass from the neighbouring mountains.   Okaïder,
who was a keen huntsman, ordered horse and lance, and sallied
forth to the chase, accompanied by his brother Hassan and several
of his people.   The wild ass proved to be a decoy.   They had not
ridden far before Khaled and his men rushed from ambush and
attacked them.   They were too lightly armed to make much
resistance.   Hassan was killed on the spot, and Okaïder taken

prisoner; the rest fled back to the castle; which, however, was soon surrendered. The prince was ultimately set at liberty on paying a heavy ransom and becoming a tributary.

As a trophy of the victory, Khaled sent to Mahomet the vest stripped from the body of Hassan. It was of silk, richly embroidered with gold. The Moslems gathered round, and examined it with admiration. "Do you admire this vest?" said the prophet. "I swear by him in whose hands is the soul of Mahomet, the vest which Saad, the son of Maadi, wears at this moment in paradise, is far more precious." This Saad was the judge who passed sentence of death on seven hundred Jewish captives at Medina, at the conclusion of a former campaign.

His troops being now refreshed by the sojourn at Tabuc, and the neighbouring country being brought into subjection, Mahomet was bent upon prosecuting the object of his campaign, and pushing forward into the heart of Syria. His ardour, however, was not shared by his followers. Intelligence of immense bodies of hostile troops, assembled on the Syrian borders, had damped the spirits of the army. Mahomet remarked the general discouragement, yet was loth to abandon the campaign when but half completed. Calling a council of war, he propounded the question whether or not to continue forward. To this Omar replied, dryly, "If thou hast the command of God to proceed further, do so." "If I had the command of God to proceed further," observed Mahomet, "I should not have asked thy counsel."

Omar felt the rebuke. He then, in a respectful tone, represented the impolicy of advancing in the face of the overwhelming force said to be collected on the Syrian frontier; he represented, also, how much Mahomet had already effected in this campaign. He had checked the threatened invasion of the imperial arms, and had received the homage and submission of various tribes and people, from the head of the Red Sea to the Euphrates: he advised him, therefore, to be content for the present year with what he had achieved, and to defer the completion of the enterprise to a future campaign.

His counsel was adopted: for, whenever Mahomet was not under strong excitement, or fancied inspiration, he was rather prone to yield up his opinion in military matters to that of his generals. After a sojourn of about twenty days, therefore, at Tabuc, he broke up his camp, and conducted his army back to Medina.

CHAPTER XXXIV.

Triumphal entry into Medina.—Punishment of those who had refused to join the campaign.—Effects of excommunication.—Death of Abdallah Ibn Obba.—Dissensions in the prophet's harem.

The entries of Mahomet into Medina on returning from his war like triumphs, partook of the simplicity and absence of parade, which characterized all his actions. On approaching the city, when his household came forth with the multitude to meet him, he would stop to greet them, and take up the children of the house behind him on his horse. It was in this simple way he entered Medina, on returning from the campaign against Tabuc.

The arrival of an army laden with spoil, gathered in the most distant expedition ever undertaken by the soldiers of Islam, was an event of too great moment, not to be hailed with triumphant exultation by the community. Those alone were cast down in spirit, who had refused to march forth with the army, or had deserted it when on the march. All these were at first placed under an interdict; Mahomet forbidding his faithful followers to hold any intercourse with them. Mollified, however, by their contrition or excuses, he gradually forgave the greater part of them. Seven of those who continued under interdict, finding themselves cut off from communion with their acquaintance, and marked with opprobrium amid an exulting community, became desperate, and chained themselves to the walls of the mosque; swearing to remain there until pardoned. Mahomet, on the other hand, swore he would leave them there unless otherwise commanded by God. Fortunately he received the command in a revealed verse of the Koran; but, in freeing them from their self-imposed fetters, he exacted one-third of their possessions, to be expended in the service of the faith.

Among those still under interdict were Kaab Ibn Malec, Murara Ibn Rabia, and Hilal Ibn Omeya. These had once been among the most zealous of professing Moslems; their defection was, therefore, ten times more heinous in the eyes of the prophet, than that of their neighbours, whose faith had been lukewarm and dubious. Toward them, therefore, he continued implacable. Forty days they remained interdicted, and the interdict extended to communication with their wives.

The account given by Kaab Ibn Malec of his situation, while thus excommunicated, presents a vivid picture of the power of Mahomet over the minds of his adherents. Kaab declared that every body shunned him, or regarded him with an altered mien. His two companions in disgrace did not leave their homes; he, however, went about from place to place, but no one spoke to him. He sought the mosque, sat down near the prophet, and saluted him, but his salutation was not returned. On the forty-first day came a command, that he should separate from his wife. He now left the city, and pitched a tent on the hill of Sala, determined there to undergo in its severest rigour the punishment meted out to him. His heart, however, was dying away; the wide world, he said, appeared to grow narrow to him. On the fifty-first day came a messenger holding out the hope of pardon. He hastened to Medina, and sought the prophet at the mosque, who received him with a radiant countenance, and said that God had forgiven him. The soul of Kaab was lifted up from the depths of despondency, and in the transports of his gratitude, he gave a portion of his wealth in atonement of his errour.

Not long after the return of the army to Medina, Abdallah Ibn Obba, the Khazradite, "the chief of the Hypocrites," fell ill, so that his life was despaired of. Although Mahomet was well aware of the perfidy of this man, and the secret arts he had constantly practised against him, he visited him repeatedly during his illness; was with him at his dying hour, and followed his body to the grave. There, at the urgent entreaty of the son of the deceased, he put up prayers that his sins might be forgiven.

Omar privately remonstrated with Mahomet for praying for a hypocrite; reminding him how often he had been slandered by Abdallah; but he was shrewdly answered by a text of the Koran; " Thou mayest pray for the 'Hypocrites' or not, as thou wilt; but though thou shouldest pray seventy times, yet will they not be forgiven."

The prayers at Abdallah's grave, therefore, were put up out of policy, to win favour with the Khazradites, and the powerful friends of the deceased; and in this respect the prayers were successful, for most of the adherents of the deceased became devoted to the prophet, whose sway was thenceforth undisputed in Medina. Subsequently he announced another revelation, which forbade him to pray by the death-bed or stand by the grave of any one who died in unbelief.

But though Mahomet exercised such dominion over his disciples, and the community at large, he had great difficulty in governing his wives, and maintaining tranquillity in his harem. He appears to have acted with tolerable. equity in his connubial concerns, assigning to each of his wives a separate habitation, of which she was sole mitress, and passing the twenty-four hours with them by turns. It so happened, that on one occasion, when he was sojourning with Hafsa, the latter left her dwelling to visit her father. Returning unexpectedly, she surprised the prophet with his favourite and forturnate slave Mariyah, the mother of his son Ibrahim. The jealousy of Hafsa was vociferous. Mahomet endeavoured to pacify her, dreading lest her outcries should rouse his whole harem to rebellion; but she was only to be appeased by an oath on his part never more to cohabit with Mariyah. On these terms she forgave the past and promised secrecy.

She broke her promise, however, and revealed to Ayesha the infidelity of the prophet; and in a little while it was known throughout the harem. His wives now united in a storm of reproaches; until, his patience being exhausted, he repudiated Hafsa and renounced all intercourse with the rest. For a month he lay alone on a mat in a separate apartment; but Allah, at length, in consideration of his lonely state, sent down the first and sixth chapters of the Koran, absolving him from the oath respecting Mariyah, who forthwith became the companion of his solitary chamber.

The refractory wives were now brought to a sense of their errour, and apprized by the same revelation, that the restrictions imposed on ordinary men did not apply to the prophet. In the end he took back Hafsa, who was penitent; and he was reconciled to Ayesha whom he tenderly loved, and all the rest were in due time received into favour; but he continued to cherish Mariyah, for she was fair to look upon, and was the mother of his only son.

CHAPTER XXXV.

Abu Beker conducts the yearly pilgrimage to Mecca.—Mission of Ali to announce
a revelation.

The sacred month of yearly pilgrimage was now at hand, but Mahomet was too much occupied with public and domestic concerns to absent himself from Medina: he deputed Abu Beker, therefore, to act in his place as emir or commander of the pilgrims, who were to resort from Medina to the holy city. Abu Beker accordingly departed at the head of three hundred pilgrims, with twenty camels for sacrifice.

Not long afterwards Mahomet summoned his son-in-law and devoted disciple Ali, and, mounting him on Al Adha, or the slit-eared, the swiftest of his camels, urged him to hasten with all speed to Mecca, there to promulgate before the multitude of pilgrims assembled from all parts, an important sura, or chapter of the Koran, just received from heaven.

Ali executed his mission with his accustomed zeal and fidelity. He reached the sacred city in the height of the great religious festival. On the day of sacrifice, when the ceremonies of pilgrimage were completed by the slaying of the victims in the valley of Mina, and when Abu Beker had preached and instructed the people in the doctrines and rites of Islamism, Ali rose before an immense multitude assembled at the hill Al Akaba, and announced himself a messenger from the prophet, bearing an important revelation. He then read the sura, or chapter of the Koran, of which he was the bearer; in which the religion of the sword was declared in all its rigour. It absolved Mahomet from all truce or league with idolatrous and other unbelievers, should they in any wise have been false to their stipulations, or given aid to his enemies. It allowed unbelievers four months of toleration from the time of this announcement, during which months they might "go to and fro about the earth securely," but at the expiration of that time all indulgence would cease; war would then be made in every way, at every time and in every place, by open force or by stratagem, against those who persisted in unbelief: no alternative would be left them but to embrace the faith, or pay tribute. The holy months and the holy places would no longer afford them protection. "When the months wherein ye are not allowed to attack them shall be passed," said the revelation, "kill the idolatrous wherever ye shall find them, or take them prisoners; besiege them, or lay in wait for them." The ties of blood and friendship were to be alike disregarded; the faithful were to hold no communion with their nearest relatives and dearest friends, should they persist in idolatry. After the expiration of the current year, no unbeliever was to be permitted to tread the sacred bounds of Mecca, nor to enter the temple of Allah, a prohibition which continues to the present day.

This stringent chapter of the Koran is thought to have been provoked, in a great measure, by the conduct of some of the Jewish and idolatrous Arabs, with whom Mahomet had made covenants, who had repeatedly played him false, and even made treacherous attempts upon his life. It evinces, however, the increased confidence he felt in consequence of the death of his insidious and powerful foe, Abdallah Ibn Obba, and the rapid conversion or subjugation of the Arab tribes. It was, in fact, a decisive blow for the exclusive domination of his faith.

When Abu Beker and Ali returned to Mecca, the former expressed surprise and dissatisfaction that he had not been made the promulgator of so important a revelation, as it seemed to be connected with his recent mission, but he was pacified by the assurance that all new revelations must be announced by the prophet himself, or by some one of his immediate family.

CHAPTER XXXVI.

Mahomet sends his captains on distant enterprises.—Appoints lieutenants to govern in Arabia Felix.—Sends Ali to suppress an insurrection in that province.—Death of the prophet's only son Ibrahim.—His conduct at the death-bed and the grave.—His growing infirmities.—His valedictory pilgrimage to Mecca, and his conduct and preaching while there.

The promulgation of the last-mentioned chapter of the Koran, with the accompanying denunciation of exterminating war against all who should refuse to believe or submit, produced hosts of converts and tributaries; so that, towards the close of the month, and in the beginning of the tenth year of the Hegira, the gates of Medina were thronged with envoys from distant tribes and princes. Among those who bowed to the temporal power of the prophet was Farwa, lieutenant of Heraclius, in Syria, and governor of Ammon, the ancient capital of the Ammonites. His act of submission, however, was disavowed by the emperor, and punished with imprisonment.

Mahomet felt and acted more and more as a sovereign, but his grandest schemes as a conqueror were always sanctified by his zeal as an apostle. His captains were sent on more distant expeditions than formerly, but it was always with a view to destroy idols, and bring idolatrous tribes to subjection; so that his temporal power but kept pace with the propagation of his faith. He appointed two lieutenants to govern in his name in Arabia Felix; but a portion of that rich and important country having shown itself refractory, Ali was ordered to repair thither at the head of three hundred horsemen; and bring the inhabitants to reason.

The youthful disciple expressed a becoming diffidence to undertake a mission where he would have to treat with men far older and wiser than himself; but Mahomet laid one hand upon his lips, and the other upon his breast, and raising his eyes to heaven, exclaimed, " Oh, Allah! loosen his tongue and guide his heart!" He

gave him one rule for his conduct as a judge. "When two parties come before thee, never pronounce in favour of one until thou
hast heard the other."   Then giving into his hands the standard
of the faith, and placing the turban on his head, he bade him
farewell.

When the military missionary arrived in the heretical region of
Yemen, his men, indulging their ancient Arab propensities, began
to sack, to plunder, and destroy.   Ali checked their excesses, and
arresting the fugitive inhabitants, began to expound to them the
doctrines of Islam.   His tongue, though so recently consecrated
by the prophet, failed to carry conviction, for he was answered by
darts and arrows; whereupon he returned to the old argument of
the sword, which he urged with such efficacy, that, after twenty
unbelievers had been slain, the rest avowed themselves thoroughly
convinced.   This zealous achievement was followed by others of a
similar kind, after each of which he despatched messengers to the
prophet, announcing a new triumph of the faith.

While Mahomet was exulting in the tidings of success from every
quarter, he was stricken to the heart by one of the severest of domestic bereavements.   Ibrahim, his son, by his favourite concubine Maryah, a child but fifteen months old, his only male issue,
on whom reposed his hope of transmitting his name to posterity,
was seized with a mortal malady, and expired before his eyes.
Mahomet could not control a father's feelings as he bent in agony
over this blighted blossom of his hopes.   Yet even in this trying
hour he showed that submission to the will of God which formed
the foundation of his faith.   "My heart is sad," murmured he,
"and mine eyes overflow with tears at parting with thee, oh my
son!   And still greater would be my grief, did I not know that I
must soon follow thee; for we are of God; from him we came,
and to him we must return."

Abda'lrahman seeing him in tears, demanded : "Hast thou not
forbidden us to weep for the dead?"   "No," replied the prophet.
"I have forbidden ye to utter shrieks and outcries, to beat your
faces, and rend your garments; these are suggestions of the evil
one; but tears shed for a calamity are as balm to the heart, and
are sent in mercy."

He followed his child to the grave, where amidst the agonies of
separation, he gave another proof that the elements of his religion
were ever present to his mind.   "My son! my son!" exclaimed
he as the body was committed to the tomb, "say God is my Lord!
the prophet of God was my father, and Islamism is my faith!"
This was to prepare his child for the questioning by examining
angels, as to religious belief, which, according to Moslem creed,
the deceased would undergo while in the grave. [1]

[1] One of the funeral rites of the Moslems is for the Mulakken or priest, to address the
deceased when in the grave, in the following words : "Oh servant of God! O son of a
handmaid of God! know that, at this time, there will come down to thee two angels
commissioned respecting thee and the like of thee ; when they say to thee, 'Who is thy
Lord?" answer them, 'God is my Lord;' in truth, and when they ask thee concerning
thy prophet, or the man who hath been sent unto you, say to them, 'Mahomet is the
apostle of God,' with veracity, and when they ask thee concerning thy religion, say to
them, 'Islamism is my religion.' And when they ask thee concerning thy book of

An eclipse of the sun which happened about that time, was interpreted by some of his zealous followers as a celestial sign of mourning for the death of Ibrahim; but the afflicted father rejected such obsequious flattery. "The sun and the moon," said he "are among the wonders of God, through which at times he signifies his will to his servants; but their eclipse has nothing to do either with the birth or death of any mortal."

The death of Ibrahim was a blow which bowed him toward the grave. His constitution was already impaired by the extraordinary excitements and paroxysms of his mind, and the physical trials to which he had been exposed; the poison too, administered to him at Khaïbar, had tainted the springs of life, subjected him to excruciating pains, and brought on a premature old age. His religious zeal took the alarm from the increase of bodily infirmities, and he resolved to expend his remaining strength in a final pilgrimage to Mecca; intended to serve as a model for all future observances of the kind.

The announcement of his pious intention brought devotees from all parts of Arabia, to follow the pilgrim-prophet. The streets of Medina were crowded with the various tribes from the towns and cities, from the fastnesses of the mountains, and the remote parts of the desert, and the surrounding valleys were studded with their tents. It was a striking picture of the triumph of a faith, these recently disunited, barbarous, and warring tribes brought together as brethren, and inspired by one sentiment of religious zeal.

Mahomet was accompanied on this occasion by his nine wives, who were transported on litters. He departed at the head of an immense train, some say of fifty-five, others ninety, and others a hundred and fourteen thousand pilgrims. There was a large number of camels also, decorated with garlands and fluttering streamers, intended to be offered up in sacrifice.

The first night's halt was a few miles from Medina, at the village of Dhu'l Holaïfa, where, on a former occasion, he and his followers had laid aside their weapons, and assumed the pilgrim garb. Early on the following morning after praying in the mosque, he mounted his camel Al Aswa, and entering the plain of Baïda, uttered the prayer or invocation called in Arabic Talbijah, in which he was joined by all his followers. The following is the import of this solemn invocation: "Here am I in thy service, oh God! Here am I in thy service! Thou hast no companion. To thee alone belongeth worship. From thee cometh all good. This alone is the kingdom. There is none to share it with thee."

This prayer, according to Moslem tradition, was uttered by the patriarch Abraham, when, from the top of the hill of Kubeis, near Mecca, he preached the true faith to the whole human race, and so wonderful was the power of his voice, that it was heard by every living being throughout the world: insomuch, that the

direction, say to them, 'the Koran is my book of direction, and the Moslems are my brothers;' and when they ask thee concerning thy Kebla, say to them, 'the Caaba is my Kebla, and I have lived and died in the assertion that there is no deity but God, and Mahomet is God's apostle,' and they will say, 'Sleep, O servant of God, in the protection of God!'"—See *Lane's Modern Egyptians*, vol. ii. p. 338.

very child in the womb reponded, "Here am I in thy service,
oh God!"

In this way the pilgrim host pursued its course, winding in a
lengthened train of miles, over mountain and valley, and making
the deserts vocal at times with united prayers and ejaculations.
There were no longer any hostile armies to impede or molest it,
for by this time the Islam faith reigned serenely over all Arabia.
Mahomet approached the sacred city over the same heights which
he had traversed in capturing it, and he entered through the
gate Beni Scheiba, which still bears the name of The Holy.

A few days after his arrival, he was joined by Ali, who had
hastened back from Yemen; and who brought with him a number
of camels to be slain in sacrifice.

As this was to be a model pilgrimage, Mahomet rigorously observed all the rites which he had continued in compliance with
patriarchal usage, or introduced in compliance with revelation.
Being too weak and infirm to go on foot, he mounted his camel,
and thus performed the circuits round the Caaba, and the journeyings to and fro, between the hills of Safa and Merwa.

When the camels were to be offered up in sacrifice, he slew
sixty-three with his own hand, one for each year of his age, and
Ali, at the same time, slew thirty-seven on his own account.

Mahomet then shaved his head, beginning on the right side and
ending on the left. The locks thus shorn away were equally divided
among his disciples, and treasured up as sacred relics. Khaled ever
afterwards wore one in his turban, and affirmed that it gave him
supernatural strength in battle.

Conscious that life was waning away within him, Mahomet,
during this last sojourn in the sacred city of his faith, sought to
engrave his doctrines deeply in the minds and hearts of his followers. For this purpose he preached frequently in the Caaba
from the pulpit, or in the open air from the back of his camel.
"Listen to my words," would he say, "for I know not whether,
after this year, we shall ever meet here again. Oh, my hearers,
I am but a man like yourselves; the angel of death may at any
time appear, and I must obey his summons."

He would then proceed to inculcate not merely religious doctrines and ceremonies, but rules for conduct in all the concerns of
life, public and domestic; and the precepts laid down and enforced
on this occasion, have had a vast and durable influence on the mo-
rals, manners, and habitudes of the whole Moslem world.

It was doubtless in view of his approaching end, and in solicitude
for the welfare of his relatives and friends after his death, and especially of his favourite Ali, who, he perceived, had given dissatisfaction in the conduct of his recent campaign in Yemen, that he took
occasion, during a moment of strong excitement and enthusiam
among his hearers, to address to them a solemn adjuration.

"Ye believe," said he, "that there is but one God; that Mahomet is his prophet and apostle; that paradise and hell are truths;
that death and the resurrection are certain; and that there is an
appointed time when all who rise from the grave must be brought
to judgment."

They all answered, " We believe these things. " He then adjured them solemnly by these dogmas of their faith ever to hold his family, and especially Ali, in love and reverence. " Whoever loves me," said he, " let him receive Ali as his friend. May God uphold those who befriend him, and may he turn from his enemies."

It was at the conclusion of one of his discourses in the open air, from the back of his camel, that the famous verse of the Koran is said to have come down from heaven in the very voice of the Deity. " Evil to those, this day, who have denied your religion. Fear them not; fear me. This day I have perfected your religion, and accomplished in you my grace. It is my good pleasure that Isla- mism be your faith."

On hearing these words, say the Arabian historians, the camel Al Karwa, on which the prophet was seated, fell on its knees in adoration. The words, add they, were the seal and conclusion of the law, for after them there were no further revelations.

Having thus fulfilled all the rites and ceremonies of pilgrimage, and made a full exposition of his faith, Mahomet bade a last farewell to his native city, and, putting himself at the head of his pilgrim army, set out on his return to Medina.

As he came in sight of it, he lifted up his voice, and exclaimed, " God is great! God is great! There is but one God; he has no companion. His is the kingdom. To him alone belongeth praise. He is almighty. He hath fulfilled his promise. He has stood by his servant, and alone dispersed his enemies. Let us return to our homes, and worship and praise him!"

Thus ended what has been termed the valedictory pilgrimage, being the last made by the prophet.

CHAPTER XXXVII.

Of the two false prophets Al Aswad and Moseïlma. .

The health of Mahomet continued to decline after his return to Medina; nevertheless his ardour to extend his religious empire was unabated, and he prepared, on a great scale, for the invasion of Syria and Palestine. While he was meditating foreign conquest, however, two rival prophets arose to dispute his sway in Arabia. One was named Al Aswad, the other Moseïlma; they received from the faithful the well-merited appellation of " The two Liars. "

Al Aswad, a quick-witted man, and gifted with persuasive elo- quence, was originally an idolater, then a convert to Islamism, from which he apostatized to set up for a prophet, and establish a religion of his own. His fickleness in matters of faith gained him the appellation of Ailhala, or " The Weathercock. " In emulation of Mahomet he pretended to receive revelations from heaven through the medium of two angels. Being versed in juggling arts and natural magic, he astonished and confounded the multitude with spectral illusions, which he passed off as miracles, insomuch that certain Moslem writers believe he was really assisted by two evil genii or demons. His schemes, for a time, were crowned with great success, which shows how unsettled the Arabs were in those days in matters of religion, and how ready to adopt any new faith.

Budhân, the Persian whom Mahomet had continued as viceroy of Arabia Felix, died in this year; whereupon Al Aswad, now at the head of a powerful sect, slew his son and successor, espoused his widow after putting her father to death, and seized upon the reins of government. The people of Najran invited him to their city; the gates of Sanaa, the capital of Yemen, were likewise thrown open to him, so that, in a little while, all Arabia Felix submitted to his sway.

The news of this usurpation found Mahomet suffering in the first stages of a dangerous malady, and engrossed by preparations for the Syrian invasion. Impatient of any interruption to his plans, and reflecting that the whole danger and difficulty in question depended upon the life of an individual, he sent orders to certain of his adherents, who were about Al Aswad, to make way with him openly or by stratagem, either way being justifiable against enemies of the faith, according to the recent revelation promulgated by Ali. Two persons undertook the task, less, however, through motives of religion than revenge. One, named Rais had received a mortal offence from the usurper; the other, named Firuz the Dailemite, was cousin to Al Aswad's newly espoused wife and nephew of her murdered father. They repaired to the woman, whose marriage with the usurper had probably been compulsory, and urged upon her the duty, according to the Arab law of blood, of avenging the deaths of her father and her former husband. With much difficulty they prevailed upon her to facilitate their entrance at the dead of night into the chamber of Al Aswad, who was asleep. Firuz stabbed him in the throat with a poniard. The blow was not effectual. Al Aswad started up, and his cries alarmed the guard. His wife, however, went forth and quieted them. "The prophet," said she, "is under the influence of divine inspiration." By this time the cries had ceased, for the assassins had stricken off the head of their victim. When the day dawned the standard of Mahomet floated once more on the walls of the city, and a herald proclaimed, by sound of trumpet, the death of Al Aswad, otherwise called the Liar and Impostor. His career of power began, and was terminated, within the space of four months. The people, easy of faith, resumed Islamism with as much facility as they had abandoned it.

Moseïlma, the other impostor, was an Arab of the tribe of Honcifa, and ruled over the city and province of Yamama, situated between the Red Sea and the Gulf of Persia. In the ninth year of the Hegira he had come to Mecca at the head of an embassy from his tribe, and had made profession of faith between the hands of Mahomet; but, on returning to his own country, had proclaimed that God had gifted him likewise with prophecy, and appointed him to aid Mahomet in converting the human race. To this effect he likewise wrote a Koran, which he gave forth as a volume of inspired truth. His creed was noted for giving the soul a humiliating residence in the region of the abdomen.

Being a man of influence and address, he soon made hosts of converts among his credulous countrymen. Rendered confident by success, he addressed an epistle to Mahomet, beginning as follows:

"From Moseïlma the prophet of Allah, to Mahomet the prophet of Allah! Come, now, and let us make a partition of the world, and let half be thine and half be mine."

This letter came also to the hands of Mahomet, while bowed down by infirmities and engrossed by military preparations. He contented himself for the present with the following reply:

"From Mahomet the prophet of God, to Moseïlma the Liar! The earth is the Lord's and he giveth it as an inheritance to such of his servants as find favour in his sight. Happy shall those be who live in his fear."

In the urgency of other affairs, the usurpation of Moseïlma remained unchecked. His punishment was reserved for a future day.

CHAPTER XXXVIII.

An army prepared to march against Syria.—Command given to Osama —The prophet's farewell address to the troops.—His last illness.—His sermons in the mosque.— His death and the attending circumstances.

It was early in the eleventh year of the Hegira that, after unusual preparations, a powerful army was ready to march for the invasion of Syria. It would almost seem a proof of the failing powers of Mahomet's mind, that he gave the command of such an army, on such an expedition, to Osama, a youth but twenty years of age, instead of some one of his veteran and well-tried generals. It seems to have been a matter of favour, dictated by tender and grateful recollections. Osama was the son of Zeid, Mahomet's devoted freedman, who had given the prophet such a signal and acceptable proof of devotion in relinquishing to him his beautiful wife Zeinab. Zeid had continued to the last the same zealous and self-sacrificing disciple, and had fallen bravely fighting for the faith in the battle of Muta.

Mahomet was aware of the hazard of the choice he had made, and feared the troops might be insubordinate under so young a commander. In a general review, therefore, he exhorted them to obedience, reminding them that Osama's father, Zeid, had commanded an expedition of this very kind, against the very same people, and had fallen by their hands; it was but a just tribute to his memory, therefore, to give his son an opportunity of avenging

his death.   Then placing his banner in the hands of the youthful
general, he called upon him to fight valiantly the fight of the
faith against all who should deny the unity of God.   The army
marched forth that very day, and encamped at Djorf, a few miles
from Medina ; but circumstances occurred to prevent its further
progress.

That very night Mahomet had a severe access of the malady which
for some time past had affected him, and which was ascribed by
some to the lurking effects of the poison given to him at Khaïbar.
It commenced with a violent pain in the head, accompanied by
vertigo, and the delirium which seems to have mingled with all his
paroxysms of illness.   Starting up in the mid-watches of the night
from a troubled dream, he called upon an attendant slave to accompany him ; saying he was summoned by the dead who lay interred
in the public burying-place of Medina to come and pray for them.
Followed by the slave, he passed through the dark and silent city,
where all were sunk in sleep, to the great burying-ground, outside
of the walls.

Arrived in the midst of the tombs, he lifted up his voice and
made a solemn apostrophe to their tenants.   " Rejoice, ye dwellers
in the grave !" exclaimed he, "More peaceful is the morning to which
ye shall awaken, than that which attends the living.   Happier is your
condition than theirs.   God has delivered you from the storms with
which they are threatened and which shall follow one another like
the watches of a stormy night, each darker than that which went
before."

After praying for the dead, he turned and addressed his slave.
" The choice is given me," said he, " either to remain in this
world to the end of time, in the enjoyment of all its delights, or
to return sooner to the presence of God ; and I have chosen the
latter."

From this time his illness rapidly increased, though he endeavoured to go about as usual, and shifted his residence from day to
day, with his different wives, as he had been accustomed to do.
He was in the dwelling of Maïmona, when the violence of his
malady became so great, that he saw it must soon prove fatal.
His heart now yearned to be with his favourite wife Ayesha, and
pass with her the fleeting residue of life.   With his head bound
up, and his tottering frame supported by Ali and Fadhl, the son
of Al Abbas, he repaired to her abode.   She, likewise, was suffering with a violent pain in the head, and entreated of him a
remedy.

" Wherefore a remedy ?" said he.   " Better that thou shouldst
die before me.   I could then close thine eyes ; wrap thee in thy
funeral garb ; lay thee in the tomb, and pray for thee."

" Yes," replied she, " and then return to my house and dwell
with one of thy other wives, who would profit by my death."

Mahomet smiled at this expression of jealous fondness, and
resigned himself into her care.   His only remaining child, Fatima,
the wife of Ali, came presently to see him.   Ayesha used to say that
she never saw any one resemble the prophet more in sweetness of
temper, than this his daughter.   He treated her always with

respectful tenderness. When she came to him, he used to rise up, go towards her, take her by the hand, and kiss it, and would seat her in his own place. Their meeting on this occasion is thus related by Ayesha, in the traditions preserved by Abulfeda.

"'Welcome, my child,' said the prophet, and made her sit beside him. He then whispered something in her ear, at which she wept. Perceiving her affliction, he whispered something more, and her countenance brightened with joy. 'What is the meaning of this?' said I to Fatima. ' The prophet honours thee with a mark of confidence never bestowed on any of his wives.' ' I cannot disclose the secret of the prophet of God,' replied Fatima. Nevertheless, after his death she declared that at first he announced to her his impending death; but seeing her weep, consoled her with the assurance that she would shortly follow him, and become a princess in heaven, among the faithful of her sex."

In the second day of his illness Mahomet was tormented by a burning fever, and caused vessels of water to be emptied on his head and over his body; exclaiming, amidst his paroxysms, " Now I feel the poison of Khaïbar rending my entrails."

When somewhat relieved, he was aided in repairing to the mosque, which was adjacent to his residence. Here, seated in his chair, or pulpit, he prayed devoutly; after which, addressing the congregation, which was numerous, "If any of you," said he, "have aught upon his conscience, let him speak out, that I may ask God's pardon for him."

Upon this a man, who had passed for a devout Moslem, stood forth and confessed himself a hypocrite, a liar, and a weak disciple. " Out upon thee!" cried Omar, "why dost thou make known what God had suffered to remain concealed?" But Mahomet turned rebukingly to Omar. "Oh son of Khattab," said he, " better is it to blush in this world, than suffer in the next." Then lifting his eyes to heaven, and praying for the self-accused, "Oh God," exclaimed he, " give him rectitude and faith, and take from him all weakness in fulfilling such of thy commands as his conscience dictates."

Again addressing the congregation, "Is there any one among you," said he, " whom I have stricken; here is my back, let him strike me in return. Is there any one whose character I have aspersed; let him now cast reproach upon me. Is there any one from whom I have taken aught unjustly; let him now come forward and be indemnified."

Upon this, a man among the throng reminded Mahomet of a debt of three dinars of silver, and was instantly repaid with interest. " Much easier is it," said the prophet, " to bear punishment in this world than throughout eternity."

He now prayed fervently for the faithful, who had fallen by his side in the battle of Ohod, and for those who had suffered for the faith in other battles; interceding with them in virtue of the pact which exists between the living and the dead.

After this he addressed the Mohajerins or Exiles, who had accompanied him from Mecca, exhorting them to hold in honour the Ansarians, or allies of Medina. " The number of believers," said he, " will increase, but that of the allies never can. They were my family with whom I found a home. Do good to those who do good to them, and break friendship with those who are hostile to them."

He then gave three parting commands :

First.—Expel all idolaters from Arabia.

Second.—Allow all proselytes equal privileges with yourselves.

Third.—Devote yourselves incessantly to prayer.

His sermon and exhortation being finished, he was affectionately supported back to the mansion of Ayesha, but was so exhausted on arriving there that he fainted.

His malady increased from day to day, apparently with intervals of delirium ; for he spoke of receiving visits from the angel Gabriel, who came from God to inquire after the state of his health ; and told him that it rested with himself to fix his dying moment ; the angel of death being forbidden by Allah to enter his presence without his permission.

In one of his paroxysms he called for writing implements, that he might leave some rules of conduct for his followers. His attendants were troubled, fearing he might do something to impair the authority of the Koran. Hearing them debate among themselves, whether to comply with the request, he ordered them to leave the room, and when they returned said nothing more on the subject.

On Friday, the day of religious assemblage, he prepared, notwithstanding his illness, to officiate in the mosque, and had water again poured over him to refresh and strengthen him, but on making an effort to go forth, fainted. On recovering, he requested Abu Beker to perform the public prayers ; observing, " Allah has given his servant the right to appoint whom he pleases in his place." It was afterwards maintained by some that he thus intended to designate this long tried friend and adherent as his successor in office ; but Abu Beker shrank from construing the words too closely.

Word was soon brought to Mahomet, that the appearance of Abu Beker in the pulpit had caused great agitation, a rumour being circulated that the prophet was dead. Exerting his remaining strength, therefore, and leaning on the shoulders of Ali and Al Abbas, he made his way into the mosque, where his appearance spread joy throughout the congregation. Abu Beker ceased to pray, but Mahomet bade him proceed, and taking his seat behind him in the pulpit, repeated the prayers after him. Then addressing the congregation, '·I have heard," said he, "that a rumour of the death of your prophet filled you with alarm ; but has any prophet before me lived for ever, that ye think I would never leave you ? Every thing happens according to the will of God, and has its appointed time, which is not to be hastened nor avoided. I return to him who sent me ; and my last command to you is, that ye remain united ; that ye love, honour, and uphold each other ; that ye exhort each other to faith and constancy in belief, and to the performance of pious deeds ; by these alone men prosper ; all else leads to destruction."

In concluding his exhortation, he added, " I do but go before you; you will soon follow me. Death awaits us all; let no one then seek to turn it aside from me. My life has been for your good; so will be my death."

These were the last words he spake in public; he was again conducted back by Ali and Abbas to the dwelling of Ayesha.

On a succeeding day there was an interval during which he appeared so well that Ali, Abu Beker, Omar, and the rest of those who had been constantly about him, absented themselves for a time, to attend to their affairs. Ayesha alone remained with him. The interval was but illusive. His pains returned with redoubled violence. Finding death approaching he gave orders that all his slaves should be restored to freedom, and all the money in the house distributed among the poor; then raising his eyes to heaven, "God be with me, in the death struggle," exclaimed he.

Ayesha now sent in haste for her father and Hafza. Left alone with Mahomet, she sustained his head on her lap, watching over him with tender assiduity, and endeavouring to soothe his dying agonies. From time to time he would dip his hand in a vase of water, and with it feebly sprinkle his face. At length raising his eyes and gazing upward for a time with unmoving eyelids, "Oh Allah!" ejaculated he, in broken accents, "be it so!—among the glorious associates in paradise!"

"I knew by this," said Ayesha, who related the dying scene, "that his last moment had arrived, and that he had made choice of supernal existence."

In a few moments his hands were cold, and life was extinct. Ayesha laid his head upon the pillow, and beating her head and breast, gave way to loud lamentations. Her outcries brought the other wives of Mahomet, and their clamorous grief soon made the event known throughout the city. Consternation seized upon the people, as if some prodigy had happened. All business was suspended. The army which had struck its tents was ordered to halt, and Osama, whose foot was in the stirrup for the march, turned his steed to the gates of Medina, and planted his standard at the prophet's door.

The multitude crowded to contemplate the corpse, and agitation and dispute prevailed even in the chamber of death. Some discredited the evidence of their senses. "How can he be dead?" cried they. "Is he not our mediator with God? How then can he be dead? Impossible! He is but in a trance, and carried up to heaven like Isa (Jesus) and the other prophets."

The throng augmented about the house, declaring with clamour that the body should not be interred; when Omar, who had just heard the tidings, arrived. He drew his scimetar, and pressing through the crowd, threatened to strike off the hands and feet of any who should affirm that the prophet was dead. "He has but departed for a time," said he, "as Musa (Moses) the son of Imram went up forty days into the mountain; and like him he will return again."

Abu Beker, who had been in a distant part of the city, arrived in time to soothe the despair of the people and calm the transports of Omar. Passing into the chamber he raised the cloth which covered the corpse, and kissing the pale face of Mahomet, "Oh thou!" exclaimed he, "who wert to me as my father and my mother, sweet art thou even in death, and living odours dost thou exhale! Now livest thou in everlasting bliss, for never will Allah subject thee to a second death."

Then covering the corpse he went forth, and endeavoured to silence Omar, but finding it impossible, he addressed the multitude : "Truly if Mahomet is the sole object of your adoration, he is dead ; but if it be God you worship, he cannot die. Mahomet was but the prophet of God, and has shared the fate of the apostles and holy men who have gone before him. Allah, himself, has said in his Koran that Mahomet was but his ambassador, and was subject to death. What then! will you turn the heel upon him, and abandon his doctrine because he is dead ? Remember your apostacy harms not God, but insures your own condemnation ; while the blessings of God will be poured out upon those who continue faithful to him."

The people listened to Abu Beker with tears and sobbings, and as they listened their despair subsided. Even Omar was convinced but not consoled, throwing himself on the earth, and bewailing the death of Mahomet, whom he remembered as his commander and his friend.

The death of the prophet, according to the Moslem historians Abulfeda and Al Jannabi, took place on his birthday, when he had completed his sixty-third year. It was in the eleventh year of the Hegira, and the 632d year of the Christian era.

The body was prepared for sepulture by several of the dearest relatives and disciples. They affirmed that a marvellous fragrance which, according to the evidence of his wives and daughters, emanated from his person during life, still continued; so that to use the words of Ali, "it seemed as if he were, at the same time, dead and living."

The body having been washed and perfumed, was wrapped in three coverings; two white, and the third of the striped cloth of Yemen. The whole was then perfumed with amber, musk, aloes, and odoriferous herbs. After this it was exposed in public, and seventy-two prayers were offered up.

The body remained three days unburied, in compliance with oriental custom, and to satisfy those who still believed in the possibility of a trance. When the evidences of mortality could no longer be mistaken, preparations were made for interment. A dispute now arose as to the place of sepulture. The Mohadjerins or disciples from Mecca contended for that city, as being the place of his nativity ; the Ansarians claimed for Medina, as his asylum and the place of his residence during the last ten years of his life. A third party advised that his remains should be transported to Jerusalem, as the place of sepulture of the prophets. Abu Beker, whose word had always the greatest weight, declared it to have been the expressed opinion of Mahomet that a prophet should be buried in the place where he died. This in the present instance was complied with to the very letter, for a grave was digged in the house of Ayesha, beneath the very bed on which Mahomet had expired.

NOTE.—The house of Ayesha was immediately adjacent to the mosque; which was at that time a humble edifice with clay walls, and a roof thatched with palm-leaves, and supported by the trunks of trees. It has since been included in a spacious temple, on the plan of a colonnade, inclosing an oblong square, 165 paces by 130, open to the heavens, with four gates of entrance. The colonnade, of several rows of pillars of various sizes covered with stucco, and gaily painted, s pports a succession of small white cupolas on the four sides of the square. At the four corners are lofty and tapering minarets.

Near the southeast corner of the square is an inclosure, surrounded by an iron railing, painted green, wrought with filagree work and interwoven with brass and gilded wire; admitting no view of the interior excepting through small windows, about six inches square. This inclosure, the great resort of pilgrims, is called the Hadgira, and contains the tombs of Mahomet, and his two friends and early successors, Abu Beker and Omar. Above this sacred inclosure rises a lofty dome surmounted with a gilded globe and crescent, at the first sight of which, pilgrims, as they approach Medina, salute the tomb of the prophet with profound inclinations of the body and appropriate prayers. The marvellous tale, so long considered veritable, that the coffin of Mahomet remained suspended in the air without any support, and which Christian writers accounted for by supposing that it was of iron, and dexterously placed midway between two magnets, is proved to be an idle fiction.

The mosque has undergone changes. It was at one time partially thrown down and destroyed in an awful tempest, but was rebuilt by the Soldan of Egypt. It has been enlarged and embellished by various Caliphs, and in particular by Waled I., under whom Spain was invaded and conquered. It was plundered of its immense votive treasures by the Wahabees when they took and pillaged Medina. It is now maintained, though which diminished splendour, under the care of about thirty Agas, whose chief is called Sheikh al Haram, or chief of the Holy House. He is the principal personage in Medina. Pilgrimage to Medina, though considered a most devout and meritorious act, is not imposed on Mahometans, like pilgrimage to Mecca, as a religious duty, and has much declined in modern days.

The foregoing particulars are from Burckhardt, who gained admission into Medina, as well as into Mecca, in disguise and at great peril; admittance into those cities being prohibited to all but Moslems.

CHAPTER XXXIX.

Person and character of Mahomet, and speculations on his prophetic career.

Mahomet, according to accounts handed down by tradition from his contemporaries, was of the middle stature, square built and sinewy, with large hands and feet. In his youth he was uncommonly strong and vigorous; in the latter part of his life he inclined to corpulency. His head was capacious, well shaped and well set on a neck which rose like a pillar from his ample chest. His forehead was high, broad at the temples and crossed by veins extending down to the eyebrows, which swelled whenever he was angry or excited. He had an oval face, marked and expressive features, an aquiline nose, black eyes, arched eyebrows which nearly met, a mouth large and flexible, indicative of eloquence; very white teeth, somewhat parted and irregular; black hair which waved without a curl on his shoulders, and a long and very full beard.

His deportment, in general, was calm and equable; he sometimes indulged in pleasantry, but more commonly was grave and
dignified; though he is said to have possessed a smile of captivating sweetness. His complexion was more ruddy than is usual
with Arabs, and in his excited and enthusiastic moments there was
a glow and radiance in his countenance, which his disciples magnified into the supernatural light of prophecy.

His intellectual qualities were undoubtedly of an extraordinary
kind. He had a quick apprehension, a retentive memory, a vivid
imagination, and an inventive genius. Owing but little to education, he had quickened and informed his mind by close observation, and stored it with a great variety of knowledge concerning
the systems of religion current in his day, or handed down by tradition from antiquity. His ordinary discourse was grave and sententious, abounding with those aphorisms and apologues so popular
among the Arabs; at times he was excited and eloquent, and his
eloquence was aided by a voice musical and sonorous.

He was sober and abstemious in his diet, and a rigorous observer
of fasts. He indulged in no magnificence of apparel, the ostentation of a petty mind; neither was his simplicity in dress affected;
but the result of a real disregard to distinction from so trivial a
source. His garments were sometimes of wool; sometimes of the
striped cotton of Yemen, and were often patched. He wore a
turban, for he said turbans were worn by the angels: and in ar-
ranging it he let one end hang down between his shoulders, which
he said was the way they wore it. He forbade the wearing of
clothes entirely of silk; but permitted a mixture of thread and silk.
He forbade also red clothes and the use of gold rings. He wore a
seal ring of silver, the engraved part under his finger close to the
palm of his hand, bearing the inscription "Mahomet the messenger
of God." He was scrupulous as to personal cleanliness, and observed frequent ablutions. In some respects he was a voluptuary.
"There are two things in this world," would he say, "which
delight me, women and perfumes. These two things rejoice my
eyes, and render me more fervent in devotion." From his extreme
cleanliness, and the use of perfumes and of sweet-scented oil for
his hair, probably arose that sweetness and fragrance of person,
which his disciples considered innate and miraculous. His passion
for the sex had an influence over all his affairs. It is said that when
in the presence of a beautiful female, he was continually smoothing
his brow and adjusting his hair, as if anxious to appear to advantage.

The number of his wives is uncertain. Abulfeda, who writes
with more caution than other of the Arabian historians, limits it to
fifteen, though some make it as much as twenty-five. At the time
of his death he had nine, each in her separate dwelling, and all in
the vicinity of the mosque at Medina. The plea alleged for his
indulging in a greater number of wives than he permitted to his
followers, was a desire to beget a race of prophets for his people.
If such indeed were his desire, it was disappointed. Of all his
children, Fatima the wife of Ali alone survived him, and she died
within a short time after his death. Of her descendants, none ex-

cepting her eldest son Hassan ever sat on the throne of the Caliphs.

In his private dealings he was just. He treated friends and strangers, the rich and poor, the powerful and the weak, with equity, and was beloved by the common people for the affability with which he received them, and listened to their complaints.

He was naturally irritable, but had brought his temper under great control, so that even in the self-indulgent intercourse of domestic life he was kind and tolerant. "I served him from the time I was eight years old," said his servant Anas, "and he never scolded me for any thing, though things were spoiled by me."

The question now occurs, was he the unprincipled impostor that he has been represented? Were all his visions and revelations deliberate falsehoods, and was his whole system a tissue of deceit? In considering this question we must bear in mind, that he is not chargeable with many extravagancies which exist in his name. Many of the visions and revelations handed down as having been given by him are spurious. The miracles ascribed to him are all fabrications of Moslem zealots. He expressly and repeatedly disclaimed all miracles excepting the Koran; which, considering its incomparable merit, and the way in which it had come down to him from heaven, he pronounced the greatest of miracles. And here we must indulge a few observations on this famous document. While zealous Moslems and some of the most learned doctors of the faith draw proofs of its divine origin from the inimitable excellence of its style and composition, and the avowed illiteracy of Mahomet, less devout critics have pronounced it a chaos of beauties and defects; without method or arrangement; full of obscurities, incoherencies, repetitions, false versions of scriptural stories, and direct contradictions. The truth is that the Koran as it now exists is not the same Koran delivered by Mahomet to his disciples, but has undergone many corruptions and interpolations. The revelations contained in it were given at various times, in various places, and before various persons; sometimes they were taken down by his secretaries or disciples on parchment, on palm-leaves, or the shoulder-blades of sheep, and thrown together in a chest, of which one of his wives had charge; sometimes they were merely treasured up in the memories of those who heard them. No care appears to have been taken to systematize and arrange them during his life; and at his death they remained in scattered fragments, many of them at the mercy of fallacious memories. It was not until some time after his death that Abu Beker undertook to have them gathered together and transcribed. Zeid Ibn Thabet, who had been one of the secretaries of Mahomet, was employed for the purpose. He professed to know many parts of the Koran by heart, having written them down under the dictation of the prophet; other parts he collected piecemeal from various hands, written down in the rude way we have mentioned, and many parts he took down as repeated to him by various disciples who professed to have heard them uttered by the prophet himself. The heterogeneous fragments thus collected were thrown together without selection; without chronological order, and without system of any kind. The volume thus formed during the Caliphat of Abu Beker was transcribed by different hands, and many professed copies put in circulation and dispersed throughout the Moslem cities. So many errors, interpolations, and contradictory readings, soon crept into these copies, that Othman, the third Caliph, called in the various manuscripts, and forming what he pronounced the genuine Koran, caused all the others to be destroyed.

This simple statement may account for many of the incoherencies, repetitions, and other discrepancies charged upon this singular document. Mahomet, as has justly been observed, may have given the same precepts, or related the same apologue at different times, to different persons in different words; or various persons may have been present at one time, and given various versions of his words; and reported his apologues and scriptural stories in different ways, according to their imperfect memoranda or fallible recollections. Many revelations given by him as having been made in foregone times to the prophets, his predecessors, may have been reported as having been given as relations made to himself. It has been intimated that Abu Beker, in the early days of his Caliphat, may have found it politic to interpolate many things in the Koran, calculated to aid him in emergencies, and confirm the empire of Islamism. What corruptions and interpolations may have been made by other and less scrupulous hands, after the prophet's death, we may judge by the daring liberties of the kind taken by Abdallah Ibn Saad, one of his secretaries, during his lifetime.

From all these circumstances it will appear, that even the documentary memorials concerning Mahomet abound with vitiations, while the traditional are full of fable. These increase the difficulty of solving the enigma of his character and conduct. His history appears to resolve into itself two grand divisions. During the first part, up to the period of middle life, we cannot perceive what adequate object he had [to gain by the impious and stupendous imposture with which he stands charged. Was it riches? His marriage with Cadijah had already made him wealthy, and for years preceding his pretended vision he had manifested no desire to increase his store. Was it distinction? He already stood high in his native place, as a man of intelligence and probity. He was of the illustrious tribe of Koreish, and of the most honoured branch of that tribe. Was it power? The guardianship of the Caaba, and with it the command of the sacred city, had been for generations in his immediate family, and his situation and circumstances entitled him to look forward with confidence to that exalted trust. In attempting to subvert the faith in which he had been brought up, he struck at the root of all these advantages. On that faith were founded the fortunes and dignities of his family. To assail it must draw on himself the hostility of his kindred, the indignation of his fellow-citizens, and the horror and odium of all his countrymen, who were worshippers at the Caaba.

Was there any thing brilliant in the outset of his prophetic career to repay him for these sacrifices, and to lure him on? On the contrary, it was begun in doubt and secrecy. For years it was not attended by any material success. In proportion as he made known his doctrines and proclaimed his revelations, they subjected him to ridicule, scorn, obloquy, and finally to an inveterate persecution; which ruined the fortunes of himself and his friends, compelled some of his family and followers to take refuge in a foreign land; obliged him to hide from sight in his native city, and finally drove him forth a fugitive to seek an uncertain home elsewhere. Why should he persist for years in a course of imposture which was thus prostrating all his worldly fortunes, at a time of life when it was too late to build them up anew?

In the absence of sufficient worldly motives, we are compelled to seek some other explanation of his conduct in this stage of his most enigmatical history; and this we have endeavoured to set forth in the early part of this work; where we have shown his enthusiastic and visionary spirit gradually wrought up by solitude, fasting, prayer, and meditation, and irritated by bodily disease into a state of temporary delirium, in which he fancies he receives a revelation from heaven, and is declared a prophet of the Most High. We cannot but think there was self-deception in this instance; and that he believed in the reality of the dream or vision; especially after his doubts had been combated by the zealous and confiding Cadijah and the learned and crafty Waraka.

Once persuaded of his divine mission to go forth and preach the faith, all subsequent dreams and impulses might be construed to the same purport; all might be considered intimations of the divine will, imparted in their several ways to him as a prophet. We find him repeatedly subject to trances and ecstasies in times of peculiar agitation and excitement, when he may have fancied himself again in communication with the Deity, and these were almost always followed by revelations.

The general tenor of his conduct up to the time of his flight from Mecca, is that of an enthusiast acting under a species of mental delusion; deeply imbued with a conviction of his being a divine agent for religious reform: and there is something striking and sublime in the luminous path which his enthusiastic spirit struck out for itself through the bewildering maze of adverse faiths and wild traditions; the pure and spiritual worship of the one true God, which he sought to substitute for the blind idolatry of his childhood.

All the parts of the Koran supposed to have been promulgated by him at this time, incoherently as they have come down to us, and marred as their pristine beauty must be in passing through various hands, are of a pure and elevated character, and breathe poetical, if not religious, inspiration. They show that he had drunk deep of the living waters of Christianity, and if he had failed to imbibe them in their crystal purity, it might be because he had to drink from broken cisterns, and streams troubled and perverted by those who should have been their guardians. The faith he had hitherto inculcated was purer than that held forth by some of the pseudo Christians of Arabia, and his life, so far, had been regulated according to its tenets.

Such is our view of Mahomet and his conduct during the early part of his career, while he was a persecuted and ruined man in Mecca. A signal change, however, took place, as we have shown

10

in the foregoing chapters, after his flight to Medina, when, in place
of the mere shelter and protection which he sought, he finds himself revered as a prophet, implicitly obeyed as a chief, and at the
head of a powerful, growing, and warlike host of votaries.   From
this time worldly passions and worldly schemes too often give the
impulse to his actions, instead of that visionary enthusiasm which,
even if mistaken, threw a glow of piety on his earlier deeds.   The
old doctrines of forbearance, long-suffering, and resignation, are
suddenly dashed aside; he becomes vindictive towards those who
have hitherto oppressed him, and ambitious of extended rule.
His doctrines, precepts, and conduct, become marked by contradictions, and his whole course is irregular and unsteady.   His revelations, henceforth, are so often opportune, and fitted to particular emergencies, that we are led to doubt his sincerity, and that
he is any longer under the same delusion concerning them.   Still,
it must be remembered, as we have shown, that the records of
these revelations are not always to be depended upon.   What he
may have uttered as from his own will, may have been reported
as if given as the will of God.   Often, too, as we have already
suggested, he may have considered his own impulses as divine intimations; and that, being an agent ordained to propagate the
faith, all impulses and conceptions toward that end might be part
of a continued and divine inspiration.

If we are far from considering Mahomet the gross and impious
impostor that some have represented him; so also are we indisposed
to give him credit for vast forecast, and for that deeply concerted
scheme of universal conquest which has been ascribed to him.
He was, undoubtedly, a man of great genius and a suggestive imagination, but it appears to us that he was, in a great degree, the
creature of impulse and excitement, and very much at the mercy
of circumstances.   His schemes grew out of his fortunes, and not
his fortunes out of his schemes.   He was forty years of age before
he first broached his doctrines. He suffered year after year to
steal away before he promulgated them out of his own family.
When he fled from Mecca thirteen years had elapsed from the
announcement of his mission, and from being a wealthy merchant
he had sunk to be a ruined fugitive. When he reached Medina he
had no idea of the worldly power that awaited him; his only
thought was to build a humble mosque where he might preach;
and his only hope that he might be suffered to preach with impunity.   When power suddenly broke upon him, he used it for a
time in petty forays and local feuds. His military plans expanded
with his resources, but were by no means masterly; and were
sometimes unsuccessful.   They were not struck out with boldness,
nor executed with decision; but were often changed in deference
to the opinions of warlike men about him, and sometimes at the
suggestion of inferior minds, who occasionally led him wrong.
Had he, indeed, conceived from the outset the idea of binding up
the scattered and conflicting tribes of Arabia into one nation by a
brotherhood of faith, for the purpose of carrying out a scheme of
external conquest, he would have been one of the first of military
projectors; but the idea of extended conquest seems to have been

an after-thought, produced by success. The moment he proclaimed the religion of the sword, and gave the predatory Arabs a taste of foreign plunder, that moment he was launched in a career of conquest, which carried him forward with its own irresistible impetus. The fanatic zeal with which he had inspired his followers did more for his success than his military science; their belief in his doctrine of predestination produced victories which no military calculation could have anticipated. In his dubious outset, as a prophet, he had been encouraged by the crafty counsels of his scriptural oracle Waraka; in his career as a conqueror, he had Omar, Khaled, and other fiery spirits by his side to urge him on, and to aid him in managing the tremendous power which he had evoked into action. Even with all their aid, he had occasionally to avail himself of his supernatural machinery as a prophet, and in so doing may have reconciled himself to the fraud by considering the pious end to be obtained.

His military triumphs awakened no pride nor vainglory, as they would have done had they been effected for selfish purposes. In the time of his greatest power, he maintained the same simplicity of manners and appearance as in the days of his adversity. So far from affecting regal state, he was displeased if, on entering a room, any unusual testimonial of respect were shown him. If he aimed at universal dominion, it was the dominion of the faith : as to the temporal rule which grew up in his hands, as he used it without ostentation, so he took no step to perpetuate it in his family.

The riches which poured in upon him from tribute and the spoils of war, were expended in promoting the victories of the faith, and in relieving the poor among its votaries ; insomuch that his treasury was often drained of its last coin. Omar Ibn Al Hareth declares that Mahomet, at his death, did not leave a golden dinar nor a silver dirhem, a slave nor a slave girl, nor any thing but his gray mule Daldal, his arms, and the ground which he bestowed upon his wives, his children, and the poor. "Allah," says an Arabian writer, " offered him the keys of all the treasures of the earth ; but he refused to accept them."

It is this perfect abnegation of self, connected with this apparently heartfelt piety, running throughout the various phases of his fortune, which perplex one in forming a just estimate of Mahomet's character. However he betrayed the alloy of earth after he had worldly power at his command, the early aspirations of his spirit continually returned and bore him above all earthly things. Prayer, that vital duty of Islamism, and that infallible purifier of the soul, was his constant practice. " Trust in God," was his comfort and support in times of trial and despondency. On the clemency of God, we are told, he reposed all his hopes of supernal happiness. Ayesha relates that on one occasion she inquired of him, " Oh prophet, do none enter paradise but through God's mercy?" " None—none—none !" replied he, with earnest and emphatic repetition. " But you, oh prophet, will not *you* enter excepting through his compassion?" Then Mahomet put his hand upon his head, and replied three times, with great solemnity,

"Neither shall I enter paradise unless God cover me with his mercy!"

When he hung over the death-bed of his infant son Ibrahim, resignation to the will of God was exhibited in his conduct under this keenest of afflictions; and the hope of soon rejoining his child in paradise was his consolation. When he followed him to the grave, he invoked his spirit, in the awful examination of the tomb, to hold fast to the foundations of the faith, the unity of God, and his own mission as a prophet. Even in his own dying hour, when there could be no longer a worldly motive for deceit, he still breathed the same religious devotion, and the same belief in his apostolic mission. The last words that trembled on his lips ejaculated a trust of soon entering into blissful companionship with the prophets who had gone before him.

It is difficult to reconcile such ardent, persevering piety, with an incessant system of blasphemous imposture; nor such pure and elevated and benignant precepts as are contained in the Koran, with a mind haunted by ignoble passions, and devoted to the grovelling interests of mere mortality; and we find no other satisfactory mode of solving the enigma of his character and conduct, than by supposing that the ray of mental hallucination which flashed upon his enthusiastic spirit during his religious ecstasies in the midnight cavern of Mount Hara, continued more or less to bewilder him with a species of monomania to the end of his career, and that he died in the delusive belief of his mission as a prophet.

APPENDIX.

OF THE ISLAM FAITH.

In an early chapter of this work we have given such particulars of the faith inculcated by Mahomet as we deemed important to the understanding of the succeeding narrative : we now, though at the expense of some repetition, subjoin a more complete summary, accompanied by a few observations.

The religion of Islam, as we observed on the before-mentioned occasion, is divided into two parts; FAITH and PRACTICE :—and first of Faith. This is distributed under six different heads, or articles, viz. : 1st, faith in God; 2d, in his angels; 3d, in his Scriptures or Koran; 4th, in his prophets; 5th, in the resurrection and final judgment; 6th, in predestination. Of these we will briefly treat in the order we have enumerated them.

FAITH IN GOD.—Mahomet inculcated the belief that there is, was, and ever will be, one only God, the creator of all things ; who is single, immutable, omniscient, omnipotent, all merciful and eternal. The unity of God was specifically and strongly urged, in contradistinction to the Trinity of the Christians. It was designated, in the profession of faith, by raising one finger, and exclaiming, " La illaha il Allah!" There is no God but God—to which was added, " Mohamed Resoul Allah ! " Mahomet is the prophet of God.

FAITH IN ANGELS.—The beautiful doctrine of angels, or ministering spirits, which was one of the most ancient and universal of oriental creeds, is interwoven throughout the Islam system. They are represented as ethereal beings, created from fire, the purest of elements, perfect in form and radiant in beauty, but without sex ; free from all gross or sensual passion, and all the appetites and infirmities of frail humanity; and existing in perpetual and unfading youth. They are various in their degrees and duties, and in their favour with the Deity. Some worship around the celestial throne ; others perpetually hymn the praises of Allah ; some are winged messengers to execute his orders, and others intercede for the children of men.

The most distinguished of this heavenly host are four Archangels. Gabriel, the angel of revelations, who writes down the divine decrees; Michael, the champion, who fights the battles of the faith ; Azrail, the angel of death ; and Israfil, who holds the awful commission to sound the trumpet on the day of resurrection. There was another angel named Azazil, the same as Lucifer, once the most glorious of the celestial band ; but he became proud and rebellious. When God commanded his angels to worship Adam, Azazil refused, saying, " Why should I, whom thou hast created of fire, bow down to one whom thou hast formed of clay?" For this offence he was accursed and cast forth from paradise, and his name changed to Eblis, which signifies despair. In revenge of his abasement, he works all kinds of mischief against the children of men, and inspires them with disobedience and impiety.

Among the angels of inferior rank is a class called Moakkibat; two of whom keep watch upon each mortal, one on the right hand, the other on the left, taking note of every word and action. At the close of each day they fly up to heaven with a written report, and are replaced by two similar angels on the following day. According to Mahometan tradition, every good action is recorded ten times by the angel on the right; and if the mortal commit a sin, the same benevolent spirit says to the angel on the left, "Forbear for seven hours to record it; peradventure he may repent and pray and obtain forgiveness."

Beside the angelic orders Mahomet inculcates a belief in spiritual beings called Gins or Genii, who, though likewise created of fire, partake of the appetites and frailties of the children of the dust, and like them are ultimately liable to death. By beings of this nature, which haunt the solitudes of the desert, Mahomet, as we have shown, professed to have been visited after his evening orisons in the solitary valley of Al Naklah.

When the angel Azazil rebelled and fell and became Satan or Eblis, he still maintained sovereignty over these inferior spirits; who are divided by Orientalists into Dives and Peri : the former ferocious and gigantic; the latter delicate and gentle, subsisting on perfumes. It would seem as if the Peri were all of the female sex, though on this point there rests obscurity. From these imaginary beings it is supposed the European fairies are derived.

Besides these there are other demi-spirits called Tacwins or Fates; being winged females of beautiful forms, who utter oracles and defend mortals from the assaults and machinations of evil demons.

There is vagueness and uncertainty about all the attributes given by Mahomet to these half-celestial beings; his ideas on the subject having been acquired from various sources. His whole system of intermediate spirits has a strong, though indistinct infusion of the creeds and superstitions of the Hebrews, the Magians, and the Pagans or Sabeans.

The third article of faith is a belief in the KORAN , as a book of divine revelation. According to the Moslem creed a book was treasured up in the seventh heaven, and had existed there from all eternity, in which were written down all the decrees of God and all events, past, present, or to come. Transcripts from these tablets of the divine will were brought down to the lowest heaven by the angel Gabriel, and by him revealed to Mahomet from time to time, in portions adapted to some event or emergency. Being the direct words of God, they were all spoken in the first person.

Of the way in which these revelations were taken down or treasured up by secretaries and disciples, and gathered together by Abu Beker after the death of Mahomet, we have made sufficient mention. The compilation, for such in fact it is, forms the Moslem code of civil and penal as well as religious law, and is treated with the utmost reverence by all true believers. A zealous pride is shown in having copies of it splendidly bound and ornamented. An inscription on the cover forbids any one to touch it who is unclean, and it is considered irreverent, in reading it, to hold it below the girdle. Moslems swear by it, and take omens from its pages, by opening it and reading the first text that meets the eye. With all its errours and discrepancies, if we consider it mainly as the work of one man, and that an unlettered man, it remains a stupendous monument of solitary legislation.

Beside the Koran or written law, a number of precepts and apologues which casually fell from the lips of Mahomet were collected after his death from ear-witnesses, and transcribed into a book called the Sonna or Oral Law. This is held equally sacred with the Koran by a sect of Mahometans thence called Sonnites; others reject it as apocryphal; these last are termed Schiites. Hostilities and persecutions have occasionally taken place between these sects almost as virulent as those which, between Catholics and Protestants, have disgraced Christianity. The Sonnites are distinguished by white, the Schiites by red turbans; hence the latter have received from their antagonists the appellation of Kussil-bachi, or Red Heads.

It is remarkable that circumcision, which is invariably practised by the Mahometans and forms a distinguishing rite of their faith, to which all proselytes must conform, is neither mentioned in the Koran nor the Sonna. It seems to have been a general usage in Arabia, tacitly adopted from the Jews, and is even said to have been prevalent throughout the East before the time of Moses.

It is said that the Koran forbids the making likenesses of any living thing, which has prevented the introduction of portrait-painting among Mahometans. The passage of the Koran, however, which is thought to contain the prohibition, seems merely an echo of the second commandment, held sacred by Jews and Christians, not to form images or pictures for worship. One of Mahomet's standards was a black eagle. Among the most distinguished Moslem ornaments of the Alhambra at Granada is a fountain supported by lions carved of stone, and some Moslem monarchs have had their effigies stamped on their coins.

Another and an important mistake with regard to the system of Mahomet, is the idea that it denies souls to the female sex, and excludes them from paradise. This errour arises from his omitting to mention their enjoyments in a future state, while he details those of his own sex with the minuteness of a voluptuary. The beatification of virtuous females is alluded to in the 56th Sura of the Koran, and also in other places, although from the vagueness of the language a cursory reader might suppose the Houris of paradise to be intended.

The fourth article of faith relates to the PROPHETS. Their number amounts to two hundred thousand, but only six are super-eminent, as having brought new laws and dispensations upon earth, each abrogating those previously received wherever they varied or were contradictory. These six distinguished prophets were Adam, Noah, Abraham, Moses, Jesus, and Mahomet.

The fifth article of Islam faith is on the RESURRECTION and the FINAL JUDGMENT. On this awful subject Mahomet blended some of the Christian belief with certain notions current among the Arabian Jews. One of the latter is the fearful tribunal of the Sepulchre. When Azrail, the angel of death, has performed his office, and the corpse has been consigned to the tomb, two black angels, Munkar and Nakeer, of dismal and appalling aspect, present themselves as inquisitors; during whose scrutiny the soul is reunited to the body. The defunct, being commanded to sit up, is interrogated as to the two great points of faith, the unity of God and the divine mission of Mahomet, and likewise as to the deeds done by him during life; and his replies are recorded in books against the day of judgment. Should they be satisfactory, his soul is gently drawn forth from his lips, and his body left to its repose; should they be otherwise, he is beaten about the brows with iron clubs, and his soul wrenched forth with racking tortures. For the convenience of this awful inquisition, the Mahometans generally deposit their dead in hollow or vaulted sepulchres; merely wrapped in funeral clothes, but not placed in coffins.

The space of time between death and resurrection is called Berzak, or the Interval. During this period the body rests in the grave, but the soul has a foretaste, in dreams or visions, of its future doom.

The souls of prophets are admitted at once into the full fruition of paradise. Those of martyrs, including all who die in battle, enter into the bodies or crops of green birds, who feed on the fruits and drink of the streams of paradise. Those of the great mass of true believers are variously disposed of, but, acording to the most received opinion, they hover, in a state of seraphic tranquillity, near the tombs. Hence the Moslem usage of visiting the graves of their departed friends and relatives, in the idea that their souls are the gratified witnesses of these testimonials of affection.

Many Moslems believe that the souls of the truly faithful assume the forms of snow-white birds, and nestle beneath the throne of Allah; a belief in accordance with an ancient superstition of the Hebrews, that the souls of the just will have a place in heaven under the throne of glory.

With regard to the souls of infidels, the most orthodox opinion is that they will be repulsed by angels both from heaven and earth, and cast into the cavernous bowels of the earth, there to await in tribulation the day of judgment.

THE DAY OF RESURRECTION will be preceded by signs and portents in heaven and earth. A total eclipse of the moon; a change in the course of the sun, rising in the west instead of the east; wars and tumults; a universal decay of faith; the advent of Antichrist; the issuing forth of Gog and Magog to desolate the world; a great smoke, covering the whole earth : these and many more prodigies and omens affrighting and harassing the souls of men, and producing a wretchedness of spirit and a weariness of life; insomuch that a man passing by a grave shall envy the quiet dead, and say, ": Would to God I were in thy place!"

The last dread signal of the awful day will be the blast of a trumpet · by the archangel Izrafil. At the sound thereof the earth will tremble; castles and towers will be shaken to the ground, and mountains levelled with the plains. The face of heaven will be darkened; the firmament will melt away, and the sun, the moon, and stars will fall into the sea. The ocean will be either dried up, or will boil and roll in fiery billows.

At the sound of that dreadful trump a panic will fall on the human race; men will fly . from their brothers, their parents, and their wives; and mothers, in frantic terrour, abandon the infant at the breast. The savage beasts of the forests, and the tame animals of the pasture, will forget their fierceness and their anti-pathies, and herd together in affright.

The second blast of the trumpet is the blast of extermination. At that sound, all creatures in heaven and on earth and in the waters under the earth, angels and genii and men and animals, all will die; excepting the chosen few especially reserved by Allah. The last to die will be Azraïl, the angel of death !

Forty days, or, according to explanations, forty years of continued rain will follow this blast of extermination ; then will be sounded for the third time the trumpet of the archangel Izrafil ; it is the call to judgment! At the sound of this blast, the whole space between heaven and earth will be filled with the souls of the dead flying in quest of their respective bodies. Then the earth will open ; and there will be a rattling of dry bones, and a gathering together of scattered limbs; the very hairs will congregate together, and the whole body be reunited, and the soul will re-enter it, and the dead will rise from mutilation, perfect in every part, and naked as when born. The infidels will grovel with their faces on the earth, but the faithful will walk erect; as to the truly pious, they will be borne aloft on winged camels, white as milk, with saddles of fine gold.

Every human being will then be put upon his trial as to the manner in which he has employed his faculties, and the good and evil actions of his life. A mighty balance will be poised by the angel Gabriel ; in one of the scales, termed Light, will be placed his good actions; in the other, termed Darkness, his evil deeds. An atom or a grain of mustard-seed will suffice to turn this balance; and the nature of the sentence will depend on the preponderance of either scale. At that moment retribution will be exacted for every wrong and injury. He who has wronged a fellow mortal will have to repay him with a portion of his own good deeds, or, if he have none to boast of, will have to take upon himself a proportionate weight of the other's sins.

The trial of the balance will be succeeded by the ordeal of the bridge. The whole assembled multitude will have to follow Mahomet across the bridge Al Serát, as fine as the edge of a scimetar, which crosses the gulf of Jehennam or Hell. Infidels and sinful Moslems will grope along it darkling and fall into the abyss; but the faithful, aided by a beaming light, will cross with the swiftness of birds and enter the realms of paradise. The idea of this bridge, and of the dreary realms of Jehennam, is supposed to have been derived partly from the Jews, but chiefly from the Magians.

Jehennam is a region fraught with all kinds of horrours. The very trees have writhing serpents for branches, bearing for fruit the heads of demons. We for-bear to dwell upon the-particulars of this [dismal abode, which are given with painful and often disgusting minuteness. It is described as consisting of seven stages, one below the other, and varying in the nature and intensity of torment. The first stage is alloted to Atheists, who deny creator and creation, and believe the world to be eternal. The second for Manicheans and others that admit two divine principles; and for the Arabian idolaters of the era of Mahomet. The third is for the Brahmins of India; the fourth for the Jews; the fifth for Christians; the sixth for the Magians or Ghebers of Persia; the seventh for hypocrites, who profess without believing in religion.

The fierce angel Thabeck, that is to say, the Executioner, presides over this region of terror.

We must observe that the general nature of Jehennam, and the distribution of its punishments, have given rise to various commentaries and expositions among the Moslem doctors. It is maintained by some, and it is a popular doctrine, that none of the believers in Allah and his prophets will be condemned to eternal punishment. Their sins will be expiated by proportionate periods of suffering, varying from nine hundred to nine thousand years.

Some of the most humane among the Doctors contend against eternity of punishment to any class of sinners, saying that, as God is all merciful, even infidels will eventually be pardoned. Those who have an intercessor, as the Christians have in Jesus Christ, will be first redeemed. The liberality of these worthy commentators, however, does not extend so far as to admit them into paradise among true believers; but concludes that, after long punishment, they will be relieved from their torments by annihilation.

Between Jehennam and paradise is Al Araf or the Partition, a region destitute of peace or pleasure, destined for the reception of infants, lunatics, idiots, and such other beings as have done neither good nor evil. For such too whose good and evil deeds balance each other; though these may be admitted to paradise through the intercession of Mahomet, on performing an act of adoration, to turn the scales in their favour. It is said that the tenants of this region can converse with their neighbours on either hand, the blessed and the condemned; and that Al Araf appears a paradise to those in hell and a hell to those in paradise.

AL JANNAT, OR THE GARDEN.—When the true believer has passed through all his trials, and expiated all his sins, he refreshes himself at the Pool of the Prophet. This is a lake of fragrant water, a month's journey in circuit, fed by the river Al Cauther, which flows from paradise. The water of this lake is sweet as honey, cold as snow, and clear as crystal; he who once tastes of it will never more be tormented by thirst; a blessing dwelt upon with peculiar zest by Arabian writers, accustomed to the parching thirst of the desert.

After the true believer has drunk of this water of life, the gate of paradise is opened to him by the angel Rushvan. The same prolixity and minuteness which occur in the description of Jehennam, are lavished on the delights of paradise, until the imagination is dazzled and confused by the details. The soil is of the finest wheaten-flour, fragrant with perfumes, and strewed with pearls and hyacinths instead of sands and pebbles.

Some of the streams are of crystal purity, running between green banks enamelled with flowers; others are of milk, of wine and honey; flowing over beds of musk, between margins of camphire, covered with moss and saffron! The air is sweeter than the spicy gales of Sabea, and cooled by sparkling fountains. Here, too, is Taba, the wonderful tree of life, so large that a fleet horse would need a hundred years to cross its shade. The boughs are laden with every variety of delicious fruit, and bend to the hand of those who seek to gather.

The inhabitants of this blissful garden are clothed in raiment sparkling with jewels; they wear crowns of gold enriched with pearls and diamonds, and dwell in sumptuous palaces or silken pavilions, reclining on voluptuous couches. Here every believer will have hundreds of attendants, bearing dishes and goblets of gold, to serve him with every variety of exquisite viand and beverage. He will eat without satiety, and drink without inebriation; the last morsel and the last drop will be equally relished with the first: he will feel no repletion, and need no evacuation.

The air will resound with the melodious voice of Izrafil, and the songs of the daughters of paradise; the very rustling of the trees will produce ravishing harmony, while myriads of bells, hanging among their branches, will be put in dulcet motion by airs from the throne of Allah.

Above all, the faithful will be blessed with female society to the full extent even of oriental imaginings. Beside the wives he had on earth, who will rejoin him in all their pristine charms, he will be attended by the Húr al Oyûn, or Houris; so called from their large black eyes; resplendent beings, free from every human defect or frailty; perpetually retaining their youth and beauty, and renewing their virginity. Seventy-two of these are allotted to every believer. The intercourse with them will be fruitful or not according to their wish, and the offspring will grow within an hour to the same stature with the parents.

That the true believer may be fully competent to the enjoyments of this blissful region, he will rise from the grave in the prime of manhood, at the age of thirty, of the stature of Adam, which was thirty cubits; with all his faculties improved to a state of preternatural perfection, with the abilities of a hundred men, and with desires and appetites quickened rather than sated by enjoyment.

These and similar delights are promised to the meanest of the faithful; there are gradations of enjoyment, however, as of merit; but, as to those prepared for the most deserving, Mahomet found the powers of description exhausted, and was fain to make use of the text from Scripture, that they should be such things " as eye hath not seen, ear hath not heard, neither hath it entered into the heart of man to conceive."

The expounders of the Mahometan law differ in their opinions as to the whole meaning of this system of rewards and punishments. One set understanding every thing in a figurative, the other in a literal sense. The former insist that the prophet spake in parable, in a manner suited to the coarse perceptions and sensual natures of his hearers; and maintain that the joys of heaven will be mental as well as corporeal; the resurrection being of both soul and body. The soul will revel in a supernatural development and employment of all its faculties; in a knowledge of all the arcana of nature; the full revelation of every thing past, present, and to come. The enjoyments of the body will be equally suited to its various senses, and perfected to a supernatural degree.

The same expounders regard the description of Jehennam as equally figurative; the torments of the soul consisting in the anguish of perpetual remorse for past crimes, and deep and ever increasing despair for the loss of heaven; those of the body in excruciating and never-ending pain.

The other doctors, who construe every thing in a literal sense, are considered the most orthodox, and their sect is beyond measure the most numerous. Most of the particulars in the system of rewards and punishments, as has been already observed, have close affinity to the superstitions of the Magians and the Jewish Rabbins. The Houri, or black-eyed nymphs, who figure so conspicuously in the Moslem's paradise, are said to be the same as the Huram Behest of the Persian Magi, and Mahomet is accused by Christian investigators of having purloined much of his description of heaven from the account of the New Jerusalem in the Apocalypse; with such variation as is used by knavish jewellers, when they appropriate stolen jewels to their own use.

The sixth and last article of the Islam faith is PREDESTINATION, and on this Mahomet evidently reposed his chief dependence for the success of his military enterprises. He inculcated that every event had been predetermined by God, and written down in the eternal tablet previous to the creation of the world. That the destiny of every individual, and the hour of his death, were irrevocably fixed, and could neither be varied nor invaded by any effort of human sagacity or foresight. Under this persuasion, the Moslems engaged in battle without risk; and, as death in battle was equivalent to martyrdom, and entitled them to an immediate admission into paradise, they had in either alternative, death or victory, a certainty of gain.

This doctrine, according to which men by their own free will can neither avoid sin nor avert punishment, is considered by many Mussulmen as derogatory to the justice and clemency of God; and several sects have sprung up, who endeavour to soften and explain away this perplexing dogma; but the number of these doubters is small, and they are not considered orthodox.

The doctrine of Predestination was one of those timely revelations to Mahomet, that were almost miraculous from their seasonable occurrence. It took place immediately after the disastrous battle of Ohod, in which many of his followers, and among them his uncle Hamza, were slain. Then it was, in a moment of gloom and despondency, when his followers around him were disheartened, that he promulgated this law, telling them that every man must die at the appointed hour, whether in bed or in the field of battle. He declared, moreover, that the angel Gabriel had announced to him the reception of Hamza into the seventh heaven, with the title of Lion of God and of the Prophet. He added, as he contemplated the dead bodies, "I am witness for these, and for all who have been slain for the cause of God, that they shall appear in glory at the resurrection, with their wounds brilliant as vermilion and odoriferous as musk."

What doctrine could have been devised more calculated to hurry forward, in a wild career of conquest, a set of ignorant and predatory soldiers, than this assurance of booty if they survived, and paradise if they fell? [1] It rendered almost irresistible the Moslem arms; but it likewise contained the poison that was to destroy their dominion. From the moment the successors of the prophet ceased to be aggressors and conquerors, and sheathed the sword definitively, the doctrine of predestination began its baneful work. Enervated by peace, and the sensuality permitted by the Koran—which so distinctly separates its doctrines from the pure and self-denying religion of the Messiah—the Moslem regarded every reverse as preordained by Allah, and inevitable; to be borne stoically, since human exertion and foresight were vain. "Help thyself and God will help thee," was a precept never in force with the followers of Mahomet, and its reverse has been their fate. The crescent has waned before the cross, and exists in Europe, where it was once so mighty, only by the suffrage, or rather the jealousy of the great Christian powers, probably ere long to furnish another illustration, that "they that take the sword shall perish with the sword."

RELIGIOUS PRACTICE.

The articles of religious practice are fourfold : Prayer, including ablution, Alms, Fasting, Pilgrimage.

ABLUTION is enjoined as preparative to PRAYER, purity of body being considered emblematical of purity of soul. It is prescribed in the Koran with curious precision. The face, arms, elbows, feet, and a fourth part of the head, to be washed once; the hands, mouth and nostrils, three times; the ears to be moistened with the residue of the water used for the head, and the teeth to be cleaned with a brush. The ablution to commence on the right and terminate on the left; in washing the hands and feet to begin with the fingers and toes; where water is not to be had, fine sand may be used.

PRAYER is to be performed five times every day, viz. : the first in the morning before sunrise; the second at noon; the third in the afternoon before sunset; the fourth in the evening between sunset and dark; the fifth between twilight and the first watch, being the vesper prayer. A sixth prayer is volunteered by many between the first watch of the night and the dawn of day. These prayers are but repetitions of the same laudatory ejaculation, "God is great! God is powerful! God is all powerful!" and are counted by the scrupulous upon a string of beads. They may be performed at the mosque, or in any clean place. During prayer

---

[1] The reader may recollect that a belief in predestination, or destiny, was encouraged by Napoleon, and had much influence on his troops.

the eyes are turned to the Kebla, or point of the heaven in the direction of Mecca; which is indicated in every mosque by a niche called Al Mehrab, and externally by the position of the minarets and doors.   Even the postures to be observed in prayer are prescribed, and the most solemn act of adoration is by bowing the forehead to the ground.   Females in praying are not to stretch forth their arms, but to fold them on their bosoms.   They are nót to make as profound inflexions as the men. They are to pray in a low and gentle tone of voice. They are not permitted to accompany the men to the mosque, lest the minds of the worshippers should be drawn from their devotions.   In addressing themselves to God, the faithful are enjoined to do so with humility; putting aside costly ornaments and sumptuous apparel.

Many of the Mahometan observances with respect to prayer were similar to those previously maintained by the Sabeans; others agreed with the ceremonials prescribed by the Jewish Rabbins. Such were the postures, inflexions and pros- trations, and the turning of the face towards the Kebla, which, however, with the Jews was in the direction of the temple at Jerusalem.

Prayer, with the Moslem, is a daily exercise: but on Friday there is a sermon in the mosque. This day was generally held sacred among oriental nations as the day on which man was created. The Sabean idolaters consecrated it to As- tarte, or Venus, the most beautiful of the planets and brightest of the stars. Mahomet adopted it as his Sabbath, partly perhaps from early habitude, but chiefly to vary from the Saturday of the Jews and Sunday of the Christians.

The *second article* of religious practice is CHARITY, or the giving of alms. There are two kinds of alms, viz. : those prescribed by law, called Zacat, like tithes in the Christian church, to be made in specified proportions, whether in money, wares, cattle, corn, or fruit; and voluntary gifts termed Sadakat, made at the discretion of the giver. Every Moslem is enjoined, in one way or the other, to dispense a tenth of his revenue in relief of the indigent and distressed.

The *third article* of practice is FASTING, also supposed to have been derived from the Jews. In each year for thirty days, during the month Rhamadan, the true believer is to abstain rigorously, from the rising to the setting of the sun from meat and drink, baths, perfumes, the intercourse of the sexes, and all other gratifications and delights of the senses. This is considered a great triumph of self-denial, mortifying and subduing the several appetites, and purifying both body and soul. Of these three articles of practice the Prince Abdalasis used to say, "Prayer leads us half way to God; fasting conveys us to his threshold, but alms conduct us into his presence."

PILGRIMAGE is the *fourth grand practical* duty enjoined upon Moslems. Every true believer is bound to make one pilgrimage to Mecca in the course of his life, either personally or by proxy. In the latter case, his name must be mentioned in every prayer offered up by his substitute.

Pilgrimage is incumbent only on free persons of mature age, sound intellect, and who have health and wealth enough to bear the fatigues and expenses of the journey.   The pilgrim before his departure from home arranges all his affairs, public and domestic, as if preparing for his death.

On the appointed day, which is either Tuesday, Thursday, or Saturday, as being propitious for the purpose, he assembles his wives, children, and all his household, and devoutly commends them and all his concerns to the care of God during his holy enterprise.   Then passing one end of his turban beneath his chin to the opposite side of his head, like the attire of a nun; and grasping a stout staff of bitter almonds he takes leave of his household, and sallies from the apartment, exclaiming, "In the name of God I undertake this holy work, con- fiding in his protection. I believe in him, and place in his hands my actions and my life."

On leaving the portal he turns his face toward the Kebla, repeats certain pas- sages of the Koran, and adds, "I turn my face to the Holy Caaba, the throne of God, to accomplish the pilgrimage commanded by his law, and which shall draw me near to him."

He finally puts his foot in the stirrup, mounts into the saddle, commends himself again to God, almighty, all wise, all merciful, and sets forth on his pilgrimage. The time of departure is always calculated so as to insure an arrival at Mecca at the beginning of the pilgrim month Dhu'l-hajji.

Three laws are to be observed throughout this pious journey.

1. To commence no quarrel.
2. To bear meekly all harshness and reviling.
3. To promote peace and good-will among his companions in the caravan.

He is, moreover, to be liberal in his donations and charities throughout his pilgrimage.

When arrived at some place in the vicinity of Mecca, he allows his hair and nails to grow, strips himself to the skin, and assumes the Ihram or pilgrim garb, consisting of two scarfs, without seams or decorations, and of any stuff excepting silk. One of these is folded round the loins, the other thrown over the neck and shoulders, leaving the right arm free. The head is uncovered, but the aged and infirm are permitted to fold something round it in consideration of alms given to the poor. Umbrellas are allowed as a protection against the sun, and indigent pilgrims supply their place by a rag on the end of a staff.

The instep must be bare; and peculiar sandals are provided for the purpose, or a piece of the upper leather of the shoe is cut out. The pilgrim, when thus attired, is termed Al Mohrem.

The Ihram of females is an ample cloak and veil, enveloping the whole person, so that, in strictness, the wrists, the ankles, and even the eyes should be concealed.

When once assumed, the Ihram must be worn until the pilgrimage is completed, however unsuited it may be to the season or the weather. While wearing it, the pilgrim must abstain from all licentiousness of language; all sensual intercourse; all quarrels and acts of violence; he must not even take the life of an insect that infests him; though an exception is made in regard to biting dogs, to scorpions, and birds of prey.

On arriving at Mecca, he leaves his baggage in some shop, and, without attention to any worldly concern, repairs straightway to the Caaba, conducted by one of the Metowefs or guides, who are always at hand to offer their services to pilgrims.

Entering the mosque by the Bab el Salam, or Gate of Salutation, he makes four prostrations, and repeats certain prayers as he passes under the arch. Approaching the Caaba, he makes four prostrations opposite the Black Stone, which he then kisses; or, if prevented by the throng, he touches it with his right hand, and kisses that. Departing from the Black Stone, and keeping the building on his left hand, he makes the seven circuits, the three first quickly, the latter four with slow and solemn pace. Certain prayers are repeated in a low voice, and the Black Stone kissed, or touched, at the end of every circuit.

The Towaf, or procession, round the Caaba was an ancient ceremony, observed long before the time of Mahomet, and performed by both sexes entirely naked. Mahomet prohibited this exposure, and prescribed the Ihram, or pilgrim dress. The female Hajji walk the Towaf generally during the night; though occasionally they perform it mingled with the men in the daytime. [1]

The seven circuits being completed, the pilgrim presses his breast against the wall between the Black Stone and the door of the Caaba, and with outstretched arms, prays for pardon of his sins.

He then repairs to the Makam, or station of Abraham, makes four prostrations, prays for the intermediation of the Patriarch, and thence to the well Zem Zem, and drinks as much of the water as he can swallow.

During all this ceremonial, the uninstructed Hajji has his guide or Metowef close at his heels, muttering prayers for him to repeat. He is now conducted out of the mosque by the gate Bab el Zafa to a slight ascent about fifty paces distant,

---

· Burckhardt's Travels in Arabia, vol. I, p. 260, Lond. edit., 1829.

called the Hill of Zafa, when, after uttering a prayer with uplifted hands, he commences the holy promenade, called the Saa or Say. This lies through a straight and level street, called Al Mesaa, six hundred paces in length, lined with shops like a bazaar, and terminating at a place called Merowa. The walk of the Say is in commemoration of the wandering of Hagar over the same ground, in search of water for her child Ishmael. The pilgrim, therefore, walks at times slowly, with an inquisitive air, then runs in a certain place, and again walks gravely, stopping at times and looking anxiously back.

Having repeated the walk up and down this street seven times, the Hajji enters a barber's shop at Merowa; his head is shaved, his nails pared, the barber muttering prayers and the pilgrim repeating them all the time. The paring and shearing are then buried in consecrated ground, and the most essential duties of the pilgrimage are considered as fulfilled. 1

On the ninth of the month Al Dhu'l-hajji, the pilgrims make a hurried and tumultuous visit to Mount Arafat, where they remain until sunset; then pass the night in prayer at an Oratory, called Mozdalifa, and before sunrise next morning repair to the valley of Mena, where they throw seven stones at each of three pillars, in imitation of Abraham, and some say also of Adam, who drove away the devil from this spot with stones, when disturbed by him in his devotions.

Such are the main ceremonies which form this great Moslem rite of pilgrimage; but, before concluding this sketch of Islam faith, and closing this legendary memoir of its founder, we cannot forbear to notice one of his innovations, which has entailed perplexity on all his followers, and particular inconvenience on pious pilgrims.

The Arabian year consists of twelve lunar months, containing alternately thirty and twenty-nine days, and making three hundred and fifty-four in the whole, so that eleven days were lost in every solar year. To make up the deficiency, a thirteenth or wandering month was added to every third year, previous to the era of Mahomet, to the same effect as one day is added in the Christian calendar to every leap-year. Mahomet, who was uneducated and ignorant of astronomy, retrenched this thirteenth or intercalary month, as contrary to the divine order of revolutions of the moon, and reformed the calendar by a divine revelation during his last pilgrimage. This is recorded in the ninth sura or chapter of the Koran, to the following effect :

"For the number of months is twelve, as was ordained by Allah, and recorded on the eternal tables 2 on the day wherein he created the heaven and the earth."

"Transfer not a sacred month unto another month, for verily it is an innovation of the infidels."

The number of days thus lost amount in 33 years to 363. It becomes necessary, therefore, to add an intercalary year at the end of each thirty-third year to reduce the Mahometan into the Christian era.

One great inconvenience arising from this revelation of the prophet is, that the Moslem months do not indicate the season; as they commence earlier by eleven days every year. This at certain epochs is a sore grievance to the Devotees at Mecca, as the great pilgrim month Dhu'l-hajji, during which they are compelled to wear the Ihram, or half-naked pilgrim garb, runs the round of the

---

1 The greater part of the particulars concerning Mecca and Medina, and their respective pilgrimages, are gathered from the writings of that accurate and indefatigable traveller, Burckhardt; who, in the disguise of a pilgrim, visited these shrines, and complied with all the forms and ceremonials. His works throw great light upon the manners and customs of the East, and practice of the Mahometan faith.

2 The facts related by Burckhardt have been collated with those of other travellers and writers, and many particulars have been interwoven with them from other sources.

The eternal tables or tablet was of white pearl, extended from east to west and from earth to heaven. All the decrees of God were recorded on it, and all events past, present, and to come, to all eternity. It was guarded by angels.

seasons, occurring at one time in the depth of winter, at another in the fervid heat of summer.

Thus Mahomet, though according to legendary history he could order the moon from the firmament and make her revolve about the sacred house, could not control her monthly revolutions; and found that the science of numbers is superior even to the gift of prophecy, and sets miracles at defiance.

END OF THE LIFE OF MAHOMET.

LIVES

OF THE

SUCCESSORS OF MAHOMET.

PREFACE.

It is the intention of the author in the following pages, to trace the progress of the Moslem dominion from the death of Mahomet, A.D. 622, to the invasion of Spain, A.D. 710. In this period, of less than fourscore and ten years, which passed within the lifetime of many an aged Arab, the Moslems extended their empire and their faith over the wide regions of Asia and Africa, subverting the empire of the Khosrus; subjugating great territories in India; establishing a splendid seat of power in Syria; dictating to the conquered kingdom of the Pharaohs; overrunning the whole northern coast of Africa; scouring the Mediterranean with their ships; carrying their conquests in one direction to the very walls of Constantinople, and in another to the extreme limits of Mauritania; in a word, trampling down all the old dynasties which once held haughty and magnificent sway in the East. The whole presents a striking instance of the triumph of fanatic enthusiasm over disciplined valour, at a period when the invention of fire-arms had not reduced war to a matter of almost arithmetical calculation. There is also an air of wild romance about many of the events recorded in this narrative, owing to the character of the Arabs, and their fondness for stratagems, daring exploits, and individual achievements of an extravagant nature. These have some-

times been softened, if not suppressed, by cautious historians; but the author has found them so in unison with
the people and the times, and with a career of conquest,
in itself out of the bounds of common probability, that he
has been induced to leave them in all their graphic force.

Those who have read the life of Mahomet, will find in
the following pages most of their old acquaintances again
engaged, but in a vastly grander field of action; leading
armies, subjugating empires, and dictating from the palaces
and thrones of deposed potentates.

In constructing his work, which is intended merely for
popular use, the author has adopted a form somewhat
between biography and chronicle, admitting of personal
anecdote, and a greater play of familiar traits and peculia-
rities, than is considered admissible in the stately walk of
history. His ignorance of the oriental languages has
obliged him to take his materials at second-hand, where he
could have wished to read them in the original; such, for
instance, has been the case with the accounts given by the
Arabian writer, Al Wákidi, of the conquest of Syria, and
especially of the siege of Damascus, which retain much of
their dramatic spirit even in the homely pages of Ockley.
To this latter writer, the author has been much indebted,
as well as to the Abbé de Marigny's History of the Arabians,
and to D'Herbelot's Bibliothèque Orientale. In fact, his
pages are often a mere digest of facts already before the
public, but divested of cumbrous diction and uninteresting
details. Some, however, are furnished from sources recently laid open, and not hitherto wrought into the regular
web of history.

In his account of the Persian conquest, the author has

been much benefited by the perusal of the Gemäldesaal of the learned Von Hammer-Purgstall, and by a translation of the Persian historian Tabari, recently given to the public in the Journal of the American Oriental Society, by Mr. John P. Brown, dragoman of the United States Legation at Constantinople.

In the account of the Moslem conquests along the northern coast of Africa, of which so little is known, he has gleaned many of his facts from Conde's Domination of the Arabs in Spain; and from the valuable work on the same subject, recently put forth under the sanction of the Oriental Translation Fund of Great Britain and Ireland, by his estimable friend, Don Pascual de Gayangos, formely Professor of Arabic in the Athenæum of Madrid.

The author might cite other sources whence he has derived scattered facts; but it appears to him that he has already said enough on this point, about a work written more from inclination than ambition; and which, as before intimated, does not aspire to be consulted as authority, but merely to be read as a digest of current knowledge, adapted to popular use.

SUNNYSIDE, 1850

MAHOMET AND HIS SUCCESSORS.

CHAPTER I.

Election of Abu Beker, first Caliph, Hegira 11th, A. D. 632.

The death of Mahomet left his religion without a head and his people without a sovereign; there was danger, therefore, of the newly formed empire falling into confusion. All Medina, on the day of his death, was in a kind of tumult, and nothing but the precaution of Osama Ibn Zeid in planting the standard before the prophet's door, and posting troops in various parts, prevented popular commotions. The question was, on whom to devolve the reins of government? Four names stood prominent as having claims of affinity; Abu Beker, Omar, Othman, and Ali. Abu Beker was the father of Ayesha, the favorite wife of Mahomet. Omar was father of Hafsa, another of his wives, and the one to whose care he had confided the coffer containing the revelations of the Koran. Othman had married successively two of his daughters, but they were dead, and also their progeny. Ali was cousin-german of Mahomet and husband of Fatima, his only daughter. Such were the ties of relationship to him of these four great captains. The right of succession, in order of consanguinity, lay with Ali; and his virtues and services eminently entitled him to it. On the first burst of his generous zeal, when Islamism was a derided and persecuted faith, he had been pronounced by Mahomet his brother, his vicegerent; he had ever since been devoted to him in word and deed, and had honoured the cause by his magnanimity as signally as he had vindicated it by his valour. His friends, confiding in the justice of his claims, gathered round him in the dwelling of Fatima his wife, to consult about means of putting him quietly in possession of the government.

Other interests, however, were at work, operating upon the public mind. Abu Beker was held up, not merely as connected by marriage ties with the prophet, but as one of the first and most zealous of his disciples; as the voucher for the truth of his night journey; as his fellow-sufferer in persecution; as the one who accompanied him in his flight from Mecca; as his companion in the cave when they were miraculously saved from discovery; as his counsellor and co-operator in all his plans and undertakings; as the one in fact whom the prophet had plainly pointed out as his successor, by deputing him to officiate in his stead in the religious ceremonies during his last illness. His claims were strongly urged by his daughter Ayesha, who had great influence among the faithful; and who was stimulated not so much by zeal for her father, as by hatred of Ali, whom she had never forgiven for having inclined his ear to the charge of incontinence against her in the celebrated case entitled The False Accusation.

Omar also had a powerful party among the populace, who admired him for his lion-like demeanour; his consummate military skill; his straight-forward simplicity and dauntless courage. He also had an active female partisan in his daughter Hafsa.

. While therefore Ali and his friends were in quiet counsel in the house of Fatima, many of the principal Moslems gathered together without their knowledge, to settle the question of succession. The two most important personages in this assemblage were Abu Beker and Omar.   The first measure was to declare the supreme power not hereditary but elective ; a measure which at once destroyed the claims of Ali on the score of consanguinity, and left the matter open to the public choice. This has been ascribed to the jealousy of the Koreishites of the line of Abd Schems; who feared, should Ali's claims be recognized, that the sovereign power, like the guardianship of the Caaba, might be perpetuated in the haughty line of Haschem. Some, however, pretend to detect in it the subtle and hostile influence of Ayesha.

A dispute now arose between the Mohadjerins or refugees from Mecca and the Ansarians or Helpers of Medina, as to the claims of their respective cities to nominate a successor to Mahomet. The former founded the claims of Mecca on its being the birth-place of the prophet. and the first in which his doctrines had been divulged; they set forward their own claims also as his townsmen, his relatives, and the companions of his exile. The Ansarians, on the other hand, insisted on the superior claims of Medina, as having been the asylum of the prophet, and his chosen residence; and on their own claims as having supported him in his exile, and enabled him to withstand and overcome his persecutors.

The dispute soon grew furious and scimetars flashed from their scabbards, when one of the people of Medina proposed as a compromise, that each party should furnish a ruler and the government have two heads. Omar derided the proposition with scorn. "Two blades," said he, "cannot go into one sheath." Abu Beker also remonstrated against a measure calculated to weaken the empire in its very infancy. He conjured the Moslems to remain under one head, and named Omar and Abu Obeidah as persons worthy of the office. and between whom they should choose. Abu Obeidah was one of the earliest disciples of Mahomet, he had accompanied him in his flight from Mecca, and adhered to him in all his fortunes.

The counsel of Abu Beker calmed for a time the turbulence of the assembly, but it soon revived with redoubled violence. Upon this Omar suddenly rose, advanced to Abu Beker and hailed him as the oldest, best, and most thoroughly-tried of the adherents of the prophet, and the one most worthy to succeed him. So saying, he kissed his hand in token of allegiance, and swore to obey him as his sovereign.

This sacrifice of his own claims in favour of a rival struck the assembly with surprise, and opened their eyes to the real merits of Abu Beker. They beheld in him the faithful companion of the prophet, who had always been by his side. They knew his wisdom and moderation and venerated his gray hairs. It appeared but reasonable that the man whose counsels had contributed to establish the government, should be chosen to carry it on. The example of Omar, therefore, was promptly followed, and Abu Beker was hailed as chief.

Omar now ascended the pulpit. "Henceforth," said he, "if any one shall presume to take upon himself the sovereign power without the public voice, let him suffer death; as well as all who may nominate or uphold him." This measure was instantly adopted, and thus a bar was put to the attempts of any other candidate.

The whole policy of Omar in these measures, which at first sight appears magnanimous, has been cavilled at as crafty and selfish. Abu Beker, it is observed, was well-stricken in years, being about the same age with the prophet; it was not probable he would long survive. Omar trusted, therefore, to succeed in a little while to the command. His last measure struck at once at the hopes of Ali, his most formidable competitor; who, shut up with his friends in the dwelling of Fatima, knew nothing of the meeting in which his pretensions were thus demolished. Craft, however, we must observe, was not one of Omar's characteristics, and was totally opposed to the prompt, stern, and simple course of his conduct on all occasions; nor did he ever show any craving lust for power. He seems ever to have been a zealot in the cause of Islam, and to have taken no indirect measures to promote it.

His next movement was indicative of his straight-forward cut-and-thrust policy. Abu Beker, wary and managing, feared there might be some outbreak on the part of Ali and his friends when they should hear of the election which had taken place. He requested Omar, therefore, to proceed with an armed band to the mansion of Fatima, and maintain tranquillity in that quarter. Omar surrounded the house with his followers; announced to Ali the election of Abu Beker, and demanded his concurrence.' Ali attempted to remonstrate, alleging his own claims; but Omar proclaimed the penalty of death, decreed to all who should attempt to usurp the sovereign power in defiance of public will; and threatened to enforce it by setting fire to the house and consuming its inmates.

"Oh son of Khattâb!" cried Fatima reproachfully, "thou wilt not surely commit such an outrage!"

"Aye will I in very truth!" replied Omar, "unless ye all make common cause with the people."

The friends of Ali were fain to yield, and to acknowledge the sovereignty of Abu Beker. Ali, however, held himself apart in

proud and indignant reserve until the death of Fatima, which happened in the course of several months. He then paid tardy homage
to Abu Beker, but, in so doing, upbraided him with want of open-
ness and good faith in managing the election without his privity;
a reproach which the reader will probably think not altogether
unmerited.   Abu Beker, however, disavowed all intrigue, and
declared- he had accepted the sovereignty merely to allay the
popular commotion; and was ready to lay it down whenever a more
worthy candidate could be found who would unite the wishes of the
people.

Ali was seemingly pacified by this explanation ; but he spurned
it in his heart, and retired in disgust into the interior of Arabia,
taking with him his two sons Hassan and Hosein ; the only descendants of the prophet. From these have sprung a numerous progeny,
who to this day are considered noble, and wear green turbans as the
outward sign of their illustrious lineage.

CHAPTER II.

Moderation of Abu Beker.—Traits of his character.—Rebellion of Arab tribes.—Defeat
and death of Malec Ibn Nowirah.—Harsh measures of Khaled condemned by Omar,
but excused by Abu Beker.—Khaled defeats Moseïlma the false prophet.—Compilation
of the Koran.

On assuming the supreme authority, Abu Beker refused to take
the title of king or prince ; several of the Moslems hailed him as
God's vicar on earth, but he rejected the appellation; he was not the
vicar of God, he said, but of his prophet, whose plans and wishes it
was his duty to carry out and fulfil. "In so doing," added he, "I
will endeavour to avoid all prejudice and partiality. Obéy me only
so far as I obey God and the prophet. If I go beyond these bounds,
I have no authority over you. If I err, set me right, I shall be open to
conviction."

He contented himself, therefore, with the modest title of Caliph,
that is to say, successor, by which the Arab sovereigns have ever
since been designated. They have not all, however, imitated the
modesty of Abu .Beker, in calling themselves successors of the
prophet; but many, in after times, arrogated to themselves the
title of Caliphs and Vicars of God, and his Shadow upon Earth.
The supreme authority, as when exercised by Mahomet, united
the civil and religious functions : the Caliph was sovereign and
pontiff.

It may be well to observe, that the original name of the newly
elected Caliph was Abdallah Athek Ibn Abu Kahafa.   He was
also, as we have shown, termed Al Seddek, or The Testifier
to the Truth; from having maintained the verity of Mahomet's
nocturnal journey; but he is always named in Moslem histories,

Abu Beker; that is to say, The Father of the Virgin; his daughter Ayesha being the only one of the prophet's wives that came a virgin to his arms; the others having previously been in wedlock.

At the time of his election Abu Beker was about sixty-two years of age; tall, and well formed, though spare; with a florid complexion and thin beard, which would have been gray, but that he tinged it after the oriental usage. He was a man of great judgment and discretion, whose wariness and management at times almost amounted to craft; yet his purposes appear to have been honest and unselfish; directed to the good of the cause, not to his own benefit. In the administration of his office he betrayed nothing of sordid worldliness. Indifferent to riches, and to all pomps, luxuries, and sensual indulgencies, he accepted no pay for his services but a mere pittance, sufficient to maintain an Arab establishment of the simplest kind, in which all his retinue consisted of a camel and a black slave. The surplus funds accruing to his treasury he dispensed every Friday; part to the meritorious, the rest to the poor; and was ever ready, from his own private means, to help the distressed. On entering office he caused his daughter Ayesha to take a strict account of his private patrimony, to stand as a record against him should he enrich himself while in office.

Notwithstanding all his merits, however, his advent to power was attended by public commotions. Many of the Arabian tribes had been converted by the sword, and it needed the combined terrors of a conqueror and a prophet to maintain them in allegiance to the faith. On the death of Mahomet, therefore, they spurned at the authority of his successor, and refused to pay the Zacat, or religious contributions of tribute, tithes, and alms. The signal of revolt flew from tribe to tribe, until the Islam empire suddenly shrank to the cities of Mecca, Medina, and Tayef.

A strong body of the rebels even took the field and advanced upon Medina. They were led on by a powerful and popular Sheikh named Malec Ibn Nowirah. He was a man of high birth and great valour, an excellent horseman, and a distinguished poet; all great claims on Arab admiration. To these may be added the enviable fortune of having for wife the most beautiful woman in all Arabia.

Hearing of the approach of this warrior poet and his army, Abu Beker hastened to fortify the city, sending the women and children, the aged and infirm, to the rocks and caverns of the neighbouring mountains.

But though Mahomet was dead, the sword of Islam was not buried with him; and Khaled Ibn Waled now stood forward to sustain the fame acquired by former acts of prowess. He was sent out against the rebels at the head of a hasty levy of four thousand five hundred men and eleven banners. The wary Abu Beker, with whom discretion kept an equal pace with valour, had a high opinion of the character and talents of the rebel chief, and hoped, notwithstanding his defection, to conquer him by kindness. Khaled was instructed, therefore, should Malec fall into his power, to treat him with great respect; to be lenient to the vanquished, and to endeavour, by gentle means, to win all back to the standard of Islam.

Khaled, however, was a downright soldier, who had no liking for gentle means. Having overcome the rebels in a pitched battle, he overran their country, giving his soldiery permission to seize upon the flocks and herds of the vanquished, and make slaves of their children.

Among the prisoners brought into his presence were Malec and his beautiful wife. The beauty of the latter dazzled the eyes even of the rough soldier, but probably hardened his heart against her husband.

"Why," demanded he of Malec, "do you refuse to pay the Zacat?"

"Because I can pray to God without paying these exactions," was the reply.

"Prayer, without alms, is of no avail," said Khaled.

"Does your master say so?" demanded Malec, haughtily.

"My master!" echoed Khaled, "and is he not thy master likewise? By Allah, I have a mind to strike off thy head!"

"Are these also the orders of your master?" rejoined Malec, with a sneer.

"Again!" cried Khaled, in a fury—"smite off the head of this rebel."

His officers interfered, for all respected the prisoner; but the rage of Khaled was not to be appeased.

"The beauty of this woman kills me," said Malec, significantly, pointing to his wife.

"Nay!" cried Khaled, "it is Allah who kills thee because of thine apostacy."

"I am no apostate," said Malec, "I profess the true faith——"

It was too late; the signal of death had already been given. Scarce had the declaration of faith passed the lips of the unfortunate Malec, when his head fell beneath the scimetar of Derar Ibn al Azwar, a rough soldier after Khaled's own heart.

This summary execution, to which the beauty of a woman was alleged as the main excitement, gave deep concern to Abu Beker, who remarked, that the prophet had pardoned even Wacksa, the Ethiop, the slayer of his uncle Hamza, when the culprit made profession of the faith. As to Omar, he declared that Khaled, according to the laws of the Koran, ought to be stoned to death for adultery, or executed for the murder of a Moslem. The politic Abu Beker, however, observed that Khaled had sinned through errour rather than intention. "Shall I," added he, "sheathe the sword of God? The sword which he himself has drawn against the unbelieving?"

So far from sheathing the sword, we find it shortly afterwards employed in an important service. This was against the false prophet Moseïlma; who, encouraged by the impunity with which, during the illness of Mahomet, he had been suffered to propagate his doctrines, had increased greatly the number of his proselytes and adherents, and held a kind of regal and sacerdotal sway over the important city and fertile province of Yamama, between the Red Sea and the Gulf of Persia.

There is quite a flavour of romance in the story of this impostor. Among those dazzled by his celebrity and charmed by his rhapsodical effusions, was Sedjah, wife of Abu Cahdla, a poetess of the tribe of Tamim, distinguished among the Arabs for her personal and mental charms. She came to see Moseïlma in like manner as the Queen of Sheba came to witness the wisdom and grandeur of King Solomon. They were inspired with a mutual passion at the first interview, and passed much of their time together in tender, if not religious intercourse. Sedjah became a convert to the faith of her lover, and caught from him the imaginary gift of prophecy. He appears to have caught, in exchange, the gift of poetry, for certain amatory effusions, addressed by him to his beautiful visitant, are still preserved by an Arabian historian, and breathe all the warmth of the Song of Solomon.

This dream of poetry and prophecy was interrupted by the approach of Khaled at the head of a numerous army. Moseïlma sallied forth to meet him with a still greater force. A battle took place at Akreba, not far from the capital city of Yamama. At the onset the rebels had a transient success, and twelve hundred Moslems bit the dust. Khaled, however, rallied his forces; the enemy were overthrown, and ten thousand cut to pieces. Moseïlma fought with desperation, but fell covered with wounds. It is said his death-blow was given by Wacksa, the Ethiopian, the same who had killed Hamza, uncle of Mahomet, in the battle of Ohod, and that he used the self-same spear. Wacksa, since his pardon by Mahomet, had become a zealous Moslem.

The surviving disciples of Moseïlma became promptly converted to Islamism under the pious but heavy hand of Khaled; whose late offence in the savage execution of Malec was completely atoned for by his victory over the false prophet. He added other services of the same military kind in this critical juncture of public affairs; reinforcing and co-operating with certain commanders who had been sent in different directions to suppress rebellions; and it was chiefly through his prompt and energetic activity that, before the expiration of the first year of the Caliphat, order was restored, and the empire of Islam re-established in Arabia.

It was shortly after the victory of Khaled over Moseïlma, that Abu Beker undertook to gather together, from written and oral sources, the precepts and revelations of the Koran, which hitherto had existed partly in scattered documents, and partly in the memories of the disciples and companions of the prophet. He was greatly urged to this undertaking by Omar, that ardent zealot for the faith. The latter had observed with alarm the number of veteran companions of the prophet who had fallen in the battle of Akreba. "In a little while," said he, "all the living testifiers to the faith, who bear the revelations of it in their memories, will have passed away, and with them so many records of the doctrines of Islam." He urged Abu Beker, therefore, to collect from the surviving disciples all that they remembered; and to gather together from all quarters whatever parts of the Koran existed in

writing.   The manner in which Abu Beker proceeded to execute
this pious task has been noticed in the preceding volume ; it was
not, however, completed until under a succeeding Caliph.

CHAPTER III.

Campaign against Syria.—Army sent under Yezed Ibn Abu Sofian.—Successes.—Another
army under Amru Ibn al Aass.—Brilliant achievements of Khaled in Irak.

The rebel tribes of Arabia being once more brought into allegiance, and tranquillity established at home, Abu Beker turned his
thoughts to execute the injunction of the prophet, to propagate
the faith throughout the world, until all nations should be converted to Islamism, by persuasion or the sword.   The moment was
auspicious for such a gigantic task.   The long and desolating wars
between the Persian and Byzantine emperors, though now at an
end, had exhausted those once mighty powers, and left their frontiers open to aggression.   In the second year of his reign, therefore, Abu Beker prepared to carry out the great enterprise contemplated by Mahomet in his latter days ; the conquest of Syria.
Under this general name, it should be observed, were com-
prehended the countries lying between the Euphrates and the
Mediterranean, including Phœnicia and Palestine [1].   These countries, once forming a system of petty states and kingdoms, each
with its own government and monarch, were now merged into the
great Byzantine empire, and acknowledged the sway of the emperor Heraclius at Constantinople.
Syria had long been a land of promise to the Arabs.   They had
known it for ages by the intercourse of the caravans, and had
drawn from it their chief supplies of corn.   It was a land of abundance.   Part of it was devoted to agriculture and husbandry,
covered with fields of grain, with vineyards and trees producing
the finest fruits ; with pastures well stocked with flocks and herds.
On the Arabian borders it had cities, the rich marts of internal
trade ; while its seaports, though declined from the ancient splendour
and pre-eminence of Tyre and Sidon, still were the staples of an
opulent and widely extended commerce.
In the twelfth year of the Hegira, the following summons was
sent by Abu Beker to the chiefs of Arabia Petrea, and Arabia Felix.
"In the name of the Most Merciful God !   Abdallah Athek Ibn Ka-
hafato all true believers, health, happiness, and the blessing of God.
Praise be to God, and to Mahomet his prophet !   This is to inform
you that I intend to send an army of the faithful into Syria, to deliver

[1] Syria, in its widest oriental acceptation, included likewise Mesopotamia, Chaldea,
and even Assyria, the whole forming what in Scriptural geography was denominated
Aram.

that country from the infidels, and I remind you that to fight for the true faith is to obey God!"

There needed no further inducement to bring to his standard every Arab that owned a horse or a camel, or could wield a lance. Every day brought some Sheikh to Medina at the head of the fighting men of his tribe, and before long the fields round the city were studded with encampments. The command of the army was given to Yezed Ibn Abu Sofian. The troops soon became impatient to strike their sunburnt tents and march. "Why do we loiter?" cried they; "all our fighting men are here; there are none more to come. The plains of Medina are parched and bare, there is no food for man or steed. Give us the word, and let us march for the fruitful land of Syria."

Abu Beker assented to their wishes. From the brow of a hill he reviewed the army on the point of departure. The heart of the Caliph swelled with pious exultation as he looked down upon the stirring multitude; the glittering array of arms; the squadrons of horsemen; the lengthening line of camels; and called to mind the scanty handful that used to gather round the standard of the prophet. Scarce ten years had elapsed since the latter had been driven a fugitive from Mecca, and now a mighty host assembled at the summons of his successor, and distant empires were threatened by the sword of Islam. Filled with these thoughts, he lifted up his voice and prayed to God to make these troops valiant and victorious. Then giving the word to march, the tents were struck, the camels laden, and in a little while the army poured in a long continuous train over hill and valley.

Abu Beker accompanied them on foot on the first day's march. The leaders would have dismounted and yielded him their steeds. "Nay," said he, "ride on. You are in the service of Allah. As for me, I shall be rewarded for every step I take in his cause."

His parting charge to Yezed, the commander of the army, was a singular mixture of severity and mercy.

"Treat your soldiers with kindness and consideration; be just in all your dealings with them, and consult their feelings and opinions. Fight valiantly, and never turn your back upon a foe. When victorious harm not the aged, and protect women and children. Destroy not the palm-tree, nor fruit-trees of any kind; waste not the cornfield with fire; nor kill any cattle excepting for food. Stand faithfully to every covenant and promise; respect all religious persons who live in hermitages, or convents, and spare their edifices. But should you meet with a class of unbelievers of a different kind, who go about with shaven crowns, and belong to the synagogue of Satan, be sure you cleave their skulls unless they embrace the true faith, or render tribute."

Having received this summary charge, Yezed continued his march toward Syria, and the pious Caliph returned to Medina.

The prayers which the latter had put up for the success of the army appeared to be successful. Before long a great cavalgada of horses, mules and camels laden with booty poured into the gates of Medina. Yezed had encountered, on the confines of Syria, a body of troops detached by the emperor Heraclius to observe him, and had defeated them, killing the general and twelve hundred men. He had been equally successful in various subsequent skirmishes. All the booty gained in these actions had been sent to the Caliph, as an offering by the army of the first fruits of the harvest of Syria.

Abu Beker sent tidings of this success to Mecca, and the surrounding country, calling upon all true believers to press forward in the career of victory, thus prosperously commenced. Another army was soon set on foot, the command of which was given to Seid Ibn Khaled. This appointment, however, not being satisfactory to Omar, whose opinions and wishes had vast weight at Medina, Ayesha prevailed on her father to invite Seid to resign, and to appoint in his place Amru Ibn al Aass; the same who in the early days of the faith ridiculed Mahomet and his doctrines in satirical verses; but who, since his conversion to Islamism, had risen to eminence in its service and was one of its most valiant and efficient champions.

Such was the zeal of the Moslems in the prosecution of this holy war, that Seid Ibn Khaled cheerfully resigned his command and enlisted under the standard which he had lately reared.

At the departure of the army Abu Beker, who was excellent at counsel, and fond of bestowing it, gave Amru a code of conduct for his government; admonishing him to live righteously, as a dying man in the presence of God, and accountable for all things in a future state. That he should not trouble himself about the private concerns of others; and should forbid his men all religious disputes about events and doctrines of the "times of ignorance;" that is to say, the times antecedent to Mahomet; but should enforce the diligent reading of the Koran, which contained all that was necessary for them to know.

As there would now be large bodies of troops in Syria, and various able commanders, Abu Beker in maturing the plan of his campaign assigned them different points of action. Amru was to draw toward Palestine; Abu Obeidah to undertake Emessa; Seid Ibn Abu Sofian, Damascus; and Serhil Ibn Hasan, the country about the Jordan. They were all to act as much as possible in concert, and to aid each other in case of need. When together they were all to be under the orders of Abu Obeidah, to whom was given the general command in Syria. This veteran disciple of the prophet stood high, as we ave shown, in the esteem and confidence of Abu Beker, having been one of the two whom he had named as worthy of the Caliphat. He was now about fifty years of age; zealously devoted to the cause, yet one with whom the sword of faith was sheathed in meekness and humanity; perhaps the cautious Abu Beker thought his moderation would be a salutary check to the headlong valour of the fanatical soldiers of Islam.

While this grand campaign was put in operation against the Roman possessions in Syria, a minor force was sent to invade Irak. This province, which included the ancient Chaldea and the Babylonia of Ptolemy, was bounded on the east by Susiana or Khurzestan and the mountains of Assyria and Medea, on the north by part of Mesopotamia, on the west and south by the Deserts of Sham or

Syria and by a part of Arabia Deserta. It was a region tributary to the Persian monarch, and so far a part of his dominions. The campaign in this quarter was confided to Khaled, of whose prowess Abu Beker had an exalted opinion, and who was at this time at the head of a moderate force in one of the rebellious provinces which he had brought into subjection. The Caliph's letter to him was to the following effect. " Turn thee toward Arabian Irak! The conquest of Hira and Cufa is intrusted to thee. After the subjection of those lands, turn thee against Aila and subdue it with God's help ! "

Hira was a kingdom to the west of Babylonia, on the verge of the Syrian Desert : it had been founded by a race of Arabs, descendants of Kahtan, and had subsisted upwards of six hundred years; the greater part of the time it had been under a line of princes of the house of Mondar ; who acknowledged allegiance to the kings of Persia, and acted as their lieutenants over the Arabs of Irak.

During the early part of the third century many Jacobite Christians had been driven, by the persecutions and disorders of the Eastern Church, to take refuge among the Arabs of Hira. Their numbers had been augmented in subsequent times by fugitives from various quarters, until, shortly before the birth of Mahomet, the king of Hira and all his subjects had embraced Christianity.

Much was said of the splendour of the capital, which bore the same name with the kingdom. Here were two palaces of extraordinary magnificence, the beauty of one of which, if Arabian legends speak true, was fatal to the architect; for the king, fearing that he might build one still more beautiful for some other monarch, had him thrown headlong from the tower.

Khaled acted with his usual energy and success in the invasion of this kingdom. With ten thousand men he besieged the city of Hira ; stormed its palaces ; slew the king in battle ; subdued the kingdom ; imposed on it an annual tribute of seventy thousand pieces of gold, the first tribute ever levied by Moslems on a foreign land, and sent the same, with the son of the deceased king, to Medina.

He next carried his triumphant arms against Aila, defeated Hormuz, the Persian governor, and sent his crown, with a fifth part of the booty, to the Caliph. The crown was of great value, being one of the first class of those worn by the seven vicegerents of the Persian " King of Kings." Among the trophies of victory sent to Medina was an elephant. Three other Persian generals and governors made several attempts, with powerful armies, to check the victorious career of Khaled, but were alike defeated. City after city fell into his hands; nothing seemed capable of withstanding his arms. Planting his victorious standard on the bank of the Euphrates, he wrote to the Persian monarch, calling upon him to embrace the faith or pay tribute. " If you refuse both," added he, " I will come upon you with a host who love death as much as you do life."

The repeated convoys of booty sent by Khaled to Medina after his several victories, the sight of captured crowns and captured princes, and of the first tribute imposed on foreign lands, had excited the public exultation to an uncommon degree.   Abù Beker especially took pride in his achievements; considering them proofs of his own sagacity and foresight, which he had shown in refusing to punish him with death when strongly urged to do so by Omar. As victory after victory was announced, and train after train laden with spoils crowded the gates of Medina, he joyed to see his anti- cipations so far outstripped by the deeds of this headlong warrior. "By Allah," exclaimed he, in an ecstasy, "womankind is too weak to give birth to another Khaled."

CHAPTER IV.

Incompetency of Abu Obeidah to the general command in Syria.— Khaled sent to supersede him.—Peril of the Moslem army before Bosra.—Timely arrival of Khaled— His exploits during the siege.—Capture of Bosra.

The exultation of the Caliph over the triumphs in Irak was checked by tidings of a different tone from the army in Syria.   Abu Obeidah, who had the general command, wanted the boldness and enterprise requisite to an invading general.   A partial defeat of some of his troops discouraged him, and he heard with disquiet of vast hosts which the emperor Heraclius was assembling to over- whelm him.   His letters to the Caliph partook of the anxiety and perplexity of his mind.   Abu Beker, whose generally sober mind was dazzled at the time by the daring exploits of Khaled, was annoyed at finding that, while the latter was dashing forward in a brilliant career of conquest in Irak, Abu Obeidah was merely standing on the defensive in Syria.   In the vexation of the moment, he regretted that he had intrusted the invasion of the latter country to one who appeared to him a nerveless man ; and he forthwith sent missives to Khaled ordering him to leave the prosecution of the war in Irak to his subordinate generals, and repair, in all haste, to aid the ar- mies in Syria, and take the general command there.   Khaled obeyed the orders with his usual promptness.   Leaving his army under the charge of Mosenna Ibn Haris, he put himself at the head of fifteen hundred horse, and spurred over the Syrian borders to join the Moslem host, which he learned, while on the way, was drawing toward the Christian city of Bosra.

This city, the reader will recollect, was the great mart on the Syrian frontier, annually visited by the caravans, and where Maho- met, when a youth, had his first interview with Sergius, the Nesto- rian monk, from whom he was said to have received instructions in the Christian faith.   It was a place usually filled with merchan- dise, and held out a promise of great booty; but it was strongly walled, its inhabitants were inured to arms, and it could at any time pour forth twelve thousand horse.   Its very name, in the Sy- rian tongue, signified a tower of safety.   Against this place Abu

Obeidah had sent Serjabil Ibn Hasanah, a veteran secretary of Mahomet, with a troop of ten thousand horse. On his approach, Romanus, the governor of the city, notwithstanding the strength of the place and of the garrison, would fain have paid tribute, for he was dismayed by the accounts he had received of the fanatic zeal and irresistible valour of the Moslems, but his people were stout of heart, and insisted on fighting.

The venerable Serjabil, as he drew near to the city, called upon Allah to grant the victory promised in his name by his apostle ; and to establish the truth of his unity by confounding its opposers. His prayers apparently were of no avail. Squadron after squadron of horsemen wheeled down from the gates of Bosra, attacked the Moslems on every side, threw them into confusion, and made great slaughter. Overwhelmed by numbers, Serjabil was about to order a retreat, when a great cloud of dust gave notice of another army at hand.

There was a momentary pause on both sides, but the shout of Allah Achbar ! Allah Achbar ! resounded through the Moslem host, as the eagle banner of Khaled was descried through the cloud. That warrior came galloping to the field, at the head of his troop of horsemen, all covered with dust. Charging the foe with his characteristic impetuosity, he drove them back to the city, and planted his standard before the walls.

The battle over, Serjabil would have embraced his deliverer, who was likewise his ancient friend, but Khaled regarded him reproachfully. " What madness possessed thee, " said he, " to attack with thy handful of horsemen a fortress girt with stone walls and thronged with soldiers?"

"I acted," said Serjabil, "not for myself, but at the command of Abu Obeidah."

"Abu Obeidah," replied Khaled, bluntly, "is a very worthy man, but he knows little of warfare."

In effect the army of Syria soon found the difference between the commanders. The soldiers of Khaled, fatigued with a hard march, and harder combat, snatched a hasty repast, and throwing themselves upon the ground, were soon asleep. Khaled alone took no rest ; but, mounting a fresh horse, prowled all night round the city and the camp, fearing some new irruption from the foe.

At daybreak he roused his army for the morning prayer. Some of the troops performed their ablutions with water, others with sand. Khaled put up the matin prayer : then every man grasped his weapon and sprang to horse, for the gates of Bosra were already pouring forth their legions. The eyes of Khaled kindled as he saw them prancing down into the plain, and glittering in the rising sun. "These infidels," said he, "think us weary and wayworn, but they will be confounded. Forward to the fight, for the blessing of Allah is with us!"

As the armies approached each other, Romanus rode in advance of his troops, and defied the Moslem chief to single combat. Khaled advanced on the instant. Romanus, however, instead of levelling his lance, entered into a parley in an under tone of voice. He declared that he was a Mahometan at heart, and had incurred great odium among the people of the place by endeavouring to persuade them to pay tribute.   He now offered to embrace Islamism, and to return and do his best to yield the city into the hands of the Moslems, on condition of security for life, liberty, and property.

Khaled readily assented to the condition, but suggested that they should exchange a few dry blows, to enable Romanus to return to the city with a better grace, and prevent a suspicion of collusion. Romanus agreed to the proposal, but with no great relish, for he was an arrant craven.   He would fain have made a mere feint and flourish of weapons; but Khaled had a heavy hand and a kindling spirit, and dealt such hearty blows, that he would have severed the other in twain, or cloven him to the saddle, had he struck with the edge instead of the flat of the sword.

"Softly, softly," cried Romanus.   "Is this what you call sham fighting ; or do you mean to slay me?"

"By no means," replied Khaled, "but we must lay on our blows a little roughly, to appear in earnest."

Romanus, battered and bruised, and wounded in several places, was glad to get back to his army with his life.   He now extolled the prowess of Khaled, and advised the citizens to negotiate a sur- render; but they upbraided him with his cowardice, stripped him of his command, and made him a prisoner in his own house : substi- tuting in his place the general who had come to them with rein- forcements from the emperor Heraclius.

The new governor, as his first essay in command, sallied in ad- vance of the army, and defied Khaled to combat.   Abda-'lrahman, son of the Caliph, a youth of great promise, begged of Khaled the honour of being his champion.   His request being granted, he rode forth, well armed, to the encounter.   The combat was of short duration.   At the onset the governor was daunted by the fierce countenance of the youthful Moslem, and confounded by the ad- dress with which he managed his horse and wielded his lance.   At the first wound he lost all presence of mind, and turning the reins, endeavoured to escape by dint of hoof.   His steed was swiftest, and he succeeded in throwing himself into the midst of his forces. The impetuous youth spurred after him, cutting and slashing, right and left, and hewing his way with his scimetar.

Khaled, delighted with his valour, but alarmed at his peril, gave the signal for a general charge.   To the fight! to the fight! Para- dise! Paradise! was the maddening cry.   Horse was spurred against horse; man grappled man.   The desperate conflict was witnessed from the walls, and spread dismay through the city. The bells rang alarums, the shrieks of women and children mingled with the prayers and chants of priests and monks moving in pro- cession through the streets.

The Moslems, too, called upon Allah for succour, mingling prayers and execrations as they fought.   At length the troops of Bosra gave way : the squadrons that had sallied forth so gloriously in the morning, were driven back in broken and headlong masses to the city; the gates were hastily swung to and barred after them ; and, while they panted with fatigue and terror behind their bulwarks, the standards and banners of the cross were planted on the battlements, and couriers were sent off imploring reinforcements from the emperor.

Night closed upon the scene of battle. The stifled groans of wounded warriors, mingled with the wailings of women, and the prayers of monks and friars, were heard in the once joyful streets of Bosra ; while sentinels walked the rounds of the Arab camp to guard it against the desperation of the foe.

Abda'lrahman commanded one of the patrols. Walking his round beneath the shadow of the city walls, he beheld a man come stealthily forth, the embroidery of whose garments, faintly glittering in the starlight, betrayed him to be a person of consequence. The lance of Abda'lrahman was at his breast, when he proclaimed himself to be Romanus, and demanded to be led to Khaled. On entering the tent of that leader, he inveighed against the treatment he had experienced from the people of Bosra, and invoked vengeance. They had confined him to his house, but it was built against the wall of the city. He had caused his sons and servants, therefore, to break a hole through it, by which he had issued forth, and by which he offered to introduce a band of soldiers, who might throw open the city gates to the army.

His offer was instantly accepted, and Abda'lrahman was intrusted with the dangerous enterprise. He took with him a hundred picked men, and, conducted by Romanus, entered in the dead of night, by the breach in the wall, into the house of the traitor. Here they were refreshed with food, and disguised to look like the soldiers of the garrison. Abda'lrahman then divided them into four bands of twenty-five men each ; three of which he sent in different directions, with orders to keep quiet until he and his followers should give the signal-shout of Allah Achbar! He then requested Romanus to conduct him to the quarters of the governor, who had fled the fight with him that day. Under the guidance of the traitor, he and his twenty-five men passed with noiseless steps through the streets. Most of the unfortunate people of Bosra had sunk to sleep; but now and then the groan of some wounded warrior, or the lament of some afflicted woman, broke the stillness of the night and startled the prowlers.

Arrived at the gate of the citadel they surprised the sentinels, who mistook them for a friendly patrol, and made their way to the governor's chamber. Romanus entered first, and summoned the governor to receive a friend.

"What friend seeks me at this hour of the night ?"

"Thy friend Abda'lrahman," cried Romanus with malignant triumph ; "who comes to send thee to hell!"

The wretched poltroon would have fled. "Nay," cried Abda'lrahman, "you escape me not a second time!" and with a blow of his scimetar laid him dead at his feet. He then gave the signal shout of Allah Achbar! It was repeated by his followers at the portal; echoed by the other parties in different quarters; the city gates were thrown open, the legions of Khaled and Serbajil rushed in, and the whole city resounded with the cries of Allah Achbar! The inhabitants, startled from their sleep, hastened forth to know the meaning of the uproar, but were cut down at their thresholds.

and a horrible carnage took place until there was a general cry for quarter. Then, in compliance with one of the precepts of Mahomet, Khaled put a stop to the slaughter, and received the survivors under the yoke. .

The savage tumult being appeased, the unhappy inhabitants of Bosra inquired as to the mode in which they had been surprised. Khaled hesitated to expose the baseness of Romanus; but the traitor gloried in his shame, and in the vengeance he had wreaked upon former friends. "'Twas I!" cried he with demoniac exultation. "I renounce ye both in this world and the next. I deny him who was crucified and despise his worshippers. I choose Islam for my faith; the Caaba for my temple; the Moslems for my brethren; Mahomet for my prophet; and I bear witness that there is but one only God, who has no partner in his power and glory."

Having made this full recantation of his old faith and profession of his new, in fulfilment of his traitorous compact the apostate departed from Bosra, followed by the execrations of its inhabitants, among whom he durst no longer abide; and Khaled, although he despised him in his heart, appointed a guard to protect his property from plunder.

CHAPTER V.

Khaled lays siege to Damascus.

The capture of Bosra increased the ambition and daring of the Moslems, and Khaled now aspired to the conquest of Damascus. This renowned and beautiful city, one of the largest and most magnificent of the East, and reputed to be the oldest in the world, stood in a plain of wonderful richness and fertility, covered with groves and gardens, and bounded by an amphitheatre of hills, the skirts of Mount Lebanon. A river called by the ancients Chrysorrhoa, or the stream of gold, flows through this plain, feeding the canals and water-courses of its gardens, and the fountains of the city. .

The commerce of the place bespoke the luxuriance of the soil; dealing in wines, silks, wool, prunes, raisins, figs of unrivalled flavour, sweet-scented waters and perfumes. The fields were covered with odoriferous flowers, and the rose of Damascus has become famous throughout the world. This is one of the few, the very few, cities famous in ancient times, which still retain a trace of ancient delights. "The citron," says a recent traveller, "perfumes the air for many miles round the city; and the fig-trees are of vast size. The pomegranate and orange grow in thickets. There is the trickling of water on every hand. Wherever you go there is a trotting brook, or a full and silent stream beside the track; and you have frequently to cross from one vivid green meadow to another by fording, or by little bridges. These streams are all from the river beloved by Naaman of old. He might well ask whether the Jordan was better than Pharpar and Abana, the rivers of Damascus."

In this city too were invented those silken stuffs called damask from the place of their origin, and those swords and scimetars proverbial for their matchless temper.

When Khaled resolved to strike for this great prize, he had but fifteen hundred horse, which had followed him from Irak, in addition to the force which he found with Serjabil; having, however, the general command of the troops in Syria, he wrote to Abu Obeidah to join him with his army, amounting to thirty-seven thousand men.

The Moslems, accustomed to the aridity of the desert, gazed with wonder and delight upon the rich plain of Damascus. As they wound in lengthening files along the banks of the shining river, through verdant and flowery fields, or among groves and vineyards and blooming gardens, it seemed as if they were already realizing the paradise promised by the prophet to true believers; but when the fanes and towers of Damascus rose to sight from among tufted bowers, they broke forth into shouts of transport.

Heraclius the emperor was at Antioch, the capital of his Syrian dominions, when he heard of the advance of the Arabs upon the city of Damascus. He supposed the troops of Khaled, however, to be a mere predatory band, intent as usual on hasty ravage, and easily repulsed when satisfied with plunder; and he felt little alarm for the safety of the city, knowing it to be very populous, strongly fortified, and well garrisoned. He contented himself, therefore, with despatching a general named Caloüs with five thousand men to reinforce it.

In passing through the country, Caloüs found the people flying to castles and other strongholds and putting them in a state of defence. As he approached Baalbec, the women came forth with dishevelled hair, wringing their hands and uttering cries of despair. "Alas!" cried they, "the Arabs overrun the land, and nothing can withstand them. Aracah and Sachnah, and Tadmor and Bosra, have fallen, and who shall protect Damascus!"

Caloüs inquired the force of the invaders.

They knew but of the troops of Khaled, and answered, "fifteen hundred horse."

"Be of good cheer," said Caloüs; "in a few days I will return with the head of Khaled on the point of this good spear."

He arrived at Damascus before the Moslem army came in sight, and the same self-confidence marked his proceedings. Arrogating to himself the supreme command, he would have deposed and expelled the former governor Azrail, a meritorious old soldier, well beloved by the people. Violent dissensions immediately arose, and the city, instead of being prepared for defence, was a prey to internal strife.

In the height of these tumults, the army of Khaled, forty thousand strong, being augmented by that of Abu Obeidah, was descried marching across the plain. The sense of danger calmed the fury of contention, and the two governors sallied forth, with a great part of the garrison, to encounter the invaders.

Both armies drew up in battle array. Khaled was in front of the Moslem line, and with him was his brother in arms, Derar Ibn al Azwar. The latter was mounted on a fine Arabian mare, and poised a ponderous lance, looking a warrior at all points. Khaled regarded him with friendly pride , and resolved to give him an opportunity of distinguishing himself. For this purpose he detached him with a small squadron of horse to feel the pulse of the enemy. "Now is the time, Derar," cried he, "to show thyself a man, and emulate the deeds of thy father and other illustrious soldiers of the faith. Forward in the righteous cause, and Allah will protect thee."

Derar levelled his lance, and at the head of his handful of followers charged into the thickest of the foe. In the first encounter four horsemen fell beneath his arm; then wheeling off, and soaring as it were into the field to mark a different quarry, he charged with his little troop upon the foot soldiers, slew six with his own hand, trampled down others, and produced great confusion. The Christians, however, recovered from a temporary panic, and opposed him with overwhelming numbers and Roman discipline. Derar saw the inequality of the fight, and having glutted his martial fury, showed the Arab dexterity at retreat, making his way back safely to the Moslem army by whom he was received with acclamation.

Abda'lrahman gave a similar proof of fiery courage; but his cavalry was received by a battalion of infantry arranged in phalanx with extended spears, while stones and darts hurled from a distance galled both horse and rider. He also, after, making a daring assault and sudden carnage, retired upon the spur and rejoined the army.

Khaled now emulated the prowess of his friends, and careering in front of the enemy, launched a general defiance to single combat.

The jealousies of the two Christian commanders continued in the field. Azraïl, turning to Caloüs, taunted him to accept the challenge as a matter of course; seeing he was sent to protect the country in this hour of danger.

The vaunting of Caloüs was at an end. He had no inclination for so close a fight with such an enemy, but pride would not permit him to refuse. He entered into the conflict with a faint heart, and in a short time would have retreated, but Khaled wheeled between him and his army. He then fought with desperation, and the contest was furious on both sides, until Caloüs beheld his blood streaming down his armour. His heart failed him at the sight; his strength flagged; he fought merely on the defensive. Khaled perceiving this, suddenly closed with him, shifted his lance to his left hand, grasped Caloüs with the right, dragged him out of the saddle, and bore him off captive to the Moslem host, who rent the air with triumphant shouts.

Mounting a fresh horse Khaled prepared again for battle.

"Tarry, my friend," cried Derar; "repose thyself for a time, and I will take thy place."

"Oh Derar," replied Khaled, "he who labours to-day shall rest to-morrow. There will be repose sufficient amidst the delights of paradise!"

When about to return to the field Caloüs demanded a moment's audience, and making use of the traitor Romanus as an interpreter, advised Khaled to bend all his efforts against Azraïl, the former governor of the city, whose death he said would be the surest means of gaining the victory. Thus a spirit of envy induced him to sacrifice the good of his country to the desire of envy induced him to sacrifice the good of his country to the desire of injuring a rival.

Khaled was willing to take advice even from an enemy, especially when it fell in with his own humour; he advanced, therefore, in front, challenging Azraïl loudly by name. The latter quickly appeared, well armed and mounted, and with undaunted bearing.

The contest was long and obtinate. The combatants paused for breath. Khaled could not but regard his adversary with admiration.

"Thy name," said he, "is Azraïl?" (This is the Arabic name for the angel of death.)

"Azraïl is my name," replied the other.

"By Allah!" replied Khaled, "thy namesake is at hand, waiting to carry thy soul to the fire of Jehennam!"

They renewed the fight. Azraïl, who was the most fleetly mounted, being sorely pressed, made use of an Arabian stratagem, and giving the reins to his steed pretended to fly the field. Having distanced his adversary and fatigued his horse, he suddenly wheeled about and returned to the charge. Khaled, however, was not to be outdone in stratagem. Throwing himself lightly from his saddle just as his antagonist came galloping upon him, he struck at the legs of his horse, brought him to the ground and took his rider prisoner.

The magnanimity of Khaled was not equal to his valour; or rather his fanatical zeal overcame all generous feelings. He admired Azraïl as a soldier; but detested him as an infidel. Placing him beside his late rival Caloüs, he called upon both to renounce Christianity and embrace the faith of Islam. They persisted in a firm refusal, upon which he gave the signal, and their heads were struck off and thrown over the walls into the city, a fearful warning to the inhabitants.

CHAPTER VI.

Siege of Damascus continued.—Exploits of Derar.—Defeat of the imperial army.

The siege of Damascus continued with increasing rigour. The inhabitants were embarrassed and dismayed by the loss of their two governors, and the garrison was thinned by frequent skirmishes, in which the bravest warriors were sure to fall. At length the soldiers ceased to sally forth, and the place became strictly invested. Khaled, with one half of the army, drew near to the walls on the east side; while Abu Obeidah, with the other half, was stationed on the west. The inhabitants now attempted to corrupt Khaled, offering him a thousand ounces of gold, and two hundred magnificent damask robes to raise the siege. His reply was, that they must embrace the Islam faith, pay tribute, or fight unto the death.

While the Arabs lay thus encamped round the city, as if watching its expiring throes, they were surprised one day by the unusual sound of shouts of joy within its walls. Sending out scouts, they soon learnt the astounding intelligence that a great army was marching to the relief of the place.

The besieged, in fact, in the height of their extremity, had lowered a messenger from the walls in the dead of the night, bearing tidings to the emperor at Antioch of their perilous condition, and imploring prompt and efficient succour. Aware for the first time of the real magnitude of the danger, Heraclius despatched an army of a hundred thousand men to their relief, led on by Werdan, prefect of Emessa, an experienced general.

Khaled would at once have marched to meet the foe; alleging that so great a host could come only in divisions, which might be defeated in detail; the cautious and quiet Abu Obeidah, however, counselled to continue the siege, and send some able officer with a detachment to check and divert the advancing army. His advice was adopted, and Derar, the cherished companion in arms of Khaled, was chosen for the purpose. That fiery Moslem was ready to march at once and attack the enemy with any handful of men that might be assigned him; but Khaled rebuked his inconsiderate zeal. "We are expected," said he, "to fight for the faith, but not to throw ourselves away." Allotting to his friend, therefore, one thousand chosen horsemen, he recommended to him to hang on the flanks of the enemy and impede their march.

The fleetly mounted band of Derar soon came in sight of the van of Werdan's army, slowly marching in heavy masses. They were for hovering about it and harassing it in the Arab manner, but the impetuous valour of Derar was inflamed, and he swore not to draw back a step without hard fighting. He was seconded by Rafi Ibn Omeirah, who reminded the troops that a handful of the faithful was sufficient to defeat an army of infidels.

The battle cry was given. Derar, with some of his choicest troops, attacked the centre of the army, seeking to grapple with the general, whom he beheld there, surrounded by his guard. At the very onset he struck down the prefect's right-hand man, and then his standard-bearer. Several of Derar's followers sprang from their steeds to seize the standard, a cross richly adorned with precious stones, while he beat off the enemy, who endeavoured to regain it. The captured cross was borne off in triumph; but at the same moment Derar received a wound in the left arm from a javelin, launched by a son of Werdan. Turning upon the youth, he thrust his lance into his body, but, in withdrawing it, the iron head remained in the wound. Thus left, unarmed, he defended himself for a time with the mere truncheon of the lance, but was over-powered and taken prisoner. The Moslems fought furiously to rescue him, but in vain, and he was borne captive from the field. They would now have fled, but were recalled by Rafi Ibn Omeirah. "Whoever flies," cried he, " turns his back upon God and his pro-phet. Paradise is for those who fall in battle. If your captain be dead, God is living, and sees your actions."

They rallied and stood at bay. The fortune of the day was against them; they were attacked by tenfold their number, and though they fought with desperation, they would soon have been cut to pieces, had not Khaled, at that critical moment, arrived at the scene of action with the greater part of his forces; a swift horse-man having brought him tidings of the disastrous affray, and the capture of his friend.

On arriving, he stopped not to parley, but charged into the thickest of the foe, where he saw most banners, hoping there to find his captive friend. Wherever he turned he hewed a path be-fore him, but Derar was not to be found. At length a prisoner told him that the captive had been sent off to Emessa under a strong escort. Khaled instantly despatched Rafi Ibn Omeirah with a hun-dred horse in pursuit. They soon overtook the escort, attacked them furiously, slew several, and put the rest to flight, who left Derar, bound with cords, upon his charger.

By the time that Rafi and Derar rejoined the Moslem army, Khaled had defeated the whole forces of Werdan, division after di-vision, as they arrived successively at the field of action. In this manner a hundred thousand troops were defeated, in detail, by less than a third of their number, inspired by fanatic valour, and led on by a skilful and intrepid chief. Thousands of the fugitives were killed in the pursuit; an immense booty in treasure, arms, baggage, and horses fell to the victors, and Khaled led back his army, flushed with conquest, but fatigued with fighting and bur-thened with spoil, to resume the siege of Damascus.

CHAPTER VII.

Siege of Damascus continued.—Sally of the garrison.—Heroism of the Moslem women.

The tidings of the defeat of Werdan and his powerful army, made the Emperor Heraclius tremble in his palace at Antioch, for the safety of his Syrian kingdom. Hastily levying another army of seventy thousand men, he put them under the command of Werdan, at Aiznadin, with orders to hasten to the relief of Damascus, and attack the Arab army, which must be diminished and enfeebled by the recent battle.

Khaled took counsel of Abu Obeidah how to avoid the impend-ing storm. It was determined to raise the siege of Damascus, and seek the enemy promptly at Aiznadin. Conscious, however, of the inadequacy of his forces, Khaled sent missives to all the Moslem generals within his call.

"In the name of the merciful God! Khaled Ibn al Walid to Amru Ibn al Aass, health and happiness. The Moslem brethren are about to march to Aiznadin to do battle with seventy thousand Greeks who are coming to extinguish the light of God. But Allah will preserve his light in despite of all the infidels. Come to Aiznadin with thy troops; for, God willing, thou shalt find me there." These missives sent, he broke up his encampment before Damascus, and marched, with his whole force, toward Aiznadin. He would have placed Abu Obeidah at the head of the army; but the latter modestly remarked, that as Khaled was now commander-in-chief that station appertained to him. Abu Obeidah, therefore, brought up the rear, where were the baggage, the booty, the women, and the children.

When the garrison of Damascus saw their enemy on the march, they sallied forth under two brothers named Peter and Paul. The former led ten thousand infantry, the latter six thousand horse. Overtaking the rear of the Moslems, Paul with his cavalry charged into the midst of them, cutting down some, trampling others under foot, and spreading wide confusion. Peter in the meantime, with his infantry, made a sweep of the camp equipage, the baggage, and the accumulated booty, and capturing most of the women, made off with his spoils towards Damascus.

Tidings of this onset having reached Khaled in the van, he sent Derar, Abda'lrahman, and Rafi Ibn Omeirah, scouring back, each at the head of two hundred horse, while he followed with the main force.

Derar and his associates soon turned the tide of battle, routing Paul and his cavalry with such slaughter, that of the six thousand but a small part escaped to Damascus. Paul threw himself from his horse, and attempted to escape on foot, but was taken prisoner. The exultation of the victors, however, was damped by the intelligence that their women had been carried away captive, and great was the grief of Derar, on learning that his sister Caulah, a woman of great beauty, was among the number.

In the meantime, Peter and his troops, with their spoils and captives, had proceeded on the way to Damascus, but halted under some trees beside a fountain, to refresh themselves and divide their booty. In the division, Caulah the sister of Derar was allotted to Peter. This done, the captors went into their tents to carouse and make merry with the spoils, leaving the women among the baggage, bewailing their captive state.

Caulah, however, was the worthy sister of Derar. Instead of weeping and wringing her hands, she reproached her companions with their weakness. "What!" cried she, "shall we, the daughters of warriors and followers of Mahomet, submit to be the slaves and paramours of barbarians and idolaters? For my part, sooner will I die!"

Among her fellow-captives were Hamzarite women, descendants as it is supposed of the Amalekites of old, and others of the tribe of

Himiar, all bold viragos, accustomed from their youth to mount the horse, ply the bow, and launch the javelin. They were roused by the appeal of Caulah. "What, however, can we do," cried they, "having neither sword nor lance nor bow?"

"Let us each take a tent pole," replied Caulah, "and defend ourselves to the utmost. God may deliver us; if not, we shall die and be at rest, leaving no stain upon our country." She was seconded by a resolute woman named Offeirah. Her words prevailed. They all armed themselves with tent poles, and Caulah placed them closely side by side in a circle. "Stand firm," said she. "Let no one pass between you; parry the weapons of your assailants, and strike at their heads."

With Caulah, as with her brother, the word was accompanied by the deed; for scarce had she spoken, when a Greek soldier happening to approach, with one blow of her staff she shattered his skull.

The noise brought the carousers from the tents. They surrounded the women, and sought to pacify them; but whoever came within reach of their staves was sure to suffer. Peter was struck with the matchless form and glowing beauty of Caulah, as she stood fierce and fearless, dealing her blows on all who approached. He charged his men not to harm her, and endeavoured to win her by soothing words and offers of wealth and honour; but she reviled him as an infidel, a dog, and rejected with scorn his brutal love. Incensed at length by her taunts and menaces, he gave the word, and his followers rushed upon the women with their scimetars. The unequal combat would soon have ended, when Khaled and Derar came galloping with their cavalry to the rescue. Khaled was heavily armed; but Derar was almost naked, on a horse without a saddle, and brandishing a lance.

At sight of them Peter's heart quaked; he put a stop to the assault on the women, and would have made a merit of delivering them up unharmed. "We have wives and sisters of our own," said he, "and respect your courageous defence. Go in peace to your countrymen."

He turned his horse's head, but Caulah smote the legs of the animal and brought him to the ground; and Derar thrust his spear through the rider as he fell. Then alighting and striking off the head of Peter, he elevated it on the point of his lance. A general action ensued. The enemy were routed and pursued with slaughter to the gates of Damascus, and great booty was gained of horses and armour.

The battle over, Paul was brought a prisoner before Khaled, and the gory head of his brother was shown to him. "Such," cried Khaled, "will be your fate unless you instantly embrace the faith of Islam." Paul wept over the head of his brother, and said he wished not to survive him. "Enough," cried Khaled; the signal was given, and the head of Paul was severed from his body.

The Moslem army now retired to their old camp, where they found Abu Obeidah, who had rallied his fugitives and intrenched himself, for it was uncertain how near Werdan and his army might be. Here the weary victors reposed themselves from their dangers and fatigues; talked over the fortunes of the day, and exulted in the courage of their women.

CHAPTER VIII.

Battle of Aiznadin.

The army of the prefect Werdan, though seventy thousand in number, was for the most part composed of newly levied troops. It lay encamped at Aiznadin, and ancient historians speak much of the splendid appearance of the imperial camp, rich in its sumptuous furniture of silk and gold, and of the brilliant array of the troops in burnished armour, with glittering swords and lances.

While thus encamped, Werdan was surprised one day to behold clouds of dust rising in different directions, from which as they advanced broke forth the flash of arms and din of trumpets. These were in fact the troops which Khaled had summoned by letter from various parts, and which, though widely separated, arrived at the appointed time with a punctuality recorded by the Arabian chroniclers as miraculous.

The Moslems were at first a little daunted by the number and formidable array of the imperial host; but Khaled harangued them in a confident tone. "You behold," said he, "the last stake of the infidels. This army vanquished and dispersed, they can never muster another of any force, and all Syria is ours."

The armies lay encamped in sight of each other all night, and drew out in battle array in the morning.

"Who will undertake," said Khaled, "to observe the enemy near at hand, and bring me an account of the number and disposition of his forces?"

Derar immediately stepped forward. "Go," said Khaled, "and Allah go with thee. But I charge thee, Derar, not to strike a blow unprovoked, nor to expose thy life unnecessarily."

When Werdan saw a single horseman prowling in view of his army and noting its strength and disposition, he sent forth thirty horsemen to surround and capture him. Derar retreated before them until they became separated in the eagerness of pursuit, then suddenly wheeling, he received the first upon the point of his lance, and so another and another, thrusting them through or striking them from their saddles, until he had killed or unhorsed seventeen, and so daunted the rest, that he was enabled to make his retreat in safety.

Khaled reproached him with rashness and disobedience of orders.

"I sought not the fight," replied Derar. "They came forth against me, and I feared that God should see me turn my back. He doubtless aided me, and had it not been for your orders, I should not have desisted when I did."

Being informed by Derar of the number and positions of the

enemy's troops, Khaled marshalled his army accordingly.   He
gave command of the right wing to Mead and Noman; the left to
Saad Ibn Abu Wakkas and Serjabil, and took charge of the centre
himself, accompanied by Amru, Abda'lrahman, Derar, Kais, Rafi,
and other distinguished leaders.   A body of four thousand horse,
under Yezed Ebn Abu Sofian, was posted in the rear to guard the
baggage and the women.

But it was not the men alone that prepared for this momentous
battle.   Caulah and Offeirah, and their intrepid companions, among
whom were women of the highest rank, excited by their recent
success, armed themselves with such weapons as they found at
hand, and prepared to mingle in the fight.   Khaled applauded their
courage and devotion, assuring them that, if they fell, the gates of
paradise would be open to them.   He then formed them into two
battalions, giving command of one to Caulah, and of the other to
Offeirah ; and charged them, besides defending themselves against
the enemy, to keep a strict eye upon his own troops; and whenever
they saw a Moslem turn his back upon the foe, to slay him as a
recreant and an apostate.   Finally he rode through the ranks of
his army, exhorting them all to fight with deseperation, since they
had wives, children, honour, religion, every thing at stake : and
no place of refuge should they be defeated.

The war cries now arose from either army ; the Christians shouting for "Christ and for the faith;" the Moslems, "La I'laha illa
Allah, Mohammed Resoul Allah !"   "There is but one God! Mahomet is the prophet of God !"

Just before the armies engaged, a venerable man came forth
from among the Christians, and, approaching Khaled, demanded,
"Art thou the general of this army?"   "I am considered such,"
replied Khaled, "while I am true to God, the Koran, and the
prophet."

"Thou art come unprovoked," said the old man, "thou and
thy host, to invade this Christian land.   Be not too certain of success.   Others who have heretofore invaded this land, have found
a tomb instead of a triumph.   Look at this host.   It is more numerous, and perhaps better disciplined than thine.   Why wilt thou
tempt a battle which may end in thy defeat, and must at all events
cost thee most lamentable bloodshed ?   Retire, then, in peace, and
spare the miseries which must otherwise fall upon either army.
Shouldst thou do so, I am authorized to offer, for every soldier in
thy host, a suit of garments, a turban, and a piece of gold; for
thyself a hundred pieces and ten silken robes, and for thy Caliph,
a thousand pieces and a hundred robes."

"You proffer a part," replied Khaled, scornfully, "to one who
will soon possess the whole.   For yourselves there are but three
conditions; embrace the faith, pay tribute, or expect the sword."
With this rough reply the venerable man returned sorrowfully to
the Christian host.

Still Khaled was unusually wary.   "Our enemies are two to
one," said he, "we must have patience and outwind them.   Let
us hold back until nightfall, for that with the prophet was the propitious time of victory."

The enemy now threw their Armenian archers in the advance, and several Moslems were killed and wounded with flights of arrows. Still Khaled restrained the impatience of his troops, ordering that no man should stir from his post. The impetuous Derar at length obtained permission to attack the insulting band of archers, and spurred vigorously upon them with his troop of horse. They faltered, but were reinforced : troops were sent to sustain Derar; many were slain on both sides, but success inclined to the Moslems.

The action was on the point of becoming general, when a horseman from the advance army galloped up, and inquired for the Moslem general. · Khaled, considering it a challenge, levelled his lance for the encounter. "Turn, thy lance aside, I pray thee," cried the Christian, eagerly; "I am but a messenger, and seek a parley."

Khaled quietly reined up his steed, and laid his lance athwart the pommel of his saddle : " Speak to the purpose," said he, " and tell no lies."

"I will tell the naked truth; dangerous for me to tell, but most important for thee to hear.; but first promise protection for myself and family."

Having obtained this promise, the messenger, whose name was David, proceeded : "I am sent by Werdan to entreat that the battle may cease, and the blood of brave men be spared; and that thou wilt meet him to-morrow morning, singly, in sight of either army, to treat of terms of peace. Such is my message; but beware, oh Khaled! for treason lurks beneath it. Ten chosen men, well armed, will be stationed in the night close by the place of conference, to surprise and seize, or kill thee, when defenceless and off thy guard."

He then proceeded to mention the place appointed for the conference, and all the other particulars. "Enough," said Khaled. "Return to Werdan, and tell him I agree to meet him."

The Moslems were astonished at hearing a retreat sounded, when the conflict was inclining in their favour; they withdrew reluctantly from the field, and Abu Obeidah and Derar demanded of Khaled the meaning of this conduct. He informed them of what had just been revealed to him. "I will keep this appointment," said he. "I will go singly, and will bring back the heads of all the assassins," Abu Obeidah, however, remonstrated against his exposing himself to such unnecessary danger. "Take ten men with thee," said he, "man for man." "Why defer the punishment of their perfidy until morning?" cried Derar. "Give me the ten men, and I will counterplot these lurkers this very night."

Having obtained permission, he picked out ten men of assured coolness and courage, and set off with them in the dead of the night for the place of ambush. As they drew near Derar caused his companions to halt, and, putting off his clothes to prevent all rustling noise, crept warily with his naked scimetar to the appointed ground. Here he beheld the ten men fast asleep, with their weapons beneath their heads. Returning silently, and beckoning his companions, they singled out each his man, so that the whole were despatched at a blow. They then stripped the dead, disguised themselves in their clothes, and awaited the coming day.

The rising sun shone on the two armies, drawn out in battle array, and awaiting the parley of the chiefs. Werdan rode forth on a white mule, and was arrayed in rich attire, with chains of gold and precious stones. Khaled was clad in a yellow silk vest and green turban. He suffered himself to be drawn by Werdan towards the place of ambush; then, alighting, and seating themselves on the ground, they entered into a parley. Their conference was brief and boisterous. Each considered the other in his power, and conducted himself with haugtiness and acrimony. Werdan spoke of the Moslems as needy spoilers, who lived by the sword, and invaded the fertile territories of their neighbours in quest of plunder. "We, on the other hand," said he, "are wealthy, and desire peace. Speak, what do you require to relieve your wants and satisfy your rapacity?"

"Miserable infidel!" replied Khaled. "We are not so poor as to accept alms at your hands. Allah provides for us. You offer us a part of what is all our own; for Allah has put all that you have into our hands; even to your wives and children. But do you desire peace? We have already told you our conditions. Either acknowledge that there is no other God but God, and that Mahomet is his prophet, or pay us such tribute as we may impose. Do you refuse? For what, then have you brought me here? Yow knew our terms yesterday, and that all your propositions were rejected. Do you entice me here alone for single combat? Be it so, and let our weapons decide between us."

So saying, he sprang upon his feet. Werdan also rose, but expecting instant aid, neglected to draw his sword. Khaled seized him by the throat, upon which he called loudly to his men in ambush. The Moslems in ambush rushed forth, and, deceived by their Grecian dresses, Werdan for an instant thought himself secure. As they drew near, he discovered his mistake, and shrank with horror at the sight of Derar, who advanced, almost naked, brandishing a scimetar, and in whom he recognized the slayer of his son. "Mercy! Mercy!" cried he to Khaled, at finding himself caught in his own snare.

"There is no mercy," replied Khaled, "for him who has no faith. You came to me with peace on your lips, but murder in your heart. Your crime be upon your head."

The sentence was no sooner pronounced, than the powerful sword of Derar performed its office, and the head of Werdan was struck off at a blow. The gory trophy was elevated on the point of a lance and borne by the little band toward the Christian troops, who, deceived by the Greek disguises, supposed it the head of Khaled and shouted with joy. Their triumph was soon turned to dismay as they discovered their errour. Khaled did not suffer them to recover from their confusion, but bade his trumpets sound a general charge. What ensued was a massacre rather than a battle. The imperial army broke and fled in all directions; some toward Cæsarea, others to Damascus, and others to Antioch. The booty was immense; crosses of silver and gold, adorned with precious

13

stones, rich chains and bracelets, jewels of price, silken robes, armour and weapons of all kinds, and numerous banners all which Khaled declared should not be divided until after the capture of Damascus.

Tidinds of this great victory was sent to the Caliph at Medina, by his brave and well beloved son Abda'lrahman. On receiving it, Abu Beker prostrated himself and returned thanks to God. The news spread rapidly throughout Arabia. Hosts of adventurers hurried to Medina from all parts, and especially from Mecca. All were eager to serve in the cause of the faith, now they found it crowned with conquest and rewarded with riches.

The worthy Abu Beker was disposed to gratify their wishes, but Omar on being consulted sternly objected. " The greater part of these fellows," said he, " who are so eager to join us now that we are successful, are those who sought to crush us when we were few and feeble. They care not for the faith, but they long to ravage the rich fields of Syria, and share the plunder of Damascus. Send them not to the army to make brawls and dissensions. Those already there are sufficient to complete what they have begun. They have won the victory; let them enjoy the spoils."

In compliance with this advice, Abu Beker refused the prayer of the applicants. Upon this the people of Mecca, and especially those of the tribe of Koreish, sent a powerful deputation, headed by Abu Sofian, to remonstrate with the Caliph. " Why are we denied permission," said they, " to fight in the cause of our religion ? It is true, that in the days of darkness and ignorance we made war on the disciples of the prophet, because we thought we were doing God service. Allah, however, has blessed us with the light ; we have seen and renounced our former errours. We are your brethren in the faith, as we have ever been your kindred in blood, and hereby take upon ourselves to fight in the common cause. Let there then no longer be jealousy and envy between us."

The heart of the Caliph was moved by these remonstrances. He consulted with Ali and Omar, and it was agreed that the tribe of Koreish should be permitted to join the army. Abu Beker accordingly wrote to Khaled congratulating him on his success, and informing him that a large reinforcement would join him conducted by Abu Sofian. This letter he sealed with the seal of the prophet, and despatched it by his son Abda'lrahman.

CHAPTER IX.

Occurrences before Damascus.—Exploits of Thomas.—Abán Ibn Zeid and his Amazonian wife.

The fugitives from the field of Aiznadin carried to Damascus the dismal tidings that the army was overthrown, and the last hope of succour destroyed. Great was the consternation of the inhabitants, yet they set to work, with desperate activity, to prepare for the coming storm. The fugitives had reinforced the garrison with several thousand effective men. New fortifications were hastily erected. The walls were lined with engines to discharge stones and darts, which were managed by Jews skilled in their use.

In the midst of their preparation, they beheld squadron after squadron of Moslem cavalry emerging from among distant groves, while a lengthening line of foot soldiers poured along between the gardens. This was the order of march of the Moslem host. The advance guard, of upwards of nine thousand horsemen, was led by Amru. Then came two thousand Koreishite horse, led by Abu Sofian. Then a like number under Serjabil. Then Omar Ibn Rabiyah with a similar division; then the main body of the army led by Abu Obeidah, and lastly the rear-guard displaying the black eagle, the fateful banner of Khaled, and led by that invincible warrior.

Khaled now assembled his captains, and assigned to them their different stations. Abu Sofian was posted opposite the southern gate. Serjabil opposite that of St. Thomas. Amru before that of Paradise, and Kais Ibn Hobeirah before that of Kaisan. Abu Obeidah encamped at some distance, in front of the gate of Jabiyah, and was charged to be strict and vigilant, and to make frequent assaults, for Khaled knew his humane and easy nature. As to Khaled himself, he took his station and planted his black eagle before the eastern gate.

There was still a southern gate, that of St. Mark, so situated that it was not practicable to establish posts or engage in skirmishes before it; it was, therefore, termed the Gate of Peace. As to the the active and impetuous Derar, he was ordered to patrol round the walls and scour the adjacent plain at the head of two thousand horse, protecting the camp from surprise and preventing supplies and reinforcements to the city. "If you should be attacked," said Khaled, "send me word, and I will come to your assistance." "And must I stand peaceably until you arrive?" said Derar, in recollection of former reproofs of his rash contests. "Not so," rejoined Khaled, "but fight stoutly, and be assured I will not fail you." The rest of the army were dismounted to carry on the siege on foot.

The Moslems were now better equipped for war than ever, having supplied themselves with armour and weapons taken in repeated battles. As yet, however, they retained their Arab frugality and plainness, neglecting the delicate viands, the sumptuous raiment, and other luxurious indulgences of their enemies. Even Abu Obeidah, in the humility of his spirit, contented himself with his primitive Arab tent of camel's hair; refusing the sumptuous tents of the Chistian commanders, won in the recent battle. Such were the stern simple-minded invaders of the effeminate and sensual nations of the East.

The first assaults of the Moslems were bravely repelled, and many were slain by darts and stones hurled by the machines from the wall. The garrison even ventured to make a sally, but were driven back with signal slaughter. The siege was then pressed with unremitting rigour, until no one dared to venture beyond the bulwarks. The principal inhabitants now consulted together whether it were not best to capitulate, while there was yet a chance of obtaining favourable terms.

There was at this time living in Damascus, a noble Greek, named Thomas, who was married to a daughter of the emperor Heraclius. He held no post, but was greatly respected, for he was a man of talents and consummate courage. In this moment of general depression, he endeavoured to rouse the spirits of the people; representing their invaders as despicable, barbarous, naked, and poorly armed, without discipline or military service, and formidable only through their mad fanaticism, and the panic they had spread through the country.

Finding all arguments in vain, he offered to take the lead himself, if they would venture upon another sally. His offer was accepted, and the next morning appointed for the effort.

Khaled perceived a stir of preparation throughout the night, lights gleaming in the turrets and along the battlements, and exhorted his men to be vigilant, for he anticipated some desperate movement. "Let no man sleep," said he. "We shall have rest enough after death; and sweet will be the repose that is never more to be followed by labour."

The Christians were sadly devout in this hour of extremity. At early dawn the bishop, in his robes, proceeded at the head of the clergy to the gate by which the sally was to be made; where he elevated the cross, and laid beside it the New Testament. As Thomas passed out at the gate, he laid his hand upon the sacred volume. "Oh God!" exclaimed he, "if our faith be true, aid us, and deliver us not into the hands of its enemies."

The Moslems, who had been on the alert, were advancing to attack just at the time of the sally, but were checked by a general discharge from the engines on the wall. Thomas led his troops bravely to the encounter, and the conflict was fierce and bloody. He was a dexterous archer, and singled out the most conspicuous of the Moslems, who fell one after another beneath his shafts. Among others he wounded Abân Ibn Zeid with an arrow tipped with poison. The latter bound up the wound with his turban, and continued in the field, but being overcome by the venom, was conveyed to the camp. He had but recently been married to a beautiful woman of the intrepid race of the Himiar; one of those Amazons accustomed to use the bow and arrow, and to mingle in warfare.

Hearing that her husband was wounded, she hastened to his tent, but before she could reach it he had expired. She uttered no lamentation, nor shed a tear, but, bending over the body, "Happy art thou, oh my beloved," said she, "for thou art with Allah, who joined us but to part us from each other. But I will avenge thy death, and then seek to join thee in paradise. Henceforth shall no man touch me more, for I dedicate myself to God!"

Then grasping her husband's bow and arrows, she hastened to the field in quest of Thomas, who, she had been told, was the slayer of her husband. Pressing toward the place where he was fighting, she let fly a shaft, which wounded his standard-bearer in the hand. The standard fell, and was borne off by the Moslems. Thomas pursued it, laying about him furiously, and calling upon his men to rescue their banner. It was shifted from hand to hand until it came into that of Serjabil. Thomas assailed him with his scimetar : Serjabil threw the standard among his troops and closed with him. They fought with equal ardour, but Thomas was gaining the advantage, when an arrow, shot by the wife of Abân, smote him in the eye. He staggered with the wound, but his men, abandoning the contested standard, rushed to his support, and bore him off to the city. He refused to retire to his home, and, his wound being dressed on the ramparts, would have returned to the conflict, but was overruled by the public. He took his station, however, at the city gate, whence he could survey the field and issue his orders. The battle continued with great fury ; but such showers of stones and darts and other missiles were discharged by the Jews from the engines on the walls, that the besiegers were kept a distance. Night terminated the conflict. The Moslems returned to their camp wearied with a long day's fighting ; and, throwing themselves on the earth, were soon buried in profound sleep.

Thomas, finding the courage of the garrison roused by the stand they had that day made, resolved to put it to further proof. At his suggestion, preparations were made in the dead of the night for a general sally at daybreak from all the gates of the city. At the signal of a single stroke upon a bell at the first peep of dawn, all the gates were thrown open, and from each rushed forth a torrent of warriors upon the nearest encampment.

So silently had the preparations been made, that the besiegers were completely taken by surprise. The trumpets sounded alarms, the Moslems started from sleep and snatched up their weapons, but the enemy were already upon them, and struck them down before they had recovered from their amazement. For a time it was a slaugter rather than a fight, at the various stations. Khaled is said to have shed tears at beholding the carnage. "Oh thou, who never sleepest ! " cried he, in the agony of his heart, "aid thy faithful servants ; let them not fall beneath the weapons of these infidels." Then, followed by four hundred horsemen, he spurred about the field wherever relief was most needed.

The hottest of the fight was opposite the gate whence Thomas had sallied. Here Serjabil had his station, and fought with undaunted valour. Near him was the intrepid wife of Abân, doing deadly execution with her shafts. She had expended all but one, when a Greek soldier attempted to seize her. In an instant the arrow was sped through his throat, and laid him dead at her feet; but she was now weaponless, and was taken prisoner.

At the same time Serjabil and Thomas were again engaged hand to hand with equal valour ; but the scimetar of Serjabil broke on the buckler of his adversary, and he was on the point of being slain or captured, when Khaled and Abda'lrahman galloped up with a troop of horse. Thomas was obliged to take refuge in the city, and Serjabil and the Amazonian widow were rescued.

The troops who sallied out at the gate of Jabeyah, met with the severest treatment. The meek Abu Obeidah was stationed in front of that gate, and was slumbering quietly in his hair tent at the time of the sally. His first care in the moment of alarm was to repeat the morning prayer. He then ordered forth a body of chosen men to keep the enemy at bay, and while they were fighting, led another detachment, silently but rapidly, round between the combatants and the city. The Greeks thus suddenly found themselves assailed in front and rear; they fought desperately, but so successful was the stratagem, and so active the valour of the meek Abu Obeidah, when once aroused, that never a man, says the Arabian historian, that sallied from that gate, returned again.

The battle of the night was almost as sanguinary as that of the day; the Christians were repulsed in all quarters, and driven once more within their walls, leaving several thousand dead upon the field. The Moslems followed them to the very gates, but were compelled to retire by the deadly shower hurled by the Jews from the engines on the walls.

CHAPTER X.

Surrender of Damascus.—Disputes of the Saracen generals.—Departure of Thomas and the exiles.

For seventy days had Damascus been besieged by the fanatic legions of the desert : the inhabitants had no longer the heart to make further sallies, but again began to talk of capitulating. It was in vain that Thomas urged them to have patience until he should write to the emperor for succour; they listened only to their fears, and sent to Khaled begging a truce, that they might have time to treat of a surrender. That fierce warrior turned a deaf ear to their prayer : he wished for no surrender, that would protect the lives and property of the besieged; he was bent upon taking the city by the sword, and giving it up to be plundered by his Arabs.

In their extremity the people of Damascus turned to the good Abu Obeidah, whom they knew to be meek and humane. Having first treated with him by a messenger who understood Arabic, and received his promise of security, a hundred of the principal inhabitants, including the most venerable of the clergy, issued privately one night by the gate of Jabiyah, and sought his presence. They found this leader of a mighty force, that was shaking the empire of the Orient, living in a humble tent of hair-cloth, like a mere wanderer of the desert. He listened favourably to their propositions, for his object was conversion rather than conquest; tribute rather than plunder. A covenant was soon written, in which he engaged that hostilities should cease on their delivering the city.

into his hands; that such of the inhabitants as pleased might depart in safety with as much of their effects as they could carry, and those who remained as tributaries should retain their property, and have seven churches allotted to them. This covenant was not signed by Abu Obeidah, not being commander-in-chief, but he assured the envoys it would be held sacred by the Moslems.

The capitulation being arranged, and hostages given for the good faith of the besieged, the gate opposite to the encampment of Abu Obeidah was thrown open, and the venerable chief entered at the head of a hundred men to take possession.

While these transactions were taking place at the gate of Jabiyah, a different scene occurred at the eastern gate. Khaled was exasperated by the death of a brother of Amru, shot from the walls with a poisoned arrow. In the height of his indignation, an apostate priest, named Josias, undertook to deliver the gate into his hands, on condition of security of person and property for himself and his relatives.

By means of this traitor, a hundred Arabs were secretly introduced within the walls, who, rushing to the eastern gate, broke the bolts and bars and chains by which it was fastened, and threw it open with the signal shout of Allah Achbar!

Khaled and his legions poured in at the gate with sound of trumpet and tramp of steed; putting all to the sword, and deluging the streets with blood. " Mercy! Mercy!" was the cry. " No mercy for infidels!" was Khaled's fierce response.

He pursued his career of carnage into the great square before the church of the Virgin Mary. Here, to his astonishment, he beheld Abu Obeidah and his attendants, theirs swords sheathed, and marching in solemn procession with priests and monks and the principal inhabitants, and surrounded by women and children.

Abu Obeidah saw fury and surprise in the looks of Khaled, and hastened to propitiate him by gentle words. " Allah in his mercy," said he, " has delivered this city into my hands by peaceful surrender; sparing the effusion of blood and the necessity of fighting."

" Not so," cried Khaled in a fury. " I have won it with this sword, and I grant no quarter."

" But I have given the inhabitants a covenant written with my own hand."

" And what right had you," demanded Khaled, " to grant a capitulation without consulting me? Am not I the general? Yes, by Allah! and to prove it I will put every inhabitant to the sword."

Abu Obeidah felt that in point of military duty he had erred, but he sought to pacify Khaled, assuring him he had intended all for the best, and felt sure of his approbation; entreating him to respect the covenant he had made in the name of God and the prophet, and with the approbation of all the Moslems present at the transaction.

Several of the Moslem officers seconded Abu Obeidah, and endeavoured to persuade Khaled to agree to the capitulation. While he hesitated, his troops, impatient of delay, resumed the work of massacre and pillage.

The patience of the good Abu Obeidah was at an end. " By

Allah!" cried he, "my word is treated as nought, and my covenant is trampled under foot!"

Spurring his horse among the marauders, he commanded them,
in the name of the prophet, to desist until he and Khaled should
have time to settle their dispute. The name of the prophet had
its effect; the soldiery paused in their bloody career, and the two
generals with their officers retired to the church of the Virgin.

Here, after a sharp altercation, Khaled, callous to all claims of
justice and mercy, was brought to listen to policy. It was represented to him that he was invading a country where many cities
were yet to be taken; that it was important to respect the capitulations of his generals, even though they might not be altogether
to his mind; otherwise the Moslem word would cease to be trusted,
and other cities, warned by the fate of Damascus, instead of surrendering on favourable terms, might turn a deaf ear to all offers
of mercy and fight to the last extremity.

It was with the utmost difficulty that Abu Obeidah wrung from the
iron soul of Khaled a slow consent to his capitulation, on condition
that the whole matter should be referred to the Caliph. At every
article he paused and murmured. He would fain have inflicted
death upon Thomas, and another leader named Herbis, but Abu
Obeidah insisted that they were expressly included in the covenant.

Proclamation was then made that such of the inhabitants as
chose to remain tributaries to the Caliph should enjoy the exercise
of their religion; the rest were permitted to depart. The greater
part preferred to remain; but some determined to follow their
champion Thomas to Antioch. The latter prayed for a passport
or a safe-conduct through the country controlled by the Moslems.
After much difficulty, Khaled granted them three days' grace,
during which they should be safe from molestation or pursuit;
on condition they took nothing with them but provisions.

Here the worthy Abu Obeidah interfered, declaring that he had
covenanted to let them go forth with bag and baggage. "Then,"
said Khaled, "they shall go unarmed." Again Abu Obeidah interfered, and Khaled at length consented that they should have
arms sufficient to defend themselves against robbers and wild
beasts; he, however, who had a lance, should have no sword;
and he who had a bow, should have no lance.

Thomas and Herbis, who were to conduct this unhappy caravan,
pitched their tents in the meadow adjacent to the city, whither all
repaired who were to follow them into exile; each laden with
plate, jewels, silken stuffs, and whatever was most precious and
least burdensome. Among other things was a wardrobe of the
emperor Heraclius, in which there were above three hundred
loads of costly silks and cloth of gold.

All being assembled, the sad multitude set forth on their way-
faring. Those who from pride, from patriotism, or from religion,
thus doomed themselves to poverty and exile, were among the
noblest and most highly bred of the land; people accustomed to
soft and luxurious life, and to the silken abodes of palaces. Of
this number was the wife of Thomas, a daughter of the emperor
Heraclius, who was attended by her maidens. It was a piteous

sight to behold aged men, delicate and shrinking women, and helpless children, thus setting forth on a wandering journey through wastes and deserts, and rugged mountains, infested by savage hordes. Many a time did they turn to cast a look of fondness and despair on those sumptuous palaces and delightful gardens, once their pride and joy; and still would they turn and weep, and beat their breasts, and gaze through their tears on the stately towers of Damascus, and the flowery banks of the Pharpar.

Thus terminated the hard-contested siege of Damascus, which Voltaire has likened for its stratagems, skirmishes, and single combats, to Homer's siege of Troy. More than twelve months elapsed between the time the Saracens first pitched their tents before it and the day of its surrender.

CHAPTER XI.

Story of Jonas and Eudocea.—Pursuit of the exiles.—Death of the Caliph Abu Beker.

It is recorded that Derar gnashed his teeth with rage at seeing the multitude of exiles departing in peace, laden with treasures, which he considered as so much hard-earned spoil, lost to the faithful; but what most incensed him was, that so many unbelievers should escape the edge of the scimetar. Khaled would have been equally indignant, but that he had secretly covenanted with himself to regain this booty. For this purpose he ordered his men to refresh themselves and their horses, and be in readiness for action, resolving to pursue the exiles when the three days of grace should have expired.

A dispute with Abu Obeidah concerning a quantity of grain, which the latter claimed for the citizens, detained him one day longer, and he was about to abandon the pursuit as hopeless, when a guide presented himself who knew all the country, and the shortest passes through the mountains. The story of this guide is worthy of notice, as illustrating the character of these people and these wars.

During the siege, Derar, as has been related, was appointed to patrol round the city and the camp, with two thousand horse. As a party of these were one night going their rounds, near the walls, they heard the distant neighing of a horse, and looking narrowly round, descried a horseman coming stealthily from the gate Keisan. Halting in a shadowy place, they waited until he came close to them, when, rushing forth, they made him prisoner. He was a youthful Syrian, richly and gallantly arrayed, and apparently a person of distinction. Scarcely had they seized him when they beheld another horseman issuing from the same gate, who in a soft voice called upon their captive, by the name of Jonas. They commanded the latter to invite his companion to advance. He seemed to reply, and called out something in Greek: upon hearing which, the other turned bridle and galloped back into the city. The Arabs, ignorant of Greek, and suspecting the words to be a warning, would have slain their prisoner on the spot; but, upon second thoughts, conducted him to Khaled.

The youth avowed himself a nobleman of Damascus, and betrothed to a beautiful maiden named Eudocea; but her parents, from some capricious reason, had withdrawn their consent to his nuptials; whereupon the lovers had secretly agreed to fly from Damascus. A sum of gold had bribed the sentinels who kept watch that night at the gate. The damsel, disguised in male attire, and accompanied by two domestics, was following her lover at a distance, as he sallied in advance. His reply in Greek, when she called upon him, was, " the bird is caught! " a warning at the hearing of which she had fled back to the city.

Khaled was not the man to be moved by a love tale ; but he gave the prisoner his alternative. " Embrace the faith of Islam," said he, " and when Damascus falls into our power, you shall have your betrothed ; refuse, and your head is forfeit."

The youth paused not between a scimetar and a bride. He made immediate profession of faith between the hands of Khaled, and thenceforth fought zealously for the capture of the city, since its downfall was to crown his hopes.

When Damascus yielded to its foes, he sought the dwelling of Eudocea, and learnt a new proof of her affection. Supposing, on his capture by the Arabs, that he had fallen a martyr to his faith, she had renounced the world, and shut herself up in a convent. With throbbing heart he hastened to the convent, but when the lofty-minded maiden beheld in him a renegade, she turned from him with scorn, retired to her cell, and refused to see him more. She was among the noble ladies who followed Thomas and Herbis into exile. Her lover, frantic at the thoughts of losing her, reminded Khaled of his promise to restore her to him, and entreated that she might be detained; but Khaled pleaded the covenant of Abu Obeidah, according to which all had free leave to depart.

When Jonas afterwards discovered that Khaled meditated a pursuit of the exiles, but was discouraged by the lapse of time, he offered to conduct him by short and secret passes through the mountains, which would insure his overtaking them. His offer was accepted. On the fourth day after the departure of the exiles, Khaled set out in pursuit, with four thousand chosen horsemen; who, by the advice of Jonas, were disguised as Christian Arabs. For some time they traced the exiles along the plains, by the numerous foot-prints of mules and camels, and by articles thrown away to enable them to travel more expeditiously. At length, the foot-prints turned towards the mountains of Lebanon, and were lost in their arid and rocky defiles. The Moslems began to falter. "Courage!" cried Jonas, "they will be entangled among the mountains. They cannot now escape."

They continued their weary course, stopping only at the stated hours of prayer. They had now to climb the high and cragged passes of Lebanon, along rifts and glens worn by winter torrents. The horses struck fire at every tramp ; they cast their shoes, their hoofs were battered on the rocks, and many of them were lamed and disabled. The horsemen dismounted and scrambled up on foot, leading their weary and crippled steeds. Their clothes were worn to shreds, and the soles of their iron-shod boots were torn from the upper leathers. The men murmured and repined; never in all their marches had they experienced such hardships;—they insisted on halting, to rest and to bait their horses. Even Khaled, whose hatred of infidels furnished an impulse almost equal to the lover's passion, began to flag, and reproached the renegade as the cause of all this trouble.

Jonas still urged them forward : he pointed to fresh footprints and tracks of horses that must have recently passed. After a few hours' refreshment they resumed the pursuit; passing within sight of Jabalah and Laodicea, but without venturing within their gates, lest the disguise of Christian Arabs, which deceived the simple peasantry, might not avail with the shrewder inhabitants of the towns.

Intelligence received from a country boor increased their perplexity. The emperor Heraclius, fearing that the arrival of the exiles might cause a panic at Antioch, had sent orders for them to proceed along the sea-coast to Constantinople. This gave their pursuers a greater chance to overtake them : but Khaled was startled at learning, in addition, that troops were assembling to be sent against him, and that but a single mountain separated him from them. He now feared they might intercept his return, or fall upon Damascus in his absence. A sinister dream added to his uneasiness, but it was favourably interpreted by Abda'lrahman, and he continued the pursuit.

A tempestuous night closed on them : the rain fell in torrents, and man and beast was ready to sink with fatigue : still they were urged forward : the fugitives could not be far distant, the enemy was at hand : they must snatch their prey and retreat. The morning dawned; the storm cleared up, and the sun shone brightly on the surrounding heights. They dragged their steps wearily, however, along the defiles, now swept by torrents or filled with mire, until the scouts in the advance gave joyful signal from the mountain brow. It commanded a grassy meadow, sprinkled with flowers, and watered by a running stream.

On the borders of the rivulet was the caravan of exiles, reposing in the sunshine from the fatigues of the recent storm. Some were sleeping on the grass, others were taking their morning repast; while the meadow was gay with embroidered robes and silks of various dyes spread out to dry upon the herbage. The weary Moslems, worn out with the horrors of the mountains, gazed with delight on the sweetness and freshness of the meadow; but Khaled eyed the caravan with an eager eye, and the lover only stretched his gaze o catch a glimpse of his betrothed among the females reclining on the margin of the stream.

Having cautiously reconnoitred the caravan without being perceived, Khaled disposed of his band in four squadrons; the first commanded by Derar, the second by Rafi Ibn Omeirah, the third by Abda'lrahman, and the fourth led by himself. He gave orders that the squadrons should make their appearance successively, one at a time, to deceive the enemy as to their force, and that there should be no pillaging until the victory was complete.

· Having offered up a prayer, he gave the word to his division, "In the name of Allah and the prophet!" and led to the attack. The Christians were roused from their repose on beholding a squadron rushing down from the mountain. They were deceived at first by the Greek dresses, but were soon aware of the truth; though the small number of the enemy gave them but little dread. Thomas hastily marshalled five thousand men to receive the shock of the onset, with such weapons as had been left them. Another and another division came hurrying down from the mountain; and the fight was furious and well contested. Thomas and Khaled fought hand to hand; but the Christian champion was struck to the ground. Abda'lrahman cut off his head, elevated it on the spear of the standard of the cross which he had taken at Damascus, and called upon the Christians to behold the head of their leader.

Rafi Ibn Omeirah penetrated with his division into the midst of the encampment to capture the women. They stood courageously on the defensive, hurling stones at their assailants. Among them was a female of matchless beauty, dressed in splendid attire, with a diadem of jewels. It was the reputed daughter of the emperor, the wife of Thomas. Rafi attempted to seize her, but she hurled a stone that struck his horse in the head and killed him. The Arab drew his scimetar, and would have slain her, but she cried for mercy, so he took her prisoner, and gave her in charge to a trusty follower.

In the midst of the carnage and confusion, Jonas hastened in search of his betrothed. If she had treated him with disdain as a renegade, she now regarded him with horror, as the traitor who had brought this destruction upon his unhappy countrymen. All his entreaties for her to forgive and be reconciled to him, were of no avail. She solemnly vowed to repair to Constantinople and end her days in a convent. Finding supplication fruitless, he seized her, and after a violent struggle, threw her on the ground and made her prisoner. She made no further resistance, but submitting to captivity, seated herself quietly on the grass. The lover flattered himself that she relented; but, watching her opportunity, she suddenly drew forth a poniard, plunged it in her breast, and fell dead at his feet.

While this tragedy was performing the general battle, or rather carnage, continued. Khaled ranged the field in quest of Herbis, but, while fighting pell-mell among a throng of Christians, that commander came behind him and dealt a blow that severed his helmet, and would have cleft his skull but for the folds of his turban. The sword of Herbis fell from his hand with the violence of the blow, and before he could recover it, he was cut in pieces by the followers of Khaled. The struggle of the unhappy Christians was at an end: all were slain, or taken prisoners, except one, who was permitted to depart, and who bore the dismal tidings of the massacre to Constantinople.

The renegade Jonas was loud in his lamentations for the loss of his betrothed, but his Moslem comrades consoled him with one of the doctrines of the faith he had newly embraced. "It was written in the book of fate," said they, "that you should never possess that woman; but be comforted, Allah has doubtless greater blessings in store for you;" and, in fact, Rafi Ibn Omeirah, out of compassion for his distress, presented him with the beautiful princess he had taken captive. Khaled consented to the gift, provided the emperor did not send to ransom her.

There was now no time to be lost. In this headlong pursuit they had penetrated above a hundred and fifty miles into the heart of the enemy's country, and might be cut off in their retreat. "To horse and away," therefore, was the word. The plunder was hastily packed upon the mules, the scanty number of surviving exiles were secured, and the marauding band set off on a forced march for Damascus. While on their way they were one day alarmed by a cloud of dust, through which their scouts descried the banner of the cross. They prepared for a desperate conflict. It proved, however, a peaceful mission. An ancient bishop, followed by a numerous train, sought from Khaled, in the emperor's name, the liberation of his daughter. The haughty Saracen released her without ransom. "Take her," said he, "but tell your master I intend to have him in exchange; never will I cease this war until I have wrested from him every foot of territory."

To indemnify the renegade for this second deprivation, a large sum of gold was given him, wherewith to buy a wife from among the captives; but he now disclaimed for ever all earthly love, and, like a devout Mahometan, looked forward for consolation among the black-eyed Houris of paradise. He continued more faithful to his new faith and new companions than he had been to the religion of his fathers and the friends of his infancy; and after serving the Saracens in a variety of ways, earned an undoubted admission to the paradise of the prophet, being shot through the breast at the battle of Yermouk.

Thus perished this apostate, says the Christian chronicler; but Alwakedi, the venerable Cadi of Bagdad, adds a supplement to the story, for the encouragement of all proselytes to the Islam faith. He states that Jonas, after his death, was seen in a vision by Rafi Ibn Omeirah, arrayed in rich robes and golden sandals, and walking in a flowery mead; and the beatified renegade assured him that, for his exemplary services, Allah had given him seventy of the black-eyed damsels of paradise, each of resplendent beauty, sufficient to throw the sun and moon in the shade. Rafi related his vision to Khaled, who heard it with implicit faith. "This it is," said that Moslem zealot, "to die a martyr to the faith. Happy the man to whose lot it falls!" [1]

Khaled succeeded in leading his adventurous band safely back to Damascus, where they were joyfully received by their companions

---

[1] The story of Jonas and Eudocea has been made the subject of an English tragedy by Hughes, entitled The Siege of Damascus; but the lover's name is changed to Phocyas, the incidents are altered, and the catastrophe is made entirely different.

in arms, who had entertained great fears for their safety. He now divided the rich spoils taken in his expedition; four parts were given to the officers and soldiers, a fifth he reserved for the public treasury, and sent it off to the Caliph, with letters informing him of the capture of Damascus; of his disputes with Abu Obeidah as to the treatment of the city and its inhabitants, and lastly of his expedition in pursuit of the exiles, and his recovery of the wealth they were bearing away. These missives were sent in the confident expectation that his policy of the sword would far outshine, in the estimation of the Caliph, and of all true Moslems, the more peaceful policy of Abu Obeidah.

It was written in the book of fate, say the Arabian historians, that the pious Abu Beker should die without hearing of the brightest triumph of the Islam faith; the very day that Damascus surrendered, the Caliph breathed his last at Medina. Arabian authors differ as to the cause of his death. Abulfeda asserts that he was poisoned by the Jews, in his frugal repast of rice; but his daughter Ayesha, with more probability, ascribes his death to bathing on an unusually cold day, which threw him into a fever. While struggling with his malady, he directed his chosen friend Omar to perform the religious functions of his office in his stead.

Feeling his end approaching, he summoned his secretary, Othman Ibn Affân, and in presence of several of the principal Moslems, dictated as follows: "I, Abu Beker Ibn Abu Kahafa, being on the point of leaving this world for the next, and at that moment when infidels believe, when the wicked cease to doubt, and when liars speak the truth, do make this declaration of my will to the Moslems. I nominate, as my successor,"——Here he was overtaken with faintness so that he could not speak. Othman, who knew his intentions, added the name of Omar Ibn al Khattâb. When Abu Beker came to himself, and saw what his secretary had written, "God bless thee," said he, "for this foresight!" He then continued to dictate. "Listen to him, and obey him, for, as far as I know him, and have seen him, he is integrity itself. He is competent to every thing he undertakes. He will rule with justice; if not, God, who knows all secrets, will reward him according to his works. I mean all for the best, but I cannot see into the hidden thoughts of men. Farewell. Act uprightly, and the blessing of Allah be upon you."

He ordered this testament to be sealed with his seal, and copies of it to be sent to the principal authorities, civil and military. Then, having sent for Omar, he told him of his having nominated him as his successor.

Omar was a stern and simple-minded man; unambitious of posts and dignities. "Oh successor to the apostle of God!" said he, "spare me from this burthen. I have no need of the Caliphat." "But the Caliphat has need of you!" replied the dying Abu Beker.

He went on to claim his acceptance of the office as a proof of friendship to himself, and of devotion to the public good, for he considered him eminently calculated to maintain an undivided rule over the restless people so newly congregated into an empire.

Having brought him to accept, he gave him much dying counsel, and after he had retired, prayed fervently for his success, and that the dominion of the faith might be strengthened and extended during his reign. Having thus provided for a quiet succession to his office, the good Caliph expired in the arms of his daughter Ayesha, in the sixty-fourth year of his age, having reigned two years, three months, and nine days. At the time of his death his father and mother were still living, the former ninety-seven years of age. When the ancient Moslem heard of the death of his son, he merely said, in Scriptural phrase: "The Lord hath given, and the Lord hath taken away. Blessed be the name of the Lord!"

Abu Beker had four wives; the last had been the widow of Jaafar, who fell in the battle of Muta. She bore him two sons after his sixtieth year. He does not appear, however, to have had the same fondness for the sex as the prophet, notwithstanding his experience in wedlock. "The women," he used to say, "are all an evil; but the greatest evil of all is, that they are necessary."

Abu Beker was universally lamented by his subjects, and he deserved their lamentations, for he had been an excellent ruler, just, moderate, temperate, frugal, and disinterested. His reign was too short to enable him to carry out any extensive schemes; but it was signalized by the promptness and ability with which, through the aid of the sword, he quelled the wide-spreading insurrections on the death of the prophet, and preserved the scarcely launched empire of Islam from perfect shipwreck. He left behind him a name dear to all true Moslems, and an example which, Omar used to say, would be a difficult pattern for his successors to imitate.

CHAPTER XII.

Election of Omar, second Caliph.—Khaled superseded in command by Obeidah.—Magnanimous conduct of those generals.—Expedition to the convent of Abyla.

The nomination of Omar to the succession was supported by Ayesha, and acquiesced in by Ali, who saw that opposition would be ineffectual. The election took place on the day of the decease of Abu Beker. The character of the new Caliph has already, through his deeds, been made known in some measure to the reader; yet a sketch of him may not be unacceptable. He was now about fifty-three years of age; a tall dark man, with a grave demeanour and a bald head. He was so tall, says one of his biographers, that when he sat, he was higher than those who stood. His strengh was uncommon, and he used the left as adroitly as the right hand. Though so bitter an enemy of Islamism at first as to seek the life of Mahomet, he became from the moment of his conversion one of its most sincere and strenuous champions. He had taken an active part in the weightiest and most decisive events of the prophet's career. His name stands at the head of the weapon companions at Beder, Ohod, Khaïbar, Honein, and Tabuc, at the defence of Medina, and the capture of Mecca, and indeed he appears to have been the soul of most of the early military enterprises of the faith. His zeal was prompt and almost fiery in its operations. He expounded and enforced the doctrines of Islam like a soldier; when a question was too knotty for his logic, he was ready to sever it with the sword, and to strike off the head of him who persisted in false arguing and unbelief.

In the administration of affairs, his probity and justice were proverbial. In private life he was noted for abstinence and frugality, and a contempt for the false grandeur of the world. Water was his only beverage. His food a few dates, or a few bits of barley bread and salt; but in time of penance, even salt was retrenched as a luxury. His austere piety and self-denial, and the simplicity and almost poverty of his appearance, were regarded with reverence in those primitive days of Islam. He had shrewd maxims on which he squared his conduct, of which the following is a specimen. "Four things come not back: the spoken word; the sped arrow; the past life, and the neglected opportunity."

During his reign mosques were erected without number for the instruction and devotion of the faithful, and prisons for the punishment of delinquents. He likewise put in use a scourge with twisted thongs for the correction of minor offences, among which he included satire and scandal, and so potently and extensively was it plied, that the word went round, "Omar's twisted scourge is more to be feared than his sword."

On assuming his office, he was saluted as Caliph of the Caliph of the apostle of God, in other words, successor to the successor of the prophet. Omar objected, that such a title must lengthen with every successor, until it became endless; upon which it was proposed and agreed that he should receive the title of Emir-al-Moumenin, that is to say, Commander of the Faithful. This title altered into Miramamolin, was subsequently borne by such Moslem sovereigns as held independent sway, acknowledging no superior, and is equivalent to that of emperor.

One of the first measures of the new Caliph was with regard to the army in Syria. His sober judgment was not to be dazzled by daring and brilliant exploits in arms, and he doubted the fitness of Khaled for the general command. He acknowledged his valour and military skill, but considered him rash, fiery and prodigal; prone to hazardous and extravagant adventure, and more fitted to be a partisan than a leader. He resolved, therefore, to take the principal command of the army out of such indiscreet hands, and restore it to Abu Obeidah, who, he said, had proved himself worthy of it by his piety, modesty, moderation, and good faith. He accordingly wrote on a skin of parchment, a letter to Abu Obeidah, informing him of the death of Abu Beker, and his own elevation as Caliph, and appointing him commander-in-chief of the army of Syria.

The letter was delivered to Abu Obeidah at the time that Khaled was absent in pursuit of the caravan of exiles. The good Obeidah was surprised, but sorely perplexed by the contents. His own modesty made him unambitious of high command, and his opinion of the signal valour and brilliant services of Khaled made him loth to supersede him, and doubtful whether the Caliph would not feel disposed to continue him as commander-in-chief when he should hear of his recent success at Damascus. He resolved, therefore, to keep for the present, the contents of the Caliph's letter to himself; and accordingly on Khaled's return to Damascus continued to treat him as commander, and suffered him to write his second letter to Abu Beker, giving him an account of his recent pursuit and plundering of the exiles.

Omar had not been long installed in office, when he received the first letters of Khaled announcing the capture of Damascus. These tidings occasioned the most extravagant joy at Medina, and the valour of Khaled was extolled by the multitude to the very skies. In the midst of their rejoicings they learnt with astonishment, that the general command had been transferred to Abu Obeidah. The admirers of Khaled were loud in their expostulations. "What!" cried they, "dismiss Khaled when in the full career of victory? Remember the reply of Abu Beker, when a like measure was urged upon him. 'I will not sheathe the sword of God, drawn for the promotion of the faith.'"

Omar revolved their remonstrances in his mind, but his resolution remained unchanged. "Abu Obeidah," said he, "is tender and merciful; yet brave. He will be careful of his people, not lavishing their lives in rash adventures and plundering inroads; nor will he be the less formidable in battle for being moderate when victorious."

In the meantime came the second despatches of Khaled, addressed to Abu Beker, announcing the success of his expedition in pursuit of the exiles; and requesting his decision of the matters in dispute between him and Abu Obeidah. The Caliph was perplexed by this letter, which showed that his election as Caliph was yet unknown to the army, and that Abu Obeidah had not assumed the command. He now wrote again to the latter reiterating his appointment; and deciding upon the matters in dispute. He gave it as his opinion, that Damascus had surrendered on capitulation, and had not been taken by the sword, and directed that the stipulations of the covenant should be fulfilled. He declared the pursuit of the exiles iniquitous and rash; and that it would have proved fatal, but for the mercy of God. The dismissal of the emperor's daughter free of ransom, he termed a prodigal action; as a large sum might have been obtained and given to the poor. He counselled Abu Obeidah, of whose mild and humane temper he was well aware, not to be too modest and compliant, but at the same time, not to risk the lives of the faithful in the mere hope of plunder. This latter hint was a reproof to Khaled.

Lest this letter should likewise be suppressed through the modesty of Abu Obeidah, he despatched it by an officer of distinction, Shaded Ibn Aass, whom he appointed his representative in Syria, with orders to have the letter read in presence of the Moslems, and to cause him to be proclaimed Caliph at Damascus.

Shaded made good his journey, and found Khaled in his tent,

still acting as commander-in-chief, and the army ignorant of the death of Abu Beker. The tidings he brought struck every one with astonishment. The first sentiment expressed was grief at the death of the good Abu Beker, who was universally lamented as a father; the second was surprise at the deposition of Khaled from the command, in the very midst of such signal victories; and many of his officers and soldiers were loud in expressing their indignation.

If Khaled had been fierce and rude in his career of triumph, he proved himself magnanimous in this moment of adversity. "I know," said he, "that Omar does not love me; but since Abu Beker is dead, and has appointed him his successor, I submit to his commands." . He accordingly caused Omar to be proclaimed Caliph at Damascus, and resigned his command to Abu Obeidah. The latter accepted it with characteristic modesty; but evinced a fear that Khaled would retire in disgust, and his signal services be lost to the cause of Islam. Khaled, however, soon let him know, that he was as ready to serve as to command, and only required an occasion to prove that his zeal for the faith was unabated. His personal submission extorted admiration even from his enemies, and gained him the fullest deference, respect, and confidence of Abu Obeidah.

About this time one of the Christian tributaries, a base-spirited wretch, eager to ingratiate himself with Abu Obeidah, came and informed him of a fair object of enterprise. "At no great distance from this, between Tripoli and Harran there is a convent called Daiz Abil Kodos, or the monastery of the Holy Father, from being inhabited by a Christian hermit, so eminent for wisdom, piety and mortification of the flesh, that he is looked up to as a saint; so that young and old, rich and poor, resort from all parts to seek his advice and blessing, and not a marriage takes place among the nobles of the country, but the bride and bridegroom repair to receive from him the nuptial benediction. At Easter there is an annual fair held at Abyla in front of the convent, to which are brought the richest manufactures of the surrounding country; silken stuffs, jewels of gold and silver, and other precious productions of art; and as the fair is a peaceful congregation of people, unarmed and unguarded, it will afford ample booty at little risk or trouble."

Abu Obeidah announced the intelligence to his troops. "Who," said he, "will undertake this enterprise?" His eye glanced involuntarily upon Khaled; it was just such a foray as he was wont to delight in; but Khaled remained silent. Abu Obeidah could not ask a service from one so lately in chief command; and while he hesitated, Abdallah Ibn Jaafar, step-son to Abu Beker, came forward. A banner was given him, and five hundred veteran horsemen, scarred in many a battle, sallied with him from the gates of Damascus, guided by the traitor Christian. They halted to rest before arriving at Abyla, and sent forward the Christian as a scout. As he approached the place he was astonished to see it crowded with an immense concourse of Greeks, Armenians, Copts and Jews, in their various garbs; beside these there was a grand procession of nobles and courtiers in rich attire, and priests in religious dresses, with a guard of five thousand horse; all, as he learned, escorting the daughter of the prefect of Tripoli, who was lately married, and had come with her husband to receive the blessing of the venerable hermit. The Christian scout hastened back to the Moslems, and warned them to retreat.

"I dare not," said Abdallah, promptly; "I fear the wrath of Allah, should I turn my back. I will fight these infidels. Those who help me, God will reward; those whose hearts fail them, are welcome to retire." Not a Moslem turned his back. "Forward!" said Abdallah to the Christian, and thou shalt behold what the companions of the prophet can perform." The traitor hesitated, however, and was with difficulty persuaded to guide them on a service of such peril.

Abdallah led his band near to Abyla, where they lay close until morning. At the dawn of day, having performed the customary prayer, he divided his host into five squadrons of a hundred each; they were to charge at once in five different places, with the shout of Allah Achbar! and to slay or capture without stopping to pillage until the victory should be complete. He then reconnoitred the place. The hermit was preaching in front of his convent to a multitude of auditors; the fair teemed with people in the variegated garbs of the Orient. One house was guarded by a great number of horsemen, and numbers of persons, richly clad, were going in and out, or standing about it. In this house evidently was the youthful bride.

Abdallah encouraged his followers to despise the number of these foes. "Remember," cried he, "the words of the prophet. 'Paradise is under the shadow of swords!' If we conquer, we shall have glorious booty; if we fall, paradise awaits us!"

The five squadrons charged as they had been ordered, with the well-known war-cry. The Christians were struck with dismay, thinking the whole Moslem army upon them. There was a direful confusion; the multitude flying in all directions; women and children shrieking and crying; booths and tents overturned, and precious merchandise scattered about the streets. The troops, however, seeing the inferior number of the assailants, plucked up spirits and charged upon them. The merchants and inhabitants recovered from their panic and flew to arms, and the Moslem band, hemmed in among such a host of foes, seemed, say the Arabian writers, like a white spot on the hide of a black camel. A Moslem trooper, seeing the peril of his companions, broke his way out of the throng, and throwing the reins on the neck of his steed, scoured back to Damascus for succour.

In this moment of emergency Abu Obeidah forgot all scruples of delicacy, and turned to the man he had superseded in office. "Fail us not," cried he, "in this moment of peril; but, for God's sake, hasten to deliver thy brethren from destruction."

"Had Omar given the command of the army to a child," replied the gracious Khaled, "I should have obeyed him; how much more thee, my predecessor in the faith of Islam!"

He now arrayed himself in a coat of mail, the spoil of the false prophet Moseilma; he put on a helmet of proof, and over it a skull-cap, which he called the blessed cap, and attributed to it wonderful virtues, having received the prophet's benediction. Then springing on his horse, and putting himself at the head of a chosen band, he scoured off towards Abyla, with the bold Derar at his side.

In the meantime the troops, under Abdallah, had maintained throughout the day a desperate conflict; heaps of the slain testified their prowess; but their ranks were sadly thinned, scarce one of the survivors but had received repeated wounds, and they were ready to sink under heat, fatigue, and thirst. Towards sunset a cloud of dust is seen: is it a reinforcement of their enemies? A troop of horsemen emerge. They bear the black eagle of Khaled. The air resounds with the shout of Allah Achbar. The Christians are assailed on either side; some fly and are pursued to the river by the unsparing sword of Khaled; others rally round the monastery. Derar engages hand to hand with the prefect of Tripoli; they grapple; they struggle; they fall to the earth; Derar is uppermost, and, drawing a poniard, plunges it into the heart of his adversary. He springs upon his feet; vaults into the saddle of the prefect's horse, and, with the shout of Allah Achbar, gallops in quest of new opponents.

The battle is over. The fair is given up to plunder. Horses, mules, and asses are laden with silken stuffs, rich embroidery, jewels of gold and silver, precious stones, spices, perfumes, and other wealthy plunder of the merchants; but the most precious part of the spoil is the beautiful bride, with forty damsels, who formed her bridal train.

The monastery was left desolate, with none but the holy anchorite to inhabit it. Khaled called upon the old man, but received no answer; he called again, but the only reply was, to invoke the vengeance of heaven upon his head for the Christian blood he had spilt. The fierce Saracen paused as he was driving off the spoil, and laying his hand upon the hilt of his scimetar, looked back grimly upon the hermit. "What we have done," said he, "is in obedience to the law of God, who commands us to slay all unbelievers; and had not the apostle of God commanded us to let such men as thee alone, thou shouldst have shared the fate of thy fellow-infidels!"

The old man saw his danger in time, and discreetly held his peace, and the sword of Islam remained within its scabbard.

The conquerors bore their booty and their captives back in triumph to Damascus. One-fifth of the spoil was set apart for the public treasury: the rest was distributed among the soldiery. Derar, as a trophy of his exploit, received the horse of the prefect of Tripoli, but he made it a present to his Amazonian sister Caulah. The saddle and trappings were studded with precious stones; these she picked out and distributed among her female companions.

Among the spoils was a cloth curiously wrought with a likeness of the blessed Saviour; which, from the exquisite workmanship or the sanctity of the portrait, was afterwards sold in Arabia Felix for ten times its weight in gold.

Abdallah, for his part of the spoil, asked for the daughter of the prefect, having been smitten with her charms. His demand was referred to the Caliph Omar and granted, and the captive beauty lived with him many years. Obeidah, in his letters to the Caliph, generously set forth the magnanimous conduct and distinguished prowess of Khaled on this occasion; and entreated Omar to write a letter to that general expressive of his sense of his recent services; as it might soothe the mortification he must experience from his late deposition. The Caliph, however, though he replied to every other part of the letter of Obeidah, took no notice, either by word or deed, of that relating to Khaled, from which it was evident that, in secret, he entertained no great regard for the unsparing sword of Islam.

CHAPTER XIII.

Moderate measures of Abu Obeidah.—Reproved by the Caliph for his slowness.

The alertness and hardihood of the Saracens in their rapid campaigns, have been attributed to their simple and abstemious habits. They knew nothing of the luxuries of the pampered Greeks, and were prohibited the use of wine. Their drink was water, and their food principally milk, rice, and the fruits of the earth, and their dress the coarse raiments of the desert. An army of such men was easily sustained; marched rapidly from place to place; and was fitted to cope with the vicissitudes of war. The interval of repose, however, in the luxurious city of Damascus, and the general abundance of the fertile regions of Syria began to have their effect upon the Moslem troops, and the good Abu Obeidah was especially scandalized at discovering that they were lapsing into the use of wine, so strongly forbidden by the prophet. He mentioned the prevalence of this grievous sin in his letter to the Caliph, who read it in the mosque in presence of his officers. "By Allah, exclaimed the abstemious Omar; "these fellows are only fit for poverty and hard fare; what is to be done with these wine-bibbers?"

"Let him who drinks wine," replied Ali, promptly, "receive twenty bastinadoes on the soles of his feet."

"Good, it shall be so," rejoined the Caliph: and he wrote to that effect to the commander-in-chief. On receiving the letter, Abu Obeidah forthwith summoned the offenders, and had the punishment publicly inflicted for the edification of his troops; he took the occasion to descant on the enormity of the offence, and to exhort such as had sinned in private to come forward like good Moslems, make public confession, and submit to the bastinado in token of repentance; whereupon many, who had indulged in secret potations, moved by his paternal exhortation, avowed their crime and their repentance, and were set at ease in their consciences by a sound bastinadoing and the forgiveness of the good Abu Obeidah.

That worthy commander now left a garrison of five hundred horse at Damascus, and issued forth with his host to prosecute the

subjugation of Syria.   He had a rich field of enterprise before him.
The country of Syria, from the amenity of its climate, tempered
by the vicinity of the sea and the mountains, from the fertility of
its soil, and the happy distribution of woods and streams, was peculiarly adapted for the vigorous support and prolific increase of
animal life; it accordingly teemed with population, and was
studded with ancient and embattled cities and fortresses.   Two of
the proudest and most splendid of these were Emessa (the modern
Hems), the capital of the plains; and Baalbec, the famous city of
the Sun, situated between the mountains of Lebanon.

These two cities, with others intermediate, were the objects of
Abu Obeidah's enterprise, and he sent Khaled in advance, with
Derar and Rafi Ibn Omeirah, at the head of a third of the army,
to scour the country about Emessa.   In his own slower march,
with the main body of the army, he approached the city of Jusheyah, but was met by the governor, who purchased a year's truce
with the payment of four hundred pieces of gold and fifty silken
robes; and the promise to surrender the city at the expiration of
a year, if in that interval Baalbec and Emessa should have been
taken.

When Abu Obeidah came before Emessa he found Khaled in
active operation.   The governor of the place had died on the day
on which the Moslem force appeared, and the city was not fully provisioned for a siege.   The inhabitants negotiated a truce for one
year by the payment of ten thousand pieces of gold and two hundred suits of silk, with the engagement to surrender at the end of
that term, provided he should have taken Aleppo, Alhâdir, and
Kennesrin, and defeated the army of the emperor.   Khaled would
have persevered in the siege, but Abu Obeidah thought it the
wisest policy to agree to these golden terms, by which he provided
himself with the sinews of war, and was enabled to proceed more
surely in his career.

The moment the treaty was concluded, the people of Emessa
threw open their gates; held a market or fair beneath the walls,
and began to drive a lucrative trade; for the Moslem camp was
full of booty, and these marauding warriors, flushed with sudden
wealth, squandered plunder of all kinds, and never regarded the
price of any thing that struck their fancy.   In the meantime predatory bands foraged the country both far and near, and came
driving in sheep and cattle, and horses and camels, laden with
household booty of all kinds; besides multitudes of captives.   The
piteous lamentations of these people, torn from their peaceful
homes and doomed to slavery, touched the heart of Abu Obeidah.
He told them that all who would embrace the Islam faith should
have their lives and property.   On such as chose to remain in infidelity, he imposed a ransom of five pieces of gold a head, besides
an annual tribute ; caused their names and places of abode to be
registered in a book, and then gave them back their property, their
wives, and children, on condition that they should act as guides
and interpreters to the Moslems in case of need.

The merciful policy of the good Abu Obeidah promised to promote the success of Islam, even more potently than the sword.

The Syrian Greeks came in, in great numbers, to have their names enregistered in the book of tributaries; and other cities capitulated for a year's truce on the terms granted to Emessa. Khaled, however, who was no friend to truces and negotiations, murmured at these peaceful measures, and offered to take these cities in less time than it required to treat with them; but Abu Obeidah was not to be swerved from the path of moderation; thus, in a little time the whole territories of Emessa, Alhâdir and Kennesrin were rendered sacred from maraud. The predatory warriors of the desert were somewhat impatient at being thus hemmed in by prohibited boundaries, and on one occasion had well nigh brought the truce to an abrupt termination. A party of Saracen troopers, in prowling along the confines of Kennesrin, came to where the Christians, to mark their boundary, had erected a statue of the emperor Heraclius, seated on his throne. The troopers, who had a Moslem hatred of images, regarded this with derision, and amused themselves with careering round and tilting at it, until one of them, either accidentally or in sport, struck out one of the eyes with his lance.

The Greeks were indignant at this outrage. Messengers were sent to Abu Obeidah, loudly complaining of it as an intentional breach of the truce, and a flagrant insult to the emperor. Abu Obeidah mildly assured them that it was his disposition most rigorously to observe the truce; that the injury to the statue must have been accidental, and that no indignity to the emperor could have been intended. His moderation only increased the arrogance of the ambassadors; their emperor had been insulted; it was for the Caliph to give redress according to the measure of the law: "an eye for an eye, a tooth for a tooth." "What!" cried some of the over-zealous Moslems; "do the infidels mean to claim an eye from the Caliph?" In their rage they would have slain the messengers on the spot; but the quiet Abu Obeidah stayed their wrath. "They speak but figuratively," said he; then taking the messengers aside, he shrewdly compromised the matter, and satisfied their wounded loyalty, by agreeing that they should set up a statue of the Caliph, with glass eyes, and strike out one of them in retaliation.

While Abu Obeidah was pursuing this moderate course, and subduing the country by clemency rather than by force of arms, missives came from the Caliph, who was astonished at receiving no tidings of further conquests, reproaching him with his slowness, and with preferring worldly gain to the pious exercise of the sword. The soldiers when they heard of the purport of this letter, took the reproaches to themselves, and wept with vexation. Abu Obeidah himself was stung to the quick, and repented him of the judicious truces he had made. In the excitement of the moment, he held a council of war, and it was determined to lose not a day, although the truces had but about a month to run. He accordingly left Khaled with a strong force in the vicinity of Emessa to await the expiration of the truce, while he marched with the main host, against the city of Baalbec.

CHAPTER XIV.

Siege and capture of Baalbec.

Baalbec, so called from Baal, the Syrian appellation of the·Sun, or Apollo, to which deity it was dedicated, was one of the proudest cities of ancient Syria. It was the metropolis of the great and fertile valley of Bekaa, lying between the mountains of Lebanon, and Anti Lebanon. During the Grecian domination it was called Heliopolis, which likewise means the City of the Sun. It was famous for its magnificent temple of Baal, which, tradition affirms, was built by Solomon the Wise, to please one of his wives, a native of Sidon and a worshipper of the·Sun. The immense blocks of stone of which it was constructed, were said to have been brought by the genii, over whom Solomon had control by virtue of his talismanic seal. Some of them remain to this day objects of admiration to the traveller, and perplexity to the modern engineer. [1]

On his march against Baalbec, Abu Obeidah intercepted a caravan of four hundred camels laden with silks and sugars, on the way to that city. With his usual clemency he allowed the captives to ransom themselves; some of whom carried to Baalbec the news of his approach, and of the capture of the caravan. Herbis, the governor, supposing the Saracens to be a mere marauding party, sallied forth with six thousand horse and a multitude of irregular foot, in hope to recover the spoils, but found to his cost that he had an army to contend with, and was driven back to the city with great loss, after receiving seven wounds.

Abu Obeidah set himself down before the city, and addressed a letter to the inhabitants, reminding them of the invincible arms of the faithful, and inviting them to profess Islamism, or pay tribute. This letter he gave in charge to a Syrian peasant, and with it a reward of twenty pieces of silver, "for Allah forbid," said the conscientious general, "that I should employ thee without pay. The labourer is worthy of his hire."

The messenger was drawn up by a cord to the battlements, and delivered the letter to the inhabitants, many of whom, on hearing the contents, were inclined to surrender. Herbis, the governor, however, who was still smarting with his wounds, tore the letter in pieces, and dismissed the messenger without deigning a reply.

Abu Obeidah now ordered his troops to the assault, but the garrison made brave defence, and did such execution with their engines from the walls, that the Saracens were repulsed with considerable loss. The weather was cold; so Abu Obeidah, who was ever mindful of the welfare of his men, sent a trumpeter round the camp·next morning, forbidding any man to take the field until he

---

[1] Among these huge blocks some measure fifty-eight, and one sixty-nine feet in length.

had made a comfortable meal. All were now busy cooking, when, in the midst of their preparations, the city gates were thrown open, and the Greeks came scouring upon them, making great slaughter. They were repulsed with some difficulty, but carried off prisoners and plunder.

Abu Obeidah now removed his camp out of reach of the engines, and where his cavalry would have more room. He threw out detachments also, to distract the attention of the enemy and oblige them to fight in several places. Saad Ibn Zeid, with five hundred horse and three hundred foot, was to show himself in the valley opposite the gate looking towards the mountains; while Derar, with three hundred horse and two hundred foot, was stationed in front of the gate on the side toward Damascus.

Herbis, the governor, seeing the Saracens move back their tents, supposed them to be intimidated by their late loss. "These Arabs," said he, "are half-naked vagabonds of the desert, who fight without object; we are locked up in steel, and fight for our wives and children, our property and our lives." He accordingly roused his troops to make another sally, and an obstinate battle ensued. One of the Moslem officers, Sohail Ibn Sabah, being disabled by a sabre cut in the right arm, alighted from his horse, and clambered a neighbouring hill which overlooked the field, the city and its vicinity. Here he sat watching the various fortunes of the field. The sally had been made through the gate before which Abu Obeidah was posted, who of course received the whole brunt of the attack. The battle was hot, and Sohail perceived from his hill that the Moslems in this quarter were hard pressed, and that the general was giving ground, and in imminent danger of being routed; while Derar and Saad remained inactive at their distant posts; no sally having been made from the gates before which they were stationed. Upon this Sohail gathered together some green branches, and set fire to them, so as to make a column of smoke; a customary signal by day among the Arabs, as fire was by night. Derar and Saad beheld the smoke and galloped with their troops in that direction. Their arrival changed the whole fortune of the field. Herbis, who had thought himself on the eve of victory, now found himself beset on each side and cut off from the city! Nothing but strict discipline and the impenetrable Grecian phalanx saved him. His men closed shield to shield, their lances in advance, and made a slow and defensive retreat, the Moslems wheeling around and charging incessantly upon them. Abu Obeidad, who knew nothing of the arrival of Derar and Saad, imagined the retreat of the Christians a mere feint, and called back his troops; Saad, however, who heard not the general's order, kept on in pursuit, until he drove the enemy to the top of a hill, where they ensconced themselves in an old deserted monastery.

When Abu Obeidah learnt the secret of this most timely aid, and that it was in consequence of a supposed signal from him, he acknowledged that the smoke was an apt thought, and saved his camp from being sacked; but he prohibited any man from repeating such an act without orders from the general.

In the meantime Herbis, the governor, finding the small number that invested the convent, sallied forth with his troops, in hopes of cutting his way to the city. Never did men fight more va- liantly, and they had already made great havoc, when the arrival of a fresh swarm of Moslems drove them back to their forlorn fortress, where they were so closely watched, that not a Grecian eye could peer from the old walls without being the aim of a Moslem arrow.

Abu Obeidah now invested the city more closely than ever, leaving Saad, with his forces, to keep the governor encaged in the monastery. The latter perceived it would be impossible to hold out longer in this shattered edifice, destitute of provisions. His proud spirit was completely broken, and, throwing off his silken robes, and clothing him in a worn woollen garb, as suited to his humble situation, he sought a conference with Saad to treat on terms of capitulation. The Moslem captain replied, that he could only treat for the party in the convent, whom he would re- ceive as brothers, if they would acknowledge God and the pro- phet, or would let them free on the pledge not to bear arms against the Moslems. He proffered to lead Herbis to the general, if he wished to treat for the city also; and added, that, should the ne- gotiation fail, he and his Greeks might return into their convent, and let God and the sword decide.

Herbis was accordingly led through the besieging camp into the presence of Abu Obeidah, and gnawed his lip when he saw the in- considerable number of the Moslem host. He offered, as a ransom for the city, one thousand ounces of gold, two thousand of silver, and one thousand silken robes; but Abu Obeidah demanded that he should double the amount, and add thereto one thousand sabres, and all the arms of the soldiers in the monastery; as well as engage in behalf of the city to pay an annual tribute; to engage to erect no more Christian churches, nor ever more act in hostility against the Moslem power.

These harsh terms being conceded, Herbis was permitted to en- ter the city alone, and submit them to the inhabitants, all his atten- dants being detained as hostages. The townsmen at first refused to capitulate, saying their city was the strongest in all Syria; but Herbis offered to pay down one-fourth of the ransom himself, and they at length complied. One point was conceded to the people of Baalbec to soothe their wounded pride. It was agreed that Rafi Ibn Abdallah, who was to remain with five hundred men, acting as lieutenant of Baalbec for Abu Obeidah, should encamp without the walls, and not enter the city. These matters being arranged, Abu Obeidah marched with his host on other enter- prises.

The Saracen troops, under Rafi Ibn Abdallah, soon ingratiated themselves with the people of Baalbec. They pillaged the surrounding country, and sold their booty for low prices to the townsfolk, who thus grew wealthy on the spoils of their own countrymen. Herbis, the governor, felt a desire to participate in these profits. He re- minded his fellow-citizens how much he had paid for their ransom, and what good terms he had effected for them; and then pro- posed that he should have one-tenth of what they gained in traffic

with the Moslems, to reimburse him.' They consented, though with
extreme reluctance. In a few days he found the gain so sweet
that he thirsted for more; he therefore told them that his reim-
bursement would be tedious at this rate, and proposed to receive
one-fourth. The people, enraged at his cupidity, rushed on him
with furious outcries, and killed him on the spot. The noise of the
tumult reached the camp of Rafi Ibn Abdallah, and a deputation of
the inhabitants coming forth, entreated him to enter the city and
govern it himself. He scrupled to depart from the terms of the
treaty until he had written to Abu Obeidah; but on receiving permission from the general, he entered and took command. Thus
did the famous Baalbec, the ancient Heliopolis, or City of the Sun,
fall under the Saracen sway on the 20th of January, A. D. 636,
being the fifteenth year of the Hegira.

CHAPTER XV.

Siege of Emessa.—Stratagems of the Moslems.—Fanatic devotion of Ikremah.—Surrender of the city.

The year's truce with the city of Emessa having now expired,
Abu Obeidah appeared before that place, and summoned it in the
following form:
"In the name of the most merciful God. Abu Obeidah Ibn
Aljerah, general of the armies of the Commander of the Faithful,
Omar al Khattâb, to the people of Emessa. Let not the loftiness
of your walls, the strength of your bulwarks, nor the robustness of
your bodies, lead you into errour. Allah hath conquered stronger
places through the means of his servants. Your city would be of
no more consideration against us than a kettle of pottage set in the
midst of our camp.
"I invite you to embrace our holy faith, and the law revealed to
our prophet Mahomet; and we will send pious men to instruct you,
and you shall participate in all our fortunes.
"If you refuse, you shall still be left in possession of all your
property on the payment of annual tribute. If you reject both
conditions, come forth from behind your stone walls, and let
Allah, the supreme judge, decide between us."
This summons was treated with scorn; and the garrison made a
old s ally, and handled their besiegers so roughly, that they were
glad when night put an end to the conflict. In the evening a crafty
old Arab sought the tent of Abu Obeidah; he represented the strength
of the place, the intrepidity of the soldiers, and the ample stock of
provisions, which would enable it to stand a weary siege. He
suggested a stratagem, however, by which it might be reduced:
and Abu Obeidah adopted his counsel. Sending a messenger into
the city, he offered to the inhabitants to strike his tents, and lead
his troops to the attack of other places, provided they would
furnish him provisions for five days' march. His offer was promptly
accepted, and the provisions were furnished. Abu Obeidah now

pretended that, as his march would be long, a greater supply would be necessary: he continued to buy, therefore, as long as the Christians had provisions to sell, and in this manner exhausted their magazines; and as the scouts from other cities beheld the people of Emessa throw open their gates and bring forth provisions, it became rumoured throughout the country that the city had surrendered.

Abu Obeidah, according to promise, led his host against other places. The first was Arrestan, a fortified city, well watered, provisioned, and garrisoned. His summons being repeated, and rejected, he requested the governor of the place to let him leave there twenty chests of cumbrous articles, which impeded him in his movements. The request was granted with great pleasure at getting clear so readily of such marauders. The twenty chests, secured with padlocks, were taken into the citadel, but every chest had a sliding bottom, and contained an armed man. Among the picked warriors thus concealed, were Derar, Abda'lrahman, and Abdallah Ibn Jaafar; while Khaled, with a number of troops, was placed in ambush to co-operate with those in the chests.

The Moslem host departed. The Christians went to church to return thanks for their deliverance, and the sounds of their hymns of triumph reached the ears of Derar and his comrades. Upon this they issued forth from their chests, seized the wife of the governor, and obtained from her the keys of the gates. Abdallah, with fourteen men, hastened to the church and closed the doors upon the congregation; while Derar, with four companions, threw open the gates with the cry of Allah Achbar; upon which Khaled and his forces rushed from their ambuscade, and the city was taken almost without bloodshed.

The city of Shaizar was next assailed, and capitulated on favourable terms; and now Abu Obeidah returned before Emessa, and once more summoned it to surrender. The governor remonstrated loudly, reminding the Moslem general of his treaty, by which he engaged to depart from Emessa, and carry the war against other places. " I engaged to depart," replied Abu Obeidah, " but I did not engage not to return. I have carried the war against other places, and have subdued Arrestan and Shaizar."

The people of Emessa now perceived how they had been circumvented. Their magazines had been drained of provisions, and they had not wherewithal to maintain them against a siege. The governor, however, encouraged them to try the chance of a battle as before. They prepared for the fight by prayers in the churches; and the governor took the sacrament in the church of St. George: but he sought to enhearten himself by grosser means, for we are told he ate the whole of a roasted kid for his supper, and caroused on wine until the crowing of the cock. In the morning, early, he arrayed himself in rich apparel, and sallied forth at the head of five thousand horsemen, all men of strength and courage, and well armed. They charged the besiegers so bravely, and their archers so galled them from the walls, that the Moslem force gave way.

Khaled now threw himself in front of the battle, and enacted wondrous feats to rally his soldiers and restore the fight. In an encounter, hand to hand, with a Greek horseman, his scimetar broke, and he was weaponless, but closing with his adversary, he clasped him in his arms, crushed his ribs, and drawing him from his saddle, threw him dead to the earth. The imminent peril of the fight roused a frantic valour in the Moslems. In the heat of enthusiasm Ikremah, a youthful cousin of Khaled, galloped about the field, fighting with reckless fury, and raving about the joys of paradise promised to all true believers who fell in the battles of the faith. "I see," cried he, "the black-eyed Houris of Paradise. One of them, if seen on earth, would make mankind die of love. They are smiling on us. One of them waves a handkerchief of green silk, and holds a cup of precious stones. She beckons me; come hither quickly, she cries, my well-beloved!" In this way he went, shouting Al Jennah! Al Jennah! Paradise! Paradise! charging into the thickest of the Christians, and making fearful havoc, until he reached the place where the governor was fighting, who sent a javelin through his heart, and despatched him in quest of his vaunted Elysium.

Night alone parted the hosts, and the Moslems retired exhausted to their tents, glad to repose from so rude a fight. Even Khaled counselled Abu Obeidah, to have recourse to stratagem, and make a pretended fight the next morning; to draw the Greeks, confident through this day's success, into disorder, for while collected, their phalanx presented an impenetrable wall to the Moslem horsemen.

Accordingly, at the dawning of the day, the Moslems retreated; at first with a show of order; then with a feigned confusion, for it was an Arab stratagem of war to scatter and rally again in the twinkling of an eye. The Christians, thinking their flight unfeigned, broke up their steady phalanx, some making headlong pursuit, while others dispersed to plunder the Moslem camp.

Suddenly the Moslems faced about, surrounded the confused mass of Christians, and fell upon it, as the Arabian-historian says, "like eagles upon a carcass." Khaled and Derar and other chiefs spirited them on with shouts of Allah Achbar, and a terrible rout and slaughter ensued. The number of Christian corpses on that field exceeded sixteen hundred. The governor was recognized among the slain by his enormous bulk, his bloated face, and his costly apparel, fragrant with perfumes.

The city of Emessa surrendered as a sequel to that fight, but the Moslems could neither stay to take possession, nor afford to leave a garrison. Tidings had reached them of the approach of an immense army, composed of the heavily armed Grecian soldiery and the light troops of the desert, that threatened completely to overwhelm them. Various and contradictory were the counsels in this moment of agitation and alarm. Some advised that they should hasten back to their native deserts, where they would be reinforced by their friends, and where the hostile army could not find sustenance; but Abu Obeidah objected that such a retreat would be attributed to cowardice. Others cast a wistful eye upon the stately dwellings, the delightful gardens, the fertile fields, and green pastures, which they had just won by the sword, and chose rather to stay and fight for this land of pleasure and abundance, than return to famine and the desert. Khaled decided the question. It would not do to linger there, he said; Constantine, the emperor's son, being not far off, at Cæsarea, with forty thousand men; he advised, therefore, that they should march to Yermouk, on the borders of Palestine and Arabia, where they would be within reach of assistance from the Caliph, and might await, with confidence, the attack of the Imperial army. The advice of Khaled was adopted.

CHAPTER XVI.

Advance of a powerful Imperial army.—Skirmishes of Khaled.—Capture of Derar.—
Interview of Khaled and Manuel.

The rapid conquests of the Saracens, had alarmed the emperor Heraclius for the safety of his rich province of Syria. Troops had been levied both in Europe and Asia, and transported by sea and land to various parts of the invaded country. The main body, consisting of eighty thousand men, advanced to seek the Moslem host, under the command of a distinguished general, called Mahan, by the Arabian writers, and Manuel by the Greeks. On its way, the Imperial army was joined by Jabalah Ibn al Aynham, chief or king of the Christian tribe of Gassan. This Jabalah had professed the Mahometan faith, but had apostatized in consequence of the following circumstance. He had accompanied the Caliph Omar on a pilgrimage to Mecca, and was performing the religious ceremony of the Towah, or sacred walk seven times round the Caaba, when an Arab of the tribe of Fezarah accidentally trod on the skirt of his Ihram or pilgrim scarf, so as to draw it from his shoulders. Turning fiercely upon the Arab, " Woe be unto thee," cried he, " for uncovering my back in the sacred house of God." The pilgrim protested it was an accident, but Jabalah buffeted him in the face, bruising him sorely, and beating out four of his teeth. The pilgrim complained to Omar, but Jabalah justified himself, stating the indignity he had suffered. " Had it not been for my reverence for the Caaba, and for the prohibition to shed blood within the sacred city, I would have slain the offender on the spot." " Thou hast confessed thy fault," said Omar, " and unless forgiven by thy adversary, must submit to the law of retaliation, ' an eye for an eye, and a tooth for a tooth.'" " I am a king," replied Jabalah, proudly, " and he is but a peasant." " Ye are both Moslems," rejoined Omar, " and in the sight of Allah, who is no respecter of persons, ye are equal." The utmost that Jabalah could obtain from the rigid justice of Omar was, that the execution of the sentence might be postponed until the next day. In the night he made his escape and fled to Constantinople, were be abjured Islamism, resumed the Christian faith, and went over to the service of the emperor Heraclius. He had now brought sixty thousand Arabs to the aid of Manuel. Such was the powerful host, the approach of which had compelled the Moslems to abandon Emessa on the very moment of surrender. They had marched to Yermouk, a place noted for its pleasant groves, and the sweet salubrity of its air, and lay encamped on the banks of a little stream of the same name, heretofore obscure, but now destined to become famous by a battle decisive of the fate of Syria.

Manuel advanced slowly and deliberately with his heavily armed Grecian soldiery; but he sent Jabalah in the advance, to scour the country with his light Arab troops, as best fitted to cope with the skirmishing warriors of the desert; thus, as he said, " using diamond to cut diamond." The course of these combined armies was marked with waste, rapine, and outrage, and they inflicted all kinds of injuries and indignities on those Christian places which had made treaties with or surrendered to the Moslems.

While Manuel with his main army was yet at a distance, he sent proposals of peace to Abu Obeidah, according to the commands of the emperor. His proposals were rejected; but Obeidah sent several messengers to Jabalah, reproaching him with his apostasy, and his warfare against his countrymen, and endeavouring to persuade him to remain neutral in the impending battle. Jabalah replied, however, that his faith was committed to the emperor, and he was resolved to fight in his cause.

Upon this Khaled came forward, and offered to take this apostate in his own hands. " He is far in the advance of the main army," said he, " let me have a small body of picked men chosen by myself, and I will fall upon him and his infidel Arabs before Manuel can come up to their assistance."

His proposal was condemned by many as rash and extravagant. " By no means," cried Khaled, with zealous zeal; " this infidel force is the army of the devil, and can do nothing against the army of Allah, who will assist us with his angels."

So pious an argument was unanswerable. Khaled was permitted to choose his men, all well-seasoned warriors whose valour he had proved. With them he fell upon Jabalah, who was totally unprepared for so hair-brained an assault, threw his host into complete confusion, and obliged him, after much slaughter to retreat upon the main body. The triumph of Khaled, however, was damped by the loss of several valiant officers, among whom were Yezed, Rafi, and Derar, who were borne off captives by the retreating Christians.

In the meantime a special messenger, named Abdallah Ibn Kort, arrived at Medina, bringing letters to the Caliph from Abu Obeidah, describing the perilous situation of the Moslem army, and entreating reinforcements. The Caliph ascended the pulpit of Mahomet, and preached up the glory of fighting the good fight of faith for God and the prophet. He then gave Abdallah an epistle for Abu Obeidah, filled with edifying texts from the Koran, and ending with an assurance that he would pray for him, and would, moreover, send him a speedy reinforcement. This done, he pronounced a blessing on Abdallah, and bade him depart with all speed.

Abdallah was well advanced on his return, when he called to

mind that he had omitted to visit the tomb of the prophet. Shocked at his forgetfulness, he retraced his steps, and sought the dwelling of Ayesha, within which the prophet lay interred. He found the beautiful widow reclining beside the tomb, and listening to Ali and Abbas, who were reading the Koran, while Hassan and Hosein, the two sons of Ali and grandsons of the prophet, were sitting on their knees.

Having paid due honours to the prophet's tomb, the considerate messenger expressed his fears that this pious visit might prevent his reaching the army before the expected battle; whereupon the holy party lifted up their hands to heaven, and Ali put up a prayer for his speedy journey. Thus inspirited, he set out anew, and travelled with such unusual and incredible speed, that the army looked upon it as miraculous, and attributed it to the blessing of Omar and the prayer of Ali.

The promised reinforcement was soon on foot. It consisted of eight thousand men under the command of Seid Ibn Amir; to whom the Caliph gave a red silk banner, and a word of advice at parting; cautioning him to govern himself as well as his soldiers, and not to let his appetites get the better of his self-command.

Seid, with Moslem frankness, counselled him, in return, to fear God and not man; to love all Moslems equally with his own kindred; to cherish those at a distance equally with those at hand; finally to command nothing but what was right and to forbid nothing but what was wrong. The Caliph listened attentively, his forehead resting on his staff and his eyes cast upon the ground. When Seid had finished, he raised his head and the tears ran down his cheek. " Alas !" said he, who can do all this without the aid of God!"

Seid Ibn Amir led his force by the shortest route across the deserts, and hurrying forward with more rapidity than heed, lost his way. While he halted one night, in the vicinity of some springs, to ascertain his route, he was apprised by his scouts, that the prefect of Ammon, with five thousand men, was near at hand. He fell upon him instantly, and cut the infantry to pieces. The prefect fled with his cavalry, but encountered a foraging party from the Moslem camp, the leader of which, Zobeir, thrust a lance through his body, and between the two parties not a man of his troop escaped. The Moslems then placed the heads of the Christians on their lances, and arrived with their ghastly trophies at the camp; to the great encouragement of Abu Obeidah and his host.

The imperial army had now drawn near, and Manuel, the general, attempted again to enter into negotiations. Khaled offered to go and confer with him; but his real object was to attempt the release of his friends and brethren in arms, Abu Sofian, Derar, Rafi, and the two other officers captured in the late skirmish with the apostate Jabalah.

When Khaled reached the outpost of the Christian army, he was required to leave his escort of one hundred chosen wariors, and proceed alone to the presence of the general; but he refused. He equally refused a demand that he and his men should dismount and deliver up their scimetars. After some parley, he was permitted to enter into the presence of the general in his own way.

Manuel was seated in state on a kind of throne, surrounded by his officers, all splendidly arrayed, while Khaled entered with his hundred war-worn veterans, clad in the simplest guise. Chairs were set out for him and his principal companions, but they pushed them aside and seated themselves cross-legged on the ground, after the Arabic manner. When Manuel demanded the reason, Khaled replied by quoting a verse from the twentieth chapter of the Koran. "Of earth ye are created, from earth ye came, and unto earth ye must return." "God made the earth," added he, "and what God has made for men to sit upon, is more precious than your silken tapestries.'"

The conference was begun by Manuel, who expostulated on the injustice of the Moslems in making an unprovoked inroad into the territories of their neighbours, molesting them in their religious worship, robbing them of their wives and property, and seizing on their persons as slaves. Khaled retorted, that it was all owing to their own obstinacy, in refusing to acknowledge that there was but one God, without relation or associate, and that Mahomet was his prophet. Their discussion grew violent, and Khaled, in his heat, told Manuel that he should one day see him dragged into the presence of Omar with a halter round his neck, there to have his head struck off as an example to all infidels and for the edification of true believers.

Manuel replied in wrath, that Khaled was protected by his character of ambassador; but that he would punish his insolence by causing the five Moslem captives, his friends, to be instantly beheaded. Khaled defied him to execute his threat, swearing by Allah, by his prophet, and by the holy Caaba, that if a hair of their heads were injured, he would slay Manuel with his own hand on the spot, and that each of his Moslems present, should slay his man. So saying, he rose and drew his scimetar, as did likewise his companions.

The imperial general was struck with admiration at his intrepidity. He replied calmly, that what he had said was a mere threat, which his humanity and his respect for the mission of Khaled would not permit him to fulfil. The Saracens were pacified and sheathed their swords, and the conference went on calmly.

In the end, Manuel gave up the five prisoners to Khaled as a token of his esteem; and in return Khaled presented him with a beautiful scarlet pavilion, which he had brought with him, and pitched in the Christian camp, and for which Manuel had expressed a desire. Thus ended this conference, and both parties retired from it with soldier-like regard for each other.

CHAPTER XVII.

The Battle of Yermouk.

The great battle was now at hand that was to determine the fate of Syria, for the emperor had staked the fortunes of this favourite province on a single, but gigantic blow. Abu Obeidah, conscious of the momentous nature of the conflict, and diffident of his abilities in the field, gave a proof of his modesty and magnanimity, by restoring to Khaled the command of the whole army. For himself, he took his station with the women in the rear, that he might rally the Moslems should any of them be inclined to fly the field. Here he erected his standard, a yellow flag, given him by Abu Beker, being the same which Mahomet had displayed in the battle of Khaïbar.

Before the action commenced Khaled rode among his troops, making a short but emphatic speech. "Paradise," cried he, "is before you; the devil and hell behind. Fight bravely, and you will secure the one; fly, and you will fall into the other."

The armies closed, but the numbers of the Christians and the superiority of Greek and Roman discipline bore down the right wing of the Moslems. Those, however, who turned their backs and attempted to fly, were assailed with reproaches and blows by the women, so that they found it easier to face the enemy than such a storm. Even Abu Sofian himself received a blow over the face with a tent-pole from one of those viragos, as he retreated before the enemy.

Thrice were the Moslems beaten back by the steady bearing of the Grecian phalanx, and thrice were they checked and driven back to battle by the women. Night at length brought a cessation of the bloody conflict; when Abu Obeidah went round among the wounded, ministering to them with his own hands, while the women bound up their wounds with tender care.

The battle was renewed on the following morning, and again the Moslems were sorely pressed. The Christian archers made fearful havoc, and such was their dexterity, that, among the great number of Moslems who suffered from their arrows on that day, seven hundred lost one or both eyes. Hence it was commemorated as "the Day of the Blinding;" and those who had received such wounds gloried in them, in after years, as so many trophies of their having struggled for the faith in that day of hard fighting. There were several single combats of note; among others, Serjabil was engaged hand to hand with a stout Christian; but Serjabil, having signalized his piety by excessive watching and fasting, was so reduced in flesh and strength, that he was no match for his adversary, and would infallibly have been overpowered, had not Derar come behind the Christian, and stabbed him to the heart. Both warriors claimed the spoil, but it was adjudged to him who slew the enemy. In the course of this arduous day, the Moslems more than once wavered, but were rallied back by the valour of the women. Caulah, the heroic sister of Derar, mingling in the fight, was wounded and struck down; but Offeirah, her female friend, smote off the head of her opponent, and rescued her. The battle lasted as long as there was light enough to distinguish friend from foe; but the night was welcome to the Moslems, who needed all their enthusiasm and reliance on the promises of the prophet to sustain them, so hard was the struggle and so overwhelming the numbers of the enemy. On this night, the good Abu Obeidah repeated at once the prayers belonging to two separate hours, that his weary soldiers might enjoy uninterruted sleep.

For several successive days this desperate battle, on which hung the fate of Syria, was renewed with various fortunes. In the end the fanatic valour of the Moslems prevailed; the Christian host was completely routed and fled in all directions. Many were overtaken and slain in the difficult passes of the mountains; others perished in a deep part of the river to which they were decoyed by one of their own people, in revenge for an injury. Manuel, the imperial general, fell by the hand of a Moslem named Noman Ibn Alkamah.

Abu Obeidah went over the battle-field in person, seeing that the wounded Moslems were well taken care of, and the slain decently interred. He was perplexed for a time on finding some heads without bodies, to know whether they were Moslems or infidels, but finally prayed over them at a venture and had them buried like the rest.

In dividing the spoils; Abu Obeidah, after setting aside one-fifth for the Caliph and the public treasury, allotted to each foot soldier one portion and to each horseman three; two for himself and one for his steed; but for each horse of the pure Arabian breed, he allowed a double portion. This last allotment met with opposition, but was subsequently confirmed by the Caliph, on account of the superior value of true Arabian horses.

Such was the great battle fought on the banks of the Yermouk, near the city of that name, in the month of November, A. D. 636, and in the 15th year of the Hegira.

CHAPTER XVIII.

Siege and capture of Jerusalem.

The Moslem invaders reposed for a month at Damascus from the toil of conquest, during which time Abu Obeidah sent to the Caliph to know whether he should undertake the siege of Cæsarea, or Jerusalem. Ali was with Omar at the time, and advised the instant siege of the latter; for such, he said, had been the intention of the prophet. The enterprise against Jerusalem was as a holy war to the Moslems, for they reverenced it as an ancient seat of prophecy and revelation, connected with the histories of Moses, Jesus, and Mahomet, and sanctified by containing the tombs of several of the ancient prophets. The Caliph adopted the advice of Ali, and ordered Abu Obeidah to lead his army into Palestine, and lay siege to Jerusalem.

On receiving these orders, Abu Obeidah sent forward Yezed Abu Sofian, with five thousand men, to commence the siege, and for five successive days detached after him considerable reinforcements. The people of Jerusalem saw the approach of these portentous invaders, who were spreading such consternation throughout the East, but they made no sally to oppose them, nor sent out any one to parley, but planted engines on their walls, and prepared for vigorous defence. Yezed approached the city and summoned it by sound of trumpet, propounding the customary terms, profession of the faith or tribute : both were rejected with disdain. The Moslems would have made instant assault, but Yezed had no such instructions : he encamped, therefore, and waited until orders arrived from Abu Obeidah to attack the city, when he made the necessary preparations.

At cock-crow in the morning the Moslem host was marshalled, the leaders repeated the matin prayer each at the head of his battalion, and all, as if by one consent, with a loud voice gave the verse from the Koran :[1] "Enter ye, oh people ! into the holy land which Allah hath destined for you."

For ten days they made repeated but unavailing attacks; on the eleventh day Abu Obeidah brought the whole army to their aid. He immediately sent a written summons requiring the inhabitants to believe in the unity of God, the divine mission of Mahomet, the resurrection and final judgment : or else to acknowledge allegiance, and pay tribute to the Caliph : " otherwise," concluded the letter, " I will bring men against you, who love death better than you love wine or swine's flesh; nor will I leave you, God willing, until I have destroyed your fighting men, and made slaves of your children."

The summons was addressed to the magistrates and principal inhabitants of Ælia, for so Jerusalem was named after the emperor Ælius Adrian, when he rebuilt that city.

Sophronius, the Christian patriarch, or bishop of Jerusalem, replied that this was the holy city, and the holy land, and that whoever entered either, for a hostile purpose, was an offender in the eyes of God. He felt some confidence in setting the invaders at defiance, for the walls and towers of the city had been diligently strengthened, and the garrison had been reinforced by fugitives from Yermouk, and from various parts of Syria. The city, too, was strong in its situation, being surrounded by deep ravines and a broken country; and above all there was a pious incentive to courage and perseverance in defending the sepulchre of Christ.

Four wintry months elapsed ; every day there were sharp skirmishings; the besiegers were assailed by sallying parties, annoyed

---

[1] These words are from the fifth chapter of the Koran, where Mahomet puts them into the mouth of Moses, as addressed to the children of Israel.

by the engines on the walls, and harassed by the inclement weather; still they carried on the siege with undiminished spirit. At length the Patriarch Sempronius held a parley from the walls with Abu Obeidah. "Do you not know," said he, "that this city is holy; and that whoever offers violence to it, draws upon his head the vengeance of heaven?"

"We know it," replied Abu Obeidah, "to be the house of the prophets, where their bodies lie interred; we know it to be the place whence our prophet Mahomet made his nocturnal ascent to heaven; and we know that we are more worthy of possessing it than you are, nor will we raise the siege until Allah has delivered it into our hands, as he has done many other places."

Seeing there was no further hope, the patriarch consented to give up the city, on condition that the Caliph would come in person to take possession and sign the articles of surrender.

When this unusual stipulation was made known to the Caliph, he held a council with his friends. Othman despised the people of Jerusalem, and was for refusing their terms, but Ali represented the sanctity and importance of the place in the eyes of the Christians, which might prompt them to reinforce it, and to make a desperate defence if treated with indignity. Besides, he added, the presence of the Caliph would cheer and inspirit the army in their long absence, and after the hardships of a wintry campaign.

The words of Ali had their weight with the Caliph: though certain Arabian writers' pretend that he was chiefly moved by a tradition handed down in Jerusalem from days of yore, which said, that a man of his name, religion, and personal appearance, should conquer the holy city. Whatever may have been his inducements, the Caliph resolved to receive, in person, the surrender of Jerusalem. He accordingly appointed Ali to officiate in his place during his absence from Medina; then, having prayed at the mosque, and paid a pious visit to the tomb of the prophet, he set out on his journey.

The progress of this formidable potentate, who already held the destinies of empires in his grasp, and had the plunder of the Orient at his command, is characteristic of the primitive days of Mahometanism, and reveals, in some measure, the secret of its success. He travelled on a red or sorrel camel, across which was slung an alforja, or wallet, with a huge sack or pocket at each end, something like the modern saddle-bags. One pocket contained dates and dried fruits, the other a provision called sawik, which was nothing more than barley, rice, or wheat, parched or sodden. Before him hung a leathern bottle, or sack, for water, and behind him a wooden platter. His companions, without distinction of rank, ate with him out of the same dish, using their fingers according to Oriental usage. He slept at night on a mat spread out under a tree, or under a common Bedouin tent of hair-cloth, and never resumed his march until he had offered up the morning prayer.

As he journeyed through Arabia in this simple way, he listened to the complaints of the people, redressed their grievances, and administered justice with sound judgment and a rigid hand. Information was brought to him of an Arab who was married to two sisters, a practice not unusual among idolaters, but the man was now a Mahometan.   Omar cited the culprit and his two wives into his presence, and taxed him roundly with his offence; but he declared his ignorance that it was contrary to the law of the prophet.

"Thou liest!" said Omar, "thou shalt part with one of them instantly, or lose thy head."

" Evil was the day that I embraced such a religion," muttered the culprit.   "Of what advantage has it been to me?"

"Come nearer to me," said Omar : and on his approaching, the Caliph bestowed two wholeshome blows on his head with his walking-staff.

"Enemy of God and of thyself," cried he, "let these blows reform thy manners, and teach thee to speak with more reverence of a religion ordained by Allah, and acknowledged by the best of his creatures."

He then ordered the offender to choose between his wives, and finding him at a loss which to prefer, the matter was determined by lot, and he was dismissed by the Caliph with this parting admonition : "Whoever professes Islam, and afterwards renounces it, is punishable with death; therefore take heed to your faith.   And as to your wife's sister, whom you have put away, if ever I hear that you have meddled with her, you shall be stoned."

At another place he beheld a number of men exposed to the burning heat of the sun by their Moslem conquerors, as a punishment for failing to pay their tribute.   Finding, on inquiry, that they were entirely destitute of means, he ordered them to be released ; and turning reproachfully to their oppressors, "Compel no men," said he, " to more than they can bear; for I heard the apostle of God say, he who afflicts his fellowman in this world, will be punished with the fire of Jehennam."

While yet within a day's journey of Jerusalem, Abu Obeidah came to meet him and conduct him to the camp. - The Caliph proceeded with due deliberation, never forgetting his duties as a priest and teacher of Islam.   In the morning he said the usual prayers, and preached a sermon, in which he spoke of the security of those whom God should lead in the right way; but added, that there was no help for such as God should lead into errour.

A gray-headed Christian priest, who sat before him, could not resist the opportunity to criticise the language of the Caliph preacher. " God leads no man into errour," said he aloud.

Omar deigned no direct reply, but, turning to those around, "Strike off that old man's head," said he, " if he repeats his words."

The old man was discreet, and held his peace.   There was no arguing against the sword of Islam.

On his way to the camp Omar beheld a number of Arabs, who had thrown by the simple garb of their country, and arrayed themselves in the silken spoils of Syria.   He saw the danger of this luxury and effeminacy, and ordered that they should be dragged with their faces in the dirt, and their silken garments torn from their backs.

When he came in sight of Jerusalem he lifted up his voice and exclaimed, "Allah Achbar! God is mighty! God grant us an easy conquest!" Then commanding his tent to be pitched, he dismounted from his camel and sat down within it on the ground. The Christians thronged to see the sovereign of this new and irresistible people, who were overrunning and subduing the earth. The Moslems, fearful of an attempt at assassination, would have kept them at a distance, but Omar rebuked their fears. "Nothing will befall us but what God hath decreed. Let the faithful trust in him."

The arrival of the Caliph was followed by immediate capitulation. When the deputies from Jerusalem were admitted to a parley, they were astonished to find this dreaded potentate a bald-headed man, simply clad, and seated on the ground in a tent of hair-cloth.

The articles of surrender were drawn up in writing by Omar, and served afterwards as a model for the Moslem leaders in other conquests. The Christians were to build no new churches in the surrendered territory. The church doors were to be set open to travellers, and free egress permitted to Mahometans by day and night. The bells should only toll, and not ring, and no crosses should be erected on the churches, nor shown publicly in the streets. The Christians should not teach the Koran to their children; nor speak openly of their religion; nor attempt to make proselytes; nor hinder their kinsfolk from embracing Islam. They should not assume the Moslem dress, either caps, slippers, or turbans, nor part their hair like Moslems, but should always be distinguished by girdles. They should not use the Arabian language in inscriptions on their signets, nor salute after the Moslem manner, nor be called by Moslem surnames. They should rise on the entrance of a Moslem, and remain standing until he should be seated. They should entertain every Moslem traveller three days gratis. They should sell no wine, bear no arms, and use no saddle in riding; neither should they have any domestic who had been in Moslem service.

Such were the degrading conditions imposed upon the proud city of Jerusalem, once the glory and terror of the East, by the leader of a host of wandering Arabs. They were the conditions generally imposed by the Moslems in their fanatical career of conquest. Utter scorn and abhorrence of their religious adversaries formed one of the main pillars of their faith.

The Christians having agreed to surrender on these terms, the Caliph gave them under his own hand, an assurance of protection in their lives and fortunes, the use of their churches, and the exercise of their religion.

Omar entered the once splendid city of Solomon on foot, in his simple Arab garb, with his walking-staff in his hand, and accompanied by the venerable Sophronius, with whom he talked familiarly, inquiring about the antiquities and public edifices. The worthy patriarch treated the conqueror with all outward deference, but, if we may trust the words of a Christian historian, he loathed the dirty Arab in his heart, and was particulary disgusted with his garb of coarse woollen, patched with sheepskin. His disgust was almost irrepressible when they entered the church of the Resurrection, and Sophronius beheld the Caliph in his filthy attire, seated in the midst of the sacred edifice. "This, of a truth," exclaimed he, " is the abomination of desolation predicted by Daniel the prophet, standing in the holy place."

It is added that, to pacify the cleanly scruples of the patriarch, Omar consented to put on clean raiment which he offered him, until his own garments were washed.

An instance of the strict good faith of Omar is related as occurring on this visit to the Christian temples. While he was standing with the patriarch in the church of the Resurrection, one of the stated hours for Moslem worship arrived, and he demanded where he might pray. "Where you now are," replied the patriarch. Omar, however, refused, and went forth. The patriarch conducted him to the church of Constantine, and spread a mat for him to pray there; but again he refused. On going forth, he knelt, and prayed on the flight of steps leading down from the east gate of the church. This done, he turned to the patriarch, and gave him a generous reason for his conduct. "Had I prayed in either of the churches," said he, " the Moslems would have taken possession of it, and consecrated it as a mosque."

So scrupulous was he in observing his capitulations respecting the churches, that he gave the patriarch a writing, forbidding the Moslems to pray upon the steps where he had prayed, except one person at a time. The zeal of the faithful, however, outstripped their respect for his commands, and one-half of the steps and porch was afterwards included in a mosque built over the spot which he had accidentally sanctified.

The Caliph next sought the place where the temple of Solomon had stood, where he founded a mosque; which, in after times, being enlarged and enriched by succeeding Caliphs, became one of the noblest edifices of Islam worship, and second only to the magnificent mosque of Cordova.

The surrender of Jerusalem took place in the seventeeth year of the Hegira, and the six hundred and thirty-seventh year of the Christian era.

CHAPTER XIX.

Progress of the Moslem arms in Syria.—Siege of Aleppo.—Obstinate defence by Youkenna.—Exploit of Damas.—Capture of the castle.—Conversion of Youkenna.

The Caliph Omar remained ten days in Jerusalem, regulating the great scheme of Islam conquest. To complete the subjugation of Syria, he divided it into two parts. Southern Syria, consisting of Palestine and the maritime towns, he gave in charge to Yezed Ibn Abu Sofian, with a considerable portion of the army to enable him to master it; while Abu Obeidah, with a larger force, had orders promptly to reduce all Northern Syria, comprising the country lying between Hauran and Aleppo. At the same time, Amru Ibn al Aass, with a body of Moslem troops, was ordered to invade Egypt, which venerable and once mighty empire was then in a state of melancholy decline. Such were the great plans of Islam conquest in these regions; while at the same time, Saad Ibn Abi Wakkâs, another of Omar's generals, was pursuing a career of victories in the Persian territories.

The return of Omar to Medina was hailed with joy by the inhabitants, for they had regarded with great anxiety and apprehension his visit to Jerusalem. They knew the salubrity of the climate, the fertility of the country, and the sacred character of the city; containing the tombs of the prophets, and being the place, according to Moslem belief, where all mankind were to be assembled in the day of the resurrection. They had feared, therefore, that he would be tempted to fix his residence, for the rest of his days, in that consecrated city. Great was their joy, therefore, when they saw their Caliph re-enter their gates in his primitive simplicity, clad in his coarse Arab garb, and seated on his camel with his wallets of dried fruits and sodden corn; his leathern bottle and his wooden platter.

Abu Obeidah departed from Jerusalem shortly after the Caliph, and marched with his army to the north, receiving in the course of his process through Syria, the submission of the cities of Kennesrin and Alhâdir, the inhabitants of which ransomed themselves and their possessions, for five thousand ounces of gold, the like quantity of silver, two thousand suits of silken raiment, and as much figs and aloes as would load five hundred mules; he then proceeded towards the city of Aleppo, which the Caliph had ordered him to besiege. The inhabitants of this place were much given to commerce, and had amassed great wealth; they trembled, therefore, at the approach of these plundering sons of the desert, who had laid so many cities under contribution.

The city of Aleppo was walled and fortified; but it depended chiefly for defence upon its citadel, which stood without the walls and apart from the city, on an artificial hill or mound, shaped like a truncated cone or sugar-loaf, and faced with stone. The citadel was of great size, and commanded all the adjacent country; it was encompassed by a deep moat, which could be filled from springs of water, and was considered the strongest castle in all Syria. The governor, who had been appointed to this place by the emperor Heraclius, and who had held all the territory between Aleppo and the Euphrates, had lately died, leaving two sons, Youkenna and Johannas, who resided in the castle and succeeded to his command. They were completely opposite in character and conduct. Youkenna, the elder of the two, was a warrior and managed the government, while Johannas passed his life in almost monkish retirement, devoting himself to study, to religious exercices, and to acts of charity. On the approach of the Moslems Johannas sympathized with the fears of the wealthy merchants, and advised his brother to compound peaceably with the enemy for a ransom in

money. "You talk like a monk," replied the fierce Youkenna;
"you know nothing that is due to the honour of a soldier. Have
we not strong walls, a brave garrison, and ample wealth to sustain
us, and shall we meanly buy a peace without striking a blow?
Shut yourself up with your books and beads; study and pray, and
leave the defence of the place to me." .

The next day he summoned his troops, distributed money among
them, and having thus roused their spirit, "The Arabs," said he,
"have divided their forces; some are in Palestine, some have gone
to Egypt, it can be but a mere detachment that is coming against
us; I am for meeting them on the way, and giving them battle before they come near to Aleppo." His troops answered his harangue
with shouts, so he put himself at the head of twelve thousand men,
and sallied forth to encounter the Moslems on their march.

Scarcely had this reckless warrior departed with his troops, when
the timid and trading part of the community. gathered together, and
took advantage of his absence to send thirty of the most important
and opulent of the inhabitants to Abu Obeidah, with an offer of a
ransom for the city. These worthies, when they entered the
Moslem camp, were astonished at the order and tranquillity that
reigned throughout, under the wise regulations of the commander-
in-chief. They were received by Abu Obeidah with dignified
composure, and informed him that they had come without the
knowledge of Youkenna, their warlike governor, who had sallied
out on a foray, and whose tyranny they found insupportable
After much discussion, Abu Obeidah offered indemnity to the city
of Aleppo, on condition that they should pay a certain sum of money,
furnish provisions to his army, make discovery of every thing within
their knowledge prejudicial to his interests, and prevent Youkenna
from returning to the castle. They agreed to all the terms except
that relating to the castle, which it was impossible for them to
execute.

Abu Obeidah dispensed with that point, but exacted from them
all an oath to fulfil punctually the other conditions; assuring them
of his protection and kindness, should they observe it; but adding
that, should they break it, they need expect no quarter. He then
offered them an escort, which they declined, preferring to return
quietly by the way they had come.

In the meantime Youkenna, on the day after his sallying forth,
fell in with the advance guard of the Moslem army, consisting of
one thousand men under Caab Ibn Damarrah. He came upon them
by surprise while watering their horses, and resting themselves on
the grass in negligent security. A desperate fight was the consequence; the Moslems at first were successful, but were overpowered by numbers. One hundred and seventy were slain, most of
the rest wounded, and their frequent cries of "Ya Mahommed!
Ya Mahommed!" (Oh Mahomet! Oh Mahomet!) showed the extremity of their despair. Night alone saved them from total massacre; but Youkenna resolved to pursue the work of extermination
with the morning light. In the course of the night, however, one
of his scouts brought him word of the peaceful negotiation carried
on by the citizens of Aleppo during his absence. Boiling with rage,

he gave up all further thought about Caab and his men, and hastening back to Aleppo, drew up his forces, and threatened to put every thing to fire and sword unless the inhabitants renounced the treaty, joined him against the Moslems and gave up the devisers of the late traitorous schemes. On their hesitating to comply with his demands, he charged on them wite his troops, and put three hundred to the sword. The cries and lamentations of the multitude reached the pious Johannas in his retirement in the castle. He hastened to the scene of carnage, and sought by prayers and supplications, and pious remonstrances, to stay the fury of his brother. "What!" cried the fierce Youkenna, "shall I spare traitors who are leagued with the enemy, and selling us for gold?"

"Alas!" replied Johannas, "they have only sought their own safety; they are not fighting men."

"Base wretch!" cried Youkenna in a frenzy, "'tis thou hast been the contriver of this infamous treason."

His naked sword was in his hand; his actions were even more frantic than his words, and in an instant the head of his meek and pious brother rolled on the pavement.

The people of Aleppo were in danger of suffering more from the madness of the army than they had apprehended from the sword of the invader, when a part of the Moslem army appeared in sight led on by Khaled. A bloody battle ensued before the walls of the town, three thousand of Youkenna's troops were slain, and he was obliged to take refuge with a considerable number within the castle, where he placed engines on the walls, and prepared to defend himself to the last extremity.

A council was held in the Moslem camp. Abu Obeidah was disposed to besiege the citadel, and starve out the garrison, but Khaled. with his accustomed promptness, was for instant assault, before the emperor could send reinforcements and supplies. As usual his bold counsel prevailed : the castle was stormed, and he headed the assault. The conflict was one of the fiercest in the wars of Syria. The besieged hurled huge stones from the battlements ; many of the assailants were slain, many maimed, and Khaled was compelled to desist from the attack.

In the dead of that very night, when the fires of the camp were extinguished, and the Moslems were sleeping after their hard-fought battle, Youkenna sallied forth with his troops, fell on the enemy sword in hand, killed sixty, and bore off fifty prisoners : Khaled, however, was hard on his traces, and killed above a hundred of his men before they could shelter themselves within the castle. On the next morning Youkenna paraded his fifty prisoners on the walls of the citadel, ordered them to be beheaded, and threw their heads among the besiegers.

Learning from his spies that a detachment of Moslems were foraging the country, Youkenna sent out, secretly, a troop of horse in the night, who fell upon the foragers, killed nearly seven score of them, slew or hamstrung their camels, mules, and horses, and then hid themselves in the recesses of the mountains, awaiting the night to get back to the castle.

Some fugitives carried tidings of this skirmish to the camp, and

Khaled and Derar, with a troop of horse, were soon at the scene of combat. They found the ground strewed with the dead bodies of men and animals, learnt from some peasants whither the enemy had retreated, and were informed of a narrow defile by which they must return to the castle. Khaled and Derar stationed their troops in ambush in this defile. Late in the night they perceived the enemy advancing. They suffered them to get completely entangled in the defile, when, closing suddenly upon them on every side, they slew a number on the spot, and took three hundred prisoners. These were brought in triumph to the Moslem camp, where they would have redeemed themselves with ample ransom, but their heads were all stricken off in front of the castle, by way of retaliation.

For five months did the siege of this fortress continue; all the attacks of the Moslems were repulsed, all their stratagems discovered and circumvented; for Youkenna had spies in the very camp of the enemy, who gave him intelligence by word, or signal, of every plan and movement. Abu Obeidah despaired of reducing this impregnable castle, which impeded him in his career of conquest, and wrote to the Caliph, proposing to abandon the siege and proceed against Antioch. The Caliph, in reply, ordered him by no means to desist, as that would give courage to the enemy, but to press the siege hard, and trust the event to God. As an additional reliance, he sent him a reinforcement of horse and foot, with twenty camels to facilitate the march of the infantry. Notwithstanding all this aid, the siege was continued for seven-and-forty days, with no greater prospect of success.

While in this state of vexatious impediment and delay, Abu Obeidah was one day accosted by one of the newly arrived soldiers, who told him that, if he would give him thirty men, all strong and valiant, he would pledge his head to put him in possession of the castle. The man who made this singular application was named Damâs; he was of herculean strength and gigantic size, a brave soldier, and of great natural sagacity, although unimproved by education, as he was born a slave. Khaled backed his application, having heard of great exploits performed by him in Arabia. Abn Obeidah, in his perplexities, was willing to adopt any expedient to get possession of this obstinate castle, and the Arabs were always prone to strange and extravagant stratagems in their warfare. He accordingly placed thirty of his bravest men under command of Damâs, charging them to obey him implicitly, notwithstanding his base condition; at the same time, in compliance with his request, he removed with his army to the distance of a league, as though about to abandon the siege.

It was now night, and Damâs concealed his thirty men near to the castle, charging them not to stir, nor utter a sound. He then went out alone and brought in six Christian prisoners, one after another. He questioned them in Arabic, but they were ignorant of the language, and replied in their own tongue. "The curse of Allah on these Christian dogs and their barbarous jargon, which no man can understand," cried the rude Arab, and in his rage he smote off their heads.

He went forth again, and saw a man sliding down the wall, whom he seized the moment he touched the ground. He was a Christian Arab, and was endeavouring to escape from the tyranny of Youkenna, and from him Damâs obtained the information he desired. He instantly despatched two men to Abu Obeidah, requesting him to send him some horse about sunrise. He then took a goat-skin from his wallet, with which he covered his back and shoulders, and a dry crust of bread in his hand, and crept on all-fours close to the wall of the castle. His men crept silently after him. When he heard a noise he gnawed his crust with a sound like that of a dog gnawing a bone, and his followers remained motionless. In this way he reached a part of the castle wall which was easiest of access. Then seating himself on the ground, he made one of his men seat himself on his shoulders, and so on until seven were thus mounted on each other. Then he who was uppermost stood upright, and so did the others in succession, until Damâs rose from the ground upon his feet, and sustained the whole by his wondrous strength, each rendering such aid as he could by bearing against the wall. The uppermost man was now enabled to scramble upon the battlement, where he found a Christian sentinel drunk and asleep. He seized and threw him down to the Moslems below the wall, who instantly despatched him. He then unfolded his turban and drew up the man below him, and they two the next, and so on until Damâs was also on the wall.

Damâs now enjoined silence on them all and left them. He found two other sentinels sleeping, whom he despatched with his dagger, and then made his way to an aperture for the discharge of arrows, looking through which he beheld Youkenna in a spacious chamber, richly clad, seated on tapestry of scarlet silk, flowered with gold, drinking and making merry with a large company; for it would seem as if, on the apparent departure of the besieging army, the whole castle had been given up to feasting and carousing.

Damâs considered the company too numerous to be attacked; returning to his men, therefore, he explored cautiously with them the interior of the castle. Coming suddenly upon the guards at the main entrance, who had no apprehension of danger from within, they killed them, threw open the gate, let down the draw-bridge, and were joined by the residue of their party. The castle was by this time alarmed : the garrison, half drunk and half asleep, came rushing from all quarters in wild confusion. The Moslems defended themselves stoutly on the draw-bridge and in the narrow pass of the barbican until the dawn of day, when a shout of Allah Achbar was heard, and Khaled, with a troop of horse, came thundering through the gate.

The Christians threw down their arms and cried for mercy. Khaled offered them their choice, death or the faith of Islam. Youkenna was the first to raise his finger and pronounce the formula; his example was followed by several of his leading men, whereupon their wives and children and property were secured to them. The castle having been taken by storm, was completely plundered, and the spoils were divided among the army, excepting the usual fifth part reserved for the Caliph. Damâs and his brave companions, who had been almost cut to pieces in the fight, were praised to the skies, nor would Abu Obeidah stir with his host until those of them who survived were out of danger from their wounds.

CHAPTER XX.

Perfidy of Youkenna to his former friends.—Attempts the castle of Aazaz by treachery —Capture of the castle.

· It is a circumstance worthy of remark in the history both of Mahomet and his successors, that the most inveterate enemies of the Islam faith, when once converted to it, even though their conversion were by the edge of the sword, that great Moslem instrument of persuasion, became its faithful defenders. Such was the case with Youkenna, who, from the time he embraced Islam with the Arab scimetar at his throat, became as determined a champion of its doctrines as he had before been an opponent. Like all new converts, he was anxious to give striking proofs of his zeal : he had slain a brother in supporting his old faith, he now proposed to betray a cousin in promoting the interests of the new. This cousin, whose name was Theodorus, was governor of an important town and fortress, named Aazaz, situated at no great distance from Aleppo, and which it was necessary for the Moslems to secure before they left that neighbourhood. The castle was of great strength, and had a numerous garrison, but Youkenna offered to put it into the hands of Abu Obeidah by stratagem. His plan was, to have one hundred Moslems disguised as Christian soldiers : with these he would pretend to fly to the fortress of Aazaz for refuge; being pursued at a distance by a large body of Arabs, who, after coming in sight of the place, would appear to retire in despair, but would conceal themselves in the neighbourhood. His cousin Theodorus, who knew nothing of his conversion, would receive him with perfect confidence : at a concerted hour of the night he and his men would fall suddenly upon the garrison, and at the same time throw open the gates to the party without the walls, and between them both, he had no doubt of carrying the place without difficulty. ·

Abu Obeidah held counsel with Khaled, who pronounced the stratagem apt and feasible, provided the sincerity of Youkenna's conversion might be depended upon. The new proselyte managed to obtain their confidence, and was despatched on his enterprise with one hundred chosen men, selected by tens from ten tribes of Arabs. After they had departed a sufficient time, one thousand men were sent in pretended pursuit, headed by Malec Alashtar, who was instructed in the whole stratagem.

These Moslem wars were always a tissue of plot and counterplot, of which this whole story of Youkenna is a striking example. Scarce had this scheme of treachery been devised in the Moslem camp, when the distant governor of Aazaz was apprised of it, with a success and celerity that almost seemed like magic. He had at that time a spy in the Moslem camp, an Arab of the tribe of Gassan, who sent him a letter, tied under the wing of a carrier pigeon, informing him of the apostasy of Youkenna, and of his intended treachery; though the spy was ignorant of that part of the plan relating to the thousand men under Malec Alashtar. On receiving this letter, Theodorus put his town and castle in a posture of defence, called in the Christian Arabs of the neighbouring villages capable of bearing arms, and despatched a messenger named Tarik al Gassani to Lucas the prefect of Arrawendân, urging him to repair with troops to his assistance.

Before the arrival of the latter, Youkenna appeared with his pretended fugitives before the gates of Aazaz, announcing that his castle was taken, and that he and his band were flying before pursuers. Theodorus sallied forth on horseback, at the head of many of his troops, as if to receive his cousin with all due honours. He even alighted from his steed, and, approaching Youkenna in a reverential manner, stooped as if to kiss his stirrup ; but suddenly cutting the saddle girth, he pulled him with his face on the ground, and in an instant his hundred followers were likewise unhorsed and made prisoners. Theodorus then spat in the face of the prostrate Youkenna, and reproached him with his apostasy and treachery ; threatening to send him to answer for his crimes before the emperor Heraclius, and to put all his followers to the sword.

In the meantime Tarik al Gassani, the Christian Arab, who had been sent by Theodorus to summon the prefect of Arrawendân to his aid, had executed his errand, but on the way back fell into the hands of Malec, who was lying in ambuscade with his thousand men. The sight of a naked scimetar drew from Tarik information that the plot of Youkenna had been discovered ; that he had been sent after aid, and that Lucas, the prefect of Arrawendân, must be actually on his way with five hundred cavalry.

Profiting by this information, Malec placed his thousand men so advantageously, as completely to surprise and capture Lucas and his reinforcement, as they were marching in the night. He then devised a stratagem still to outwit the governor of Aazaz. First he disguised his five hundred men in dresses taken from their Christian prisoners, and gave them the Christian standard of the prefect of Arrawendân. Then summoning Tarik the messenger before him, and again displaying the scimetar, he exhorted him most earnestly to turn Mahometan. There was no resisting his arguments, and Tarik made a full and hearty profession of the faith. Malec then ordered him to prove his zeal for the good cause by proceeding to Aazaz and informing Theodorus, that the prefect of Arrawendân was at hand with a reinforcement of five hundred men. The double-faced courier departed on his errand, accompanied by a trusty Moslem, who had secret orders to smite off his head, if he should be found to waver; but there were still other plots at work in this tissue of stratagems.

As Tarik and his companion approached Aazaz, they heard great shouting and the sound of trumpets, and this was the cause of the change.   Theodorus, the governor, had committed Youkenna and his men into the custody of his son Leon.   Now it so happened, that the youth having frequently visited his father's kinsmen at the castle of Aleppo, had become violently enamoured of the daughter of Youkenna, but had met strong opposition to his love.   The present breach between his father and Youkenna, threatened to place an inseparable barrier between him and the gratification of his passion.   Maddened by his desires, the youth now offered to Youkenna, if he would give him his daughter to wife, to embrace Mahometanism, and to set him and his companions at liberty.   The offer was accepted.   At the dead of the night, when the prisoners were armed and liberated, they fell upon the sleeping garrison; a tumultuous fight ensued, in the course of which Theodorus was slain, by the hand, it is said, of his unnatural son.

It was in the height of this conflict, that Tarik and his companion arrived at the place, and learning the situation of affairs, hastened back to Malec Alashtar with the news.   The latter hurried on with his troops and came in time to complete the capture of the place. He bestowed greet praises on Youkenna, but the latter taking him by the hand, exclaimed, "Thank Allah and this youth."   He then related the whole story.   The pious Malec lifted up his eyes and hands in wonder.   "When Allah wills a thing," exclaimed he, "he prepares the means."

Leaving Seid Ibn Amir in command of the place, with Youkenna's band of a hundred men, as a garrison, Malec Alashtar returned to the main army with great booty and many prisoners.   Youkenna, however, refused to accompany him.   He was mortified at the questionable result of his undertaking against Aazaz, the place having been taken by other means than his own, and vowed not to show himself in the Moslem camp until he had retrieved his credit by some signal blow.   Just at this time, there arrived at Aazaz, a foraging party of a thousand Moslems, that had been ravaging the neighbouring country; among them were two hundred renegades, who had apostatized with Youkenna, and whose families and effects were in the castle of Aleppo.   They were the very men for his purpose, and with these he marched off to execute one of his characteristic stratagems at Antioch.

CHAPTER XXI.

Intrigues of Youkenna at Antioch.—Siege of that city by the Moslems.—Flight of the emperor to Constantinople.—Surrender of Antioch.

The City of Antioch was at that time the capital of Syria and the seat of the Roman government in the East.   It was of great extent, surrounded by stone walls and numerous towers, and stood in the midst of a fertile country, watered by wells and fountains and abundant streams.   Here Heraclius held his court, and here the

Greeks, sunk in luxury and effeminacy, had lost all the military discipline and heroism that had made them conquerors in Asia.

Towards this capital Youkenna proceeded with his band of two hundred men; but in the second watch of the night he left them, after giving them orders to keep on in the high way of the caravans, and on arriving at Antioch, to give themselves out as fugitives from Aleppo. In the meantime, he with two of his relatives, struck into a by-road, and soon fell into the hands of one of the emperor's outposts. On announcing himself Youkenna, late governor of Aleppo, he was sent under a guard of horse to Antioch.

The emperor Heraclius, broken in spirit by his late reverses and his continual apprehensions, wept at the sight of Youkenna, and meekly upbraided him with his apostasy and treason, but the latter, with perfect self-possession and effrontery, declared that whatever he had done was for the purpose of preserving his life for the emperor's service; and cited the obstinate defence he had made at Aleppo, and his present voluntary arrival at Antioch, as proofs of his fidelity. The emperor was easily deceived by a man he had been accustomed to regard as one of his bravest and most devoted officers; and indeed the subtle apostate had the address to incline most of the courtiers in his favour. To console him for what was considered his recent misfortunes, he was put in command of the two hundred pretended fugitives of his former garrison, as soon as they arrived at Antioch; he had thus a band of kindred renegades, ready to aid him in any desperate treachery. Furthermore, to show his entire confidence in him, the emperor sent him with upwards of two thousand men, to escort his youngest daughter from a neighbouring place to the court at Antioch. He performed his mission with correctness; as he and his troop were escorting the princess about midnight, the neighing of their horses put them on the alert, and sending out scouts they received intelligence of a party of Moslems asleep, with their horses grazing near them. They proved to be a body of a thousand Christian Arabs, under Haim, son of the apostate Jabalah Ibn al Ayam, who had made captives of Derar Ibn al Azwar and a foraging party of two hundred Moslems. They all proceeded together to Antioch, where the emperor received his daughter with great joy, and made Youkenna one of his chief counsellors.

. Derar and his men were brought into the presence of the emperor, and commanded to prostrate themselves before him, but they held themselves erect and took no heed of the command. It was repeated more peremptorily. "We bow to no created being," replied Derar, "the prophet bids us to yield adoration to God alone."

The emperor, struck with this reply, propounded several questions touching Mahomet and his doctrines, but Derar, whose province did not lie in words, beckoned to Kais Ibn Amir, an old gray-headed Moslem, to answer them. A long and edifying conference ensued, in which. in reply to the searching questions of the emperor, the venerable Kais went into a history of the prophet, and of the various modes in which inspiration came upon him. Sometimes like the sound of a bell; sometimes in the likeness of an

16

angel in human shape; sometimes in a dream; sometimes like the brightness of the dawning day; and that when it was upon him great drops of sweat rolled from his forehead, and a tremor seized upon his limbs. He furthermore descanted with eloquence upon the miracles of Mahomet, of his nocturnal journey to heaven, and his conversation with the Most High. The emperor listened with seeming respect to all these matters, but they roused the indignation of a bishop who was present, and who pronounced Mahomet an impostor. Derar took fire in an instant; if he could not argue, he could make use of a soldier's vocabulary, and he roundly gave the bishop the lie, and assailed him with all kinds of epithets. Instantly a number of Christian swords flashed from their scabbards, blows were aimed at him from every side; and according to Moslem accounts, he escaped death only by miracle; though others attribute it to the hurry and confusion of his assailants, and to the interference of Youkenna. The emperor was now for having him executed on the spot; but here the good offices of Youkenna again saved him, and his execution was deferred.

In the meantime Abu Obeidah, with his main army, was making his victorious approaches, and subjecting all Syria to his arms. The emperor, in his miserable imbecility and blind infatuation, put the treacherous Youkenna in full command of the city and army. He would again have executed Derar and his fellow-prisoners, but Youkenna suggested that they had better be spared to be exchanged for any Christians that might be taken by the enemy. They were then, by advice of the bishops, taken to one of the churches, and exhorted to embrace the Christian faith, but they obstinately refused. The Arabian writers, as usual, give them sententious replies to the questions put to them. "What hinders ye," demanded the patriarch, "from turning Christians?" "The truth of our religion," replied they. Heraclius had heard of the mean attire of the Caliph Omar, and asked them why, having gained so much wealth by his conquests, he did not go richly clad like other princes? They replied, that he cared not for this world, but for the world to come, and sought favour in the eyes of God alone. "In what kind of a palace does he reside?" asked the emperor. "In a house built of mud." "Who are his attendants?" "Beggars and the poor." "What tapestry does he sit upon?" "Justice and equity." "What is his throne?" "Abstinence and true knowledge." "What is his treasure?" "Trust in God." "And who are his guard?" "The bravest of the Unitarians."

Of all the prisoners one only could be induced to swerve from his faith; and he was a youth fascinated by the beauty and the unveiled charms of the Greek women. He was baptized with triumph; the bishops strove who most should honour him, and the emperor gave him a horse, a beautiful damsel to wife, and enrolled him in the army of Christian Arabs, commanded by the renegade Jabálah; but he was upbraided in bitter terms by his father, who was one of the prisoners, and ready to die in the faith of Islam.

The emperor now reviewed his army, which was drawn up outside of the walls, and at the head of every battalion was a wooden oratory with a crucifix; while a precious crucifix out of the main church, exhibited only on extraordinary occasions, was borne as a sacred standard, before the treacherous Youkenna. One of the main dependencies of Heraclius for the safety of Antioch, was in the Iron Bridge, so called from its great strength. It was a bridge of stone across the river Orontes, guarded by two towers and garrisoned by a great force, having not less than three hundred officers. The fate of this most important pass shows the degeneracy of Greek discipline and the licentiousness of the soldiery, to which in a great measure has been attributed the rapid successes of the Moslems. An officer of the court was charged to visit this fortress each day, and see that every thing was in order. On one of his visits, he found those who had charge of the towers, drinking and revelling, whereupon he ordered them to be punished with fifty stripes each. They treasured the disgrace in their hearts; the Moslem army approached to lay siege to that formidable fortress, and when the emperor expected to hear of a long and valiant resistance, he was astonished by the tidings that the Iron Bridge had been surrendered without a blow.

Heraclius now lost heart altogether. Instead of calling a council of his generals, he assembled the bishops and wealthiest citizens in the cathedral, and wept over the affairs of Syria. It was a time for dastard counsel; the apostate Jabalah proposed the assassination of the Caliph Omar, as a means of throwing the affairs of the Saracens into confusion. The emperor was weak enough to consent, and Vathek Ibn Mosapher, a bold young Arab of the tribe of Jabalah, was despatched to Medina to effect the treacherous deed. The Arabian historians give a miraculous close to this undertaking. Arriving at Medina, Vathek concealed himself in a tree, without the walls, at a place where the Caliph was accustomed to walk after the hour of prayers. After a time Omar approached the place, and lay down to sleep near the foot of the tree. The assassin drew his dagger, and was descending, when he beheld a lion walking round the Caliph, licking his feet and guarding him as he slept. When he woke the lion went away, upon which Vathek, convinced that Omar was under the protection of heaven, hastened down from the tree, kissed his hand in token of allegiance, revealed his treacherous errand and avowed his conversion to the Islam faith.

The surrender of the Iron Bridge had laid open Antioch to the approach of Abu Obeidah, and he advanced in battle array to where the Christian army was drawn up beneath its walls. Nestorius, one of the Christian commanders, sallied forth from among the troops and defied the Moslems to single combat. Damâs, the herculean warrior, who had taken the castle of Aleppo, spurred forward to meet him, but his horse stumbled and fell with him, and he was seized as the prisoner of Nestorius, and conveyed to his tent, where he was bound hand and foot. Dehac, another Moslem, took his place, and a brave fight ensued between him and Nestorius. The parties, however, were so well matched, that, after fighting for a long time until both were exhausted, they parted by mutual consent. While this fight was going on the soldiers, horse and foot, of either army, thronged to see it, and in the tumult, the tent of Nestorius was thrown down. There were but three servants left in charge of it. Fearful of the anger of their master, they hastened to set it up again, and loosened the bands of Damâs that he might assist them; but the moment he was free, he arose in his giant strength, seized two of the attendants, one in each hand dashed their heads against the head of the third, and soon laid them all lifeless on the ground. Then opening a chest he arrayed himself in a dress belonging to Nestorius, armed himself with a sabre, sprang on a horse that stood ready saddled, and cut his way through the Christian Arabs of Jabalah to the Moslem host.

While these things were happening without the walls, treason was at work in the city. Youkenna, who commanded there, set free Derar and his fellow-prisoners, furnished them with weapons, and joined to them his own band of renegadoes. The tidings of this treachery, and the apprehension of revolt among his own troops, struck despair to the heart of Heraclius. He had been terrified by a dream, in which he had found himself thrust from his throne, and his crown falling from his head; the fulfilment appeared to be at hand. Without waiting to withstand the evil, he assembled a few domestics, made a secret retreat to the sea-shore, and set sail for Constantinople.

The generals of Heraclius, more brave than their emperor, fought a pitched battle beneath the walls: but the treachery of Youkenna, and the valour of Derar and his men, who fell on them unawares, rendered their gallant struggle unavailing; the people of Antioch seeing the battle lost, capitulated for the safety of their city at the cost of three hundred thousand golden ducats, and Abu Obeidah entered the ancient capital of Syria in triumph. This event took place on the 21st of August, in the year of redemption 638.

CHAPTER XXII.

Expedition into the mountains of Syria.—Story of a miraculous cap.

The discreet Abu Obeidah feared to expose his troops to the enervating delights of Antioch, and to the allurements of the Greek women, and, after three days of repose and refreshment, marched forth from that luxurious city. He wrote a letter to the Caliph, relating his important conquest, and the flight of the emperor Heraclius; and added, that he discovered a grievous propensity among his troops to intermarry with the beautiful Grecian females, which he had forbidden them to do, as contrary to the injunctions of the Koran.

Te epistle was delivered to Omar, just as he was departing on a pilgrimage to Mecca, accompanied by the widows of the prophet. When he had read the letter, he offered prayers and thanksgiving to Allah, but wept over Abu Obeidah's rigour to his soldiers. Seating himself upon the ground, he immediately wrote a reply to his general, expressing his satisfaction at his success, but exhorting him to more indulgence to his soldiers. Those who had fought the good fight ought to be permitted to rest themselves, and to enjoy the good things they had gained. Such as had no wives at home, might marry in Syria, and those who had a desire for female slaves, might purchase as many as they chose.

While the main army reposed after the taking of Antioch, the indefatigable Khaled, at the head of a detachment, scoured the country as far as to the Euphrates; took Membege, the ancient Hierapolis, by force, and Berah and Bales, and other places, by capitulation, receiving a hundred thousand pieces of gold by way of ransom, besides laying the inhabitants under annual tribute.

' Abu Obeidah, in an assemblage of his officers, now proposed an expedition to subdue the mountains of Syria; but no one stepped forward to volunteer. The mountains were rugged and sterile, and covered with ice and snow for the greater part of the year, and the troops already began to feel the effects of the softening climate and delights of Syria. At length a candidate presented himself, named Meisara Ibn Mesroud; a numerous body of picked men was placed under his command, and a black flag was given him, bearing the inscription, "There is no God but God. Mahomet is the messenger of God." Damâs accompanied him at the head of one thousand black Ethiopian slaves. The detachment suffered greatly in the mountains, for they were men of sultry climates, unaccustomed to ice and snow, and they passed suddenly from a soft Syrian summer to the severity of frozen winter, and from the midst of abundance to regions of solitude and sterility. The inhabitants, too, of the scanty villages, fled at their approach. At length they captured a prisoner, who informed them that an imperial army of many thousand men was lying in wait for them in a valley about three leagues distant, and that all the passes behind them were guarded. A scout, despatched in search of intelligence, confirmed this news : whereupon they intrenched themselves in a commanding position, and despatched a fleet courier to Abu Obeidah, to inform him of their perilous situation.

The courier made such speed, that when he reached the presence of Obeidah, he fainted through exhaustion. Khaled, who had just returned from his successful expedition to the Euphrates, instantly hastened to the relief of Meisara with three thousand men, and was presently followed by Ayad Ibn Ganam, with two thousand more.

Khaled found Meisara and his men making desperate stand against an overwhelming force. At the sight of this powerful reinforcement, with the black eagle of Khaled in the advance, the Greeks gave over the attack and returned to their camp, but secretly retreated in the night, leaving their tents standing, and bearing off captive Abdallah Ibn Hodafa, a near relative of the prophet, and a beloved friend to the Caliph Omar, whom they straightway sent to the emperor at Constantinople.

The Moslems forbore to pursue the enemy through these difficult mountains, and, after plundering the deserted tents, returned to the main army. When the Caliph Omar received tidings from

Abu Obeidah of the capture of Abdallah Ibn Hodafa, he was grieved at heart, and despatched instantly an epistle to the emperor Heraclius at Constantinople.

"Bismillah!" In the name of the all merciful God!

"Praise be to Allah, the Lord of this world, and of that which is to come, who has neither companion, wife, nor son; and blessed be Mahomet his apostle. Omar Ibn all Khattâb, servant of God, to Heraclius, emperor of the Greeks. As soon as thou shalt receive this epistle, fail not to send to me the Moslem captive, whose name is Abdallah Ibn Hodafa. If thou doest this, I shall have hope that Allah will conduct thee in the right path. If thou dost refuse, I will not fail to send thee such men as traffic and merchandise have not turned from the fear of God. Health and happiness to all those who tread in the right way!"

In the meantime the emperor had treated his prisoner with great distinction, and as Abdallah was a cousin-german to the prophet, the son of one of his uncles, he was an object of great curiosity at Constantinople. The emperor proffered him liberty if he would only make a single sign of adoration to the crucifix, and magnificent rewards if he would embrace the Christian faith; but both proposals were rejected. Heraclius, say the Arab writers, then changed his treatment of him; shut him up for three days, with nothing to eat and drink but swine's flesh and wine, but on the fourth day found both untouched. The faith of Abdallah was put to no further proof, as by this time the emperor received the stern letter from the Caliph. The letter had its effect. The prisoner was dismissed, with costly robes and rich presents, and Heraclius sent to Omar a diamond of great size and beauty: but no jeweller at Medina could estimate its value. The abstemious Omar refused to appropriate it to his own use, though urged to do so by the Moslems. He placed it in the public treasury, of which, from his office, he was the guardian and manager. It was afterwards sold for a great sum.

A singular story is related by a Moslem writer, but not supported by any rumour or surmise among Christian historians. It is said that the emperor Heraclius wavered in his faith, if he did not absolutely become a secret convert of Mahometanism, and this is stated as the cause. He was afflicted with a violent pain in the head, for which he could find no remedy, until the Caliph Omar sent him a cap of mysterious virtue. So long as he wore this cap he was at ease, but the moment he laid it aside the pain returned. Heraclius caused the cap to be ripped open, and found within the lining a scrap of paper, on which was written, in Arabic character, Bismillah! Arrahmany Arrahimi! In the name of the all-merciful God. This cap is said to have been preserved among the Christians until the year 833, when it was given up by the governor of a besieged town to the Caliph Almotassem, on condition of his raising the siege. It was found still to retain its medicinal virtues, which the pious Arabians ascribed to the efficacy of the devout inscription. An unbelieving Christian will set it down among the charms and incantations which have full effect on imaginative persons inclined to credulity, but upon none others; such persons abounded among the Arabs.

CHAPTER XXIII.

Expedition of Amru Ibn al Aass against Prince Constantine in Syria.—Their conference.
—Capture of Tripoli and Tyre.—Flight of Constantine.—Death of Khaled.

The course of our history now turns to record the victories of Amru Ibn al Aass, to whom, after the capture of Jerusalem, the Caliph had assigned the invasion and subjugation of Egypt. Amru, however, did not proceed immediately to that country, but remained for some time with his division of the army, in Palestine, where some places still held out for the emperor. The natural and religious sobriety of the Arabs was still sorely endangered among the temptations of Syria. Several of the Moslem officers being seized while on the march, with chills and griping pains in consequence of eating unripe grapes, were counselled by a crafty old Christian Arab, to drink freely of wine which he produced, and which he pronounced a sovereign remedy. They followed his prescriptions so lustily, that they all came reeling into the camp to the great scandal of Amru. The punishment for drunkenness, recommended by Ali and adopted by the Caliph, was administered to the delinquents; who each received a sound bastinado on the soles of the feet. This sobered them completely, but so enraged them with the old man who had recommended the potations, that they would have put him to death, had it not been represented to them that he was a stranger and under Moslem protection.

Amru now advanced upon the city of Cæsarea, where Constantine, son of the emperor, was posted with a large army. The Moslems were beset by spies, sent by the Christian commander to obtain intelligence. These were commonly Christian Arabs, whom it was almost impossible to distinguish from those of the faith of Islam. One of these, however, after sitting one day by the camp fires, as he rose trod on the end of his own robe and stumbled; in his vexation, he uttered an oath "by Christ!" He was immediately detected by his blasphemy to be a Christian and a spy, and was cut to pieces by the bystanders. Amru rebuked them for their precipitancy, as he might have gained information from their victim; and ordered that in future all spies should be brought to him.

The fears of Constantine increased with the approach of the army, and he now despatched a Christian priest to Amru, soliciting him to send some principal officer to confer amicably with him. An Ethiopian negro named Belal Ibn Rebah, offered to undertake the embassy. He was a man of powerful frame and sonorous voice, and had been employed by Mahomet as a Muezzin or crier, to summon the people to prayers. Proud of having officiated under the prophet, he retired from office at his death, and had raised his voice but once since that event, and that was on the taking possession of Jerusalem, the city of the prophets, when at the Caliph Omar's command, he summoned the true believers to prayers with a force of lungs, that astonished the Jewish inhabitants.

Amru would have declined the officious offer of the vociferous Ethiopian, representing to him that such a mission required a smooth-spoken Arab, rather than one of his country; but, on Belal conjuring him in the name of Allah and the prophet, to let him go, he reluctantly consented. When the priest saw who was to accompany him back to Constantine, he objected stoutly to such an ambassador, and glancing contemptuously at the negro features of the Ethiopian, observed that Constantine had not sent for a slave but for an officer. The negro ambassador, however, persisted in his diplomatic errand, but was refused admission and returned mortified and indignant.

Amru now determined to undertake the conference in person. Repairing to the Christian camp, he was conducted to Constantine, whom he found seated in state, and who ordered a chair to be placed for him; but he put it aside, and seated himself cross-legged on the ground after the Arab fashion, with his scimetar on his thigh and his lance across his knees. The curious conference that ensued is minutely narrated by that pious Iman and Cadi, the Moslem historian Alwakedi, in his chronicle of the conquest of Syria.

Constantine remonstrated against the invasion, telling Amru that the Romans and Greeks and Arabs were brethren, as being all the children of Noah, although, it was true, the Arabs were misbegotten, as being the descendants of Ishmael, the son of Hagar, a slave and a concubine, yet being thus brethren, it was sinful for them to war against each other.

Amru replied that what Constantine had said was true, and that the Arabs gloried in acknowledging Ishmael as their progenitor, and envied not the Greeks their forefather Esau, who had sold his birthright for a mess of pottage. He added that their difference related to their religion, upon which ground even brothers were justified in warfare.

Amru proceeded to state that Noah, after the deluges divided the earth into three parts, between his sons Shem, Ham, and Japhet, and that Syria was in the portion assigned to Shem, which continued down through his descendants Kathan and Tesm, and Jodais to Amalek, the father of the Amelekite Arabs; but that the Arabs had been pushed from their fertile inheritance of Syria into the stony and thorny deserts of Arabia.

"We come now," continued Amru, "to claim our ancient inheritance, and resume the ancient partition. Take you the stones and the thorns and the barren deserts we have occupied, and give us back the pleasant land of Syria, with its groves, its pastures, its fair cities and running streams."

To this Constantine replied, that the partition was already made; that time and possession had confirmed it; and that the groves had been planted, and the cities built by the present inhabitants. Each, therefore, ought to be contented with the lot that had fallen to him.

"There are two conditions," rejoined Amru, "on which the

land may remain with its present inhabitants. Let them profess the religion of Islam, or pay tribute to the Caliph, as is due from all unbelievers."

"Not so," said Constantine, "but let each continue to possess the land he has inhabited, and enjoy the produce of his own toil, and profess the faith he believes,in his own conscience, to be true."

Upon this Amru sternly rose. "One only alternative," said he, "remains. ·Since you obstinately refuse the conditions I propose, even as your ancestor Esau refused obedience to his mother, let God and the sword decide between us."

As he was about to depart, he added : "We will acknowledge no kindred with you, while ye continue unbelievers. Ye are the children of Esau, we of Ishmael, through whom alone the seal and gift of prophecy descended from father to son, from our great forefather Adam, until it reached the prophet Mahomet. Now Ishmael was the best of the sons of his father, and made the tribe of Kenanah, the best tribe of Arabia; and the family of Koreish is the best of the tribe of Kenanah; and the children of Haschem are the best of the family of Koreish; and Abdallah Motâlleb, grandsire of Mahomet, was the best of the sons of Haschem; and Abdallah, the youngest and best of the thirteen sons of Abu Motâlleb, was the father of Mahomet, (on whom be peace!) who was the best and only issue of his sire; and to him the angel Gabriel descended from Allah, and inspired him with the gift of prophecy."

Thus terminated this noted conference, and Amru returned to his host. The armies now remained in sight of each other, prepared for battle, but without coming to action. One day an officer richly arrayed came forth from the Christian camp, defying the Moslems to single combat. Several were eager to accept the challenge in hopes of gaining such glittering spoil; but Amru rebuked their sordid motives. "Let no man fight for gain," said he, "but for the truth. He who loses his life fighting for the love of God, will have paradise as a reward; but he who loses it fighting for any other object, will lose his life and all that he fights for."

A stripling now advanced, an Arab from Yemen, or Arabia the Happy, who had sought these wars not, as he said, for the delights of Syria, or the fading enjoyments of this world, but to devote himself to the service of God and his apostle. His mother and sister had in vain opposed his leaving his peaceful home, to seek a life of danger. "If I fall in the service of Allah," said he, "I shall be a martyr; and the prophet has said, that the spirits of the martyrs shall dwell in the crops of the green birds that eat of the fruits and drink of the rivers of paradise." Finding their remonstrances of no avail, his mother and sister had followed him to the wars, and they now endeavoured to dissuade him from fighting with an adversary so much his superior in strength and years; but the youthful enthusiast was not to be moved. "Farewell, mother and sister!" cried he, "we shall meet again by that river of joy provided in paradise, for the apostle and his followers."

The youth rushed to the combat, but obtained almost instantly the crown of martyrdom he sought. Another, and another succeeded him, but shared the same fate. Serjabil Ibn Hasanah stepped forth. As on a former occasion, in purifying the spirit, he had reduced the flesh ; and a course of watching and fasting had rendered him but little competent to face his powerful adversary. After a short combat the Christian bore him to the earth, and setting his foot upon his breast, was about to take his life, when his own hand was suddenly severed from his body. The prostrate Serjabil looked up with surprise at his deliverer; for he was in Grecian attire, and had come from the Grecian host. He announced himself as the unhappy Tuleïa Ibn Chowailed, formerly a pretended prophet and an associate of Moseïlma. After the death of that impostor, he had repented of his false prophecies, and become a Moslem in heart, and had sought an opportunity of signalizing his devotion to the Islam cause.

"Oh brother!" cried Serjabil, "the mercy of Allah is infinite, and repentance wipes away all crimes.".

Serjabil would now have taken him to the Moslem host, but Tuleïa hung back ; and at length confessed that he would long since have joined the standard of Islam, but that he was afraid of Khaled, that terror and scourge of false prophets, who had killed his friend Moseïlma, and who might put him to death out of resentment for past misdeeds. Serjabil quieted his fears, by assuring him that Khaled was not in the Moslem camp; he then conducted him to Amru, who received him with great favour, and afterwards gave him a letter to the Caliph setting forth the signal service he had performed, and his sincere devotion to the cause of Islam. He was subsequently employed in the wars of the Moslems against the Persians.

The weather was cold and tempestuous, and the Christians disheartened by repeated reverses, began daily to desert their colours. The prince Constantine dreaded, with his diminished and discouraged troops, to encounter an enemy flushed with success, and continually augmenting in force. Accordingly, he took advantage of a tempestuous night, and abandoning his camp, to be plundered by the Moslems, retreated with his army to Cæsarea, and shut himself up within its walls. Hither he was soon followed by Amru, who laid close siege to the place, but the walls were strong, the garrison was numerous, and Constantine hoped to be able to hold out until the arrival of reinforcements. The tidings of further disasters and disgraces to the imperial cause, however, destroyed this hope; and these were brought about by the stratagems and treacheries of that arch deceiver Youkenna. After the surrender of Antioch, that wily traitor still kept up his pretended devotion to the Christian cause, and retreated with his band of renegadoes to the town of Tripoli, a sea-port in Syria, situated on the Mediterranean. Here he was cordially admitted, as his treachery was still unknown. Watching his opportunity, he rose with his devoted band, seized on the town and citadel without noise or tumult, and kept the standard of the cross still flying, while he sent secret intelligence of his exploit to Abu Obeidah. Just at this time, a fleet of fifty ships from Cyprus and Crete put in there, laden with arms and provisions for Constantine's army. Before notice

could be given of the posture of affairs, Youkenna gained possession of the ships, and embarked on board of them with his renegadoes and other troops, delivering the city of Tripoli into the hands
of the force sent by Abu Obeidah to receive it.

Bent on new treacheries, Youkenna now sailed with the fleet to
Tyre, displaying the Christian flag, and informing the governor that
he was come with a reinforcement for the army of the emperor.
He was kindly received, and landed with nine hundred of his troops,
intending to rise on the garrison in the night. One of his own
men, however, betrayed the plot, and Youkenna and his followers
were seized and imprisoned in the citadel.

In the meantime Yezed Ibn Abu Sofian, who had marched with
two thousand men against Cæsarea, but had left Amru to subdue
it, came with his troops into the neighbourhood of Tyre, in hopes to
find it in possession of Youkenna. The governor of the city de-
spising so slender a force, sallied forth with the greater part of his
garrison, and the inhabitants mounted on the walls to see the battle.

It was the fortune of Youkenna, which he derived from his consummate skill in intrigue, that his failure and captivity on this
occasion, as on a former one in the castle of Aazaz, served only as
a foundation for his success. He contrived to gain over a Christian
officer named Basil, to whose keeping he and the other prisoners
were intrusted, and who was already disposed to embrace the
Islam faith ; and he sent information of his plan by a disguised
messenger to Yezed, and to those of his own followers who remained on board of the fleet. All this was the work of a few hours,
while the opposing forces were preparing for action.

The battle was hardly begun when Youkenna and his nine hundred men, set free by the apostate Basil, and conducted to the
arsenal, armed themselves and separated in different parties. Some
scoured the streets, shouting La ilaha Allah! and Allah Achbar!
Others stationed themselves at the passages by which alone the guard
could descend from the walls. Others ran to the port, where they
were joined by their comrades from the fleet, and others threw
wide the gates to a detachment of the army of Yezed. All this was
suddenly effected, and with such co-operation from various points,
that the place was presently in the hands of the Moslems. Most of
the inhabitants embraced the Islam faith ; the rest were pillaged
and made slaves.

It was the tidings of the loss of Tripoli and Tyre, and of the capture of the fleet, with its munitions of war, that struck dismay into
the heart of the prince Constantine, and made him quake within the
walls of Cæsarea. He felt as if Amru and his besieging army were
already within the walls, and, taking disgraceful counsel from his
fears, and example from his father's flight from Antioch, he removed
furtively from Cæsarea with his family and vast treasure, gained
promptly a convenient port, and set all sail for Constantinople.

The people of Cæsarea finding one morning that the son of their
sovereign had fled in the night, capitulated with Amru, offering to
deliver up the city, with all the wealth belonging to the family of
the late emperor, and two hundred thousand pieces of silver, as
ransom for their own property. Their terms were promptly ac-

cepted, Amru being anxious to depart on the invasion of Egypt.

The surrender of Cæsarea was followed by the other places in the province which had still held out, and thus, after a war of six years, the Moslem conquest of Syria was completed, in the 5th year of the Caliph Omar, the 29th, of the reign of the emperor Heraclius, the 17th of the Hegira, and the 639th year of our redemption.

The conquest was followed by a pestilence, one of the customary attendants upon war. Great numbers of the people of Syria perished, and with them twenty-five thousand of their Arabian conquerors. Among the latter was Abu Obeidah, the commander-in-chief, then fifty-eight years of age ; also Yezed Ibn Abu Sofian, Serjabil, and other distinguished generals, so that the 18th year of the Hegira became designated as " The year of the mortality."

In closing this account of the conquest of Syria, we must note the fate of one of the most efficient of its conquerors, the invincible Khaled. He had never been a favourite of Omar, who considered him-rash and headlong ; arrogant in the exercise of command ; unsparing in the use of the sword, and rapacious in grasping the spoils of victory. His brilliant achievements in Irak and Syria, and the magnanimity with which he yielded the command to Abu Obeidah, and zealously fought under his standard, had never sufficed to efface the prejudice of Omar.

After the capture of Emessa, which was mainly effected by the bravery of Khaled, he received congratulations on all hands as the victor. Eschaus, an Arabian poet, sang his exploits in lofty verse, making him the hero of the whole Syrian conquest. Khaled, who was as ready to squander as to grasp, rewarded the adulation of the poet with thirty thousand pieces of silver. All this, when reported to Omar, excited his quick disgust ; he was indignant at Khaled for arrogating to himself, as he supposed, all the glory of the war ; and he attributed the lavish reward of the poet to gratified vanity. "Even if the money came from his own purse," said he, "it was shameful squandering ; and God, says the Koran, loves not a squanderer."

He now gave faith to a charge made against Khaled of embezzling the spoils set apart for the public treasury, and forthwith sent orders for him to be degraded from his command in presence of the assembled army ; it is even said his arms were tied behind his back with his turban.

A rigid examination proved the charge of embezzlement to be unfounded, but Khaled was subjected to a heavy fine. The sentence causing great dissatisfaction in the army, the Caliph wrote to the commanders : "I have punished Khaled not on account of fraud or falsehood, but for his vanity and prodigality ; paying poets for ascribing to him alone all the successes of the holy war. Good and evil come from God, not from Khaled !"

These indignities broke the heart of the veteran, who was already infirm from the wounds and hardships of his arduous campaigns, and he gradually sank into the grave, regretting in his last moments that he had not died in the field of battle. He left a name idolized by the soldiery, and beloved by his kindred ;

at his sepulture, all the women of his race cut off their hair
in token of lamentation.   When it was ascertained, at his death,
that instead of having enriched himself by the wars, his whole property consisted of his war-horse, his arms, and a single slave,
Omar became sensible of the injustice he had done to his faithful
general, and shed tears over his grave.

CHAPTER XXIV.

Invasion of Egypt by Amru.—Capture of Memphis.—Siege and surrender of Alexandria.
—Burning of the Alexandrian library.

A proof of the religious infatuation, or the blind confidence in
destiny, which hurried the Moslem commanders of those days into
the most extravagant enterprises, is furnished in the invasion of
the once proud empire of the Pharaohs, the mighty, the mysterious
Egypt, with an army of merely five thousand men.   The Caliph,
himself, though he had suggested this expedition, seems to have
been conscious of its rashness ; or rather to have been chilled by
the doubts of his prime counsellor Othman ; for, while Amru was
on the march, he despatched missives after him to the following
effect : "If this epistle reach thee before thou hast crossed the
boundary of Egypt, come instantly back; but if it find thee within
the Egyptian territory, march on with the blessing of Allah, and be
assured I will send thee all necessary aid."
    The bearer of the letter overtook Amru while yet within the
bounds of Syria ; that wary general either had secret information,
or made a shrewd surmise, as to the purport of his errand, and
continued his march across the border without admitting him to an
audience.   Having encamped at the Egyptian village of Arish, he
received the courier with all due respect, and read the letter aloud
in the presence of his officers.   When he had finished, he demanded
of those about him whether they were in Syria or Egypt.   "In
Egypt," was the reply.   "Then," said Amru, "we will proceed,
with the blessing of Allah, and fulfil the commands of the
Caliph."
    The first place to which he laid siege was Farwak, or Pelusium
situated on the shores of the Mediterranean, on the Isthmus which
separates that sea from the Arabian Gulf, and connects Egypt with
Syria and Arabia. It was therefore considered the key to Egypt.
A month's siege put Amru in possession of the place ; he then examined the surrounding country with more forethought than was
generally manifested by the Moslem conquerors, and projected a
canal across the Isthmus, to connect the waters of the Red Sea and
the Mediterranean.   His plan, however, was condemned by the
Caliph, as calculated to throw open Arabia to a maritime invasion
of the Christians.
    Amru now proceeded to Misrah, the Memphis of the ancients,

and residence of the early Egyptian kings.   This city was at that
time the strongest fortress in Egypt, except Alexandria, and still
retained much of its ancient magnificence.   It stood on the western bank of the Nile, above the Delta, and a little east of the
Pyramids.   The citadel was of great strength, and well garrisoned,
and had recently been surrounded with a deep ditch, into which
nails and spikes had been thrown, to impede assailants.

The Arab armies, rarely provided with the engines necessary
for the attack of fortified places, generally beleaguered them; cut off
all supplies; attacked all foraging parties that sallied forth, and thus
destroyed the garrison in detail, or starved it to a surrender.   This
was the reason of the long duration of their sieges.   This of Misrah,
or Memphis, lasted seven months : in the course of which the little
army of Amru was much reduced by frequent skirmishings.   At
the end of this time he received a reinforcement of four thousand
men, sent to him at his urgent entreaties by the Caliph.   Still his
force would have been insufficient for the capture of the place,
had he not been aided by the treachery of its governor Mokawkas.

This man, an original Egyptian, or Copt, by birth, and of noble
rank, was a profound hypocrite.   Like most of the Copts he was
of the Jacobite sect, who denied the double nature of Christ.   He
had dissembled his sectarian creed, however, and deceived the emperor Heraclius by a show of loyalty; so as to be made prefect of
his native province, and governor of the city.   Most of the inhabitants of Memphis were Copts and Jacobite Christians; and held
their Greek fellow-citizens, who were of the regular Catholic church
of Constantinople, in great antipathy.

Mokawkas, in the course of his administration, had collected,
by taxes and tribute, an immense amount of treasure, which he
had deposited into citadel.   He saw that the power of the emperor
was coming to an end in this quarter, and thought the present a
good opportunity to provide for his own fortune. Carrying on a
secret correspondence with the Moslem general, he agreed to
betray the place into his hands, on condition of receiving the treasure as a reward for his treason.   He accordingly, at an appointed
time, removed the greater part of the garrison from the citadel to
an island in the Nile.   The fortress was immediately assailed by
Amru, at the head of his fresh troops, and was easily carried by
assault, the Copts rendering no assistance.   The Greek soldiery,
on the Moslem standard being hoisted on the citadel, saw through
the treachery, and, giving up all as lost, escaped in their ships to
the main land; upon which the prefect surrendered the place by
capitulation.   An annual tribute of two ducats a head was levied
on all the inhabitants of the district, with the exception of old
men, women, and boys under the age of sixteen years.   It was
further conditioned, that the Moslem army should be furnished with
provisions, for which they would pay, and that the inhabitants of
the country should, forthwith, build bridges over all the streams
on the way to Alexandria.   It was also agreed that every Mussulman travelling through the country should be entitled to three
days' hospitality, free of charge.

The traitor Mokawkas was put in possession of his ill-gotten wealth. He begged of Amru to be taxed with the Copts, and always to be enrolled among them; declaring his abhorrence of the Greeks and their doctrines; urging Amru to persecute them with unremitting violence. He extended his sectarian bigotry even into the grave, stipulating that, at his death, he should be buried in the Christian Jacobite church of St. John, at Alexandria.

Amru, who was politic as well as brave, seeing the irreconcilable hatred of the Coptic or Jacobite Christians to the Greeks, shewed some favour to that sect, in order to make use of them in his conquest of the country. He even prevailed upon their patriarch Benjamin to emerge from his desert and hold a conference with him; and subsequently declared that "he had never conversed with a Christian priest of more innocent manners or venerable aspect." This piece of diplomacy had its effect, for we are told that all the Copts above and below Memphis swore allegiance to the Caliph.

Amru now pressed on for the city of Alexandria, distant about one hundred and twenty-five miles. According to stipulation, the people of the country repaired the roads and erected bridges to facilitate his march; the Greeks, however, driven from various quarters by the progress of their invaders, had collected at different posts on the island of the Delta, and, the channels of the Nile, and disputed with desperate but fruitless obstinacy, the onward course of the conquerors. The severest check was given at Keram al Shoraik, by the late garrison of Memphis, who had fortified themselves there after retreating from the island of the Nile. For three days did they maintain a gallant conflict with the Moslems, and then retired in good order to Alexandria. With all the facilities furnished to them on their march, it cost the Moslems two-and-twenty days to fight their way to that great city.

Alexandria now lay before them, the metropolis of wealthy Egypt, the emporium of the East, a place strongly fortified, stored with all the munitions of war, open by sea to all kinds of supplies and reinforcements, and garrisoned by Greeks, aggregated from various quarters, who here were to make the last stand for their Egyptian empire. It would seem that nothing short of an enthusiasm bordering on madness, could have led Amru and his host on an enterprise against this powerful city.

The Moslem leader, on planting his standard before the place, summoned it to surrender on the usual terms, which being promptly refused, he prepared for a vigorous siege. The garrison did not wait to be attacked, but made repeated sallies, and fought with desperate valour. Those who gave greatest annoyance to the Moslems, were their old enemies, the Greek troops from Memphis. Amru, seeing that the greatest defence was from a main tower, or citadel, made a gallant assault upon it, and carried it sword in hand. The Greek troops, however, rallied to that point from all parts of the city; the Moslems, after a furious struggle, gave way, and Amru, his faithful slave Werdan, and one of his generals, named Moslema Ibn al Mokalled, fighting to the last, were surrounded, overpowered, and taken prisoners.

The Greeks, unaware of the importance of their captives, led them before the governor. He demanded of them, haugtily, what was their object in thus overrunning the world and disturbing the quiet of peaceable neighbours. Amru made the usual reply. that they came to spread the faith of Islam; and that it was their intention, before they laid by the sword, to make the Egyptians either converts or tributaries. The boldness of his answer, and the loftiness of his demeanour, awakened the suspicions of the governor, who, supposing him to be a warrior of note among the Arabs, ordered one of his guards to strike off his head. Upon this Werdan, the slave, understanding the Greek language, seized his master by the collar, and, giving him a buffet on the cheek, called him an impudent dog, and ordered him to hold his peace, and let his superiors speak. Moslema, perceiving the meaning of the slave, now interposed, and made a plausible speech to the governor; telling him that Amru had thoughts of raising the siege, having received a letter to that effect from the Caliph, who intended to send ambassadors to treat for peace, and assuring the governor that, if permitted to depart, they would make a favourable report to Amru.

The governor, who, if Arabian chronicles may be believed on this point, must have been a man of easy faith, ordered the prisoners to be set at liberty; but the shouts of the besieging army on the safe return of their general soon showed him how completely he had been duped.

But scanty details of the siege of Alexandria have reached the Christian reader, yet it was one of the longest, most obstinately contested and sanguinary, in the whole course of the Moslem wars. It endured fourteen months with various success; the Moslem army was repeatedly reinforced, and lost twenty-three thousand men; at length their irresistible ardour and perseverance prevailed; the capital of Egypt was conquered, and the Greek inhabitants were dispersed in all directions. Some retreated in considerable bodies into the interior of the country, and fortified themselves in strongholds; others took refuge in the ships, and put to sea.

Amru, on taking possession of the city, found it nearly abandoned; he prohibited his troops from plundering; and leaving a small garrison to guard the place, hastened with his main army in pursuit of the fugitive Greeks. In the meantime the ships which had taken off a part of the garrison were still lingering on the coast, and tidings reached them that the Moslem general had departed, and had left the captured city nearly defenceless. They immediately made sail back for Alexandria, and entered the port in the night. The Greek soldiers surprised the sentinels, got possession of the city, and put most of the Moslems they found there to the sword.

Amru was in full pursuit of the Greek fugitives, when he heard of the recapture of the city. Mortified at his own negligence in leaving so rich a conquest with so slight a guard, he returned in all haste, resolved to retake it by storm. The Greeks, however, had fortified themselves strongly in the castle, and made stout resistance. Amru was obliged, therefore, to besiege it a second time, but the siege was short. The castle was carried by assault; many of the Greeks were cut to pieces, the rest escaped once more to their ships, and now gave up the capital as lost. All this occurred in the nineteenth year of the Hegira, and the year 640 of the Christian era.

On this second capture of the city by force of arms, and without capitulation, the troops were clamorous to be permitted to plunder. Amru again checked their rapacity, and commanded that all persons and property in the place, should remain inviolate, until the will of the Caliph could be known. So perfect was his command over his troops, that not the most trivial article was taken. His letter to the Caliph shows what must have been the population and splendour of Alexandria, and the luxury and effeminacy of its inhabitants, at the time of the Moslem conquest. It states the city to have contained four thousand palaces; five thousand baths; four hundred theatres and places of amusement; twelve thousand gardeners which supply it with vegetables, and forty thousand tributary Jews. t was impossible, he said, to do justice to its riches and magnificence. He had hitherto held it sacred from plunder, but his troops having won it by force of arms, considered themselves entitled to the spoils of victory.

The Caliph Omar in reply, expressed a high sense of his important services, but reproved him for even mentioning the desire of the soldiery to plunder so rich a city, one of the greatest emporiums of the East. He charged him, therefore, most rigidly to watch over the rapacious propensities of his men; to prevent all pillage, violence and waste; to collect and make out an account of all moneys, jewels, household furniture, and every thing else that was valuable, to be appropriated towards defraying the expenses of this war of the faith. He ordered the tribute also, collected in the conquered country, to be treasured up at Alexandria, for the supplies of the Moslem troops.

The surrender of all Egypt followed the capture of its capital. A tribute of two ducats was laid on every male of mature age, beside a tax on all lands in proportion to their value, and the revenue which resulted to the Caliph is estimated at twelve millions of ducats.

We have shown that Amru was a poet in his youth; and throughout all his campaigns he manifested an intelligent and inquiring spirit, if not more highly informed, at least more liberal and extended in its views than was usual among the early Moslem conquerors. He delighted, in his hours of leisure, to converse with learned men, and acquire through their means such knowledge as had been denied to him by the deficiency of his education. Such a companion he found at Alexandria in a native of the place, a Christian of the sect of the Jacobites, eminent for his philological researches, his commentaries on Moses and Aristotle, and his laborious treatises of various kinds, surnamed Philoponus from his love of study, but commonly known by the name of John the Grammarian. An intimacy soon arose between the Arab conqueror and the Christian philologist; an intimacy honourable to Amru, but destined to be

17

lamentable in its result to the cause of letters. In an evil hour, John the Grammarian, being encouraged by the favour shown him by the Arab general, revealed to him a treasure hitherto unnoticed, or rather unvalued by the Moslem conquerors. This was a vast collection of books or manuscripts, since renowned in history as the ÁLEXANDRIAN LIBRARY. Perceiving that in taking an account of every thing valuable in the city, and sealing up all its treasures, Amru had taken no notice of the books, John solicited that they might be given to him. Unfortunately, the learned zeal of the Grammarian gave a consequence to the books in the eyes of Amru, and made him scrupulous of giving them away without permission of the Caliph. He forthwith wrote to Omar, stating the merits of John, and requesting to know whether the books might be given to him. The reply of Omar was laconic, but fatal. "The contents of those books," said he, "are in conformity with the Koran, or they are not. If they are, the Koran is sufficient without them; if they are not, they are pernicious. Let them, therefore, be destroyed.

Amru, it is said, obeyed the order punctually. The books and manuscripts were distributed as fuel among the five thousand baths of the city; but so numerous were they that it took six months to consume them. This act of barbarism, recorded by Abulpharagius, is considered somewhat doubtful by Gibbon, in consequence of its not being mentioned by two of the most ancient chroniclers, Elmacin in his Saracenic history, and Eutychius in his annals, the latter of whom was patriarch of Alexandria, and has detailed the conquest of that city. It is inconsistent, too, with the character of Amru, as a poet and a man of superior intelligence; and it has recently been reported, we know not on what authority, that many of the literary treasures thus said to have been destroyed, do actually exist in Constantinople. Their destruction, however, is generally credited and deeply deplored by historians. Amru, as a man of genius and intelligence, may have grieved at the order of the Caliph; while, as a loyal subject and faithful soldier, he felt bound to obey it.[1]

The fall of Alexandria decided the fate of Egypt and likewise that of the emperor Heraclius. He was already afflicted with a dropsy, and took the loss of his Syrian, and now that of his Egyptian dominions, so much to heart, that he underwent a paroxysm, which ended in his death, about seven weeks after the loss of his Egyptian capital. He was succeeded by his son Constantine.

While Amru was successfully extending his conquests, a great

[1] The Alexandrian Library was formed by Ptolemy Soter, and placed in a building called the Bruchion. It was augmented in successive reigns to 400,000 volumes, and an additional 300,000 volumes were placed in a temple called the Serapeon. The Bruchion, with the books it contained, was burnt in the war of Cæsar, but the Serapeon was preserved. Cleopatra, it is said, added to it the library of Pergamas, given to her by Marc Antony, consisting of 200,000 volumes   t sustained repeated injuries during various subsequent revolutions, but was always restored to its ancient splendour, and numerous additions made to it. Such was its state   the capture of Alexandria by the Moslems.

dearth and famine fell upon all Arabia, insomuch that the Caliph Omar had to call upon him for supplies from the fertile plains of Egypt; whereupon Amru despatched such a train of camels laden with grain, that it is said, when the first of the line had reached the city of Medina, the last had not yet left the land of Egypt. But this mode of conveyance proving too tardy, at the command of the Caliph, he dug a canal of communication from the Nile to the Red Sea, a distance of eighty miles; by which provisions might be conveyed to the Arabian shores. This canal had been commenced by Trajan, the Roman emperor.

The able and indefatigable Amru went on in this manner, executing the commands and fulfilling the wishes of the Caliph; and governed the country he had conquered, with such sagacity and justice, that he rendered himself one of the most worthily renowned among the Moslem generals.

CHAPTER XXV.

Enterprises of the Moslems in Persia.—Defence of the kingdom by Queen Arzemia.—Her death.—Elevation of Yezdegird to the throne.—Battle of the Bridge.

For the sake of perspicuity, we have recorded the Moslem conquests in Syria and Egypt in a continued narrative, without pausing to notice events which were occurring at the same time in other quarters; we now recede several years, to take up the course of affairs in Persia, from the time that Khaled, in the thirteenth year of the Hegira, in obedience to the orders of Abu Beker, left his victorious army on the banks of the Euphrates, to take the general command in Syria. The victories of Khaled had doubtless been owing in part to the distracted state of the Persian empire. In the course of an inconsiderable number of years, the proud sceptre of the Khosrus had passed from hand to hand; Khosru II, surnamed Parviz, having been repeatedly defeated by Heraclius, was deposed in 628, by a party of his nobles, headed by his own son Siroes (or Shiruyah), and was put to death by the latter in a vault under the palace, among the treasures he had amassed. To secure possession of the throne, Siroes followed up the parricide by the massacre of seventeen of his brothers. It was not ambition alone that instigated these crimes. He was enamoured of a sultana in the harem of his father; the matchless Shireen. While yet reeking with his father's blood, he declared his passion to her. She recoiled from him with horror, and when he would have used force, gave herself instant death to escape from his embraces. The disappointment of his passion; the upbraidings of his sisters for the murders of their father and their brothers; and the stings of his own conscience, threw Siroes into a moody melancholy, and either caused, or added acuteness to a malady, of which he died in the course of eight months.

His infant son Ardisheer, was placed on the throne about the end of 628, but was presently slain, and the throne usurped by Sheriyar a Persian noble, who was himself killed after a very short reign. Turan-Docht, a daughter of Khosru Parviz, was now crowned and reigned eighteen months, when she was set aside by her cousin Shah Shenandeh, who was himself deposed by the nobles, and Arzemi-Docht [1] or Arzemia, as the name is commonly given, another daughter of Khosru Parviz, was placed on the throne in the year 632 of the Christian era. The Persian seat of government, which had been often changed, was at this time held in the magnificent city of Madain or Madayn, on the Tigris, where was the ancient Ctesiphon.

Arzemia was distinguished alike for masculine talents and feminine beauty; she had been carefully instructed under her father Khosru, and had acquired sad experience, during the series of conspiracies and assassinations which had beset the throne for the last four years. Rejecting from her council the very traitors who had placed the crown upon her head, she undertook to wield the sceptre without the aid of a vizir, thereby giving mortal offence to the most powerful nobles of her realm. She was soon called upon to exert her masculine spirit by the continued aggressions of the Moslems.

The reader will recollect that the Moslem army on the Euphrates, at the departure of Khaled, was left under the command of Mosenna Ibn Haris (or Muthenna Ibn Hârith, as the name is sometimes rendered). On the accession of Omar to the Caliphat, he appointed Mosenna emir or governor of Sewad, the country recently conquered by Khaled, lying about the lower part of the Euphrates and the Tigris, forming a portion of the Persian province of Irak-Arabi. This was in compliance with the wishes and intentions of Abu Beker; though Omar does not appear to have had great confidence in the military talents of Mosenna, the career of conquest having languished in his hands since the departure of Khaled. He accordingly sent Abu Obeidah Sakfi, one of the most important disciples of the prophet, at the head of a thousand chosen men, to reinforce the army under Mosenna, and to take the lead in military enterprises. [2] He was accompanied by Sabit Ibn Kais, one of the veterans of the battle of Beder.

The Persian Queen, hearing of the advance of the Moslem army thus reinforced, sent an able general, Rustam Ibn Ferukh-Zad (or Feruchsad), with thirty thousand more, to repel them. Rustam halted on the confines of Irak, and sent forward strong detachments under a general named Dschaban, and a Persian prince named Narsi (or Narsis). These were so roughly handled by the Moslems, that Rustam found it necessary to hasten with his main force to

---

[1] Docht or Dokht, diminutive of dukhter, signifies the unmarried or maiden state.
[2] This Abu Obeidah has sometimes been confounded with the general of the same name, who commanded in Syria; the latter, however, was Abu Obeidah *Ibn Aljerah* (the son of Aljerah).

their assistance. He arrived too late; they had been severally defeated and put to flight, and the whole country of Sewad was in the hands of the Moslems.

Queen Arzemia, still more aroused to the danger of her kingdom, sent Rustam a reinforcement led by Behman Dschadu, surnamed the Veiled, from the shaggy eyebrows which overshadowed his visage. He brought with him three thousand men and thirty elephants. These animals, of little real utility in warfare, were formidable in the eyes of those unaccustomed to them, and were intended to strike terror into the Arabian troops.. One of them was the white elephant Mahmoud, famous for having been ridden by Abraha, the Ethiopian king, in foregone times, when he invaded Mecca and assailed the Caaba. It was considered a harbinger of victory, all the enterprises in which it had been employed having proved successful.

With Behman, the heavy-browed, came also the standard of Kaoh, the sacred standard. It was originally the leathern apron of the blacksmith Kaoh, which he reared as a banner when he roused the people, and delivered Persia from the tyranny of Sohak. It had been enlarged from time to time, with costly silk, embroidered with gold, until it was twenty-two feet long and fifteen broad; and was decorated with gems of inestimable value. With this standard the fate of the kingdom was believed, by superstitious Persians, to be connected.

The Moslem forces, even with the reinforcement brought by Abu Obeidah Sakfi, did not exceed nine thousand in number; the Persians, encamped near the ruins of Babylon, were vastly superior. It was the counsel of Mosenna and the veteran Sabit, that they should fall back into the deserts, and remain encamped there until reinforcements could be obtained from the Caliph. Abu Obeidah, however, was for a totally different course. He undervalued the prowess of the Persians; he had heard Mosenna censured for want of enterprise, and Khaled extolled to the skies for his daring achievements in this quarter. He was determined to emulate them, to cross the Euphrates and attack the Persians in their encampment. In vain Mosenna and Sabit remonstrated. He caused a bridge of boats to be thrown across the Euphrates, and led the way to the opposite bank. His troops did not follow, with their usual alacrity, for they felt the rashness of the enterprise. While they were yet crossing the bridge, they were severely galled by a body of archers, detached in the advance by Rustam; and were met at the head of the bridge by that warrior with his vanguard of cavalry.

The conflict was severe. The banner of Islam passed from hand to hand of seven brave champions, as one after another fell in its defence. The Persians were beaten back, but now arrived the main body of the army with the thirty elephants. Abu Obeidah breasted fearlessly the storm of war which he had so rashly provoked. He called to his men not to fear the elephants, but to strike at their trunks. He himself severed, with a blow of his scimetar, the trunk of the famous white elephant, but in so doing his foot slipped, he fell to the earth, and was trampled to death by the enraged animal.

The Moslems, disheartened by his loss, and overwhelmed by numbers, endeavoured to regain the bridge. The enemy had thrown combustibles into the boats on which it was constructed, and had set them on fire. Some of the troops were driven into the water and perished there ; the main body retreated along the river, protected in the rear by Mosenna, who now displayed the skill of an able general, and kept the enemy at bay until a slight bridge could be hastily thrown across another part of the river. He was the last to cross the bridge, and caused it to be broken behind him.

Four thousand Moslems were either slain or drowned in this rash affair : two thousand fled to Medina, and about three thousand remained with Mosenna; who encamped and intrenched them, and sent a fleet courier to the Caliph, entreating instant aid. Nothing saved this remnant of the army from utter destruction but a dissension which took place between the Persian commanders ; who, instead of following up their victory, returned to Madayn, the Persian capital.

This was the severest and almost the only severe check that Moslem audacity had for a long time experienced. It took place in the 13th year of the Hegira, and the year 634 of the Christian era ; and was long and ruefully remembered by the Arabs as the battle of "El Jisir," or The Battle of the Bridge.

CHAPTER XXVI.

Mosenna Ibn Haris ravages the country along the Euphrates.—Death of Arzemia.— Yezdegird III. raised to the throne.—Saad Ibn Abu Wakkás given the general command.—Death of Mosenna.—Embassy to Yezdegird.—Its reception.

Having received moderate reinforcements, Mosenna again took the field in Arab style, hovering about the confines of Babylonia, and sending detachments in different directions to plunder and lay waste the country bordering on the Euphrates. It was an instance of the vicissitude of human affairs, and the instability of earthly grandeur, that this proud region, which once held the world in awe, should be thus marauded and insulted by a handful of predatory Arabs.

To check their ravages, Queen Arzemia sent out a general named Mahran, with twelve thousand chosen cavalry. Mosenna, hearing of their approach, called in his plundering parties and prepared for battle. The two hosts met near Hirah, on the borders of the desert. Mosenna, who in the battle of the bridge had been the last man to retire, was now the foremost man to charge. In the fury of the fight he made his way, almost alone, into the heart of the

Persian army, and with difficulty fought his way out again and back to his own men. The Persians, as we have noted, were chosen troops, and fought with unusual spirit. The Moslems, in some parts of the field, began to give way. Mosenna galloped up and threw himself before them; he expostulated, he threatened, he tore his beard in the agony of his feelings; he succeeded in leading them back to the fight; which endured from noon until sunset; and still continued doubtful. At the close of the day Mosenna encountered Mahran hand to hand, in the midst of his guards, and received a powerful blow, which might have proved fatal, but for his armour. In return he smote the Persian commander with his scimetar just where the neck joins to the shoulder, and laid him dead. The Persians, seeing their leader fall, took to flight, nor stopped until they reached Madayn.

The Moslems next made a plundering expedition to Bagdad, at that time a mere village, but noted for a great fair, the resort of merchants from various parts of the East. An Arab detachment pounced upon it at the time of the fair, and carried off many captives and immense booty.

The tidings of the defeat of Mahran, and the plundering of the fair, spread consternation in the Persian capital. The nobles and priests, who had hitherto stood in awe of the spirit of the queen, now raised a tumult. "These are the fruits," said they, "of having a woman to reign over us."

The fate of the beautiful Arzemia was hastened by private revenge. Faruch-Zad, one of the most powerful of her nobles, and governor of Khorassan, incited by love and ambition, had aspired to her hand. At first, it is said, she appeared to favour his addresses, fearing to provoke his enmity, but afterwards slighted them; whereupon he entered the palace by night, and attempted to get possession of her person. His attempt failed, and, by her command, he received instant death at the hands of her guards, accompanied by some indignities.

His son, Rustam, who had been left by him in the government of Khorassan, hastened, at the head of an armed force, to avenge his death. He arrived in the height of the public discontent; entered the city without opposition, stormed the palace, captured the young and beautiful queen, subjected her to degrading outrages, and put her to death in the most cruel manner. She was the sixth of the usurping sovereigns, and had not yet reigned a year.

A remaining son of Khosru Parviz was now brought forward and placed on the slippery throne, but was poisoned within forty days, some say by his courtiers, others by a slave.

The priests and nobles now elevated a youth about fifteen years of age to this perilous dignity. He was a grandson of Khosru Parviz, and had been secluded, during the late period of anarchy and assassination, in the city of Istakar, the ancient Persepolis. He is known by the name of Yezdegird III, though some historians call him Hermisdas IV, from his family, instead of his personal appellation. He was of a good natural disposition, but weak and irresolute, and apt, from his youth and inexperience, to become a passive instrument in the hands of the faction which had placed him on the throne.

One of the first measures of the new reign was to assemble a powerful army and place it under the command of Rustam, the same general who had so signally revenged the death of his father. It was determined, by a signal blow, to sweep the Arabian marauders from the land.

Omar, on his part, hearing of the changes and warlike preparations in the Persian capital, made a hasty levy of troops, and would have marched in person to carry the war into the heart of Persia. It was with great difficulty he was dissuaded from this plan by his discreet counsellors, Othman and Ali, and induced to send in his place Saad Ibn Abu Wakkâs. This was a zealous soldier of the faith who used to boast that he was the first who had shed the blood of the unbelieving : and, moreover, that the prophet, in the first holy war, had intrusted to him the care of his household during his absence; saying, "To you, oh Saad, who are to me as my father and my mother, I confide my family." To have been a favoured and confidential companion of the prophet, was fast growing to be a title of great distinction among the faithful.

Saad was invested with the general command of the forces in Persia; and Mosenna, though his recent good conduct and signal success entitled him to the highest consideration, was ordered to serve under him.

Saad set out from Medina with an army of but six or seven thousand men; among these, however, were one thousand well-tried soldiers who had followed the prophet in his campaigns, and one hundred of the veterans of Beder. They were led on also by some of the most famous champions of the faith. The army was joined on its march by recruits from all quarters, so that by the time it joined the troops under Mosenna, it amounted to upwards of thirty thousand men.

Mosenna died three days after the arrival of his successor in the camp; the cause and nature of his death are not mentioned. He left behind him a good name, and a wife remarkable for her beauty. The widow was easily brought to listen to the addresses of Saad, who thus succeeded to Mosenna in his matrimonial as well as his military capacity.

The Persian force, under Rustam, lay encamped at Kadesia (or Khâdesîyah), on the frontier of Sawâd or Irak-Arabi, and was vastly superior in numbers to the Moslems. Saad sent expresses to the Caliph entreating reinforcements. He was promised them, but exhorted in the meantime to doubt nothing; never to regard the number of the foe, but to think always that he vas fighting under the eye of the Caliph He was instructed, however, before commencing hostilities, to send a delegation to Yezdegird inviting him to embrace the faith.

Saad accordingly sent several of his most discreet and veteran officers on this mission. They repaired to the magnificent city of Madayn, and were ushered through the sumptuous halls and saloons of the palace of the Khosrus, crowded with guards and attendants all richly arrayed, into the presence of the youthful monarch, whom they found seated in state on a throne, supported by silver columns, and surrounded by the dazzling splendour of an Oriental Court.

The appearance of the Moslem envoys, attired in simple Arab style, in the striped garments of Yemen, amidst the gorgeous throng of nobles arrayed in jewels and embroidery, was but little calculated to inspire deference in a young and inconsiderate prince, brought up in pomp and luxury, and accustomed to consider dignity inseparable from splendour. He had no doubt, also, been schooled for the interview by his crafty counsellors.

The audience opened by a haughty demand on his part, through his interpreter, as to the object of their embassy. Upon this, one of their number, Na'man Ibn Muskry, set forth the divine mission of the prophet and his dying command to enforce his religion by the sword, leaving no peaceable alternative to unbelievers, but conversion or tribute. He concluded by inviting the king to embrace the faith; if not, to consent to become a tributary; if he should refuse both, to prepare for battle.

Yezdegird restrained his indignation, and answered in words which had probably been prepared for him. "You Arabs," said he, "have hitherto been known to us by report, as wanderers of the desert; your food dates, and sometimes lizards and serpents; your drink brackish water; your garments coarse hair cloth. Some of you, who by chance have wandered into our realms, have found sweet water, savoury food, and soft raiment. They have carried back word of the same to their brethren in the desert, and now you come in swarms to rob us of our goods and our very land. Ye are like the starving fox, to whom the husbandman afforded shelter in his vineyard, and who in return, brought a troop of his brethren to devour his grapes. Receive from my generosity whatever your wants require; load your camels with corn and dates, and depart in peace to your native land; but if you tarry in Persia, beware the fate of the fox who was slain by the husbandman."

The most aged of the Arab envoys, the Sheikh Mukair Ibn Zarrarah, replied with great gravity and decorum, and an unaltered countenance. "Oh king! all thou hast said of the Arabs is most true. The green lizard of the desert was their sometime food; the brackish water of wells their drink; their garments were of hair cloth, and they buried their infant daughters to restrain the increase of their tribes. All this was in the days of ignorance. They knew not good from evil. They were guilty, and they suffered. But Allah in his mercy sent his apostle Mahomet, and his sacred Koran among them. He rendered them wise and valiant. He commanded them to war with infidels until all should be converted to the true faith. On his behest we come. All we demand of thee is to acknowledge that there is no God but God, and that Mahomet is his apostle, and to pay from thy income the customary contribution of the Zacat, paid by all true believers, in charity to the poor, and for the support of the family of the prophet. Do this, and not a Moslem shall enter the Persian dominions, without thy leave; but if thou refuse it, and refuse to pay the tribute exacted from all unbelievers, prepare for the subjugation of the sword."

The forbearance of Yezdegird was at an end. "Were it not unworthy of a great Padischah," said he, "to put ambassadors to death, the sword should be the only tongue with which I would reply to your insolence. Away! ye robbers of the lands of others! take with ye a portion of the Persian soil ye crave." So saying, he caused sacks of earth to be bound upon their shoulders; to be delivered by them to their chiefs as symbols of the graves they would be sure to find at Kadesia.

When beyond the limits of the city, the envoys transferred the sacks of earth to the backs of their camels, and returned with them to Saad Ibn Abu Wakkâs; shrewdly interpreting into a good omen what had been intended by the Persian monarch as a scornful taunt. "Earth," said they, "is the emblem of empire. As surely, oh Saad, as we deliver thee these sacks of earth, so surely will Allah deliver the empire of Persia into the hands of true believers."

CHAPTER XXVII.

The Battle of Kadesia.

The hostile armies came in presence of each other on the plains of Kadesia (or Kâdesîyah), adjacent to a canal derived from the Euphrates. The huge mass of the Persian army would have been sufficient to bear down the inferior number of the Moslems, had it possessed the Grecian or Roman discipline; but it was a tumultuous multitude, unwieldy from its military pomp, and encumbered by its splendid trappings. The Arabs, on the contrary, were veteran skirmishers of the desert; light and hardy horsemen; dexterous with the bow and lance, and skilled to wheel and retreat, and to return again to the attack. Many individual acts of prowess took place between champions of either army, who dared each other to single combat in front of the hosts when drawn out in battle array. The costly armour of the Persians, wrought with gold, and their belts or girdles studded with gems, made them rich prizes to their Moslem victors; while the Persians, if victorious, gained nothing from the rudely clad warriors of the desert, but honour and hard blows.

Saad Ibn Abu Wakkâs was in an unfortunate plight for a leader of an army on such a momentous occasion. He was grievously afflicted with boils in his reins, so that he sat on his horse with extreme difficulty. Still he animated his troops by his presence, and gave the *tekbir* or battle-cry — Allah Achbar!

The Persian force came on with great shouts; their elephants in the van. The horses of the Moslem cavalry recoiled at sight of the latter, and became unmanageable. A great number of the horse-men dismounted; attacked the unwieldy animals with their swords, and drove them back upon their own host. Still the day went hard with the Moslems; their force being so inferior, and their general unable to take the lead and mingle in the battle. The arrival of a reinforcement from Syria, put them in new heart, and they fought on until the approach of night, when both parties desisted, and drew off to their encampments. Thus ended the first day's fight, which the Persians called the battle of Armâth; but the Moslems. The Day of Succour, from the timely arrival of reinforcements.

On the following morning the armies drew out again in battle ar-ray, but no general conflict took place. Saad was unable to mount his horse and. lead his troops into action, and the Persians, aware of the reinforcements received by the Moslems, were not disposed to provoke a battle. The day passed in light skirmishes and single combats between the prime warriors of either host, who defied each other to trials of skill and prowess. These combats, of course, were desperate, and commonly cost the life of one, if not both of the combatants.

Saad overlooked the field from the shelter of a tent, where he sat at a repast with his beautiful bride beside him. Her heart swelled with grief at seeing so many gallant Moslems laid low; a thought of the valiant husband she had lost passed across her mind, and the unwary ejaculation escaped her, "Alas! Mosenna Ibn Haris, where art thou?" Saad was stung to the quick by what he con-ceived a reproach on his courage or activity, and, in the heat of the moment, struck her on the face with his dagger. "To-Mor-row," muttered he to himself, "I will mount my horse."

In the night he secretly sent out a detachment in the direction of Damascus, to remain concealed until the two armies should be en-gaged on the following day, and then to come with banners dis-played, and a great sound of drum and trumpet, as though they were a reinforcement hurrying to the field of action.

The morning dawned, but still, to his great mortification, Saad was unable to sit upon his horse, and had to intrust the conduct of the battle to one of his generals. It was a day of bloody and obstinate conflict; and from the tremendous shock of the encoun-tering hosts, was celebrated among the Arabs as "The day of the Concussion."

The arrival of the pretended reinforcement inspirited the Mos-lems, who were ignorant of the stratagem, and dismayed the enemy. Rustam urged on his elephants to break down the Arab host, but they had become familiar with those animals, and attacked them so vigorously that, as before, they turned upon their own em-ployers, and trampled them down in their unwieldy flight from the field.

The battle continued throughout the day with varying fortune; nor did it cease at nightfall, for Rustam rode about among his troops urging them to fight until morning. That night was called by some the night of delirium; for in the dark and deadly struggle the comba-tants struck at random, and often caught each other by the beard:

by others it was called the night of howling and lamentation, from the cries of the wounded.

The battle ceased not even at the dawning, but continued until the heat of the day. A whirlwind of dust hid the armies from each other for a time, and produced confusion on the field, but it aided the Moslems, as it blew in the faces of the enemy. During a pause in the conflict, Rustam, panting with heat and fatigue, and half blinded with dust, took shelter from the sun under a tent which had been pitched near the water, and was surrounded by camels laden with treasure, and with the luxurious furniture of the camp. A gust of wind whirled the tent into the water. He then threw himself upon the earth in the shade of one of the camels. A band of Arab soldiers came upon him by surprise. One of them, Hellâl Ibn Alkameh by name, in his eagerness for plunder, cut the cords which bound the burthen on the camel. A package of silver fell upon Rustam and broke his spine. In his agony he fell, or threw himself into the water, but was drawn out by the leg, his head stricken off, and elevated on the lance of Hellâl. The Persians recognized the bloody features, and fled amain, abandoning to the victors their camp, with all its rich furniture and baggage, and scores of beasts of burden, laden with treasure and with costly gear. The amount of booty was incalculahle.

The sacred standard, too, was among the spoils. To the soldier who had captured it, thirty thousand pieces of gold are said to have been paid at Saad's command; and the jewels, with which it was studded, were put with the other booty, to be shared according to rule. Hellâl, too, who brought the head of Rustam to Saad, was allowed as a reward, to strip the body of his victim. Never did Arab soldier make richer spoil. The garments of Rustam were richly embroidered, and he wore two gorgeous belts, ornamented with jewels, one worth a thousand pieces of gold, the other seventy thousand dirhems of silver.

Thirty thousand Persians are said to have fallen in this battle, and upwards of seven thousand Moslems. The loss most deplored by the Persians, was that of their sacred banner, with which they connected the fate of the realm.

This battle took place in the fifteenth year of the Hegira, and the six hundred and thirty-sixth year of the Christian era, and is said to be as famous among the Arabs as that of Arbela among the Greeks.

Complaints having circulated among the troops that Saad had not mingled in the fight, he summoned several of the old men to his tent, and, stripping himself, showed the boils by which he was so grievously afflicted; after which there were no further expressions of dissatisfaction. It is to be hoped he found some means, equally explicit, of excusing himself to his beautiful bride for the outrage he had committed upon her.

CHAPTER XXVIII.

Founding of Bassora.—Capture of the Persian capital.—Flight of Yezdegird to Holwán.

After the signal victory of Kadesia, Saad Ibn Abu Wakkâs, by command of the Caliph, remained for some months in the neighbourhood, completing the subjugation of the conquered country, collecting tax and tribute, and building mosques in every direction for the propagation of the faith. About the same time Omar caused the city of Basra, or Bassora, to be founded in the lower part of Irak Arabi, on that great river formed by the junction of the Euphrates and the Tigris. This city was intended to protect the region conquered by the Moslems about the mouth of the Euphrates; to cut off the trade of India from Persia, and to keep a check upon Ahwâz (a part of Susiana or Khusestan), the prince or satrap of which, Hormusân by name, had taken an active part in the late battle of Kadesia. The city of Bassora was founded in the fourteenth year of the Hegira, by Orweh Ibn Otbeh. It soon gathered. within its walls great numbers of inhabitants from the surrounding country; rose rapidly in importance, and has ever since been distinguished as a mart for the Indian commerce.

Having brought all the country in the neighbourhood of Kadesia into complete subjection, Saad Ibn Abu Wakkâs, by command of the Caliph, proceeded in the conquest of Persia. The late victories, and the capture of the national banner, had struck despair into the hearts of the Persians. They considered the downfall of their religion and empire at hand, and for a time made scarcely any resistance to the invaders. Cities and strongholds surrendered almost without a blow. Babel is incidentally enumerated among the captured places; but the once all-powerful Babylon was now shrunk into such insignificance, that its capture seemed not worthy of a boast. Saad crossed the Tigris and advanced upon Madayn, the Persian capital. His army, on departing from Kadesia, had not exceeded twenty thousand men, having lost many by battle, and more by disease. Multitudes, however, from the subjugated cities, and from other parts, joined his standard while on the march, so that, as he approached Madayn, his forces amounted to sixty thousand men.

There was abundance of troops in Madayn, the wrecks of vanquished armies and routed garrisons, but there was no one capable or willing to take the general command. All seemed paralyzed by their fears. The king summoned his counsellors about him, but their only advice was to fly. "Khorasan and Kerman are still yours," said they, "let us depart while we may do so in safety; why should we remain here to be made captives?"

Yezdegird hesitated to take this craven advice; but more from weakness and indecision of character than from any manly repugnance. He wavered and lingered, until what might have been an orderly retreat became a shameful flight. When the invaders were within one day's march of his capital, he ordered his valuables to be packed upon beasts of burthen, and set off, with a worthless retinue of palace minions, attendants, and slaves, male and female, for Holwân, at the foot of the Medean hills. His example was followed throughout the city. There was hurry and tumult in every part. Fortunate was he who had a camel, or a horse, or an ass, to load with his most valuable effects; such as were not so provided, took what they could on their shoulders; but, in such a hasty and panic-striken flight, where personal safety was the chief concern, little could be preserved; the greater part of their riches remained behind. Thus the wealthy Madayn, the once famous Ctesiphon, which had formerly repulsed a Roman army, though furnished with battering rams and other warlike engines, was abandoned without a blow at the approach of these nomad warriors.

As Saad entered the deserted city, he gazed with wonder and admiration at its stately edifices, surrounded by vineyards and gardens, all left to his mercy by the flying owners. In pious exultation he repeated aloud a passage of the Koran, alluding to the abandonment by Pharaoh and his troops of their habitations, when they went in pursuit of the children of Israel. "How many gardens and fountains, and fields of corn and fair dwellings, and other sources of delight did they leave behind them! Thus we dispossessed them thereof, and gave the same for an inheritance to another people. Neither heaven nor earth wept for them. They were unpitied." [1]

The deserted city was sacked and pillaged. One may imagine the sacking of such a place by the ignorant hordes of the desert. The rude Arabs beheld themselves surrounded by treasures beyond their conception; works of art, the value of which they could not appreciate, and articles of luxury which moved their ridicule rather than their admiration. In roving through the streets they came to the famous palace of the Khosrus, begun by Kobâd Ibn Firuz, and finished by his son Nushirwan, constructed of polished marble, and called the white palace, from its resplendent appearance. As they gazed at it in wonderment, they called to mind the prediction of Mahomet, when he heard that the haughty monarch of Persia had torn his letter: "Even so shall Allah rend his empire in pieces." "Behold the white palace of Khosru," cried the Moslems to one another! "This is the fulfilment of the prophecy of the apostle of God!"

Saad entered the lofty portal of the palace with feelings of devotion. His first act was to make his salaam and prostrations, and

.[1] Koran, chapter xxiv.

pronounce the confession of faith in its deserted halls. He then took note of its contents, and protected it from the ravage of the soldiery, by making it his headquarters. It was furnished throughout with oriental luxury. It had wardrobes filled with gorgeous apparel. In the armory were weapons of all kinds, magnificently wrought : a coat of mail and sword, for state occasions, bedecked with jewels of incalculable value; a silver horseman on a golden horse, and a golden rider on a silver camel, all likewise studded with jewels.

In the vaults were treasures of gold and silver and precious stones; with money, the vast amount of which, though stated by Arabian historians, we hesitate to mention.

In some of the apartments were gold and silver vessels filled with oriental perfumes. In the magazines were stored exquisite spices, odoriferous gums, and medicinal drugs. Among the latter were quantities of camphor, which the Arabs mistook for salt, and mixed with their food.

In one of the chambers was a silken carpet of great size, which the king used in winter. Art and expense had been lavished upon it. It was made to represent a garden. The leaves of the plants were emeralds; the flowers were embroidered in their natural colours, with pearls and jewels and precious stones; the fountains were wrought with diamonds and sapphires, to represent the sparkling of their waters. The value of the whole was beyond calculation.

The hall of audience surpassed every other part in magnificence. The vaulted roof, says D'Herbelot, resembled a firmament decked with golden spheres, each with a corresponding movement, so as to represent the planets and the signs of the Zodiac. The throne was of prodigious grandeur, supported on silver columns. Above it was the crown of Khosru Nushirwan, suspended by a golden chain to bear the immense weight of its jewels, but contrived to appear as if on the head of the monarch when seated.

A mule is said to have been overtaken, on which a trusty officer of the palace was bearing away some of the jewels of the crown, the tiara or diadem of Yezdegird, with his belt and scimetar and bracelets.

Saad appointed Omar Ibn Muskry to take charge of all the spoils for regular distribution, and criers were sent about to make proclamation that the soldiers should render in their booty to that officer. Such was the enormous amount that, after a fifth had been set apart for the Caliph, the remainder, divided among sixty thousand men, gave each of them twelve hundred dirhems of silver.

It took nine hundred heavily laden camels to convey to Medina the Caliph's fifth of the spoil, among which the carpet, the clothing, and regalia of the king were included. The people of Medina, though of late years accustomed to the rich booty of the armies, were astonished at such an amount of treasure. Omar ordered that a mosque should be built of part of the proceeds. A consultation was held over the royal carpet, whether it should be stored away in the public treasury to be used by the Caliph on state occasions, or whether it should be included in the booty to be shared.

Omar hesitated to decide with his usual promptness, and referred the matter to Ali. "Oh prince of true believers!" exclaimed the latter; "how can one of thy clear perception doubt in this matter. In the world nothing is thine but what thou expendest in well-doing. What thou wearest will be worn out; what thou eatest will be consumed; but that which thou expendest in well-doing, is sent before thee to the other world."

Omar determined that the carpet should be shared among his chiefs. He divided it literally, with rigid equity, cutting it up without regard to the skill and beauty of the design, or its value as an entire piece of workmanship. Such was the richness of the materials, that the portion alloted to Ali alone, sold for eight thousand dirhems of silver.

This signal capture of the capital of Persia took place in the month Safar, in the sixteenth year of the Hegira, and the year 637 of the Christian era; the same year with the capture of Jerusalem. The fame of such immense spoil, such treasures of art in the hands of ignorant Arab soldiery, summoned the crafty and the avaricious from all quarters. All the world, it is said, flocked from the West, from Yemen, and from Egypt, to purchase the costly stuffs captured from the Persians. It was like the vultures, winging their way from all parts of the heavens, to gorge on the relics of a hunting camp.

CHAPTER XXIX.

Capture of Jálulá.—Flight of Yezdegird to Rei.—Founding of Cufa.—Saad receives a severe rebuke from the Caliph for his magnificence.

Saad Ibn Abu Wakkâs would fain have pursued Yezdegird to Holwân, among the hills of ancient Media, where he had taken refuge; but he was restrained by the Caliph Omar, who kept a cautious check from Medina upon his conquering generals; fearful that in the flush and excitement of victory, they might hurry forward beyond the reach of succour. By the command of Omar, therefore, he remained with his main army in Madayn, and sent his brother Hashem with twelve thousand men in pursuit of the fugitive monarch. Hashem found a large force of Persians, relics of defeated armies, assembled in Jálulá, not far from Holwân, where they were disposed to make a stand. He laid siege to the place, but it was of great strength and maintained a brave and obstinate defence for six months, during which there were eighty assaults. At length, the garrison being reduced by famine and incessant fighting, and the commander slain, it surrendered.

Yezdegird on hearing of the capture of Jálulá abandoned the city of Holwân, leaving troops there under a general named Habesh, to check the pursuit of the enemy. The place of refuge which he now sought was the city of Rei, or Raî, the Rhages of Arrian; the Rhaga and Rhageia of the Greek geographers; a city of remote antiquity, contemporary, it is said, with Nineveh and Ecbatana, and mentioned in the book of Tobit; who, we are told, travelled from Nineveh to Rages, a city of Medea. It was a favourite residence of the Parthian kings in days of yore. In his flight through the mountains, the monarch was borne on a chair or litter between mules; travelling a station each day, and sleeping in the litter. Habesh, whom he had left behind, was soon defeated, and followed him in his flight.

Saad again wrote to the Caliph, urging that he might be permitted to follow the Persian king to his place of refuge among the mountains, before he should have time to assemble another army; but he again met with a cautious check. "You have this year," said the Caliph, "taken Sawaad and Irak; for Holwân is at the extremity of Irak. That is enough for the present. The welfare of true believers, is of more value than booty." So ended the sixteenth year of the Hegira.

The climate of Madayn proving unhealthy to his troops, and Saad wishing to establish a fortified camp in the midst of his victories, was ordered by the Caliph to seek some favourable site on the western side of the Euphrates, where there was good air, a well watered plain and plenty of grass for the camels; things highly appreciated by the Arabs.

Saad chose for the purpose the village of Cufa, which, according to Moslem tradition, was the spot where Noah embarked in the Ark. The Arabs further pretend that the serpent after tempting Eve was banished to this place. Hence, they say, the guile and treachery for which the men of Cufa are proverbial. This city became so celebrated that the Euphrates was at one time generally denominated Nahar Cufa, or the river of Cufa. The most ancient characters of the Arabic alphabet are termed Cufic to the present day.

In building Cufa, much of the stone, marble and timber for the principal edifices were furnished from the ruins of Madayn; there being such a scarcity of those materials in Babylonia and its vicinity, that the houses were generally constructed of bricks baked in the sun and cemented with bitumen. It used to be said, therefore, that the army on its remove took with it all the houses of Sawad. Saad Ibn- Abu Wakkâs, who appears to have imbibed a taste for Persian splendour, erected a sumptuous Kiosk or summer residence, and decorated it with a grand portal taken from the palace of the Khosrus at Madayn. When Omar heard of this he was sorely displeased, his great apprehension being that his generals would lose the good old Arab simplicity of manners in the luxurious countries they were conquering. He forthwith despatched a trusty envoy, Mahomet Ibn Muslemah, empowered to give Saad a salutary rebuke. On arriving at Cufa, Mahomet caused a great quantity of wood to be heaped against the door of the Kiosk, and set fire to

18

It. When Saad came forth in amazement at this outrage, Mahomet put into his hands, the following letter from the Caliph :

"I am told thou hast built a lofty palace, like to that of the Khosrus, and decorated it with a door taken from the latter; with a view to have guards and chamberlains stationed about it to keep off those who may come in quest of justice or assistance, as was the practice of the Khosrus before thee. In so doing thou hast departed from the ways of the prophet (on whom be benedictions), and hast fallen into the ways of the Persian monarchs. Know that the Khosrus have passed from their palace to the tomb ; while the prophet, from his lowly habitation on earth, has been elevated to the highest heaven. I have sent Mahomet Ibn Muslemah to burn thy palace. In this world two houses are sufficient for thee ; one to dwell in, the other to contain the treasure of the Moslems."

Saad was too wary to make any opposition to the orders of the stern-minded Omar ; so he looked on without a murmur as his stately Kiosk was consumed by the flames. He even offered Mahomet presents, which the latter declined, and returned to Medina. Saad removed to a different part of the city, and built a more modest mansion for himself, and another for the treasury.

In the same year with the founding of Cufa, the Caliph Omar married Omm Kolsam, the daughter of Ali and Fatima, and granddaughter of the prophet. This drew him in still closer bonds of friendship and confidence with Ali; who with Othman shared his councils, and aided him in managing from Medina the rapidly accumulating affairs of the Moslem empire.

It must be always noted, that however stern and strict may appear the laws and ordinances of Omar, he was rigidly impartial in enforcing them ; and one of his own sons, having been found intoxicated, received the twenty bastinadoes on the soles of the feet, which he had decreed for offences of the kind.

CHAPTER XXX.

War with Hormuzân, the Satrap of Ahwâz.—His conquest and conversion.

The founding of the city of Bassora had given great annoyance and uneasiness to Hormuzân, the satrap or viceroy of Ahwâz, or Susiana. His province lay between Babylonia and Farsistan, and he saw that this rising city of the Arabs was intended as a check upon him. His province was one of the richest and most important of Persia, producing cotton, rice, sugar, and wheat. It was studded with cities, which the historian Tabari compared to a cluster of stars. In the centre stood the metropolis Susa; one of the royal resorts of the Persian kings, celebrated in scriptural history, and said to possess the tomb of the prophet Daniel. It was once adorned with palaces and courts, and parks of prodigious extent, though now all is a waste, "echoing only to the roar of the lion, or yell of the hyæna."

Here Hormuzân, the satrap, emulated the state and luxury of a king. He was of a haughty spirit, priding himself upon his descent, his ancestors having once sat on the throne of Persia. For this reason his sons, being of the blood royal, were permitted to wear crowns, though of smaller size than those worn by kings, and his family was regarded with great deference by the Persians.

This haughty satrap, not rendered wary by the prowess of the Moslem arms, which he had witnessed and experienced at Kadesia, made preparations to crush the rising colony of Bassora. The founders of that city called on the Caliph for protection, and troops were marched to their assistance from Medina, and from the head-quarters of Saad at Cufa. Hormuzân soon had reason to repent his having provoked hostilities. He was defeated in repeated battles, and at length was glad to make peace with the loss of half of his territories, and all but four of his cluster of cities. He was not permitted long to enjoy even this remnant of domain. Yezdegird, from his retreat at Rei, reproached Hormuzân and the satrap of the adjacent province of Farsistan, for not co-operating to withstand the Moslems. At his command they united their forces, and Hormuzân broke the treaty of peace which he had so recently concluded.

The devotion of Hormuzân to his fugitive sovereign ended in his ruin. The Caliph ordered troops to assemble from the different Moslem posts, and complete the conquest of Ahwâz. Hormuzân disputed his territory bravely, but was driven from place to place, until he made his last stand in the fortress of Ahwâz, or Susa. For six months he was beleaguered, during which time there were many sallies and assaults, and hard fighting on both sides. At length, Barâ Ibn Mâlek was sent to take command of the besiegers. He had been an especial favourite of the prophet, and there was a superstitious feeling concerning him. He manifested at all times an indifference to life or death; always pressed forward to the place of danger, and every action in which he served was successful.

On his taking the command, the troops gathered round him. "Oh Barâ! swear to overthrow these infidels, and the Most High will favour us."

Barâ swore that the place would be taken, and the infidels put to flight, but that he would fall a martyr.

In the very next assault, he was killed by an arrow sped by Hormuzân. The army took his death as a good omen. "One-half of his oath is fulfilled," said they, "and so will be the other."

Shortly afterward a Persian traitor came to Abu Shebrah, who had succeeded to the Moslem command, and revealed a secret entrance by a conduit under the castle, by which it was supplied with water. A hundred Moslems entered it by night, threw open the outward gates, and let in the army into the court-yards. Hormuzân was ensconced, however, in a strong tower, or keep, from the battlements of which he held a parley with the Moslem commander. "I have a thousand expert archers with me," said he, "who never miss their aim. By every arrow they discharge, you will lose a man. Avoid this useless sacrifice. Let me depart in honour; give me safe conduct to the Caliph, and let him dispose of me as he pleases."

It was agreed. Hormuzân was treated with respect as he issued from his fortress, and was sent under an escort to Medina. He maintained the air of one not conducted as a prisoner, but attended by a guard of honour. As he approached the city he halted, arrayed himself in sumptuous apparel, with his jewelled belt and regal crown, and in this guise entered the gates. The inhabitants gazed in astonishment at such unwonted luxury of attire.

Omar was not at his dwelling; he had gone to the mosque. Hormuzân was conducted thither. On approaching the sacred edifice, the Caliph's cloak was seen hanging against the wall, while he himself, arrayed in patched garments, lay asleep with his staff under his head. The officers of the escort seated themselves at a respectful distance until he should awake. "This," whispered they to Hormuzân, "is the prince of true believers."

"This the Arab king!" said the astonished satrap; "and is this his usual attire?" "It is." "And does he sleep thus without guards?" "He does; he comes and goes alone; and lies down and sleeps where he pleases." "And can he administer justice, and conduct affairs without officers and messengers and attendants?" "Even so," was the reply. "This," exclaimed Hormuzân, at length, "is the condition of a prophet, but not of a king." "He is not a prophet," was the reply, "but he acts like one."

As the Caliph awoke he recognized the officers of the escort. "What tidings do you bring?" demanded he. —"But who is this so extravagantly arrayed?" rubbing his eyes as they fell upon the embroidered robes and jewelled crown of the satrap. "This is Hormuzân, the king of Ahwâz." "Take the infidel out of this place," cried he, turning away his head. "Strip him of his riches, and put on him the riches of Islam."

Hormuzân was accordingly taken forth, and in a little time was brought again before the Caliph, clad in a simple garb of the striped cloth of Yemen.

The Moslem writers relate various quibbles by which Hormuzân sought to avert the death with which he was threatened, for having slain Barâ Ibn Mâlek. He craved water to allay his thirst. A vessel of water was brought. Affecting to apprehend immediate execution: "Shall I be spared until I have drunk this?" Being answered by the Caliph in the affirmative, he dashed the vessel to the ground. "Now," said he, "you cannot put me to death, for I can never drink the water."

The straightforward Omar, however, was not to be caught by a quibble. "Your cunning will do you no good," said he. "Nothing will save you but to embrace Islamism." The haughty Hormuzân was subdued. He made the profession of faith in due style, and was at once enrolled among true believers.

He resided thenceforth in Medina; received rich presents from the Caliph, and subsequently gave him much serviceable information and advice in his prosecution of the war with Persia. The conquest of Ahwâz was completed in the nine teenth year of the Hegira.

CHAPTER XXXI.

Saad suspended from the command.—A Persian army assembled at Nehâvend.— Council at the mosque of Medina.— Battle of Nehâvend.

Omar, as we have seen, kept a jealous and vigilant eye upon his distant generals; being constantly haunted by the fear that they would become corrupted in the rich and luxurious countries they were invading, and lose that Arab simplicity which he considered inestimable in itself, and all-essential to the success of the cause of Islam. Notwithstanding the severe reproof he had given to Saad Ibn Abu Wakkâs in burning down his palace at Cufa, complaints still reached him that the general affected the pomp of a Caliph, that he was unjust and oppressive; unfair in the division of spoils, and slow in conducting military concerns. These charges proved, for the most part, unfounded, but they caused Saad to be suspended from his command until they could be investigated.

When the news reached Yezdegird at Rei that the Moslem general who had conquered at Kadesia, slain Rustam, captured Madayn, and driven himself to the mountains, was deposed from the command, he conceived fresh hopes, and wrote letters to all the provinces yet unconquered, calling on the inhabitants to take up arms and make a grand effort for the salvation of the empire. Nehâvend was appointed as the place where the troops were to assemble. It was a place of great antiquity, founded, says tradition, by Noah, and called after him, and was about fifteen leagues from Hamadân, the ancient Ecbatana. Here troops gathered together to the number of one hundred and fifty thousand.

Omar assembled his counsellors at the mosque of Medina, and gave them intelligence, just received, of this great armament. "This," said he, "is probably the last great effort of the Persians. If we defeat them now they will never be able to unite again." He expressed a disposition, therefore, to take the command in person. Strong objections were advanced. "Assemble troops from various parts," said Othman; "but remain, yourself, either at Medina, Cufa, or Holwân, to send reinforcements if required, or to form a rallying point for the Moslems, if defeated." Others gave different counsel. At length the matter was referred to Abbas Ibn Abd al Motâlleb, who was considered one of the sagest heads for counsel in the tribe of Koreish. He gave it as his opinion that the Caliph should remain in Medina, and give the command of the campaign to Nu'mân Ibn Mukry, who was already in Ahwâz, where he had been ever since Saad had sent him thither from Irak. It is singular to see the fate of the once mighty and magnificent empires of the Orient, Syria, Chaldea, Babylonia, and the dominions of the Medes and Persians, thus debated and decided in the mosque of Medina, by a handful of gray-headed Arabs, who but a few years previously had been homeless fugitives.

Orders were now sent to Nu'mân to march to Nehâvend, and reinforcements joined him from Medina, Bassora, and Cufa. His force, when thus collected, was but moderate, but it was made up of men hardened and sharpened by incessant warfare, rendered daring and confident by repeated victory, and led by able officers. He was afterwards joined by ten thousand men from Sawad, Holwân, and other places, many of whom were tributaries.

The Persian army now collected at Nehâvend was commanded by Firuzân ; he was old and infirm, but full of intelligence and spirit, and the only remaining general considered capable of taking charge of such a force, the best generals having fallen in battle. The veteran, knowing the impetuosity of the Arab attack, and their superiority in the open field, had taken a strong position, fortified his camp, and surrounded it with a deep moat filled with water. Here he determined to tire out the patience of the Moslems, and await an opportunity to strike a decisive blow.

Nu'mân displayed his forces before the Persian camp, and repeatedly offered battle, but the cautious veteran was not to be drawn out of his intrenchments. Two months elapsed without any action, and the Moslem troops, as Firuzân had foreseen, began to grow discontented, and to murmur at their general.

A stratagem was now resorted to by Nu'mân to draw out the enemy. Breaking up his camp, he made a hasty retreat, leaving behind him many articles of little value. The stratagem succeeded. The Persians sallied, though cautiously, in pursuit. Nu'mân continued his feigned retreat for another day, still followed by the enemy. Having drawn them to a sufficient distance from their fortified camp, he took up a position at nightfall. "To-morrow," said he to his troops, "before the day reddens, be ready for battle. I have been with the prophet in many conflicts, and he always commenced battle after the Friday prayer."

The following day, when the troops were drawn out in order of battle, he made this prayer in their presence. - "Oh Allah! sustain this day the cause of Islamism ; give us victory over the infidels, and grant me the glory of martyrdom." Then turning to his officers, he expressed a presentiment that he should fall in the battle, and named the person who, in such case, should take the command.

He now appointed the signal for battle. "Three times," said he, "I will cry the tekbîr, and each time will shake my standard. At the third time let every one fall on as I shall do. ' He gave the signal, Allah Achbar ! Allah Achbar ! Allah Achbar ! At the third shaking of the standard, the tekbîr was responded by the army, and the air was rent by the universal shout of Allah Achbar !

The shock of the two armies was terrific; they were soon enveloped in a cloud of dust, in which the sound of scimetars and battle-axes told the deadly work that was going on ; while the shouts of Allah Achbar continued, mingled with furious cries and execrations of the Persians, and dismal groans of the wounded. In an hour the Persians were completely routed. "Oh Lord!" exclaimed Nu'mân in pious ecstasy, "my prayer for victory has been heard; may that for martyrdom be likewise favoured!"

He advanced his standard in pursuit of the enemy, but at the same moment a Parthian arrow from the flying foe gave him the death he coveted. His body, with the face covered, was conveyed to his brother, and his standard given to Hadîfeh, whom he had named to succeed him in the command.

The Persians were pursued with great slaughter. Firuzân fled towards Hamadân, but was overtaken at midnight as he was ascending a steep hill, embarrassed among a crowd of mules and camels laden with the luxurious superfluities of a Persian camp. Here he and several thousand of his soldiers and camp-followers were cut to pieces. The booty was immense. Forty of the mules were found to be laden with honey; which made the Arabs say with a sneer, that Firuzân's army was clogged with its own honey, until overtaken by the true believers. The whole number of Persians slain in this battle, which sealed the fate of the empire, is said to have amounted to one hundred thousand. It took place in the twenty-first year of the Hegira, and the year 641 of the Christian era, and was commemorated among Moslems, as "The Victory of Victories."

On a day subsequent to the battle, a man mounted on an ass, rode into the camp of Hadîfeh. He was one who had served in the temples of the fire-worshippers, and was in great consternation, fearing to be sacrificed by the fanatic Moslems. "Spare my life," said he to Hadîfeh, "and the life of another person whom I shall designate, and I will deliver into your hands a treasure put under my charge by Yezdegird when he fled to Rei." His terms being promised, he produced a sealed box. On breaking the seal, Hadîfeh found it filled with rubies and precious stones of various colours, and jewels of great price. He was astonished at the sight of what appeared to him incalculable riches. "These jewels," said he, "have not been gained in battle, nor by the sword; we have, therefore, no right to any share in them." With the concurrence of his officers, therefore, he sent the box to the Caliph to be retained by himself or divided among the true believers as he should think proper. The officer who conducted the fifth part of the spoils to Medina, delivered the box, and related its history to Omar. The Caliph, little skilled in matters of luxury, and holding them in supreme contempt, gazed with an ignorant or scornful eye at the imperial jewels, and refused to receive them. "You know not what these things are," said he. "Neither do I; but they justly belong to those who slew the infidels, and to no one else." He ordered the officer, therefore, to depart forthwith and carry the box back to Hadîfeh. The jewels were sold by the latter to the merchants who followed the camp, and when the proceeds were divided among the troops, each horseman received for his share four thousand pieces of gold.

Far other was the conduct of the Caliph when he received the letter giving an account of the victory at Nehâvend. His first inquiry

was after his old companion in the faith, Nu'mân. "May God grant
you and him mercy!" was the reply. "He has become a martyr!"
   Omar, it is said, wept. He next inquired who also were martyrs. Several were named with whom he was acquainted; but
many who were unknown to him. "If I know them not," said he,
piously quoting a text of the Koran, "God does!"

CHAPTER XXXII.

Capture of Hamadân; of Rei.—Subjugation of Tabaristan; of Azerbîjân.—Campaign
among the Caucasian mountains.

   The Persian troops who had survived the signal defeat of Firuzân,
assembled their broken forces near the city of Hamadân; but were
soon routed again by a detachment sent against them by Hadîfeh,
who had fixed his headquarters at Nehâvend. They then took
refuge in Hamadân, and ensconced themselves in its strong fortress
or citadel.
   Hamadân was the second city in Persia for grandeur, and
was built upon the site of Ecbatana, in old times the principal
city of the Medes. There were more Jews among its inhabitants
than were to be found in any other city of Persia, and it boasted
of possessing the tombs of Esther and Mordecai. It was situated
on a steep eminence, down the sides of which it descended into
a fruitful plain, watered by streams gushing down from the lofty
Orontes, now Mount Elwand. The place was commanded by
Habesh, the same general who had been driven from Holwân after
the flight of Yezdegird. Habesh sought an interview with Hadîfeh,
at his encampment at Nehâvend, and made a treaty of peace with
him; but it was a fraudulent one, and, 'intended merely to gain
time. Returning to Hamadân, he turned the whole city into a fortress, and assembled a strong garrison, being reinforced from the
neighbouring province of Azerbîjân.
   On being informed of this want of good faith on the part of the
governor of Hamadân, the Caliph Omar despatched a strong force
against the place, led by an able officer named Nu'haim Ibn Mukrin.
Habesh had more courage than caution. Confident in the large
force he had assembled, instead of remaining within his strongly
fortified city, he sallied forth and met the Moslems in open field.
The battle lasted for three days and was harder fought than even
that of Nehâvend, but ended in leaving the Moslems triumphant
masters of the once formidable capital of Media.
   Nu'haim now marched against Rei, late the place of refuge of
Yezdegird. That prince, however, had deserted it on the approach of danger, leaving it in charge of a noble named Siyâwesh
Ibn Barham. Hither the Persian princes had sent troops from the
yet unconquered provinces, for Siyâwesh had nobly offered to
make himself as a buckler to them, and conquer or fall in their
defence. His patriotism was unavailing; treachery and corruption

were too prevalent among the Persians. Zain, a powerful noble resident in Rei, and a deadly enemy of Siyâwesh, conspired to admit two thousand Moslems in at one gate of the city, at the time when its gallant governor was making a sally by another. A scene of tumult and carnage took place in the streets, where both armies engaged in deadly conflit. The patriot Siyâwesh was slain with a great part of his troops; the city was captured and sacked, and its citadel destroyed, and the traitor Zain was rewarded for his treachery by being made governor of the ruined place.

Nu'haim now sent troops in different directions against Kumish, and Dameghân, and Jurgan (the ancient Hircania), and Tabaristan. They met with feeble resistance. The national spirit was broken; even the national religion was nearly at an end. " This Persian religion of ours has become obsolete," said Farkham, a military sage, to an assemblage of commanders, who asked his advice; "the new religion is carrying every thing before it; my advice is to make peace and pay tribute." His advice was adopted. All Tabaristan became tributary in the annual sum of five hundred thousand dirhems, with the condition that the Moslems should levy no troops in that quarter.

Azerbîjân was next invaded; the country which had sent troops to the aid of Hamadân. This province lay north of Rei and Hamadân, and extended to the Rocky Caucasus. It was the stronghold of the Magians or Fire-worshippers, where they had their temples, and maintained their perpetual fire. Hence the name of the country, Azer signifying fire. The princes of the country made an ineffectual stand; their army was defeated; the altars of the fire-worshippers were overturned; their temples destroyed, and Azerbîjân won.

The arms of Islam had now been carried triumphantly to the very defiles of the Caucasus; those mountains were yet to be subdued. Their rocky sierras on the east separated Azerbîjân from Haziz and the shores of the Caspian, and on the north from the vast Sarmatian regions. The passes through these mountains were secured of yore, by fortresses and walls and iron gates, to bar against irruptions from the shadowy land of Gog and Magog, the terror of the olden time, for by these passes had poured in the barbarous hordes of the north, "a mighty host all riding upon horses," who lived in tents, worshipped the naked sword planted in the earth, and decorated their steeds with the scalps of their enemies slain in battle.[1]

---

[1] By some Gog and Magog are taken in an allegorical sense, signifying the princes of heathendom, enemies of saints and the church.

According to the prophet Ezekiel, Gog was the king of Magog; Magog signifying the people, and Gog the king of the country. They are names that loom vaguely and fearfully in the dark denunciations of the prophets; and in the olden time inspired awe throughout the eastern world.

The Arabs, says Lane, call Gog and Magog, Yâjûj and Mâjûj, and say they are two nations or tribes descended from Japhet, the son of Noah; or, as others write, Gog is a tribe of the Turks, and Magog those of Gilan; the Geli and the Gelæ of Ptolemy and Strabo. They made their irruptions into the neighbouring countries in the spring, and carried off all the fruits of the earth.—Sale's Koran, note to ch. 18.

According to Moslem belief, a great irruption of Gog and Magog is to be one of the signs of the latter days, forerunning the resurrection and final judgment. They are to

Detachments of Moslems under different leaders penetrated the defiles of these mountains and made themselves masters of the Derbends, or mountain barriers. One of the most important, and which cost the greatest struggle, was a city or fortress called by the Persians Der-bend; by the Turks Demir-Capi or the Gate of Iron, and by the Arabs Bab-el-abwâb (the Gate of Gates). It guards a defile between a promontory of Mount Caucasus and the Caspian Sea. A superstitious belief is still connected with it by the Moslems. Originally it had three gates; two only are left; one of these has nearly sunk into the earth; they say when it disappears the day of judgment will arrive.

Abda'lrahman Ibn Rabiah, one of the Moslem commanders who penetrated the defiles of the Caucasus, was appointed by Omar to the command of the Derbends or passes, with orders to keep vigilant watch over them; for the Caliph was in continual solicitude about the safety of the Moslems on these remote expeditions, and was fearful that the Moslem troops might be swept away by some irruption from the north.

Abda'lrahman, with the approbation of the Caliph, made a compact with Shahr-Zad, one of the native chiefs, by which the latter, in consideration of being excused from paying tribute, undertook to guard the Derbends against the northern hordes. The Arab general had many conversations with Shahr-Zad about the mountains, which are favoured regions of Persian romance and fable. His imagination was fired with what he was told about the people beyond the Derbends, the Allâni and the Rus; and about the great wall or barrier of Yâjûj and Mâjûj, built to restrain their inroads.

In one of the stories told by Shahr-Zad, the reader will perceive the germ of one of the Arabian tales of Sindbad the Sailor. It is recorded to the following purport, by Tabari, the Persian historian: " One day as Abda'lrahman was seated by Sharh-Zad, conversing

come from the north in a mighty host, covering the land as a cloud; so that when subdued, their shields and bucklers, their bows and arrows and quivers, and the staves of their spears, shall furnish the faithful with fuel for seven years.—All which is evidently derived from the book of the prophet Ezekiel; with which Mahomet had been made acquainted by his Jewish instructors.

The Koran makes mention of a wall built as a protection against these fearful people of the north by Dhu'lkarneim, or the Two Horned; by whom some suppose is meant Alexander the Great, others a Persian king of the first race, contemporary with Abraham.

And they said, O Dhu'lkarneim, verily, Gog and Magog waste the land. . . . . He answered, I will set a strong wall between you and them. Bring me iron in large pieces, until it fill up the space between the two sides of these mountains. And he said to the workmen, Blow with your bellows until it make the iron red hot; and bring me molten brass, that I may pour upon it. Wherefore, when this wall was finished, Gog and Magog could not scale it, neither could they dig through it.—*Sale's Koran*, chap. 18

The Czar Peter the Great, in his expedition against the Persians, saw in the neighbourhood of the city of Derbend, which was then besieged, the ruins of a wall which went up hill and down dale, along the Caucasus, and was said to extend from the Euxine to the Caspian. It was fortified from place to place, by towers or castles. It was eighteen Russian stades in height; built of stones laid up dry; some of them three ells long and very wide. The colour of the stones, and the traditions of the country, showed it to be of great antiquity. The Arabs and Persians said that it was built against the invasions of Gog and Magog.—See *Travels in the East, by Sir William Ousley*.

with him, he perceived upon his finger a ring decorated with a ruby, which burned like fire in the daytime, but at night was of dazzling brilliancy. ' ' It came,' said Shahr-zad, ' from the wall of Yâjûj and Mâjûj ; from a king whose dominions between the mountains is traversed by the wall. I sent him many presents, and asked but ony ruby in return." Seeing the curiosity of Abda'lrahman aroused, he sent for the man who had brought the ring, and commanded him to relate the circumstances of his errand.

" ' When I delivered the presents and the letter of Shahr-Zad to that king,' said the man, ' he called his chief falconer, and ordered him to procure the jewel required. The falconer kept an eagle for three days without food, until he was nearly starved ; he then took him up into the mountains near the wall, and I accompanied him. From the summit of one of these mountains, we looked down into a deep dark chasm like an abyss. The falconer now produced a piece of tainted meat ; threw it into the ravine, and let loose the eagle. He swept down after it ; pounced upon it as it reached the ground, and returning with it, perched upon the hand of the falconer. The ruby which now shines in that ring was found adhering to the meat.'

" Abda'lrahman asked an account of the wall. ' It is built,' replied the man, ' of stone, iron, and brass, and extends down one mountain and up another.' ' This,' said the devout and all-believing Abda'lrahman, ' must be the very wall of which the Almighty makes mention in the Koran.'

" He now inquired of Shahr-Zad what was the value of the ruby. ' No one knows its value.' was the reply ; ' though presents to an immense amount had been made in return for it.' Sharh-Zad now drew the ring from his finger, and offered it to Abda'lrahman, but the latter refused to accept it, saying that a gem of that value was not suitable to him. ' Had you been one of the Persian kings', said Shahr-Zad, ' you would have taken it from me by force ; but men who conduct like you will conquer all the world.' "

The stories which he had heard, had such an effect upon Abda'lrahman, that he resolved to make a foray into the mysterious country beyond the Derbends. Still it could only be of a partial nature, as he was restrained from venturing far by the cautious injunctions of Omar. " Were I not fearful of displeasing the Caliph," said he, " I would push forward even to Yâjûj and Mâjûj, and make converts of all the infidels."

On issuing from the mountains, he found himself among a barbarous people, the ancestors of the present Turks, who inhabited a region of country between the Euxine and the Caspian seas. A soldier who followed Abda'lrahman in this foray gave the following account of these people to the Caliph on his return to Medina. " They were astonished." said he, " at our appearance, so different from their old enemies the Persians, and asked us, ' Are you angels, or the sons of Adam ?' to which we replied, we are sons of Adam ; but the angels of heaven are on our side and aid us in our warfare."

The infidels forbore to assail men thus protected ; one, however, more shrewd or dubious than the rest, stationed himself behind a tree, sped an arrow and slew a Moslem. The delusion was at an end ; the Turks saw that the strangers were mortal, and from that time there was hard fighting. Abda'Irahman laid siege to a place called Belandscher, the city or strong-hold of the Bulgarians or Huns, another semi-barbarous and warlike people like the Turks, who, like them had not yet made themselves world-famous by their conquering migrations. The Turks came to the aid of their neighbours ; a severe battle took place, the Moslems were defeated, and Abda'Irahman paid for his daring enterprise and romantic curiosity with his life. The Turks, who still appear to have retained a superstitious opinion of their unknown invaders, preserved the body of the unfortunate general as a relic, and erected a shrine in honour of it, at which they used to put up their prayers for rain in time of drought.

The troops of Abda'Irahman retreated within the Derbends ; his brother Selman Ibn Rabiah was appointed to succeed him in the command of the Caucasian passes, and thus ended the unfortunate foray into the land of God and Magog.

CHAPTER XXXIII.

The Caliph Omar assassinated by a fire-worshipper.—His character.—Othman elected Caliph.

The life and reign of the Caliph Omar, distinguished by such great and striking events, were at length brought to a sudden and sanguinary end. Among the Persians who had been brought as slaves to Medina, was one named Firuz, of-the sect of the Magi, or fire-worshippers. Being taxed daily by his master two pieces of silver out of his earnings he complained of it to Omar as an extortion. The Caliph inquired into his condition, and, finding that he was a carpenter, and expert in the construction of windmills, replied, that the man who excelled in such a handicraft could well afford to pay two dirhems a day. " Then, muttered Firuz, " I'll construct a windmill for you that shall keep grinding until the day of judgment." Omar was struck with his menacing air. " The slave threatens me," said he, calmly. " If I were disposed to punish any one on suspicion, I should take off his head ;" he suffered him, however, to depart without further notice.

Three days afterwards, as he was praying in the mosque, Firuz entered suddenly and stabbed him thrice with a dagger. The attendants rushed upon the assassin. He made furious resistance, slew some and wounded others, until one of his assailants threw his vest over him and seized him, upon which he stabbed himself to the heart and expired. Religion may have had some share in prompting this act of violence ; perhaps revenge for the ruin brought upon his native country. " God be thanked," said Omar, " that he by whose hand it was decreed I should fall, was not a Moslem !"

The Caliph gathered strength sufficient to finish the prayer in which he had been interrupted; "for he who deserts his prayers," said he, "is not in Islam." Being taken to his house, he languished three days without hope of recovery, but could not be prevailed upon to nominate a successor. "I cannot presume to do that," said he, "which the prophet himself did not do." Some suggested that he should nominate his son Abdallah. "Omar's family," said he, "has had enough in Omar, and needs no more." He appointed a council of six persons to determine as to the succession after his decease; all of whom he considered worthy of the Caliphat; though he gave it as his opinion that the choice would be either Ali or Othman. "Shouldst thou become Caliph," said he to Ali, "do not favour thy relatives above all others, nor place the house of Haschem on the neck of all mankind;" and he gave the same caution to Othman in respect to the family of Omeya.

Calling for ink and paper, he wrote a letter as his last testament, to whosoever might be his successor, full of excellent counsel for the upright management of affairs, and the promotion of the faith. He charged his son Abdallah in the most earnest manner, as one of the highest duties of Islamism, to repay eighteen thousand dirhems which he had borrowed out of the public treasury. All present protested against this as unreasonable, since the money had been expended in relief of the poor and destitute, but Omar insisted upon it as his last will. He then sent to Ayesha and procured permission of her to be buried next to her father Abu Beker.

Ibn Abbas and Ali now spoke to him in words of comfort, setting forth the blessings of Islam, which had crowned his administration, and that he would leave no one behind him who could charge him with injustice. "Testify this for me," said he, earnestly, "at the day of judgment." They gave him their hands in promise: but he exacted that they should give him a written testimonial, and that it should be buried with him in the grave.

Having settled all his worldly affairs, and given directions about his sepulture, he expired, the seventh day after his assassination, in the sixty-third year of his age, after a triumphant reign of ten years and six months.

His death was rashly and bloodily revenged. Mahomet Ibn Abu Beker, the brother of Ayesha, and imbued with her mischief-making propensity, persuaded Abdallah, the son of Omar, that his father's murder was the result of a conspiracy; Firuz having been instigated to the act by his daughter Lulu, a Christian named Dschofeine, and Hormuzân, the once haughty and magnificent Satrap of Susiana. In the transport of his rage, and instigated by the old Arab principle of blood revenge, Abdallah slew all three of the accused; without reflecting on the improbability of Hormuzân, at least, being accessory to the murder; being, since his conversion, in close friendship with the late Caliph; and his adviser, on many occasions, in the prosecution of the Persian war.

The whole history of Omar shows him to have been a man of great powers of mind, inflexible integrity, and rigid justice. He was, more than any one else, the founder of the Islam empire; confirming and carrying out the inspirations of the prophet; aiding

Abu Beker with his counsels during his brief Caliphat; and establishing wise regulations for the strict administration of the laws throughout the rapidly-extending bounds of the Moslem conquests. The rigid hand which he kept upon his most popular generals in the midst of their armies, and in the most distant scenes of their triumphs, give signal evidence of his extraordinary capacity to rule. In the simplicity of his habits, and his contempt for all pomp and luxury, he emulated the example of the prophet and Abu Beker. He endeavoured incessantly to impress the merit and policy of the same in his letters to his generals. "Beware," he would say, "of Persian luxury both in food and raiment. Keep to the simple habits of your country, and Allah will continue you victorious; depart from them, and he will reverse your fortunes." It was his strong conviction of the truth of this policy, which made him so severe in punishing all ostentatious style and luxurious indulgence in his officers.

Some of his ordinances do credit to his heart as well as his head. He forbade that any female captive who had borne a child should be sold as a slave. In his weekly distributions of the surplus money of his treasury, he proportioned them to the wants, not the merits of the applicants. "God," said he, "has bestowed the good things of this world to relieve our necessities, not to reward our virtues: those will be rewarded in another world."

One of the early measures of his reign was the assigning pensions to the most faithful companions of the prophet, and those who had signalized themselves in the early service of the faith. Abbas, the uncle of the prophet, had a yearly pension of 200,000 dirhems; others of his relatives in graduated proportions; those veterans who had fought in the battle of Beder 5000 dirhems; pensions of less amount to those who had distinguished themselves in Syria, Persia, and Egypt. Each of the prophet's wives was allowed ten thousand dirhems yearly, and Ayesha twelve thousand. Hasan and Hoscin, the sons of Ali and grandsons of the prophet, had each a pension of five thousand dirhems. On any one who found fault with these disbursements out of the public wealth, Omar invoked the curse of Allah.

He was the first to establish a chamber of accounts or exchequer; the first to date events from the Hegira or flight of the prophet; and the first to introduce a coinage into the Moslem dominions; stamping the coins with the name of the reigning Caliph, and the words, "There is no God but God."

During his reign, we are told, there were thirty-six thousand towns, castles, and strong-holds taken; but he was not a wasteful conqueror. He found new cities; established important marts; built innumerable mosques, and linked the newly acquired provinces into one vast empire by his iron inflexibility of purpose. As has well been observed, "his Caliphat, crowned with the glories of its triple conquest of Syria, Persia, and Egypt, deserves to be distinguished as the heroic age of Saracen history. The gigantic foundations of the Saracenic power were perfected in the short space of less than ten years." Let it be remembered, moreover, that this great conqueror, this great legislator, this magnanimous sovereign, was originally a rude half-instructed Arab of Mecca. Well may we say in regard to the early champions of Islam, "there were giants in those days."

After the death of Omar, the six persons met together whom he had named as a council to elect his successor. They were Ali, Othman, Telha, Ibn Obeid'allah (Mahomet's son-in-law), Zobeir, Abda'lrahman Ibn Awf, and Saad Ibn Abu Wakkâs. They had all been personally intimate with Mahomet, and were therefore styled THE COMPANIONS.

After much discussion and repeated meetings the Caliphat was offered to Ali, on condition that he would promise to govern according to the Koran and the traditions of Mahomet, and the regulations established by the two seniors or elders; meaning the two preceding Caliphs Abu Beker and Omar.

Ali replied, that he would govern according to the Koran and the authentic traditions; but would, in all other respects, act according to his own judgment, without reference to the example of the seniors. This reply not being satisfactory to the council, they made the same proposal to Othman Ibn Affân, who assented to all the conditions, and was immediately elected, and installed three days after the death of his predecessor. He was seventy years of age at the time of his election. He was tall and swarthy, and his long gray beard was tinged with henna. He was strict in his religious duties; fasting, meditating, and studying the Koran; not so simple in his habits as his predecessors, but prone to expense and lavish of his riches. His bountiful spirit, however, was evinced at times in a way that gained him much popularity. In a time of famine he had supplied the poor of Medina with corn. He had purchased at great cost the ground about the mosque of Medina, to give room for houses for the prophet's wives. He had contributed six hundred and fifty camels and fifty horses for the campaign against Tabuc.

He derived much respect among zealous Moslems for having married two of the prophet's daughters; and for having been in both of the Hegiras, or flights, the first into Abyssinia, the second, the memorable flight to Medina. Mahomet used to say of him, "Each thing has its mate, and each man his associate : my associate in paradise is Othman."

Scarcely was the new Caliph installed in office, when the retaliatory punishment prescribed by the law was invoked upon Obeid'allah, the son of Omar, for the deaths so rashly inflicted on those whom he had suspected of instigating his father's assassination. Othman was perplexed between the letter of the law and the odium of following the murder of the father by the execution of the son. He was kindly relieved from his perplexity by the suggestion, that as the act of Obeid'allah took place in the interregnum between the Caliphats of Omar and Othman, it did not come under the cognizance of either. Othman gladly availed himself of the quibble; Obeid'allah escaped unpunished, and the sacrifice of the once magnificent Hormuzân and his fellow-victims remained unavenged,

CHAPTER XXXIV.

Conclusion of the Persian conquest.—Flight and death of Yezdegird.

The proud empire of the Khosrus had received its death-blow during the vigorous Caliphat of Omar; what signs of life it yet gave were but its dying struggles. The Moslems, led by able generals, pursued their conquests in different directions. Some, turning to the west, urged their triumphant way through ancient Assyria; crossed the Tigris by the bridge of Mosul, passing the ruins of mighty Nineveh as unheedingly as they had passed those of Babylon; completed the subjugation of Mesopotamia, and planted their standards beside those of their brethren who had achieved the conquest of Syria.

Others directed their course into the southern and eastern provinces, following the retreating steps of Yezdegird. A fiat issued by the late Caliph Omar had sealed the doom of that unhappy monarch. "Pursue the fugitive king wherever he may go, until you have driven him from the face of the earth!"

Yezdegird, after abandoning Rei, had led a wandering life, shifting from city to city and province to province, still flying at the approach of danger. At one time we hear of him in the splendid city of Ispahan; next among the mountains of Farsistan, the original Persis, the cradle of the conquerors of Asia; and it is another of the lessons furnished by history, to see the last of the Khosrus a fugitive among those mountains whence, in foregone times, Cyrus had led his hardy but frugal and rugged bands to win, by force of arms, that vast empire which was now falling to ruin through its effeminate degeneracy.

For a time the unhappy monarch halted in Istakar, the pride of Persia, where the tottering remains of Persepolis, and its hall of a thousand columns, speak of the ancient glories of the Persian kings. Here Yezdegird had been fostered and concealed during his youthful days, and here he came near being taken among the relics of Persian magnificence.

From Farsistan he was driven to Kerman, the ancient Carmania; thence into Korassan; in the northern part of which vast province he took breath at the city of Merv, or Merou, on the remote boundary of Bactriana. In all his wanderings he was encumbered by the shattered pageant of an oriental court, a worthless throng which had fled with him from Madayn, and which he had no means of supporting. At Merv he had four thousand persons in his train; all minions of the palace, useless hangers-on, porters, grooms, and slaves; together with his wives and concubines, and their female attendants.

In this remote halting-place he devoted himself to building a fire-temple; in the meantime he wrote letters to such of the cities and provinces as were yet unconquered, exhorting his governors and generals to defend, piece by piece, the fragments of empire which he had deserted.

The city of Ispahan, one of the brightest jewels of his crown, was well garrisoned by wrecks of the army of Nehavend, and might have made brave resistance; but its governor, Kadeskan, staked the fortunes of the place upon a single combat with the Moslem commander who had invested it, and capitulated at the first shock of lances; probably through some traitorous arrangement.

Ispahan has never recovered from that blow. Modern travellers speak of its deserted streets, its abandoned palaces, its silent bazaars. " I have ridden for miles among its ruins," says one, " without meeting any living creature, excepting, perhaps, a jackal peeping over a wall, or a fox running into his hole. Now and then an inhabited house was to be seen, the owner of which might be assimilated to Job's forlorn man dwelling in desolate cities, and in houses which no man inhabiteth ; which are ready to become heaps."

Istakar made a nobler defence. The national pride of the Persians was too much connected with this city, once their boast, to let it fall without a struggle. There was another gathering of troops from various parts; one hundred and twenty thousand are said to have united under the standard of Shah-reg, the patriotic governor. It was all in vain. The Persians were again defeated in a bloody battle; Shah-reg was slain, and Istakar, the ancient Persepolis, once almost the mistress of the Eastern world, was compelled to pay tribute to the Arabian Caliph

The course of Moslem conquest now turned into the vast province of Khorassan; subdued one part of it after another, and approached the remote region where Yezdegird had taken refuge. Driven to the boundaries of his dominions, the fugitive monarch crossed the Oxus (the ancient Gihon) and the sandy deserts beyond, and threw himself among the shepherd hordes of Scythia. His wanderings are said to have extended to the borders of Tshin, or China, from the emperor of which he sought assistance.

- Obscurity hangs over this part of his story : it is affirmed that he succeeded in obtaining aid from the great Khan of the Tartars, and, re-crossing the Gihon, was joined by the troops of Balkh or Bactria, which province was still unsubdued and loyal. With these he endeavoured to make a stand against his unrelenting pursuers. A slight reverse, or some secret treachery, put an end to the adhesion of his barbarian ally. The Tartar chief returned with his troops to Turkestan.

Yezdegird's own nobles, tired of following his desperate fortunes, now conspired to betray him and his treasures into the hands of the Moslems as a price for their own safety. He was at that time at Merv, or Merou, on the Oxus, called Merou al Roud, or ' Merou of the River,' to distinguish it from Merou in Khorassan. Discovering the intended treachery of his nobles, and of the governor of the place, he caused his slaves to let him down with cords from a window of his palace, and fled, alone and on foot, under cover of the night. At the break of day he found himself near a mill, on the banks of the river, only eight miles from the city, and offered the miller his ring and bracelets, enriched with gems, if he would ferry him across the stream.   The boor, who knew nothing of jewels, demanded four silver oboli, or drachms, the amount of a day's earnings, as a compensation for leaving his work. . While they were debating, a party of horsemen, who were in pursuit of the king, came up and clove him with their scimetars.   Another account states that, exhausted and fatigued with the weight of his embroidered garments, he sought rest and concealment in the mill, and that the miller spread a mat, on which he laid down and slept. His rich attire, however, his belt of gold studded with jewels, his rings and bracelets, excited the avarice of the miller, who slew him with an axe while he slept, and, having stripped the body, threw it into the water.   In the morning several horsemen, in search of him, arrived at the mill, where discovering, by his clothes and jewels, that he had been murdered, they put the miller to death.

This miserable catastrophe to a miserable career is said to have occurred on the 23d August, in the year 651 of the Christian era.   Yezdegird was in the thirty-fourth year of his age ; having reigned nine years previous to the battle of Nehâvend, and since that event having been ten years a fugitive.   History lays no crimes to his charge, yet his hard fortunes and untimely end have failed to awaken the usual interest and sympathy.   He had been schooled in adversity from his early youth, yet he failed to profit by it.   Carrying about with him the wretched relics of an effeminate court, he sought only his personal safety, and wanted the courage and magnanimity to throw himself at the head of his armies, and battle for his crown and country like a great sovereign and a patriot prince.

Empires, however, like all other things, haver their allotted time, and die, if not by violence, at length of imbecility and old age.   That of Persia had long since lost its stamina, and the energy of a Cyrus would have been unable to infuse new life into its gigantic but palsied limbs.   At the death of Yezdegird it fell under the undisputed sway of the Caliphs, and became little better than a subject province. [1]

---

[1] According to popular traditions in Persia, Yezdegird, in the course of his wanderings, took refuge for a time in the castle of Fahender, near Schiraz, and buried the crown jewels and treasures of Nushirwan, in a deep pit or well under the castle, where they still remain guarded by a talisman, so that they cannot be found or drawn forth. Others say that he had them removed and deposited in trust with the Khacan, or emperor of Chin or Tartary. After the extinction of the royal Persian dynasty, those treasures and the crown remained in Chin.—*Sir William Ouseley's Travels in the East*, vol. ii. p. 34.

CHAPTER XXXV.

Amru displaced from the government of Egypt.—Revolt of the inhabitants.—Alexandria retaken by the imperialists.—Amru reinstated in command.—Retakes Alexandria, and tranquillizes Egypt.—Is again displaced.—Abdallah Ibn Saad invades the north of Africa.

" In the conquests of Syria, Persia, and Egypt," says a modern writer, " the fresh and vigorous enthusiasm of the personal companions and proselytes of Mahomet was exercised and expended, and the generation of warriors whose simple fanaticism had been inflamed by the preaching of the pseudo prophet, was in a great measure consumed in the sanguinary and perpetual toils of ten arduous campaigns."

We shall now see the effect of those conquests on the national character and habits; the avidity of place and power and wealth, superseding religious enthusiasm; and the enervating luxury and soft voluptuousness of Syria and Persia sapping the rude but masculine simplicity of the Arabian desert. Above all, the single-mindedness of Mahomet and his two immediate successors is at end. Other objects beside the mere advancement of Islamism distract the attention of its leading professors; and the struggle for worldly wealth and worldly sway, for the advancement of private ends, and the aggrandizement of particular tribes and families, destroy the unity of the empire, and beset the Caliphat with intrigue, treason, and bloodshed.

It was a great matter of reproach against the Caliph Othman that he was injudicious in his appointments, and had an inveterate propensity to consult the interests of his relatives and friends before that of the public. One of his greatest errours in this respect was the removal of Amru Ibn Al Aass from the government of Egypt, and the appointment of his own foster brother Abdallah Ibn Saad in his place This was the same Abdallah who, in acting as amanuensis to Mahomet, and writing down his revelations, had interpolated passages of his own, sometimes of a ludicrous nature. For this, and for his apostasy, he had been pardoned by Mahomet at the solicitation of Othman, and had ever since acted with apparent zeal; his interest coinciding with his duty.

He was of a courageous spirit, and one of the most expert horsemen of Arabia; but what might have fitted him to command a horde of the desert, was insufficient for the government of a conquered province. He was new and inexperienced in his present situation; whereas Amru had distinguished himself as a legislator as well as a conqueror, and had already won the affections of the Egyptians by his attention to their interests, and his respect for their customs and habitudes. His dismission was, therefore, resented by the people, and a disposition was manifested to revolt against the new governor.

The emperor Constantine, who had succeeded to his father Heraclius, hastened to take advantage of these circumstances. A fleet and army were sent against Alexandria under a prefect named Manuel. The Greeks in the city secretly co operated with him, and the metropolis was, partly by force of arms, partly by treachery, recaptured by the imperialists without much bloodshed.

Othman, made painfully sensible of the errour he had committed, hastened to revoke the appointment of his foster brother, and reinstated Amru in the command in Egypt. That able general went instantly against Alexandria with an army, in which were many Copts, irreconcilable enemies of the Greeks. Among these was the traitor Makawkas, who, from his knowledge of the country, and his influence among its inhabitants, was able to procure abundant supplies for the army.

The Greek garrison defended the city bravely and obstinately. Amru, enraged at having thus again to lay siege to a place which he had twice already taken, swore, by Allah, that if he should master it a third time, he would render it as easy of access as a brothel. He kept his word, for when he took the city he threw down the walls and demolished all the fortifications. He was merciful, however, to the inhabitants, and checked the fury of the Saracens, who were slaughtering all they met. A mosque was afterwards erected on the spot at which he stayed the carnage, called the Mosque of Mercy. Manuel, the Greek general, found it expedient to embark with all speed with such of his troops as he could save, and make sail for Constantinople.

Scarce, however, had Amru quelled every insurrection and secured the Moslem domination in Egypt, when he was again displaced from the government, and Abdallah Ibn Saad appointed a second time in his stead.

Abdallah had been deeply mortified by the loss of Alexandria, which had been ascribed to his incapacity; he was emulous too of the renown of Amru, and felt the necessity of vindicating his claims to command by some brilliant achievement. The north of Africa presented a new field for Moslem enterprise. We allude to that vast tract extending west from the desert of Libya or Barca, to Cape Non, embracing more than two thousand miles of sea-coast; comprehending the ancient divisions of Mamarica, Cyrenaica, Carthage, Numidia, and Mauritania; or, according to modern geographical designations, Barca, Tripoli, Tunis, Algiers, and Morocco.

A few words respecting the historical vicissitudes of this once powerful region may not be inappropriate. The original inhabitants are supposed to have come at a remote time from Asia ; or rather, it is said that an influx of Arabs drove the original inhabitants from the sea-coast to the mountains, and the borders of the interior desert, and continued their nomade and pastoral life along the shores of the Mediterranean. About nine hundred years before the Christian era, the Phœnicians of Tyre founded colonies along the coast; of these Carthage was the greatest. By degrees it extended its influence along the African shores and the opposite coast of Spain, and rose in prosperity and power until it became a rival republic to Rome. On the wars between Rome and Carthage it is needless to dilate. They ended in the downfall of the Carthaginian republic and the domination of Rome over Northern Africa.

This domination continued for about four centuries, until the Roman prefect Bonifacius invited over the Vandals from Spain to assist him in a feud with a political rival. The invitation proved fatal to Roman ascendency. The Vandals, aided by the Moors and Berbers, and by numerous Christian sectarians recently expelled from the Catholic church, aspired to gain possession of the country, and succeeded. Genseric, the Vandal general, captured and pillaged Carthage, and having subjugated Northern Africa, built a navy, invaded Italy and sacked Rome. The domination of the Vandals by sea and land lasted above half a century. In 533 and 534, Africa was regained by Belisarius for the Roman empire, and the Vandals were driven out of the land. After the departure of Belisarius, the Moors rebelled and made repeated attempts to get the dominion, but were as often defeated with great loss, and the Roman sway was once more established.

All these wars and changes had a disastrous effect on the African provinces. The Vandals had long disappeared; many of the Moorish families had been extirpated ; the wealthy inhabitants had fled to Sicily and Constantinople, and a stranger might wander whole days over regions, once covered with towns and cities, and teeming with population, without meeting a human being.

For near a century the country remained sunk in apathy and inaction, until now it was to be roused from its torpor by the all-pervading armies of Islam.

Soon after the reappointment of Abdallah to the government of Egypt, he set out upon the conquest of this country, at the head of forty thousand Arabs. After crossing the western boundary of Egypt he had to traverse the desert of Libya, but his army was provided with camels accustomed to the sandy wastes of Arabia, and, after a toilsome march, he encamped before the walls of Tripoli ; then as now, one of the most wealthy and powerful cities of the Barbary coast. The place was well fortified and made good resistance. A body of Greek troops which were sent to reinforce it, were surprised by the besiegers on the sea-coast, and dispersed with great slaughter.

The Roman prefect Gregorius having assembled an army of one hundred and twenty thousand men, a great proportion of whom were the hastily levied and undisciplined tribes of Barbary, advanced to defend his province. He was accompanied by an Amazonian daughter of wonderful beauty, who had been taught to manage the horse, to draw the bow and wield the scimetar, and who was always at her father's side in battle.

Hearing of the approach of this army, Abdallah suspended the siege and advanced to meet it. A brief parley took place between the hostile commanders. Abdallah proposed the usual alternatives, profession of Islamism, or payment of tribute Both were indignantly rejected. The armies engaged before the walls of Tripoli. Abdallah, whose fame was staked on this enterprise, stimulated his troops by word and example, and charged the enemy repeatedly at the head of his squadrons. Wherever he pressed, the fortune of the day would incline in favour of the Moslems; but on the other hand Gregorius fought with desperate bravery, as the fate of the province depended on this conflict; and wherever he appeared, his daughter was at his side, dazzling all eyes by the splendour of her armour and the heroism of her achievements. The contest was long, arduous, and uncertain. It was not one drawn battle, but a succession of conflicts, extending through several days, beginning at early dawn, but ceasing toward noon, when the intolerable heat of the sun obliged both armies to desist, and seek the shade of their tents.

The prefect Gregorius was exasperated at being in a manner held at bay by an inferior force, which he had expected to crush by the superiority of numbers. Seeing that Abdallah was the life and soul of his army, he proclaimed a reward of one hundred thousand pieces of gold and the hand of his daughter to the warrior who should bring him his head.

The excitement caused among the Grecian youth by this tempting prize, made the officers of Abdallah tremble for his safety. They represented to him the importance of his life to the army and the general cause, and prevailed upon him to keep aloof from the field of battle. His absence, however, produced an immediate change, and the valour of his troops, hitherto stimulated by his presence, began to languish.

Zobeir, a noble Arab of the tribe of Koreish, arrived at the field of battle with a small reinforcement, in the heat of one of the engagements. He found the troops fighting to a disadvantage, and looked round in vain for the general. Being told that he was in . his tent, he hastened thither and reproached him with his inactivity. Abdallah blushed, but explained the reason of his remaining passive. "Retort on the infidel commander his perfidious bribe," cried Zobeir; "proclaim that his daughter as a captive, and one hundred thousand pieces of gold, shall be the reward of the Moslem who brings his head." The advice was adopted, as well as the following stratagem suggested by Zobeir. On the next morning, Abdallah sent forth only sufficient force to keep up a defensive fight; but, when the sun had reached its noontide height, and the panting troops retired as usual to their tents, Abdallah and Zobeir sallied forth at the head of the reserve, and charged furiously among the fainting Greeks. Zobeir singled out the prefect, and slew him after a well contested fight. His daughter pressed forward to avenge his death, but was surrounded and made prisoner. The Grecian army was completely routed, and fled to the opulent town of Safetula, which was taken and sacked by the Moslems.

The battle was over, Gregorius had fallen, but no one came forward to claim the reward set upon his head. His captive daughter, however, on beholding Zobeir, broke forth into tears and exclamations, and thus revealed the modest victor. Zobeir refused to accept the maiden or the gold. He fought, he said, for the faith, not for earthly objects; and looked for his reward in paradise. In honour of his achievements, he was sent with tidings of this victory to the Caliph; but when he announced it, in the great . mosque at Medina, in presence of the assembled people, he made

no mention of his own services. , His modesty enhanced his merits in the eyes of the public, and his name was placed by the Moslems beside those of Khaled and Amru.

, Abdallah found his forces too much reduced and enfeebled by
battle and disease to enable him to maintain possession of the
country he had subdued; and, after a campaign of fifteen months,
he led back his victorious, but diminished army into Egypt, encumbered with captives and laden with booty.

He afterwards, by the Caliph's command, assembled an army in
the Thebaid or Upper Egypt, and thence made numerous successful
excursions into Nubia, the Christian king of which was reduced to
make a humiliating treaty, by which he bound himself to send annually to the Moslem commander in Egypt a great number of Nu-
bian or Ethiopian slaves by way of tribute.

CHAPTER XXXVI.

Moawyah, Emir of Syria.--His naval victories.—Othman loses the prophet's ring.—
Suppresses erroneous copies of the Koran.—Conspiracies against him.—His death.

Among the distinguished Moslems who held command of the distant provinces during the Caliphat of Othman, was Moawyah Ibn
Abu Sofian. As his name denotes, he was the son of Abu Sofian,
the early foe and subsequent, proselyte of Mahomet. On his
father's death he had become chief of the tribe of Koreish, and head
of the family of Omeya or Ommiah. The late Caliph Omar, about
four years before his death, had appointed him emir, or governor
of Syria, and he was continued in that office by Othman. He was
between thirty and forty years of age, enterprising, courageous, of
quick sagacity, extended views, and lofty aims. , Having the maritime coast and ancient ports of Syria under his command, he aspired to extend the triumphs of the Moslem arms by sea as well as
land. He had repeatedly endeavoured, but in vain, to obtain permission from Omar to make a naval expedition, that Caliph being
always apprehensive of the too wide and rapid extension of the enterprises of his generals. Under Othman he was more successful,
and in the twenty-seventh year of the Hegira was permitted to fit
out a fleet, with which he launched forth on the sea of Tarshish, or
the Phœnician Sea, by both which names the eastern part of the
Mediterranean Sea was designated in ancient times.

His first enterprise was against the island of Cyprus, which was
still held in allegiance to the emperor of Constantinople. The Christian garrison was weak and the inhabitants of the island soon submitted to pay tribute to the Caliph.

His next enterprise was against the island of Aradus, where he
landed his troops and besieged the city or fortress; battering it with
military engines. The inhabitants made vigorous resistance, repelled him from the island, and it was only after he had come a se-

cond time, with superior force that he was able to subdue it. He then expelled the natives, demolished the fortifications, and set fire to the city.

His most brilliants achievement, however, was a battle with a large fleet, in which the emperor was cruising in the Phœnician Sea. It was called in Arab history The Battle of Masts, from the forest of masts in the imperial fleet. The Christians went into action singing psalms and elevating the cross; the Moslems repeating texts of the Koran, shouting Allah Achbar, and waving the standard of Islam. The battle was severe; the imperial fleet dispersed, and the emperor escaped by dint of sails and oars.

Moawyah now swept the seas victoriously, made landings on Crete and Malta, captured the island of Rhodes, demolished its famous colossal statue of brass, and, having broken it to pieces, transported the fragments to Alexandria, where they were sold to a Jewish merchant of Edissa, and were sufficient to load nine hundred camels. He had another fight with a Christian fleet in the bay of Fencke, by Castel Rosso, in which both parties claimed the victory. He even carried his expeditions along the coasts of Asia Minor, and to the very port of Constantinople.

These naval achievements, a new feature in Arab warfare, rendered Moawyah exceedingly popular in Syria, and laid the foundation for that power and importance to which he subsequently attained.

It is worthy of remark how the triumphs of an ignorant people, who had heretofore dwelt obscurely in the midst of their deserts, were overrunning all the historical and poetical regions of antiquity. They had invaded and subdued the once mighty empires on land, they had now launched forth from the old Scriptural ports of Tyre and Sidon, swept the Sea of Tarshish and were capturing the isles rendered famous by classic fable.

In the midst of these foreign successes an incident, considered full of sinister import, happened to Othman. He accidentally dropped in a brook a silver ring, on which was inscribed, "Mahomet the apostle of God." It had originally belonged to Mahomet, and since his death had been worn by Abu Beker, Omar and Othman, as the symbol of command, as rings had been considered throughout the East from the earliest times. The brook was searched with the most anxious care, but the ring was not to be found. This was an ominous loss in the eyes of the superstitious Moslems.

It happened about this time that, scandalized by the various versions of the Koran, and the disputes that prevailed concerning their varying texts, he decreed, in a council of the chief Moslems, that all copies of the Koran which did not agree with the genuine one in the hands of Hafza, the widow of Mahomet, should be burnt. Seven copies of Hafza's Koran were accordingly made; six were sent to Mecca, Yemen, Syria, Bahrein, Bassora, and Cufa, and one was retained in Medina. All copies varying from these were to be given to the flames. This measure caused Othman to be called the Gatherer of the Koran. It, at any rate, prevented any further vitiation of the sacred Scripture of Islam, which has remained unchanged from that time to the present. Besides this pious act, Othman caused a wall to be built round the sacred house of the Caaba, and enlarged and beautified the mosque of the prophet in Medina.

Notwithstanding all this, disaffection and intrigue were springing up round the venerable Caliph in Medina. He was brave, open-handed, and munificent, but he wanted shrewdness and discretion; was prone to favoritism; very credulous and easily deceived.

Murmurs rose against him on all sides, and daily increased in virulence. His conduct, both public and private, was reviewed, and circumstances, which had been passed by as trivial, were magnified into serious offences. He was charged with impious presumption in having taken his stand, on being first made Caliph, on the uppermost step of the pulpit, where Mahomet himself used to stand, whereas Abu Beker had stood one step lower, and Omar two. A graver accusation, and one too well merited, was that he had displaced men of worth, eminent for their services, and given their places to his own relatives and favourites: This was especially instanced in dismissing Amru Ibn al Aass from the government of Egypt, and appointing in his stead his own brother Abdallah Ibn Saad, who had once been proscribed by Mahomet. Another accusation was, that he had lavished the public money upon parasites, giving one hundred thousand dinârs to one, four hundred thousand to another, and no less than five hundred and four thousand upon his secretary of state, Merwân Ibn Hakem, who had, it was said, an undue ascendency over him; and was, in fact, the subtle and active spirit of his government. The last sum, it was alleged, was taken out of a portion of the spoils of Africa, which had been set apart for the family of the prophet.

The ire of the old Caliph was kindled at having his lavish liberality thus charged upon him as a crime. He mounted the pulpit and declared that the money in the treasury belonged to God, the distribution to the Caliph at his own discretion, as successor of the prophet; and he prayed God to confound whoever should gainsay what he had set forth.

Upon this Ammar Ibn Yaser, one of the primitive Moslems, of whom Mahomet himself had said that he was filled with faith from the crown of his head to the sole of his foot, rose and disputed the words of Othman, whereupon some of the Caliph's kindred of the house of Ommiah fell upon the venerable Ammar and beat him until he fainted.

The outrage offered to the person of one of the earliest disciples and especial favourites of the prophet was promulgated far and wide, and contributed to the general discontent which now assumed the aspect of rebellion. The ringleader of the disaffected, was Ibn Caba, formerly a Jew. This son of mischief made a factious tour from Yemen to Hidschaf, thence to Bassora, to Cufa, to Syria and Egypt, decrying the Caliph and the emirs he had appointed; declaring that the Caliphat had been usurped by Othman from Ali, to whom it rightly belonged, as the nearest relative of the prophet and suggesting by word of mouth and secret correspondence, that the malcontents should assemble simultaneously in various parts under pretext of a pilgrimage to Mecca.

The plot of the renegade Jew succeeded.   In the fulness of time deputations arrived from all parts.   One mounting to a hundred and fifty persons from Bassora; another of two hundred under Malec Alashtar from Cufa; a third of six hundred from Egypt headed by Mahomet, the son of Abu Beker, and brother of Ayesha, together with numbers of a sect of zealots called Karegites, who took the lead.   These deputies encamped like an army within a league of Medina, and summoned the Caliph by message either to redress their grievances or to abdicate.

Othman in consternation applied to Ali to go forth and pacify the multitude.   He consented on condition that Othman would previously make atonement for his errours from the pulpit.   Harassed and dismayed, the aged Caliph mounted the pulpit, and with a voice broken by sobs and tears, exclaimed, "My God, I beg pardon of thee, and turn to thee, with penitence and sorrow." The whole assemblage were moved and softened, and wept with the Caliph.

Merwân, the intriguing and well-paid secretary of Othman, and the soul of his government, had been absent during these occurrences, and on returning reproached the Caliph with what he termed an act of weakness.   Having his permission, he addressed the populace in a strain that soon roused them to tenfold ire. Ali, hereupon, highly indignant, renounced any further interference in the matter.

Naile, the wife of Othman, who had heard the words of Merwân, and beheld the fury of the people, warned her husband of the storm gathering over his head, and prevailed upon him again to solicit the mediation of Ali.   The latter suffered himself to be persuaded and went forth, among the insurgents.   Partly by good words and liberal donations from the treasury, partly by a written promise from the Caliph to redress all their grievances, the insurgents were quieted, all but the deputies from Egypt who came to complain against the Caliph's foster-brother Abdallah Ibn Saad, who they said had oppressed them with exactions, and lavished their blood in campaigns in Barbary, merely for his own fame and profit, without retaining a foothold in the country.   To pacify these complainants, Othman displaced Abdallah from the government, and left them to name his successor.   They unanimously named Mahomet, the brother of Ayesha; who had in fact been used by that intriguing woman as a firebrand to kindle this insurrection; her object being to get Telha appointed to the Caliphat.

The insurgent camp now broke up.   Mahomet with his followers set out to take possession of his post, and the aged Caliph flattered himself he would once more be left in peace.

Three days had Mahomet and his train been on their journey, when they were overtaken by a black slave on a dromedary.   They demanded who he was, and whither he was travelling so rapidly. He gave himself out as a slave of the secretary Merwân bearing a message from the Caliph to his emir in Egypt.   "I am the emir," said Mahomet.   "My errand," said the slave, "is to the emir Abdallah

Ibn Saad." He was asked if he had a letter, and on his prevaricating was searched. A letter was found concealed in a water-flask. It was from the Caliph, briefly ordering the emir, on the arrival of Mahomet Ibn Abu Beker, to make way with him secretly, destroy his diploma, and imprison, until further orders, those who had brought complaints to Medina.

Mahomet Ibn Abu Beker returned furious to Medina, and showed the perfidious letter to Ali, Zobeir, and Telha, who repaired with him to Othman. The latter denied any knowledge of the letter. It must then, they said, be a forgery of Merwân's, and requested that he might be summoned. Othman would not credit such treason on the part of his secretary, and insisted it must have been a treacherous device of one of his enemies. Medina was now in a ferment. There was a gathering of the people. All were incensed at such an atrocious breach of faith, and insisted that if the letter originated with Othman, he should resign the Caliphat, if with Merwân, that he should receive the merited punishment. Their demands had no effect upon the Caliph.

Mahomet Ibn Abu Beker now sent off swift messengers to recall the recent insurgents from the provinces, who were returning home, and to call in aid from the neighbouring tribes. The dwelling of Othman was beleaguered; the alternative was left him to deliver up Merwân or to abdicate. He refused both. His life was now threatened. He barricadoed himself in his dwelling. The supply of water was cut off. If he made his appearance on the terraced roof, he was assailed with stones. Ali, Zobeir, and Telha, endeavoured to appease the multitude, but they were deaf to their entreaties. Saad Ibn al Aass advised the Caliph, as the holy month was at hand, to sally forth on a pilgrimage to Mecca, as the piety of the undertaking and the sanctity of the pilgrim garb would protect him. Othman rejected the advice. " If they seek my life," said he, " they will not respect the pilgrim garb."

Ali, Zobeir, and Telha, seeing the danger imminent, sent their three sons, Hassan, Abdallah, and Mahomet, to protect the house. They stationed themselves by the door, and for some time kept the rebels at bay ; but the rage of the latter knew no bounds. They stormed the house ; Hassan was wounded in its defence. The rebels rushed in ; among the foremost was Mahomet, the brother of Ayesha, and Ammar Ibn Yaser, whom Othman had ordered to be beaten. They found the venerable Caliph seated on a cushion, his beard flowing on his breast ; the Koran open on his lap, and his wife Naïle beside him.

One of the rebels struck him on the head, another stabbed him repeatedly with a sword, and Mahomet Ibn Abu Beker thrust a javelin into his body after he was dead. His wife was wounded in endeavouring to protect him, and her life was only saved through the fidelity of a slave. His house was plundered, as were some of the neighbouring houses, and two chambers of the treasury.

As soon as the invidious Ayesha heard that the murder was accomplished, she went forth in hypocritical guise loudly bewailing the death of a man to whom she had secretly been hostile, and joining with the Ommiah family in calling for blood revenge.

The noble and virtuous Ali with greater sincerity, was incensed at his sons for not sacrificing their lives in defence of the Caliph, and reproached the sons of Telha and Zobeir with being lukewarm. " Why are you so angry, father of Hassan?" said Telha; ."had Othman given up Merwân this evil would not have happened."

In fact it has been generally affirmed that the letter really was written by Merwân without the knowledge of the Caliph, and was intended to fall into the hands of Mahomet, and produce the effect which resulted from it. Merwân, it is alleged having the charge of the correspondence of the Caliphat, had repeatedly abused the confidence of the weak and superannuated Othman in like manner, but not with such a nefarious aim. Of late he had secretly joined the cabal against the Caliph.

The body of Othman lay exposed for three days, and was then buried in the clothes in which he was slain, unwashed and without any funeral ceremony. He was eighty-two years old at the time of his death, and had reigned nearly twelve years. The event happened in the thirty-fifth year of the Hegira, in the year 655 of the Christian era. Notwithstanding his profusion and the sums lavished upon his favourites, immense treasures were found in his dwelling, a considerable part of which he had set apart for charitable purposes.

CHAPTER XXXVII.

Candidates for the Caliphat.—Inauguration of Ali, fourth Caliph.—He undertakes measures of reform.—Their consequences.—Conspiracy of Ayesha.—She gets possession of Bassora.

We have already seen that the faith of Islam had begun to lose its influence in binding together the hearts of the faithful, and uniting their feelings and interests in one common cause. The factions which sprang up at the very death of Mahomet, had increased with the election of every successor, and candidates for the succession multiplied as the brilliant successes of the Moslem arms elevated victorious generals to popularity and renown. On the assassination of Othman, four candidates were presented for the Caliphat; and the fortuitous assemblage of deputies from the various parts of the Moslem empire threatened to make the election difficult and tumultuous.

The most prominent candidate was Ali, who had the strongest natural claim, being cousin and son-in-law of Mahomet, and his children by Fatima being the only posterity of the prophet. He was of the noblest branch of the noble race of Koreish. He possessed the three qualities most prized by Arabs : courage, eloquence, and munificence. His intrepid spirit had gained him from the prophet, the appellation of The Lion of God; specimens of his eloquence remain in some verses and sayings preserved among the Arabs; and his munificence was manifested in sharing among others, every Friday, what remained in the treasury. Of his magnanimity, we have given repeated instances; his noble scorn of every thing false and mean, and the absence in his conduct of every thing like selfish intrigue.

His right to the Caliphat was supported by the people of Cufa, the Egyptians, and a great part of the Arabs who were desirous of a line of Caliphs of the blood of Mahomet. He was opposed, however, as formely, by the implacable Ayesha, who, though well-stricken in years, retained an unforgiving recollection of his having once questioned her chastity.

A second candidate was Zobeir, the same warrior who distinguisheld himself by his valour, in the campaign of Barbary, by his modesty in omitting to mention his achievements, and in declining to accept their reward. His pretensions to the Caliphat were urged by the people of Bassora.

A third candidate was Telha, who had been one of the six electors of Othman; and who had now the powerful support of Ayesha.

A fourth candidate was Moawyah, the military governor of Syria, and popular from his recent victories by sea and land. He had, moreover, immense wealth to back his claims, and was head of the powerful tribe of Koreish; but he was distant from the scene of election, and in his absence, his partisans could only promote confusion and delay.

It was a day of tumult and trouble in Medina. The body of Othman was still unburied. His wife Naile, at the instigation of Ayesha, sent off his bloody vest to be carried through the distant provinces, a ghastly appeal to the passions of the inhabitants.

The people, apprehending discord and disunion, clamoured for the instant nomination of a Caliph. The deputations, which had come from various parts with complaints against Othman became impatient. There were men from Babylonia, and Mesopotamia, and other parts of Persia; from Syria and Egypt, as well as from the three divisions of Arabia; these assembled tumultuously, and threatened the safety of the three candidates, Ali, Telha, and Zobeir, unless an election were made in four and twenty hours.

In this dilemma, some of the principal Moslems repaired to Ali, and entreated him to accept the office. He consented with reluctance, but would do nothing clandestinely, and refused to take their hands, the Moslem mode at that time of attesting fealty, unless it were in public assembly at the mosque; lest he should give cause of cavil or dispute to his rivals. He refused, also, to make any promises or conditions. "If I am elected Caliph," said he, "I will administer the government with independence, and deal with you all according to my ideas of justice. If you elect another, I will yield obedience to him, and be ready to serve him as his vizier." They assented to every thing he said, and again entreated him to accept, for the good of the people and of the faith.

On the following morning there was a great assemblage of the people at the mosque, and Ali presented himself at the portal. He appeared in simple Arab style, clad in a thin cotton garb girded round his loins, a coarse turban, and using a bow as a walking-staff. He took off his slippers in reverence of the place, and entered the mosque bearing them in his left hand.

Finding that Telha and Zobeir were not present, he caused them to be sent for. They came, and knowing the state of the public mind, and that all immediate opposition would be useless, offered their hands in token of allegiance. Ali paused, and asked them if their hearts went with their hands; "speak frankly," said he; "if you disapprove of my election, and will accept the office, I will give my hand to either of you." They declared their perfect satisfaction, and gave their hands. Telha's right arm had been maimed in the battle of Ohod, and he stretched it forth with difficulty. The circumstance struck the Arabs as an evil omen. "It is likely to be a lame business, that is begun with a lame hand," muttered a bystander. Subsequent events seemed to justify the foreboding.

Moawyah, the remaining candidate, being absent at his government in Syria, the whole family of Ommiah, of which he was the head, withdrew from the ceremony. This, likewise, boded future troubles.

After the inauguration, Telha and Zobeir, with a view, it is said, to excite disturbance, applied to Ali to investigate and avenge the death of Othman. Ali, who knew that such a measure would call up a host of enemies, evaded the insidious proposition. It was not the moment, he said, for such an investigation. The event had its origin in old enmities and discontents instigated by the devil, and when the devil once gained a foothold, he never relinquished it willingly. The very measure they recommended was one of the devil's suggesting, for the purpose of fomenting disturbances. However," added he, "if you will point out the assassins of Othman, I will not fail to punish them according to their guilt."

While Ali thus avoided the dangerous litigation, he endeavoured to cultivate the good will of the Koreishites, and to strengthen himself against apprehended difficulties with the family of Ommiah. Telha and Zobeir, being disconcerted in their designs, now applied for important commands. Telha for the government of Cufa, and Zobeir for that of Bassora; but Ali again declined complying with their wishes; observing that he needed such able counsellors at hand in his present emergencies. They afterwards separately obtained permission from him to make a pilgrimage to Mecca; and set off on that devout errand with piety on their lips, but crafty policy in their breasts; Ayesha had already repaired to the holy city, bent upon opposition to the government of the man she hated.

Ali was now Caliph, but did not feel himself securely fixed in his authority. Many abuses had grown up during the dotage of his predecessor, which called for redress, and most of the governments of provinces were in the hands of persons in whose affection and fidelity he felt no confidence. He determined upon a general reform; and as a first step, to remove from office all the governors who had been appointed by the superannuated Othman. This measure was strongly opposed by some of his counsellors. They represented to him that he was not yet sufficiently established to venture upon such changes; and that he would make powerful enemies of men, who, if left in office, would probably hasten to declare allegiance to him, now that he was Caliph.

Ali was not to be persuaded. "Sedition," he said, "like fire, is easily extinguished at the commencement; but the longer it burns the more fiercely it blazes."

He was advised, at least, to leave his formidable rival Moawyah, for the present, in the government of Syria, as he was possessed of great wealth and influence, and a powerful army, and might rouse that whole province to rebellion; and in such case might be joined by Telha and Zobeir, who were both disappointed and disaffected men. He had recently shown his influence over the feelings of the people under his command; when the bloody vest of Othman arrived in the province, he had displayed it from the pulpit of the mosque in Damascus. The mosque resounded with lamentations mingled with clamours for the revenge of blood; for Othman had won the hearts of the people of Syria by his munificence. Some of the noblest inhabitants of Damascus swore to remain separate from their wives, and not to lay their heads on a pillow until blood for blood had atoned for the death of Othman. Finally the vest had been hoisted as a standard, and had fired the Syrian army with a desire for vengeance.

Ali's counsellor represented all these things to him. "Suffer Moawyah, therefore," added he, "to remain in command until he has acknowledged your government, and then he may be displaced without turmoil. Nay, I will pledge myself to bring him bound hand and foot into your presence."

Ali spurned at this counsel, and swore he would practise no such treachery, but would deal with Moawyah with the sword alone. He commenced immediately his plan of reform, with the nomination of new governors devoted to his service. Abdallah Ibn Abbas was appointed to Arabia Felix, Ammar Ibn Sahel to Cufa, Othman Ibn Hanif to Bassora, Sahel Ibn Hanif to Syria, and Saad Ibn Kais to Egypt. These generals lost no time in repairing to their respective governments, but the result soon convinced Ali that he had been precipitate.

Jaali, the governor of Arabia Felix, readily resigned his post to Abdallah Ibn Abbas, and retired to Mecca; but he took with him the public treasure, and delivered it into the hands of Ayesha, and her confederates Telha and Zobeir, who were already plotting rebellion.

Othman Ibn Hanif on arriving at Bassora to take the command, found the people discontented and rebellious, and having no force to subjugate them, esteemed himself fortunate in escaping from their hands and returning to the Caliph.

When Ammar Ibn Sahel reached the confines of Cufa, he learnt that the people were unanimous in favour of Abu Musa Alashari, their present governor, and determined to support him by fraud or force. Ammar had no disposition to contend with them, the Cufians being reputed the most treacherous and perfidious people of the East; so he turned the head of his horse. and journeyed back mortified and disconcerted to Ali.

Saad Ibn Kais was received in Egypt with murmurs by the inhabitants, who were indignant at the assassination of Othman, and refused to submit to the government of Ali, until justice was done upon the perpetrators of that murder. Saad prudently, therefore, retraced his steps to Medina.

Sahel Ibn Hanif had no better success in Syria, he was met at Tabuc, by a body of cavalry, who demanded his name and business. "For my name," said he, "I am Sahel, the son of Hanif; and for my business. I am governor of this province, as lieutenant of the Caliph Ali, Commander of the Faithful." They assured him in reply, that Syria had already an able governor in Moawyah, son of Abu Sofian, and that to their certain knowledge there was not room in the province for the sole of his foot; so saying, they unsheated their scimetars.

The new governor, who was not provided with a body of troops sufficient to enforce his authority, returned also to the Caliph with this intelligence. Thus of the five governors, so promptly sent forth by Ali in pursuance of his great plan of reform, Abdallah Ibn Abbas was the only one permitted to assume his post.

When Ali received tidings of the disaffection of Syria, he wrote a letter to Moawyah, claiming his allegiance, and transmitted it by an especial messenger. The latter was detained many days by the Syrian commander, and then sent back, accompanied by another messenger, bearing a sealed letter superscribed, "From Moawyah to Ali." The two couriers, arrived at Medina in the cool of the evening, the hour of concourse, and passed through the multitude bearing the letter aloft on a staff, so that all could see the superscription. The people thronged after the messengers into the presence of Ali. On opening the letter it was found to be a perfect blank, in token of contempt and defiance.

Ali soon learned that this was no empty bravado. He was apprised by his own courier that an army of sixty thousand men was actually on foot in Syria, and that the bloody garment of Othman, the standard of rebellion, was erected in the mosque at Damascus. Upon this he solemny called Allah and the prophet to witness that he was not guilty of that murder; but made active preparations to put down the rebellion by force of arms; sending missives into all the provinces, demanding the assistance of the faithful.

The Moslems were now divided into two parties: those who adhered to Ali, among whom were the people of Medina generally; and the Motazeli, or Separatists, who were in the opposition. The latter were headed by the able and vindictive Ayesha, who had her headquarters at Mecca, and with the aid of Telha and Zobeir, was busy organizing an insurrection. She had induced the powerful family of Ommiah to join her cause, and had sent couriers to all the governors of provinces whom Ali had superseded, inviting them to unite in the rebellion. The treasure brought to her by Jaali, the displaced governor of Arabia Felix, furnished her with the means of war, and the bloody garment of Othman proved a powerful auxiliary.

A council of the leaders of this conspiracy was held at Mecca. Some inclined to join the insurgents in Syria, but it was objected, that Moawyah was sufficiently powerful in that country without their aid. The intrepid Ayesha was for proceeding immediately to Medina and attacking Ali in his capital, but it was represented that the people of Medina were unanimous in his favour, and too powerful to be assailed with success. It was finally determined to march for Bassora, Telha assuring them that he had a strong party in that city, and pledging himself for its surrender.

A proclamation was accordingly made by sound of trumpet through the streets of Mecca to the following effect:

"In the name of the most high God. Ayesha, Mother of the Faithful, accompanied by the chiefs Telha and Zobeir, is going in person to Bassora. All those of the faithful who burn with a desire to defend the faith and avenge the death of the Caliph Othman, have only to present themselves and they shall be furnished with all necessaries for the journey."

Ayesha sallied forth from one of the gates of Mecca, borne in a litter placed on the back of a strong camel named Alascar. Telha and Zobeir attended her on each side, followed by six hundred persons of some note, all mounted on camels, and a promiscuous multitude of about six thousand on foot.

After marching some distance, the motley host stopped to refresh themselves on the bank of a rivulet near a village. Their arrival aroused the dogs of the village, who surrounded Ayesha and barked at her most clamorously. Like all Arabs, she was superstitious, and considered this an evil omen. Her apprehensions were increased on learning that the name of the village was Jowab. "My trust is in God," exclaimed she, solemnly. "To him do I turn in time of trouble,"—a text from the Koran, used by Moslems in time of extreme danger. In fact, she called to mind some proverb of the prophet about the dogs of Jowab, and a prediction that one of his wives would be barked at by them when in a situation of imminent peril. "I will go no further," cried Ayesha, "I will halt here for the night." So saying, she struck her camel on the leg to make him kneel that she might alight.

Telha and Zobeir, dreading any delay, brought some peasants whom they had suborned to assign a different name to the village, and thus quieted her superstitious fears. About the same time some horsemen, likewise instructed by them, rode up with a false report that Ali was not far distant with a body of troops. Ayesha hesitated no longer, but mounting nimbly on her camel, pressed to the head of her little army, and they all pushed forward with increased expedition towards Bassora. Arrived before the city, they had hoped, from the sanguine declarations of Telha, to see it throw open its gates to receive them; the gates, however, remained closely barred. Othman Ibn Hanef, whom Ali had sent without success to assume the government of Cufa, was now in command at Bassora, whither he had been invited by a part of the inhabitants.

Ayesha sent a summons to the governor to come forth and join the standard of the faithful, or at least to throw open his gates; but he was a timid, undecided man, and confiding the defence of the city to his lieutenant Ammar, retired in great tribulation within his own dwelling in the citadel, and went to prayers.

Ammar summoned the people to arms, and called a meeting of the principal inhabitants in the mosque. He soon found out, to his great discouragement, that the people were nearly equally divided into two factions, one for Ali, since he was regularly elected Caliph, the other composed of partisans of Telha. The parties, instead of deliberating, fell to reviling, and ended by throwing dust in each others' faces.

In the meantime Ayesha and her host approached the walls, and many of the inhabitants went forth to meet her. Telha and Zobeir alternately addressed the multitude, and were followed by Ayesha, who harangued them from her camel. Her voice, which she elevated that it might be heard by all, became shrill and sharp, instead of intelligible, and provoked the merriment of some of the crowd. A dispute arose as to the justice of her appeal; mutual revilings again took place between the parties; they gave each other the lie, and again threw dust in each others' faces. One of the men of Bassora then turned and reproached Ayesha. "Shame on thee, oh Mother of the Faithful!" said he. "The murder of the Caliph was a grievous crime, but was a less abomination than thy forgetfulness of the modesty of thy sex. Wherefore dost thou abandon thy quiet home, and thy protecting veil, and ride forth like a man barefaced on that accursed camel, to foment quarrels and dissensions among the faithful?"

Another of the crowd scoffed at Telha and Zobeir. "You have brought your mother with you," cried he, "why did you not also bring your wives?"

Insults were soon followed by blows, swords were drawn, a skirmish ensued, and they fought until the hour of prayer separated them.

Ayesha sat down before Bassora with her armed host, and some days passed in alternate skirmishes and negotiations. At length a truce was agreed upon, until deputies could be sent to Medina to learn the cause of these dissensions among the Moslems, and whether Telha and Zobeir agreed voluntarily to the election of Ali, or did so on compulsion : if the former, they should be considered as rebels; if the latter, their partisans in Bassora should be considered justified in upholding them.

The insurgents, however, only acquiesced in this agreement to get the governor in their power, and so gain possession of the city. They endeavoured to draw him to their camp by friendly messages, but he apparently suspected their intentions, and refused to come forth until the answer should be received from Medina. Upon this Telha and Zobeir, taking advantage of a stormy night, gained an entrance into the city with a chosen band, and surprised the governor in the mosque, where they took him prisoner, after killing forty of his guard. They sent to Ayesha to know what they should do with their captive. "Let him be put

to death," was her fierce reply.   Upon this one of her women
interceded.   "I adjure thee," said she, "in the name of Allah and
the companions of the apostle, do not slay him."   Ayesha was
moved by this adjuration, and commuted his punishment into forty
stripes and imprisonment.   He was doomed, however, to suffer
still greater evils before he escaped from the hands of his captors.
His beard was plucked out hair by hair, one of the most disgraceful
punishments that can be inflicted on an Arab.   His eyebrows were
served in the same manner, and he was then contemptuously set
at liberty.

   The city of Bassora was now taken possession of without further
resistance.   Ayesha entered it in state, supported by Telha and
Zobeir, and followed by her troops and adherents.   The inhabitants
were treated with kindness, as friends who had acted through
errour; and every exertion was made to secure their good-will, and
to incense them against Ali, who was represented as a murderer
and usurper.

CHAPTER XXXVIII.

Ali defeats the rebels under Ayesha.—His treatment of her.

   When Ali heard of the revolt at Mecca, and the march against
Bassora, he called a general meeting in the mosque, and endeavoured to stir up the people to arm and follow him in pursuit
of the rebels: but, though he spoke with his usual eloquence, and
was popular in Medina, a coldness and apathy pervaded the assembly.   Some dreaded a civil war; others recollected that the
leader of the rebels, against whom they were urged to take up
arms, was Ayesha, the favourite wife of the prophet, the Mother
of the Faithful; others doubted whether Ali might not, in some
degree, be implicated in the death of Othman, which had been so
artfully charged against him.

   At length a Moslem of distinction, Ziyad Ibn Hantelah, rose with
generous warmth, and, stepping up to Ali, " Let whosoever will,
hold back," cried he, " we will go forward."

   At the same time two Ansars, or doctors of the law, men of
great weight, pronounced with oracular voice, " The Imam
Othman, master of the two testimonies, did not die by the hand of
the master of the two testimonies; " [1] that is to say, " Othman was
not slain by Ali."

   The Arabs are a mercurial people, and acted upon by sudden
impulses.   The example of Ziyad, and the declaration of the two
Ansars, caused an immediate excitement.   Abu Kotadà, an Ansar

---

[1] The two testimonies mean the two fundamental beliefs of the Moslem creed : "There
is but one God.   Mahomet is the apostle of God."   The Caliph, as Imam or pontiff of
the Mussulman religion, is master of the two testimonies.

of distinction, drew his sword. " The apostle of God," said he, " upon whom be peace, girt me with this sword. ·It has long been sheathed. I now devote it to the destruction of these deceivers of the faithful."

A matron in a transport of enthusiasm exclaimed, " Oh Commander of the Faithful, if it were permitted by our law, I myself would go with thee; but here is my cousin, dearer to me than my own life, he shall follow thee and partake of thy fortunes."

Ali profited by the excitement of the moment, and making a hasty levy, marched out of Medina at the head of about nine hundred men, eager to overtake the rebels before they should reach Bassora. Hearing, however, that Ayesha was already in possession of that city, he halted at a place called Arrabdah until he should be joined by reinforcements : sending messengers to Abu Musa Alashair, governor of Cufa, and to various other commanders, ordering speedy succour. He was soon joined by his eldest son Hassan, who undertook to review his conduct, and lecture him on his policy. " I told you," said he, " when the Caliph Othman was besieged, to go out of the city, lest you should be implicated in his death. I told you not to be inaugurated until deputies from the Arabian tribes were present. Lastly, I told you when Ayesha and her two confederates took the field, to keep at home until they should be pacified; so that, should any mischief result, you might not be made responsible. You have not heeded my advice, and the consequence is that you may now be murdered to-morrow, with nobody to blame but yourself."

Ali listened with impatience to this filial counsel, or rather, censure : when it was finished, he replied, " Had I left the city when Othman was besieged, I should myself have been surrounded. Had I waited for my inauguration until all the tribes came in, I should have lost the votes of the people of Medina, the ' Helpers,' who have the privilege of disposing of the government. Had I remained at home after my enemies had taken the field, like a wild beast lurking in its hole, I should like a wild beast have been digged out and destroyed. If I do not look after my own affairs, who will look after them? If I do not defend myself, who will defend me? Such are my reasons for acting as I have acted; and now, my son, hold your peace." We hear of no further counsels from Hassan.

Ali had looked for powerful aid from Abu Musa Alashair, governor of Cufa, but he was of a lukewarm spirit, and cherished no good will to the Caliph, from his having sent Othman Ibn Hanef to supplant him, as has been noticed. He therefore received his messengers with coldness, and sent a reply full of evasions. Ali was enraged at this reply; and his anger was increased by the arrival about the same time of the unfortunate Othman Ibn Hanef, who had been so sadly scourged and maltreated and ejected from his government at Bassora. What most grieved the heart of the ex-governor was the indignity that had been offered to his person. " Oh Commander of the Faithful," said he, " mournfully, " when you sent me to Bassora I had a beard, and now, alas, I have not a hair on my chin!"

All commiserated the unfortunate man who thus deplored the loss of his beard more than of his government; but comforted him with the assurance that his sufferings would be counted to him as merits. He then spoke of his own case; the Caliphs, his predecessors, had reigned without opposition; but, for his own part, those who had joined in electing him, had proved false to him. "Tellha and Zobeir," said he, "have submitted to Abu Beker, Omar, and Othman, why have they arrayed themselves against me? By Allah they shall find that I am not one jot inferior to my predecessors!"

Ali now sent more urgent messages to Abu Musa, governor of Cufa, by his son Hassan and Ammar Ibn Yaser, his general of the horse, a stern old soldier, ninety years of age, the same intrepid spokesman who, for his hardihood of tongue, had been severely maltreated by order of the Caliph Othman. They were reinforced by Alashtar, a determined officer, who had been employed in the previous mission, and irritated by the prevarications of Abu Musa.

Hassan and Ammar were received with ceremonious respect by the governor, and their mission was discussed, according to usage, in the mosque, but Alashtar remained with the guard that had escorted them. The envoys pressed their errand with warmth, urging the necessity of their sending immediate succour to the Caliph. Abu Musa, however, who prided himself more upon words than deeds, answered them by an evasive harangue; signifying his doubts of the policy of their proceeding; counselling that the troops should return to Medina, that the whole matter in dispute should be investigated, and the right to rule amicably adjusted. "It is a bad business," added he, "and he that meddles least with it, stands less chance of doing wrong. For what says the prophet touching an evil affair of the kind? He who sleepeth in it is more secure than he that waketh; he that lyeth than he that sitteth; he that sitteth than he that standeth; he that standeth than he that walketh; and he that walketh than he that rideth. Sheathe, therefore, your swords, take the heads from your lances, and the strings from your bows, and receive him that is injured into your dwellings, until all matters are adjusted and reconciled. »

The ancient general, Ammar, replied to him tartly, that he had misapplied the words of the prophet, which were meant to rebuke such servants as himself, who were better sitting than standing, and sleeping than awake. Abu Musa would have answered him with another long harangue in favour of non-resistance, but was interrupted by the sudden entrance of a number of his soldiers, bearing evidence of having been piteously beaten. While Abu Musa had been holding forth at the mosqne, Alashtar, the hardy officer who remained with the escort, had seized upon the castle of Cufa, caused the garrison to be soundly scourged, and sent them to the mosque to cut short the negotiation. This prompt measure of Alashtar placed the cold-spirited conduct of Abu Musa in so ridiculous a light that the feelings of the populace were instantly turned against him. Hassan, the son of Ali, seized upon the moment to address the assembly. He maintained the innocence of his father in regard to the assassination of Othman. "His father," he said, " had either done wrong, or had suffered wrong.. If he had done wrong, God would punish him. If he had suffered wrong, God would help him. The case was in the hand of the Most High. Telha and Zobeir, who were the first to inaugurate him, were the first to turn against him. What had he done, as Caliph, to merit such opposition? What injustice had he committed? What covetous or selfish propensity had he manifested? " I am going back to my father," added Hassan, " those who are disposed to render him assistance, may follow me."

His eloquence was powerfully effective, and the people of Cufa followed him to the number of nearly nine thousand. In the meantime the army of Ali had been reinforced from other quarters, and now amounted to thirty thousand men, all of whom had seen service. When he appeared with his force before Bassora, Ayesha and her confederates were dismayed, and began to treat of conciliation. Various messages passed between the hostile parties, and Telha and Zobeir, confiding in the honourable faith of Ali, had several interviews with him.

When these late deadly enemies were seen walking backward and forward together, in sight of either army, and holding long conversations, it was confidently expected that a peace would be effected; and such would have been the case had no malign influence interfered; for Ali, with his impressive eloquence, touched the hearts of his opponents when he reproached them with their breach of faith, and warned them against the judgments of heaven. " Dost thou not remember," said he to Zobeir, " how Mahomet once asked thee if thou didst not love his dear son Ali? and when thou answered yea, dost thou not remember his reply : ' Nevertheless a day will come when thou wilt rise up against him, and draw down miseries upon him and upon all the faithful?'"

" I remember it well," replied Zobeir, " and had I remembered it before, never would I have taken up arms against you."

He returned to his camp determined not to fight against Ali, but was overruled by the vindictive Ayesha. Every attempt at pacification was defeated by that turbulent woman, and the armies were at length brought to battle. Ayesha took the field on that memorable occasion, mounted in a litter on her great camel Alascar, and rode up and down among her troops, animating them by her presence and her voice. The fight was called, from that circumstance, The Battle of the Camel, and also The Battle of Karibah, from the field on which it was fought.

It was an obstinate and bloody conflict, for Moslem was arrayed against Moslem, and nothing is so merciless and unyielding as civil war. In the heat of the fight Merwan Ibn Hakem, who stood near Ali, noticed Telha endeavouring to goad on the flagging valour of his troops. " Behold the traitor Telha," cried he, " but lately one of the murderers of Othman now the pretended avenger of his blood." So saying, he let fly an arrow and wounded him in the leg. Telha writhed with the pain, and at the same moment his horse reared and threw him. In the dismay and anguish of the moment, he imprecated the vengeance of Allah upon his own head for the death of Othman. Seeing his boot full of blood, he made one of his followers take him up behind him on his horse and convey him to Bassora. Finding death approaching, he called to one of Ali's men who happened to be present, " Give me your hand," said the dying penitent, " that I may put mine in it, and thus renew my oath of fealty to Ali." With these words he expired. His dying speech was reported to Ali, and touched his generous heart. " Allah," said he, " would not call him to heaven until he had blotted out his first breach of his word by this last vow of fidelity."

Zobeir, the other conspirator, had entered into the battle with a heavy heart. His previous conversation with Ali had awakened compunction in his bosom. He now saw that old Ammar Ibn Yaser, noted for probity and rectitude, was in the Caliph's host; and he recollected hearing Mahomet say that Ammar Ibn Yaser would always be found on the side of truth and justice. With a boding spirit he drew out of the battle and took the road towards Mecca. As he was urging his melancholy way, he came to a valley crossed by the brook Sabaa, where Hanef Ibn Kais was encamped with a horde of Arabs, awaiting the issue of the battle, ready to join the conqueror and share the spoil. Hanef knew him at a distance. " Is there no one," said he, " to bring me tidings of Zobeir?" One of his men, Amru Ibn Jarmuz, understood the hint, and spurred to overtake Zobeir. The latter suspecting his intentions, bade him keep at a distance. · A short conversation put them on friendly terms, and they both dismounted and conversed together. · The hour of prayers arrived. " Salat" (to prayers!) cried Zobeir. " Salat" replied Amru; but as Zobeir prostrated himself in supplication, Amru struck off his head, and hastened with it, as a welcome trophy, to Ali. That generous conqueror shed tears over the bleeding head of one who was once his friend. Then turning to his slayer, " Hence, miscreant!" cried he, " and carry thy tidings to Ben Safiah in hell." So unexpected a malediction, where he expected a reward, threw Amru into a transport of rage and desperation; he uttered a rhapsody of abuse upon Ali, and then, drawing his sword, plunged it into his own bosom.

Such was the end of the two leaders of the rebels. As to Ayesha, the implacable soul of the revolt, she had mingled that day in the hottest of the fight. Tabari, the Persian historian, with national exaggeration, declares that the heads of threescore and ten men were cut off that held the bridle of her camel, and that the inclosed litter in which she rode, was bristled all over with darts and arrows. At last her camel was hamstringed, and sank with her to the ground, and she remained there until the battle was concluded.

Ayesha might have looked for cruel treatment at the hands of Ali, having been his vindictive and persevering enemy, but he was too magnanimous to triumph over a fallen foe. It is said some reproachful words passed between them, but he treated her with respect; gave her an attendance of forty females, and sent his sons Hassan and Hosein to escort her a day's journey toward Medina;

where she was confined to her own house and forbidden to inter-
meddle any more with affairs of state. He then divided the spoils
among the heirs of his soldiers who were slain, and appointed
'Abdallah Ibn Abbas governor of Bassora. This done, he repaired
to Cufa, and in reward of the assistance he had received from its
inhabitants, made that city the seat of his Caliphat. These occurrences took place in the thirty-fifth year of the Hegira, the 655th
of the Christian era.

CHAPTER XXXIX.

Battles between Ali and Moawyah.—Their claims to the Caliphat left to arbitration; the
result.—Decline of the power of Ali—Loss of Egypt.

The victory at Karibah had crushed the conspiracy of Ayesha,
and given Ali quiet dominion over Egypt, Arabia, and Persia;
still his most formidable adversary remained unsubdued. Moawyah
Ibn Abu Sofian held sway over the wealthy and populous province
of Syria; he had immense treasures and a powerful army at his
command; he had the prejudices of the Syrians in his favour, who
had been taught to implicate Ali in the murder of Othman, and
refused to acknowledge him as Caliph. Still further to strengthen
himself in defiance of the sovereign power, he sought the alliance
of Amru, who had been displaced from the government of Egypt
by Ali, and was now a discontented man in Palestine. Restoration
to that command, was to be the reward of his successful co-operation with Moawyah in deposing Ali : the terms were accepted :
Amru hastened to Damascus at the head of a devoted force; and
finding the public mind ripe for his purpose, gave the hand of
allegiance to Moawyah in presence of the assembled army, and
proclaimed him Caliph, amid the shouts of the multitude.
Ali had in vain endeavoured to prevent the hostility of Moawyah,
by all conciliatory means; when he heard of this portentous alliance, he took the field and marched for Syria, at the head of
ninety thousand men. The Arabians, with their accustomed fondness for the marvellous, signalize his entrance into the confines of
Syria with an omen. Having halted his army in a place where
there was no water, he summoned a Christian hermit, who lived
in a neighbouring cave, and demanded to be shown a well. The
anchorite assured him that there was nothing but a cistern, in which
there were scarce three buckets of rain water. Ali maintained
that certain prophets of the people of Israel had abode there in
times of old, and had digged a well there. The hermit replied,
that a well did indeed exist there, but it had been shut up for ages,
and all traces of it lost, and it was only to be discovered and
reopened by a predestined hand. He then, says the Arabian tradition, produced a parchment scroll written by Simeon ben Safa
Simon Cephas), one of the greatest apostles of Jesus Christ, pre-

dicting the coming of Mahomet, the last of the prophets, and that this well would be discovered and reopened by his lawful heir and successor.

Ali listened with becoming reverence to this prediction; then turning to his attendants and pointing to a spot, "Dig there," said he. They digged, and after a time came to an immense stone, which having removed with difficulty, the miraculous well stood revealed, affording a seasonable supply to the army, and an unquestionable proof of the legitimate claim of Ali to the Caliphat. The venerable hermit was struck with conviction; he fell at the feet of Ali, embraced his knees, and never afterwards vould leave him.

It was on the first day of the thirty-seventh year of the Hegira (18th June, A. D. 657), that Ali came in sight of the army of Moawyah, consisting of eighty thousand men, encamped on the plain of Seffein, on the banks of the Euphrates, on the confines of Babylonia and Syria. Associated with Moawyah was the redoubtable Amru, a powerful ally both in council and in the field. The army of Ali was superior in number; in his host, too, he had several veterans who had fought under Mahomet in the famous battle of Beder, and thence prided themselves in the surname of Shahabah; that is to say, Companions of the Prophet. The most distinguished of these was old Ammar Ibn Yaser, Ali's general of horse, who had fought repeatedly by the side of Mahomet. He was ninety years of age, yet full of spirit and activity, and idolized by the Moslem soldiery.

The armies lay encamped in sight of each other, but as it was the first month of the Moslem year, a sacred month, when all warfare is prohibited, it was consumed in negotiations; for Ali still wished to avoid the effusion of kindred blood. His efforts were in vain, and in the next month hostilities commenced; still Ali drew his sword with an unwilling hand; he charged his soldiers never to be the first to fight; never to harm those who fled, and never to do violence to a woman. · Moawyah and Amru were likewise sensible of the unnatural character of this war; the respective leaders, therefore, avoided any general action, and months passed in mere, skirmishings. These, however, were sharp and sanguinary, and in the course of four months Moawyah is said to have lost five and forty thousand men, and Ali more than half that number.

Among the slain on the part of Ali, were five and twenty of the Shahabah, the veterans of Beder, and companions of the prophet. Their deaths were deplored even by the enemy; but nothing caused greater grief than the fall of the brave old Ammar Ibn Yaser, Ali's general of horse, and the patriarch of Moslem chivalry. Moawyah and Amru beheld him fall. "Do you see," cried Moawyah, "What precious lives are lost in our dissensions?" "See," exclaimed Amru; "would to God I had died twenty years since!"

Ali forgot his usual moderation on beholding the fate of his brave old general of the horse; and putting himself at the head of twelve thousand cavalry, made a furious charge to avenge his death. The ranks of the enemy were broken by the shock; but the heart of Ali soon relented at the sight of carnage. Spurring within call of

Moawyah, "How long," cried he, "shall Moslem blood be shed like water in our strife? Come forth, and let Allah decide between us. Which ever is victor in the fight, let him be ruler."

Amru was struck with the generous challenge, and urged Moawyah to accept it; but the latter shunned an encounter with an enemy surnamed "The Lion," for his prowess, and who had always slain his adversary in single fight. Amru hinted at the disgrace that would attend his refusal; to which Moawyah answered with a sneer, "You do wisely to provoke a combat that may make you governor of Syria."

A desperate battle at length took place, which continued throughout the night. Many were slain on both sides; but most on the part of the Syrians. Alashtar was the hero of this fight; he was mounted upon a piebald horse, and wielded a two-edged sword; every stroke of that terrible weapon clove down a warrior, and every stroke was accompanied by the shout of Allah Achbar! He was heard to utter that portentous exclamation, say the Arabian historians, four hundred times during the darkness of the night.

The day dawned disastrously upon the Syrians. Alashtar was pressing them to their very encampment, and Moawyah was in despair; when Amru suggested an expedient, founded on the religious scruples of the Moslems. On a sudden, the Syrians elevated the Koran on the points of their lances. "Behold the book of God," cried they. "Let that decide our differences." The soldiers of Ali instantly dropped the points of their weapons. It was in vain Ali represented that this was all a trick, and endeavoured to urge them on. "What!" cried they, "do you refuse to submit to the decision of the book of God!"

Ali found that to persist would be to shock their bigot prejudices, and to bring a storm upon his own head; reluctantly, therefore, he sounded a retreat; but it required repeated blasts to call off Alashtar, who came, his scimetar dripping with blood, and murmuring at being, as he said, tricked out of so glorious a victory.

Umpires were now appointed to settle this great dispute according to the dictates of the Koran. Ali would have nominated on his part Abdallah Ibn Abbas, but he was objected to, as being his cousin german. He then named the brave Alashtar, but he was likewise set aside, and Abu Musa pressed upon him; an upright, but simple and somewhat garrulous man, as has already been shown. As to Moawyah, he managed on his part to have Amru Ibn al Aass appointed, the shrewdest and most sagacious man in all Arabia. The two rival leaders then retired, Ali to Cufa, and Moawyah to Damascus, leaving generals in command of their respective armies.

The arbitrators met several months afterwards at Jumat al Joudel in presence of both armies, who were pledged to support their decision. Amru, who understood the weak points of Musa's character, treated him with great deference, and after having won his confidence, persuaded him that, to heal these dissensions, and prevent the shedding of kindred blood, it would be expedient to set aside both candidates and let the faithful elect a third. This beeing agreed upon, a tribunal was erected between the armies,

and Amru, through pretended deference, insisted that Musa should
be the first to ascend it and address the people. Abu Musa accordingly ascended, and proclaimed with a loud voice, " I depose Ali
and Moawyah from the office to which they pretend, even as I draw
this ring from my finger." So saying he descended.

Amru now mounted in his turn. " You have heard," said he,
" how Musa on his part has deposed Ali ; I on my part depose him
also ; and I adjuge the Caliphat to Moawyah, and invest him with
it, as I invest my finger with this ring : and I do it with justice, for
he is the rightful successor and avenger of Othman."

Murmurs succeeded from the partisans of Ali, and from Abu
Musa, who complained of the insincerity of Amru. The Syrians applauded the decision, and both parties, being prevented from
hostilities by a solemn truce, separated without any personal violence ; but with mutual revilings and augmented enmity. A kind
of religious feud sprang up, which continued for a long time between
the house of Ali and that of Ommiah ; they never mentioned each
other without a curse, and pronounced an excommunication upon
each other whenever they harangued the people in the mosque.

The power of Ali now began to wane ; the decision pronounced
against him influenced many of his own party, and a revolt was at
length stirred up among his followers, by a set of fanatic zealots
called Karigites or seceders ; who insisted that he had done wrong
in referring to the judgment of men what ought to be decided by
God alone ; and. that he had refused to break the truce and massacre his ennemies when in his power, though they had proved
themselves to be the enemies of God ; they therefore renounced
allegiance to him ; appointed Abdallah Ibn Waheb as their leader,
and set up their standard at Naharwan, a few miles from Bagdad,
whither the disaffected repaired from all quarters, until they
amounted to twenty-five thousand.

The appearance of Ali with an army brought many of them to
their senses. Willing to use gentle measures, he caused a standard
to be erected outside of his camp, and proclaimed a pardon to such
of the malcontents as should rally round it. The rebel army immediately began to melt away, until Abdallah Ibn-Waheb was left
with only four thousand adherents. These, however, were fierce
enthusiasts, and their leader was a fanatic. Trusting that Allah and
the prophet would render him miraculous assistance, he attacked
the army of Ali with his handful of men, who fought with such
desperation that nine only escaped. These served as firebrands
to enkindle future mischief.

Moawyah had now recourse to a stratagem to sow troubles in
Egypt, and ultimately to put it in the hands of Amru. Ali, on assuming the Caliphat, had appointed Saad Ibn Kais to the government of that province, who administered its affairs with ability.
Moawyah now forged a letter from Saad to himself, professing
devotion to his interests, and took measures to let it fall into the
hands of Ali. The plan was successful. The suspicions of Ali were
excited ; he recalled Saad and appointed in his place Mahomet,
son of Abu Beker, and brother of Ayesha. Mahomet began to
govern with a high hand ; proscribing and exiling the leaders of the

Othman faction, who made the murder of the late Caliph a question of party. This immediately produced commotions and insurrections, and all Egypt was getting into a blaze. Ali again sought to remedy the evil by changing the governor, and despatched Malec Shutur, a man of prudence and ability, to take the command. In the course of his journey Malec lodged one night at the house of a peasant, on the confines of Arabia and Egypt. The peasant was a creature of Moawyah's, and poisoned his unsuspecting guest with a pot of honey. Moawyah followed up this treacherous act by sending Amru with six thousand horse to seize upon Egypt in its present stormy state. Amru hastened with joy to the scene of his former victories, made his way rapidly to Alexandria, united his force with that of Ibn Sharig, the leader of the Othman party, and they together routed Mahomet Ibn Abu Beker and took him prisoner. The avengers of Othman reviled Mahomet with his assassination of that Caliph, put him to death, enclosed his body in the carcass of an ass, and burnt both to ashes. Then Amru assumed the government of Egypt as lieutenant of Moawyah.

When Ayesha heard of the death of her brother, she knelt down in the mosque, and in the agony of her heart invoked a curse upon Moawyah and Amru, an invocation which she thenceforth repeated at the end of all her prayers. Ali, also, was afflicted at the death of Mahomet, and exclaimed, " The murderers will answer for this before God."

CHAPTER XL.

Preparations of Ali for the invasion of Syria.—His Assassination.

The loss of Egypt was a severe blow to the fortunes of Ali, and he had the mortification subsequently to behold his active rival make himself master of Hejaz, plant his standard on the sacred cities of Mecca and Medina, and ravage the fertile province of Yemen. The decline of his power affected his spirits, and he sank at times into despondency. His melancholy was aggravated by the conduct of his own brother Okail, who, under pretence that Ali did not maintain him in suitable style, deserted him in his sinking fortunes, and went over to Moawyah, who rewarded his unnatural desertion with ample revenues.

Still Ali meditated one more grand effort. Sixty thousand devoted adherents pledged themselves to stand by him to the death, and with these he prepared to march into Syria. While preparations were going on, it chanced that three zealots, of the sect of Karigites, met as pilgrims in the mosque of Mecca, and fell into conversation about the battle of Naharwan, wherein four thousand of their brethren had lost their lives. This led to lamentations over the dissensions and dismemberment of the Moslem empire, all which they attributed to the ambition of Ali, Moawyah, and Amru. The

Karigites were a fanatic sect, and these men were zealots of that dangerous kind who are ready to sacrifice their lives in the accomplishment of any bigot plan. In their infuriate zeal they determined that the only way to restore peace and unity to Islam, would be to destroy those three ambitious leaders, and they devoted themselves to the task, each undertaking to despatch his victim. The several assassinations were to be effected at the same time, on Friday, the seventeenth of the month Ramadan, at the hour of prayer ; and that their blows might be infallibly mortal, they were to use poisoned weapons.

The names of the conspirators were Barak Ibn Abdallah, Amru Ibn Asi, and Abda'lrahman Ibn Melgem. Barak repaired to Damascus and mingled in the retinue of Moawyah on the day appointed, which was the Moslem Sabbath ; then, as the usurper was officiating in the mosque as pontiff, Barak gave him what he considered a fatal blow. The wound was desperate, but the life of Moawyah was saved by desperate remedies ; the assassin was mutilated of hands and feet and suffered to live ; but was slain in after years by a friend of Moawyah.

Amru Ibn Asi, the second of these fanatics, entered the mosque in Egypt on the same day and hour, and with one blow killed Karijah the Imam, who officiated, imagining him to be Amru Ibn al Aass, who was prevented from attending the mosque through illness. The assassin being led before his intended victim, and informed of his errour, replied with the resignation of a predestinarian : "I intended Amru ; but Allah intended Karijah." He was presently executed.

Abda'lrahman, the third assassin, repaired to Cufa, where Ali held his court. Here he lodged with a woman of the sect of the Karigites, whose husband had been killed in the battle of Neharwân. To this woman he made proposals of marriage, but she replied she would have no man who could not bring her, as a dowry, three thousand drachms of silver, a slave, a maid-servant, and the head of Ali. He accepted the conditions, and joined two other Karigites, called Derwan and Shabib, with him in the enterprise. They stationed themselves in the mosque to await the coming of the Caliph.

Ali had recently been afflicted with one of his fits of despondency, and had uttered ejaculations which were afterwards considered presages of his impending fate. In one of his melancholy moods he exclaimed, with a heavy sigh, "Alas, my heart! there is need of patience, for there is no remedy against death!" In parting from his house to go to the mosque, there was a clamour among his domestic fowls, which he interpreted into a fatal omen. As he entered the mosque the assassins drew their swords, and pretended to be fighting among themselves; Derwan aimed a blow at the Caliph, but it fell short, and struck the gate of the mosque ; a blow from Abda'lrahman was better aimed, and wounded Ali in the head. The assassins then separated and fled. Derwan was pursued and slain at the threshold of his home ; Shabib distanced his pursuers and escaped. Abda'lrahman, after some search, was discovered hidden in a corner of the mosque, his sword still in his

hand.   He was dragged forth and brought before the Caliph.
The wound of Ali was pronounced mortal; he consigned his murderer to the custody of his son Hassan, adding, with his accustomed
clemency, "Let him want for nothing; and, if I die of my wound,
let him not be tortured; let his death be by a single blow."   His
orders, according to the Persian writers, were strictly complied
with, but the Arabians declare that he was killed by piecemeal;
and the Moslems opposed to the sect of Ali hold him up as a
martyr.

The death of Ali happened within three days after receiving his
wound : it was in the fortieth year of the Hegira, A. D. 660.   He
was about sixty-three years of age, of which he had reigned not
quite five.   His remains were interred about five miles from Cufa;
and, in after times, a magnificent tomb, covered by a mosque,
with a splendid dome, rose over his grave, and it became the site
of a city called Meshed Ali, or, the Sepulchre of Ali, and was
enriched and beautified by many Persian monarchs.

We make no concluding comments on the noble and generous
character of Ali, which has been sufficiently illustrated throughout
all the recorded circumstances of his life.   He was one of the last
and worthiest of the primitive Moslems, who imbibed his religious
enthusiasm from companionship with the prophet himself; and who
followed, to the last, the simplicity of his example.   He is honourably spoken of as the first Caliph who accorded some protection
to Belles-Lettres.   He indulged in the poetic vein himself, and
many of his maxims and proverbs are preserved, and have been
translated into various languages.   His signet bore this inscription :
"The kingdom belongs to God."   One of his sayings shows the
little value he set upon the transitory glories of this world.   "Life
is but the shadow of a cloud; the dream of a sleeper."

By his first wife, Fatima, the daughter of Mahomet, he had three
sons, Mohassan, who died young, and Hassan and Hosein, who
survived him.   After her death he had eight other wives, and his
issue, in all, amounted to fifteen sons and eighteen daughters.
His descendants, by Fatima, are distinguished among Moslems as
descendants of the prophet, and are very numerous, being reckoned
both by the male and female line.   They wear turbans of a peculiar fashion, and twist their hair in a different manner from other
Moslems.   They are considered of noble blood, and designated in
different countries by various titles, such as Sheriffs, Fatimites,
and Emirs.   The Persians venerate Ali as next to the prophet, and
solemnize the anniversary of his martyrdom.   The Turks hold him
in abhorrence, and, for a long time, in their prayers, accompanied
his name with execrations; but subsequently abated in their violence.   It is said that Ali was born in the Caaba, or holy temple
of Mecca, where his mother was suddenly taken in labour, and
that he was the only person of such distinguished birth.

CHAPTER XLI.

Succession of Hassan, fifth Caliph.—He abdicates in favour of Moawyah.

In his dying moments Ali had refused to nominate a successor, but his eldest son Hassan, then in his 37th year, was elected without opposition. He stood high in the favour of the people, partly from his having been a favourite with his grandfather, the prophet, to whom in his features he bore a strong resemblance; but chiefly from the moral excellence of his character, for he was upright, sincere, benevolent and devout. He lacked, however, the energy and courage necessary to a sovereignty, where the sceptre was a sword; and he was unfitted to command in the civil wars which distracted the empire, for he had a horror of shedding Moslem blood. He made a funeral speech over his father's remains, showing that his death was coincident with great and solemn events. "He was slain," said he, "on the same night of the year, in which the Koran was transmitted to earth; in which Isa (Jesus) was taken up to heaven, and in which Joshua, the son of Nun, was killed. By Allah! none of his predecessors surpassed him, nor will he ever be equalled by a successor."

Then Kais, a trusty friend of the house of Ali, commenced the inauguration of the new Caliph. "Stretch forth thy hand," said he to Hassan, "in pledge that thou wilt stand by the book of God, and the tradition of the apostle, and make war against all opposers." Hassan complied with the ceremonial, and was proclaimed Caliph, and the people were called upon to acknowledge allegiance to him, and engage to maintain peace with his friends, and war with his enemies. Some of the people, however, with the characteristic fickleness of Babylonians, murmured at the suggestion of further warfare, and said, we want no fighting Caliph.

Had Hassan consulted his own inclination, he would willingly have clung to peace, and submitted to the usurpations of Moawyah; but he was surrounded by valiant generals eager for action, and stimulated by his brother Hosein, who inherited the daring character of their father; beside, there were sixty thousand fighting men, all ready for the field, and who had been on the point of marching into Syria under Ali. Unwillingly, therefore, he put himself at the head of this force and commenced his march. Receiving intelligence that Moawyah had already taken the field and was advancing to meet him, he sent Kais in the advance, with 12,000 light troops, to hold the enemy in check, while he followed with the main army. Kais executed his commission with spirit, had a smart skirmish with the Syrians, and having checked them in their advance, halted and put himself in a position to await the coming of the Caliph.

Hassan, however, had already become sensible of his incompetency to military command. There was disaffection among some of his troops, who were people of Irak or Babylonia, disinclined to this war. On reaching the city of Madayn, an affray took place among the soldiers in which one was slain; a fierce tumult succeeded; Hassan attempted to interfere, but was jostled and wounded in the throng, and obliged to retire into the citadel. He had taken refuge from violence, and was in danger of treason, for the nephew of the governor of Madayn proposed to his uncle, now that he had Hassan within his castle, to make him his prisoner, and send him in chains to Moawyah. "A curse upon thee for a traitor and an infidel!" cried the honest old governor; "wouldst thou betray the son of the daughter of the Apostle of God!"

The mild-tempered Caliph, who had no ambition of command, was already disheartened by its troubles. He saw that he had an active and powerful enemy to contend with, and fickleness and treachery among his own people; he sent proposals to Moawyah, offering to resign the Caliphat to him, on condition that he should be allowed to retain the money in the public treasury at Cufa, and the revenues of a great estate in Persia, and that Moawyah would desist from all evil-speaking against his deceased father. Moawyah assented to the two former of these stipulations, but would only consent to refrain from speaking evil of Ali in presence of Hassan; and indeed, such was the sectarian hatred already engendered against Ali, that, under the sway of Moawyah, his name was never mentioned in the mosques without a curse, and such continued to be the case for several generations under the dominion of the house of Ommiah.

Another condition exacted by Hassan, and which ultimately proved fatal to him, was that he should be entitled to resume the Caliphat on the death of Moawyah, who was above a score of years his senior. These terms being satisfactorily adjusted. Hassan abdicated in favour of Moawyah, to the great indignation of his brother Hosein, who considered the memory of their father Ali dishonoured by this arrangement. The people of Cufa refused to comply with that condition relative to the public treasury; insisting upon it that it was their property. Moawyah, however, allowed Hassan an immense revenue, with which he retired with his brother to Medina, to enjoy that ease and tranquillity which he so much prized. His life was exemplary and devout, and the greater part of his revenue was expended in acts of charity.

Moawyah seems to have been well aware of the power of gold in making the most distasteful things palatable. An old beldame of the lineage of Haschem, and branch of Ali, once reproached him with having supplanted that family, who were his cousins, and with having acted toward them as Pharaoh did toward the children of Israel. Moawyah gently replied, "May Allah pardon what is past," and inquired what were her wants. She said two thousand pieces of gold for her poor relations, two thousand as a dower for her children, and two thousand as a support for herself. The money was given instantly, and the tongue of the clamorous virago was silenced.

CHAPTER XLII.

Reign of Moawyah I., sixth Caliph.—Account of his illegitimate brother Ziyad.—Death of Amru.

Moawyah now, in the forty-first year of the Hegira, assumed legitimate dominion on the whole Moslem empire. The Karigites, it is true, a fanatic sect opposed to all regular government, spiritual or temporal, excited an insurrection in Syria, but Moawyah treated them with more thorough rigour than his predecessors, and finding the Syrians not sufficient to cope with them, called in his new subjects, the Babylonians, to show their allegiance by rooting out this pestilent sect; nor did he stay his hand, until they were almost exterminated.

With this Caliph commenced the famous dynasty of the Ommiades or Omeyades, so called from Ommiah his great-grandfather; a dynasty which lasted for many generations, and gave some of the most brilliant names to Arabian history. Moawyah himself gave indications of intellectual refinement. He surrounded himself with men distinguished in science or gifted with poetic talent, and from the Greek provinces and islands which he had subdued, the Greek sciences began to make their way, and under his protection to exert their first influence on the Arabs.

One of the measures adopted by Moawyah to strengthen himself in the Caliphat excited great sensation, and merits particular detail. At the time of the celebrated flight of Mahomet, Abu Sofian, father of Moawyah, at that time chief of the tribe of Koreish, and as yet an inveterate persecutor of the prophet, halted one day for refreshment at the house of a publican in Tayef. Here he became intoxicated with wine, and passed the night in the arms of the wife of a Greek slave, named Somyah, who in process of time made him the father of a male child. Abu Sofian, ashamed of this amour, would not acknowledge the child, but left him to his fate; hence he received the name of Ziyad Ibn Abihi, that is to say, Ziyad the son of nobody.

The boy, thus deserted, gave early proof of energy and talent. When scarce arrived at manhood, he surprised Amru Ibn al Aass, by his eloquence and spirit in addressing a popular assembly. Amru, himself illegitimate, felt a sympathy in the vigour of this spurious offset. "By the prophet!" exclaimed he, "if this youth were but of the noble race of Koreish, he would drive all the tribes of Arabia before him with his staff!"

Ziyad was appointed cadi or judge, in the reign of Omar, and was distinguished by his decisions. On one occasion, certain witnesses came before him accusing Mogeirah Ibn Seid, a distinguished person of unblemished character, with incontinence, but failed to establish the charge; whereupon, Ziyad dismissed the accused with honour, and caused his accusers to be scourged with rods for bearing false witness. This act was never forgotten by Mogeirah, who, becoming afterwards one of the counsellors of the Caliph Ali, induced him to appoint Ziyad lieutenant or governor of Persia, an arduous post of high trust, the duties of which he discharged with great ability.

After the death of Ali and the abdication of Hassan, events which followed hard upon each other, Ziyad, who still held sway over Persia, hesitated to acknowledge Moawyah as Caliph. The latter was alarmed at this show of opposition, fearing lest Ziyad should join with the family of Haschem, the kindred of the prophet, who desired the elevation of Hosein; he, therefore, sent for Mogeirah, the former patron of Ziyad, and prevailed upon him to mediate between them. Mogeirah repaired to Ziyad in person, bearing a letter of kindness and invitation from the Caliph, and prevailed on him to accompany him to Cufa. On their arrival Moawyah embraced Ziyad, and received him with public demonstrations of respect and affection, as his brother by the father's side. The fact of their consanguinity was established on the following day, in full assembly, by the publican of Tayef, who bore testimony to the intercourse between Abu Sofian and the beautiful slave.

This decision, enforced by the high hand of authority, elevated Ziyad to the noblest blood of Koreish, and made him eligible to the highest offices; though in fact, the strict letter of the Mahometan law would have pronounced him the son of the Greek slave, who was husband of his mother.

The family of the Ommiades were indignant at having the base-born offspring of a slave, thus introduced among them; but Moawyah disregarded these murmurs; he had probably gratified his own feelings of natural affection, and he had firmly attached to his interest, a man of extensive influence, and one of the ablest generals of the age.

Moawyah found good service in his valiant, though misbegotten brother. Under the sway of incompetent governors the country round Bassora had become overrun with thieves and murderers, and disturbed by all kinds of tumults. Ziyad was put in the command, and hastened to take possession of his turbulent post. He found Bassora a complete den of assassins; not a night but was disgraced by riot and bloodshed, so that it was unsafe to walk the streets after dark. Ziyad was an eloquent man, and he made a public speech terribly to the point. He gave notice that he meant to rule with the sword, and to wreak unsparing punishment on all offenders; he advised all such, therefore, to leave the city. He warned all persons from appearing in public after evening prayers, as a patrol would go the rounds and put every one to death who should be found in the streets. He carried this measure into effect. Two hundred persons were put to death by the patrol during the first night, only five during the second, and not a drop of blood was shed afterwards, nor was there any further tumult or disturbance.

Moawyah then employed him to effect the same reforms in Korassan and many other provinces, and the more he had to execute, the more was his ability evinced; until his mere name would quell commotion, and awe the most turbulent into quietude. Yet he was not sanguinary nor cruel, but severely rigid in his discipline, and inflexible in the dispensation of justice. It was his custom, wherever he held sway, to order the inhabitants to leave their doors open at night, with merely a hurdle at the entrance to exclude cattle, engaging to replace any thing that should be stolen : and so effective was his police, that no robberies were committed.

Though Ziyad had whole provinces under his government, he felt himself not sufficiently employed; he wrote to the Caliph, therefore, complaining that, while his left hand was occupied in governing Babylonia, his right hand was idle; and he requested the government of Arabia Petrea also, which the Caliph gladly granted him, to the great terror of its inhabitants, who dreaded so stern a ruler. But the sand of Ziyad was exhausted. He was attacked with the plague when on the point of setting out for Arabia. The disease made its appearance with an ulcer in his hand, and the agony made him deliberate whether to smite it off. As it was a case of conscience among predestinarians, he consulted a venerable cadi. "If you die," said the old expounder of the law, "you go before God without that hand, which you have cut off to avoid appearing in his presence. If you live, you give a bye-name to your children, who will be called the sons of the cripple. I advise you, therefore, to let it alone." The intensity of the pain, however, made him determine on amputation, but the sight of the fire and cauterizing irons again deterred him. He was surrounded by the most expert physicians, but, say the Arabians, "It was not in their power to reverse the sealed decree." He died in the forty-fifth year of the Hegira and of his own age, and the people he had governed with so much severity, considered his death a deliverance. His son Obeidallah, though only twenty-five years of age, was immediately invested by the Caliph with the government of Korassan, and gave instant proofs of inheriting the spirit of his father. On his way to his government he surprised a large Turkish force, and put them to such sudden flight, that their queen left one of her buskins behind, which fell into the hands of her pursuers, and was estimated, from the richness of its jewels, at two thousand pieces of gold.

Ziyad left another son named Salem, who was, several years afterwards, when but twenty-four years of age, appointed to the government of Korassan, and rendered himself so beloved by the people, that upwards of twenty thousand children were named after him. He had a third son called Kameil, who was distinguished for sagacity and ready wit, and he furthermore left from his progeny a dynasty of princes in Arabia Felix, who ruled under the denomination of the children of Ziyad.

The wise measures of Moawyah produced a calm throughout his empire, although his throne seemed to be elevated on the surface of a volcano. He had reinstated the famous Amru Ibn al Aass in the government of Egypt, allowing him to enjoy the revenues of that opulent province, in gratitude for his having proclaimed him Caliph during his contest with Ali ; but stipulating that he should maintain the forces stationed there.   The veteran general did not long enjoy this post, as he died in the forty-third year of the He-gira, A. D. 663, as full of honours as of years.   In him the cause of Islam lost one of its wisest men and most illustrious conquerors. "Show me," said Omar to him on one occasion, "the sword with which you have fought so many battles and slain so many infidels," The Caliph expressed surprise when he unsheathed an ordinary scimetar.   "Alas!" said Amru, "the sword, without the arm of the master, is no sharper nor heavier than the sword of Farezdak the poet"

Mahomet, whose death preceded that of Amru upwards of thirty years, declared that there was no truer Moslem than he would prove to be; nor one more steadfast in the faith.   Although Amru passed most of his life in the exercise of arms, he found time to cultivate the softer arts which belong to peace.   We have already shown that he was an orator and a poet.   The witty lampoons, however, which he wrote against the prophet in his youth, he deeply regretted in his declining age.   He sought the company of men of learning and science, and delighted in the conversation of philosophers.   He has left some proverbs distinguished for pithy wisdom, and some beautiful poetry, and his dying advice to his children was celebrated for manly sense and affecting pathos.

CHAPTER XLIII.

Siege of Constantinople.—Truce with the emperor.—Murder of Hassan.—Death of Ayesha.

The Caliph Moawyah being thoroughly established in his sov-ereignty, was ambitious of foreign conquests, which might shed lustre on his name, and obliterate the memory of these civil wars. He was desirous, also, of placing his son Yezid in a conspicuous light, and gaining for him the affections of the people; for he secretly entertained hopes of making him his successor.   He de-termined, therefore, to send him with a great force to attempt the conquest of Constantinople, at that time the capital of the Greek and Roman empire.   This indeed was a kind of holy war; for it was fulfilling one of the most ardent wishes of Mahomet; who had looked forward to the conquest of the proud capital of the Cæsars as one of the highest triumphs of Islam; and had promised full pardon of all their sins to the Moslem army that should achieve it.

The general command of the army in this expedition was given to a veteran named Sophian, and he was accompanied by several of those old soldiers of the faith, battered in the wars, and almost broken down by years, who had fought by the side of the prophet at Beder and Ohod, and were, therefore, honoured by the title of "Companions," and who now showed, among the ashes of age, the sparks of youthful fire, as they girded on their swords for this sacred enterprise.

Hosein, the valiant son of Ali, also accompanied this expedition; in which, in fact, the flower of Moslem chivalry engaged. Great preparations were made by sea and land, and sanguine hopes entertained of success; the Moslem troops were numerous and hardy, inured to toil and practised in warfare, and they were animated by the certainty of paradise, should they be victorious. The Greeks, on the other hand, were in a state of military decline, and their emperor, Constantine, a grandson of Heraclius, disgraced his illustrious name by indolence and incapacity.

It is singular and to be lamented, that of this momentous expedition we have very few particulars, notwithstanding that it lasted long, and must have been checkered by striking vicissitudes. The Moslem fleet passed without impediment through the Dardanelles, and the army disembarked within seven miles of Constantinople. For many days they pressed the siege with vigour, but the city was strongly garrisoned by fugitive troops from various quarters, who had profited by sad experience in the defence of fortified towns; the walls were strong and high; and the besieged made use of Greek fire, to the Moslems a new and terrific agent of destruction.

Finding all their efforts in vain, the Moslems consoled themselves by ravaging the neighbouring coasts of Europe and Asia, and on the approach of winter retired to the island of Cyzicus, about eighty miles from Constantinople, where they had established their headquarters.

Six years were passed in this unavailing enterprise; immense sums were expended; thousands of lives were lost by disease; ships and crews, by shipwreck and other disasters, and thousands of Moslems were slain, gallantly fighting for paradise under the walls of Constantinople. The most renowned of these was the venerable Abu Ayub, in whose house Mahomet had established his quarters when he first fled to Medina, and who had fought by the side of the prophet at Beder and Ohod. He won an honoured grave; for though it remained for ages unknown, yet nearly eight centuries after this event, when Constantinople was conquered by Mahomet II, the spot was revealed in a miraculous vision, and consecrated by a mausoleum and mosque, which exist to this day, and to which the grand seignors of the Ottoman empire repair to be belted with the scimetar on their accession to the throne.

The protracted war with the Greeks revived their military ardour, and they assailed the Moslems in their turn. Moawyah found the war which he had provoked threatening his own security. Other enemies were pressing on him; age, also, had sapped his bodily and mental vigour, and he became so anxious for safety and repose, that he in a manner purchased a truce of the emperor for thirty years, by agreeing to pay an annual tribute of three thousand pieces of gold, fifty slaves, and fifty horses of the noblest Arabian blood.

Yezid, the eldest son of Moawyah, and his secretly-intended successor, had failed to establish a renown in this enterprise, and if Arabian historians speak true, his ambition led him to a perfidious act sufficient to stamp his name with infamy. He is accused of instigating the murder of the virtuous Hassan, the son of Ali, who had abdicated in favour of Moawyah, but who was to resume the Caliphat on the death of that potentate. It is questionable whether Hassan would ever have claimed this right, for he was of quiet, retired habits, and preferred the security and repose of a private station. He was strong, however, in the affection of the people, and to remove out of the way so dangerous a rival, Yezid, it is said, prevailed upon one of his wives to poison him, promising to marry her in reward of her treason. The murder took place in the forty-ninth year of the Hegira, A. D. 669, when Hassan was forty-seven years of age. In his last agonies, his brother Hosein inquired at whose instigation he supposed himself to have been poisoned, that he might avenge his death, but Hassan refused to name him. "This world," said he, "is only a long night; leave him alone until he and I shall meet in open daylight, in the presence of the Most High."

Yezid refused to fulfil his promise of taking the murderess to wife, alleging that it would be madness to intrust himself to the embraces of such a female; he, however, commuted the engagement for a large amount in money and jewels. Moawyah is accused, of either countenancing; or being pleased with a murder, which made his son more eligible to the succession, for it is said that when he heard of the death of Hassan, "he fell down and worshipped."

Hassan had been somewhat uxorious; or rather, he had numerous wives, and was prone to change them when attracted by new beauties. One of them was the daughter of Yezdegird, the last king of the Persians, and she bore him several children. He had, altogether, fifteen sons and five daughters, and contributed greatly to increase the race of Sheriffs, or Fatimites, descendants from the prophet. In his testament he left directions that he should be buried by the sepulchre of his grandsire Mahomet; but Ayesha, whose hatred for the family of Ali went beyond the grave, declared that the mansion was hers, and refused her consent; he was, therefore, interred in the common burial-ground of the city.

Ayesha, herself, died some time afterwards, in the fifty-eighth year of the Hegira, having survived the prophet forty-seven years. She was often called the Prophetess, and generally denominated the Mother of the Faithful, although she had never borne any issue to Mahomet, and had employed her widowhood in intrigues to prevent Ali and his children, who were the only progeny of the prophet, from sitting on the throne of the Caliphs. All the other wives of Mahomet who survived him, passed the remainder of their lives in widowhood; but none, save her, seem to have been held in especial reverence.

CHAPTER XLIV.

Moslem conquests in Northern Africa.—Achievements of Acbah ; his death.

The conquest of Northern Africa, so auspiciously commenced by Abdallah Ibn Saad, had been suspended for a number of years by the pressure of other concerns, and particularly by the siege of Constantinople, which engrossed a great part of the Moslem forces ; in the meantime Cyrene had shaken off the yoke, all Cyrenaica was in a state of insurrection, and there was danger that the places which had been taken, and the post which had been established by the Arab conquerors would be completely lost.

The Caliph Moawyah now looked round for some active and able general, competent to secure and extend his sway along the African sea-coast. Such a one he found in Acbah Ibn Nafe el Fehri, whom he despatched from Damascus with ten thousand horse. Acbah made his way with all speed into Africa, his forces augmenting as he proceeded, by the accession of barbarian troops. He passed triumphantly through Cyrenaica ; laid close siege to the city of Cyrene, and retook it, notwithstanding its strong walls and great population ; but in the course of the siege many of its ancient and magnificent edifices were destroyed.

Acbah continued his victorious course westward , traversing wildernesses sometimes barren and desolate ; sometimes entangled with forests, and infested by serpents and savage animals, until he reached the domains of ancient Carthage, the present territory of Tunis. Here he determined to found a city to serve as a stronghold, and a place of refuge in the heart of these conquered regions. The site chosen was a valley closely wooded, and abounding with lions, tigers, and serpents. The Arabs give a marvellous account of the founding of the city. Acbah, say they, went forth into the forest, and adjured its savage inhabitants. " Hence ! avaunt ! wild beasts and serpents ! Hence, quit this wood and valley !" This solemn adjuration he repeated three several times, on three several days, and not a lion, tiger, leopard, nor serpent, but departed from the place.

Others, less poetic, record that he cleared away a forest which had been a lurking place not merely for wild beasts and serpents, but for rebels and barbarous hordes ; that he used the wood in constructing walls for his new city, and when these were completed, planted his lance in the centre, and exclaimed to his followers, " This is your Caravan." Such was the origin of the city of Kairwan or Caerwan, situated thirty-three leagues southeast of Carthage, and twelve from the sea on the borders of the great desert. Here Acbah fixed his seat of government, erecting mosques and other public edifices, and holding all the surrounding country in subjection.

While Acbah was thus honourably occupied, the Caliph Moawyah, little aware of the immense countries embraced in these recent conquests, united them with Egypt under one command, as if they had been two small provinces, and appointed Muhegir Ibn Omm Dinar, one of the Ansari, as emir or governor. Muhegir was an ambitious, or rather an envious and perfidious man. Scarce had he entered upon his government, when he began to sicken with envy of the brilliant fame of Acbah and his vast popularity, not merely with the army, but throughout the country; he accordingly made such unfavourable reports of the character and conduct of that general, in his letters to the Caliph, that the latter was induced to displace him from the command of the African army, and recall him to Damascus.

The letter of recall being sent under cover to Muhegir, he transmitted it by Muslama Ibn Machlad, one of his generals, to Acbah, charging his envoy to proceed with great caution, and to treat Acbah with profound deference, lest the troops, out of their love for him, should resist the order for his deposition. Muslama found Acbah in his camp at Cyrene, and presented him the Caliph's letter of recall, and a letter from Muhegir as governor of the province, letting him know that Muslama and the other generals were authorized to arrest him should he hesitate to obey the command of the Caliph.

There was no hesitation on the part of Acbah. He at once discerned whence the blow proceeded. "Oh God!" exclaimed he, "spare my life until I can vindicate myself from the slanders of Muhegir Ibn Omm Dinar." He then departed instantly, without even entering his house; made his way with all speed to Damascus, and appeared before Moawyah in the presence of his generals and the officers of his court. Addressing the Caliph with noble indignation, "I have traversed deserts," said he, "and encountered savage tribes; I have conquered towns and regions, and have brought their infidel inhabitants to the knowledge of God and his law. I have built mosques and palaces, and fortified our dominion over the land, and in reward I have been degraded from my post, and summoned hither as a culprit. I appeal to your justice, whether I have merited such treatment?"

Moawyah felt rebuked by the magnanimous bearing of his general, for he was aware that he had been precipitate in condemning him on false accusations. "I am already informed," said he, "of the true nature of the case. I now know who is Muhegir, and who is Acbah; return to the command of the army, and pursue your glorious career of conquest."

Although it was not until the succeeding Caliphat, that Acbah resumed the command in Africa, we will anticipate dates in order to maintain unbroken the thread of his story. In passing through Egypt he deposed Muslama from a command, in which he had been placed by Muhegir, and ordered him to remain in one of the Egyptian towns a prisoner at large.

He was grieved to perceive the mischief that had been done in Africa, during his absence, by Muhegir, who, out of mere envy and jealousy, had endeavoured to mar and obliterate all traces of his good deeds; dismantling the cities he had built; destroying his public edifices at Caerwan, and transferring the inhabitants to another place. Acbah stripped him of his command, placed him in irons, and proceeded to remedy the evils he had perpetrated. The population was restored to Caerwan; its edifices were rebuilt, and it rose from its temporary decline more prosperous and beautiful than ever. Acbah then left Zohair Ibn Kais in command of this metropolis, and resumed his career of western conquest, carrying Muhegir with him in chains. He crossed the kingdom of Numidia, now Algiers, and the vast regions of Mauritania, now Morocco, subduing their infidel inhabitants or converting them with the sword, until coming to the western shores of Africa, he spurred his charger into the waves of the Atlantic, until they rose to his saddle girths; then raising his scimetar towards heaven, "Oh Allah!" cried the zealous Moslem, "did not these profound waters prevent me, still further would I carry the knowledge of thy law, and the reverence of thy holy name!"

While Acbah was thus urging his victorious way to the uttermost bounds of Mauritania, tidings overtook him that the Greeks and barbarians were rising in rebellion in his rear; that the mountains were pouring down their legions, and that his city of Caerwan was in imminent danger. He had in fact incurred the danger against which the late Caliph Omar had so often cautioned his too adventurous generals. Turning his steps he hastened back, marching at a rapid rate. As he passed through Zab or Numidia, he was harassed by a horde of Berbers or Moors, headed by Aben Cahina, a native chief of daring prowess, who had descended from the fastnesses of the mountains, in which he had taken refuge from the invaders. This warrior, with his mountain band, hung on the rear of the army, picking off stragglers, and often carrying havoc into the broken ranks, but never venturing on a pitched battle. He gave over his pursuit as they crossed the bounds of Numidia.

On arriving at Caerwan, Acbad found every thing secure; the rebellion having been suppressed by the energy and bravery of Zohair, aided by an associate warrior, Omar Ibn Ali, of the tribe of Koreish.

Acbah now distributed a part of his army about the neighbourhood, formed of the residue a flying camp of cavalry, and leaving Zohair and his brave associate to maintain the safety of the metropolis, returned to scour the land of Zab, and take vengeance on the Berber chief, who had harassed and insulted him when on the march.

He proceeded without opposition as far as a place called Téhuda; when in some pass or defile, he found himself surrounded by a great host of Greeks and Berbers, led on by the mountain chief Aben Cahina. In fact, both Christians and Moors, who had so often been in deadly conflict in these very regions, had combined to drive these new intruders from the land.

Acbah scanned the number and array of the advancing enemy, and saw there was no retreat, and that destruction was inevitable. He marshalled his little army of horsemen, however, with great calmness; put up the usual prayers, and exhorted his men to fight valiantly. Summoning Muhegir to his presence, "This," said he, "is a day of liberty and gain for all true Moslems, for it is a day of martyrdom. I would not deprive you of so great a chance for paradise." So saying, he ordered his chains to be taken off.

Muhegir thanked him for the favour, and expressed his determination to die in the cause of the faith. Acbah then gave him arms and a horse, and both of them drawing their swords, broke the scabbards in token that they would fight until victory or death. The battle was desperate, and the carnage terrible. Almost all the Moslems fought to the very death, asking no quarter. Acbah was one of the last of his devoted band, and his corpse was found scimetar in hand, upon a heap of the enemy whom he had slain.

CHAPTER XLV.

Moawyah names his successor.— His last acts and death.—Traits of his character.

Moawyah was now far advanced in years, and aware that he had not long to live; he sought therefore, to accomplish a measure which he had long contemplated, and which was indicative of his ambitious character and his pride of family. It was to render the Caliphat hereditary, and to perpetuate it in his line. For this purpose he openly named his son Yezid as his successor, and requested the different provinces to send deputies to Damascus to perform the act of fealty to him. The nomination of a successor was what the prophet himself had not done, and what Abu Beker, Omar, and Othman had therefore declined to do; the attempt to render the Caliphat hereditary was in direct opposition to the public will manifested repeatedly in respect to Ali; Yezid, to whom he proposed to bequeath the government, was publicly detested, yet, notwithstanding all these objections, such influence had Moawyah acquired over the public mind, that delegates arrived at Damascus from all parts, and gave their hands to Yezid in pledge of future fealty. Thus was established the dynasty of the Ommiades, which held the Caliphat for nearly a hundred years. There were fourteen Caliphs of this haughty line, known as the Pharaohs of the house of Omaya (or rather Ommiah). The ambition of rule manifested in Moawyah, the founder of the dynasty, continued even among his remote descendants, who exercised sovereignty nearly four centuries afterwards in Spain. One of them, anxious to ascend the throne in a time of turbulence and peril, exclaimed: "Only make me king to-day, and you may kill me to-morrow!"

The character of the Caliph had much changed in the hands of Moawyah, and in the luxurious city of Damascus assumed more and more the state of the oriental sovereigns which it superseded. The frugal simplicity of the Arab, and the stern virtues of the primitive disciples of Islam, were softening down and disappearing among the voluptuous delights of Syria. Moawyah, however, endeavoured to throw over his favourite city of Damascus some of the sanctity with which Mecca and Medina were invested. For this purpose he sought to transfer to it, from Medina, the pulpit of the prophet, as also his walking-staff; " for such precious relics of the apostle of God," said he, " ought not to remain among the murderers of Othman."

The staff was found after great search, but when the pulpit was about to be removed, there occurred so great an eclipse of the sun, that the stars became visible. The superstitious Arabs considered this a signal of divine disapprobation, and the pulpit was suffered to remain in Medina.

Feeling his end approaching, Moawyah summoned his son Yezid to his presence, and gave advice full of experience and wisdom. " Confide in the Arabs," said he, " as the sure foundation of your power. Prize the Syrians, for they are faithful and enterprising, though prone to degenerate when out of their own country. Gratify the people of Irak in all their demands, for they are restless and turbulent, and would unsheath a hundred thousand scimetars against thee on the least provocation."

" There are four rivals, my son," added he, " on whom thou must keep a vigilant eye; the first is Hosein, the son of Ali, who has great influence in Irak, but he is upright and sincere, and thy own cousin; treat him, therefore, with clemency, if he fall within thy power. The second is Abdallah Ibn Omar ; but he is a devout man, and will eventually come under allegiance to thee. The third is Abda'lrahman ; but he is a man of no force of mind, and merely speaks from the dictates of others; he is, moreover, incontinent, and a gambler; he is not a rival to be feared. The fourth is Abdallah Ibn Zobeir; he unites the craft of the fox with the strength and courage of the lion. If he appear against thee, oppose him valiantly; if he offer peace, accept it, and spare the blood of thy people. If he fall within your power, cut him to pieces ! "

Moawyah was gathered to his fathers in the sixtieth year of the Hegira, A. D. 679, at the age of seventy, or, as some say, seventy-five years, of which he had reigned nearly twenty. He was interred in Damascus, which he had made the capital of the Moslem empire, and which continued to be so during the dynasty of the Ommiades. The inscription of his signet was, " Every deed hath its meed ; " or, according to others, " All power rests with God."

Though several circumstances in his reign savour of crafty, and even treacherous policy, yet he bears a high name in Moslem history. His courage was undoubted, and of a generous kind; for though fierce in combat, he was clement in victory. He prided himself greatly upon being of the tribe of Koreish, and was highly aristocratical before he attained to sovereign power ; yet he was affable and accessible at all times, and made himself popular among his people. His ambition was tempered with some considerations of justice. He assumed the throne, it is true, by the aid of the scimetar, without regular election; but he subsequently bought off the right of his rival Hassan, the legitimate Caliph ; and transcended munificently all the stipulations of his purchase, presenting him, at one time, with four million pieces of gold. One almost regards with incredulity the stories of immense sums passing from hand to hand among these Arab conquerors, as freely as bags of dates in their native deserts; but it must be recollected they had the plundering of the rich empires of the East, and as yet were flush with the spoils of recent conquests.

The liberality of Moawyah is extolled as being beyond all bounds; one instance on record of it, however, savours of policy. He gave Ayesha a bracelet valued at a hundred thousand pieces of gold, that had formerly, perhaps, sparkled on the arm of some Semiramis; but Ayesha, he knew, was a potent friend and a dangerous enemy.

Moawyah was sensible to the charms of poetry, if we may judge from the following anecdotes:

A robber, who had been condemned by the Cadi to have his head cut off, appealed to the Caliph in a copy of verses, pleading the poverty and want by which he had been driven. Touched by the poetry, Moawyah reversed the sentence, and gave the poet a purse of gold, that he might have no plea of necessity for repeating the crime.

Another instance was that of a young Arab, who had married a beautiful damsel, of whom he was so enamoured, that he lavished all his fortune upon her. The governor of Cufa happening to see her, was so struck with her beauty, that he took her from the youth by force. The latter made his complaint to the Caliph in verse, poured forth with Arab eloquence, and with all the passion of a lover, praying redress or death. Moawyah, as before, was moved by the poetic appeal. and sent orders to the governor of Cufa to restore the wife to her husband. The governor, infatuated with her charms, entreated the Caliph to let him have the enjoyment of her for one year, and then to take his head. The curiosity of the Caliph was awakened by this amorous contest; and he caused the female to be sent to him. Struck with her ravishing beauty, with the grace of her deportment, and the eloquence of her expressions, he could not restrain his admiration; and in the excitement of the moment told her to choose between the young Arab, the governor of Cufa, and himself. She acknowledged the honour proffered by the Caliph to be utterly beyond her merit; but avowed that affection and duty still inclined her to her husband. Her modesty and virtue delighted Moawyah even more than her beauty; he restored her to her husband, and enriched them both with princely munificence.

CHAPTER XLVI.

Succession of Yezid, seventh Caliph.—Final fortunes of Hosein, the son of Ali.

Yezid, the son of Moawyah, succeeded to the Caliphat without the ceremony of an election. His inauguration took place in the new moon of the month Rajeb, in the sixtieth year of the Hegira; coincident with the seventh day of April, in the year of our Lord 680. He was thirty-four years of age, and is described as tall and thin; with a ruddy countenance pitted with the small-pox, black eyes, curled hair, and a comely beard. He was not deficient in talent, and possessed the popular gift of poetry. The effect of his residence among the luxuries and refinements of Syria, was evinced in a fondness for silken raiment and the delights of music;-but he was stigmatized as base-spirited, sordid and covetous; grossly sensual, and scandalously intemperate.

Notwithstanding all this, he was readily acknowledged as Caliph throughout the Moslem empire, excepting by Mecca, Medina, and some cities of Babylonia. His first aim was to secure undisputed possession of the Caliphat. The only competitors from whom he had danger to apprehend, were Hosein, the son of Ali, and Abdallah, the son of Zobeir. They were both at Medina, and he sent orders to Waled Ibn Otbah, the governor of that city, to exact from them an oath of fealty. Waled, who was of an undecided character, consulted Merwân Ibn Hakem, formerly secretary of Othman, and suspected of forging the letter which effected the ruin of that Caliph. He was in fact one of the most crafty, as well as able men of the age. His advice to the governor was to summon Hosein and Abdallah to his presence, before they should hear of the death of Moawyah, and concert any measures of opposition; then to tender to them the oath of fealty to Yezid, and, should they refuse, to smite off their heads.

Hosein and Abdallah discovered the plot in time to effect their escape with their families to Mecca; where they declared themselves openly in opposition to Yezid. In a little while Hosein received secret messages from the people of Cufa, inviting him to their city, assuring him not merely of protection, but of joyful homage as the son of Ali, the legitimate successor of the prophet. He had only, they said, to show himself in their city, and all Babylonia would rise in arms in his favour.

Hosein sent his cousin, Muslim Ibn Okail, to ascertain the truth of these representations, and to foment the spirit of insurrection should it really exist among the people of Cufa. Muslim made his way, almost unattended, and with great peril and hardship across the deserts of Irak. On arriving at Cufa, he was well received by the party of Hosein; they assured him that eighteen thousand men were ready to sacrifice their blood and treasure in casting down the usurper and upholding the legitimate Caliph. Every day augmented the number of apparent zealots in the cause, until it amounted to one hundred and forty thousand. Of all this, Muslim sent repeated accounts to Hosein; urging him to come on, and assuring him that the conspiracy had been on with such secrecy, that Nu'mân Ibn Baschir, the governor of Cufa, had no suspicion of it.

But though the conspiracy had escaped the vigilance of Nu'mân, intimation of it had reached the Caliph Yezid at Damascus, who sent instant orders to Obeid'allah, the Emir of Bassora, to repair with all speed to Cufa, displace its negligent governor, and take that place likewise under his command.

Obeid'allah was the son of Ziyad, and inherited all the energy of his father. Aware that the moment was critical, he set off from Bassora with about a score of fleet horsemen. The people of Cufa were on the look out for the arrival of Hosein, which was daily expected, when Obeid'allah rode into the city in the twilight at the head of his troopers. He wore a black turban, as was the custom likewise with Hosein. The populace crowded round him, hailing the supposed grandson of the prophet.

"Stand off!" cried the horsemen fiercely. "It is the emir Obeid'allah."

The crowd shrank back abashed and disappointed, and the emir rode on to the castle. The popular chagrin increased when it was known that he had command of the province; for he was reputed a second Ziyad in energy and decision. His measures soon proved his claims to that character. He discovered and disconcerted the plans of the conspirators; drove Muslim to a premature outbreak; dispersed his hasty levy, and took him prisoner. The latter shed bitter tears on his capture; not on his own account, but on the account of Hosein, whom he feared his letters and sanguine representations had involved in ruin, by inducing him to come on to Cufa. The head of Muslim was struck off and sent to the Caliph.

His letters had indeed produced the dreaded effect. On receiving them Hosein prepared to comply with the earnest invitation of the people of Cufa. It was in vain his friends reminded him of the proverbial faithlessness of these people; it was in vain they urged him to wait until they had committed themselves, by openly taking the field. It was in vain that his near relative Abdallah Ibn Abbas urged him at least, to leave the females of his family at Mecca; lest he should be massacred in the midst of them, like the Caliph Othman. Hosein in the true spirit of a Moslem and predestinarian declared he would leave the event to God; and accordingly set out with his wives and children, and a number of his relatives, escorted by a handful of Arab troops.

Arrived in the confines of Babylonia, he was met by a body of a thousand horse, led on by Harro, an Arab of the tribe of Temimah. He at first supposed them to be a detachment of his partisans, sent to meet him, but was soon informed by Harro, that he came from the emir Obeid'allah to conduct him and all the people with him to Cufa.

Hosein haughtily refused to submit to the emir's orders; and represented that he came in peace, invited by the inhabitants of Cufa, as the rightful Caliph. He set forth at the same time, the justice of his claims, and endeavoured to enlist Harro in his cause, but the latter, though in no wise hostile to him, avoided committing himself, and urged him to proceed quietly to Cufa under his escort.

While they were yet discoursing, four horsemen rode up accompanied by a guide. One of these named Thirmah was known to Hosein, and was reluctantly permitted by Harro to converse with him apart. Hosein inquired about the situation of things at Cufa. "The nobles," replied the other, "are now against you to a man; some of the common people are still with you, by to-morrow, however, not a scimetar but will be unsheathed against you."

Hosein inquired about Kais, a messenger whom he had sent in advance to apprise his adherents of his approach. He had been seized on suspicion; ordered as a test by Obeid'allah to curse Hosein and his father Ali, and on his refusing had been thrown headlong from the top of the citadel. ·

Hosein shed tears at hearing the fate of his faithful messenger. "There be some," said he, in the words of the Koran, "who are already dead, and some who living expect death. Let their mansions, Oh God, be in the gardens of paradise, and receive us with them to thy mercy."

Thirmah represented to Hosein that his handful of followers would be of no avail against the host prepared to oppose him in the plains of Cufa, and offered to conduct him to the impregnable mountains of Aja, in the province of Naja, where ten thousand men of the tribe of Tay might soon be assembled to defend him. He declined his advice, however, and advanced towards Kadesia, the place famous for the victory over the Persians. Harro and his cavalry kept pace with him, watching every movement, but offering no molestation. The mind of Hosein, however, was darkened by gloomy forebodings. A stupor at times hung over his faculties as he rode slowly along ; he appeared to be haunted with a presentiment of death. "We belong to God and to God we must return," exclaimed he as he roused himself at one time from a dream or reverie. He had beheld in his phantasy, a horseman who had addressed him in warning words, "men travel in the night, and their destiny travels in the night to meet them." This he pronounced a messenger of death.

In this dubious and desponding mood he was brought to a halt, near the banks of the Euphrates, by the appearance of four thousand men, in hostile array, commanded by Amar Ibn Saad. These, likewise, had been sent out by the emir Obeid'allah, who was full of uneasiness lest there should be some popular movement in favour of Hossein. The latter, however, was painfully convinced by this repeated appearance of hostile troops, without any armament in his favour, that the fickle people of Cufa were faithless to him. He held a parley with Amar, who was a pious and good man, and had come out very unwillingly against a descendant of the prophet, stated to him the manner in which he had been deceived by the people of Cufa, and now offered to return to Mecca. Amar despatched a fleet messenger to apprise the emir of this favourable offer, hoping to be excused from using violence against Hosein. Obeid'-allah wrote in reply: "Get between him and the Euphrates, cut him off from the water as he did Othman; force him to acknowledge allegiance to Yezid, and then we will treat of terms."

Amar obeyed these orders with reluctance, and the little camp of Hosein suffered the extremities of thirst. Still he could not be brought to acknowledge Yezid as Caliph. He now offered three things, either to go to Damascus and negotiate matters personally with Yezid; to return into Arabia; or to repair to some frontier post in Khorassan and fight against the Turks. These terms were likewise transmitted by Amar to Obeid'allah.

The emir was exasperated at these delays, which he considered as intended to gain time for tampering with the public feeling. His next letter to Amar was brief and explicit. "If Hosein and his men submit and take the oath of allegiance, treat them kindly; if they refuse, slay them — ride over them — trample them under the feet of thy horses!" This letter was sent by Shamar, a warrior of note, and of a fierce spirit. He had private instructions. "If Amar fail to do as I have ordered, strike off his head and take command of his troops." He was furnished also with a letter of protection, and passports for four of the sons of Ali, who had accompanied their brother Hosein.

Amar, on receiving the letter of the emir, had another parley with Hosein. He found him in front of his tent conversing with his brother Al Abbas, just after the hour of evening prayer, and made known to him the peremptory demand of the emir and its alternative. He also produced the letter of protection and the passports for his brothers, but they refused to accept them.

Hosein obtained a truce until the morning to consider the demand of the emir; but his mind was already made up. He saw that all hope of honourable terms was vain, and he resolved to die.

After the departure of Amar, he remained seated alone at the door of his tent, leaning on his sword, lost in gloomy cogitation on the fate of the coming day. A heaviness again came over him, with the same kind of portentous fantasies that he had already experienced. The approach of his favourite sister, Zenaid, roused him. He regarded her with mournful significance. "I have just seen," said he, "in a dream, our grandsire the prophet, and he said, ' Thou wilt soon be with me in paradise.'"

., The boding mind of Zenaib interpreted the portent. "Woe unto us and our family," cried she, smiting her breast; "our mother Fatima is dead, and our father Ali and our brother Hassan! Alas for the desolation of the past and the destruction that is to come!" So saying her grief overcame her, and she fell into a swoon. Hosein raised her tenderly, sprinkled water in her face, and restored her to consciousness. He entreated her to rely with confidence on God, reminding her that all the people of the earth must die, and every thing that exists must perish, but that God, who created them, would restore them and take them to himself. "My father, and my mother, and my brother," said he, "were better than I, yet they died, and every Moslem has had an example in the death of the apostle of God." Taking her then by the hand, he led her into the tent, charging her, in case of his death, not to give way thus to immoderate sorrow.

He next addressed his friends and followers. "These troops by whom we are surrounded," said he, "seek no life but mine, and will be contented with my death. Tarry not with me, therefore, to your destruction, but leave me to my fate."

"God forbid," cried Al Abbas, "that we should survive your fall;" and his words were echoed by the rest.

Seeing his little band thus determined to share his desperate fortunes, Hosein prepared to sell their lives dear, and make their deaths a memorable sacrifice. By his orders all the tents were disposed in two lines, and the cords interwoven so as to form barriers on both sides of the camp, while a deep trench in the rear was filled with wood, to be set on fire in case of attack. It was assailable, therefore, only in front. This done, the devoted band, conscious that the next day was to be their last, passed the night in prayer; while a troop of the enemy's horse kept riding round to prevent their escape.

When the morning dawned, Hosein prepared for battle. His whole force amounted only to two-score foot soldiers, and two-and-thirty horse; but all were animated with the spirit of martyrs. Hosein and several of his chief men washed, anointed, and perfumed themselves; "for in a little while," said they, "we shall be with the blackeyed Houris of paradise."

His steadfastness of soul, however, was shaken by the loud lamentations of his sisters and daughters, and the thought of the exposed and desolate state in which his death would leave them. He called to mind, too, the advice which he had neglected of Abdallah Ibn Abbas, to leave his women in safety at Mecca. "God will reward thee, Abdallah!" exclaimed he in the fulness of his feelings.

A squadron of thirty horse, headed by Harro, now wheeled up, but they came as friends and allies. Harro repented him of having given the first check to Hosein, and now came in atonement to fight and die for him. "Alas for you, men of Cufa!" cried he, as Amar and his troops approached; "you have invited the descendant of the prophet to your city, and now you come to fight against him. You have cut off from him and his family the waters of the Euphrates, which are free even to infidels and the beasts of the field, and have shut him up like a lion in the toils."

Amar began to justify himself and to plead the orders of the emir; but the fierce Shamar cut short all parley by letting fly an arrow into the camp of Hosein; calling all to witness that he struck the first blow. A skirmish ensued, but the men of Hosein kept within their camp, where they could only be reached by the archers. From time to time there were single combats in defiance, as was customary with the Arabs. In these the greatest loss was on the side of the enemy, for Hosein's men fought with the desperation o men resolved on death.

Amar now made a general assault, but the camp being open only in front, was successfully defended. Shamar and his fol-

22

lowers attempted to pull down the tents, but met with vigorous resistance. He thrust his lance through the tent of Hosein, and called for fire to burn it. The women ran out shrieking. "The fire of Jehennam be thy portion!" cried Hosein "wouldst thou destroy my family?"

Even the savage Shamar stayed his hand at the sight of defenceless women, and he and his band drew off with the loss of several of their number.

Both parties desisted from the fight at the hour of noontide prayer; and Hosein put up the prayer of Fear, which is only used in time of extremity.

When the prayers were over the enemy renewed the assault, but chiefly with arrows from a distance. The faithful followers of Hosein were picked off one by one, until he was left almost alone; yet no one ventured to close upon him. An arrow from a distance pierced his little son Abdallah, whom he had upon his knee. Hosein caught his blood in the hollow of his hand and threw it toward heaven. "Oh God," exclaimed he, "if thou withholdest help from us, at least take vengeance on the wicked for this innocent blood."

His nephew, a beautiful child with jewels in his ears, was likewise wounded in his arms. "Allah will receive thee, my child," said Hosein; "thou wilt soon be with thy forefathers in paradise."

At this moment Zeinab rushed forth imprecating the vengeance of Heaven upon the murderers of her family. Her voice was overpowered by the oaths and curses of Shamar, who closed with his men upon Hosein. The latter fought desperately, and laid many dead around him, but his strength was failing him; it became a massacre rather than a fight; he sank to the earth, and was stripped ere life was extinct. Thirty wounds were counted in his body, and four-and-thirty bruises. His head was then cut off to be sent to Obeid'allah, and Shamar, with his troops, rode forward and backward over the body, as he had been ordered, until it was trampled into the earth.

Seventy-two followers of Hosein were slain in this massacre; seventeen of whom were descendants from Fatima. Eighty-eight of the enemy were killed, and a great number wounded. All the arms and furniture of Hosein and his family were taken as lawful spoils, although against the command of Amar.

Shamar despatched one of his troopers to bear the head of Hosein to the emir Obeid'allah. He rode with all speed, but arrived at Cufa after the gates of the castle were closed. Taking the gory trophy to his own house until morning, he showed it with triumph to his wife; but she shrank from him with horror, as one guilty of the greatest outrage to the family of the prophet; and from that time forward renounced all intercourse with him.

When the head was presented to Obeid'allah, he smote it on the mouth with his staff. A venerable Arab present was shocked at his impiety. "By Allah!" exclaimed he, "I have seen those lips pressed by the sacred lips of the prophet!"

As Obeid'allah went forth from the citadel, he beheld several women, meanly attired and seated disconsolately on the ground at the threshold. He had to demand three times who they were, before he was told that it was Zeinab, sister of Hosein, and her maidens. "Allah be praised," cried he with ungenerous exultation, "who has brought this proud woman to shame, and wrought death upon her family." "Allah be praised," retorted Zeinab haughtily, "who hath glorified our family by his holy apostle Mahomet. As to my kindred, death was decreed to them, and they have gone to their resting-place ; but God will bring you and them together, and will judge between you."

The wrath of the emir was inflamed by this reply, and his friends, fearful he might be provoked to an act of violence, reminded him that she was a woman and unworthy of his anger. "Enough," cried he, "let her revile ; Allah has given my soul full satisfaction in the death of her brother, and the ruin of her rebellious race."

"True !" replied Zeinab, "you have indeed destroyed our men, and cut us up root and branch. If that be any satisfaction to your soul, you have it."

The emir looked at her with surprise. "Thou art indeed," said he, "a worthy descendant of Ali, who was a poet and a man of courage."

"Courage," replied Zeinab, "is not a woman's attribute ; but what my heart dictates, my tongue shall utter."

The emir cast his eyes on Ali, the son of Hosein, a youth just approaching manhood, and ordered him to be beheaded. The proud heart of Zeinab now gave way. Bursting into tears she flung her arms round her nephew. "Hast thou not drunk deep enough of the blood of our family?" cried she to Obeid'allah ; "and dost thou thirst for the blood of this youth? Take mine too with it ; and let me die with him."

The emir gazed on her again, and with greater astonishment ; he mused for awhile, debating with himself, for he was disposed to slay the lad ; but was moved by the tenderness of Zeinab. At length his better feelings prevailed, and the life of Ali was spared.

The head of Hosein was transmitted to the Caliph Yezid, at Damascus, in charge of the savage-hearted Shamar ; and with it were sent Zeinab and her women, and the youth Ali. The latter had a chain round his neck, but the youth carried himself proudly, and would never vouchsafe a word to his conductors.

When Shamar presented the head with the greetings of Obeid'allah, the Caliph shed tears, for he recalled the dying counsel of his father with respect to the son of Ali. "Oh Hosein!" ejaculated he, "hadst thou fallen into my hands thou wouldst not have been slain." Then giving vent to his indignation against the absent Obeid'allah, "The curse of God," exclaimed he, "be upon the son of Somyah." [1]

He had been urged by one of his courtiers to kill Ali, and extinguish the whole generation of Hosein, but milder counsels prevailed. When the women and children were brought before him,

---

[1] A sneer at Obeid'allah's illegitimate descent from Somyah, the wife of a Greek slave.

in presence of the Syrian nobility, he was shocked at their mean attire, and again uttered a malediction on Obeid'allah. In conversing with Zeinab, he spoke with disparagement of her father Ali and her brother Hosein, but the proud heart of this intrepid woman again rose to her lips, and she replied with a noble scorn and just invective, that shamed him to silence.

Yezid now had Zeinab and the other females of the family of Hosein treated with proper respect ; baths were provided for them, and apparel suited to their rank; they were entertained in his palace, and the widowed wives of his father Moawyah came and kept them company, and joined with them in mourning for Hosein. Yezid acted also with great kindness toward Ali and Amru, the sons of Hosein, taking them with him in his walks. Amru was as yet a mere child. Yezid asked him one day jestingly, " Wilt thou fight with my son Khaled ? " The urchin's eye flashed fire. " Give him a knife," cried he, " and give me one!" "Beware of this child," said a crafty old courtier who stood by, and who was an enemy to the house of Ali. " Beware of this child, depend upon it, one serpent is the parent of another."

After a time when the family of Hosein wished to depart for Medina, Yezid furnished them abundantly with every comfort for the journey, and a safe convoy under a careful officer, who treated them with all due deference. When their journey was accomplished, Zeinab and Fatima, the young daughter of Hosein, would have presented their conductor with some of their jewels, but the worthy Syrian declined their offer. "Had I acted for reward," said he, less than these jewels would have sufficed; but what I have done, was for the love of God, and for the sake of your relationship to the prophet."

The Persians hold the memory of Hosein in great veneration, entitling him Shaded or the Martyr, and Seyejed or Lord ; and he and his lineal descendants for nine generations are enrolled among the twelve Imams or Pontiffs of the Persian creed. The anniversary of his martyrdom is called Rus Hosein (the day of Hosein), and is kept with great solemnity. A splendid monument was erected in after years on the spot where he fell, and was called in Arabic Meshed Hosein, The Sepulchre of Hosein. The Shyites, or sectaries of Ali, relate divers prodigies as having signalized his martyrdom. The sun withdrew his light, the stars twinkled at noonday and clashed against each other, and the clouds rained showers of blood. A supernatural light beamed from the head of the martyr, and a flock of white birds hovered around it. These miracles, however, are all stoutly denied by the sect of Moslems called Sonnites, who hold Ali and his race in abomination.

CHAPTER XLVII.

Insurrection of Abdallah Ibn Zobeir.—Medina taken and sacked.—Mecca besieged.—
Death of Yezid.

The death of Hosein had removed one formidable rival of Yezid;
but gave strength to the claims of another, who was scarcely less
popular. This was Abdallah, the son of Zobeir; honoured for his
devotion to the faith; beloved for the amenity of his manners, and
of such adroit policy, that he soon managed to be proclaimed Caliph, by the partisans of the house of Haschem, and a large portion
of the people of Medina and Mecca. The martyrdom, as he termed
it, of Hosein furnished him a theme for public harangues, with
which, after his inauguration, he sought to sway the popular
feelings. He called to mind the virtues of that grandson of the
prophet, his pious watchings, fastings, and prayers; the perfidy of
the people of Cufa, to which he had fallen a victim; the lofty heroism of his latter moments, and the savage atrocities which had
accompanied his murder. The public mind was heated by these
speeches; the enthusiasm awakened for the memory of Hosein was
extended to his politic eulogist. An Egyptian soothsayer, famed
for skill in divination, and who had studied the prophet Daniel,
declared that Abdallah would live and die a king; and this operated
powerfully in his favour among the superstitious Arabs, so that his
party rapidly increased in numbers.

The Caliph Yezid, although almost all the provinces of the empire were still in allegiance to him, was alarmed at the movements
of this new rival. He affected, however to regard him with contempt, and sent a silver collar to Merwân Ibn Hakem, then governor of Medina, directing him to put it round the neck of the
" mock Caliph," should he persist in his folly, and send him in
chains to Damascus. Merwân, however, who was of a wily character himself, and aware of the craft and courage of Abdallah and
his growing popularity in Medina, evaded the execution of the
order.

Yezid had no better success in his endeavours to crush the
rising power of Abdallah at Mecca. In vain he repeatedly changed
his governors of that city; each in his turn was outwitted by the
superior sagacity of Abdallah, or overawed by the turbulent discontent of the people.

Various negotiations took place between Yezid and these disaffected cities, and despatches were sent from the latter to Damascus;
but these only rendered the schism in the Caliphat more threatening
The deputies brought back accounts of the dissolute life of Yezid,
which shocked the pious and abstemious Arabs of the sacred cities.
They represented him as destitute of religion and morality; neglectful of the hours of worship; a gross sensualist addicted to

wine and banqueting; an effeminate voluptuary, passing his time amid singing and dancing women, listening to music and loose minstrelsy, and surrounded by dogs and eunuchs.

The contempt and loathing caused by their representations were fomented by the partisans of Abdallah Ibn Zobeir, and extended to the whole house of Ommiah, of which Yezid was a member. Open rebellion at length broke out in a manner characteristic of the Arabs. During an assemblage in the mosque of Medina, one of the conspirators threw his turban on the ground, exclaiming, " I cast off Yezid as I cast off this turban." Another seconded him with the exclamation, " I cast off Yezid as I cast off this shoe." Heaps of shoes and turbans soon showed that the feeling was unanimous.

The next move was to banish the house of Ommiah and all its dependents; but these, to the number of a thousand, took refuge in the palace of Merwân Ibn Hakem, the governor, who was of that race. Here they were closely besieged and sent off to Yezid, imploring instant succour.

. It was with difficulty Yezid could prevail upon any of his generals to engage in so unpopular a cause. Meslem Ibn Okbah, a stout-hearted but infirm old general, at length undertook it; but observed, with contempt, that a thousand men who suffered themselves to be cooped up like fowls, without fighting, scarce deserved assistance.

When the troops were about to depart, Yezid rode about among them, his scimetar by his side, and an Arab bow across his shoulder, calling upon them to show their loyalty and courage. His instructions to Meslem were to summon the city of Medina, three days in succession, before he made any assault; if it refused to surrender, he should, after taking it, give it up to three days' pillage. He charged him, however, to be careful of the safety of the youth Ali, son of Hosein, who was in the city, but had taken no part in the rebellion.

Meslem departed at the head of twelve thousand horse and five thousand foot. When he arrived before Medina he found a huge trench digged round the city, and great preparations made for defence. On three successive days he summoned it to surrender, and on each day received a refusal. On the fourth day he attacked it by storm, making his assault on the east side, that the besieged might be blinded by the rising sun. The city held out until most of its prime leaders were slain; it would then have capitulated, but the stern old general compelled an unconditional surrender.

Meslem entered the city sword in hand, and sent instantly for Ali, the youthful son of Hosein, whom he placed on his own camel, and furnished with a trusty guard. His next care was to release the thousand men of the house of Ommiah from confinement, lest they should be involved in the sacking of the city; this done, he abandoned the place for three days to his soldiery, and a scene of slaughter, violence, and rapine ensued, too horrible to be detailed. Those of the inhabitants who survived the massacre were compelled to submit as slaves and vassals of Yezid. The rigid severity of old Meslem, which far surpassed his orders, gained him the appellation of Musreph, or, The Extortionate. His memory has ever been held in odium by the Moslems, for the outrages which he permitted in this sacred city. This capture of Medina took place at night, in the sixty-third year of the Hegira, and the year 682 of the Christian era.

The old general now marched on to wreak the same fate upon Mecca; but his fires were burnt out; he died on the march of fatigue, infirmity, and old age, and the command devolved on a Syrian general named Hozein Ibn Thamir. The latter led his force up to the walls of Mecca, where Abdallah Ibn Zobeir commanded in person. For the space of forty days he besieged the city; battering the walls with engines brought from Syria. In the course of the siege a part of the Caaba was beaten down and the rest burnt. Some ascribe the fire to the engines of the besiegers; others affirm that Abdallah, hearing a shouting in the night, caused a flaming brand to be elevated on a lance to discover the cause, and that the fire communicated to the veil which covered the edifice.

Mecca was reduced to extremity, and the inhabitants began to dread the fate of Medina, when a swift messenger brought to Abdallah Ibn Zobeir the joyful tidings of the death of Yezid. He immediately mounted the walls and demanded of the besiegers why they continued to fight, seeing that their master Yezid was no more. They regarded his words as a mere subterfuge, and continued the attack with increased vigour. The intelligence, however, was speedily confirmed.

Hozein now held a conference with Abdallah; he expressed an ardent desire to put an end to all further effusion of kindred blood; and proffered the allegiance of himself and his army, in which were some of the leading men of Syria. Abdallah, for once, was too cautious for his own good. He shrank from trusting himself with Hozein and his army; he permitted them, however, at their earnest request, to walk in religious procession round the ruins of the Caaba, of course without arms; after which Hozein and his host departed on the march homeward; and the late beleaguered family of Ommiah accompanied them to Syria.

The death of the Caliph Yezid took place at Hawwarin, in Syria, in the sixty-fourth year of the Hegira, A. D. 683, in the thirty-ninth year of his age, after a reign of three years and six months. He was cut down in the flower of his days, say the Moslem writers, in consequence of his impiety in ordering the sacking of Medina, the burial-place of the prophet; for the latter had predicted, "Whoever injureth Medina, shall melt away even as salt melteth in water." The Persian writers also, sectarians of Ali, hold the memory of Yezid in abhorrence, charging him with the death of Hassan and Hosein, and accompany his name with the imprecation, "May he be accursed of God!"

CHAPTER XLVIII.

Inauguration of Moawyah II, eighth Caliph.—His abdication and death.—Merwân Ibn Hakem and Abdallah Ibn Zobeir, rival Caliphs.—Civil wars in Syria.

On the death of Yezid, his son, Moawyah II, was proclaimed at Damascus, being the third Caliph of the house of Ommiah. He was in the twenty-first year of his age, feeble in mind and body, and swayed in his opinions and actions by his favourite teacher Omar Almeksus, of the sect of the Kadarii, who maintain the free-will of men, and that a contrary opinion would make God the author of sin.

Moawyah assumed the supreme authority with extreme re-luctance, and felt his incompetency to its duties; for the state of his health obliged him to shun daylight, and keep in dark-ened rooms; whence the Arabs, in their propensity to bynames, gave him the derisive appellation of Abuleilah, "Father of the Night."

He abdicated at the end of six months, alleging his incom-petency. The Ommiades were indignant at his conduct; they at-tributed it, and probably with reason, to the counsels of the sage Omar Almeksus, on whom they are said to have wreaked their rage by burying him alive.

Moawyah refused to nominate a successor. His grandfather Moawyah, he said, had wrested the sceptre from the hands of a better man; his father Yezid had not merited so great a trust, and he himself, being unworthy and unfit to wield it, was equally unworthy to appoint a successor; he left the election, therefore, to the chiefs of the people. In all which he probably spake accord-ing to the dictates of the sage Omar Almeksus.

As soon as he had thrown off the cares of government, he shut himself up in the twilight gloom of his chamber, whence he never stirred until his death; which happened soon after : caused, some say, by the plague, others by poison. His own diseased frame and morbid temperament, however, account sufficiently for his dis-solution.

The election of a Caliph again distracted the Moslem empire. The leading men at Damascus determined upon Merwân Ibn Hakem, of the family of Ommiah, and once the secretary of state of Othman, who had so craftily managed the correspondence of that unfortunate Caliph. He was now well stricken in years; tall and meagre, with a pale face and yellow beard, doubtless tinged according to oriental usage. Those who elected him took care to stipulate that he should not nominate any of his posterity as his successor; but should be succeeded by Khaled, the son of Yezid; as yet a minor. Mervân, in his eagerness for power, pledged himself without hesitation; how faithfully he redeemed his pledge will be seen hereafter.

While this election was held at Damascus, Abdallah Ibn Zobeir was acknowledged as Caliph in Mecca, Medina, and throughout Arabia; as also in Korassan, in Babylonia, and in Egypt.

Another candidate for the supreme power unexpectedly arose in Obeid'allah Ibn Ziyad, the emir of Bassora ; the same who had caused the massacre of Hosein. He harangued an assemblage of the people of Bassora on the state of the contending factions in Syria and Arabia; the importance of their own portion of the empire, so capable of sustaining itself in independence, and the policy of appointing some able person as a protector to watch over the public weal, until these dissensions should cease, and a Caliph be unanimously appointed. The assembly was convinced by his reasoning, and urged him to accept the appointment. He declined it repeatedly with politic grace, but was at length prevailed upon ; and the leaders gave him their hands, promising allegiance to him as a provisional chief, until a Caliph should be regurlarly elected. His authority, however, was but of short duration. The people of Cufa, who had experienced his tyranny as governor, rejected with scorn his election as protector; their example reacted upon the fickle Bassorians, who suddenly revoked their late act of allegiance, rose in tumultuous opposition to the man they had so recently honoured, and Obeid'allah was fain to disguise himself in female attire, and take refuge in the house of an adherent. During his sway, however, he had secured an immense amount of gold from the public treasury. This he now shared among his partisans, and distributed by handsful among the multitude : but though he squandered in this way above two hundred thousand pieces of gold upon the populace, and raised a few transient tumults in his favour, he was ultimately obliged to fly for his life, and his effects were pillaged by the rabble. So fared it with the temporary tyrant who smote the gory head of the virtuous Hosein.

He fled by night at the head of only a hundred men; after a time weariness compelled him to exchange the camel on which he was mounted for an ass. In this humble plight, with drooping head, and legs dangling to the ground, journeyed the imperious Obeid'allah, who, but the day before, was governor of Babylonia, and aspired to the throne of the Caliphs. One of his attendants noticing his dejection, and hearing him mutter to himself, supposed him smitten with contrition, and upbraiding himself with having incurred these calamities, as a judgment for the death of Hosein : he ventured to suggest his thoughts and to offer consolation ; but Obeid'allah quickly let him know that his only repentance and self-reproach were for not having attacked the faithless Bassorians, and struck off their heads at the very outbreak of their revolt. Obeid'allah effected his escape into Syria, and arrived at Damascus in time to take an active part in the election of Merwân to the Caliphat : in the meantime Bassora declared its allegiance to Abdallah Ibn Zobeir.

The claims of Merwân to the Caliphat were acknowledged in Syria alone, but Syria, if undivided, was an empire in itself. It was divided, however. A powerful faction headed by Dehac Ibn Kais, late governor of Cufa, disputed the pretensions of Merwân, and declared for Abdallah. They appeared in arms in the plain near Damascus. Merwân took the field against them in person; a great and sanguinary battle took place; Dehac and fourscore of the flower of Syrian nobility were slain, and an immense number of their adherents. Victory declared for Merwân. He called off his soldiers from the pursuit, reminding them that the fugitives were their brethren.

When the head of Dehac was brought to him he turned from it with sorrow. "Alas!" exclaimed he, "that an old and worn-out man like myself, should occasion the young and vigorous to be cut to pieces!"

His troops hailed him as Caliph beyond all dispute; and bore him back in triumph to Damascus. He took up his abode in the palace of his predecessors Moawyah and Yezid; but now came a harder part of his task. It had been stipulated that at his death, Khaled the son of Yezid should be his successor; it was now urged that he should marry the widow of Yezid, the mother of the youth, and thus make himself his legitimate guardian.

The aged Merwân would fain have evaded this condition, but it was forced upon him as a measure of policy, and he complied; no sooner, however, was the marriage solemnized than he left his capital and his bride, and set off with an army for Egypt, to put down the growing ascendency of Abdallah in that region. He sent in advance, Amru Ibn Saad, who acted with such promptness and vigour, that while the Caliph was yet on the march, he received tidings that the lieutenant of Abdallah had been driven from the province, and the Egyptians brought under subjection; whereupon, Merwân turned his face again toward Damascus.

Intelligence now overtook him that an army under Musab, brother of Abdallah, was advancing upon Egypt. The old Caliph again faced about, and resumed his march in that direction, but again was anticipated by Amru, who routed Musab in a pitched battle, and completely established the sway of Merwân over Egypt. The Caliph now appointed his son Abd'alaziz to the government of that important country, and once more returned to Damascus, whither he was soon followed by the victorious Amru.

CHAPTER XLIX.

State of affairs in Khorassan.—Conspiracy at Cufa.—Faction of the Penitents; their fortunes.—Death of the Caliph Merwân.

In the present divided state of the Moslem empire, the people of Khorassan remained neuter, refusing to acknowledge either Caliph. They appointed Salem, the son of Ziyad, to act as regent, until the unity of the Moslem government should be restored. He continued for a length of time in this station, maintaining the peace of the province, and winning the hearts of the inhabitants by his justice, equity, and moderation.

About this time, there was a sudden awakening among the sect of Ali, in Babylonia. The people of Cufa, proverbially fickle and faithless, were seized with tardy remorse for the fate of Hosein, of which they were conscious of being the cause. Those who had not personally assisted in his martyrdom, formed an association to avenge his death. Above a hundred of the chief men of the country joined them; they took the name of The Penitents, to express their contrition for having been instrumental in the death of the martyr, and they chose for their leader one of the veteran companions of the prophet, the venerable Solyman Ibn Sorâd, who devoted his gray hairs to this pious vengeance.

The awakening spread far and wide; in a little while upwards of sixteen thousand names were enrolled; a general appeal to arms was anticipated throughout the country, and the veteran Solyman called upon all true Moslems disposed to prosecute this "holy war," to assemble at a place called Nochaila. Before the appointed time, however, the temporary remorse of the people of Cufa had subsided; the enthusiasm for the memory of Hosein had cooled throughout the province; intriguing meddlers, jealous of the appointment of Solyman, had been at work, and when the veteran came to the place of assemblage, he found but an inconsiderable number prepared for action.

He now despatched two horsemen to Cufa, who arrived there at the hour of the last evening prayer, galloped through the streets to the great mosque, rousing the Penitents with the war cry of "Vengeance for Hosein." The call was not lost on the real enthusiasts; a kind of madness seized upon many of the people, who thronged after the couriers, echoing the cry of vengeance. The cry penetrated into the depths of the houses. One man tore himself from the arms of a beautiful and tenderly beloved wife, and began to arm for battle. She asked him if he were mad. "No!" cried he, "but I hear the summons of the herald of God, and I fly to avenge the death of Hosein." "And in whose protection do you leave our child?" "I commend him and thee to the protection of Allah!" So saying he departed.

Another called for a lance and steed; told his daughter that he fled from crime to penitence; took a hurried leave of his family and galloped to the camp of Solyman.

Still, when the army of Penitents was mustered on the following day it did not exceed four thousand. Solyman flattered himself, however, that reinforcements, promised him from various quarters would join him when on the march. He harangued his scanty host, roused their ardour, and marched them to the place of Hosein's murder, where they passed a day and night in prayer and lamentation. They then resumed their march. Their intention was to depose both Caliphs, Merwân and Abdallah; to overthrow the family of Ommiah, and restore the throne to the house of Ali; but their first object was vengeance on Obeid'allah, the son of Ziyad, to whom they chiefly ascribed the murder of Hosein. The aged Solyman led his little army of enthusiasts through Syria, continually disappointed of recruits, but unabated in their expectation of aid from heaven, until they were encountered by Obeid'allah with an army of twenty thousand horsemen, and cut in pieces.

In the midst of these internal feuds and dissensions, a spark of the old Saracen spirit was aroused by the news of disastrous reverses in Northern Africa. We have recorded in a former chapter, the heroic but disastrous end of Acbah on the plains of Numidia, where he and his little army were massacred by a Berber host, led on by Aben Cahina. That Moorish chieftain, while flushed with victory, had been defeated by Zohair before the walls of Caerwan, and the spirits of the Moslems had once more revived; especially on the arrival of reinforcements sent by Abd'alaziz from Egypt. A sad reverse, however, again took place. A large force of imperialists, veteran and well armed soldiers from Constantinople, were landed on the African coast to take advantage of the domestic troubles of the Moslems, and drive them from their African possessions. Being joined by the light troops of Barbary, they attacked Zobeir in open field. He fought long and desperately, but being deserted by the Egyptian reinforcements, and overpowered by numbers, was compelled to retreat to Barca, while the conquering foe marched on to Caerwan, captured that city, and made themselves masters of the surrounding country.

It was the tidings of this disastrous reverse, and of the loss of the great outpost of Moslem conquest in Northern Africa, that roused the Saracen spirit from its domestic feuds. Abd'almâlec, the eldest son of the Caliph Merwân, who had already served in Africa, was sent with an army to assist Zobeir. He met that general in Barca, where he was again collecting an army. They united their forces; retraced the westward route of victory, defeated the enemy in every action, and replaced the standard of the faith on the walls of Caerwan. Having thus wiped out the recent disgraces, Abd'almâlec left Zobeir in command of that region, and returned covered with glory to sustain his aged father in the Caliphat at Damascus.

The latter days of Merwân had now arrived. He had been intriguing and faithless in his youth; he was equally so in his age. In his stipulations on receiving the Caliphat, he had promised the succession to Khaled, the son of Yezid; he had since promised it to his nephew Amru, who had fought his battles and confirmed his power; in his latter days he caused his own son Abd'almâlec, fresh from African exploits, to be proclaimed his successor, and allegiance to be sworn to him. Khaled, his step-son, reproached him with his breach of faith; in the heat of reply, Merwân called the youth by an opprobrious epithet; which brought in question the chastity of his mother. This unlucky word, is said to have caused the sudden death of Merwân. His wife, the mother of Khaled, is charged with having given him poison; others say that she threw a pillow on his face while he slept, and sat on it until he was suffocated. He died in the 65th year of the Hegira, A. D. 684, after a brief reign of not quite a year.

CHAPTER L.

Inauguration of Abd'almâlec, the eleventh Caliph.—Story of Al Moktâr, the Avenger.

On the death of Merwân, his son Abd'almâlec was inaugurated Caliph at Damascus, and acknowledged throughout Syria and Egypt, as well as in the newly-conquered parts of Africa. He was in the full vigour of life, being about forty years of age; his achievements in Africa testify his enterprise, activity, and valour, and he was distinguished for wisdom and learning. From the time of his father's inauguration he had been looking forward to the probability of becoming his successor, and ambition of sway had taken place of the military ardour of his early youth. When the intelligence of his father's death reached him, he was sitting cross-legged, in oriental fashion, with the Koran open on his knees. He immediately closed the sacred volume and rising exclaimed, "Fare thee well, I am called to other matters."

The accession to sovereign power is said to have wrought a change in his character. He had always been somewhat superstitious; he now became attentive to signs, omens and dreams, and grew so sordid and covetous, that the Arabs, in their propensity to give characteristic and satirical surnames, used to call him Raf-hol Hejer, that is to say, Sweat-Stone; equivalent to our vulgar epithet of skin-flint.

Abdallah Ibn Zobeir was still acknowledged as Caliph by a great portion of the Moslem dominions, and held his seat of government at Mecca ; this gave him great influence over the true believers, who resorted in pilgrimage to the Caaba. Abd'almâlec determined to establish a rival place of pilgrimage within his own dominions. For this purpose he chose the temple of Jerusalem, sacred in the eyes of the Moslems, as connected with the acts and revelations of Moses, of Jesus, and of Mahomet, and as being surrounded by the tombs of the prophets. He caused this sacred edifice to be enlarged so as to include within its walls the steps upon which the Caliph Omar prayed on the surrender of that city. It was thus converted into a mosque, and the venerable and sanctified stone called Jacob's pillow, on which the patriarch is said to have had his dream, was presented for the kisses of pilgrims, in like manner as the black stone of the Caaba.

There was at this time a general of bold, if not ferocious character, who played a sort of independent part in the troubles and commotions of the Moslem empire. He was the son of Abu Obeidah, and was sometimes called Al Thakifi, from his native city Thayef, but won for himself the more universal appellation of Al Moktâr, or the Avenger. The first notice we find of him is during the short reign of Hassan, the son of Ali, being zealously devoted to the family of that Caliph. We next find him at Cufa, harbouring and assisting Muslem, the emissary of Hosein, and secretly fomenting the conspiracy in favour of the latter.   When the emir Obeid'allah came to Cufa, he was told of the secret practices of Al Moktâr, and questioned him on the subject.   Receiving a delusive reply, he smote him over the face with his staff and struck out one of his eyes.   He then cast him into prison, where he lay until the massacre of Hosein.   Intercessions were made in his favour with the Caliph Yezid, who ordered his release.   The emir executed the order, but gave Al Moktâr notice, that if, after the expiration of three days, he were found within his jurisdiction, his life should be forfeit.

Al Moktâr departed, uttering threats and maledictions.   One of his friends who met him, inquired concerning the loss of his eye. " It was the act of that son of a wanton, Obeid'allah," said he, bitterly, " but may Allah confound me if I do not one day cut him in pieces."   Blood revenge for the death of Hosein became now his ruling thought.   " May Allah forsake me," he would say, " if I do not kill as many in vengeance of that massacre, as were destroyed to avenge the blood of John, the son of Zacharias, on whom be peace ! "

He now repaired to Mecca, and presented himself before Abdallah Ibn.Zobeir, who had recently been inaugurated; but he would not take the oath of allegiance until the Caliph had declared his disposition to revenge the murder of Hosein.   " Never," said he, " will the affairs of Abdallah prosper, until I am at the head of his army taking revenge for that murder."

Al Moktâr fought valiantly in defence of the sacred city while besieged; but when the siege was raised in consequence of the death of Yezid, and Abdallah became generally acknowledged, he found the Caliph growing cold towards him, or towards the constant purpose of his thoughts; he left him therefore, and set out for Cufa, visiting all the mosques on the way haranguing the people on the subject of the death of Hosein and declaring himself his avenger.

On arriving at Cufa, he found his self-appointed office of avenger likely to be forestalled by the veteran Solyman, who was about to depart on his mad enterprise with his crazy Penitents.   Calling together the sectaries of Ali, he produced credentials from Mahomet, the brother of Hosein, which gained for him their confidence; and then represented to them the rashness and futility of the proposed expedition; and to his opposition may be ascribed the diminished number of volunteers that assembled at the call of Solyman.

While thus occupied he was arrested on a charge of plotting an insurrection with a view to seize upon the province, and was thrown into the same prison in which he had been confined by Obeid'allah.   During his confinement he kept up a correspondence with the sectaries of Ali by letters conveyed in the lining of a cap. On the death of the Caliph Merwân he was released from prison, and found himself head of the Alians, or powerful sect of Ali; who even offered their adhesion to him as Caliph, on condition that he would govern according to the Koran, and the Sonna or traditions, and would destroy the murderers of Hosein and his family.

Al Moktâr entered heartily upon the latter part of his duties, and soon established his claim to the title of Avenger. The first on whom he wreaked his vengeance was the ferocious Shamar, who had distinguished himself in the massacre of Hosein. Him he overcame and slew. The next was Caulah, who cut off the head of Hosein and conveyed it to the emir Obeid'allah. Him he beleaguered in his dwelling, and killed, and gave his body to the flames. His next victim was Amar Ibn Saad, the commander of the army that surrounded Hosein; with him he slew his son; and sent both of their heads to Mahomet, the brother of Hosein. He then seized Adi Ibn Hathem, who had stripped the body of Hosein while the limbs were yet quivering with life. Him he handed over to some of the sect of Ali, who stripped him, set him up as target, and discharged arrows at him until they stood out from his body like the quills of a porcupine. In this way Al Moktâr went on, searching out the murderers of Hosein wherever they were to be found, and inflicting on them a diversity of deaths.

Sustained by the Alians, or sect of Ali, he now maintained a military sway in Cufa, and held, in fact, a sovereign authority over Babylonia; he felt, however, that his situation was precarious; an army out of Syria, sent by Abd'almâlec, was threatening him on one side; and Musab, brother of the Caliph Abdallah, was in great force at Bassora menacing him on the other. He now had recourse to stratagems to sustain his power, and accomplish his great scheme of vengeance. He made overtures to Abdallah, offering to join him with his forces. The wary Caliph suspected his sincerity, and required, as proofs of it, the oath of allegiance from himself and his people, and a detachement to proceed against the army of Abd'almâlec.

Al Moktâr promptly sent off an officer, named Serjabil, with three thousand men, with orders to proceed to Medina. Abdallah, still wary and suspicious, despatched a shrewd general, Abbas Ibn Sahel, with a competent force to meet Serjabil and sound his intentions, and if he were convinced there was lurking treachery, to act accordingly.

Abbas and Serjabil encountered at the head of their troops on the highway to Medina. They had an amicable conference, in which Abbas thought he discovered sufficient proof of perfidy. He took measures accordingly. Finding the little army of Serjabil almost famished for lack of provisions, he killed a great number of fat sheep and distributed them among the hungry troops. A scene of hurry and glad confusion immediately took place. Some scattered themselves about the neighbourhood in search of fuel; some were cooking, some feasting. In this unguarded moment Abbas set upon them with his troops, slew Serjabil, and nearly four hundred of his men; but gave quarter to the rest, most of whom enlisted under his standard.

Al Moktâr, finding that his good faith was doubted by Abdallah, wrote privately to Mahomet, brother of Hosein, who was permitted by the Caliph to reside in Mecca, where he led a quiet, inoffensive life, offering to bring a powerful army to his assistance if he would take up arms.' Mahomet sent a verbal reply, assuring Al Moktâr of his belief in the sincerity of his offers; but declining all appeal to arms, saying he was resolved to bear his lot with patience, and leave the event to God. As the messenger was departing he gave him a parting word : "Bid Al Moktâr fear God and abstain from shedding blood."

The pious resignation and passive life of Mahomet were of no avail. The suspicious eye of Abdallah was fixed upon him. The Cufians of the sect of Ali, and devotees to the memory of Hosein, who yielded allegiance to neither of the rival Caliphs, were still permitted to make their pilgrimages to the Caaba, and when in Mecca, did not fail to do honour to Mahomet Ibn Ali and his family. The secret messages of Al Moktâr to Mahomet were likewise known. The Caliph Abdallah, suspecting a conspiracy, caused Mahomet and his family, and seventeen of the principal pilgrims from Cufa, to be arrested, and confined in the edifice by the sacred well Zem Zem, threatening them with death, unless by a certain time they gave the pledge of allegiance.

From their prison they contrived to send a letter to Al Moktâr, apprising him of their perilous condition. He assembled the Alians or sect of Ali, at Cufa and read the letter. "This comes," said he, "from Mahomet, the son of Ali, and brother of Hosein. He and his family, the purest of the house of your prophet, are shut up like sheep destined for the slaughter. Will you desert them in their extremity, and leave them to be massacred as you did the martyr Hosein and his family?"

The appeal was effectual; the Alians cried out to be led to Mecca. Al Moktâr marshalled out seven hundred and fifty men, bold riders, hard fighters, well armed and fleetly mounted, arranged them in small troops to follow each other at considerable intervals, troop after troop like the waves of the sea; the leader of the first troop, composed of a hundred and fifty men, was Abu Abdallah Aljodali. He set off first; the others followed at sufficient distance to be out of sight, but all spurred forward, for no time was to be lost.

Abu Abdallah was the first to enter Mecca. His small troop awakened no alarm. He made his way to the well of Zem Zem, crying "Vengeance for Hosein;" drove off the guard and broke open the prison' house, where he liberated Mahomet Ibn Ali and his family.

The tumult brought the Caliph and his guard. Abu Abdallah would have given them battle, but Mahomet interfered, and represented that it was impious to fight within the precincts of the Caaba. The Caliph, seeing the small force that was with Abdallah, would on his part have proceeded to violence, when lo, the second troop of hard riders spurred up; then the third, and presently all the rest; shouting "Allah Achbar," and "Vengeance for Hosein."

The Caliph, taken by surprise, lost all presence of mind. He knew the popularity of Mahomet Ibn Ali and his family, and dreaded an insurrection. Abu Abdallah in the moment of triumph would have put him to death, but his hand was stayed by the pious and humane Mahomet. The matter was peaceably adjusted. The Caliph was left unmolested; Mahomet distributed among his friends and adherents a great sum of money, which had been sent to him by Al Moktâr, and then with his family departed in safety from Mecca.

Al Moktâr had now to look to his safety at home; his old enemy Obeid'allah, former emir of Cufa, was pressing forward at the head of an army of the Caliph Abd'almâlec, to recover that city, holding out to his troops a promise of three days' sack and pillage. Al Moktâr called on the inhabitants to take arms against their former tyrant and the murderer of Hosein. A body of troops sallied forth headed by Ibrahim, the son of Alashtar. To give a mysterious sanctity to the expedition, Al Moktâr caused a kind of throne covered with a veil to be placed on a mule, and led forth with the army; to be to them what the ark was to the children of Israel, a sacred safeguard. On going into battle, the following prayer was to be offered up at it : " Oh God ! keep us in obedience to thee; and help us in our need." To which all the people were to respond, "Amen !"

The army of Ibrahim encountered the host of Obeid'allah on the plains, at some distance from Cufa. They rushed forward with a holy enthusiasm inspired by the presence of their ark. "Vengeance for Hosein !" was their cry, and it smote upon the heart of Obeid'allah. The battle was fierce and bloody; the Syrian force, though greatly superior, was completely routed; Obeid'allah was killed, fighting with desperate valour, and more of his soldiers were drowned in the flight than were slaughtered in the field. This signal victory was attributed, in a great measure, to the presence of the ark or veiled throne, which thenceforward was regarded almost with idolatry.

Ibrahim caused the body of Obeid'allah to be burnt to ashes, and sent his head to Al Moktâr. The gloomy heart of the Avenger throbbed with exultation, as he beheld this relic of the man who had oppressed, insulted, and mutilated him; he recollected the blow over the face which had deprived him of an eye, and smote the gory head of Obeid'allah, even as he had been smitten.

Thus, says the royal and pious historian Abulfeda, did Allah make use of the deadly hate of Al Moktâr, to punish Obeid'allah, the son of Ziyad, for the martyrdom of Hosein.

The triumph of Al Moktâr was not of long duration. He ruled over a fickle people, and he ruled them with a rod of iron. He persecuted all who were not, or whom he chose to consider as not, of the Hosein party, and he is charged with fomenting an insurrection of the slaves against the chief men of the city of Cufa. A combination was at length formed against him, and an invitation was sent to Musab Ibn Zobeir, who had been appointed emir of Bassora, by his brother, the Caliph Abdallah.

The invitation was borne by one Shebet, an enthusiast who made his entrance into Bassora on a mule with cropt ears and tail, his clothes rent, exclaiming with a loud voice, " Ya gautha ! Ya gautha ! Help ! help !" He delivered his message in a style suited to his garb, but accompanied it by letters from the chief men of Cufa, which stated their grievances in a more rational manner. Musab wrote instantly to Al Mohalleb, the emir of Persia, one of

23

the ablest generals of the time, to come to his aid with men and money; and on his arrival, joined forces with him to attack the Avenger in his seat of power.

Al Moktâr did not wait to be besieged. He took the field with his accustomed daring, and gave battle beneath the walls of his capital. It was a bloody fight; the presence of the mysterious throne had its effect upon the superstitious minds of the Cufians, but Al Moktâr had become hateful from his tyranny, and many of the first people were disaffected to him. His army was routed; he retreated into the royal citadel of Cufa, and defended it bravely and skilfully, until he received a mortal wound. Their chief being killed, the garrison surrendered at discretion, and Musab put every man to the sword, to the number of seven thousand.

Thus fell Al Moktâr Ibn Abu Obeidah, in his sixty-seventh year, after having defeated the ablest generals of three Caliphs, and by the sole power of his sword, made himself the independent ruler of all Babylonia. He is said never to have pardoned an enemy; to have persecuted with inveterate hate all who were hostile to the family of Ali, and in vengeance of the massacre of Hosein, to have shed the blood of nearly fifty thousand men, exclusive of those who were slain in battle. Well did he merit the title of the Avenger.

CHAPTER LI.

Musab Ibn Zobeir takes possession of Babylonia.—Usurpation of Amru Ibn Saad ; his death.—Expedition of Abd'almâlec against Musab.—The result.—Omens ; their effect upon Abd'almâlec.—Exploits of Al Mohalleb.

The death of Al Moktâr threw the province of Babylonia, with its strong capital, Cufa, into the hands of Musab Ibn Zobeir, brother to the Caliph Abdallah. Musab was well calculated to win the favour of the people. He was in the flower of his days, being but thirty-six years of age, comely in person, engaging in manners, generous in spirit, and of consummate bravery, though not much versed in warfare. He had been an intimate friend of Abd'almâlec before the latter was made Caliph, but he was brother to the rival Caliph, and connected by marriage with families in deadly opposition to the house of Ommiah. Abd'almâlec, therefore, regarded him as a formidable foe, and warned by the disasters of his army under Obeid'allah, resolved now to set out at the head of a second expedition in person; designed for the invasion of Babylonia.

In setting forth on this enterprise, he confided the government of Damascus to his cousin, Amru Ibn Saad; he did this in consideration of the military skill of Amru, though secretly there was a long nourished hate between them. The origin of this hatred shows the simplicity of Saracen manners in those days. When boys, Abd'almâlec and Amru were often under the care of an old beldame of their family, who used to prepare their meals, and produce quarrels between them in the allotment of their portions. These childish disputes became fierce quarrels and broils as they grew up together, and were rivals in their youthful games and exercises. In manhood they ripened into deadly jealousy and envy, as they became conquering generals; but the elevation of Abd'almâlec to the Caliphat, sank deep into the heart of Amru, as a flagrant wrong; the succession having been promised to him by his uncle, the late Caliph Merwân, as a reward for having subjugated Egypt. As soon, therefore, as Abd'almâlec had departed from Damascus, Amru, not content with holding the government of the city, aspired to the sovereignty of Syria, as his rightful dominion.

Abd'almâlec heard of the usurpation while on the march, returned rapidly in his steps, and a bloody conflict ensued between the forces of the rival cousins in the streets of Damascus. The women rushed between them; held up their children and implored the combatants to desist from this unnatural warfare. Amru laid down his arms and articles of reconciliation were drawn up and signed by the cousins.

Abd'almâlec proved faithless to his engagements. Getting Amru into his power by an artful stratagem, he struck off his head; put to death the principal persons who had supported him in his usurpation, and banished his family. As the exiles were about to depart, he demanded of the widow of Amru, the written articles of pacification which he had exchanged with her husband. She replied that she had folded them up in his winding sheet, to be at hand at the final day of judgment.

Abd'almâlec now resumed his march for Babylonia. He had sent agents before him to tamper with the fidelity of the principal persons. One of these, Ibrahim Ibn Alashtar, he had offered to make emir if he would serve his cause. Ibrahim, who was of incorruptible integrity, showed the letter to Musab, warned him that similar attempts must have been made to sap the fidelity of other persons of importance and advised him to use the scimetar freely, wherever he suspected disaffection; but Musab was too just and merciful to act thus upon mere suspicion. The event showed that Ibrahim understood the fickle and perfidious nature of the people of Irak.

A battle took place on the margin of the desert, not far from Palmyra. It commenced with a gallant charge of cavalry, headed by Ibrahim Ibn Alashtar, which broke the ranks of the Syrians and made great havoc. Abd'almâlec came up with a reinforcement, and rallied his scattered troops. In making a second charge, however, Ibrahim was slain, and now the perfidy of the Cufians became apparent. Musab's general of horse wheeled round and spurred ignominiously from the field; others of the leaders refused to advance. Musab called loudly for Ibrahim; but seeing his lifeless body on the ground, "Alas!" he exclaimed, "there is no Ibrahim for me this day."

Turning to his son Isa, a mere stripling, yet who had fought with manly valour by his side, "Fly my son," cried he; "fly to thy uncle Abdallah at Mecca; tell him of my fate, and of the perfidy of the men of Irak." Isa, who inherited the undaunted spirit of the family of Zobeir, refused to leave his father. "Let us retreat," said he, "to Bassora, where you will still find friends, and may thence make good your return to Mecca.

"No, my son!" replied Musab, "never shall it be said among the men of Koreish, that I fled the field of battle, or entered the temple of Mecca, a vanquished general!"

During an interval of the battle, Abd'almâlec sent Musab an offer of his life. His reply was, he had come to conquer or to die. The conflict was soon at an end. The troops who adhered to Musab were cut to pieces, his son Isa was slain by his side, and he himself, after being repeatedly wounded with arrows was stabbed to the heart, and his head struck off.

When Abd'almâlec entered Cufa in triumph, the fickle inhabitants thronged to welcome him and take the oath of allegiance, and he found himself in quiet possession of both Babylonia and Persian Irak. He distributed great sums of money to win the light affections of the populace, and gave a sumptuous banquet in the citadel to which all were welcome.

In the height of the banquet, when all was revelry, a thought passed through the mind of the Caliph, as to the transient duration of all human grandeur. "Alas!" he ejaculated, "how sweetly we might live, if a shadow would but last!" The same vein of melancholy continued when the banquet was over, and he walked about the castle with an old gray-headed inhabitant, listening to his account of its antiquities and traditions. Every reply of the old man to his questions about things or persons, began with the words, "This was,—That was,—He was."

"Alas!" sighed the Caliph, repeating a verse from an Arabian poet; "every thing new soon runneth to decay, and of every one that is, it is soon said, He was!"

While thus conversing, the head of Musab was brought to him, and he ordered a thousand dinars of gold to the soldier who brought it, but he refused the reward. "I slew him," he said, "not for money, but to avenge a private wrong." The old chronicler of the castle now broke forth on the wonderful succession of events. "I am fourscore and ten years old," said he, "and have outlived many generations. In this very castle I have seen the head of Hosein presented to Obeid'allah, the son of Ziyad; then the head of Obeid'allah to Al Moktâr; then the head of Al Moktâr to Musab, and now that of Musab to yourself." The Caliph was superstitious, and the words of the old man sounded ominously as the presage of a brief career to himself. He determined that his own head should not meet with similar fate within that castle's walls, and gave orders to raze the noble citadel of Cufa to the foundation.

Abd'almâlec now appointed his brother Besher Ibn Merwân to the government of Babylonia; and as he was extremely young, he gave him, as chief counsellor, or vizier, a veteran named Musa Ibn Nosseyr, who had long enjoyed the confidence of the family of Merwân, as had his father before him. It is said by some that his

father Nosseyr was a liberated slave of the Caliph's brother
Abd'alaziz, and employed by him in high functions. So great was
the confidence of the Caliph in Musa, that he intrusted him with
all the military rolls of the province, and signified to him that in
future the responsibility would rest upon him. On taking possession of his government, Besher delivered his seal of office into the
hands of Musa, and intrusted him with' the entire management of
affairs. This Musa, it will be found, rose afterwards to great.
renown.

The Caliph also appointed Khaled Ibn Abdallah to the command
at Bassora, after which he returned to his capital of Damascus.
The province of Babylonia, however, was not destined to remain
long at peace. There was at this time a powerful Moslem sect in
Persia, a branch of the Motalazites, called Azarakites from the
name of their founder Ibn Al Azarak, but known also by the name
of Separatists. They were enemies of all regular government, and
fomenters of sedition and rebellion. During the sway of the unfortunate Musab, they had given him great trouble by insurrections
in various parts of the country, accompanied by atrocious cruel-
ties. They had been kept in check, however, by Mohalleb, the
lieutenant of Musab, and one of the ablest generals of the age;
who was incessantly on the alert at the head of the army, and never
allowed their insurrections to come to any head.

Mohalleb was on a distant command at the time of the invasion
and conquest. As soon as he heard of the defeat and death of
Musab, and the change in the government of Irak, he hastened to
Bassora to acknowledge allegiance to Abd'almâlec. Khaled accepted his services, in the name of the Caliph, but instead of
returning him to the post he had so well sustained at the head of
the army, appointed him supervisor or collector of tributes, and
gave the command of the forces to his own brother, named
Abd'alaziz. The change was unfortunate. The Azarakites had
already taken breath, and acquired strength during the temporary
absence of their old adversary, Mohalleb; but as soon as they
heard he was no longer in command, they collected all their forces
and made a rapid inroad into Irak.

Abd'alaziz advanced to meet them; but he was new to his own
troops, being a native of Mecca, and he knew little of the character
of the enemy. He was entirely routed, and his wife, a woman of
great beauty, taken captive. A violent dispute arose among the
captors as to the ransom of their prize, some valuing her at one
hundred thousand dinars : until a furious zealot, indignant that
her beauty should cause dissension among them, struck off her
head.

The Caliph Abd'almâlec was deeply grieved when he heard of
this defeat, and wrote to Khaled, emir of Bassora, reproving him
for having taken the command of the army from Mohalleb, a man
of penetrating judgment, and hardened in war, and given it to
Abd'alaziz, "a mere Arab of Mecca." He ordered him, therefore,
to replace Mohalleb forthwith, and wrote also to his brother,
Besher, emir of Babylonia, to send the general reinforcements.

Once more Mohalleb proved his generalship, by defeating the

Azarakites in a signal and bloody battle near the city of Ahwâz; nor did he suffer them to rally, but pursued them over the borders and into the heart of the mountains, until his troops lost almost all their horses, and returned crowned with victory, but wayworn and almost famished.

The effect of all these internal wars was to diminish, for a time, the external terror of the Moslem name. The Greek emperor, during the recent troubles, had made successful incursions into Syria; and Abd'almâlec, finding enemies enough among those of his own faith, had been fain to purchase a humiliating truce of the Christian potentate by an additional yearly tribute of fifty thousand ducats.

CHAPTER LII.

Abd'almâlec makes war upon his rival Caliph in Mecca.—Siege of the sacred city.—
Death of Abdallah.—Demolition and reconstruction of the Caaba.

Abd'almâlec, by his recent victories, had made himself sovereign of all the eastern part of the Moslem dominions; he had protected himself also from the Christian emperor by a disgraceful augmentation of tribute; he now determined to carry a war against his rival, Abdallah, to the very gates of Mecca; and make himself sovereign of an undivided empire.

The general chosen for this important enterprise was Al Hejagi (or Hedjadgi) Ibn Yusef, who rose to renown as one of the ablest and most eloquent men of that era. He set off from Damascus with but two thousand men; but was joined by Taric Ibn Amar with five thousand more. Abd'almâlec had made proclamations beforehand, promising protection and favour to such of the adherents of Abdallah as should come unto his allegiance, and he trusted that many of the inhabitants of Mecca would desert to the standard of Al Hejagi.

Abdallah sent forth troops of horse to waylay and check the advance of the army, but they were easily repulsed, and Al Hejagi arrived without much difficulty before the sacred city. Before proceeding to hostilities he discharged arrows over the walls carrying letters, in which the inhabitants were assured that he came merely to release them from the tyranny of Abdallah; and were invited to accept the most favourable terms, and abandon a man who would fain die with the title of Caliph, though the ruins of Mecca should be his sepulchre.

The city was now assailed with battering-rams and catapultas; breaches were made in the walls; the houses within were shattered by great stones, or set on fire by flaming balls of pitch and naphtha.

A violent storm of thunder and lightning killed several of the besiegers, and brought them to a pause. "Allah is wreaking his anger upon us," said they, "for assailing his holy city."   Al Hejagi rebuked their superstitious fears and compelled them to renew the attack; setting them an example by discharging a stone with his own hands.

On the following day there was another storm which did most injury to the garrison. "You perceive," said Al Hejagi, "the thunder strikes your enemies as well as yourselves."

The besieged held out valiantly, and repulsed every assault. Abdallah, though now aged and infirm, proved himself a worthy son of Zobeir. During the early part of the siege, he resided chiefly in the Caaba; that sacred edifice, therefore, became an object of attack; a part of it was battered down by stones, and it was set on fire repeatedly by the balls of naphtha. He therefore abandoned it, and retired to his own dwelling. He was sustained throughout all this time of peril by the presence and counsels of his mother; a woman of masculine spirit and unfailing energy, though ninety years of age. · She was the granddaughter of Abu Beker, and proved herself worthy of her descent. She accompanied her son to the ramparts; caused refreshments to be distributed among the fighting men; was consulted in every emergency and present in every danger.

The siege continued with unremitting strictness; many of Abdallah's most devoted friends were killed; others became disheartened; nearly ten thousand of the inhabitants deserted to the enemy; even two of the Caliph's sons, Hamza and Koheib, forsook him, and made terms for themselves with the besiegers.

In this forlorn state, his means of defence almost exhausted, and those who ought to have been most faithful. deserting him; Abdallah was tempted by an offer of his own terms on condition of surrender.

He turned to his aged mother for advice. "Judge for yourself, my son," said the resolute descendant of Abu Beker. "If you feel that your cause is just, persevere. Your father Zobeir died for it, as did many of your friends. Do not bend your neck to the scorn of the haughty race of Ommiah. How much better an honourable death, than a dishonoured life for the brief term you have yet to live."

The Caliph kissed her venerable forehead. "Thy thoughts are my own," said he, "nor has any other motive than zeal for God induced me thus far to persevere. From this moment, consider thy son as dead; and refrain from immoderate lamentation." "My trus is in God," replied she, "and I shall have comfort in thee, my son, whether I go before or follow thee."

As she took a parting embrace, she felt a coat of mail under the outer garments of Abdallah, and told him to put it off, as unsuited to a martyr prepared to die. "I have worn it, replied he, "that I might be the better able to defend thee, my mother." He added that he had little fear of death, but a horror of the insults and exposures to which his body might be subjected after death.

"A sheep once killed, my son, feels not the flaying." With these words she gave him to rouse his spirits, a cordial draught in which was a strong infusion of musk, and Abdallah went forth a self-devoted martyr.

This last sally of the veteran Caliph struck terror and astonishment into the enemy. At the head of a handful of troops he repulsed them from the breach; drove them into the ditch, and slew an incredible number with his own hand; others, however, thronged up in their place : he fought until his followers were slain, his arrows expended, and he had no weapon but sword and lance. He now retreated, step by step, with his face to the foe, disputing every inch of ground, until he arrived in a narrow place where he could only be assailed in front. Here he made his last stand. His opponents, not daring to come within reach of his weapons, assailed him from a distance with darts and arrows, and when these missiles were expended, with bricks, and tiles and stones. A blow on the head from a stone made him totter, and the blood streamed down his face and beard. His assailants gave a shout ; but he recovered himself and uttered a verse of a poet, " The blood of our wounds falls on our instep, not on our heels ;" implying that he had not turned his back upon the foe. At length he sank under repeated wounds and bruises, and the enemy closing upon him cut off his head. Thus died Abdallah the son of Zobeir, in the seventy-third year of the Hegira, and the seventy-second year of his own age, after a stormy and disastrous reign of nine years.

Taric Ibn Amar, struck with admiration of his persevering valour, exclaimed, " Never did woman bear a braver son !" " How is this," cried Al Hejagi, " do you speak thus of an enemy of the Commander of the Faithful ?" But Abd'almâlec, when the speech was reported to him, concurred in the praise of his fallen rival. " By Allah !" exclaimed he, " what Taric hath spoken is the truth." When the tidings of Abdallah's death were brought to his aged mother, she experienced a revulsion of nature which she had not known for fifty years, and died of hemorrhage.

Abdallah was said to unite the courage of the lion with the Craftiness of the fox. He was free from any glaring vice, but reputed to be sordidly covetous and miserly, insomuch that he wore the same garment for several years. It was a saying in Arabia, that he was the first example of a man being at the same time brave and covetous; but the spoils of foreign conquest were fast corrupting the chivalrous spirit of the Arab conquerors. He was equally renowned for piety, being according to tradition so fixed and immovable in prayer, that a pigeon once perched upon his head mistaking him for a statue.

With the death of Abdallah ended the rival Caliphat, and the conquering general received the oaths of allegiance of the Arabs for Abd'almâlec. His conduct, however, toward the people of Mecca and Medina, was as cruel and oppressive as his military operations had been brilliant. He inflicted severe punishments for trivial offences, sometimes on mere suspicion; and marked many with stamps of lead upon the neck, to disgrace them in the public eye. His most popular act was the reconstruction of the dilapidated Caaba on the original form which it had borne before the era of the prophet.

For a time the people of Mecca and Medina groaned under his

tyranny, and looked back with repining to the gentler sway of Abdallah; and it was a cause of general joy throughout those cities,
when the following circumstances caused him to be removed from
their government and promoted to a distant command.

Though the death of Abdallah had rendered Abd'almâlec sole
sovereign of the Moslem empire, the emir of Khorassan, Abdallah
Ibn Hazem, who had been appointed by his rival, hesitated to give
in his allegiance. His province, so distant and great in extent,
might make him a dangerous rebel; Abd'almâlec, therefore, sent
a messenger, claiming his oath of fealty, and proffering him in
reward, the government of Khorassan for seven years, with the
enjoyment of all its revenues; at the same time, he sent him the
head of the deceased Caliph, to intimate the fate he might expect
should he prove refractory.

The emir, instead of being intimidated, was filled with horror,
and swore never to acknowledge Abd'almâlec as Commander of
the Faithful. He reverently washed and embalmed the head, folded
it in fine linen, prayed over it, and sent it to the family of the deceased Caliph at Medina. Then summoning the messenger, he made
him eat the epistle of Abd'almâlec in his presence, and dismissed
him with the assurance that his sacred character of herald alone
saved his head.

It was to go against this refractory but high-minded emir, that
Al Hejagi was called off from his commmand in Arabia. He entered
Khorassan with a powerful army, defeated the emir in repeated
battles, and at length slew him and reduced the province to
obedience.

The vigour, activity, and indomitable courage displayed by Al
Hejagi in these various services, pointed him out as the very man
to take charge of the government of Babylonia, or Irak, recently
vacated by the death of the Caliph's brother Besher; and he was
accordingly sent to break that refractory province into more
thorough obedience.

The province of Babylonia, though formerly a part of the Persian empire, had never been really Persian in character. Governed
by viceroys, it had partaken of the alien feeling of a colony:
forming a frontier between Persia and Arabia, and its population
made up from both countries, it was deficient in the virtues of
either. The inhabitants had neither the simplicity and loyalty of
the Arabs of the desert, nor the refinement and cultivation of the
Persians of the cities. Restless, turbulent, factious, they were ever
ready to conspire against their rulers; to desert old faiths, and to
adopt new sects and heresies. Before the conquest by the Moslems, when Irak was governed by a Persian Satrap, and Syria by
an imperial prefect, a spirit of rivalry and hostility existed between
these frontier provinces; the same had revived during the division
of the Caliphat; and while Syria was zealous in its devotion to the
house of Onmiah, Irak had espoused the cause of Ali. Even since
the reunion and integrity of the Caliphat, it still remained a restless, unsteady part of the Moslem empire; the embers of old sedi-
tions still lurked in its bosom, ready at any moment once more to
burst forth into flame. We shall see how Al Hejagi fared in his
government of that combustible province.

CHAPTER LIII.

Administration of Al Hejagi as Emir of Babylonia.

Al Hejagi, aware of the nature of the people over whom he was to rule, took possession of his government in military style. Riding into Cufa at the head of four thousand horse, he spurred on to the mosque, alighted at the portal, and ascending the pulpit, delivered an harangue to the multitude, that let them know the rigorous rule they were to expect. He had come, he said, "to make the wicked man bear his own burden, and wear his own shoe;" and, as he looked round on the densely-crowded assemblage, he intimated he saw before him turbaned heads ripe for mowing, and beards which required to be moistened with blood.

His sermon was carried out in practice; he ruled with a rigorous hand, swearing he would execute justice in a style that should put to shame all who had preceded, and serve as an example to all who might follow him. He was especially severe, and even cruel, towards all who had been in any way implicated in the assassination of the Caliph Othman. One person, against whom he came prepared to exercise the utmost severity, was the veteran Musa Ibn Nosseyr, who had officiated as prime minister to the deceased emir Besher. He had been accused of appropriating and squandering the taxes collected in the province, and the Caliph had lent a too ready ear to the accusation. Fortunately, the following letter, from a friend in Damascus, apprised Musa in time of his danger:

"Thy deposition is signed; orders have been despatched to Al Hejagi to seize on thy person and inflict on thee the most severe punishment: so away! away! thy safety depends on the fleetness of thy horse. If thou succeed in placing thyself under the protection of Abd'alaziz Ibn Merwân, all will go well with thee."

Musa lost no time, but mounted his steed and fled to Damascus, where Abd'alaziz was then sojourning, having arrived with the tribute of Egypt. Abd'alaziz received with protecting kindness the veteran adherent of the family, and accompanied him before the Caliph. "How darest thou show thy beard here," exclaimed Abd'almâlec?" "Why should I hide it?" replied the veteran; "what have I done to offend the Commander of the Faithful?" "Thou hast disobeyed my orders, and squandered my treasures." "I did no such thing," replied Musa, firmly; "I have always acted like a faithful subject; my intentions have been pure; my actions true." "By Allah," cried the Caliph, "thou shalt make thy defalcation good fifty times over." The veteran was about to make an angry reply, but at a sign from Abd'alaziz, he checked himself, and bowing his head, "Thy will be done," said he, "oh, Commander of the Faithful." He was fined fifty thousand dinars of gold; which, however, Abd'alaziz enabled him to pay; and, on his return to his government in Egypt, took his old favourite with him. How he further indemnified Musa for his maltreatment will be shown hereafter. ,

To resume the affairs of Al Hejagi in Irak. Having exercised the rod of government in Cufa, he proceeded to Bassora, where he was equally sharp with this tongue, and heavy with his hand. The consequence was, as usual, an insurrection. This suited his humour. He was promptly in the field; defeated the rebels in a pitched battle; sent the heads of eighteen of their leaders to the Caliph, and then returned to the administration of affairs at Bassora. He afterwards sent two of his lieutenants to suppress a new movement among the Azarakite sectaries, who were defeated and driven out of the province.

In the 76th year of the Hegira, a conspiracy was formed against the life of Abd'almâlec, by two Karegite fanatics, named Shebib Ibn Zeid and Saleh Ibn Mari. Their conspiracy was discovered and defeated, but they made their escape and repaired to the town of Daras, in Mesopotamia, where they managed to get together adherents to the number of one hundred and twenty men. Saleh was smooth-tongued and seductive; having a melodious voice and a great command of figurative language. He completely fascinated and bewildered his companion Shebib, and their infatuated followers, mingling his inflammatory harangues with pious precepts and expositions of the Koran. In the end he was hailed Commander of the Faithful by the motley crew, and gravely accepted the office. His men were all armed, but most of them were on foot; he therefore, led them, to a neighbouring village, where they seized upon the best horses in the name of Allah and the prophet, to whom they referred the owners for payment.

Mahomet, brother of Abd'almâlec, who was at that time emir of Mesopotamia, was moved to laughter when he heard of this new Caliph and his handful of rabble followers; and ordered Adi, one of his officers, to take five hundred men and sweep them from the province.

Adi shook his head doubtfully, "One madman," said he, " is more dangerous than five soldiers in their senses."

"Take one thousand then," said the emir; and with that number well armed and mounted, Adi set out in quest of the fanatics. He found them and their pseudo Caliph living in free quarters on the fat of the land, and daily receiving recruits in straggling parties of two, and three, and four at a time, armed with such weapons as they could catch up in their haste. On the approach of Adi they prepared for battle, having full confidence that a legion of angels would fight on their side.

Adi held a parley, and endeavoured to convince them of the absurdity of their proceedings, or to persuade them to carry their marauding enterprises elsewhere; but Saleh, assuming the tone of Caliph as well as sectarian, admonished Adi and his men to conform to his doctrines, and come into his allegiance. The conference ended while it was yet morning hour. Adi still forbore to attack such a handful of misguided men, and paid dearly for his

forbearance. At noontide, when he and his men were engaged
in the customary prayer, and their steeds were feeding, the enthusiast band charged suddenly upon them with the cry of Allah
Achbar! Adi was slain in the onset, and his body was trampled
under foot; his troops were slaughtered or dispersed, and his camp
and horses, with a good supply of arms, became welcome booty to
the victors.

The band of sectarians increased in numbers and in daring after
this signal exploit. Al Hejagi sent five thousand veteran troops
against them, under Al Hareth Alamdani. These came by surprise
upon the two leaders, Saleh and Shebib, with a party of only
ninety men, at a village on the Tigris not far from Mosul, the capital of Mesopotamia. The fanatic chiefs attacked the army with
a kind of frantic courage, but Saleh, the mock Caliph, was instantly
killed, with a score of his followers. Shebib was struck from his
horse, but managed to keep together the remnant of his party;
made good his retreat with them into Montbagi, a dismantled fortress, and swung to and secured the ponderous gate.

The victors kindled a great fire against the gate, and waited
patiently until it should burn down, considering their prey secure.

As the night advanced, Shebib, who from his desolate retreat
watched anxiously for some chance of escape, perceived, by the
light of the fire, that the greater part of the besiegers, fatigued by
their march, were buried in deep sleep. He now exacted from
his men an oath of implicit obedience, which they took between
his hands. He then caused them to steep most of their clothing in
a tank of water within the castle, after which, softly drawing the
bolts of the flaming gate, they threw it down on the fire kindled
against it; flung their wet garments on the burning bridge thus
suddenly formed, and rushed forth scimetar in hand.

Instead of contenting themselves with an escape, the crazy
zealots charged into the very heart of the sleeping camp, and
wounded the general before an alarm was given. The soldiers
started awake in the midst of havoc and confusion; supposing
themselves surprised by a numerous army, they fled in all directions, never ceasing their flight until they had taken refuge in
Mosul or Jukhi, or some other walled city.

Shebib established himself amid the abundance of the deserted
camp; scarce any of his men had been killed or wounded in this
midnight slaughter; he considered himself therefore invincible;
proclaimed himself Commander of the Faithful, and partisans
crowded to his standard. Strengthened by numbers, he led his
fanatic horde against Cufa, and had the address and good fortune
to make himself master of it, Al Hejagi, the emir, being absent at
Bassora. He was soon joined by his wife Gazala; established himself as Caliph with some ceremonial, and doubtless his vagabond
sway was more acceptable to the people of Cufa, than the iron
rule of Al Hejagi.

The mock Caliphat, however, was of brief duration. Al Hejagi,
reinforced by troops from Syria, marched in person against Cufa.
He was boldly met in the plains near that city by Shebib, at the
head of four thousand men. The fanatics were defeated, and Ga-

zala, the wife of the mock Caliph, who had accompanied her husband to the field, was slain. Shebib with a remnant of his force cut his way through the Syrian army; crossed and recrossed the Tigris, and sought refuge and reinforcements in the interior of Persia. He soon returned into Irak, with a force inconsiderable in numbers, but formidable for enthusiasm and desperate valour. He was encountered at the bridge of Dojail al Awaz. Here a sudden and unexpected end was put to his fanatic career. His horse struck his forefeet on some loose stones on the margin of the bridge, and threw his rider into the stream. He rose twice to the surface, and each time uttered a pious ejaculation. "What God decrees is just!" was the first exclamation. "The will of God be done!" was the second, and the waters closed over him. His followers cried with loud lamentations, "The Commander of the Faithful is no more!" and every man betook himself to flight. The water was dragged with a net, the body was found and decapitated, and the head sent to Al Hejagi, who transmitted it to the Caliph. The heart of this enthusiast was also taken out of his breast, and is said to have been as hard as stone. He was assuredly a man of extraordinary daring.

Arabian writers say that the manner of Shebib's death was predicted before his birth. His mother was a beautiful Christian captive, purchased at a public sale by Yezid Ibn Naim for his harem. Just before she gave birth so Shebib, she had a dream that a coal of fire proceeded from her, and after enkindling a flame over the firmament, fell into the sea and was extinguished. This dream was interpreted that she would give birth to a man-child, who would prove a distinguished warrior, but would eventually be drowned. So strong was her belief in this omen, that when she heard, on one occasion, of his defeat and of his alleged death on the battle-field, she treated the tidings as an idle rumour, saying it was by water only her son would die. At the time of Shebib's death he had just passed his fiftieth year.

The emir Al Hejagi was destined to have still farther commotions in his turbulent and inconstant province. A violent feud existed between him and Abda'lrahman Ibn Mohammed, a general subject to his orders. To put an end to it, or to relieve himself from the presence of an enemy, he sent him on an expedition to the frontiers against the Turks. Abda'lrahman set out on his march, but when fairly in the field, with a force at his command, conceived a project either of revenge or ambition.

Addressing his soldiers in a spirited harangue, he told them that their numbers were totally inadequate to the enterprise; that the object of Al Hejagi in sending him on such a dangerous service with such incompetent means, was to effect his defeat and ruin, and that they had been sent to be sacrificed with him.

The harangue produced the desired effect. The troops vowed devotion to Abda'lrahman and vengeance upon the emir. Without giving their passion time to cool, he led them back to put their threats in execution. Al Hejagi heard of the treason, and took the field to meet them, but probably was not well seconded by the people of Babylonia, for he was defeated in a pitched battle.

Abda'lrahman then marched to the city of Bassora; the inhabitants welcomed him as their deliverer from a tyrant, and, captivated by his humane and engaging manners, hailed him as Caliph. Intoxicated by his success, he gravely assumed the title, and proceeded toward Cufa. Encountering Al Hejagi on the way, with a hastily levied army, he gave him another signal defeat, and then entered Cufa in triumph, amid the shouts of its giddy populace, who were delighted with any change that released them from the yoke of Al Hejagi.

Abda'lrahman was now acknowledged Caliph throughout the territories bordering on the Euphrates and the Tigris, a mighty empire in ancient days, and still important from its population, for he soon had on foot an army of one hundred thousand men.

Repeated defeat had but served to rouse the energy of Al Hejagi. He raised troops among such of the people of Irak as remained faithful to Abd'almâlec; received reinforcements from the Caliph, and by dint of indefatigable exertions was again enabled to take the field.

The two generals, animated by deadly hate, encamped their armies at places not far apart. Here they remained between three and four months, keeping vigilant eye upon each other, and engaged in incessant conflicts, though never venturing upon a pitched battle.

The object of Al Hejagi was to gain an advantage by his superior military skill, and he succeeded. By an artful manœuvre he cut off Abda'lrahman, with a body of five thousand men, from his main army ; compelled him to retreat, and drove him to take refuge in a fortified town; where, being closely besieged, and having no hope of escape, he threw himself headlong from a lofty tower, rather than fall into the hands of his cruel enemy.

Thus terminated the rebellion of this second mock Caliph, and Al Hejagi, to secure the tranquillity of Irak, founded a strong city on the Tigris, called Al Wazab, or the Centre, from its lying at equal distance from Cufa, Bassora, Bagdad, and Ahwâz, about fifty leagues from each.

Al Hejagi, whom we shall have no further occasion to mention, continued emir of Irak until his death, which took place under the reign of the next Caliph, in the ninety-fifth year of the Hegira, and the fifty-fourth of his own age. He is said to have caused the death of one hundred and twenty thousand persons, independent of those who fell in battle, and that, at the time of his death, he left fifty thousand confined in different prisons. Can we wonder that he was detested as a tyrant?

In his last illness, say the Arabian historians, he sent for a noted astrologer, and asked him whether any great general was about to end his days. The learned man consulted the stars, and replied, that a great captain named Kotaib, or 'The Dog,' was at the point of death. "That," said the dying emir, "is the name my mother used to call me when a child." He inquired of the astrologer if he was assured of his prediction. The sage, proud of his art, declared that it was infallible. "Then," said the emir, I will take you with me, that I may have the benefit of your skill in the other world." So saying, he caused his head to be struck off.

The tyranny of this general was relieved at times by displays of great magnificence and acts of generosity, if not clemency. He spread a thousand tables at a single banquet, and bestowed a million dirhems of silver at a single donation.

On one occasion, an Arab, ignorant of his person, spoke of him, in his presence, as a cruel tyrant. "Do you know me?" said Al Hejagi, sternly." "I do not," replied the Arab. "I am Al Hejagi!" "That may be," replied the Arab, quickly; "but do you know me? I am of the family of Zobeir, who are fools in the full of the moon; and if you look upon the heavens you will see that this is my day." The emir laughed at his ready wit, and dismissed him with a present.

On another occasion, when separated from his party while hunting, he came to a spring where an Arab was feeding his camels, and demanded drink. The Arab bade him, rudely, to alight and help himself. It was during the rebellion of Abda'lrahman. After he had slaked his thirst, he demanded of the Arab whether he was for the Caliph Abd'almâlec. The Arab replied "no; for the Caliph had sent the worst man in the world to govern the province." Just then a bird, passing over head, uttered a croaking note. The Arab turned a quick eye upon the emir: "Who art thou?" cried he, with consternation. "Wherefore the question?" "Because I understand the language of birds, and he says that thou art chief of yon horsemen that I see approaching."

The emir smiled, and when his attendants came up, bade them to bring the camel-driver with them. On the next day, he sent for him; had meat set before him, and bade him eat. Before he complied, the Arab uttered a grace, "Allah grant that the end of this meal be as happy as the beginning."

The emir inquired if he recollected their conversation of yesterday. "Perfectly! but I entreat thee to forget it, for it was a secret which should be buried in oblivion."

"Here are two conditions for thy choice," said the emir; "recant what thou hast said and enter into my service, or abide the decision of the Caliph, to whom thy treasonable speech shall be repeated." "There is a third course," replied the Arab, "which is better than either. Send me to my own home, and let us be strangers to each other as heretofore."

The emir was amused by the spirit of the Arab, and dismissed him with a thousand dirhems of silver.

There were no further troubles in Irak during the lifetime of Al Hejagi, and even the fickle, turbulent and faithless people of Cufa became submissive and obedient. Abulfaragius says that this general died of eating dirt. It appears that he was subject to dyspepsia or indigestion, for which he used to eat Terra Lemnia, and other medicinal or absorbent earths. Whether he fell a victim to the malady or the medicine, is not clearly manifest.

CHAPTER LIV.

Renunciation of tribute to the emperor.—Battles in Northern Africa.—The prophet queen Cahina; her achievements and fate.

The seventy-second year of the Hegira, saw the Moslem dominions at length free from rebellion and civil war, and united under one Caliph. Abd'almâlec now looked abroad, and was anxious to revive the foreign glories of Islam, which had declined during the late vicissitudes. His first movement was to throw off the galling tribute to the Greek emperor. This, under Moawyah I, had originally been three thousand dinars of gold, but had been augmented to three hundred and sixty-five thousand; being one thousand for every day in the Christian year. It was accompanied by three hundred and sixty-five female slaves, and three hundred and sixty-five Arabian horses of the most generous race.

Not content with renouncing the payment of tribute, Abd'almâlec sent Alid one of his generals on a ravaging expedition into the imperial dominions, availing himself of a disaffection evinced to the new emperor Leontius. Alid returned laden with spoils. The cities of Lazuca and Baruncium were likewise delivered up to the Moslems through the treachery of Sergius, a Christian general.

Abd'almâlec next sought to vindicate the glory of the Moslem arms along the northern coast of Africa. There, also, the imperialists had taken advantage of the troubles of the Caliphat, to reverse the former successes of the Moslems, and to strengthen themselves along the sea-coast, of which their navy aided them to hold possession. Zohair, who had been left by Abd'almâlec in command of Barca, had fallen into an ambush and been slain with many of his men, and the posts still held by the Moslems were chiefly in the interior.

In the seventy-seventh year of the Hegira, therefore, Abd'-almâlec sent Hossán Ibn An-no'mán, at the head of forty thousand choice troops, to carry out the scheme of African conquest. That general pressed forward at once with his troops against the city of Carthage, which, though declined from its ancient might and glory, was still an important seaport, fortified with lofty walls, haughty towers and powerful bulwarks, and had a numerous garrison of Greeks and other Christians. Hossán proceeded according to the old Arab mode; beleaguering it and reducing it by a long siege; he then assailed it by storm, scaled its lofty walls with ladders, and made himself master of the place. Many of the inhabitants fell by the edge of the sword; many escaped by sea to Sicily and Spain. The walls were then demolished; the city was given up to be plundered by the soldiery, the meanest of whom was enriched by booty. Particular mention is made among the spoils of victory of a great number of female captives of rare beauty.

The triumph of the Moslem host was suddenly interrupted. While they were revelling in the ravaged palaces of Carthage, a fleet appeared before the port; snapped the strong chain which guarded the entrance, and sailed into the harbour. It was a combined force of ships and troops from Constantinople and Sicily; reinforced by Goths from Spain; all under the command of the prefect John, a patrician general of great valour and experience.

Hossán felt himself unable to cope with such a force; he withdrew, however, in good order, and conducted his troops laden with spoils to Tripoli and Caerwân, and having strongly posted them, he awaited reinforcements from the Caliph. These arrived in the course of time, by sea and land. Hossán again took the field; encountered the prefect John, not far from Utica, defeated him in a pitched battle, and drove him to embark the wrecks of his army, and make all sail for Constantinople.

Carthage was again assailed by the victors, and now its desolation was complete, for the vengeance of the Moslems gave that majestic city to the flames. A heap of ruins and the remains of a noble aqueduct, are all the relics of a metropolis that once valiantly contended for dominion with Rome, the mistress of the world.

The imperial forces were now expelled from the coasts of Northern Africa, but the Moslems had not yet achieved the conquest of the country. A formidable enemy remained in the person of a native and heroic queen, who was revered by her subjects as a saint or prophetess. Her real name was Dhabbá, but she is generally known in history by the surname given to her by the Moslems, of Cahina or the Sorceress. She has occasionally been confounded with her son Aben, or rather Ibn Cahina, of whom mention has been made in a previous chapter.

Under the sacred standard of this prophet queen were combined the Moors of Mauritania and the Berbers of the mountains, and of the plains bordering on the interior deserts. Roving and independent tribes, which had formerly warred with each other, now yielded implicit obedience to one common leader, whom they regarded with religious reverence. The character of marabout or saint has ever had vast influence over the tribes of Africa. Under this heroic woman the combined host had been reduced to some degree of discipline, and inspired with patriotic ardour, and were now prepared to make a more effective struggle for their native land than they had yet done under their generals.

After repeated battles, the emir Hossán was compelled to retire with his veteran but diminished army to the frontiers of Egypt. The patriot queen was not satisfied with this partial success. Calling a council of war of the leaders and principal warriors of the different hordes: " This retreat of the enemy," said she, "is but temporary; they will return in greater force. What is it that attracts to our land these Arab spoilers? The wealth of our cities; the treasures of silver and gold digged from the bowels of the earth; the fruits of our gardens and orchards; the produce of our fields. Let us demolish our cities; return these accursed treasures into the earth; fell our fruit trees; lay waste our fields, and spread

24

a barrier' of desolation between us and the country of these robbers!"

The words of the royal prophetess were received with fanatic enthusiasm by her barbarian troops; the greater part of whom, collected from the mountains and from distant parts, had little share in the property to be sacrificed. Walled towns were forthwith dismantled; majestic edifices were tumbled into ruins; groves of fruit trees were hewn down, and the whole country from Tangiers to Tripoli was converted from a populous and fertile region into a howling and barren waste. A short time was sufficient to effect a desolation, which centuries have not sufficed to remedy.

This sacrificial measure of Queen Cahina, however patriotic its intention, was fatal in the end to herself. The inhabitants of the cities and the plains, who had beheld their property laid waste by the infuriated zeal of their defenders, hailed the return of the Moslem invaders as though they had been the saviours of the land.

The Moslems, as Cahina predicted, returned with augmented forces: but when she took the field to oppose them, the ranks of her army were thinned; the enthusiasm which had formerly animated them was at an end: they were routed, after a sanguinary battle, and the heroine fell into the hands of the enemy. Those who captured her spared her life, because she was a woman and a queen. When brought into the presence of Hossán she maintained her haughty and fierce demeanor. He proposed the usual conditions, of conversion or tribute. She refused both with scorn, and fell a victim to her patriotism and religious constancy, being beheaded in presence of the emir.

Hossán Ibn An-no'mán now repaired to Damascus, to give the Caliph an account of his battles and victories; bearing an immense amount of booty, and several signal trophies. The most important of the latter was a precious box, containing the embalmed head of the slaughtered Cahina. He was received with great distinction, loaded with honours, and the government of Barca was added to his military command.

This last honour proved fatal to Hossán. Abd'alaziz Ibn Merwân, the Caliph's brother, was at that time emir of Egypt, and considered the province of Barca a part of the territories under his government. He had, accordingly, appointed one of his officers to command it as his lieutenant. He was extremely displeased and disconcerted, therefore, when he was told that Hossán had solicited and obtained the government of that province. Sending for the latter, as he passed through Egypt on his way to his post, he demanded whether it was true that in addition to his African command, he was really appointed governor of Barca. Being answered in the affirmative, he appeared still to doubt; whereupon Hossán produced the mandate of the Caliph. Finding it correct, Abd'alaziz urged him to resign the office. "Violence only," said Hossán, "shall wrest from me an honour conferred by the Commander of the Faithful." "Then I deprive thee of both governments," exclaimed the emir, in a passion, "and will appoint a better man in thy stead; and my brother will soon perceive the benefit he derives from the change." So saying, he tore the diploma in pieces.

It is added that, not content with depriving Hossán of his command, he despoiled him of all his property, and carried his persecution so far, that the conqueror of Carthage, the slayer of the patriot queen, within a brief time after her death, and almost amid the very scenes of his triumphs, died of a broken heart. His cruel treatment of the heroic Cahina reconciles us to the injustice wreaked upon himself.

CHAPTER LV.

Musa Ibn Nosseyr made emir of Northern Africa.—His campaigns against the Berbers.

The general appointed by the Caliph's brother, Abd'alaziz Ibn Merwân, to the command in Northern Africa, was Musa Ibn Nosseyr, the same old adherent of the Merwân family that had been prime counsellor of the Caliph's brother Besher, when emir of Iràk, and had escaped by dint of hoof from the clutches of Al Hejagi, when the latter was about to arrest him on a charge of squandering the public funds. Abd'alaziz, it will be remembered, assisted him to pay the fifty thousand dinars of gold, in which he was mulcted by the Caliph, and took him with him to Egypt; and it may have been with some view to self-reimbursement, that the Egyptian emir now took the somewhat bold step of giving him the place assigned to Hossán, by Abd'almâlec.

At the time of his appointment, Musa was sixty years of age. He was still active and vigorous; of noble presence, and concealed his age by tinging his hair and beard with henna. He had three brave sons who aided him in his campaigns, and in whom he took great pride. The eldest he had named Abd'alaziz, after his patron; he was brave and magnanimous, in the freshness of his youth and his father's right hand in all his enterprises. Another of his sons, he had called Merwân, the family name of Abd'alaziz and the Caliph.

Musa joined the army at its African encampment, and addressed his troops in frank and simple language. "I am a plain soldier like yourselves," said he; "whenever I act well, thank God, and endeavour to imitate me. When I do wrong, reprove me, that I may amend; for we are all sinners and liable to err. If any one has at any time a complaint to make, let him state it frankly, and it shall be attended to. I have orders from the emir Abd'alaziz (to whom God be bountiful!) to pay you three times the amount of your arrears. Take it, and make good use of it." It is needless to say, that the address, especially the last part, was received with acclamations.

While Musa was making his harangue, a sparrow fluttered into his bosom. Interpreting it as a good omen, he called for a knife; cut off the bird's head; besmeared the bosom of his vest with the

blood, and scattering. the feathers in the air above his head—
"Victory! Victory!" he cried, "by the master of the Caaba, victory is ours!"

· It is evident that Musa understood the character and foibles of his troops; he soon won their favour by his munificence, and still more by his affability; always accosting them with kind words and cheerful looks; carefully avoiding the errour of those reserved commanders, shut up in the fancied dignity of station, who looked, he said, "as if God had tied a knot in their throats, so that they could not utter a word."

"A commander," he used to say, "ought to consult wise and experienced men in every undertaking; but when he has made up his mind, he should be firm and steady of purpose. He should be brave, adventurous, at times even rash, confiding in his good fortune, and endeavouring to do more than is expected of him. He should be doubly cautious after victory; doubly brave after defeat."

' Musa found a part of Eastern Africa, [1] forming the present states of Tunis and Algiers, in complete confusion and insurrection. A Berber chief, Warkattáf by name, scoured night and day the land between Zaghwan and Caerwan. The Berbers had this advantage; if routed in the plains they took refuge in the mountains, which ran parallel to the coast, forming part of the great chain of Atlas; in the fastnesses of these mountains they felt themselves secure; but should they be driven out of these, they could plunge into the boundless deserts of the interior, and bid defiance to pursuit.

The energy of Musa rose with the difficulty of his enterprise. "Take courage," would he say to his troops. "God is on our side, and will enable us to cope with our enemies, however strong their holds. By Allah! I'll carry the war into yon haughty mountains, nor cease until we have seized upon their passes, surmounted their summits, and made ourselves masters of the country beyond."

His words were not an empty threat. Having vanquished the Berbers in the plains, he sent his sons Abd'alaziz and Merwân with troops in different directions, who attacked the enemy in their mountain-holds, and drove them beyond to the borders of the Southern·desert. Warkattáf was slain with many of his warriors, and Musa had the gratification of seeing his sons return triumphant from their different expeditions, bringing to the camp thousands of captives and immense booty. Indeed the number of prisoners of both sexes, taken in these campaigns, is said to have amounted to three hundred-thousand; of whom one-fifth, or sixty thousand, formed the Caliph's share.

Musa hastened to write an account of his victories to his patron Abd'alaziz Ibn Merwân, and as he knew covetousness to be the prime failing of the emir, he sent him, at the same time, a great share of the spoils, with choice horses and female slaves of surpassing beauty.

---

[1] Northern Africa, extending from Egypt to the extremity of Mauritania, was subdivided into Eastern and Western Africa.

The letter and the present came most opportunely. Abd'alaziz had just received a letter from his brother, the Caliph, rebuking him for having deposed Hossán, a brave, experienced and fortunate officer, and given his office to Musa, a man who had formerly incurred the displeasure of the government; and he was ordered forthwith to restore Hossán to his command.

In reply, Abd'alaziz transmitted the news of the African victories. "I have just received from Musa," writes he, "the letter which I inclose, that thou mayest peruse it, and give thanks to God."

Other tidings came to the same purport, accompanied by a great amount of booty. The Caliph's feelings toward Musa immediately changed. He at once saw his fitness for the post he occupied, and confirmed the appointment of Abd'alaziz, making him emir of Africa. He, moreover, granted yearly pensions of two hundred pieces of gold to himself and one hundred to each of his sons, and directed him to select from among his soldiers five hundred of those who had most distinguished themselves in battle, or received most wounds, and give them each thirty pieces of gold. Lastly, he revoked the fine formerly imposed upon him of fifty thousand dinars of gold, and authorized him to reimburse himself out of the Caliph's share of the spoil.

This last sum Musa declined to receive for his own benefit, but publicly devoted it to the promotion of the faith and the good of its professors. Whenever a number of captives were put up for sale after a victory, he chose from among them those who were young, vigorous, intelligent, of noble origin, and who appeared disposed to be instructed in the religion of Islam. If they were converted, and proved to have sufficient talent, he gave them their liberty, and appointed them to commands in his army; if otherwise, he returned them to the mass of captives, to be disposed of in the usual manner.

The fame of Musa's victories, and of the immense spoil collected by his troops, brought recruits to his standard from Egypt and Syria, and other distant parts; for rapine was becoming more and more the predominant passion of the Moslems. The army of Musa was no longer composed, like the primitive armies of the faith, merely of religious zealots. The campaigns in foreign countries, and the necessity, at distant points, of recruiting the diminished ranks from such sources as were at hand, had relaxed the ancient scruples, as to unity of faith, and men of different creeds now fought under the standard of Islam without being purified by conversion. The army was, therefore, a motley host of every country and kind; Arabs and Syrians, Persians and Copts, and nomadic Africans; arrayed in every kind of garb, and armed with every kind of weapon. Musa had succeeded in enlisting in his service many of the native tribes; a few of them were Christians, a greater proportion idolaters, but the greatest number professed Judaism. They readily amalgamated with the Arabs, having the same nomad habits, and the same love of war and rapine. They even traced their origin to the same Asiatic stock. According to their traditions five colonies, or tribes, came in ancient times from Sabæa, in

Arabia the Happy; being expelled thence with their king Ifrique. From these descended the five most powerful Berber tribes, the Zenhagians, Muzamudas, Zenetes, Gomeres and Hoares.

Musa artfully availed himself of these traditions; addressed the conquered Berbers as Aulad-arabi (sons of the Arabs), and so soothed their pride by this pretended consanguinity, that many readily embraced the Moslem faith, and thousands of the bravest men of Numidia enrolled themselves, of their own free will, in the armies of Islam.

Others, however, persisted in waging stubborn war with the invaders of their country, and among these, the most powerful and intrepid, were the Zenetes. They were a free, independent and haughty race. Marmol, in his description of Africa, represents them as inhabiting various parts of the country. Some leading a roving live about the plains, living in tents like the Arabs; others having castles and strongholds in the mountains; others, very troglodytes, infesting the dens and caves of Mount Atlas, and others wandering on the borders of the Libyan desert.

The Gomeres were also a valiant and warlike tribe, inhabiting the mountains of the lesser Atlas, in Mauritania, bordering the frontiers of Ceuta, while the Muzamudas lived in the more western part of that extreme province, where the great Atlas advances into the Atlantic Ocean.

In the eighty-third year of the Hegira, Musa made one of his severest campaigns against a combined force of these Berber tribes, collected under the banners of their several princes. They had posted themselves in one of the fastnesses of the Atlas mountains, to which the only approach was through different gorges and defiles. All these were defended with great obstinacy, but were carried, one after the other, after several days of severe fighting.

The armies at length found themselves in presence of each other, when a general conflict was unavoidable. As they were drawn out, regarding each other with menacing aspect, a Berber chief advanced, and challenged any one of the Moslem cavaliers to single combat. There was a delay in answering to the challenge; whereupon Musa turned to his son Merwân, who had charge of the banners, and told him to meet the Berber warrior. The youth handed his banner to his brother Abd'alaziz, and stepped forward with alacrity. The Berber, a stark and seasoned warrior of the mountains, regarded with surprise and almost scorn, an opponent scarce arrived at manhood. "Return to the camp," cried he, "I would not deprive thine aged father of so comely a son." Merwân replied but with his weapon, assailing his adversary so vigorously, that he retreated and sprang upon his horse. He now urged his steed upon the youth, and made a thrust at him with a javelin, but Merwân seized the weapon with one hand, and with the other thrust his own javelin through the Berber's side, burying it in the flanks of the steed; so that both horse and rider were brought to the ground and slain.

The two armies now closed in a general struggle; it was bloody and desperate, but ended in the complete defeat of the Berbers. Kasleyah, their king, fell, fighting to the last. A vast number of captives were taken; among them were many beautiful maidens, daughters of princes and military chiefs. At the division of the spoil, Musa caused these high-born damsels to stand before him, and bade Merwân, his son, who had so recently distinguished himself, to choose among them. The youth chose one who was a daughter of the late king Kasleyah. She appears to have found solace for the loss of her father in the arms of a youthful husband; and ultimately made Merwân the father of two sons, Musa and Abd'almâlec.

CHAPTER LVI.

Naval enterprises of Musa.—Cruisings of his son Abdolola.—Death of Abd'almâlec.

The bold and adventurous spirit of Musa Ibn Nosseyr was not content with victories on land. "Always endeavour to do more than is expected of thee," was his maxim, and he now aspired to achieve triumphs on the sea. He had ports within his province, whence the Phœnicians and Carthaginians, in the days of their power, had fitted out maritime enterprises. Why should he not do the same?

The feelings of the Arab conquerors had widely changed in regard to naval expeditions. When Amru, the conqueror of Egypt, was at Alexandria, the Caliph Omar required of him a description of the Mediterranean. "It is a great pool," replied Amru, "which some foolhardy people furrow; looking like ants on logs of wood." The answer was enough for Omar, who was always apprehensive that the Moslems would endanger their conquests by rashly-extended enterprises. He forbade all maritime expeditions. Perhaps he feared that the inexperience of the Arabs would expose them to defeat from the Franks and Romans, who were practised navigators.

Moawyah, however, as we have shown, more confident of the Moslem capacity for nautical warfare, had launched the banner of Islam on the sea from the ancient ports of Tyre and Sidon, and had scoured the eastern waters of the Mediterranean. The Moslems now had armaments in various ports of Syria and Egypt, and warred with the Christians by sea as well as by land. Abd'almâlec had even ordered Musa's predecessor, Hossân, to erect an arsenal at Tunis; Musa now undertook to carry those orders into effect; to found dock-yards, and to build a fleet for his proposed enterprise.

At the outset he was surrounded by those sage doubters who are ever ready to chill the ardour of enterprise. They pronounced the scheme rash and impracticable. A gray-headed Berber, who had been converted to Islam, spoke in a different tone. "I am one hundred and twenty years old," said he, "and I well remember hearing my father say, that when the Lord of Carthage thought of building his city, the people all, as at present, exclaimed against

it as impracticable; one alone rose and said, oh king, put thy hand
to the work and it will be achieved; for the kings thy predecessors
persévered and achieved every thing they undertook, whatever
might be the difficulty.   And I say to thee, oh emir, put thy hand
to this work, and God will help thee! "

Musa did put his hand to the work, and so effectually, that by
the conclusion of the eighty-fourth year of the Hegira, A. D. 703,
the arsenal and dock-yard were complete, and furnished with
maritime stores, and there was a numerous fleet in the port of
Tunis.

About this time a Moslem fleet, sent by Abd'alaziz, the emir of
Egypt, to make a ravaging descent on the coast of Sardinia,
entered the port of Susa, which is between Caerwan and Tunis.
Musa sent provisions to the fleet, but wrote to the commander,
Attá Ibn Rafi, cautioning him that the season was too late for his
enterprise, and advising him to remain in port until more favourable
time and weather.

Attá treated his letter with contempt, as the advice of a landsman:
and having refitted his vessels, put to sea. He landed on an island,
called by the Arab writers, Salsalah, probably Linosa or Lam-
pedosa; made considerable booty of gold, silver, and precious,
stones, and again set sail on his plundering cruise. A violent storm
arose, his ships were dashed on the rocky coast of Africa, and he
and nearly all his men were drowned.

Musa, hearing of the disaster, despatched his son, Abd'alaziz,
with a troop of horse to the scene of the shipwreck, to render all
the assistance in his power; ordering that the vessels and crews
which survived the storm, should repair to the port of Tunis; all
which was done.   At the place of the wreck Abd'alaziz found a
heavy box cast up on the sea-shore; on being opened, its contents
proved to be the share of spoil of one of the warriors of the fleet,
who had perished in the sea.

The author of the tradition from which these facts are gleaned,
adds, that one day he found an old man sitting on the sea-shore
with a reed in his hand, which he attempted to take from him.   A
scuffle ensued; he wrested the reed from his hands, and struck
him with it over his head; when lo, it broke, and out fell gold
coins and pearls and precious stones.   Whether the old man, thus
hardly treated, was one of the wrecked cruisers, or a wrecker,
seeking to profit by their misfortunes, is not specified in the tradition.   The anecdote shows in what a random way the treasures
of the earth were in those days scattered about the world by the
predatory hosts of Islam.

The surviving ships having been repaired, and added to those
recently built at Tunis, and the season having become favourable,
Musa, early in the eighty-fifth year of the Hegira, declared his
intention to undertake, in person, a naval expedition.   There was
a universal eagerness among the troops to embark; Musa selected
about a thousand of the choicest of his warriors, especially those
of rank and family, so that the enterprise was afterwards designated
The Expedition of the Nobles.   He did not, however, accompany
it as he had promised; he had done so merely to enlist his bravest

men in the undertaking; the command was given to his son, Abdo-lola, to give him an opportunity to distinguish himself; for the reputation of his sons was as dear to Musa as his own.

It was, however, a mere predatory cruise; a type of the ravaging piracies from the African ports in after ages. Abdolola coasted the fair island of Sicily with his ships, landed on the western side, and plundered a city which yielded such abundant spoil, that each of the thousand men embarked in the cruise received one hundred dinars of gold for his share. This done, the fleet returned to Africa.

Soon after the return of his ships, Musa received news of the death of his patron Abd'alaziz, which was followed soon after by tidings of the death of the Caliph. On hearing of the death of the latter, Musa immediately sent a messenger to Damascus to take the oath of allegiance, in his name, to the new Caliph; to inform him of the naval achievements of his son Abdolola, and to deliver to him his share of the immense booty gained. The effect of course was to secure his continuance in office as emir of Africa.

The malady which terminated in the death of Abd'almâlec is supposed to have been the dropsy. It was attended in its last stages with excessive thirst, which was aggraved by the prohibition of his physicians that any water should be given to him, lest it should cause certain death. In the paroxysms of his malady the expiring Caliph demanded water of his son Waled; it was withheld through filial piety. His daughter, Fatima, approached with a flagon, but Waled interfered and prevented her; whereupon the Caliph threatened him with disinheritance and his malediction. Fatima handed to him the flagon, he drained it at a draught, and almost instantly expired. He was about sixty years old at the time of his death, and had reigned about twenty years. Abulfeda gives him a character for learning, courage, and foresight. He certainly showed ability and management in reuniting, under his sway, the dismembered portions of the Moslem empire, and quelling the various sects that rose in arms against him. His foresight with regard to his family also, was crowned with success, as four of his sons succeeded him, severally, in the Caliphat.

He evinced an illiberal spirit of hostility to the memory of Ali, carrying it to such a degree that he would not permit the poet Ferazdak to celebrate in song the virtues of any of his descendants. Perhaps this may have gained for Abd'almâlec another by-name with which some of the Arab writers have signalized his memory, calling him the "Father of Flies;" for so potent, say they, was his breath, that any fly which alighted on his lips died on the spot.

CHAPTER LVII.

Inauguration of Waled, 12th Caliph.—Revival of the arts under his reign.—His taste for architecture.—Erection of mosques.—Conquests of his generals.

Waled, the eldest son of Abd'almâlec, was proclaimed Caliph at Damascus immediately on the death of his father, in the eighty-sixth year of the Hegira, and the year 705 of the Christian era. He was about thirty-eight years of age ; and is described as being tall and robust, with a swarthy complexion, a face much pitted with the small-pox, and a broad flat nose ; in other respects, which are left to our conjecture, he is said to have been of a good countenance. His habits were indolent and voluptuous, yet he was of a choleric temper, and somewhat inclined to cruelty.

During the reign of Waled the arts began to develope themselves under the Moslem sway ; finding a more genial home in the luxurious city of Damascus, than they had done in the holy cities of Mecca or Medina. Foreign conquests had brought the Arabs in contact with the Greeks and the Persians. Intercourse with them, and residence in their cities, had gradually refined away the gross habits of the desert ; had awakened thirst for the sciences, and a relish for the elegancies of cultivated life. Little skilled in the principles of government, accustomed in their native deserts to the patriarchal rule of separate tribes, without any extended scheme of policy, or combined system of union, the Arabs, suddenly masters of a vast and continually widening empire, had to study the art of governing in the political institutions of the countries they conquered. Persia, the best organized monarchy in Asia, held out a model by which they were fain to profit ; and in their system of emirs vested with the sway of distant and powerful provinces, but strictly responsible to the Caliph, we see a copy of the satraps or viceroys, the provincial depositaries of the power of the Khosrus.

Since Moawyah had moved the seat of the Caliphat to Damascus, a change had come over the style of the Moslem court. It was no longer, as in the days of Omar, the conference of a poorly clad Arab chieftain with his veteran warriors and graybeard companions, seated on their mats in the corner of a mosque : the Moslem Caliph at Damascus had now his divan, in imitation of the Persian monarch ; and his palace began to assume somewhat of oriental state and splendour.

In nothing had the Moslem conquerors showed more ignorance of affairs than in financial matters. The vast spoils acquired in their conquests, and the tribute and taxes imposed on subjugated countries, had for a time been treated like the chance booty caught up in predatory expeditions of the deserts. They were amassed in public treasuries without register or account, and shared and apportioned without judgment and often without honesty. Hence continual frauds and peculations; hence those charges so readily brought and readily believed, against generals and governors in distant stations, of enormous frauds and embezzlements, and hence that grasping avarice, that avidity of spoil and treasure, which were more and more destroying the original singleness of purpose of the soldiers of Islam.

Moawyah was the first of the Caliphs who ordered that registers of tribute and taxes, as well as of spoils, should be kept in the Islamite countries, in their respective languages; that is to say, in the Greek language in Syria, and in the Persian language in Irak; but Abd'almâlec went further, and ordered that they should all be kept in Arabic. Nothing, however, could effectually check the extortion and corruption which was prevailing more and more in the administration of the conquered provinces. Even the rude Arab soldier, who in his desert would have been content with his tent of hair-cloth, now aspired to the possession of fertile lands, or a residence amid the voluptuous pleasures of the city.

Waled had grown up amid the refinements and corruptions of the transplanted Caliphat. He was more of a Greek and Persian than an Arab in his tastes; and the very opposite of that primitive Moslem, Omar, in most of his habitudes. On assuming the sovereign power, he confirmed all the emirs or governors of provinces, and also the generals appointed by his father. On these he devolved all measures of government and warlike duties; for himself, he led a soft luxurious life amidst the delights of his harem. Yet, though he had sixty-three wives, he does not appear to have left any issue. Much of his time was devoted to the arts, and especially the art of architecture, in which he left some noble monuments to perpetuate his fame.

He caused the principal mosque at Cairo to be demolished, and one erected of greater majesty, the pillars of which had gilded capitals. He enlarged and beautified the grand mosque erected on the site of the temple of Solomon, for he was anxious to perpetuate the pilgrimage to Jerusalem established by his father. He gave command that the bounds of the mosque at Medina should be extended; so as to include the tomb of the prophet, and the nine mansions of his wives. He furthermore ordered, that all the buildings round the Caaba at Mecca should be thrown down, and a magnificent quadrangular mosque erected, such as is to be seen at the present day. For this purpose, he sent a body of skilful Syrian architects from Damascus.

Many of the faithful were grieved, particularly those well-stricken in years, the old residents of Mecca, to see the ancient simplicity established by the prophet, violated by the splendour of this edifice; especially as the dwellings of numerous individuals were demolished to furnish a vast square for the foundations of the new edifice; which now inclosed within its circuit, the Caaba, the well of Zem Zem, and the stations of different sects of Moslems, which came in pilgrimage.

All these works were carried on under the supervision of his emirs, but the Caliph attended in person to the erection of a grand mosque in his capital of Damascus. In making arrangements for this majestic pile he cast his eyes on the superb church of St. John the Baptist, which had been embellished by the Roman emperors during successive ages, and enriched with the bones and relics of saints and martyrs. He offered the Christians forty thousand dinars of gold for this holy edifice; but they replied, gold was of no value in comparison with the sacred bones enshrined within its walls.

The Caliph, therefore, took possession of the church on his own authority, and either demolished or altered it, so as to suit his purpose in the construction of his mosque, and did not allow the Christian owners a single dirhem of compensation. He employed twelve thousand workmen constantly, in this architectural enterprise, and one of his greatest regrets in his last moments was that he should not live to see it completed.

The architecture of these mosques was a mixture of Greek and Persian, and gave rise to the Saracenic style, of which Waled may be said to be founder. The slender and graceful palm-tree, may have served as a model for its columns; as the clustering trees and umbrageous forests of the north are thought to have thrown their massive forms and shadowy glooms into Gothic architecture. These two kinds of architecture have often been confounded, but the Saracenic takes the precedence; the Gothic borrowed graces and embellishments from it in the times of the Crusades.

While the Caliph Waled lived indolently and voluptuously at Damascus, or occupied himself in erecting mosques, his generals extended his empire in various directions. Moslema Ibn Abd'al-mâlec, one of his fourteen brothers, led an army into Asia Minor, invaded Cappadocia, and laid siege to Tyana, a strong city garrisoned with imperial troops. It was so closely invested, that it could receive no provisions; but the besiegers were equally in want of supplies. The contest was fierce on both sides, for both were sharpened and irritated by hunger, and it became a contest which could hold out longest against famine.

The duration of the siege enabled the emperor to send reinforcements to the place, but they were raw undisciplined recruits, who were routed by the hungry Moslems, their camp captured and their provisions greedily devoured. The defeat of these reinforcements rendered the defence of the city hopeless, and the pressure of famine hastened a capitulation, the besieged not being aware that the besiegers were nearly as much famished as themselves. Moslema is accused by Christian writers, of having violated the conditions of surrender; many of the inhabitants were driven forth into the deserts, and many of the remainder were taken for slaves. In a subsequent year Moslema made a successful incursion into Pontus and Armenia, a great part of which he subjugated, and took the city of Amasia, after a severely contested siege. He afterwards made a victorious campaign into Galatia, ravaging the whole province, and bearing away rich spoils and numerous captives.

While Moslema was thus bringing Asia Minor into subjection, his son Khatiba, a youth of great bravery, was no less successful in extending the empire of the faith toward the East. Appointed to the government of Khorassan, he did not content himself with attending to the affairs of his own province, but crossing the Oxus, ravaged the provinces of Turkistan, defeated a great army of Turks and Tartars, by which he had been beleaguered and reduced to great straits, and took the capital city of Bochara, with many others of inferior note.

He defeated also Magourek, the Khan of Charism, and drove him to take refuge in the great city of Samarcand. This city, anciently called Marcanda, was one of the chief marts of Asia, as well for the wares imported from China, and Tangut across the desert of Cobi, as of those brought through the mountains of the great Thibet, and those conveyed from India to the Caspian Sea. It was, therefore, a great resort and resting-place for caravans from all quarters. The surrounding country was renowned throughout the East for fertility, and ranked among the paradises, or gardens, of Asia.

To this city Khatiba laid siege, but the inhabitants set him at defiance, being confident of the strength of their walls, and aware that the Arabs had no battering-rams, nor other engines necessary for the attack of fortified places. A long and close siege, however, reduced the garrison to great extremity, and finding that the besiegers were preparing to carry the place by storm, they capitulated, agreeing to pay an annual tribute of one thousand dinars of gold and three thousand slaves.

Khatiba erected a magnificent mosque in that metropolis, and officiated personally in expounding the doctrines of Islam, which began soon to supersede the religion of the Magians, or Ghebers.

Extensive victories were likewise achieved in India during the reign of Waled, by Mohamed Ibn Casem, a native of Thayef, one of his generals, who conquered the kingdom of Sindia, or Sinde, killed its sovereign in battle, and sent his head to the Caliph ; overran a great part of Central India, and first planted the standard of Islam on the banks of the Ganges, the sacred river of the Hindoos.

CHAPTER LVIII.

Further triumphs of Musa Ibn Nosseyr.—Naval enterprises.—Descents in Sicily, Sardinia, and Mallorca.—Invasion of Tingitania.—Projects for the invasion of Spain.—Conclusion.

To return to affairs in Africa. During the first years of the Caliphat of Waled, the naval armaments fitted out by Musa in the ports of Eastern Africa, continued to scour the Mediterranean, and carry terror and devastation into its islands. One of them coasted the island of Sicily in the eighty-sixth year of the Hegira, and attaked the city of Syracuse ; but the object appears to have been mere plunder, not to retain possession. Another ravaged the island of Sardinia, sacked its cities, and brought off a vast number of prisoners and immense booty. Among the captives were Christian women of great beauty, and highly prized in the Eastern harems. The command of the sea was ultimately given by Musa to his son Abdolola, who added to his nautical reputation by a descent upon the island of Mallorca.

While Abdolola was rejoicing his father's heart by exploits and triumphs on the sea, Abd'alaziz contributed no less to his pride and exultation by his achievements on land. Aided by this favourite son, Musa carried the terror of the Moslem arms to the western extremity of Mount Atlas, subduing Fez, Duquella, Morocco, and Sus. The valiant tribes of the Zenetes at length made peace, and entered into compact with him; from other tribes Musa took hostages; and by degrees the sway of the Caliph was established throughout western Almagreb to Capo Non on the Atlantic.

Musa was not a ferocious conqueror. The countries subjected by his arms became objects of his paternal care. He introduced law and order; instructed the natives in the doctrines of Islam, and defended the peaceful cultivators of the fields and residents in the cities against the incursions of predatory tribes. In return they requited his protection by contributing their fruits and flocks to the support of the armies, and furnishing steeds matchless for speed and beauty.

One region, however, yet remained to be subjugated before the conquest of Northern Africa would be complete; the ancient Tingis, or Tingitania, the northern extremity of Almagreb. Here the continent of Africa protruded boldly to meet the continent of Europe; a narrow strait intervened; the strait of Hercules, the gate of the Mediterranean Sea. Two rocky promontories appeared to guard it on each side, the far-famed pillars of Hercules. Two rock-built cities, Ceuta and Tangiers, on the African coast, were the keys of this gate, and controlled the neighbouring seaboard. These had been held in ancient times by the Berber kings, who made this region their stronghold, and Tangiers their seat of power; but the keys had been wrested from their hands at widely-separated, periods, first by the Vandals, and afterwards by the Goths, the conquerors of the opposite country of Spain; and the Gothic Spaniards had now held military possession for several generations.

Musa seems to have reserved this province for his last African campaign. He stationed his son Merwân, with ten thousand men, in a fortified camp on the frontier, while Taric Ibn Zeyad a veteran general scarred in many a battle, scoured the country from the fountains or head waters of the river Moluya, to the mountains of Aldaran. The province was bravely defended by a Gothic noble, Count Julian by name; but he was gradually driven to shut himself up in Ceuta. Meantime Tangiers yielded to the Moslem arms after an obstinate defence, and was strongly garrisoned by Arab and Egyptian troops, and the command given to Taric. An attempt was made to convert the Christian inhabitants to the faith of Islam; the Berber part easily conformed, but the Gothic persisted in unbelief, and rather than give up their religion, abandoned their abodes, and crossed over to Andaluz with the loss of all their property.

Musa now advanced upon Ceuta, into which Count Julian had drawn all his troops. He attempted to carry it by storm, but was gallantly repulsed, with the loss of many of his best troops. Repeated assaults were made with no better success; the city was situated on a promontory, and strongly fortified. Musa now laid waste the surrounding country, thinking to reduce the place by famine, but the proximity of Spain enabled the garrison to receive supplies and reinforcements across the straits.

Months were expended in this protracted and unavailing siege, According to some accounts Musa retired personally from the attempt, and returned to his seat of government at Caerwan, leaving the army and province in charge of his son Merwân, and Taric in command of Tangiers.

And now occurred one of the most memorable pieces of treason, in history. Count. Julian, who had so nobly defended his post, and checked the hitherto irresistible arms of Islam, all at once made secret offers, not merely to deliver up Ceuta to the Moslem commander, but to betray Andaluz itself into his hands. The country he represented as rife for a revolt against Roderick the Gothic king, who was considered an usurper; and he offered to accompany and aid the Moslems in a descent upon the coast, where he had numerous friends ready to flock to his standard.

Of the private wrongs received by Count Julian from his sovereign, which provoked him to this stupendous act of treason, we shall here say nothing. Musa was startled by his proposition. He had long cast a wistful eye at the mountains of Andaluz, brightening beyond the strait, but hitherto the conquest of Northern Africa had tasked all his means. Even now he feared to trust too readily to a man whose very proposition showed an utter want of faith. He determined, therefore, to despatch Taric Ibn Zeyad on a reconnoitering expedition to coast the opposite shores, accompanied by Count Julian, and ascertain the truth of his representations. Taric accordingly embarked with a few hundred men in four merchant vessels, crossed the straits under the guidance of Count Julian, who, on landing, despatched emissaries to his friends and adherents, summoning them to a conference at Jesirah al Khadra, or the Green Island, now Algeziras. Here, in presence of Taric, they confirmed all that Julian had said of the rebellious disposition of the country, and of their own readiness to join the standard of an invader. A plundering cruise along the coast convinced Taric of the wealth of the country, and he returned to the African shores with ample spoils and female captives of great beauty.

A new career of conquest seemed thus opening upon Musa. His predecessor, Acbah, had spurred his steed into the waves of the Atlantic, and sighed that there were no further lands to conquer; but here was another quarter of the world inviting the triumphs of Islam. He forthwith wrote to the Caliph, giving a glowing account of the country thus held out for conquest; a country abounding in noble monuments and wealthy cities; rivalling Syria in the fertility of its soil and the beauty of its climate; Yemen, or Arabia the happy, in its temperature; India in its flowers and spices;

Hegiaz in its fruits and its productions; Cathay in its precious and abundant mines; Aden in the excellence of its ports and harbours. "With the aid of God," added he, "I have reduced to obedience the Zenetes and the other Berber tribes of Zab and Derâr, Zaara, Mazamuda, and Sus : the standard of Islam floats triumphant on the walls of Tangiers; thence to the opposite coast of Andaluz is but a space of twelve miles. Let but the Commander of the Faithful give the word, and the conquerors of Africa will cross into that land, there to carry the knowledge of the true God and the law of the Koran."

The Arab spirit of the Caliph was roused by this magnificent prospect of new conquests. He called to mind a tradition that Mahomet had promised the extension of his law to the uttermost regions of the West; and he now gave full authority to Musa to proceed in his pious enterprise, and carry the sword of Islam into the benighted land of Andaluz.

We have thus accomplished our self-allotted task. We have set forth, in simple and succinct narrative, a certain portion of this wonderful career of fanatical conquest. We have traced the progress of the little cloud which rose out of the deserts of Arabia, "no bigger than a man's hand," until it has spread out and overshadowed the ancient quarters of the world and all their faded glories. We have shown the handful of proselytes of a pseudo prophet, driven from city to city, lurking in dens and caves of the earth; but at length rising to be leaders of armies and mighty conquerors; overcoming in pitched battle the Roman cohort, the Grecian phalanx, and the gorgeous hosts of Persia; carrying their victories from the gates of the Caucasus, to the western descents of Mount Atlas; from the banks of the Ganges to the Sus, the ultimate river in Mauritania; and now planting their standard on the pillars of Hercules, and threatening Europe with like subjugation.

Here, however, we stay our hand. Here we lay down our pen. Whether it will ever be our lot to resume the theme, to cross with the Moslem hosts the strait of Hercules, and narrate their memorable conquest of Gothic Spain, is one of those uncertainties of mortal life and aspirations of literary zeal, which beguile us with agreeable dreams, but too often end in disappointment.

THE END.

PARIS.—PRINTED BY E. THUNOT AND CO., 26, RUE RACINE.

ImTheStory.com

Personalized Classic Books in many genre's

Unique gift for kids, partners, friends, colleagues

Customize:

- Character Names
- Upload your own front/back cover images (optional)
- Inscribe a personal message/dedication on the
  inside page (optional)

Customize many titles Including
- Alice in Wonderland
- Romeo and Juliet
- The Wizard of Oz
- A Christmas Carol
- Dracula
- Dr. Jekyll & Mr. Hyde
- And more...

Lightning Source UK Ltd.
Milton Keynes UK
UKOW06f0023060717
304763UK00009B/623/P